THE AMERICAN WAY OF CRIME

The American Way of Crime

Frank Browning
John Gerassi

G. P. PUTNAM'S SONS
NEW YORK

 Published simultaneously
in Canada by Academic Press Canada Limited, Toronto.

Library of Congress Cataloging in Publication Data

Browning, Frank.
The American way of crime.

Includes bibiliographical references and index.
1. Crime and criminals—United States—History.
2. Crime and criminals—United States. I. Gerassi,
John, joint author. II. Title.
HV6779.B76 1980 364'.973 79-18291
ISBN 0-399-11906-X

Printed in the United States of America

Acknowledgments

Various historians, political scientists, sociologists, journalists, and interested observers of America's mores helped us achieve our perspectives, locate our sources, and crystallize our theme. We cannot thank them all, but we would like to single out the following: Beverly Axelrod, Leonard Weinglass, Marc Raskin, Paul Jaricco, Dan Share, Sandy Close, Frank Viviano, Steve Weissman, Peter Solomon, George Wargo, Joseph Jorgensen, Judith Stanley, Edward Malefakis, Peter Dale Scott, Mary Milton, Charles Sellers, Rachell Keefe, Janet Tierney, Bill Hunt, Bonnie Sanford, Cynthia Merman, Phil Stanford, Mike Locker, and Robert Weingarten.

Our years of research and the time put in by those we hired were made possible by generous support from The Institute for Policy Studies, Howard Bray of the Fund for Investigative Journalism, W.H. and Carol Bernstein Ferry, Joseph Belden, Victor Herbert, John Thorne and Lynn Meyer of Research for Social Change.

We are especially indebted to Ned Chase, who originally contracted for this study, to Judith Wederholt, our editor, and to our agent, Joan Daves, and her assistants, especially Ruth Soika, who mothered us through it. Their patience and encouragement, more than anything else, enabled us to persevere through the long months when the size of the project threatened to overcome our energy and confidence.

Frank Browning
John Gerassi
New York City, January, 1979

The principal researchers for this book were

CHRISTINA WHITLOCK

Fernando Mechon
Alice Messing
Shoshana Rihn

Contents

PART IV: *Crime in the Superstate*

Introduction

In 1973, when the discussions that led to this book began, the authors were living and teaching in Paris. The initial dialogues began as a series of interviews with a French journalist who was struck by the extraordinary events then taking place in America and by the general malaise that followed in their wake. Drug usage was said to be epidemic, seeping out from decaying ghettos to the suburbs. Murder and assault were reported rising at an unparalleled rate. Corporate fraud and chicanery had made headlines and sent Wall Street reeling. And Watergate, the apparent crime of the century, was in full flower. The harder we struggled to place these phenomena in a cultural and political context, the more we found ourselves driven to examine the roots of American crime.

The record of crime in America is of course voluminous, and our attempt has not been to provide an encyclopedic recounting of it all. Rather we have tried to draw the lines of authority between the individual and the state, to discover how it is that particular actions are determined to be crimes, who defines them as such, how those definitions change and for what reasons, and how as a consequence America has evolved a criminal subculture unmatched anywhere in the world. It is our thesis that the rulers and leading intellectuals of the nation have through the years often diffused our most disturbing social and personal issues and redefined them as the combat between crime and social stability. Episodes of rebellion and dissent, complemented by the pervasiveness of poverty and violence, have until recently escaped public-school texts. Recent "discoveries" of these themes have themselves demonstrated the peculiar opaqueness that has so obscured the American past—an opaqueness that in large part has resulted from the way in which individual and social challenges to the dominant culture have been deflected through the mechanism of the criminal court. To challenge the established order, established customs, or established ideologies was to attack society—just as in the original Puritan settlements to act without the approval of the church "elect" was to act as an agent of the devil, and therefore as a criminal. Public preoccupation with "the crime problem," we believe, has been a recurring method by which America's social elites have defined the boundaries of acceptable moral and political behavior.

Europeans, who acknowledge a centuries-old class system, have described their social conflicts in overtly ideological terms as the combat among competing groups within society. Believing themselves free of these class conflicts, however, Americans were always convinced that challenges to the singular authority of the state resulted from flaws within the individual. A political system that declared class antagonism to be criminal on the face of it thus sought to eliminate conflict by eliminating its individual instigators, labeling them criminal. At the same time, through the invention of the penitentiary as the critical punitive device, the elites sought to reform lower-class miscreants by making them dependent and reshaping their moral deficiencies. That the courts and reformatories seldom achieved their immediate goal of reforming petty criminals has been secondary to their effect on the discourse created around crime and their symbolic importance as institutions of public order.

Control over the definition of crime and the administration of the criminal justice system has been, we argue, the dominant means by which the nation has addressed a broad range of public dilemmas. Not merely obvious crimes like murder, burglary, assault, and fraud are left to the courts, but the ever changing power relations among individuals—sex, job opportunities, family structure—are finally codified through criminal case law. Thus in 1978 a Michigan woman who burned her husband alive after he had repeatedly beaten her and denied her an independent career was acquitted of murder—largely because the movement for political and personal liberation among American women had grown powerful enough that homicide could be considered a legitimate self-defense against the crime of wife beating. Until recently, however, wife beating was considered a matter of male privilege within the family, far beyond the purview of the criminal courts. And in colonial times a woman who struck her husband could be tried for treason.

Contemporary issues of crime and social conflict are matters of ongoing debate that reflect profound cleavages within American society and that continue to be played out as issues of crime and punishment. We have attempted to reveal the antecedents to these conflicts through the development of American culture and politics and to trace the way in which criminal actions that result from broad social policies have been defined in terms of individual culpability.

There has been, however, a grand irony in the criminalization of the nonconformer and the outcast, and that is the second theme of our inquiry into the nature of America's criminal past. For while the criminal courts have been important mechanisms for diffusing class conflicts and redefining them as problems of crime and individual deviance, the structure of criminal sanction in America has also forged another kind of class system that until recently has been unique to America. Police and philanthropists of the nineteenth century frequently spoke of the dangerous classes and of the criminal classes—by which they usually meant unemployed factory hands and unassimilated immigrants. The coming of the twentieth century has brought a new meaning to those terms that is only comprehensible when set against the history of the modern representative democracies and the idea of the social estate.

The word *estate* originally denoted an organized class of society with a separate, distinct voice—a power in government. The men of the Enlightenment talked of three such estates: the nobility, the clergy, and the "commons," by which they meant the townspeople of means and property—the bourgeois or the burgesses. It was this estate, the third, that unleashed and led the French Revolution of 1789 and gained power.

The word estate has remained meaningful ever since. In the century following the revolution, the *first estate* came to refer to any ruling class that had inherited its wealth; the *second* to the politicians, judges, and custom makers who set the tone and mode of life in their society; and the *third* to the entrepreneurs and petit bourgeois who developed that society—the three groups with the power to forge the social contract in emerging Western nations. Eventually a *fourth estate* gained power because it could make or break individual members of the other three classes, though never the whole class. That fourth estate is the press.

Since the 1960s, there has been a great deal of talk about a *fifth estate,* one sometimes so powerful that the others are often forced to defer to it. Though it is supposed to carry out the wishes of the first three, in practice it has acted so independently that it has been dubbed the invisible government. To some that estate is the military, to others the intelligence agencies, and some see it as a combination of the two. Whatever final convention is adopted, by the end of the 1970s America's various intelligence agencies were certainly powerful enough to change our lives; thus they collectively are indeed the fifth estate.

Beyond these social forces, we believe, there has emerged a new estate in America, a *sixth estate,* which has exerted tremendous power on the country's government, economics, laws, police, value system, tastes, mores, and habits. It is an estate whose roots extend almost from the beginning of American history. The influence of this estate is strong, its reach wide, its might steadily growing. As it is today, America cannot and does not function without it. That sixth estate is the complex world of professional and organized crime. Firmly entrenched in both politics and business, it nevertheless maintains an independent status of its own. Professional criminals are certainly at the service of corrupt corporations and political parties; they may be responsible for and do indeed manipulate the violent street crime that Americans have come to regard as the greatest threat to their peace and security. Individual lawbreakers have come to rely upon the organized protection, the financial security, and the hierarchy of compromise by which the estate has exercised its power over American society. The estate of crime cuts across traditional classes and political alliances, almost as a subsidiary government, to represent the interests of its own members and to offer succor against the social alienation by which they have been defined as outcasts in the first place. Thus, as an estate, institutional crime in America is not just a corruption of other forces. The sixth estate is an independent force that both permeates and opposes the others and has become endemic to every element of modern life.

For all these reasons, a history of crime in America cannot help but be a history of America, in which the sagas of the outlaw and the gangster, the rebel and the mob, the crusader and the horde, are played back again and again in counterpoint to the dominant themes of unbridled progress and prosperity. Like many of the recent historical "discoveries," the narrative of American crime, the emergence of what we call the sixth estate, is a hidden history, one that so-called revisionist scholars have only begun to address. By describing the trends of crime, though certainly not each major case, in the historical development of the American nation, we have tried to discover why and how the sixth estate established itself. Our main task has been to describe the setting in which such a question must be posed. In the process, it seems to us, the evidence became overwhelming: America is run by various estates, and one of the most powerful is the sixth—crime. If America is to change, the inordinate power that all the others share with the sixth must be curtailed—by an estate not yet established.

PART I

Crime in the Colonies

The great questions that have
troubled the country are about
the authority of the magistrates
and the liberty of the people. . . .

—Governor John Winthrop
Massachusetts Bay Colony
July 3, 1645

Chapter 1

Harmony vs. Blasphemy

Three years before she was hanged in Boston in 1638, Dorothy Talbye had been a revered member of the Salem church, esteemed for her devotion to her husband and admired for her dedication to her children. Then one day she asked herself a strange question: By what right was her husband the master of her life?

In early Puritan America, the answer—as enforced by the church, the governor, and the court—was clear: by the laws of Moses. But the same Puritan code also proclaimed that any full member of the church who discovered grace was no more fallible than any minister of the colony. Thus Dorothy Talbye, having experienced spiritual revelation, suddenly considered herself equal to her husband and refused to obey him. The society that guaranteed that equality under God proclaimed her a criminal.

By 1637 Dorothy's life was a miserable torment. Her fights with her husband were severe. Her friends abandoned her. Salem's elders condemned her. And when her husband reported that she had tried to kill him, they cast her out of the church for her "melancholy or spiritual delusions." Her revelations became a daily affair, and they instructed her to starve her children and herself. Taken to the town square and flogged, she then "carried herself more dutifully toward her husband," wrote Governor John Winthrop in his journal. But it was a momentary reform. In the early fall of 1638, Dorothy Talbye, acting on a new revelation, took her daughter, Difficult, to a secluded gulley and quietly broke her neck. No one, she declared, should be forced to live in the misery suffered by women in Puritan America. Only through death, the revelation told her, might her daughter escape the torment she herself had endured.

Dorothy Talbye refused to repent. She denounced her excommunicators. She fought her executioners. Dragged to the gallows in the middle of Boston, she refused to stand, wrenched the cover from her face, grabbed vainly for the ladder. She was "possessed by Satan," Governor Winthrop wrote, as if that explained her aberrant behavior in the "citty upon a Hill" he had hoped to create in America. But the fact is that Dorothy Talbye was very much a product of that hope.[1]

Shortly before the 350-ton *Arbella* sailed into Salem harbor in June 1630, John Winthrop, a gaunt, ascetic, forty-two-year-old lawyer and self-trained physician-turned-preacher, explained that hope to his flock of ocean-weary Puritans. Swaying gently with the North Atlantic breeze, Winthrop, leader and first governor of the Masachusetts Bay Colony, said that their task would be to create a model of Christian charity, the embodiment of a covenant with God and men, a Bible society of justice and mercy—"a citty upon a Hill," where would reign pure law and pure relationships of harmony and brotherhood.[2]

Neither John Winthrop nor his Puritan herd had any intention of abandoning the Anglican church nor, for that matter, of challenging the divine powers of their king. Instead, these conquerors of North America, as the natives came to view them, believed that they had been chosen by God to form a covenant amongst themselves to purify the corrupt practices—but not the divine nature—of their homeland church. They were, arrogantly, God's "elect," but their tasks were practical, especially in a new land of wilderness and hostile heathens.

Yet to built a "citty" that would bear witness to God's great design in such a strange land could only be accomplished by total cooperation and mutual aid, by brotherhood and self-reliance. These qualities, then, had to be God's will. But if so, to live according to God's covenant with men would be precisely to empower men—collectively if not individually—with the divine insights needed to regulate concrete existence. It would mean that men were free to choose their own codes of behavior. Such liberty would challenge not only secular authority but divine morality as well. It was to eliminate the paradox that Winthrop stated in 1645:

> There is a two-fold liberty, natural (I mean as nature is now corrupt) and civil or federal. The first is common to man with beasts and other creatures. By this, man, as he stands in relation to man simply, hath liberty to do what he lists; it is a liberty to evil as well as to good. This liberty is incompatible and inconsistent with authority. . . .
>
> The other kind of liberty I call civil or federal; it may also be termed moral, . . . this liberty is the proper end and object of authority, and cannot subsist without it; and it is a liberty to that only which is good, just, and honest. This liberty you are to stand for, with the hazard not only of your goods, but of your lives, if need be. Whatsoever crosseth this is not authority, but a distemper thereof. This liberty is maintained and exercised in a way of subjection to authority; it is of the same kind of liberty where Christ has made us free.[3]

Today, Winthrop and his fellow magistrates in Boston are frequently described as narrow-minded theological tyrants who constructed their law and found biblical rationalizations in an attempt to oppress all religious dissenters. Indeed, tolerance was not high among their virtues. But their ideas of liberty, authority, and deviance were deeply rooted in their search and capacity for survival. Unlike the frontier freedoms codified and guaranteed in the U.S. Bill of Rights—freedoms derived essentially from the Virginia experiences and based on personal independence, industry, and property rights—the New England utopians proposed a far more positive and aggressive concept of freedom.

To them, freedom was never the mere right of the individual to act according to his own values, interpreting the will of God as he saw fit. The Puritans understood liberty as that paradox whereby the individual found himself through the loss of himself to divine purpose, in particular through his communal responsibility to his fellows.

But there was a further paradox that had plagued the followers of John Calvin: the same diligence required to build a godly kingdom also brought prosperity to the individual entrepreneurs. So it was within the fundamental precepts of the Puritan experiment that the seeds of its destruction were sowed. The very industry that the utopian dream required slowly devoured the communitarian principles for which it was founded, tearing rifts in the utopian structure itself. These rifts, the great cases of religious persecution in the colony, were in fact the sources of deviance, of crime as the Puritans saw it, and they were but reflections of the individualist challenge to communitarian authority.

Thus the search for purity led to its violators. Criminal behavior reflecting that alienation—drunkenness, fornication, and such challenges to authority as public criticisms of courts, governors, or kings, contempt of bailiffs, dereliction of militia duty, and the like—were at first much more common, according to the indictments before the Court of Assistants, than such premeditated crimes as theft, murder, assault, servant rebellions, or unholy or blasphemous behavior. Indeed, a reading of the court minutes from 1630 to 1643 suggests that the early colonials were far closer to the lusty swains and maids of John Barth's *Sotweed Factor* than to the dour figures of Nathaniel Hawthorne's *Scarlet Letter*. Eager young couples frequently wrestled in the hay in spite of the bare-backed lashings *both* would receive if the woman were pregnant unmarried or before marriage. Perversion, on the other hand, drew special penalties: Teague Ocrimi, for example, convicted of buggering a cow, was whipped, then displayed at the gallows with a rope around his neck. For public drunkenness, the punishment was usually a fine, although repeated conviction could bring on the whip or confinement in stocks. Defying the court, cursing the governor, resisting taxation, and seditious speeches were the most common offenses—and the most harshly punished.[4]

In England at the time, crime was far more serious. But most crimes were economic. England's cities were crammed with displaced serfs and impoverished farmers, and in such cities as London and Bristol whole neighborhoods were taken over by beggars, thieves, and pickpockets. Penalties were hence much stiffer. Pickpockets had their hands chopped off, while the death penalty was imposed for some thirty-five common offenses, ranging from petty larceny to rebellion. But in New England, where there were actually very few real victims, crime took on a special symbolic character in the maintenance of social control. By its definition and prosecution, it became a tool for the Puritan leaders in staking out the boundaries of acceptable moral and public behavior. So-called crime waves, as we came to call the crises in law and order in the nineteenth and twentieth centuries, erupted only when morality became ambiguous, when spiritual belief and political authority developed contradictions, when set patterns of life were challenged by new economic structures. Such crises led to the Quaker roundups of 1661 and to the Salem witchcraft trials of 1692.[5]

But curiously, even during these crises—and "crime waves"—the percentage of people committing crimes remained the same, or so at least concluded Yale historian Kai Erikson after examining the Essex County court records (which included Salem) for the thirty-year period from 1651 to 1680. Erikson's study did not cover the witchcraft trials, but it did include the Quaker prosecutions in which scores were jailed and at least four were hanged. Promoting Quaker ideas was then a grave criminal offense, and it became more and more troublesome as Quaker businessmen began to dominate much of colonial commerce.

Mostly due to the Quaker problem, church-related crimes rose from zero during the first five years of the 1650s to 171 during the first half of the 1660s (and then dropped just as sharply by the mid-1670s). Massachusetts can hence be said to have suffered a wave of Quaker "crimes." But the number of actual criminals remained the same; that is, other regular criminal convictions not related to the Quakers dropped during the crisis. Or as Erikson says, "Quakers who entered the scene in the late 1650s were somehow absorbed into the deviant population without affecting its size to any appreciable extent, almost as if other potential offenders had withdrawn for the moment to make room for them."[6]

The early records (1630–43) of the Massachusetts Court of Assistants tend to confirm the same pattern for the entire colony. As the population of Massachusetts grew steadily, so did the number of criminals, and in direct proportion. Later in the 1670s, as a consequence of a change in the court's jurisdiction, the percentage of people convicted by the court was slightly less. Overall, however, early New England seemed to maintain a constant pool of thieves, fighters, drunks, fornicators, and social dissidents.[7]

There are many possible explanations for this almost consistently steady percentage of crime. Until 1648, when the first *Book of General Laws and Liberties* was published, the Massachusetts judicial system underwent little change in either its size or its method of operation. To some extent the fixed number of judges and magistrates placed a limit on how many criminals could be processed. At the same time, sheriffs may have restricted the rate of arrests to the amount of jail space they had available. Yet something more profound seemed at work in the Puritan administration of crime than the simple technical limitations of the legal system. In a world where barren terrain, harsh weather, and fearsome Indians were all seen as dark, evil threats to the survival of a godly kingdom, men's internal iniquities were presented, in journals and sermons of the day, with similar consistency. God's world, even the devil within it, was seen as an orderly place. If the men and women of the New World were to remember their own personal failings as clearly as the threat from natural, external forces, it seemed reasonable that the moral administrators—the courts—should present a constant tableau of warnings, or indictments, to the citizens. The punishment of criminals was symbolically important, and thus the retention of a constant reservoir of criminals actually became a vital tool for maintaining political stability in the colony.[8]

Dorothy Talbye's real crime had not been murder, but her challenging of that political stability, the authority of church and governor, whose code of imposed harmony demanded a wife's total obedience to her husband. For all their heralding of freedom and equality in the "citty upon a Hill," Winthrop and his peers could not allow their society's way of life to be questioned. The America they had founded and used the courts to preserve was based on the dual principles of individual freedom and collective obedience to its ruling elites.

It is therefore not surprising that Puritan justice, contrary to myth, was not at all evenhanded. For men of wealth and station, punishments were usually limited to fines, and were often remitted after a demonstration of good behavior. One study has shown that of 245 sentences passed by the Court of Assistants between 1630 and 1641 almost half were eventually canceled. Those sentences included fines, banishments, disenfranchisements, and the like—penalties normally inflicted upon "gentlemen" and wealthy members of the community.[9]

The case of Sir Richard Saltonstall, ancestor to the modern Boston Brahmins, has often been cited as an example of the stern fair-handedness of Puritan justice. Yet a deeper search into the court records reveals that Saltonstall's fines (one for illegally whipping several people, another for tardy appearance in court) were continued for several years and eventually canceled. Those who actually received the harshest *and* most frequent punishments were lower-class and working people who could not afford the fines. Farm hands, laborers, sailors, and servants almost never received pardons. It was impossible to take back the thirty-nine lashes a man had received on his back or to erase the day he had been confined in stocks in the town square. Of the 121 penalties canceled by the courts in the 1630s, 44 had been imposed for crimes committed by designated "gentlemen," and most of the rest were for offenses committed by shopkeepers and tradesmen, such as improper sales, overcharging, or neglect of public duty. By 1648 propertied gentlemen were made legally exempt from whippings.[10]

Since there was always a shortage of prison space in early Massachusetts, a wide variety of physical tortures had to be devised for the commoners. One unnamed woman from Salem was brought before the court in 1638 for having boisterously demanded her right to take communion in spite of the church elders' denial. At first she was sentenced to three days in jail for disturbing the peace, then released on bond to her husband. Her outspoken, unorthodox religious statements continued, however, and eventually so irritated the magistrates she was given a public whipping. Again brought before the court in 1646 for abusing the church elders, she was ordered to wear a cleft stick on her tongue for half an hour.[11]

Punishment for the most heinous blasphemies specified that the offender's tongue was to be run through with a red-hot wire. Philip Ratcliffe, a convict servant, was not only whipped but had his ears cut off and was banished in 1631 for uttering "foul, scandalous invectives" against the church and the government. Sometimes the ears were not sliced off but merely nailed to a pillory and later cut loose in shreds.[12]

Thieves and robbers were usually whipped or branded with the letter T on their cheeks, thumbs, or foreheads and ordered to repay the stolen property sometimes at twice or three times the value. Only occasionally were drunkards whipped or jailed. Usually, in an effort to elicit shame and contrition, they were fined and ordered to repent before the church. Repeated offenders faced progressively stiffer penalties. Robert Coles came before the court four times between August 1631 and April 1634: First he was fined; then he was fined and ordered to confess publicly; next, for being drunk and "enticing" another man's wife, he was fined and directed to wear a paper on his back proclaiming him a drunkard; finally he was disenfranchised and ordered to wear a large red D on his coat for one year.[13]

Fornicators were whipped. If they were brazen, drunk, had sworn against God or the government, they normally received the maximum thirty-nine lashes and were placed in bilboes, an ingenious device whereby the prisoner was held in chains, often upside down with the weight of his own body pressing against his neck. Women were sentenced to whippings at the cart's tail, a punishment in which the prisoner was made to run behind a horse-driven cart from which a rope had been tied around her neck; each time the cart stopped she would receive several lashes.

Weybro Lovell, whose husband was a captain and therefore of high rank, was admonished to repent and "be chaste" in April 1637 for her "light and whorish behavior," while Thomas Owen and Sara Hales were ordered to the gallows four years later for adultery. Owen and Hales were not hanged. Instead they were victims of that grizzly Puritan game in which the convict was taken to the gallows, a cover placed over his head, and a noose tightened round his neck as though for hanging. At the penultimate moment the executioner would move away from the trapdoor and leave the prisoner tied to the gallows for one or two hours. Those who did not suffer heart attacks or total collapse were profoundly sobered. For poor Sara Hales, alas, punishment was still not complete; upon release from the mock hanging she was banished.[14]

Sometimes, the executions were carried out, even for the "crime" of lust. In March 1644, James Britten and Mary Latham took the full penalty. Winthrop recalled their unfortunate episode, including their hanging, with satisfaction in his journal. James, he wrote, was "a man ill-affected both to our church discipline and civil government," and Mary was "a proper young woman about 18 years of age, whose father was a godly man and had brought her up well."

Regardless of her father's upbringing Mary had proven herself rather more impetuous than godly. Rejected by the man she loved, she vowed to marry the next man who proposed, an "ancient" fellow, said Winthrop, unlikely to satisfy her unfulfilled desire. Married or not, Mary Latham was hardly ready to shrivel in the bridal bed—as the young men about town soon discovered. One of them, unfortunately for Mary, contracted a "palsy" and with it a case of conscience. Horror stricken over his sin, the "ill-affected" James Britten unburdened his soul to the court, confessing all the sordid details.

Mary fiercely denied his accusation at first. Perhaps she had acted improperly, even a little wantonly, she argued, but certainly she had never permitted actual intercourse. Reports from her neighbors and companions, however, were too damning. She had been intemperate to her husband, they said. She drank too much. She had threatened him. She had called him a cuckold. She had, in short, been grossly, crudely immoral. So she confessed. Not only had she taken James Britten to bed. At least twelve other men had enjoyed her body, she declared in a final fling of repentance. Yet her behavior was too horrible for repentance, the court decided. There could be no atonement short of hanging. According to Winthrop, both she and James died penitently, she the more hopeful since she had never criticized the church. The other twelve men denied her charges. None were indicted. Governor Winthrop was pleased that justice had been done.[15]

It was, after all, *his* justice, a justice he and a few formidable leaders of the Bible society had instituted and upheld with unyielding tenacity. Among these leaders were John Cotton, the eloquent minister of Boston's first church and one of the colony's most influential authors; Thomas Hooker, founder and first governor of Connecticut; and Thomas Shepard, a Cambridge-trained grocer's son who became one of Boston's great Congregational preachers and interpreters of the covenant. By 1652, all four were dead.

Indeed, within ten years of Winthrop's death, almost all the political and intellectual leaders who had forged the New England colonies were gone. They had been an elite set of men, utopian visionaries who, in public at least, never faltered, never betrayed doubt over the righteousness of their mission. Ruthlessly, they had fought off what they believed were false faiths, insidious forms of corruption that might have subverted their adventure in the wilderness. But in the process they had instituted a code of behavior that considered rebellion, antisocial activity, and irreverent talk as synonymous with crime. What's more, because of their emphasis on dedication to the building of a successful "citty," they established in practice a dual system of justice—those who achieved material success had proved their dedication and were treated much more leniently than those who failed—a system of justice whose underlying philosophy—"the rich deserve their wealth, the poor are lazy"—was to permeate the American way of life for generations.

Chapter 2

Common Bawds and Praying Indians

In an unjust society, criminal behavior is a form of individual rebellion. It may not change that society—nor is it meant to—but it tends not to be morally condemned by the criminal's peer group. Society under the second generation of puritans was unjust, both politically and economically. Crime in that society tended to reflect that fact.[1]

Theft, pickpocketing, burglary, trafficking in stolen goods—all relatively minor problems for New England's first generation—rose noticeably as the second generation came into adulthood. Moral and sexual offenses also went up sharply in the towns. By the 1670s Boston's continual flow of strangers included frontier adventurers, Indian fighters, sailors, pirates, fortune hunters, and newly freed servants searching for work. So high was the demand for sexual favors that the infamous "Whores of Boston" won notoriety throughout the colonies. From 1670 to 1680, no fewer than sixty-two defendants were brought before the Suffolk County court for fornication and adultery. Another fifty-one people were prosecuted on diverse sexual charges, including eleven for prostitution. From 1630 to 1643 the Court of Assistants had handled only thirty such cases in a population larger than Boston in the 1670s.[2]

Increased theft and petty violence were not restricted to Boston alone in the 1670s. Magistrates throughout the colonies were spending much more of their time prosecuting burglaries, robberies, assaults, and murders. In the early years colonial prosecutions for victimless crimes involving sex and liquor abuse had far outnumbered the victim crimes of theft and violence, usually by as much as two or three to one. But by the late 1670s, crimes involving violence or theft almost matched the victimless charges.[3]

The case of Widow Alice Thomas stands almost as a symbol for Boston's growing troubles with crime. She was "a common baud," the court declared in January 1672, a slut of a woman whose only aim was to corrupt the children of Boston's better families. Her age, how long she had been a widow, the sort of merchandising she sold in her "shop," are all details omitted in the fragmentary record of the court. Only one thing is certain: in the winter of '72 she was reviled by the proper authorities of Boston. The county court found her guilty on five counts:

—aiding and abetting theft by buying and concealing stolen goods;

—"frequent secret and unreasonable entertainment in her house to leud, lascivious and notorious persons of both sexes, giving them opportunity to commit carnal wickedness . . . ;"

—selling wine and strong waters without a license;

—entertaining servants and children;

—selling drink on the Sabbath.

For her crimes and transgressions Alice Thomas was sentenced to pay threefold restitution for the stolen property, a £50 fine, and court fees. She was ordered to stand on the gallows for one hour with a rope around her neck, after which she was stripped to the waist and whipped thirty-nine lashes at the cart's tail—all in freezing January weather. Her whipping complete, she was jailed until October when she was banished from the city of Boston.[4]

Curiously, Widow Thomas's name does not appear in any record of cases involving prostitution or adultery. Nor is there a court record showing whose property she stole. Nor were any servants convicted of drunkenness or "loose behavior" in her house. Aside from civil disputes she appears only in a 1671 divorce case between Edward Naylor and his wife, Nanny, a member of the prominent Wheelwright family, and therein may lie the source of the intense community anger she provoked.

Testimony of one John Anibal about events in her house had proven especially damning a year earlier in the Naylor divorce case.

"Jabez Salter came and asked me who was in the shop of Widow Thomas," Anibal told the court on February 2, 1671. "I answered I could not tell, but he asked me to go with him and he would see and I said I thought it best to keep to my work. Then he went to William Godfrey and told him, and he went and fetched a candle and he and the neger woman went and looked in and see who it was.

"I asked Godfrey who they were and he said he was loather to tell me but bid me guess. I guessed Naylor and Mary More and he said I was right.

"I have often seen Mary More and Mr. Naylor at the widow Thomas's house together," he added.

Reacting to the "bold and audacious presumption of some, to erect a Stews, whore-house, or Brothel House," the colony immediately enacted a new law specifying that "every such Baud, whore, or vile person shall be severely whipped at the carts-tail, through the streets, where such offense or offenses hath been committed, with 30 stripes and then to be committed to the House of Corrections . . . to be kept with hard fare and hard labor." To indulge in dalliance and theft was bad enough in old Boston, but to disgrace a fine family and humiliate the daughter of a leading citizen in the process was unpardonable. Yet in a society based on material achievement, money pardons all sins. In September 1673, Widow Thomas made substantial gifts to the city for the construction of new buildings and a harbor seawall. Three years later, in July 1676, her petition to return to Boston was accepted.[5]

Before 1670 New England had never known a case quite the measure of the Widow Thomas's, either in the depth or the diversity of its sin. Cuckolds, adulterers, and fallen women had peppered the court dockets from the very beginning; certain houses, especially those of widows, had developed salacious reputations. But the Widow Thomas brought organization to these otherwise pedestrian sins, and in so doing had diversified into lower-class crime as well, by providing a marketplace for stolen property. If not precisely the first, she is still one of the original "fences" in the history of American crime. As such she also stands as a pioneer in the saga of American enterprise.

Like Boston's other imaginative traders, Widow Thomas saw the changing character of the city's social and economic makeup, sensed a need, and moved to fill it. In skill, perception, and instinct she was probably little different from the New England mast exporters described by Harvard historian Bernard Bailyn. Just as the exporters maneuvered "with all the arts of high pressure negotiators, from cornering the supply to cultivating friendships with governmental officials," so we may suppose an operator as successful as Widow Thomas had also mastered the vagaries of a difficult market and secured friends in high places. Keen to the expanding commercial life that brought her customers, she also tapped the rootless women of the lower class desperate to find any means of survival. Thus to a large extent the new drift in crime during the sixties, seventies, and eighties came as a natural complement to the first wave of the mercantile movement.[6]

The tightly knit communities of the Puritan covenant were being challenged by new kinds of towns—those which owed their existence to the needs and desires of outside traders. Under intense pressure from the Board of Trade in London, the colonies were being pressed further into the service of the English imperial system. "It is Trade and Commerce alone that draweth store of wealth along with it, and that potency at sea by shipping which is not otherwise to be had," the earl of Shaftesbury told his colleagues on the board. As the American towns found their niche in Shaftesbury's grand imperial system, they began to require a stratum of people to supply labor and service to the travelers and traders or their local agents. Consequently the large coastal centers of New England—Newport, Boston, even Salem—were transformed by class stratification. It is to that transformation that the Widow Thomas owes her place in history.[7]

The most obvious sign of the expanding lower class was the increase in indentured servants brought to New England. Most of those who came in the sixties and seventies worked as dockhands, as apprentices to tradesmen, as household maids, or as laborers on farms owned by merchants. Usually, servants sold themselves to their American masters on seven-year contracts in exchange for free passage from England—all brokered through the ship's captain, who was actually paid by the Americans.[8]

The servants came to the colonies in part hoping to find land and higher wages. They were also pressured to leave England by its mercantilists, worried that their cities were being overrun by too many unemployed and therefore volatile workers. So began the imperial policy of skimming off excess laborers, deporting them with the convicts to the overseas colonies. Most of the convicts went to Virginia and Maryland. Most of the servants, however, went to the trading towns of New England as manpower for the developing industries. As their terms of indenture expired in the seventies and eighties and they became freemen in search of land and work, they frequently surfaced on the dockets of the criminal courts.[9]

Fifty slaves and servants were convicted of serious crimes before the Court of Assistants between October 1671 and January 1680, half on charges of theft or assault, a handful as runaways. The cumulative record of the county courts and the broader Court of Assistants shows that servant behavior was becoming a pervasive problem throughout Massachusetts. The Court of Assistants in the 1670s was sentencing twice as many servants as it had in the 1670s.* And the sentences were stiff. Nearly two-thirds, 64 percent, were whipped, and most were required to serve additional time or make special payments to their masters. Moreover, as their terms of indenture expired and it became increasingly difficult to find farmland, they emerged as New England's first class of propertyless wage earners—a class of men and women whose only stake in the New World was the money they could make in it. For them there was not even the myth of full participation, only possible salvation through the bond of the holy covenant. As America drew closer to the eighteenth century, so rich in the rhetoric of democratic principle, social life in the colonies became more and more rigidly divided, and an emerging majority of commoners felt more and more excluded from political relevance.[10]

But New England's governors had more to worry about than crime in the cities. More new settlers and more freed servants meant that without additional land properties were carved into increasingly smaller parcels as each generation succeeded. That was one of the dire dilemmas underlying the witch-hunts of Salem Village.

From 1660 to 1700 the average size of village landholdings dropped from about 245 acres to fewer than 115 acres. The search for farmland meant a push to the west, an invasion of Indian lands. The resulting conflict, as the criminal court records show, brought the Indians under direct white justice. Twenty-five Indians came before the Court of

*While it may be argued that population jumped dramatically during the intervening thirty years, the court also sharply restricted its jurisdiction. In the 1670s, misdemeanors and routine violations were generally heard by the county courts and sent to the Court of Assistants only on appeal, a luxury servants could seldom afford.

Assistants in the 1670s, sixteen on charges of theft or personal assault. As with servant offenders, almost two-thirds of the Indians were whipped. Indians had never lived far from the English settlements, but they had seldom merged into white communities. Their own ancient laws and social customs served them well. Indian criminal offenders were judged within their own tribes.[11]

Westward white expansion, however, led to more imaginative and more complex relations with the Indians. The missionary spirit, which had always been a minor theme of local sermons as well as of English charter statements, found new vigor. An "Indian College" had been established at Harvard in the 1650s, albeit under rather dubious financial circumstances. By the 1670s Christian proselytizers were elated at how many Indians they had converted to their religion and culture. In 1674 the missionaries calculated they had gathered some eleven hundred so-called praying Indians. Through them, the white settlers were able to soften the distinction between Indian and English cultures, since the best of the praying Indians were dispatched as missionaries themselves to the several tribes of western Massachusetts, Connecticut, and the Hudson Valley. The Puritan leaders hoped that these unofficial emissaries would draw the savages into Christian brotherhood.[12]

A little brotherhood, new tools, perhaps a few of God's covenants here and there, a bit of Divine Grace—and new land would become as plentiful as crackers on the communion plate. As for those poor Indians who landed in court, they had simply reverted to "savage instinct." An English Royal commissioner visiting Massachusetts in 1665 reported approvingly that the missionaries had pacified the Indians "by hiring them to hear sermons, by teaching them not to obey their heathen princes, and by appointing rulers amongst them."[13]

Modern reexamination of the New England frontier has shown how fast and thoroughly the social conquest of the Indians was accomplished, mostly through simple barter. For at least a hundred years the New England tribes had regularly traded fish, game, and corn among themselves as a means of balancing their subsistence needs. Land, while it was reserved along certain rough boundaries to demarcate political territory, was not itself a commodity to be traded. It was as immovable as the sea and the sky. It was used to create food and artifacts that could be handled, transported, and exchanged. Thus, as one recent historian has written, "When the white man offered new and, to the natives, highly desirable commodities, the red man was only too willing to revise his existing network of trade relations to accommodate the newcomers. Before long the Indian had largely discarded his old patterns. New commercial systems centering on trade with the colonists emerged, which in some instances created bitter intertribal rivalries—an unexpected and unwanted byproduct of the new prosperity."[14]

Thus, too, the incomprehension when, after the missionaries came proffering the common brotherhood of Christ, the Indians could no longer till and dwell upon their own lands, which, they were suddenly told, they had bartered away. By the 1660s the changes had become irreversible. However perfidious the white man's trading schemes were, the whole system of Indian commerce had been transformed and the northern tribes had become dependant upon it. Only one more ingredient was needed to set the stage for the bloodiest war of the colonial era.[15]

That ingredient was the persistent angling among the colonies for power, profits, and territory. Plymouth, oldest of all the northern colonies, had long been overshadowed by Massachusetts. The combination of Puritan zeal, solid capital backing, and Boston's fine harbor gave Massachusetts a firmer base and continued to provide it with enough commercial support to retain its favor among English investors. Connecticut, the Congregationalist colony, had split off under the leadership of Thomas Hooker and won a partially deserved reputation for its religious liberalism. However, it lacked any major ports, and it was mostly blanketed by farms and quiet villages. Rhode Island, born in turmoil and settled by renegades from the Puritan theocracy, was really only a loose collection of towns and villages scattered across Narragansett Bay back to the mouth of the Pawtucket River. But tiny Rhode Island, spurned for its heretical freethinkers and beset by continual threats of annihilation from Boston, had two invaluable assets: a heritage of friendly relations with the Narragansett Indians and a number of fine deep harbors. For land-hungry New England, infected by the earl of Shaftesbury's call to commerce, the appetite for Rhode Island and the Narragansett lands proved insatiable.[16]

The spirit and intent of what would follow was laid bare in a letter written to John Winthrop from his brother-in-law, Emanuel Downing, in summer 1645. Having just argued the manifest benefits of launching a just, Christian war against the Narragansetts (who had just pledged their loyalty to the king as a guarantee for their independence from the other colonies), Downing got to the point:

> . . . for I do not see how we can thrive until we get into a stock of slaves sufficient to do all our business, for our children's children will hardly see this great continent filled with people, so that our servants will still desire freedom to plant for themselves, and not stay but for very great wages. And I suppose you know very well how we shall maintain 20 Moores* cheaper than one English servant.[17]

Fifteen years later Winthrop's son, John Jr., who had become governor of Connecticut, tried again to snatch the Narragansett territory through an elegant land-fraud scheme. Working through the Atherton Company, John Jr. and a group of Connecticut and Massachusetts land speculators entertained the feeble-minded younger brother of a Narragansett sachem (chief), got him drunk, and induced him to transfer six thousand acres of the tribe's land to them. To insure the transaction, the Narragansett tribe was "fined" 595 fathoms of wampum for a variety of nonexistent crimes. In order to guarantee payment of the fines, John Atherton himself lent the tribe the money, secured by a mortgage of the entire territory on a six-month note, at just below 50 percent interest. When the Narragansetts somehow met the loan terms, Atherton refused to accept payment and foreclosed, claiming title to four hundred square miles of tribal land.[18]

A Royal commission exposed the fraud, gave the land back to the Narragansetts, and prohibited the colonies from launching any further conquest of "native lands." But greedy colonists found a way around the prohibition: Christian missionaries and their armies of praying Indians, commanded by one Rev. John Eliot, who had established the "Indian College" at Harvard. There is strong reason to suppose the Reverend Eliot may have had a hand in the first covert land operation against the Indians. It is possible that Eliot was a victim of circumstance. This much, however, is clear: It was the shadowy role of Eliot's praying Indians that finally ignited King Philip's War in 1675 and crushed the final vestiges of Indian strength in New England.[19]

Several years earlier, weapons and ammunition had been supplied to

*To many early English writers, all nonwhites, red or black, were called Moores.

Eliot and his praying Indians by wealthy English benefactors, their use to be determined only by the minister's prudent judgment. The same praying Indians then attacked the Mohawks in the Hudson Valley, which had recently caught the fancy of John Winthrop, Jr. Eliot disclaimed any responsibility for the campaign—which may have been true but was also convenient since his praying Indians were roundly defeated. Eliot, however, continued his missions and frequently drew sharp rebuke from Wampanoag sachem Philip. The Wampanoags, whose territory lay within the Plymouth jurisdiction, had retained their independence from all English settlers; in fact, since Plymouth was never formally chartered by London, its only legal status was as a protectorate for the Wampanoags. Already dwarfed by the expansion of the other colonies, Plymouth grew even more jittery as the Wampanoags began selling sections of their land to Rhode Island. Eliot's Indian missions offered the promise of pacifying any rebellious instincts the Wampanoags might harbor and of preserving the colony from piecemeal absorption by its neighbors. Philip, who took his name out of early respect for the English, held a rather different view of Eliot and his praying Indians, whom he described as mischievous, "dissemblers," and liars. Soon enough Philip would have even greater reason to distrust Eliot's missionaries.[20]

On the morning of January 29, 1675, John Sassamon was found dead, floating beneath the ice of a pond fifteen miles southwest of Plymouth. His hat and gun lay on the surface. His head was badly swollen and his neck was broken. No water spilled from his lungs or stomach, indicating that he had been dead before he entered the pond.[21]

John Sassamon had formerly been one of Philip's most trusted aides. He was also one of John Eliot's earliest protégés and a militant praying Indian, which Philip did not know. Nor is it likely that Philip knew how helpful Sassamon had been to the English forces in their earlier conquest of the Pequots.* When Sassamon came to Philip some three

*Enraged over the killing of a New England trader, the colonies had pressed a campaign of revenge which wiped out the entire Pequot nation, including a final massacre of noncombatant survivors near New Haven in May 1637. Captain John Mason, one of the Connecticut commanders of the campaign, arrived in a Pequot village at dawn, May 26. It was mostly deserted except for women, children, and the old as Mason and his men moved from hut to hut searching for the enemy. Not finding any warriors, he pointed to the wigwams, shouted "we must burn," and proceeded to lead the assault that wiped out the villages and killed its defenseless inhabitants.

decades later, it was as a wise and learned man, educated at Harvard, rich in knowledge of white customs but eager to live again among Indian people. He advised the new sachem and taught his men to read and write, not so much a missionary as a primitive Peace Corps volunteer. He did not mention that he had been personally dispatched to the Wampanoags by John Eliot.[22]

Sassamon's knowledge and skills were useful to the Wampanoags who, completely encircled by English settlements, were constrained to walk a very delicate line between the feuding colonies. At the same time the economic strain facing all the tribes was especially intense for the Wampanoags. A man of Sassamon's background proved invaluable. Sassamon rose rapidly to take his seat at the innermost circle of the tribal councils. He became Philip's personal secretary and legal adviser. He eventually wrote Philip's will. And that was his downfall. For apparently he believed he had left Philip sufficiently illiterate that the sachem would not understand a provision he had inserted leaving himself a vast amount of Wampanoag land.

When Sassamon's scheme was uncovered, he fled to John Eliot, pretended a public "reconversion" to the church, and began again preaching to other praying Indians. To the men and women of Plymouth he stood as a heroic symbol of Christian triumph over heathen savagery. Virtue had become a veritable disease with this born-again Christian whose value to the colonial government may have exceeded even Eliot's. Sassamon allied himself to Plymouth governor Edward Winslow with the same fervor he had appeared to offer Philip a few years earlier. There is no record of his precise relationship to the government, but he was close enough to be welcome in Winslow's home. One day in January 1665, he went to the governor to transmit reports that his old comrades, the Wampanoags, were planning a massive attack against the whites. On his way back home, he was killed.[23]

At first Sassamon's death was interpreted as an accident. Then a praying Indian came forward to report that he had seen Sassamon murdered. Sassamon's killers, he declared, were three Wampanoags. According to the logic of Plymouth authorities, that meant that Philip must have ordered the killing as an act of revenge, and that Sassamon's warnings of an imminent uprising were therefore correct. The theory would have been plausible but for two details: Philip went immediately to Plymouth and testified that he knew nothing of the killing, even though, as sachem, he was legally empowered to order an execution within his territory; and the witness who testified against the three Wampanoags owed them a gambling debt he had been unable to repay.[24]

These details did not impress the court at the three Wampanoags' trial. Nor have the details of the case impressed mainline historians who have stressed that the white jury's guilty verdict was confirmed by a second Indian jury—an advisory body of four Indians, each of whom was one of Eliot's praying disciples.[25]

Whether Sassamon was murdered and by whom remain unanswerable questions. Certainly by the end of the trial, white fear and hostility had been stirred to fury. Philip, whose real grievances were already piling up rapidly and who had recently lost his birthplace, Swansea Island, to white encroachment, was equally inflamed. Regardless of how reliable Sassamon's initial reports had been, war seemed inevitable after the three Wampanoags were hanged. Some fleeting efforts at mediation had been attempted by Quakers in the Rhode Island government, but those were dashed when Plymouth's governor Winslow sent word he was committed to military punishment of the Wampanoags. Rumblings of skirmishes came in daily, and rumors of Indian pilferage flew wildly about the colony. Then, one morning, an old man and a boy saw three Indians running from a house. The boy fired his musket, hit the Indian but did not stop him. Later several Wampanoags came to the Plymouth military garrison to ask why their fellow tribesman had been shot. Rhode Island Quaker chronicler John Easton tells the rest of the story:

"They [the officers] asked whether he was dead.

"The Indians said yea.

"An English lad said it was no matter. The men endeavored to inform them it was but an idle lad's words, but the Indians in haste went away and did not harken to them. The next day the lad that shot the Indian and his father and five English more were killed.

"So the war begun with Philip."[26]

Whatever the war's immediate cause, its real goal was land—without which New England could not hope to prosper. It was that economic uncertainty that had provoked the numerous challenges to political authority, the steady erosion of the Puritan covenant, the rising incidence of theft and assault, the ruthless persecutions of Quaker dissidents, and that would eventually lead to the Salem witch-hunts. Barely half a century after it had been founded under the Christian principles of "the liberty of the people" and divinely inspired authority, as Governor Winthrop had proclaimed, America was becoming a country where men of authority—including even Winthrop's own son—were replacing liberty with corruption, fraud, class oppression, and murder. As one English traveler, Edward Ward, said: The colony was run by men with neither charity nor mercy, neither loyalty nor amity.[27]

But if the "citty upon a Hill" was turning into a place where "progress" could best be achieved by an alliance of greedy mercantilists, corrupt officials, and a system of magistrates more bent on punishing dissenters and the restless poor than true criminals, those who still longed for a just and equitable Bible society were by no means silenced. Their accusations at Salem would be their first major counterattack.

Chapter 3

Poor Witches, Prosperous Devils

There could be no greater transgression in the Puritan wilderness than witchcraft. To be convicted as a witch was to be condemned as a totally depraved criminal. To suppose that the witch trials were simply the consequence of religious zeal run wild or that the town fathers were crudely suppressing their political opponents is a fundamental misunderstanding of Salem's social fabric. The witchcraft episode was primarily a record of the factional disputes and family feuds caused by the collapsing Puritan way of life, played out as a campaign of hardheaded criminal prosecution.

While it lasted, however, the "witchcraft delusion" truly possessed the village of Salem. Every tavern, every household, every barn stable was swept up by the hysterical events. No woman dared talk freely with her husband or her neighbor or even her children for fear some inconsequential aside would be recalled in court testimony and used as evidence against her. Mutable spirits and dark creatures were reported to appear from out of the shadows at any moment to inflict their spells on innocent children; a sleeping cat might instantly be transformed into the bleeding image of a long-dead mother or sister. And then there were the afflictions, horrid, painful tortures, that fulfilled all the requirements of modern occult movie scripts.

First to be afflicted were the children of the village minister, Samuel Parris, in February 1692. The Parris children began to carry themselves "after a strange and unusual manner, *viz,* as by getting into holes, and creeping under chairs and stools, and to use sundry odd postures and antick gestures, uttering foolish, rediculous speeches, which neither they nor any others could make sense of; the physicians that were called could assign no reason for this; but it seems one of them, having recourse to the old shift, told them he was afraid they were Bewitched." Before long other teenage girls of the village were complaining of invisible persecutions. Goodwife Martha Cory was accused of "afflicting them, by biting, pinching, stranglins, etc." The four-year-old daughter of a beggarwoman, Sarah Good, was accused of biting other small children who "would shew such like marks, as those of a small set of teeth upon their arms."[1]

In front of the judges and in the courtroom, the accusers would often scream that they were being taunted by evil spirits. When John Alden, son of the famous Pilgrim John Alden who arrived on the *Mayflower,* was tried for wizardry, his accusers swore that he was pinching them—even though he stood across the room from them. During Sarah Good's trial one of the witnesses cried out she was being stabbed in the breast by the defendant, and after an immediate search a knife blade was discovered on the floor. It had, however, been dropped by one of the spectators who had broken the knife the day before. So believable were these outcries that the judges and prosecutors would strike out physically at the supposed spirits. One of the favorite invisible nemeses of the accusers was a little black man who would promise great power and riches if only they would sign their names in his book. He would then return to sit on witness tables during the trials, the accusers swore. "The people would strike with swords or sticks at those places. One justice broke his cane at this exercise, and sometimes the accusers would say they struck the Spectre, and it is reported several of the accusers were hurt and wounded thereby."[2]

George Burroughs, a former village minister, was described at his trial as that black man. One of the bewitched accusers testified "that in her agonies a little black-haired man came to her, saying his name was B. and bidding set her hand unto a book," but when she refused, "he inflicted cruel pains and hurts upon her." Later in his trial, another accuser, Mercy Lewis, was even more precise about the former Salem minister, naming the exact day he had appeared to her: "Mr.

Burroughs carried me up to an exceeding mountain and shewed me all the kingdoms of the earth, and told me he would give them all to me if I would write in his book, and if not, he would throw me down and break my neck: but I told him they were none of his to give, and would not write if he throwed me on a hundred pitchforks."[3]

Twelve-year-old Ann Putnam, one of the most prolific accusers, brought further "spectral evidence" against the Reverend George Burroughs when she testified that two women had come to her in a vision: "The two women turned their faces towards me, and looked as pale as a white wall, and told me that they were Mr. Burroughs's first two wives, and he had murdered them. And one told me that she was his first wife, and he [had] stabbed her under the left arm and put a piece of sealing wax on the wound. And she pulled aside the winding sheet and showed me the place."[4]

The grotesqueries of the Salem trials test the imagination. To this day, they remain bizarre and hideous gothic tales. But they make up very real criminal prosecutions. By the end of September 1692, nineteen people—sixteen women and three men—had been hanged as witches or wizards. Hundreds more had been accused. Over a hundred were still in jail. New arrests were made daily. And then, it all stopped. The court was disbanded. Further arrests were forbidden in an order issued October 12 by Governor William Phips, a onetime Caribbean treasure hunter who owed his appointment to Increase Mather, the foremost minister of the colony and founder of a dynasty of powerful preachers. Within four months all the remaining accused witches were set free, either by acquittal under a new court or by official reprieve. The entire wave of witchcraft had appeared and disappeared in a single year.[5]

What really happened in Salem in 1692 may never be completely explained. But part of the answer surely lies in the rising and failing fortunes of two great New England families, the Putnams and the Porters.[6]

John Putnam migrated to Massachusetts from a small town outside London early in the 1640s. Over the next twenty years he and his three sons extended their original Salem land grant of a hundred acres into a thriving farm of nearly eight hundred acres. From the beginning, they were prominent and respectable church members who were frequently elected as Salem Town selectmen. They did not, however, live in the town proper, a seaport that gradually grew in commercial importance.

The Putnams' holdings were to the west, in Salem Village, the unincorporated hinterland settled almost entirely by farmers. Among their neighbors the Putnams commanded respect. While they apparently kept no servants, they lived in a large house, and by the time John's sons reached their prime, the family tax assessment was twice that of the average village farmer. They were, in short, successful. But they were not wealthy men, and in fact they were sorely frustrated by the specter of those other original farmers whose land lay closer to the sea and whose access to roads and streams tied them directly to the commercial life of the town.[7]

Such a farmer was John Porter. He too had come from an English town not far from London. But he appears always to have had a keener eye for trade than the Putnams. He first settled in Hingham, Massachusetts, then sold his farm for a handsome profit and with the proceeds acquired enough property to become the largest landholder in Salem. By 1676 his estate included almost two thousand acres, much of it near the river leading to the port in the eastern section of the village. That division between East and West Salem Village was to become as crucial as the rivalry between Salem Town and Salem Village. Not only did Porter choose the location of his land carefully. He also refused to limit himself to the narrow chores of tilling corn and wheat. Soon servants (two black and two white) had taken over the greater part of the daily drudgery while he dabbled in investments. With several other townsmen he secured a waterfront grant for harbor development. With another village family, he built a sawmill across a creek on his own land. He even speculated in sugar imports from the Caribbean during the late 1650s. By the end of his life, he ranked, though slightly in the shadows, with the great men of trade and commerce of the colony.[8]

Both John Putnam, who died in 1662, and John Porter, who lived until 1676, established themselves as patriarchs among the people of New England. Yet the two families followed profoundly different courses in the pursuit of their fortunes. Both Porter and Putnam, as well as their families, became captives of their choices, the former a sharp bargainer with the seaside merchants, the latter a self-appointed headman of the village farmers. Their paths led inevitably to conflict.

Recent inquiries into Salem Town history prior to the trials provide new insights into the crisis caused by that conflict. By 1690 Salem Village had come to desperate straits, as had the family of the late John Putnam. For twenty-five years the village had petitioned the town for the right to establish its own church since many of the villagers lived too far from the one in town. Each request had been rebuffed, leaving the village with a meetinghouse and a minister but not the right to hold full church services. The village had even petitioned to establish itself as an independent township. That too had been denied. The villagers continuously complained that the town authorities neglected their needs, that their taxes were too high, and that they had to provide too many men for the militia.[9]

After the fall of Cromwell, the Restoration reopened immigration to the colonies. But around Salem new land was very scarce and available only in the far western end of the village. It was rocky, swampy land, and it was there that the Putnams had tried to expand. Frustrated by the unyielding soil, envious of the Porter family's obvious prosperity, the Putnams tried to diversify into iron smelting in early 1670s. But that venture too was a failure: A Welshman who had been hired to run the operation produced neither iron bars for his contract customers nor rent for the Putnams and their partners. Soon a great many lawsuits were filed and the Welshman disappeared. His possessions were seized and his sons were indicted for lewd behavior (parading nude at the swimming hole in the presence of young women), but no funds were extracted from his family. Finally, on a warm Sunday morning in July 1674, the ironworks burned to the ground. Suspicion had it that the proud and aggrieved Welsh family was guilty of arson, but no proof was ever produced. Forced back to their thin farmlands at the worst possible moment, the Putnam family's second generation, with its numerous offspring, could no longer survive on the homestead which had originally provided status, church membership, and modest wealth to the family's founder. Everything appeared in jeopardy for the sons who had just been born.[10]

Such hardships were common throughout West Salem Village. Occasional bids by west villagers to marry into the wealthier eastern or town families seemed always to end in failure; either the western villager was absorbed into the richer family or his wife was incontestably disinherited. Further, the lack of good arable land combined with the arrival of new immigrants and the natural multiplication of old family members left the whole village, both east and west, in a hopeless dilemma. As the growing population in the west village began to strain their fixed resources, famine and poverty appeared certain, while the booming expansion of the townspeople seemed to provide only prosperity. Not only the laws of man but the laws of nature had conspired against the villagers.

Intrigue and manipulation ran constantly through the inner life of Salem Village during the ten years before the trials began. The villagers were constantly demanding greater autonomy. Ministers were lured into the village with promises of land and special payment (in one case negotiations stumbled over the amount of firewood to be provided) only to be turned out a year or so later.[11]

One of the worst blows to the Putnam family, and symbolically to the west village, came when second-generation Thomas remarried at age fifty-one and later willed his largest bequest to his late-born son, Joseph. Thomas's house, his furniture, his barns and farm equipment, and his most fertile land all went jointly to Joseph and his mother, while the balance of his estate was distributed among his earlier children. The elder two Putnam sons sued to break the will, charging darkly that their father's second wife had had an improper influence on the framing of the will. Some have speculated that she was indeed responsible for generating most of the hatred within the Putnam family. It certainly was because of her that villagers began talking about "wicked old women." What was worse, Israel Porter, of the rival Porter family, became the overseer of the Thomas Putnam estate until Joseph reached the age of eighteen, and Joseph married Israel's sixteen-year-old daughter, Elizabeth, when he turned twenty. A renegade Putnam at best, Joseph thus became the richest of them all, forsaking his allegiance to his family, to the west village, even to the church, and casting his lot with the family's traditional antagonists, the Porter merchants.[12]

Joseph Putnam was not oblivious to the good fortune that had drifted his way. He was already rich by the land he had inherited, but he was just as interested in power as were his uncles and brothers, who had held such sway over village life. Just as the fortunes of the other Putnams had come into doubt along with the village's own uncertain destiny, so dissident factions had begun to question their leadership. The constant debates in the village meetinghouse over ministerial appointments had provoked a generally tendentious atmosphere.

One result was that in 1691—only months before the first witchcraft accusations were made—a recall petition had been mounted against the village minister, Rev. Samuel Parris. The village became thoroughly polarized almost along east-west lines over the question of Parris's tenure, so much so that in October an entirely new set of members were elected to the local governing body, the village committee. Twenty-two-year-old Joseph Putnam led the new slate of committeemen (including two Porter in-laws) into office and undertook immediately to investigate charges that the parsonage had been fraudulently transferred to the minister a few years before. Amidst those bitter conditions began the Witchcraft Delusion in Salem.[13]

When the trials began in the spring of 1692, they were directed by Joseph Putnam's elder brothers, Thomas, Edward, John, and Nathaniel, who, as one contemporary historian wrote, "were the chief prosecutors in this business." Young Joseph found himself in the camp of the infidel, for as the year unfolded it would be the friends of the Porter family, their neighbors or the wives of their colleagues, who would be most often accused of witchcraft. And it would be the hard-pressed farmers from the west village who would point their damning fingers.

Explanations for the bizarre episode have ranged from the biophysical (a rare mold affecting the wheat from which bread was made, causing villagers to hallucinate as if on LSD trips) to psychiatric (the vicious persecution of noble dissenters by a sexually repressed clique of elders). More convincing is the analysis offered by historians Paul Boyer and Stephen Nissenbaum. They divided Salem Village into its two sections, east and west. Relying on surviving maps that showed the locations of almost all the village residents, they plotted the geography of accusers and accused. Overwhelmingly the accused witches and their defenders lived in the more prosperous eastern section of the village, while their accusers lived in the more barren west (and north). Their findings:

> There were fourteen accused witches who lived within the bounds of Salem Village. Twelve of these fourteen lived in the eastern section of the village.
>
> There were thirty-two adult villagers who testified against these accused witches. Only two of these lived in that eastern section. The other thirty lived on the western side. In other words, the alleged witches and those who accused them resided on opposite sides of the village.
>
> There were twenty-nine villagers who publicly showed their skepticism about the trials or came to the defense of

> one or more of the accused witches. Twenty-four of these lived in the eastern part of the village—the same side on which the witches lived—and only five of them in the west. Those who defended the witches were generally their neighbors, often their immediate neighbors. Those who accused them were not.[14]

Geography, as the fortunes of the Putnam and Porter families reveal, was a fine measure of wealth in Salem Village. Likewise, signers of the petitions for and against the Reverend Samuel Parris, who also tended to align themselves directly with the accusers and the defendants, were also divided according to location. Easterners opposed Parris forty-two to seven; westerners who supported Parris outnumbered his opponents thirty-six to eight. Landownership conformed to the same pattern. Prosperous eastern landowners opposed Parris, while the lands owned by Parris's supporters were almost all in the west and northwest. Salem tax records again showed the same pattern: "Of the twelve most prosperous men among the petition signers (those taxed more than twenty shillings) only four supported Parris, while eight opposed him. . . . At the other end of the scale, thirty-one of the poorer men of the Village (those taxed at under ten shillings) backed Parris, with only fifteen in opposition. In other words, the richest men in the Village opposed Parris by a margin of better than two to one, while the poorest supported him in almost precisely the same proportion." While the correlation may not be numerically exact, support for the witchcraft trials came overwhelmingly from the ranks of Reverend Samuel Parris's supporters, while the accused witches and the trial opponents were nearly all united against the minister.[15]

Not surprisingly, one of the first men charged with witchcraft was Philip English. Hardly anyone could have been a better object for the villagers' hatred. Born Phillips L'Anglais on the English isle of Guernsy, he had come to Salem as a child, married well and established himself as one of the richest men in the town. His holdings included: a wharf, more than twenty ships, a large town house and fourteen town lots. Urbane and worldly-wise, he had trading partners throughout the world. He was a man set apart from the mundane world of New England agriculture and cod fishing. And at the time of his indictment, he had just taken office as town selectman with Israel Porter and three Porter in-laws. As the summer wore on Philip English became but one of many rich and prominent New Englanders accused as agents of the devil.[16]

Through a variety of maneuvers, including a jailbreak probably engineered by his wealthy friends, English avoided trial, as did most of the upper-echelon New Englanders accused of witchcraft. Within the confines of Salem Village, however, the newly established merchants and storekeepers, as well as the so-called outsiders,* fared less well. Among those who did not escape the gallows were:

—Bridget Bishop, an unlicensed tavern keeper on Ipswich Road, the main thoroughfare dividing the village from the town. Charges had frequently been made that she slept with the men who drank her strong cider, that she disrupted decent family life by keeping the tavern open late into the night, thereby corrupting the village youth. She had come to the village after marrying Edward Bishop, her third husband, and she collected rent from her former home in Salem Town.

—John Proctor, a licensed tavern keeper just beyond the village boundary on Ipswich Road. He owned a large farm near the village and had several pieces of rental property in Ipswich, all of which brought him a handsome income and thrust him into the business life of both Salem Town and Boston.

—Reverend George Burroughs, a former village minister who had left under a cloud of conflict nine years earlier. A Harvard graduate from a family of wealth, he still owned considerable land in England and was at the time of his arrest minister of a church in Maine where he had served before coming to Salem. John Putnam, who had advanced Burroughs credit against his church salary, later sued him for the debt when the village refused to pay the salary.

—Rebecca Nurse, daughter of a modest Topsfield family. She had married a Salem Town artisan, Francis Nurse, whose fortunes had risen sharply when he bought a three-hundred acre farm near the town, some of which touched Putnam land and had been the source of an angry dispute with a Putnam brother. Francis Nurse later allied himself with the Porter family against the Putnams and the Reverend Samuel Parris in an attempt to save his economic position.

*Generally an outsider was anyone not born in the village, including spouses who had married into the village. Such outsiders frequently labored against great odds in colonial America.

—Sarah Good, a Watertown native and wife of Robert Prince, whose farm lay adjacent to John Putnam's, also faced the gallows but died in prison before her trial. After Prince's death, she had bought an Irish servant who first became her lover and then her second husband. Worse, she had then attempted to disinherit her earlier children, against the terms of Prince's will, in favor of the children by her second marriage—a move that struck at the heart of village social structure.[17]

But to conclude that the witch trials reflect nothing more than the culmination of a long class struggle between two sectors of the Salem gentry is to ignore the peculiar dynamics of Puritan social life. The villagers were not merely frustrated at their dwindling material fortunes, they were faced with the collapse of a dream: the failure of their mission to establish God's kingdom in the wilderness of America.

To the third generation of New Englanders, such a failure could mean only one thing: that God had turned away from them, had withdrawn his blessings, precisely because they had themselves permitted evil to enter their lives and pervert the new Eden that had been granted them. The final proof of their own failure lay in the fact that among the religious and intellectual leaders of England and Europe, America had dropped from sight. It had become little more than a valuable financial asset to England's vast imperial system. What had begun as a bold experiment in theocratic law—the idea of the covenant community—had been transformed by the end of the century into a tool of commercial law through the passage of the Navigation Acts.

English traveler Edward Ward recorded the effects of that transformation in his acerbic travelogue of 1699. Everywhere he found mean-minded, faithless, competitive tradesmen eager to take advantage of their neighbors. Avarice and alienation had replaced the heart of the covenant through which the first settlers had been bound together. "Bishops, Bailiffs, and Bastards, were the three terrible persecutions which chiefly drove our unhappy brethren to seek their Fortunes in our Foreign Colonies," Ward said. But in America, he found hypocritical ogres, their eyes popping with avarice, their pockets bursting with silver, their cloaks embroidered with the relics of the Lord.

"Many of the leading puritans may (without injustice) be thus characteris'd," he continued. "They are saints without religion, traders without honesty, christians without charity, magistrates without mercy, subjects without loyalty, neighbours without amity, faithless friends, implacable enemys, and rich men without money." The Puritan fathers took the brunt of Ward's broadside: "The inhabitants seem very Religious, showing many outward and visible signs of an inward and Spiritual Grace: But tho' they wear in their Faces the innocence of doves, you will find them in their dealings, as subtile as serpents. Interest is their faith, money their God, and large possessions the only Heaven they covet." And Ward concluded: "He that knows how to deal with their Traders, may deal with the Devil and fear not craft."[18]

What had become of grace and the covenant in Salem in 1692? So far as the Reverend Samuel Parris and his followers believed, the covenant was everywhere under attack. The "cement" of grace, as Thomas Shepherd had once described it, was everywhere disintegrating. John Cotton, perhaps the most notable of all the early ministers, had preached that such spiritual truth was fundamental to the survival of the *state* the Puritans were building. No distinction could exist between the church and state since the ideas of liberty and justice upon which the state was erected were derived directly from man's spiritual comprehension. To have pulled one from the other would have amounted to spiritual vivisection. As historian Perry Miller has written, Cotton believed that the possession of grace would lead men to live voluntarily according to the rules of truth and justice. "Bad men were criminals, whether their offense was theft or a belief in the 'inner light' and they should be punished."[19]

Crime in the Puritan world might just as likely be a violation of the spirit as of the body, for the social contract by which the Puritans lived was equally dependent upon both. So it was that in 1637, when Ann Hutchinson preached a doctrine of individual grace whereby each man and woman might find God alone outside the communal covenant, she was convicted as a criminal and banished. Roger Williams, the most famous of Puritan spiritual libertarians, suffered criminal sanction when he denied the ability of clay-footed human beings to rule in absolute perfection.

The Quakers possibly represented the most profound threat to human and spiritual solidarity, for their ideal of spiritual enlightenment, devoid of either liturgical rules or ministerial authority, was, in the context of the seventeenth century, almost anarchistic. Thus Quakers were hanged by their necks side by side with the most brutal of criminals. In each case the real threat posed by these religious dissenters was to the corporate unity of the Puritan community.

Living by what they preached, the Quakers quickly emerged as the most successful merchants and traders of the northern colonies. But it was, supposedly, for their heretical ideas, not their practical success, that they were hanged. The proof of such heresy, however, was precisely its practical consequence. To old-line Puritans, sin and success could be distinguished only with difficulty. Thus, the chances were that if the Quakers were so successful it was because they were aided by the devil, not God, Who is just—and hence supports equality. And so with Salem. If one sector was poor while the other prospered, it could only mean that God had removed Himself from the area. He had done so because of the graceless pursuit of money by some of its leaders. To bring Him back, Salem had to purge itself of those rich leaders.

And there lies the key to both the intensity of the Salem hysteria and its almost instantaneous reversal six months after the trials began. Since the villagers knew, through the logic of their faith, who their enemies were, is it any wonder that their "spectral visions" pointed to the oppressive trader leaders, even to the wife of Governor Phips and some of the most powerful families in Boston? It was precisely because the men of commerce—from the Porters in East Salem Village to the rum and slave traders of Boston—had taken control of the colony that Salem's remaining true Puritans had launched their attack. And for precisely the same reason, Governor Phips ordered the witch trials halted, the court disbanded, and a new court of his own choosing established to close the issue.

Within five years of the trials' end, its prosecutors had either thoroughly recanted their earlier position or disappeared. Thomas Putnam, Jr., Joseph's half-brother and chief antagonist, died in 1699, and his sons left the area permanently. Joseph Putnam lived another thirty years, grew even richer, and left behind him one of the great American families. Nineteen men and women lost their lives as witches, and their accusers lost their way of life altogether. The famous minister Cotton Mather, who advised the court during the trials but had avoided taking any strong public position, preached that it had all been a great delusion.

On February 12, 1702, Cotton Mather was forty years old. He was at the height of his intellectual and ministerial career, an aristocrat of the wilderness. Grandson of two original founders, Richard Mather and

John Cotton, he was as welcome in the governor's private chambers as he was in the crude pulpits of the hinterland. His father, Increase Mather, had personally selected the governor, Sir William Phips. Together with his father he ruled Boston's powerful Second Church. And yet Cotton Mather, the third-generation minister and perhaps the brightest, most imaginative member of his family line, found himself captive of a social order that was everywhere collapsing around him. For all his brilliance and social prominence, he failed either to understand the Salem trials or to impose his vision upon them. A variety of motivations had drawn him to the events at Salem. Occurring so near the end of the century, they exuded a certain millenarian aroma, and that alone was enough to tempt Mather's precocious mind. But there were other sources for Mather's interest.

In 1689, three years before the trials began, Mather had published his own treatise on witchcraft, *Memorable Providence, Relating to Witchcrafts and Possessions.* Filled with sinister descriptions of possessed souls, it is gothic theology at its grimmest, though it offers a surefire cure for the diabolical afflictions of witchcraft—exorcism by example. The book was a hit in Salem, but not in the way Mather had hoped. Overwhelmed by their own troubles, the Salemites saw the work not as a record of God's triumph over evil but as a diagnostician's handbook for spotting the devil's handiwork. Far from reassuring the beleaguered villagers, Mather's book only fanned the smoldering coals of hysteria.[20]

As the outcome of the trials proved more gruesome than he had ever dreamed, Mather found himself in a terrible dilemma. Although he and most New Englanders sincerely believed in the existence of witches, since crime was the tangible manifestation of evil and evil emanated directly from the powers of an absolutely real devil, nonetheless Mather did not support capital punishment for the accused witches. Rather he advanced his own "exorcism" of the four children in his book as the proper example to any community besieged by evil. By the true exercise of the covenant, by the powerful demonstration of grace among the members of the godly community, the community could rid itself of the evil scourge, and the poor souls who had been possessed would be freed of the demon. It was an idea not wholly unlike the reeducation centers for criminals proposed by certain modern utopian states. And it was an idea doomed to failure.

In what must have been a profound humiliation for the young Mather, his father, Increase, delivered the decisive sermon that stopped the trials. To a considerable degree the elder Mather was Governor Phips's personal Richelieu. Thus, when the witchcraft trials threatened to undermine the superstructure of the whole Bay Colony, it fell to him to solve the political and religious dilemma. Increase's reasoning was simple: (1) Although witches do exist and are creations of supernatural forces, they can only be tried by humans; (2) humans, even acting in a state of grace, are not divine and therefore make mistakes—as evidenced by the obvious error in calling the governor's wife a witch; (3) if mistakes can be made and human lives taken in error, then the accusers are in danger of committing a mortal sin and must be stopped. Or, as he wrote in a paper circulated to the governor and his advisers, "It were better that ten suspected witches should escape, than that one innocent person should be condemned." After that statement no witches were ever executed in the Bay Colony. There remained, however, the animus that had inspired the whole trouble, of unpious commercialism which had in fact been vindicated by the final resolution of the trials.[21]

Cotton Mather recalled the festering trouble, though not referring to the trials directly, ten years later:

> That there is a general defection in New England from primitive purity and piety in many respects is so plain as that it cannot be denied. . . . There are ministers who are not like their predecessors, not principled, nor spirited, as they were. . . . Of later times we have too much changed that which was our glory, not keeping the kingdom of God in the first place, not making religion but trade and land and earthly accommodations our interests.[22]

This analysis of provincial America could not have been more prescient.

Eighteenth-century America would be a land of commercial cities shaped around busy harbors. Its streets would be filled with lustful sailors, wanton women, sharp-eyed bankers, avaricious politicians, starving beggars, and common thieves. Its churches, which had once been so central to men's lives, would become weekend amusement places where the emotions of doubt, anxiety, and guilt could be brought out for occasional examination. America would become, from Mather's pessimistic perspective, an evil, Godless country, a country that had subconsciously discarded the covenants of mutual responsibility in favor of the opportunities of individual achievement—and where those who would not fit into the new scheme were left to find an existence outside the law. If Mather's prediction was doctrinaire, it was also prophetic. For by the end of Mather's life, America had entered a stage where crime was for the first time truly profitable.

Chapter 4

Pirates and Profiteers

No sooner had crime become profitable in America than it became organized. And no sooner did it become organized than it became a regular part of the American way of life, thanks to the cooperation and collusion of government officials. Organized crime did not begin with twentieth-century Prohibition. It began with the colonial pirates.

Though they traded with almost total impunity all along the Atlantic coast, America's pirates, originally ocean-borne mercenaries hired by the English throne to harass Spain, actually lived in the various coves and inlets that honeycombed North Carolina, Virginia, Maryland, Long Island, and the Bahamas. One of their most notable way stations, Accomac, lay just across Chesapeake Bay from Jamestown, the seat of Virginia's colonial government, which was hardly eager to undercut the only commerce that kept its people alive. But Accomac was only one of many such towns. The letters and reports of the colonial governors abound with complaints about such trading posts in Pennsylvania, Delaware, North Carolina, New York, and Rhode Island.[1]

Pirate lore reached its highest pitch in Virginia and the Carolinas but especially in Charleston. Preeminent among the southern towns, Charleston had quickly captured the West Indian trade in rum, sugar, molasses—and eventually slaves. Ambitious Englishmen as well as restless, or landless, traders from the mid-Atlantic colonies gravitated there, bringing a cosmopolitan if lusty ambience to the town.[2]

Charleston was bound to the West Indies by more than punch and profits. Separated from the northern settlements by hundreds of miles of barren coastline, Carolina was the most precarious of all the English colonies. To the west were the Indian tribes. To the south were the Spanish, who retained their desire for a grand empire in North America and hence kept the people of Charleston under constant fear of attack. By the 1680s their most reliable defenders were the pirates and privateers of the West Indies—an anomaly that finds its explanation in the original French and English colonial conquests a hundred years earlier.[3]

Since the late 1500s, Jamaica and Barbados had been the special preserve of freebooters and buccaneers commissioned privately by the English kings and queens to attack, burn, loot or otherwise decimate Spain's military and commercial ships. As one war bubbled over into the next, usually to Spain's detriment, there appeared entire fleets of privateers ranging the Baltic, the Mediterranean, the Barbary Coast and the Caribbean. Though protected by commission from their own king and therefore technically innocent of committing piracy, the privateers fought for themselves, free of any normal military control. Too far away and rugged for any effective government by either the English or French, the smaller Caribbean islands provided a natural base for these seaworthy mercenaries. Gradually through the decades, a loose nomadic population of mariners began to cover the islands. These self-styled "Brethren of the Coast," as the English privateers were sometimes called, held an almost fanatical hatred of Spain. Moreover, it was profitable hatred, for unlike the English, Spain's colonial enterprise was dedicated to the simple extraction of native wealth. Her ships were nearly always loaded with gold, silver, and precious ornaments, items vital to any fighters who must live off their plunder.[4]

In theory a privateer was commissioned only to seize enemy ships; seizure of neutral ships was piracy. That the privateer and his crew took their pay in plunder meant that the decision to seize a ship often depended upon opportunity, capability, and how desperate the crew was for supplies. Consequently the line between privateering and piracy was exceedingly fine and subject to change week by week. Among the hardiest of the lot were those called buccaneers, originally a mixture of English and French sailors who had settled on Tortuga and later Jamaica and who always seemed to be waging skirmishes with the Spanish authorities. Besides the bounty they could seize from Spanish ships, they added to their income by smuggling imports to the Spanish settlers in violation of restrictive colonial trade laws.

Contrary to the high-minded description of most colonial historians, the buccaneers were hardly groveling bands of vicious depraved men. Within their own ranks the standard of behavior tended to be both democratic and egalitarian. A direct account of the buccaneers' own rules comes from the diary of a young French surgeon, Alexander Exquemeling, who in 1668 signed on to a buccaneer ship as surgeon-barber. Wild drinking bouts and pistol play fill many pages of Exquemeling's diary. But he also described the councils formed by the crew and the rules they established jointly for life at sea:

> Having got possession of flesh sufficient for their voyage, they return to their ship. Here their allowance, twice a day to everyone, is as much as he can eat, without either weight or measure. Neither does the steward of the vessel give any greater proportion of flesh or anything else to the captain than to the meanest mariner. . . . They mention how much the captain ought to have for his ship. Next the salary of the carpenter, or shipwright, who careened, mended or rigged the vessel. . . . They stipulate in writing what recompense or reward each one ought to have, this is either wounded or mained in his body, suffering the loss of any limb, by that voyage. Thus they order for the loss of a right arm 600 pieces of eight or six slaves; for the loss of a left arm 500 pieces of eight, or five slaves; for an eye 100 pieces of eight, or one slave; for a finger of the hand the same reward as for an eye. . . . They observe among themselves very good order. For in the prizes they take it is severely prohibited to everyone to usurp anything in particular to themselves. Hence all they take is equally divided . . . . Yea, they make a common oath to each other not to abscond or conceal the least thing they find amongst the prey. If afterwards anyone is found unfaithful, who has contravened the said oath, immediately he is separated and turned out of the society.[5]

In all likelihood the buccaneers and other pirates of the Caribbean did not maintain their egalitarian relations perfectly. There is no record, from the young surgeon or elsewhere, of the kind of justice meted out to violators of the code. Indeed there were occasional accounts of pirate captains whose power was matched only by their caprice. The most notable example is that of the pirate Blackbeard, who in the middle of a card game blew out the candles, pulled his pistols and fired randomly beneath the table. Asked for an explanation by one crewman hit in the knee, he answered curtly that such displays were necessary occasionally to demonstrate who was in charge.[6]

Even flawed, the myth of brotherhood seems to have been a critical attraction for the men who became pirates. Cast against the social and political turmoil sweeping England in the late seventeenth century, the promise of such shipboard camaraderie doubtless offered a fine alternative to many a London laborer. For what inspired the strong young men to sail off to the pirate seas also led rebellious souls to fight for Oliver Cromwell's radical visions. The wild dreamers known as Diggers and Levellers, who sought to banish the king while twirling the English propertied establishment on its nose, were spiritual kinsmen to these adventurers. And of course these young men did not set out to be criminals; most pirates first went to sea as perfectly legitimate privateers.

In much of America, especially Charleston, there was no dire stigma attached to pirating and privateering. "For many years scarcely a month passed without seeing these licensed freebooters sail into Carolina, their vessels laden with the spoil of their latest expedition," one Carolina historian has written. "Not infrequently they would meet with rich prizes, ships of treasure and plate, and on coming into the colony would scatter their gold and silver about with so generous a hand that their appearance would soon come to be welcomed by the trading classes; and by means of their money they ingratiated themselves not only with the people, but with the highest officials of the government.[7]

Pirates were often simply regarded as gentlemanly outlaws. Their officers were regular guests in the city's finest homes, for it was the pirates who enabled the colonists to circumvent the English Trade and Navigation Acts. Enacted first under Cromwell's regime and later reaffirmed under the Restoration kings, the Navigation Acts forbade the colonists to buy or sell goods that had not been shipped through England and delivered on English boats. All the seaport town bristled under the restrictive laws, but the northern towns were too closely watched by the English governors to do much about them. Charleston, as the principal continental port for the Caribbean pirates and privateers, held a more advantageous position. The Charlestonians were able to buy their luxury items at prices far lower than the legal markets offered in Europe or the northern towns. Thus they graced their tables with the most elegant china and sterling, draped their windows in silk brocades, and otherwise created the veneer of sophistication—all through the services of a vast "underworld" fencing system.

For the captains, a privateer's commission could prove highly profitable. For the crew, the motive was twofold: brotherhood and profit. The adventurous English worker-turned-crewman would find his performance evaluated, for the most part, by a brotherhood of equals. And however improbable his dream of wealth, his chances were far better at sea than on the plantations of Virginia or in the slums of London.[8]

Officially, of course, Carolina authorities condemned piracy and its fruits. Strict laws were passed against trading with pirates, and as the pirates expanded their attacks against English ships, the king dispatched a regular stream of governors to crack down on them. None of the Royal emissaries achieved any real success, however, until the end of the century when the Carolinians themselves became prosperous enough, commercially and agriculturally, to produce their own exports, particularly rice. Then the tables began to turn, for the loss of sales to such a fragile community could soon have bankrupted the entire colony. Moreover, the development of exports increased the colonies' trade in general. More trade meant more ships, and more ships only heightened the pirates' appetite. Suddenly the shopkeepers, grain dealers, and bankers of colonial Charleston were no longer pleased with their former trading companions.

In the early 1700s, the West Indies—Barbados, the Bahamas, Jamaica, Tortuga, and Haiti—were teeming with freebooters, mercenaries, marooned sailors and countless unemployed fighters from the war England had just concluded with France. King William's War, the colonial name for Europe's War of the League of Ausburg, which lasted from 1688 to 1697, had mostly been fought along the colonies' northern frontiers. But it had greatly stimulated privateer and pirate activity along the Atlantic and Caribbean coasts, so much so that New York's governor, Lord Bellomont, solicited the support of Virginia in his attempt to impose the navigation laws. Virginia and Maryland were then at the edge of economic ruin, and the tight group of landholders who would eventually dominate Virginia's political and commercial life were determined to rid their busy bays and rivers of the pirate prey. "We are in a state of war with the pirates," Governor Nicholson of Virginia wrote to Lord Bellomont.[9]

In 1702, Queen Anne's War, known in Europe as the War of Spanish Succession, expanded into America. Spanish forces, usually aided by the French, repeatedly attacked Carolina settlers, while English troops tried to separate their opponents by raiding Spanish settlements in Florida. The war quickly eroded the Chesapeake colonies' tobacco and agricultural exports to England, and they were left teetering on the brink of bankruptcy. At the same time, Indians had begun to fight back against white expansion across the Blue Ridge and Great Smokey mountains, forcing the Carolinians and Virginians to use much of their military energy to crush them, in what became known as the Tuscarora War (1711–12). This effectively stopped the Carolinians and Virginians from dealing with the pirates.[10]

The Treaty of Utrecht ended Queen Anne's War in 1713. But it did not curtail the pirates. On the contrary, so bold had they become during the colonies' preoccupation with the war that they had proved a serious menace, controlling many of the shipping lanes used by the colonies. By 1718, when the pirate Blackbeard died, between fifteen hundred and two thousand pirates navigated these waters, sometimes sailing openly into Long Island Sound and the ports of Rhode Island. Understandably, it had become time for the colonies, especially Virginia, which most depended on exports and which had long coveted Carolina's land, to put an end to piracy once and for all—and occupy the pirates' sanctuaries in the process.

Alexander Spotswood, who became Virginia's governor in 1710, did not even wait for the end of the war to launch an attack on the pirate outposts. But the pirates were formidable. Among them, four of their leaders were especially courageous and colorful: Stede Bonnet, Captain Kidd, Anne Bonney, and Blackbeard. Within ten years, from 1710 to 1720, they rose to the peak of their power and wealth—and then fell to death and oblivion, sacrificed to the burgeoning commercial movement that was sweeping America.[11]

Major Stede Bonnet apparently became a pirate out of boredom. Until about 1715 he had spent his life as a rich respectable farmer who kept a large manor in Barbados. Then he shocked his equally respectable neighbors and took off "a-pirating." Charles Johnson, who in 1724 published the first encyclopedia of pirate lives and lore, believed Bonnet suffered "a Disorder in his Mind, which has been but too visible in him some time before this wicked Undertaking and which is said to have been occasioned by some Discomfort he found in a married State." Bonnet joined Blackbeard for a while, but old and inexperienced, he was soon double-crossed. He and his crew continued to prey upon the South Carolina coast alone and with considerable success until they were captured in a bloody fight led by English customs collectors. Sympathy was so widespread for Bonnet among Charlestonians, however, that he was allowed to escape before his final trial. He was eventually recaptured and executed.[12]

The saga of female pirate Anne Bonney suggests she too had friends in South Carolina. In the pamphlets and journals of the early eighteenth century, Anne Bonney and her sometime companion Mary Read took on heroic grandeur. "Bonnie," known best for her "fierce and courageous temper," was said to be the bastard daughter of an Irish lawyer who had sailed to Carolina. Banished from the household by her father for having secretly married a sailor (who in the midst of the scandal chose to disappear), Anne Bonney soon found her match in a wild and handsome pirate called Captain John ("Calico Jack") Rackam. Together they plundered the seas, she as eager as her mate to leap aboard each newly captured prize ship.[13]

Anne Bonney was not the only woman aboard Rackam's ship when they were caught under attack by an armed sloop of the Jamaican governor one October morning in 1720. Mary Read was also a full member of the crew. Her zeal was said to be exceeded only by her skill. As the Jamaican warship drew up against Rackam's sloop, the king's men leapt aboard, gaining an early advantage. But while Calico Jack and his men fell back below deck, Anne Bonney and Mary Read stood their ground, bare-breasted, their swords and cutlasses flashing through the air.[14]

Cowardice has no place in the stories of these two women. Captured alive and brought to trial, Bonney begged mercy on the grounds of pregnancy—and was spared. But her lover, the dashing Calico Jack, won no such mercy. Shortly before his hanging, the two were permitted a final meeting, where, according to Johnson, she wasted no time weeping but declared "she was sorry to see him there, but if he had fought like a Man, he need not have been hang'd like a Dog."[15]

Apparently the same court would have granted clemency to Mary Read as well had her own iron will not been revealed in a statement regarded as too brazen for forgiveness. Once, the court was told, Rackam had asked her why such a fine attractive woman could want to risk death and danger among pirates. Her fateful response: "as to hanging, she thought it no great Hardship, for, were it not for that, every cowardly Fellow would turn Pyrate and so infest the Seas, that Men of Courage must starve." Read was convicted of piracy and would have hanged with the rest had she not contracted a "fatal fever" and died in prison.[16]

Had the burghers of Charleston retained their loyalties to their old pirate friends, Edward Teach might have retired to some manorial estate on the delta, planted rice and harvested indigo, and have contributed his name to one of the grand genealogies of the aristocratic South. Instead his head, one November morning in 1718, was chopped off, and he is remembered as Blackbeard, the most notorious pirate in American history.

Blackbeard was a promoter in the grand style—mostly of himself. Improbable tales of his brutality, his wiliness, his charm, even of his birth and his dozen or more wives were repeated up and down the entire coast. He cultivated mystery and fostered a reputation for volcanic unpredictability. For he knew his ability to survive depended mostly upon his capacity to entertain, to draw out the venal interests of an ambitious and insecure population, huddled along the shores of England's least successful colony. In 1699, in order to crush piracy, the king had allowed the colonies to establish their own admiralty courts for the prosecution of pirates and other violators of the Navigation Acts. Blackbeard then decided that as long as his wild and romantic reputation preceded him, he would always find colonial allies susceptible to his charms, people whose greed so exceeded their social position that they were willing to gamble on the quick profits of the pirate's traffic.

Taller than most men of his time, he wore a great, curly, black beard which, according to one account, "like a frightful meteor, covering his whole face, frightened America more than any comet that has appeared there a long time." Under his broad leather hat, his beard, festooned with bright colored ribbons, tumbled to his waist. He kept pistols strapped to his shoulders. On occasion he achieved novel nighttime effects by attaching small lighted wicks to his hat just above his ears so that his eyes flickered in the shadow of his beard.[17]

Teach's first definitive appearance was in the Bahamas beneath a hill just east of the site that is now downtown Nassau. If the fragmentary accounts are to be believed, he maintained an invincible position aided by a great watchtower at the top of the hill from which he could survey the entire expanse of the Bahamian waters. Just as well could he maintain careful watch of the pirate denizens who swarmed about the island. "Occasionally Blackbeard would descend the tower steps and the steep, narrow trail to the pathway below, where he and some of his favorites from among the crew had set up a few tents. There, under a huge tree, he held court—trading loot, interviewing volunteers for his next cruise, planning its itinerary, and drinking more rum," according to one historian of colonial piracy.[18]

He appeared off Charleston in June 1718 with a French merchant ship he had named *Queen Anne's Revenge,* loaded with four hundred men and forty cannons, and a fleet of three lesser sloops. Within a week he had stopped at least eight outbound ships, seized what cargo he wanted, and taken several prominent Charlestonians hostage. One of them was province council member Samuel Wragg.

Blackbeard then dispatched one of his deputies to town to bring back needed medicines. Upon delivery, all hostages would be released, he said. After two days passed, Blackbeard threatened to slaughter the hostages. He relented when he learned his deputy's sloop had capsized in a squall. When the deputy did finally land in Charleston, panic swept the town. Angry citizens were itching to attack Blackbeard's fleet with sailboats and lynch the pirate's deputy. But the council and the governor, backed against the wall, quickly acceded and sent Blackbeard a cache of medicines worth between three and four hundred English pounds. Before releasing his hostages, Blackbeard stripped them to the waist, relieving council member Wragg personally of the equivalent of $6,000 in cash.[19]

The pirates had a short voyage as they sailed out of Charleston harbor. For Blackbeard's new base had become Ocracoke Inlet, near the mouth of the Pamlico River in North Carolina. He had come to North Carolina a few years earlier in the wake of a new British campaign against West Indian pirates. Devoid of much commerce or many people, the North Carolinians responded as had the people of Charleston in the 1680s. The pirates were friendly, and they brought in as much trade and fun as could be found in most of the colony. They had established thoroughly cordial relations with Charles Eden, North Carolina's governor. Six months before their Charleston raid, Blackbeard and his crew had surrendered to Eden under terms of a pirate amnesty proclamation offered by George I. Having settled along the coast in apparent legitimacy, the crew had waited until spring before getting local merchants to outfit the ships for their new exploits.[20]

After the Charleston raid, Blackbeard disbanded his company, keeping one sloop, which he called the *Revenge,* and only his most trusted men. He promised Governor Eden he would carry out only honest trading missions. But the summer had hardly ended when he returned from one such mission, a French merchant sloop in tow. He had "found the French ship at sea without a soul on board her," he reported to Governor Eden on September 24, adding that since it was such a leaky vessel it should be towed back to sea and burned to avoid any hazard to the harbor. Eden, egged on by his secretary and customs chief, Tobias Knight, agreed. Knight, who happened to be the judge of the vice-admiralty court responsible for certifying the ship abandoned, quickly convened the court and issued judgment in favor of the reformed pirate.[21]

Blackbeard of course kept the bulk of the "abandoned" ship's cargo. Sixty hogsheads of sugar, however, were delivered to Governor Eden, while twenty more, ostensibly a customs tax, were taken to Secretary Knight's personal barn. This led some North Carolinians to doubt Blackbeard's claim that he had found the ship abandoned. Before long the tale of the extraordinary episode reached Governor Spotswood's chambers in Virginia and went on to Philadelphia where that colony's angry governor issued a warrant against Teach for past depredations. Some have argued that Teach then entered his long-deferred dream of respectable "semiretirement" hobnobbing with the gentry of Ocracoke.[22]

Regardless of Blackbeard's own intentions, Alexander Spotswood was hardly ready to rest quietly on the James and miss a fine opportunity. Instead, he launched his mission against Blackbeard with care. First he had Blackbeard's former quartermaster, William Howard, arrested on the harbor docks on trumped-up charges: The governor's agents confiscated £150 from Howard, then indicted him for vagrancy.

Spotswood prevailed against adamant protests from Howard's lawyer, who was a former Speaker in the House of Burgesses and mayor of Williamsburg. Howard was then compelled at his trial to testify against Blackbeard and assist the Virginians in identifying his Ocracoke hideout.

Autumn 1718 was half over by the end of Howard's trial, and Spotswood moved fast. He appealed to the British naval commander for help in mounting an expedition, but was rebuffed. Under a blanket of total secrecy, Spotswood then solicited Captains George Gordon and Ellis Brand to lead the mission, financed privately from the governor's personal account. Only certain selected members of the governor's council were informed.

On November 13 Spotswood asked the House of Burgesses to offer a special reward for Blackbeard's capture, charging that information taken at William Howard's trial indicated the pirate was planning new revenge against the Virginians. Providing no explanation, Spotswood insisted the legislation be approved immediately. On November 24, after the bill had been rushed past the Burgesses with almost no debate, Spotswood signed into law a proclamation offering £100 reward for the capture of Blackbeard and his crew.[23]

But Blackbeard had been killed by Captain Brand's men two days earlier. Brand himself was not in command of the final assault. Instead he had led an expedition overland to Governor Eden's home at Plum Point, across Bath Creek from Blackbeard's home. Brand left his ship, the *Pearl,* under command of his lieutenant, Robert Maynard. A second sloop, commanded by Captain George Gordon, accompanied Maynard. Maynard slipped into Ocracoke Inlet at sunset on Thursday, November 21, waiting for the high tides of morning to ease him over the unmarked shoals. Just before dawn Friday he hoisted anchor. Several men were dispatched in rowboats to trace a route through the shoals. As soon as the scouts were spotted, Blackbeard fired warning shots and they retreated to the *Pearl.* Blackbeard's final battle was under way, and he chose to stand rather than retreat through the scores of obscure channels upstream.

Blackbeard grabbed a flask of liquor, so the story was told, and announced to all of Maynard's men: "Damnation seize my soul if I give you quarter or take any from you!" He cut cable and maneuvered his ship beyond a submerged sandbar upon which Maynard quickly ran aground.[24]

As Maynard's ship slid free from the sandbar and he began to close in, Blackbeard unleashed a barrage of crude grenades made of bottles filled with powder and small pieces of jagged lead and iron. But Maynard moved the *Pearl* alongside the *Revenge,* keeping his men below deck, safe from the grenades.

The pirates stormed aboard Maynard's ship, its decks slippery with the blood of twenty sailors killed by Blackbeard's earlier broadside. Blackbeard led the assault, flailing his cutlass about his head like a great razored windmill until he came face to face with Maynard.

Each man fired his pistol. Though he was hit, Blackbeard was not stopped, and the two drew their swords, Blackbeard still swinging his cutlass. It snapped Maynard's sword just below the hilt and would have cut him down when one of Maynard's men struck Blackbeard "a terrific wound in the neck and throat." Blackbeard flung his cutlass a final time, then stumbled, before several of Maynard's men closed in on him with their swords. Within minutes the other pirates surrendered, and Blackbeard's head was chopped from his body and mounted on a spike on the bow of the *Pearl.*

By battle's end, Blackbeard and nine of his men lay dead. Twenty-nine of Spotswood's expeditionary force were killed or wounded. The surviving pirates were transported back to Virginia and tried on March 12, 1719. Fourteen of the fifteen prisoners were convicted and hanged, one having persuaded the court he had only come aboard ship for a party the previous night. The seized booty sold at auction for £2,238.[25]

Evidence produced at the trial so implicated Customs Chief Tobias Knight that he too was later indicted by the North Carolina provincial council. The most damning evidence against Knight was a letter found on the *Revenge* dated November 19, addressed to Teach:

> My friend,
>
> If this finds you yet in harbor I would have you make the best of your way up as soon as possible your affairs will let you. I have something more to say to you than at present I can write; the bearer will tell you the end of our Indian war, and Ganet can tell you in part what I have to say to you, so referr you in some measure to him.
>
> I really think these three men are heartily sorry at their difference with you and will be very willing to ask your pardon; if I may advise, be friends again, it's better than falling out among your selves.

I expect the Governor this night or tomorrow, who I believe would be likewise glad to see you before you go, I have not time to add save my hearty respects to you, and am your real friend.

And servant
T. Knight

Knight was acquitted by the council of all charges, in part because the key witnesses against him were four black slaves, and testimony by blacks was never admitted into court in any of the southern colonies. Knight also argued that he had written the letter to Blackbeard on explicit instructions from Governor Eden. A member of the famed aristocratic English family from which British prime minister Sir Anthony Eden descended, Eden was already ill and died within a few months.[26]

Outside North Carolina Alexander Spotswood was lionized for having eliminated the colonies' most fearsome brigand. The North Carolinians, however, harbored more than passing resentment for his invasion of their territory, for the embarrassment he caused them, and for his refusal to recognize their legal jurisdiction after the pirates had been captured. There were also other, more profound, reasons for their antagonism toward the Virginia governor.

Before Spotswood was appointed governor (technically he was lieutenant governor as a stand-in for the English earl of Orkney), he had been a colonel in the army and acquired vast land holdings. North Carolinians complained that he had been continuously prejudiced against their province since its formal separation from South Carolina in 1712. He had discouraged adventurers and new arrivals from settling there, they said, largely because he sought to profit from the sale or lease of his own large wilderness tracts on the Virginia frontier.

Some historians partial to the Carolina viewpoint have explained Spotswood's eagerness to embarrass Governor Eden as part of a grand design to annex the colony to Virginia. If so, he obviously failed. Nonetheless by the end of his term as governor, Spotswood had accumulated more than eighty-five thousand acres in Spotsylvania County alone, much of it covered by seven-year tax exemptions from the date of transfer. He had secretly granted himself much of this land by putting it in the name of friends with whom he had special transfer agreements.[27]

If Spotswood gloated over Blackbeard's death, other powerful men wept—among them several New York and Long Island import brokers whose involvement with the pirates stretched back over an entire generation to the 1690s. Taking advantage of a corrupt colonial administration, these importers had become virtual partners with the pirates in massive smuggling schemes aimed at subverting the trade and customs laws.

The one who did most to create this corrupt administration was Benjamin Fletcher, governor of New York between 1692 and 1698. Fletcher was a man caught in a hopeless web of contradiction. Today, few standard historians ever mention him by name, or if they do, it is to note only parenthetically that he was the most corrupt governor in colonial history. Yet Fletcher did little that might not have fallen under the mantle of patriotism half a century later.

Governor Fletcher was quite simply the leading commercial courtesan for the pirate trade of the North Atlantic coast. He liked most of the pirates who visited New York. He found them clever, amusing, and worldly. They were expert sailors whose skills, and confidence in their own skills, easily distinguished them from the plodding preachers and bureaucrats of the colonial council. They were also well liked by the rising class of merchants and import brokers who were the governor's most loyal backers.[28]

Fletcher had been named governor in 1692 in the wake of a failed rebellion led by a New York shopkeeper named Jacob Leisler. A German immigrant who bitterly resented his static position in a social structure that blocked the rising middle class from political power, Leisler was not a democrat. But, as a captain in the citizen militia, he successfully led his troops into deposing the royal deputy, and afterwards he did call for a constituent assembly. Defeated by Loyalist forces, Leisler was hanged on March 30, 1691, before Fletcher became governor. Fletcher decided to wipe out whatever remained of Leisler's movement by rigging three consecutive elections for the New York Assembly. In the election of 1695, he even forced voters to cast their ballots orally in front of soldiers and sheriffs, who pistol whipped anyone who dared vote against his candidates.[29]

Once securely backed by a rubber-stamp assembly, Fletcher proceeded to develop New York as the colony's foremost trading center, for the benefit of its dominant class and, of course, himself. He realized New York would have to create an independent world of commerce, unhampered by such obstacles as the king's Navigation Acts. Fletcher encouraged the pirates and the colonial merchants to sidestep these laws, and built up his own power with the latter's support. His principal mistake was to expect that these upstart capitalists would continue to back him in his hour of need.

The charges that eventually drove Fletcher from office in 1698 were devastating: He had given protection to notorious pirates in exchange for payoffs; he had jailed his political opponents; he had armed various rogues and nonuniformed soldiers with clubs and sent them to the voting polls to intimidate dissident voters; he had offended friendly Indians; he had made huge land grants, totaling over two thousand square miles, to his friends and political cronies.[30]

While Leisler and his men had reacted spontaneously out of growing frustration with the old brazen colonial regime, Fletcher's rule fomented real polarization. He frequently alluded to his close connections at Whitehall, London, implying that he could easily open doors to new trade for those who would support him. He went out of his way to characterize the Leislerians as anarchic rogues and radicals who had no respect for law or commerce and who could not be trusted with political power. In that way he eagerly sought to ingratiate himself with the tiny elite of manorial gentry, while simultaneously cementing his alliance with the fast-rising businessmen of the coast. Thus, as historian Herbert Osgood put it, "the official, merchant and landed aristocracy of New York was again in the saddle."[31]

Fletcher made a point of displaying his taste for spectacle from the very beginning of his rule, employing a coach and six horses for his inauguration—"a pomp this place had never seen in any Governor." Fanfare and splendor were frequently his response to local crises. When Iroquois tribal leaders asked for supplies and men in their loyal battles against the French, Fletcher pleaded poverty. Responding later to charges that he had treated the Indians poorly, Fletcher answered without a trace of embarrassment:

> I have been at great pains to gain the hearts of the Heathen . . . I have taken their Chief Sachims to my table; some of the principal leading men of the Five nations came down the River to pay me a visit, whom I treated with all manner of kindness and Courtesy. I ordered them on board the greatest ships we have and guns to be fired, the King's birthday happening in that time. . . . I ordered six horses to

> be put into my coach and coachmen to drive them around the City and into the country to take the air, by which they were extremely obliged, and dismissed them with considerable presents, at which they did express great satisfaction.[32]

In his acceptance of gifts and favors, Fletcher was equally nonchalant. It had been custom in the colony for the assembly to assess a onetime tax of a penny per pound against estate owners for the newly arrived governors. Such pennies were niggardly sums, Fletcher informed the assembly, adding as one of his first statements that he would throw the estate owners in jail if they would not pay him more. "He takes a particular delight," wrote one of his opponents, "in having presents made to him, declaring he looks upon them as marks of their esteem of him, and he keeps a catalogue of persons who show that good manners as men most worthy of his favor. This knack has found employment for our silversmiths and furnished his Excellency with more plate (besides variety of other things) than all our former Governors ever received."[33]

Gift-taking was minor compared to the charge, later corroborated in court, that Governor Fletcher encouraged trafficking by pirates:

> His Excellency gives all due encouragement to these men, because they make all due acknowledgements to him; one Coats a captain of this honorable order presented his Excellency with his ship, which his Excellency sold for £800 and every one of the crew made him a suitable present of Arabian Gold for his protection; one Capt. Twoo who is gone to the Red Sea upon the same errand was before his departure highly caressed by his Excellency in his coach and six horses and presented with a gold watch to engage him to make New York his port at his return. Twoo retaliated the kindness with a present of jewells.[34]

The evidence against Fletcher was damning. Pirate Coates, for example, testified directly that he had been forced to pay Fletcher £1,300 protection money. But Fletcher seemed nonplussed and eagerly explained his behavior with imaginative tales, especially when talking about Captain Tew (Twoo), who was as notorious a pirate as Blackbeard.

"This Tew appeared to me," Fletcher said, "not only a man of courage and activity, but of the greatest sense and remembrance of what he had seen, of any seaman I had met. He was also what they call a very pleasant man; so that at some times when the labours of the day were over it was some divertisment as well as information to me to hear him talke. I wished in my mind to make him a sober man, and in particular to reclaime from him a vile habit of swearing."[35]

Meanwhile, frontier forts had fallen into disrepair. Soldiers constantly deserted from the militia because of the low pay, yet Fletcher had never failed to deduct a half penny per day from each soldier's pay. He had even inflated the payroll figures to show four hundred men on the muster rolls when at times there were hardly half that many. When these collections were added to the pirate payoffs, Fletcher's total profit became impressively large; Coates, Tew, and a certain Hoare alone paid him £6,000 for his "commissions." The assembly of 1694 had asked Fletcher for an account of the three previous years' appropriations, revenues amounting to about £40,000. The governor refused, admonishing them that theirs was to appropriate, his was to spend.[36]

The hearings against Fletcher continued at Whitehall until late 1697. Richard Coote, the earl of Bellomont, who eventually replaced Fletcher in 1698, had been given free rein two years earlier to suppress pirate traffic in the northern colonies. Bellomont's reports, combined with local testimony drawn mostly from the old Leislerian faction, finally became overwhelming and Fletcher was replaced.

Not six months after his arrival, Lord Bellomont found himself surrounded by corruption and iniquity. In September 1698, the New York Board of Trade reported, "we can not but with his Lordship conclude the great corruption of the whole body of that people, both officers and traders." They and Bellomont determined that from 1687 to 1697 the Royal revenues from customs and duties had actually decreased despite immense expansion of trade.[37]

In June 1698, Bellomont failed to secure approval from his council on an order requiring four suspected pirate ships to post security before departing for Madagascar, an infamous pirate hangout. As it turned out, at least one council member, Frederick Phillips, had warned the pirates not to sail into the harbor but to drop anchor off Delaware where he would sail out to bring in the booty on his own craft. When Bellomont did carry off successful seizures of booty and imports, he found few witnesses willing to testify in court. At one trial some twenty-two merchants conspired to block incriminating testimony, and shortly afterward, the customs agent resigned rather than effect the seizure ordered by Bellomont.[38]

Frustrated at every turn, Bellomont wrote his London superiors in July 1699 of his despair:

> Arabian Gold is in great supply [in New York], and indeed till there be a good judge or two and an honest active Attorney General to prosecute for the King, all my labor to suppress piracy will signify even just nothing. The people there are so impudent in abetting and sheltering pirates and their goods, that without such assistance as I have now proposed, I can never expect to check that vile practice of theirs.[39]

Lord Bellomont never succeeded in crushing the violators of the Navigation Acts. Eventually the same commercial instincts that lay at the root of the illegal trade became a battle cry of the American Revolution. At best Bellomont helped stop northern piracy. Some of his gambits, however, failed miserably—notably his employment of Captain William Kidd in 1695 on a privateer's commission to suppress the pirates. Two years later, having spent some £6,000 paid him by Bellomont, the famed Captain Kidd was convicted and hanged for having himself become a "notorious" pirate.[40]

Severe pressure was applied to colonial administrations in Delaware, New Jersey, and Rhode Island, where piracy had been a major problem to the English. Even in godly, pacifist Pennsylvania, certain colonial governors developed rather comfortable relations with the pirates. William Penn, by that time rather antiquated but ever mindful of his own interests, wrote to the English authorities in 1700 that he should not be forgotten in disposal of booty seized from the scurrilous pirates: "I confess I think my interest in these cases ought not wholly to be overlooked, who as Lord of the Soil, erected into a Seigneury, must needs have a royalty, and share in such seizures, else I am in much meaner circumstances than many Lords of Manors upon the seacoasts of England, Ireland and Scotland." Penn merely wanted his cut, now that the dreaded pirates had been liquidated.[41]

Piracy drew slowly to an end as the new century began. English determination to stop it had simply made the price too high; only a few colorful figures in the weaker southern colonies hung on. Within another generation they too would disappear. Naval power, however, could never have crushed the pirate fleets had the colonies themselves not entered a new era. By the eighteenth century, the coasts were no longer harsh frontiers.

Colonial America had become commercial America. Some of her industries, especially shipbuilding, rivaled England's. And crewmen on American ships were better paid than they were in England. Simple piracy—the outright seizure of commercial vessels—had become a blight against the colonists as well as the king. Smuggling was another matter, however. One might even presume the furious industry in small shipcraft construction bore a special relation to the proliferation of coastal smugglers.[42]

The deeper Lord Bellomont probed into the commercial corruption of New York, the more he began to discover that piracy was not his toughest problem:

> There is a great trade between Boston and Newfoundland and I have been told there is a constant trade between St. Sebastian and Newfoundland and that there is great store of French and Spanish wines and Spanish iron in Newfoundland. If the merchants of Boston be minded to run their goods, there's nothing to hinder them. . . . 'Tis a common thing as I have heard to unload their ships at Cape Ann and bring their goods to Boston in wooden boats.[43]

The new century was transforming pirates into patriots—and smuggling into free trade.

To say that piracy brought prosperity to North America would be facile and untrue. Nothing could have kept the lid on the whistling engine of colonial commerce once the throttle began to be opened in the late 1600s. But prosperity could not have come so rapidly or so fully without the pirate heritage.

The pirates, it is clear, were the racketeers of their day. Bribing officials, corrupting entire governments, stealing and looting to maintain a vast underworld market in forbidden goods, they held the monopoly on "big crime" during the first century of English and Spanish settlement. Today the crime syndicates offer everything from prime Colombian marijuana to bargain-priced Japanese color televisions, all free from expensive sales tax. Three hundred years ago, Charlestonians or New Yorkers bought their Madeira wines and sterling silver sets from the naval forerunners of the modern syndicates, all free from expensive customs duties.

By the end of the century, the pirate captains and crews had been organized into a coherent system of trade running the length of the Atlantic seaboard. No longer were they the free-roaming brethren of the coast who thrived on adventure, camaraderie, and plunder. They had become integrated into the system of international trade. Crime and business, crime and government, crime and freedom, had become inseparably linked.

Chapter 5

Counterfeiters and Regulators

English America in 1700 was a disjointed assemblage of farms, villages, and seaports that were only just beginning to fuse into a contradictory but dynamic society of entrepreneurs, husbandmen, and adventurers that resisted the provincial authorities' attempts to maintain social stability. Religious heretics of every color taunted the Puritan and Anglican elders. Farmers fought port merchants. Town councils jousted with the king's governors. Once friendly Indians were in a near permanent state of war against the whites. Servants and slaves were talking back to their masters. Colonial businessmen no longer viewed their interests as compatible with those of their sponsors back in London. And everywhere within these social divisions enough men and women felt alienated from the idealistic dreams of their grandparents that overt, conscious violation of the laws became, as historian Carl Bridenbaugh put it, "attractive in America for the first time."[1]

Part of the alienation, among ordinary people at least, was caused by the fact that by 1700 it had become clear that it was only the planters and merchants, and their political allies and representatives, who really profited from the system. Their disproportionate wealth, in a land where farmers and workers still had to put in sixteen-hour stints just to eke out a subsistence living, left no doubt in the popular mind that

America was neither Winthrop's "citty upon a Hill" nor Cotton Mather's New Eden, but rather a harsh, hypocritical, venal colony. Tax laws were unfair. Officials were arbitrary and contemptuous. Governors and city merchants were corrupt—Fletcher's scandalous activities were well publicized but represented only one of many such cases—and no one, it seemed, felt any sympathy for the plight of the poor. Thus, more and more they began to steal.

The more the poor stole in response to the colony's immoral treatment of them, the more they were blamed for the colony's immorality. For example, Sameul Sewell, Boston's preeminent jurist and a minor figure in the Salem witchcraft trials, deplored the rise of these "disorderly poor" who had flooded the city in the wake of the European wars, and accused them of the massive rise in petty robberies between 1704 and 1707. The items most often stolen were fine linen, silk, silverware, jewels—items that could be sold fast for cash and that had begun to pour into the city only after the merchants, import brokers, public officials and pirate-smugglers had reached their accord.

The city continued to suffer waves of theft after that, especially in 1712 and 1715. Town constables were stymied by the problem, so much so that the principal crime-fighting forces became the neighborhood committees set up by Cotton Mather. The Society for the Suppression of Disorders had three branches by 1703, but chiefly it kept watch over public morals—which meant sex, swearing, drinking, and public brawls. It did so mostly by collecting dossiers on "immoral people" who frequented "wicked houses." Thus began the long tradition of American rulers spying on American citizens.[2]

Compared to Philadelphia, Boston's petty crime remained fairly insignificant until the last years before the Revolution when thieves, muggers, and counterfeiters seemed to sweep the city. Philadelphia, however, was the crime capital of the colonies throughout the first thirty years of the 1700s. Why crime should have flourished so quickly at the site of William Penn's "holy experiment," the so-called inward colony of the Quakers, remains one of the paradoxes of Pennsylvania history. One facile analysis blames the Quakers' traditional permissiveness toward victimless crimes. A likelier explanation may be their general tolerance of their own greed and acquisitions, as well as of antagonistic political, religious, and social ideas.[3]

Because Pennsylvania and its "city of brotherly love" were well known all over Europe and America as territory free of political persecution, all kinds of people who had not the least interest in Quaker utopias settled there. The policy of toleration enabled entire towns to be built that were not populated by Quakers at all. In Philadelphia the nonreflective, possessive tendency of Quakerism soon became dominant. Since in England and in the other colonies Quakers had usually been poor and outcast, they had survived much like the Jews of the Diaspora—by becoming the cleverest traders and merchants around.

The wealthy Quakers who settled in Philadelphia came mostly from the New England colonies where they had been reviled for their efficient, sharp-eyed trading practices. Not too surprisingly, these "Quaker grandees" brought to Pennsylvania the sort of fierce competitive spirit that strained sharply against the ideals of the contemplative Friends. While the English Quakers were mostly poor laborers, artisans, and small farmers, the rich port merchant Quakers from New England traded with the pirates and promoted the smuggling traffic in plunder and stolen goods. Scrambling all these factors and tendencies together into a single city, Philadelphia emerged as something of an economic free-for-all, a booming cosmopolitan seaport where anyone with money could buy most anything, no questions asked. Before long it was the largest city on the continent, hardly the idyllic, pacifist utopia envisioned by Penn.[4]

Though greedy and acquisitive himself, William Penn was profoundly distraught over the degeneration of his colony, declaring in 1697 that Philadelphia had become the most vile, wicked city he knew, a place where deeds "so very Scandalous [were] openly committed in defiance of Law and Virtue: facts so foul, I am forbid by common modesty to relate them." By 1701 the schedule of benign criminal laws under which the colony had operated was therefore replaced by the stiffest criminal code in America. Mild prosecutions for drunkenness, petty theft, and violations of public decorum and authority were replaced by heavy charges against "burglary, highway robbery, petit treasons, rape, homicide, infanticide, and murder." In 1718, these general crimes having grown more frequent, Lieutenant Governor William Keith directed the assembly to adopt the same severe punishments as were standard in England. The Quaker dream of a peaceful society with fundamentally new ideas of law and justice had failed. To make a point of his determination, Keith refused to consider a pardon for one of the first violators condemned to die for burglary under the new law. Convict Ann Husen's "crime was a growing evil in the city of Philadelphia," he said, adding that she must be made "a proper example of the force of the law."[5]

Crime statistics for Pennsylvania paint an especially harsh picture. Having divided the colonial era into three periods, one historian found that in the first thirty-two years, from 1683 to 1715, only three serious cases came before the provincial council. One drew a fine and the two other cases were dropped. In the second period, from 1715 to 1745, twenty-four people were condemned to die on charges that included arson, burglary, counterfeiting, murder, and treason. One woman convicted of treason was drawn, then set afire. For the final period, between 1745 and 1775, 112 were sentenced to die and 66 were actually executed.[6]

New Yorkers were equally aggravated by deepening crime troubles in the mid-1700s. The city had gone through a dramatic population explosion and in the process had developed a rich ethnic diversity. Blacks, both free and slave, had moved in and developed their own community. The Dutch and Germans had their own distinct neighborhoods. And the harbor kept a steady flow of strangers roaming the streets. The most secular of all the colonial cities, New York had to confront sharp increases in the volume of crime, could draw on none of the religious tradition that the Boston and Philadelphia authorities used to assert their legitimacy. Year after year the mayor, the prosecutors, and the police waged a losing battle against the proliferation of crime and criminals until by the 1750s "law enforcement had virtually collapsed."[7]

Throughout the 1700s in New York City, the most frequent crime was theft, while in the upstate counties the primary offense was public disorder. In both the city and the country violence and personal assault accounted for about a fifth of all crimes. Confounded by the increase of crime in all categories, the judges turned to the easy solution of imposing ever harsher penalties. One historian has found that before 1750, most thieves—70.9 percent—were whipped, while fewer than 10 percent were executed. After 1750, executions rose sharply to more than 22 percent, and brandings were ordered almost 30 percent of the time. Whippings dropped to about 25 percent of the sentences.[8]

Such crimes produced hot copy for the fledgling colonial press, which appeared ironically just at the time that crime became a serious public issue. Boston, Newport, New York, Philadelphia, and Charleston all had newspapers founded between 1719 and 1733, when real gangs first emerged. By the mid-1740s, Philadelphia and New York papers regularly gave top billing to crime stories. "It seems to have now become dangerous for the good People of this City, to be out late at nights without being sufficiently strong or well armed, as several attacks and disturbances have been lately made in our streets," wrote one New York commentator. Iniquitous Philadelphia was frequently cited as the corruptor of moral New York; gangs were reported to have ridden the stage all the way from Philadelphia so they might inflict gross villanies on New Yorkers.[9]

So intractable was one "loose and profligate wretch" from Philadelphia, Mary Anderson, that she was whipped thirty-nine lashes in a Manhattan public square. "She afforded some diversion while at the Post to the mob," one paper reported, "as she was very obstinate and resisting, causing several to try the sharpness of her teeth, others to feel the weight of her hands, a third got kick'd by her." Philadelphians themselves complained loudly about their city, particularly during the French and Indian War. One reporter wrote in February 1758: "Thefts and petty robberies are now become so common in and about this city, that no less than eight persons were last Saturday chastised at a cart's tail, in the market-place, and carted about and whipt at the public corners of the town, notwithstanding the rigidness of the season."[10]

If there were any single distinguishing feature of crime at the middle of the century, it was the appearance of professional rogues. These were men—and women—who possessed skill and a certain amount of learning yet held no special allegiance either to the laws of the colonies or to existing social values. They were people who chose to be outlaws as others chose to be silversmiths. One such man was Tom Bell.

Bell's prime years lasted from 1743 to 1754. He was born in Charlestown, Massachusetts. He studied two years at Harvard, picked up a gentlemanly command of Latin, and then went to work. By 1749 Tom Bell was accounted one of the best-traveled, quickest-witted crooks in the colonies, "an old offender, who has been as great an instrument of fraud, oppression and injustice as has been known, perhaps, in any age of the world," the Charlestown court declared before it ordered his execution. His repertoire included: "confidence man, impersonator, robber, petty thief, horse thief, forger, counterfeitor, bully boy, stool pigeon, mariner, soldier, surveyor." An ingratiating and entertaining prisoner, he escaped prison in 1749 before his execution date and retired to the dull life of a schoolteacher in Hanover County, Virginia.[11]

Tom Bell may be America's first legendary outlaw, a precursor to bandits of the nineteenth century, such as Jesse James and Billy the Kid. There were also in those final days of British rule well-organized intercolonial gangs who moved from town to town, colony to colony. The greatest of these was a gang of thieves headquartered in the late 1760s in the hills of the Carolinas. Although details are necessarily sketchy, one early account said "the villains had their confederates in ev'ry colony. What Negroes, horses, and goods was stollen southwardly, was carried northerly, and the northward southward. The southward shipped off at New York and Rhode Island for the French and Dutch Island, the northward carried to Georgia and Florida where smuggling sloops would bargain with the rogues and buy great bargains." There is no proof that any of that gang were ever caught, although four men and two women arrested in Boston in 1769 were believed to be part of the same operation. "'Tis reported," the Boston account declared, "that when those concerned with them at Providence, Newport, New York, Philadelphia, etc. had got any Booty they conveyed it to their correspondents this way and likewise to them, in order to prevent being detected."[12]

Less exotic but more troublesome to the British authorities were the rings of counterfeiters working mostly in lower New England. One New York newspaper estimated in 1768 that there were at least five hundred counterfeiters scattered through the colonies. By 1776, several hundred thousand pounds in phony money had been printed.[13]

Three of the century's best-known counterfeiters were Peter Long of Philadelphia, John David of Boston, and Owen Sullivan, who lived almost everywhere in New England. Long had issued almost £6,000 in the 1730s, David £3,500 a little earlier, and Sullivan at least £24,000 in Rhode Island and New Hampshire bills during the 1650s. The counterfeiters were usually artisans and craftsmen—weavers, carpenters, tailors, bakers, teachers, even merchants, doctors and deacons—who were pressed for cash. The actual engravers were sometimes drawn into the rings by their own pride as craftsmen. Certainly there was more challenge to successfully engraving a £5 printing plate than in stamping out a dozen pewter pitchers. Or, as Connecticut silversmith Gilbert Belcher boasted in 1764, "No gain afforded me so much pleasure as that which I acquired by illicit means."[14]

The prince of colonial counterfeiters was the spry and agile Owen Sullivan, who first appeared in Boston in 1749 as a silversmith, pockets bulging with more money than his trade could have provided. He was indicted for passing false bills in 1750, the evidence drawn in part from his wife, who, on drunken binges, would pronounce him the "forty thousand pound money maker." For punishment he was taken to the pillory and given twenty lashes. Two years later he was convicted with several others in Providence of printing excellent though not quite perfect £16 Rhode Island bills. This time his ears were cropped and the letter C branded on his cheek. He escaped from his jailers a few days later, slipping through Connecticut to Dover in Dutchess County, New York. There he organized an infamous band of money-makers who came to be called the Dover Money Club.[14]

"'Tis said a large gang of villains have harboured for a considerable time past, few of which but have a crop or a brand-mark upon them," one reporter wrote of the Money Club in 1756. The club had outlets in Connecticut, Rhode Island, and of course in Dutchess County. A subsidiary of the club printed New York, Rhode Island, and Spanish dollars in Salem, New York. For a while, in 1754, Sullivan lived and worked with a gang of counterfeiters in Nottingham West, New Hampshire, where some £15,000 were printed from his plates. By then, according to the wife of his host and partner, Benjamin Winn, he had become rather surly and something of a lush. He was "a very difficult man to board," she protested to a neighbor. "He must have chicken or fresh meat every day." His tastes were so extravagant, she added, that she would not keep him a year for all Nottingham.[16]

"Damn you for a pack of fools!" he yelled to his partners in a rage one day. "I never was concerned with such a pack of damned fools before . . . ministers and ministers' sons, squires and squires' sons" were all who ever came to call, he complained. Sullivan may well have surrounded himself with fools. Through 1754 and 1755 more than a dozen of his comrades fell before the courts. Four admitted at Newport in August 1755 that they had printed £50,000 from Sullivan's plates. Faced with prison terms, mutilation, and possible death, a few of the counterfeiters began to talk. The press had already raised Sullivan to the order of a high scoundrel.[17]

To remove the embarrassment of such famous outlaws, bounty hunters were often well rewarded by the colonial authorities. Dutchess County officials had shown no particular interest in finding Sullivan, in part, one might suppose, because they had prospered by not looking. The Connecticut Assembly, however, did not hesitate a moment when approached in the fall of 1755 by one Cornet Eliphalet Beacher, a New Haven businessman who promised that with modest support he could mount an expedition to round up Owen Sullivan and all the other rogues of the Dover Money Club. That he proceeded to do, enlisting as guides both convicted counterfeiters and other suspects he had simply "seized."

Beacher's "guides" took him to a swamp in Dutchess County where, beside a stagnant stream, a carefully placed stump camouflaged the opening to a long narrow cave. Wooden facing covered the walls of a large room inside, neatly appointed with chairs, tables, and beds. A window had been installed in an opening cut higher up on the hillside. But Sullivan was not there. He had left much earlier, suspecting that some of his old accomplices would betray him.

Beacher pursued his search and initiated a sweep of the township with his eleven mounted assistants—three of whom were Beacher relatives. At 1:00 A.M. Saturday, March 12, 1756, Beacher and his posse rode into the yard of one of Sullivan's acquaintances. Armed and bearing torches, his men searched the house over the protests of the owners. They were almost ready to leave when one of Beacher's men noticed some freshly stirred dust beneath the edge of a bed. The bed and the woman in it were moved. There they found a loose board, which when removed revealed a dirt passageway to a tiny cell that had its own fireplace vented into the house chimney. Hiding in the cell was Owen Sullivan.

Owen Sullivan was hanged, though not without attempts to prevent it. His execution was scheduled for Saturday May 8, but on Friday night some of his friends took a saw to the gallows. He reckoned, in his final speech from the rebuilt gallows on May 10, that his sentence was just. He admitted counterfeiting some £24,000 in various colonial currencies. He even urged his comrades to quit counterfeiting. But he would not betray them. Taking a big bite of chewing tobacco, he said he would not reveal just which New York bills he had printed. "You must find that out by your learning," he said with a smile to his executioners. Then he begged mercy for his soul, repeated the Lord's Prayer, and was hanged.[18]

The mercy Sullivan sought was for his soul as a freeman. It was not a sign of repentance. Indeed, few criminals felt compelled to regret their deeds in a society of class conflicts and corrupt officials, for the spirit of disaffection was spreading throughout the colonies. Law and justice were becoming more and more a reflection of those class conflicts. Beacher, for example, was no better than Sullivan. His motivation in pursuing the counterfeiter was the protection of his own assets, and the profit he could reap in the process. In the end, he got Sullivan by kidnapping his guides. No government official thought that that was improper—Beacher was a proper businessman, after all. But then few officials acted as if the law applied to them either.

Governor Benjamin Fletcher might have won the record for public venality in the colonies, but his successor's successor, Lord Cornbury, was small improvement. A transvestite who delighted in generating genteel scandal, Cornbury pranced about the city in long dresses, curls, and dainty makeup, inspecting his troops and strewing favors upon his friends. The Mayor of Philadelphia, William Fishbourne, mysteriously lost £2,000 of public money in 1731; it was robbery, he claimed. The sheriffs of Philadelphia were similarly free with the money they collected. Questionable, though probably not illegal, was the policy of Philadelphia officials to rent the city's wharves and market stalls for themselves. Constables in Charleston during the 1770s took bribes and beat people who did not pay kickbacks to them. In the New York of the 1730s the police reserved the city's liquor licenses for themselves; at one point nearly half the constabulary forces kept taverns or sold liquor.[19]

Were all these governors, mayors, and lesser officials on the take, desperately lining their pockets because of an unbridled sense of greed? Traditionally American historians have been more generous with the colonial officials. These "peculations," as they were then called, were nothing more than the contemporary perquisites of power, the argument runs. Perhaps. But the fact is that such massive official corruption led many Americans to lose all respect for law and authority. This generated not only more crime; it also gave rise to some peculiar notions of self-reliance that would set the colonials apart from all other arms of the British Empire.

As English and European yeomen sought salvation on the land, killing off or pushing back the native population, their successes subjected them directly to the economic appetite of the British Empire. The growth of that empire required strict management of colonial enterprises. The Stamp Acts, the harsh taxation policies, the ever tightening trade laws, meant only one thing to the colonists: while they spoke the same language and had the same color skin as the home subjects of Mother Britain, they had become an exploited class of second-rate citizens. The grand traditions of British equity, justice, and democracy were damned: those traditions benefited only the masters of the trading companies who, through Parliament, controlled colonial policy.

When the American colonists were no longer able to deny the hypocrisy of their British social traditions, the effect was devastating. If the government was politically bankrupt, if the very system of law and justice was revealed as a fraud, and if the church no longer commanded the respect and authority upon which the whole colonial adventure had been justified, in short if there was no codified system of ethics or morality to which Americans could turn, then law had degenerated into a problem of individual pragmatism—and vigilantism.

To the poor and propertyless of Boston, Newport, New York, or Philadelphia the law had little to offer. In a land of elegant upper-class thieves who stole from the public purse, the lower classes found profit where they could. But beyond the cities, on the farms and the frontier, social outsiders followed another pattern. There, justice was a volatile affair at best, punctuated by a daily acceptance of violence and limited war.

Since the days of Bacon's Rebellion in the 1670s, the Appalachian foothills had been bathed in blood. Not only were they the preserve of Virginia's land speculators—would-be extensions of the tobacco plantations—these outbacks also provided a necessary buffer zone between the white settlements along the coastal plains and the increasingly hostile Indian tribes who had been pushed back into the mountains. The unlucky whites who populated these buffer zones were the latecomers who could find land nowhere else and who had to buy from the speculators whom they grew to despise. Not only did they pay high prices for inferior land but they were left exposed, with almost no armed protection, to the justifiable wrath of the Indians. Their settlements were turned into the front line of defense for the comfortable plantation owners who risked virtually nothing. Little wonder that these mountain people soon took the law into their own hands to initiate the American vigilante tradition—a tradition that over the last two hundred years has been a hallmark of rural crime fighting.[20]

Rebellions, insurrections, and vigilante uprisings became commonplace in the mid-1700s. The Paxton Boys swept into Philadelphia from western Pennsylvania in 1764 demanding a government more responsive to the economic plight of the frontier. Vermont's Green Mountain Boys battled against New York's jurisdictional claims in the early 1770s. Strong-willed vigilantes in western North Carolina successfully seized control of several counties in 1771 before they were crushed by the governor's militia. Even after the Revolution, beleaguered farmers in Massachusetts and Pennsylvania resorted to open fighting when they joined Shays's Rebellion and, eight years later, unleashed the Whisky Rebellion. More telling than any of these short-lived sieges, however, was the so-called Regulator movement of South Carolina.

The South Carolina Regulators were America's first true vigilantes. Small planters and shopkeepers from the villages of the South Carolina backcountry, they claimed between one thousand and three thousand members. A third of the Regulators were fairly prosperous farmers and merchants who were convinced they could never become as rich as the owners of the flatland estates. The Regulators first joined arms in the fall of 1767 to suppress what must have been the most audacious wave of thievery, pillaging, and general outlawry the colonies had ever suffered. By the mid-sixties well-organized gangs had established almost impregnable bases in the backcountry. Some had alliances with thieves and counterfeiters in the northern colonies who, on occasion, were forced to beat a hasty retreat to the remote mountain hollows. Yet most backcountry crime was the work of homegrown South Carolina outlaws, gangs of thieves and bandits whose criminal careers had developed from the colony's own internal turmoil.[21]

The most successful of these thieves had learned their business in the aftermath of the Cherokee war, waged from February 1760 through December 1761. The Cherokees were finally crushed, but it was a bitter victory for the whites as well. Hundreds had fled their homes for the protection of the forts. "Almost fifteen hundred people spent the winter of 1760–61 in the thirty forts of the area. Life in the forts was crowded and unhealthy. During 1759 and 1760 smallpox raged in the Back Country, and in early March 1760 two-thirds of the garrison of Fort Ninety Six were down with the disease, which took fourteen lives." Hundreds of farms had been abandoned, some permanently. The resulting chaos was predictable: Looting began at once.[22]

Relief appropriated by the Charleston government was inadequate and frequently diverted before it reached the impoverished victims. Militiamen, as much as anyone else, stole from the supply shipments. Even before a treaty had been signed with the Cherokees, the fighting men had begun to turn against the settlers. "These rangers instead of annoying the Enemy, fell to plundering of, and living at free quarter on the poor scattered inhabitants. The forts into which they retired were filled with whores and prostitutes and there maintained at the public expense."[23]

Chaos reigned over the backcountry after the war. Economic privation, matched by the institutional corruption, left the hill people demoralized. The small farmers who had survived faced nearly insurmountable odds. Before the Cherokee war, farming had already been a precarious enterprise—roads were mud troughs and the rivers barely navigable. By the end of the war, labor had grown even scarcer than it had been. Machinery had been stolen or destroyed, and the villages had begun to fill with penniless wanderers. Historian Richard Maxwell Brown described the situation:

> Except for certain bandit gangs, the lower people and outlaws were loose and disorganized, but they all had one thing in common: alienation from respectable Back Country society. The degree of alienation accounted for the distinction between lower people and outlaws as types. The outlaws were aggressively antisocial; their alienation was absolute. The psychic alienation of the lower people was perhaps as complete as that of the outlaws, but outwardly it was less extreme. The outlaws were actively hostile to respectable society; the lower people were marginal to it.[24]

Winslow Driggers, thought to have been the cousin of a respectable planter, had fought in the militia at age twenty and became a gang leader ten years later. Govery and George Black had inherited fine farmland from their father, which they gradually sold off before becoming full-time outlaws. Thomas and James Moon also sold their lands before they became gang leaders by the mid-1760s. The most successful outlaws seemed not to be the washouts of backcountry social life; instead they belonged to the second generation of respectable families. They had wit, skill, and imagination. By 1765 they had begun to form a distinct society of their own. According to local accounts, the outlaws even had their own villages where women, children, and grandparents lived together in fair harmony. Racial bigotry was rare in their settlements, and blacks were often accepted "as equals."[25]

In the early 1760s, the outlaws rode with impunity. "So vigorous were the gangs," historian Brown has written, "so pervasive their operations, so impregnable their strongholds that many Back Country officials and tradesmen out of fear, duress, or greed, became their secret allies." But by 1767 some planters and traders had rebuilt their lives and their fortunes so that they were no longer willing to cooperate with the gangs. The spring of 1767 had also brought a particularly vicious wave of arson, robbery, and kidnapping by the outlaws. Rising prosperity plus outrage at the new attacks spread an aura of righteous indignation among the rich. Since there were no real courts in the backcountry, serious criminal cases were tried only in Charleston. In March of 1767 six outlaws were convicted on charges of petty larceny, horse theft, and robbing houses. The five outlaws who were to be hanged were all pardoned by the governor, the sixth was whipped. The hill people began to wonder aloud just how free of corruption the provincial government was.[26]

Throughout the summer the people of the backcountry stewed over their dilemma. Frustrated by each new outlaw assault, they finally began to organize citizen posses to punish the outlaws directly. Houses were burned in villages harboring horse thieves. Other villains were simply seized and whipped. In a counterattack late during the night of October 8, the outlaws kidnapped a justice of the peace from his home and dragged him by horseback far into the countryside. From then on the violence of the citizens and of the outlaws escalated in a continuing spiral. The vigilantes chose "a thousand men to execute the laws against all villains and harborers of villains." The thousand men were called Regulators.[27]

Immediate orders from Charleston directed the citizen "mobs" to disperse and cease "committing riots and disturbances." But the Regulators were of no mind to disband or withdraw. Throughout the next month they imposed their own self-created system of law enforcement on the outlaws. All the while they kept their grievances before the colonial assembly in Charleston, demanding that courts be established to try the backwoods outlaws. In November 1767 the Regulators won: two companies of official Rangers were formed by the assembly to track down the gangs and bring law and order to the hill country. Riding side by side with the Regulators, they proved remarkably successful. "By March 1768, when the campaign came to an end, the Regulators had broken the back of the crime problem."[28]

Though the outlaws ceased to remain a serious threat after the spring of 1768, the Regulators—who by then numbered as many as three thousand—were still not satisfied. Crime had come to their settlements, they believed, through the greed and dissolute behavior of the lower classes, the drifters, hunters, squatters, and generally displaced persons who had arrived in the wake of war. If crime were not to return to their country, then sharp controls would have to be placed on the "lower people." Thus, in their Plan of Regulation of June 1768 they determined to "purge, by measures of their own, the country of all idle persons, all that have not a visible way of getting an honest living, all that are suspected or known to be guilty of mal-practices."

Strict regulations, covering morals and family life, were imposed on the people of the backcountry. For the next three years, until the colony finally reimposed its own judicial authority, the Regulators and the Rangers, who had been financed by the assembly, ruled supreme. Charleston officials exerted almost no influence over the territory and "the people were governed by their militia officers who decided all disputes over the drum head in the muster field. The country was purged of all villains. The whores were whipped and driven off. The magistrates and constables associated with the rogues, silenced and inhibited. Tranquility reigned. Industry was restored."[29]

Law and order was reestablished. But at what cost? To combat crime, a new breed of semiofficial fast-draw criminals had been organized. Condoned, then supported by the state, these new criminals epitomized justice in America: Justice had become synonymous with the swiftness of the gun.

Chapter 6

Convicts, Concubines, and Corrupt Officials

Doubt and desperation may have possessed the imaginations of Cotton Mather and his devout New England followers, but in the more worldly colonies to the south—Pennsylvania, Maryland, Virginia, the Carolinas—the eighteenth century promised tantalizing opportunities. Although there were recurring cycles of prosperity and recession, business had begun to be truly profitable. Timber, dyes, and agricultural produce, the key exports of the lower colonies, soon overshadowed New England trade. Even population growth mirrored the changing balance of prosperity and influence in the colonies. Between 1700 and 1765 Boston's population grew from 6,700 to 15,500. Philadelphia, on the other hand, blossomed from an inlet surrounded by 500 farmers in 1683 to a city of 35,000 by 1775.[1]

Changing fortunes were paralleled by the growth of the servant class in the colonies. Initially most servants were sold to the highest bidder by the shipmaster who brought them over. A small second category of "free-willers" had no contract with the ship captain but sought independently to indenture themselves to a master who would pay for their passage. Most New England servants, including those in its early Irish communities, arrived under these indentured agreements. But by 1700 the scarcity of land and the rising surplus of labor caused the northerners to reduce servant imports. Consequently, the third category of servants who came in massive numbers after 1700 went almost entirely to the South. These were "convicts, felons, vagrants, and dissolate *[sic]* persons and those kidnapped or 'spirited' away by so-called 'spirits' or 'crimps.'" Only through the importation of these "bonded colonists" did the entrepreneurs of the 1700s win their economic independence.[2]

Historian Curtis Nettels offers an apt explanation:

> The poor servant immigrants, once they had completed their terms of service, had to begin an independent life without capital assets. Obviously their labor as servants had produced a surplus to the employing capitalist groups; otherwise the system of indentured servitude would have been unprofitable. Such surplus was used in part to finance the freed servant at the expiration of his term—either by means of long-term loans which enabled him to acquire or equip a farm or through short-term credits extended by merchants for the purchase of store goods. The indebted farmers were thereupon obliged to deliver their produce to their creditors immediately after harvest, with the result that the price of farm produce fell to low levels when deliveries were made. On the other hand the prices paid by the farmers for store goods and credit remained practically constant; consequently the merchant creditors were able to extract handsome profits from their dealings with their farmer debtors. This, in fact, was the chief source of the capital accumulations of the merchant class.[3]

Most profitable of all the servants were "His Majesty's seven-year passengers," the convicts whose transportation had been paid by the king and who therefore were sold at bargain prices to the plantation owners of Maryland and Virginia. Indeed, one prison alone, London's Old Bailey, supplied just under ten thousand convicts to America between 1717 and 1775. Parliament had in 1717 approved routine transportation of convicts for seven-year terms or for fourteen years in murder cases. So great was America's reputation as a convict repository that the irascible Samuel Johnson was moved to dismiss any complaints from officials in the New World: "Sir, they are a race of convicts, and ought to be content with anything we may allow them short of hanging!"[4]

Only a few convicts—no more than forty-five hundred—had been transported to the great estates of the mid-Atlantic colonies in the late 1600s. After the turn of the century they came by the shipload to Maryland and Virginia. Columbia University historian Richard B. Morris has estimated that more than fifty thousand English convicts were shipped to the colonies before the Revolution. They were seldom identified by the crimes they had committed in England.[5]

Though offenses were seldom noted, the logs of the convict ships provide a glimpse of how grim was the transatlantic crossing. Ship mortality ran from 15 to 30 percent, while within the first five years of arrival between 35 and 50 percent of the indentured newcomers died. Port records at Annapolis show that of the sixty-one convicts put aboard the *Honour* in 1720, twenty had died before the ship arrived. Thirty of the eighty-seven convicts aboard the *Gilbert* died in 1722, and thirty-eight of ninety-five died on the voyage of the *Rappahannock Merchant* in 1725.[6]

British sea captain Jonathan Forward, who held a near monopoly in the convict trade, regularly took on prisoners even though he himself did not know where he would land; his destination could be determined by a last-minute freight order or by a change of the winds. Forward won a plum contract with the British solicitor general in 1718, renewed annually, by which he was paid £3 a head for every convict he carried. He raised his charge to £5 in 1727 and was once paid a bonus of £114 for "alleged losses" in the trade. The mortality rate aboard Forward's and other captains' ships reveals the squalor in which the convicts lived during their two-month passage. A letter from a Londoner who had visited one of the ships provides the detail: "I went on board, and to be sure, all the horror I ever had an idea of is short of what I saw this poor man in; chained to a board in a hold not above 16 feet long, more than 50 with him; a collar and padlock about his neck, and chained to five of the most dreadful creatures I ever looked on!"[7]

Nearly every convict voyage included women, although the ship logs only occasionally show the percentage. The *Snow Eugene,* which arrived in Maryland in 1658 carried 18 women and 51 men. A census of whites brought over in 1755 listed, 1,893 adult convicts of whom 386 were women; of the 88 children, one-quarter were female. During the seventeenth century, hundreds of women convicts were dispatched to

Virginia in exchange for tobacco (140 in just two years, 1619 and 1621). These "tobacco wedlocks" provided wives, or concubines, for the early settlers, and from these unions came the ancestors to much of Virginia's "aristocratic" gentry. But female convicts were dispatched to the middle and southern colonies, for the men who carved out the first settlement constantly complained of the lack of female "entertainment."[8]

French Louisiana was a rather special case and might well have been called the brothel colony. Hardly a woman landed in New Orleans in the early 1700s who had not walked the streets of Paris as a prostitute. More than twelve hundred women and girls were sent from the French prisons to New Orleans between 1717 and 1721 at a time when the settlement was still tiny, populated almost exclusively by troops from the regiment. On leaving Paris these *filles de joie* made quite a stir. One shipment, in October 1719, was driven through the Paris streets "in 30 carts, filled with these women of average virtue, each of whom had a yellow ribbon in her hair, and a like number of young men who wore cockades of the same color in their hats, but who went afoot. In crossing Paris, the wenches sang as if they had no worries and hailed by name the males they recognized from previous commerce . . . inviting the men to accompany them on their voyage to Mississippi."

The prostitutes apparently pursued the gay life even after they arrived in America, for ten years later a New Orleans nun complained that "not only debauchery, but dishonesty and all other vices reign here more than elsewhere. As for the girls of evil life, although they are watched closely and punished severely by putting them on a wooden horse and having them whipped by all the regiment that guards our city, there are more than enough to fill a refuge."[9]

Prostitution was a tough problem for the colonies' urban authorities. William Penn was said to have erupted into paroxysms of rage at the turn of the century when a devout Quaker comrade escorted him past the "caves" of the Delaware then infested by sailors and wanton women. In Virginia and Maryland, however, which had not yet built any important towns, women could not turn to prostitution for their living. As a result, throughout the prerevolutionary period, such women became far more inventive in their pursuit of a living even if they usually fared badly. One example is Sarah Wilson, who had been sentenced to death in England for stealing a jewel from her mistress, the queen's maid of honor.

Spared from the gallows, Sarah Wilson was deported to Maryland in 1771 and sold immediately upon her arrival. How she slipped away from her new master remains a mystery, but she soon surfaced in Virginia and then South Carolina posing as Princess Susanna Carolina Matilda—the queen's "lesser known" sister. Ever keen to future opportunities, Sarah Wilson had managed to smuggle elegant clothes and jewels to America. She had even brought along a medallion portrait of the queen. She might have sold such treasures on the black market after she arrived. Instead she used them to establish her credibility, then angled invitations to fancy parties where she could attach herself to handsome and desirable gentlemen. She went about Charleston "making astonishing impressions in many places, affecting the mode of royalty so inimitably that many had the honor to kiss her hand."

Had she not been so brilliant an actress, Sarah Wilson might have succeeded in her outrageous gambit. Unfortunately she began to forget the limitations of her role. Her appetite for grandeur led her into making increasingly dubious claims for herself. She began to promise colonial posts to the men who entertained her. She even dangled a colonial governorship before one ambitious fellow—in return of course for immediate large loans. Always fearful of discovery, she made her promises and moved on. Perhaps she made too many promises or borrowed too much money; eventually her young men became suspicious. Stumbling across an advertisement for a runaway servant who matched the description of the "princess," one of them contacted her former master. Her gentlemen benefactors, wistful, if somewhat poorer, saw her to the boat in Charleston where again she shipped out as a prisoner to a plantation in Maryland.[10]

Convict labor was not an unmixed blessing to the colonists. Many people, especially the new arrivals and the small farmers who drew no direct benefit from convict laborers, opposed accepting the overflow of England's prisons. Gradually, bills began to appear in the Virginia and Maryland legislatures placing restrictions on convict importation, demanding that shipmasters identify the crimes of their human cargo, or requiring that a security deposit be placed against each. Most of the provincial laws were ignored by the crown, but the debate surrounding their passage reveals how deeply the colonists associated their spreading crime problems with convict importation. "When we see our papers filled continually with accounts of the most audacious robberies, the most cruel murders, infinite other villainies perpetrated by convicts transported from Europe, what melancholy and what terrible reflections must it occasion. . . . These are some of thy favours Britain, thou art called Mother Country; but what good mother ever sent thieves and villains to accompany her children; to corrupt with their infectious vices and to murder the rest."[11]

Servants and convicts fattened the criminal dockets, especially in Virginia, Pennsylvania, and Maryland. Yet they were seldom charged with robbery, assault, or any kind of violence. Most servants were arrested simply for running away. Once caught, they were usually whipped and ordered to repay some multiple of the time they were absent from their masters. In New Jersey, Virginia, and North Carolina, for example, they usually served twice the number of days they were absent; in Pennsylvania, their added service was five times their absence; in South Carolina seven times, in Maryland ten times. In Anne Arundel County, Maryland, a maid servant was brought before the court by her master in 1719 just as she completed her term of indenture. Her master had kept account since 1714 of all her short absences, usually a few days each, but had done nothing about them until the end of her five-year term. Altogether he charged she had been gone 133 days, and the court agreed, awarding him an additional 1,330 days of extra labor from the hapless woman. Runaways were not usually caught, however. Fewer than a half dozen cases per year appear in the surviving court records, while the Maryland and Virginia *Gazettes* published in excess of a hundred and fifty ads for runaways each year.[12]

Just as a growing number of southern colonists came to regard the transportation of convicts as an oppressive imperial policy, so too there was mounting criticism against the use of indentured servants. Writing in 1724, university teacher Hugh Jones railed that servants were "the poorest, idlest, and worst of Mankind, the refuse of Great Britain and Ireland, and the outcast of the people." Worse yet, Jones complained, were the "convicts or felons" whose cheap labor the planters were only eager to purchase and who were wont to "do great mischiefs, commit robbery and murder, and spoil servants that were before very good." Though exaggeratedly rhetorical, Jones's book betrayed the economic insecurity felt not only by Virginia but by all the lower colonies as well.[13]

That insecurity was caused by the widening rift between the wealthier provincial leaders and gentry who had long ago taken the good coastal lands for their plantations, and the immigrants who, arriving in the 1700s, were forced to settle along the Piedmont or the foothills of the Appalachians. The struggle between these two forces fueled most of the political debate from 1720 to the Revolution and laid the groundwork for the wholesale corruption that marked the final decades of provincial government.

More than any other colony in North America, Virginia was the model of success for investors in England's overseas empire. After a rocky beginning in the early 1600s, it soon developed a sprawling manorial system. Neither feudal nor democratic, the first Virginia planters cleverly devised a plantation system along the tidewater river lands that obviated the need for a central trading town. Each of the huge plantations resembled a semiautonomous duchy that could provide for all the needs of its laborers and family members. The very finest tracts had their own river docks upon which English vessels could unload manufactured goods and take on tobacco or other farm produce. These same plantations acted as import brokers for those farms lacking adequate river frontage. Thus, the tidewater plantation system brought profit to the planters, work for English laborers, wealth to English merchants, a release of pressure in the home prisons, and duties and revenues to the king. The key to the cultivation of the vast tobacco fields upon which the whole system pivoted was a steady supply of cheap labor. Unlike the town-centered colonies to the north, Virginia could more easily control its flood of servants and convicts, since the dispersed farms offered them little chance to band together.[14]

Servant laborers offered still other advantages to the Virginia planters that would eventually set them apart from the later immigrants of the 1700s. Many of the founding planter families had accumulated their vast acreages by becoming servant dealers who would order scores if not an entire shipload of laborers at once. Since lands were granted to the planter based on servant headrights, the more servants he could claim, the more land he could be granted from the king. Little matter if the laborers were so poorly cared for after their miserable voyage that they died within a few months; the planter had only to prove the number of servants he had purchased. The disappearance of servants had become so scandalous that by 1700 laws were enacted prohibiting the private burial of servants by their masters. Two of the most prominent planters, William Claiborne and Peter Ashton, built most of their estates by working the servant traffic. Ashton received over forty-five hundred acres for his headright. But the most extraordinary dealer of all was Robert Beverley, a loyal militia commander during Bacon's Rebellion in 1676 who accumulated land patents in excess of twenty-five thousand acres.[15]

Bacon's Rebellion was the first clue that the plantation system was spreading rancor across the Virginia countryside. Nathaniel Bacon, a wealthy cousin of English essayist Francis Bacon, arrived in Virginia in 1674 after the plantation system had absorbed the best lands. He was immediately drawn to the plight of the frontier farmers, many of whom were freed servants with little access to the colony's governing councils. They, and Bacon, were particularly upset that in addition to getting the barest land for their farms, they paid the same tax rates as the wealthier planters and received almost no protection from the increasingly hostile Indians. First, Bacon led an illegal attack on the Pamunkey, Susquehanna, and Occaneechi Indians. Then, denounced by Virginia's governor William Berkeley (who, coincidentally, was also Bacon's cousin), Bacon and his small army moved on the capital, Jamestown, and nearly succeeded in taking it when he suddenly took ill and died. Leaderless, his men were defeated by a planter army led by Robert Beverley. Lured to surrender by promise of amnesty, the remaining rebels were tried for treason; twenty-three were hanged—the largest number of criminal executions for any year in Virginia's colonial history.[16]

That Bacon's Rebellion attracted such a following is ample indication of popular dissatisfaction with the unresponsive aristocracy. The land records themselves explain much of the underlying unhappiness. On the one hand, a few families, which controlled the government and its tax power, owned hundreds of thousands of acres. On the other, a great many people (almost 40 percent of their former servants) owned a few acres each. "In Virginia," wrote historian Philip A. Bruce, "the large landowner carried so much weight that he found no difficulty in securing the election of a son to the House [of Burgesses]. . . . The broader the plantation, and the more numerous the proprietor's slaves and herds, the more extensive was the influence exercised by him among voters belonging to his own calling, and the more easily he obtained the advancement of any person of his own blood aspiring to enter public life."[17]

The planter elite was not only interested in public office for the prestige it might afford. From the governor's council to the lowly justice of the peace, the control of public offices was a vital part of the planters' political and economic grip on the colony. County offices in particular were useful in keeping track of the disgruntled middle class, the likes of whom had fueled Bacon's Rebellion and which became ever more important in the 1700s. Public office was also highly profitable, for under the terms of public ethics in colonial Virginia, civil servants were expected to line their own pockets first. At the center of the Virginia land aristocracy, inside dealing with public money was just one way of maintaining rectitude, stability, and of course power. Bruce, a conservative apologist for the Virginia gentry, observed:

> It is not going too far to say that the members of the Council appropriated to themselves all those higher offices of the colony which were attended with the largest salaries, or presented the most numerous chances for money-getting.[18]

Bruce added that these council members deliberately

> . . . disregarded the fact that the concentration of these offices in so few hands brought about serious damage to the public interests whenever the Councillor was required by his incumbency of two separate positions to perform two sets of duties really in conflict with each other; a Councillor, for instance, was called upon to pass upon the correctness of his own accounts as collector; as collector, he was obliged, for his own enlightenment as a judge of the General Court, to inform himself of all violations of the Navigation Acts; as a farmer of the quitrents, he practically owed the success of his bed to himself as Councillor; as escheator, who was a ministerial officer, he took and returned the inquisitions of escheats to himself as a judicial officer, and as such, passed upon points of law coming up in his own inquisitions.

Land speculation, land development, and the cozy arrangements between the council and the planters is a constant theme throughout Virginia history up to the Revolution. Even the heroic, pirate-fighting governor Spotswood, it is remembered, tallied up some eighty-five thousand acres by the end of his term in 1722. At the middle of his term, in 1712, Spotswood and Robert Beverley II, whose father had fought Bacon's men, led an expedition through the Piedmont to open up the Susquehanna River Valley to speculators.

Technically Spotswood was only a lieutenant governor. He had purchased this position from the earl of Orkney, an aristocratic fop who won the governor's appointment as a financial prize and then, having never set foot in America, subcontracted the job. Spotswood was a master speculator who at first encouraged both immigration and slavery, but then quickly realized their dangers. While slave labor underwrote many Virginia fortunes in the eighteenth century, it also helped to undermine the dominance of the old planter elite, who, in the early years, had depended mostly upon indentured servants. At first, slavery only expanded their profits, freeing them of the obligation to stake their servants at the end of their indenture. But the addition of a permanent labor force also entailed fixed and often growing responsibility.[19]

More important, many smaller farmers who could not afford servants were able to keep slaves and thus increase their tobacco production. "The great number of negroes imported here and solely employed in making tobacco hath produced for some years past an increase in tobacco far disproportionate to the consumption of it . . . and consequently lowered the price of it," Spotswood warned in 1711. Within two years the effect was twofold: The great planters bore up under the strain but only with difficulty as their expanded production increased costs and reduced the margin of their profits; the free yeoman farmer who worked only with his wife and children was virtually eliminated. "The glorious promises which the country had held out to him in the first fifty years of its existence had been belied. The Virginia which had formerly been so largely the land of the little farmer, had become the land of masters and slaves."[20]

While slavery crushed the independent tidewater farmers, it did provide certain advantages to the medium-sized slave owners who could operate more efficiently than the plantation aristocrats. And as these slave owners acquired wealth and prestige, they also began to send representatives into the House of Burgesses. By the decade before the American Revolution several of the old families had not only lost economic superiority, but they also faced a profound challenge to their control of the colony's political apparatus.

In May 1766, nine years before the outbreak of the Revolution, the venerable colony of Virginia was all but bankrupt. A score or more of its oldest and most prominent families could not pay their bills. A few had been forced to sell out and even then lacked the cash to satisfy their creditors. William Byrd III, whose father and grandfather had epitomized Old Dominion gentility, was a profligate gambler, an incompetent manager, and, like every other planter, a victim of the decaying economic climate; he survived by begging loans from his friends. Bernard Moore, a member of the House of Burgesses, a colonel in the militia, holder of thousands of acres in King William and Spotsylvania counties, was a reckless speculator who finally lost his credit and barely covered his daily living expenses from the haphazard income of a pig-iron foundry. Benjamin Grymes, another burgess from Spotsylvania County who descended from an old planter family, and had married into the even older Fitzhugh clan, also dabbled in everything from tobacco exports to pig-iron production and land speculation—all endeavors requiring large quantities of cash he did not have. In the end his estate was placed in trust to pay off his debts.[21]

These men and another dozen tobacco lords gathered in the courthouse of King and Queen County some forty miles below Richmond on the second Tuesday of June 1766. Even in upper tidewater, June is a hot, humid month. They sat, weak and clammy, in the wooden courthouse, its windows open to the clamor of a Virginia Court Day outside. Court Days, then as now in much of the rural South, were not only judicial dates; they were regular public festivals where horse traders, blacksmiths, silk dealers—anyone who had something to barter—paraded into town to do business.

Little of the festivity drifted into the courtroom, however, for the court's agenda that day would prove to be the first round in the dismantling of the blue-blood aristocracy. The occasion: the appointment of administrators for the estate of the late John Robinson, Speaker of the House of Burgesses, treasurer of the colony, and personal creditor to probably every gentleman in the room. The bond required of the estate administrators was fixed at a quarter million pounds—approximately half the amount Virginia spent fighting the French and Indian War. The gravity of the case could not have been stated more dramatically.[22]

The dilemma before the court and the ruling class of Virginia was simple. John Robinson, using the public treasury of Virginia, had bailed out his failing planter friends to the tune of £138,708. He himself owed the treasury £100,000, which the planters would have to repay or else forfeit their own estates. And interest on the debt mounted daily.[23]

Shock, more than remorse, gripped Robinson's friends. Some feared they might die in debtor's prison, the result not of illegality but of Robinson's perfectly understandable gesture of friendship. Robinson had not stolen from the treasury. He had simply failed to reclaim paper money lent to the planters during the French and Indian War of the 1750s and early 1760s. Had he followed royal orders and reclaimed the war currency, the colony would have had no money at all. As one student of the case put it, "Robinson was the only considerable source of money or credit in Virginia. He could burn the paper money and bankrupt his friends, or ignore the law and make the paper available to those in desperate need. He chose to save his friends."[24]

The Robinson affair caused no end of anguish within Virginia's ruling circles. The rather pudgy, purse-lipped Robinson had been Speaker of the House since 1738 and by most accounts stood as the most powerful man in the colony. Certainly he was one of the colony's wealthiest men, acclaimed by Lieutenant Governor Fauquier "the darling of the Country." He had also been a business partner with Fauquier and the unfortunate William Byrd III. His death revealed not only the financial bankruptcy of his social coterie; his corruption of the public trust, while not technically criminal, had shattered the moral and political authority that had kept the planter elite in control.[25]

The corruption of the Virginia upper class was neither new nor exceptional in colonial America. Practically every Royal governor appointed in Virginia had taken payoffs from the good gentlemen of the House of Burgesses. Governor Robert Dinwiddie, an antagonist to the gentry, graciously pocketed a £500 "gift" voted by the burgesses and then demanded additional payment before approving their land speculation schemes in the western mountains. Lieutenant Governor Francis Nicholson had been dismissed over such improprieties at the beginning of the century and Governor William Gooch was sharply reprimanded. In Maryland the spoils of patronage were so crass that officeholders haggled with the lord proprietor over the amount he would be paid. Cecilius Calvert, secretary to the proprietor, "was accustomed to levy certain charges upon persons appointed to office in the colony, requiring judges of the colonial land office, for example, to remit to him a part of their profits."[26]

Although such gentlemen's arrangements had long existed in the coastal colonies, they were becoming more and more difficult to maintain. After 1700 new settlers had begun to move on to the colonies' western frontiers and their interests had little to do with the aims and needs of the older provincial rulers. These settlers were the middle-class people with middle-sized farms who grew tobacco more or less profitably and kept a watchful eye on sailing notices to catch the latest word on slavers arriving from Angola. Unlike the Quakers of Pennsylvania, they seldom reflected on the design of a "holy experiment." They sought new mountain gaps through which to open farming in the Piedmont, and they sought slaves to work those farms.

This new wave of settlers, most of whom arrived in the first two decades of the 1700s, were in an important sense the first American immigrants. Before 1700 there were older and newer generations by which the colonists differentiated themselves; but outside the churches of Boston, the social institutions—government, domestic commerce, even the church—had not sufficiently jelled for an old-timer to label a new arrival "immigrant." When in the early eighteenth century these immigrants did arrive, they had left Europe mostly for the opportunities that existed abroad—or were thought to exist. Wages were higher in America. The frontier was so vast, a family never needed to fear oppressive kings, bishops, and bailiffs. And, it was said, good farmland could be had for the asking. The thousands of Scots and Germans who sailed into Philadelphia harbor in search of jobs on the docks or new land in the backcountry were the people who, alongside the few successful freedmen, populated the second tier of America along the rim of the Appalachians. They felt little if any kinship to the old landed families and sea merchants who held an iron grip on the ruling provincial councils. They were interested only in success, and to succeed, especially in Virginia and the Carolinas, they needed mostly only one commodity: cheap—or better still, free—labor.

To the modern mind the institution of slavery often appears to be the most criminal enterprise undertaken by the Englishmen who came to America, a barbaric heritage that became an indelible blight on American civilization. But despite its barbarism, slavery was not criminal: It was a fully legitimate business, blessed by the church, the state, and by the best Enlightenment thinkers of the day. Indeed its very legitimacy contributed greatly to its inhumanity. For acts of brutality that were normally punished as vicious crimes were openly tolerated when they were perpetrated against black slaves. Slaves were branded, whipped, burned, and casually executed. Their limbs were hacked off, their bodies deliberately maimed, usually with the full approval of the courts. The record in some colonies was worse than in others. In South Carolina, Forrest McDonald has written, the "planters' callous disregard for human life and suffering was probably unmatched anywhere west of the Dnieper."[27]

A relatively high percentage of slaves was desperate enough to run away, even though they knew the penalty might be death. Yet "slaveholders generally believed that their slaves lived better than the great mass of peasants and industrial workers of the world." Those who ran away were judged guilty of "stealing themselves." In the annals of American crime, it is the runaway slave who is the criminal, not the sheriff or bounty hunter or vigilante who tracked him down and hanged him as an example to his peers.[28]

Nor would the slave owner tolerate or even attempt to understand the blacks' discontent. They complained about their laziness and were always suspicious of their illnesses. George Washington, America's noble father, constantly bemoaned the fact that his slaves never produced as much as he did—on his land. He often resorted to whipping women who feigned sickness and was always suspicious of slave women claiming to be pregnant, until he could actually see visible signs. He used to characterize those who tried not to work too hard during their eighteen-hour days as "idle creatures" and "deceitful."[29]

Washington, James Madison, and the other slave-owning aristocrats who went on to define freedom in America were just as responsible for the slave codes as the middle-class farmers who most often put such codes into practice. These codes, four of which were passed into law from 1705 to 1797, all said basically the same thing:

> Whereas many times slaves run away and lie hid and lurking in swamps, woods . . . two justices *(Quorum unus)* can issue a proclamation . . . if the slave does not immediately return, anyone whatsoever may kill or destroy such slaves by such ways and means as he . . . shall think fit. . . . If the slave is apprehended . . . it shall . . . be lawful for the county court, to order such punishment to the said slave, either by dismembering, or in any other way . . . as they in their discretion shall think fit, for the reclaiming any such incorrigible slave, and terrifying others from the like practices.[30]

In order to run away, indeed often in order just to survive, slaves had to steal. Washington complained that his slaves stole everything they could get their hands on. He ordered his corn and meat houses locked, his apples picked early, his sheep and pigs watched carefully, and all dogs belonging to slaves hanged because the dogs "aid them in their night robberies." Inevitably, as such thievery spread, white entrepreneurs served as fences for the stolen property. They were known as "common proprietors of orchards" and "idle scatter lopping people," but were rarely treated harshly by the courts when caught. Blacks, however, were very severely punished. Washington decreed the death penalty for hog stealing in Virginia in 1748.[31]

The viciousness of American colonists' repression of slaves was successful in keeping down the number of slave revolts. Some scholars have tried to intimate that such rebellions were extensive. The fact is that there were very few, but as Eugene Genovese has said, "the significance of the slave revolts in the United States lies neither in their frequency nor in their extent, but in their very existence as the ultimate manifestation of class war under the most unfavorable conditions."

Before the Revolution, there were two major slave rebellions. In New York in 1712 a group of skilled mechanics, craftsmen, and other privileged slaves, influenced by the democratic rhetoric of Leisler's movement, led a group of thirty blacks in an attempt to free themselves from church and state. They were quickly defeated, and their revolt brought about few changes in the repressive systems.[32]

The slave rebellion at Stono, North Carolina, in 1739, however, did bring about some important changes. Carefully planned, the rebellion began in the early hours of Sunday, September 9, when some twenty slaves, mostly Angolans, gathered near the Stono River in St. Paul's Parish. There, they broke into Hutchenson's store, killed the two shopkeepers, stole all the small arms and powder they could carry and marched southward toward St. Augustine, Florida, a Spanish stronghold where American slaves were being granted freedom. By the time the rebels stopped late that afternoon, they had killed some twenty-five whites, burned various houses and freed seventy more slaves who joined the rebellion.[33]

The militia killed most of the rebels that night. Those who escaped into the woods were eventually tracked down, their heads were cut off and exhibited "at every Mile Post they came to." Thereafter, whites kept much closer watch on their slaves. Blacks were forbidden the right to move about freely on their time off, to assemble, to raise their own food, to earn or keep money, even to learn to read English. Slave owners, while being encouraged to treat their slaves more humanely, were threatened with stiff fines for failing to keep them in line.

So shaken were Carolina whites by the Stono rebellion that they tried to minimize the possibility of another such uprising. They attacked the Spaniards, hoping to push them back from St. Augustine. And they tried to balance off the local ratio of blacks to whites by limiting slave import. But one of the results of the Stono rebellion was to dissuade new European settlers from coming to the Carolinas, and the population remained heavily black. The whites therefore felt compelled to tighten their repression, eliminating any possibility of racial equality or justice.[34]

Chapter 7

Smugglers and Conspirators

Angry, rambunctious, cantankerous, disputatious, dissatisfied, and corrupt, American Britishers in 1765 were not yet disloyal. But they would be by the end of that year—and conspiratorially so as well.

The germ for such conspiracies seems to have been one John Robinson, who bore no relation to the Virginia politician of the same name, and who arrived in America early in the spring of 1764. Assigned to the Newport customs house, he was one of a new group of agents deployed in the colonies to tighten enforcement of His Majesty's Laws of Trade—in short, to crack down on the proliferation of smugglers. A few months earlier, the governor of Rhode Island had flatly refused to install the colony's newly appointed comptroller of customs. The assembly, the governor said, had forbidden him to issue the oath of office. Then in plain view of the surveyor general of customs for all New England, a cargo ship had tied up in Providence without even acknowledging the presence of the customs officials. After the surveyor general ordered the ship seized, a disguised band of citizens returned by night, loaded the ship with export cargo, and dispatched her before dawn. The ship, it turned out, was owned by a Rhode Island judge.[1]

Genteel, urbane Newport, its broad boulevards lined by stately mansions and town houses fronting on carefully tended gardens, may have promised Robinson some hope that he would have an easier assignment than his colleagues in Providence. However, no sooner had he found quarters (with a retired British army officer) and set up office than he discovered how many of those elegant houses were built on the profits of illegal traffic in French molasses. The merchants were perfectly willing to offer him the same arrangement they had provided his predecessors—a flat annual fee of £70,000 in exchange for free license to do business as they liked, no questions asked. Unlike his predecessors, Robinson refused. Instead, he alerted the navy and began to seize the merchants' ships. But the judge of the admiralty court, a Rhode Island native sympathetic to the merchants, always seemed to call the trials on short notice whenever Robinson was too busy to appear. When the court did impose a conviction, it often auctioned off the seized ship and cargo at such ridiculously low prices that the smuggler himself repurchased his own property.[2]

Robinson's first major crisis began with the arrival of the sloop *Polly* at Newport harbor on April 2, 1765. Since the ship's home berth was Taunton, Massachusetts, a town within the Newport jurisdiction, the captain had to declare his cargo—sixty-three casks of molasses from Surinam—at Newport. Once shipowner Job Smith paid the required duty of three pence per gallon, the *Polly* weighed anchor and began to move downbay for unloading at Taunton.[3]

Surveying the ship's report two days later, Robinson decided the captain's declaration was suspiciously low. That afternoon he set out with his servant, a deputy from the customs office, and a certain Captain Antrobus of the British man-of-war *Maidstone* to stop the *Polly* for a second examination. Two days later, on April 6, the four men overtook and searched the *Polly* while she was anchored at Dighton. They found twice the amount of molasses the captain had reported. Robinson ordered the ship and her undeclared cargo seized. But he then had to enforce his order and get the ship hauled to Newport, site of the admiralty court. He tried to recruit a crew in Dighton but found no one willing to serve. He certainly could not beg the ship's captain to bring her in. Lacking other alternatives, he and Antrobus left the customs deputy and the servant on board and returned to Newport to raise a crew. The servant and the deputy then rowed to shore to take a few beers at a Dighton tavern. When they filed out of the bar at dusk, they noticed some forty men dressed in ragged clothes, their faces blackened with charcoal, milling around the waterfront. As they drew closer, it became clear that the peculiarly dressed men were boarding the *Polly* in small boats and carrying off all her molasses casks. More wise than daring, the two retreated to Newport to report what had happened.[4]

Enraged, Robinson again set out for Dighton, this time with Antrobus and a company of thirty marines and forty armed sailors. They stopped en route at Swansea, where a justice of the peace urged them against proceeding farther, advising that "the handful of men they had with them would be nothing against a whole Country." Robinson ignored the advice, asking instead for search warrants, which the justice explained he was not empowered to issue. When Robinson reached Dighton, he stood aghast at what he saw. The townspeople had not only looted the *Polly*'s cargo, but they had also stripped the ship of all her sails, riggings, and fixtures, then drilled holes in her bottom to ground her—at the behest of the shipowner Smith. What was more, when the stunned customs collector reached shore, he was served with an arrest warrant on a complaint from Job Smith, alleging improper seizure and demanding £3,000 damages for the loss of his ship and its cargo.

As a man whose public life was founded upon respect for the law, Robinson had little choice but to give himself over to the sheriff. He may also have noticed how vastly Smith's friends outnumbered the British marines. Smith's friends made the most of their captive customs collector. They forced him to march like a common criminal along the muddy eight-mile road from Dighton to Taunton, surrounded, as he later described it, by an armed "incensed Rabble" and subjected to catcalls from roadside farmers. At Taunton he was thrown in jail. Lacking any local friend to bail him out, all he could do was send a message to the surveyor general for help. "My antagonist," he wrote of Job Smith, "by his friends had made several overtures for an accomodation but as it is no more my inclination than it is in my power, to favour a wretch deserving of the severest treatment that the law can inflict, I continue inflexable, and ready to suffer anything that their malice and wickedness can suggest, tho' happy in the Consolation that the whole is the effect of my doing my duty." Robinson remained in jail two days before the surveyor general sent a man to bail him out. On advice of his superior, the surveyor general, he then had the case transferred out of New England to the admiralty court in Halifax some several hundred miles distant. The net result of the episode was to unite most Rhode Islanders in their determination to resist the Royal taxes.

The wooden-headed Robinson was lionized among a small coterie of Newporters whose principal aim was the destruction of the provincial government. These ten-odd Newport conservatives had come together but a few weeks after Robinson first arrived in Boston. Some were natives, some recent arrivals from England, but all were "of the quality," as the farmers and mechanics might have said derisively. One was an architect, another had as a young man been a companion and colleague of Bishop Berkeley, a third was a debt collector for a large English firm. The exact membership is shadowy and may even have included the attorney general of the colony. None of them projected the character of back-room conspirators; rather they appeared more like disgruntled middle nobility, well educated, and given to loquacious letter writing. And they might have been dismissed as such had they not taken into their bosom this inflexible customs collector who had the power to order Royal gunboats into the pursuit of colonial businessmen.

The members of this Newport club had a simple proposition: bring law and order back to Rhode Island by having the king revoke its charter for self-government and appoint his own royal administrator. For over a hundred years, since Roger Williams secured self-rule for the colony in 1663, they argued, Rhode Island had been plagued by anarchy, the petty bickering of politicians, and the lax authority of the crown. Not until direct royal rule was reimposed, one member insisted, could the colonies ever "be beneficial to themselves nor good subjects to Great Britain." The men of the Newport club also called for a total reordering of colonial rule and reminded Americans, in a document printed in the *Newport Mercury,* that Charles I had always reserved the right to revoke any colonial charters.[5]

Republication of such a document was a clear signal to the supporters of Royal rule that legality was on their side. The Newport conservatives were delighted when the Pennsylvania legislature recommended an end to that colony's charter. There was even talk that Benjamin Franklin favored royal intervention. Thus gaining a real following, the Newporters were so effective in provoking widespread discussion of self-rule in the colonies that other Rhode Islanders began to register alarm that the seeds of a dark plot were being sown. One writer charged that "some, if not all, of the members of this wonderful club are at this time actually conspiring against the liberties of the colony, and that they have, with other enemies of the colony, formed a petition, and sent it to the King, praying that our most valuable charter privileges may be taken away, notwithstanding their specious pretences in the newspapers of promoting the welfare of the government." Rhode Island's governor Stephen Hopkins then confirmed that such a petition had been sent to the king and denounced it, setting off a veritable pamphleteering war between the enemies and the partisans of home rule which lasted throughout 1765.[6]

None of the letters and pamphlets surpassed the rhetorical fervor of Boston firebrand James Otis. Describing the Newport club, Otis wrote: "Such is the little dirty, drinking, drabbing, contaminated knot of thieves, beggars and transports, or the worthy descendents of such, collected from the four winds of the earth, and made up of Turks, Jews and other Infidels, with a few renegade Christians and Catholics, and altogether formed into a club of scarce a dozen at N-p-t. From hence proceed Halifax-letters, petitions to alter the colony forms of government, libels upon all good colonists and subjects, and every evil work that can enter into the heart of man."[7]

Boston's James Otis certainly escalated the rhetorical warfare between the royalist conservatives and the emerging patriots. Like Governor Hopkins, he was widely known in New England for his attacks against the arbitrary policies of George III. And just at that point, another such arbitrary measure was passed by the English Parliament—the Stamp Act.

A direct tax levied against all publications and legal documents (even shipping papers) issued anywhere in the colonies, the tax was seen as grossly oppressive to all of the colonies' merchants. But these rich entrepreneurs did, after all, control the politics of the colonies. Calling themselves—and called—patriots, they succeeded in damning the act as an infringement on the liberty of all colonials. The response throughout the colonies is well known. The Virginia House of Burgesses led the resistance, adopting resolutions at the end of May 1765 that denied the Crown's right to impose the new tax. But it was the Boston patriots who reacted most vehemently, and the pivotal figure in their campaign was a South End gang boss named Ebeneezer MacIntosh.

Romance and intrigue surround MacIntosh's role in prerevolutionary politics. He emerged into sudden prominence as leader of the anti-Stamp Act riots in August. He held a minor political office as leather sealer (or inspector) for another four years. His brother-in-law was killed in the Boston Massacre of 1770. His descendants maintain he was one of the masterminds of the Boston Tea Party in 1773, though there is scant evidence to confirm their claim. By the outbreak of the Revolution, he had retired to his regular life as shoemaker and moved to New Hampshire. A slight man, not physically striking in any way, MacIntosh was born into a Scottish family that always seemed to be scrambling for survival. His father, Moses, was several times "warned out" of the towns where he had lived—an action usually taken by town fathers to get rid of those they believed might become public charges. By the time he was fourteen, Ebeneezer MacIntosh was on his own, his mother dead and his father driven out of Boston. He apparently stayed in school long enough to learn to read and write, and by his middle teens was earning a living as a shoemaker. In December 1754 he appears as a private in the "alarm list of militia" in Boston's South End—then as now a working-class quarter where young men formed loose gangs in order to survive in the rivalry with the city's North End. Although he fought in the French and Indian War on the Canadian front, MacIntosh probably established his prowess during the annual November 5 Pope's Day brawls, which brought him to the attention of Boston's "patriotic" merchant leaders.

Known in England as Guy Fawkes Day, Pope's Day was always a rowdy celebration that usually ended in fistfights between the North and South Enders. So it was on November 5, 1764, but with one big difference. In previous years, the South Enders had been roundly beaten. This time Ebeneezer MacIntosh had managed to organize his boys at strategic locations along the festival's parade route. And this time, they fought with clubs and staves as well as their fists. Bridges were sealed off, town squares turned bloody. A small child was killed as a wagon wheel crushed his head. At day's end, MacIntosh and his boys were victorious, and Ebeneezer MacIntosh won a reputation and the title "Captain."

No record shows exactly how MacIntosh the rowdy rioter was transformed in less than a year into MacIntosh the patriotic freedom fighter. He had been arrested, along with several others, for his behavior during the Pope's Day brawl, but if he received any sentence, it was at worst a slight fine and served only to boost his standing in the community, for in March he was elected to his post as leather sealer. Then in July, MacIntosh became involved in a peculiar civil suit brought by the patriot Samuel Adams for an old debt of just over twelve pounds. The suit appeared to be a perfectly ordinary affair that might have involved any merchant or tradesman in Boston. But to the conspiracy-minded English, and especially to Lieutenant Governor Thomas Hutchinson, its disposal implied a sinister plot, especially when Adams, who won the judgment, made no attempt to collect and then canceled the debt. Hutchinson concluded—and some historians agree—that MacIntosh worked for a secret group of merchants known as the Loyal Nine, who later became the part of the famous Sons of Liberty, and the Nine pressured Adams to drop the case. The fact is, that on August 14, 1765, MacIntosh turned a demonstration against the newly arrived stamp distributor into one of the most violent riots before the Revolution. The demonstration had been planned by the Loyal Nine, and while Adams was not a full member, he attended their meetings.[9]

The events of the August 14 riots are well known. Just after dawn, members of the Loyal Nine hung two effigies on the limb of a great tree on Newberry Street. Known among the patriots as the Liberty Tree, it was a gathering point for radical celebrations. The two effigies strung up that morning were of Andrew Oliver, the new stamp distributor, and a devil crawling out of a large boot. The boot, no doubt constructed by shoemaker MacIntosh, represented a pun on the name of the detested English prime minister, John Stuart, third earl of Bute; the sole of the boot was painted green, a punning reference to George Grenville, who as chancellor of the exchequer was in charge of taxes. An early attempt by Hutchinson to have the effigies cut down was dropped when the sheriff reported that he and his men would surely be killed if they tried to move against the mobs, reputedly five thousand strong.[10]

As the afternoon wore on, MacIntosh—who had been anointed "First Captain General of Liberty Tree," mocking the long pompous titles of the English officials—had his men take down the effigy of Oliver and carry it to Oliver's house. There, in grand pantomime, the mob leaders beheaded the figure as their followers stoned the stamp distributor's house. Moving to the top of Fort Hill, they then urged the people to come and "stamp" the dismembered effigy with their feet. Finally the remains of the shredded effigy were burned. Officially that was the end of the protest as planned by the Loyal Nine.

Few people, however, were in a mood to retire. Instead they marched back down the hill, destroyed an office building Oliver owned, then returned to his house. Within a few hours, the place had been ransacked, the dishes and furniture shattered, the walls ripped to shreds. Oliver had retreated at the first sound of trouble, but later, at about 11:00 P.M., Lieutenant Governor Hutchinson (who was Oliver's brother-in-law) made a grand show of braggadocio as he appeared with the sheriff and attempted to quell the crowds. Immediately the cry went up: "The governor and the sheriff!" The two were driven away by a storm of rocks.

The next day Andrew Oliver agreed to resign the job he had not yet actually begun. For the next twelve days, the city was peaceful. MacIntosh, keeping close counsel with the Loyal Nine, maintained order among his followers. On August 26 a new rally was set. After a few initial speeches beside a bonfire on King Street, the demonstrators broke into two groups. One went to the home of Justice William Story, a conservative North Ender who had tried MacIntosh in February for his role in the previous Pope's Day brawl and who had reportedly filed damning reports about the corrupt activities of Boston merchants. The other demonstrators marched to the home of the customs collector, Benjamin Hallowell. The houses of both men were ravaged. Finally, as the demonstrators reunited under MacIntosh's direction, they went on to attack the stately home of Lieutenant Governor Thomas Hutchinson, said to be one of the finest in New England.[11]

What followed is best described by Thomas Hutchinson himself in a letter he wrote to a colleague in London, August 30:

> In the evening while I was at supper and my children round me, somebody ran in and said the mob were coming. I directed my children to fly to a secure place and shut up my house as I had done before intending not to quit it, but my eldest daughter . . . would not quit the house unless I did. I could not stand this and withdrew with her to a neighboring house where I had been but a few minutes before the hellish crew fell upon my house with the rage of devils and in a moment with axes split down the door and entered. My son being in the great entry heard them cry damn him, he is upstairs we'll have him. Some ran immediately as high as the top of the house, others filled the rooms below and cellars and others remained without the house to be employed

> there. Messages soon came . . . to inform me the mob were coming in pursuit of me and I was obliged to retire thro yards and gardens to a house more remote where I remained until 4 o'clock by which time one of the best finished houses in the Province had nothing but the bare walls and floors. Not contented with tearing off all the wainscot and hangings and splitting the doors to pieces they beat down the Partition walls and altho that alone cost them near two hours they cut down the cupola or lantern and they began to take the plate [slate] and boards from the roof and were prevented only by the approaching daylight from a total destruction of the building. The garden fence was laid flat and all my trees &c broke down to the ground. Such ruins were never seen in America. Besides my plate and family pictures, household furniture of every kind, my own, my children and servants apparel, they carried off about £900 sterling in money, emptied the house of every thing whatsoever except a part of the kitchen furniture not leaving a single book or paper in it and having scattered or destroyed all the manuscript and other papers I had been collecting for 30 years together besides a great number of publick papers in my custody.[12]

A town meeting was called the next day, attended by rioters and Crown sympathizers alike. No clear call to action emerged from it. Ebeneezer MacIntosh was arrested by Sheriff Stephen Greenleaf later in the day, but he was released almost immediately when several prominent gentlemen warned Greenleaf that if MacIntosh were held, an even more devastating riot would likely result. As angry as Hutchinson understandably was, no further moves were taken against MacIntosh. A twenty-eight-year-old bachelor, riding on the unanimous support of the South End gangs, he had dared to challenge two of the highest ranking authorities in the province and had won. The city's merchants then began organizing a boycott of English goods, and the governor, Francis Bernard, was cowed. In a letter to General Gage, he confessed "that all civil power ceased in an instant, and I had not the least authority to oppose or quiet the Mob."[13]

On November 1, the day the Stamp Act was to go into effect, MacIntosh took charge of yet another demonstration. But as there now was little need to show further patriot muscle, MacIntosh proved his power by shutting off the violence, and did so again on November 5, Pope's Day. For the first time in years, the North and South End gangs marched together to the Liberty Tree, an accomplishment for which only MacIntosh could claim credit. Yet his greatest moment of glory came six weeks later. Despite Andrew Oliver's resignation and statement to the newspapers that he would not administer the Stamp Act in Boston, rumors circulated that he was planning to do so just the same. Thus he was summoned to the Liberty Tree at noon on December 17 by the very people who destroyed his house to publicly renounce his responsibility as stamp distributor. According to one contemporary account, "It happened to be a rainy and tempestuous day, and Mr. Oliver was obliged to march through the streets exposed to the weather. But what added, probably, not a little to his mortification, Mr. MacIntosh, a chief leader among the Liberty Party, attended him at his right hand to the Tree, at the head of an immense multitude."[14]

After 1765 and the subsequent passing of the Stamp Act crisis Ebeneezer MacIntosh faded into relative obscurity. He may have had a central role in the Boston Tea Party eight years later, as his son later claimed, but if so it was not well known. The fact that he did not rise into further prominence after the winter of 1765–66 may have been partial grounds for the English suspicion that he was really only a tool in the hands of a large conspiracy hatched by the gentlemen merchants of Boston whose motivation was little more than greed and personal political ambition. But though Hutchinson regarded him as little more than a jailbird from the lower-class rabble, other English officials credited MacIntosh as a man of measured integrity. Andrew Oliver's brother Peter wrote that, "He was sensible and manly, and performed their dirty Jobs for them with great Eclat." As Hutchinson reported it, MacIntosh took his orders for running the riots and demonstrations from "a superior set consisting of the master masons, carpenters &c of the town." That "superior set," Hutchinson maintained, took *their* cues from a committee of merchants. But above them all, according to Hutchinson's amazingly accurate scenario, were the master smugglers—and master strategists—Samuel Adams, James Otis, and John Hancock.[15]

Of all the wealthy prerevolutionary smugglers, John Hancock was the most notorious. At one time proprietors of the largest shipping firm in Boston, John and his father, Thomas, kept their own wharf and ran a large commercial fleet between Spain, Holland, London, the West

Indies, and Boston. The elder Hancock had built much of the firm's strength in the 1730s by flaunting the Molasses Act import tax. By the 1760s John, a better politician than he was a businessman, had publicly forbidden English customs officers to search below deck on any of his London ships. Such insolence, however, was too much for the English to ignore. One night in early June 1767, the Boston customs collector called on the captain of a recently arrived British man-of-war to help him seize the pride of the Hancock fleet, the *Liberty*. Fighting spread across the wharf as the *Liberty* was being cut loose. Several times the man-of-war's master ordered his marines to fire on the mob, but there is no report that they did. At first Hancock seemed willing to make a settlement with the customs collector, but then, on advice of Sam Adams and James Otis, he refused. His ship was taken by the court. He was indicted for smuggling £3,000 worth of wine; other fines and penalties could have totaled £100,000. Having made their stand, however, the British began to back off, realizing that a harsh judgment against a man so popular as Hancock could provoke a citywide rebellion. The attorney general dropped the remaining charges. After all, the *Liberty* had already been forfeited to the Crown. It was converted to a British revenue cutter.[16]

In organizing the actual riots, Otis and Adams and the Loyal Nine preferred to remain anonymous. As Henry Bass, one of the Nine, wrote to a friend, "We do everything in order to keep this . . . private, and are not a little pleas'd to hear that MacIntosh has the credit of the whole affair." Indeed, in Newport, Charleston, Philadelphia, the pattern was repeated: Rich merchants who did not want to pay taxes used the poor, by talking about liberty, to raise the banner of independence and got them to do so by hiring young leaders from the lower classes as intermediaries. As General Gage, commander of New York and regarded by historians as a fair observer, put it: "The whole body of merchants in general, Assembly Men, Magistrates, &c have been united in this plan of riots, and without the influence and instigation of these, inferior people would have been quiet. . . . The sailors who are the only people who may be properly stiled mob, are entirely at the command of the merchants who employ them."[17]

In fact, Gage was correct. But what he and his Royal British colleagues failed to understand was that while the lower classes were indeed being used by mostly avaricious merchants for their own ends, the lower classes were increasingly fed up. The system that oppressed them was not wholly British-made. It was also the result of the selfishness, racial and class intolerance, self-righteous corruption, oppressive superiority and immorality of that upper crust of merchants and entrepreneurs which eventually called itself the patriots and which took over economic and political control of America after the Revolution. But the exploited classes did not know it. They blamed the British. And this was not understood by the British and Loyalists. Thus, until such irreversible watershed events as the Massacre and later the Tea Party, the Loyalists seemed incapable of seeing the American resistance as a unified political rebellion of a rising nation. Regarding the Sons of Liberty as only a group of greedy manipulators conspiring for their self-interest, the English despised them as heinous criminals who not only betrayed their class by unleashing the power of the mob but were also willing to risk destroying the whole fabric of secular and divine authority. But more than simple profits were at stake. To most Americans, the notorious corruption at the court of George III, the traffic in royal appointments, and the autocratic treatment of the colonies constituted "great reason to believe that a deep-laid and desperate plan of imperial despotism has been laid, and partly executed, for the extinction of all civil liberty . . . the august and once revered fortress of English freedom—the admirable of ages—the BRITISH CONSTITUTION seems fast tottering into fatal and inevitable ruin."[18]

The American merchant-patriots of 1770 did not view themselves as venal, corrupt hustlers. Cheating on taxes imposed by a foreign power, smuggling, resisting unfair laws, even destroying Crown property or taking the life of an arbitrary despot had nothing to do with crime. Nor was their revolution launched to alleviate social and economic exploitation. The only principle involved, said the patriots, was freedom. In America, consequently, liberty became equated with the absence of corruption. As they surveyed the continents of the world, Americans found only one other country where corrupt demagogues had not oppressed the people's freedom, and that was tiny Switzerland. As Thomas Paine wrote in one of his most fervent essays, "Every spot of the old world is overrun with oppression. Freedom hath been hunted round the globe. Asia and Africa have long expelled her. Europe regards her like a stranger, and England hath given her warning to depart. O! receive the fugitive, and prepare in time an asylum for mankind." Little wonder then that the patriots and their descendants could believe that "the cause of America is in a great measure the cause of all mankind."[19]

As that cause became identified with the Revolution, actions which both sides would otherwise have regarded as vandalism, assault, and murder became accepted as legitimate acts of political warfare. Barristers and gentlemen might describe their grievances in grand language concerning the hallowed rights of Englishmen. Farmers, mechanics, tradesmen, and petty merchants, however, had been bitten by the bug of rising expectation. By July 4, 1776, there was no longer doubt in the minds of serious men and women that justice in courtrooms was secondary to politics. In a Loyalist town, "patriots" would be the criminals most aggressively prosecuted; in counties dominated by revolutionaries it would be the Loyalists.

Ordinary crime, of course, did not disappear during the Revolution any more than it has in any other American war. Horse stealing, highway robbery, and counterfeiting remained problems for the British and the rebels alike, especially in the backcountry along the Appalachian ridges. New Jersey and Pennsylvania authorities passed laws making horse theft a capital offense. As the fighting intensified, there seems to have been as much plundering of homes and shops by the Americans as by the British. Fresh, untrained volunteers in the patriot forces were especially susceptible to the iniquities of such large cities as Philadelphia and New York. In New York's "Holy Ground" district, many a clever wench lured an eager rebel lad and fleeced him of whatever money he had. As Isaac Bangs, a pious lieutenant fresh from Harvard, wrote, "When I visited them at first, I thought nothing could exceed them for imprudence and immodesty; but I found the more I was acquainted with them the more they excelled in their Brutality." Several squads of General Washington's New York troops were at one time reported infected with "the French disease" from their prowling ventures in the Holy Ground. Others were even less lucky, for not all the prostitutes sympathized with the patriot boys. Lieutenant Bangs concluded his report: "Unless there is some care taken of these horrid wretches by the General, he will soon have his Army greatly impaired, for they not only destroy men by sickness, but they sometimes inhumanly murther them; for since Monday last two men were found inhumanly murthered and concealed, besides one who was castrated in a barbarous manner."[20]

According to complaints of Loyalist Americans, particularly in the districts held by the patriots, general crime often went unpunished. Apparently, the new civil authorities—many of whom had held provincial posts under British rule—were far more concerned with establishing respect for authority than with tracking down random crooks. James Allen, a prominent Tory, wrote that "the province of Pennsylvania . . . may be divided into two classes of men, viz. those that plunder and those that are plundered. No justice had been administered, no crimes punished for 9 months. All power is in the hands of the associators, who are under no subordination to their officers." Allen became so outspoken in his criticism of the patriot cause that he was himself arrested in Philadelphia and threatened with banishment to North Carolina.[21]

What upset Allen and his fellow Tories even more than unprosecuted crimes, however, was the apparent threat from the lower classes, the rising of "all the dregs to the top," as Allen put it. The Loyalists of the Northeast were particularly concerned about class upheaval. "Everything I see," declared Boston's Jonathan Sewell, "is laughable, cursable, and damnable; my pew in the church is converted into a pork tub; my house into a den of rebels, thieves, and lice; my farm in possession of the very worst of all God's creation; my debts all gone to the devil with my debtors."[22]

To the south, along the tidewater settlements of Virginia and the Carolinas and the ridges of Appalachia, there was more than social station at stake. Neither the patriots nor the Crown officers could count on abiding loyalty from the country people. Family feuds and Indian massacres, still a residual problem, made the South a volatile and savage revolutionary front. Towns that claimed allegiance to Washington one month went over to the British the next. Moreover, the outbreak of war thoroughly dismantled the remnants of the Regulator movements, which in the 1760s had kept mountain outlaws in check. Ironically, it was the Tories—known as the party of law and order—who turned more and more to simple banditry once the revolutionary forces took control of the frontier. Turned away as outcasts by their neighbors, these poor isolated Tories had no real chance of returning to England and instead became mountain marauders. Frequently allying themselves with the increasingly disgruntled Indian tribes, they often mounted raids on the coastal cities. One of the most notorious of these Tories, Major William ("Bloody Bill") Cunningham, led a band of men on a wave of revenge murders against the Whig families of Savannah. Not only had Cunningham's father been brutally beaten by a patriot officer, his epileptic brother had been flogged to death. According to one account, Cunningham's men captured several Whig soldiers. Then, "each of Cunningham's men singled out whomsoever among the prisoners had been guilty of murdering any of his relatives, and killed him forthwith."[23]

The banditry, plundering, and random individual violence that took place during the American Revolution are almost indistinguishable from the wanton individual criminal acts that are usually encouraged by the atmosphere of war. It may be true that as the French gentleman-farmer J. Hector St. John (M.G.J. de Crèvecoeur) claimed, the backcountry violence of the revolutionary war was especially horrific. Certainly many of the gentlemen-patriots sympathized with his warnings about the consequences of civil rape, especially when they surveyed the power of urban mob actions. "When from whatever motives," he wrote, "the laws are no longer respected; when . . . all the social bonds are loosened, the same effects will follow. This is now the case with us: the son is armed against the father, the brother against the brother, family against family." But that was not the ultimate danger. For while the social bonds were indeed loosened during the Revolution, that did not lead to a new society riddled with itinerant criminals. On the contrary, there was a much worse consequence: Social bonds were drawn tight against the freedom of dissidents and malcontents, so that the suppression of crime became an important new tool in the campaign for a stable postwar society that the newly rich would govern in a manner designed to guarantee their own prosperity.[24]

PART II

Crime in the New Republic

Thronged as our city is, men are robbed in the streets. Thousands, that are arrested, go unpunished, and the defenseless and the beautiful are ravished in the day time, and no trace of the criminals is found. The man of business, in his lawful calling, at the most public corner of our city, is slaughtered in the sunshine and packed up and sent away.

—Board of Aldermen, New York City, 1842

Chapter 8

Poverty, Property, and Prisons

In less than half a century after the inauguration of George Washington, the United States became transformed from a loose alliance of farm towns and seaports to one of the most formidable political and economic powers in the Atlantic community. A generation of revolutionary heroes and philosophical idealists had been replaced by a generation of promoters, military adventurers, and party politicians. The national leadership had successfully prosecuted a war with England and was preparing for another with Mexico, both conflicts justified by America's holy destiny to create a new world free of Europe's corrupt and despotic influence. To the world beyond her borders, the stripling government of the United States was both testing its political manhood and proclaiming itself the trailblazer for freedom, justice, and domestic tranquillity. As a member of the "community of nations," the United States was conducting itself just as the Founding Fathers had envisioned it would.

The people who lived and worked in this new constitutional utopia, however, were soon forced to confront a growing and dangerous challenge at home. While generals, statesmen, and explorers were harvesting the fruits of the boundless western frontier, the artisans, shopkeepers, and petty officials of the port cities were discovering a dark new frontier of men and women who lived beyond the law. Within a generation of the Constitution's ratification, an expanding permanent population of criminals had emerged all along the eastern seaboard. Prostitution, thievery, counterfeiting, even a fairly continuous rumble of violence and killing, had seasoned daily life in this new America. Ghettos, dominated by racketeers, were now the blight of every major coastal city. Goon squads, in the hire of upstart politicians, ran roughshod over Boston, New York, Philadelphia, and Baltimore. Sooty urchins sold their bodies to the factories or street hustlers or both, and died of starvation on the doorsteps of flophouses so vile the armed police feared to enter them. Newspaper writers, politicians, ministers, and ordinary citizens were naturally upset by the specter of uncontrollable crime in their cities. The lack of public safety was a threat to everyone.

But beyond the fear of personal attack, runaway crime exposed a deeper dilemma that recalled the metaphysical roots of American society: the old problem of subconscious self-doubt that had haunted the Puritan imagination. Americans believed that after the Revolution they stood as the tangible proof that the liberal ideas of the Enlightenment could lead to a new age of progress and human brotherhood. It was to be a society of law where such corruptions as crime, poverty, and oppression would wither of their own accord. The discovery of poverty and crime, as one historian has put it, is the story of the great failure of the first age of the American Republic.[1]

"It is from ignorance, wretchedness or corrupted manners of a people that crime proceeds," Philadelphia pamphleteer William Bradford wrote in 1793. "In a country where these do not prevail, moderate punishments, strictly enforced, will be a curb as effectual as the greatest severity." That fervent hope was borrowed, at least in part, from Italian economist and criminologist Cesare Beccaria. Crime, Beccaria had written, was the result of oppressive law:

> The severity of punishment of itself emboldens men to commit the very wrongs it is supposed to prevent. They are driven to commit additional crimes to avoid the punishment for a single one. The countries and times most notorious for severity of penalties have always been those in which the bloodiest and most inhumane deeds were committed. . . . Do you want to prevent crime? See to it that the laws are clear and simple and that the entire force of a nation is united in their defense.[2]

In response to such optimism, early republican leaders moved quickly to abolish the painful punishments that had been the hallmark of colonial justice. First they restricted the death penalty, which, under English law, could be imposed for the theft of a handkerchief as easily as for murder. Whippings, stocks, the tying of "immoral" women to the cart's tail, were replaced with a new and progressive institution—prison. The theory was that if the threat of punishment would deter free citizens from violating the social contract, separation from society would definitely sober those few who violated the law. Thus, by 1800, prisons were built in Pennsylvania, New York, New Jersey, and Virginia.[3]

But it was not just the concept of punishment that was changing. It was the definition of crime itself. In Massachusetts, the "Bible Colony," sinful offenses against God and offensive public behavior had always burdened the criminal docket. By 1789, at the time of completion of the Constitution, irreverence and sexual license were of virtually no concern to the courts. A study of Middlesex County cases showed that 210 of the 370 prosecutions between 1760 and 1774 were for fornication, 3 were for cohabitation and adultery, and 27 were for violation of the Sabbath. By 1789, when a new code was put into effect, 5 people were convicted of fornication; in 1791, 1 and after that none. Clearly the courts of Middlesex County—like most of the nation's prosecutors—cared little about who went to bed with whom. Religious indictments also declined, so much so, that by 1816 a court publication noted that " thousands of violations occurred every year, with scarcely a single instance of punishment."[4]

If God had been driven from the bench by the enlightened ideas of the revolutionaries, still the courts were not left without work, for a new trend was developing—prosecution for crimes against property. Throughout the colonial decades, a gradual increase in theft and burglary had been recorded in the larger port cities. But after the revolutionary war, the increase was phenomenal. In Middlesex County, for example, the records show that theft and burglary prosecutions rose about four times from 1775 through 1784. Prosecutions remained at that level until 1790, decreasing slightly during the economic boom years of the 1790s; but during the depression of 1807 they doubled again. Those prosecuted were mostly poor laborers (75 percent during the 1780s; 71 percent after 1807) from the crowded towns along the Charles River outside Boston.[5]

According to the urban gentry, private property appeared in greater danger after the Revolution than before. Events in Middlesex County were symptomatic. Middlesex was one of the several Massachusetts counties caught up in Shays's Rebellion in 1786, a major populist challenge to the big city's control of the state government. From 1780, conservative Boston shippers and financiers used the state constitution to restrict voting rights to property holders. By controlling the legislature, they secured several tax levies for the repayment of the revolutionary war debt and, at the same time, pressed foreclosure suits against the threadbare farmers of western Massachusetts. In reaction, former militia captain Daniel Shays led an unsuccessful armed insurrection of two thousand debt-ridden farmers that shut down the courts of several counties. The rebellion smoldered for six months until it was crushed in February 1787. But Shays and his comrades aroused the anger and resentment of thousands across the Bay State, not only farmers but also poor laborers in the cities. Later, the Whisky and Fries rebellions in western and eastern Pennsylvania resurrected that anger fueled by the same issues.

The disparity between rich and poor, which the Revolution had promised to diminish, grew worse. But artisans, shopkeepers, and petty politicians profited well from the postrevolutionary economic free-for-all. The sudden exodus of between sixty to eighty thousand British Loyalists threw open the doors to thousands of small businesses and hundreds of thousands of acres of confiscated estates. Land speculation in Kentucky, Ohio, Georgia, Mississippi, and the Northwest Territory was rampant. With the former aristocracy decimated, social rank and prestige fell to those who were quickest to display the outward trappings of success. Or, as Boston Brahmin Catherine Sedgwick reflected some years later: "Wealth is the great leveling principle." Those who had it, or could get it, claimed influence. Those who could not were seen as threatening rabble.[6]

Under the guiding influence of Federalist leaders, most importantly John Adams, John Jay, and Alexander Hamilton, these materialist tendencies were canonized into law. Although the 1780s were in fact years of general prosperity, the rising class of businessmen were just as dissatisfied as the struggling poor under the loose Articles of Confederation. War creditors were unable to recover their money. Attempts by the individual states to devise protective tariffs failed. Craftsmen were fearful of a flood of English imports. American diplomacy failed to reopen British markets to northern manufacturers.

And, crucial in the long run, the southern states grew ever more anxious about their proportional representation in a Congress dominated by antislavery politicians. The haphazard confederation of states was, in short, an inadequate instrument for molding the interests of the new commercial classes. But in the eyes of the Federalist patricians, the solution was a tough national legal system to enforce order among rebellious insurgents.

Conflict among the competing commercial factions led to the call for a constitutional convention in 1787. The nation, they were convinced, could no longer function without a coherent economic structure to regulate trade and establish a unified commercial system. The deals made by these competitive commercial interests were, in the words of the eminent historian Charles Beard, "the great compromises of the constitution."[7]

Fear of lower-class rebellion against privilege and property was a central motivation of the constitutionalists, and it was not entirely new. In 1765 John Adams, the future president, had written in alarm after a "mob" had pillaged a British royal official's house:

> . . . to have his garden torn in pieces and his house broken open, his furniture destroyed . . . is a very atrocious violation of the peace and of dangerous tendency and consequence.[8]

That these attacks against property continued during the 1790s and afterward, and were aggravated during the periods of depression, was a sign of continued popular discontent. Thus, an important new function of the law became the protection of property. Massachusetts governor John Hancock said as much when he warned the state's legislature in 1793 that the object of criminal law was both the "good order" of the government and "the security" of the property. Throughout the colonial period the security of people's homes had been largely a matter of civil law enforced by order of the court. By the end of the nation's second decade, in 1810, the prosecution of assaults on private property became the primary activity of the courts. The Middlesex records show 47 percent of all prosecutions were for theft during those two decades.[9]

Just as the protection of property became the direct concern of the government, so too the relationship of each individual citizen to the government took on a new character. Under colonial law, when one citizen accused another of stealing his horses, the court and the sheriff formally took the role of Solomon—to adjudicate the fairness of claims between citizens. But as the violation of property became a violation of *law,* the court came to represent the rights of the property owner. As a result the alleged thief stood not only against his accusing neighbor; he was also pitted against the power and authority of the government. Edward Livingstone, one of the ablest civil libertarians of the postrevolutionary era, argued that these new legalistic "advances" in the law left the ordinary citizen more tyrannized than ever before. He charged: ". . . a criminal in his trial—squalid in his appearance, his body debilitated by confinement, his mind weakened by misery or conscious guilt, abandoned by all the world—stands alone to contend with the fearful odds that are arrayed against him." Such a system thus embodied the notion that a criminal was not just someone who had failed to act according to a universal moral code. He was now characterized as an enemy of the state bent on the willful destruction of its authority.[10]

Such an outlaw enemy, for example, was Michael Martin, Irish immigrant, farmhand, sometime brewer, and highway robber. He and a score of others had their lives chronicled in probably the first criminal encyclopedia published in the United States, a small volume printed in 1833 under the title *The Record of Crimes in the United States.* The exploits of Martin and the other rogues highlighted in *The Record* appeared when patrician fear of growing crime waves was being whipped into a panic by the press and politicians.

Michael Martin landed at Salem, Massachusetts, in 1819 aboard a ship he and other passengers had commandeered after the captain had announced he was changing course midway across the ocean. Throughout the account of his life in Ireland, Canada, and the United States, Martin's biographer carefully portrayed him as an avaricious, lower-class malcontent, a man who, because he was Irish, took special pride in fleecing English gentlemen of their fine watches. First, we are told, he worked as an honest man, operating a small brewery with money his brother had sent him "until he found the people too acute for him in the way of bargaining" and then "returned to his former habits of dissipation." Next, on the way to Canada, "he robbed a Connecticut peddler of seventy dollars," arguing that "he took it for granted that the peddler had obtained the cash by cheating honest men, which was probably the case, and thought that the money would be in better keeping for the transfer."

Gambler, horse thief, highway robber, con artist, Michael Martin was a man of wit and spirit who lived not only outside the law but also outside proper society, where he saw trade and commerce as simply other forms of ritualized thievery. In one gambit he paraded as an agent for a group of immigrants looking for land to buy and "was directed to the house of an old gentleman who had large tracts for sale." As he was being led about the grounds of the estate and up into the manor house, Martin pulled a pistol on the old man in an upper room, took his money, left him bound and gagged, then walked downstairs where the man's son had been writing in the parlor. "He told the young man he was waiting for his father, and desired him to bring his horse in the meantime. While the youth was gone to the stable he opened the desk and took away an hundred and seventy pounds in specie. On the son's return Martin told him that his father desired to see him upstairs, and as soon as he was out of the room mounted his horse and went off."

Crooks always met doom at the hands of the law in those early annals, and Martin, of course, found his. On October 9, 1821, two years after he arrived in America, he stood before the Cambridge Supreme Judicial Court and was convicted of stealing a watch from a "Mr. Bray, a very respectable gentleman of Boston." (Martin had declined to take the watch of Mrs. Bray, who was riding in the carriage with her husband, because, he said, he never robbed ladies.) He was sentenced to be hanged on a gibbet, a sentence he took calmly, remarking, "Well, that is the worst you can do." Though he failed in a clever escape attempt, feigning sickness so as to overcome the turnkey, Martin remained stoic to his death. The world and his life in it, he explained a few days before the execution, appeared "much like a cloud of smoke over the city, to be driven away by the first gust."[11]

The young American government certainly regarded Michael Martin as its enemy. He was the sort of fellow the aging John Adams had warned against in 1765. Yet Michael Martin was also an exceptional outlaw on the increasingly urban eastern seaboard. Most of the rangy, adventurous highwaymen like Martin were being pushed westward toward the frontiers of the Mississippi and Ohio rivers, leaving in New York, Boston, and Philadelphia their more timid cousins, the poor, hungry displaced Irish farmers who packed themselves into tenement houses and searched for work in the new factories.

Five thousand immigrants a year streamed into the United States during its first thirty years. Population jumped from 4 million to 7 million between 1790 and 1820. No country in the world claimed such a growth during any part of the nineteenth century. For a while, new factories and industries kept up with the pace. Shipyards, ironworks, cotton mills, farm-implement foundries, shoe factories—every commodity that a prosperous society could need went into production. In 1809 alone eighty-seven new cotton mills were erected. "From one end of the continent to the other, the universal roar is, Commerce! Commerce! at all events, Commerce!" boasted one well-traveled physician and commentator. It was the age of enterprise. Not merely factories, but all manner of businesses were incorporated—banks, insurance companies, canals, turnpikes, and trading combines. Over seventeen hundred incorporation charters were granted by the states in the first seventeen years of the century. To make it all work, America needed manpower. Skilled workmen from England, Scotland and Germany, especially metal workers, miners, and specialized craftsmen, were wooed and for a while commanded premium wages. But for the unskilled workers, like the displaced Irish farmers, American prosperity frequently proved fickle. When they arrived they found only tough competition—which, of course, led to strife.[12]

Strife was exactly what the new entrepreneurs wanted. Elkenah Watson, the son of a Massachusetts artisan who became a wealthy agricultural promoter, put forth the opinion that national success, as well as public welfare, could only emerge from "a general strife" fomented by competing individuals. That general strife, which replaced the village neighborliness and paternalism of the colonial years, arose from the swelling labor pool the immigrants provided. The common mill laborer became as expendable as a broken pulley. As one leading historian of the period has pointed out: "Mechanization and the factory system, by minimizing the values of traditional crafts and skills, reduced the bargaining power of the individual workman almost to the vanishing point; what little he had left was lost in contests with other men—and women and children too—for jobs which one was as competent to fill as another. The prizes in these races nearly always went to the cheapest." The result was inevitable: the depressions of 1807, 1819, and 1837. America's transient mass of poor, expendable, unskilled workers were perceived as the source of America's expanding pool of criminality.[13]

At first the discovery of crime and poverty provoked shame and embarrassment. By 1820 politicians and social reformers could no longer deny the dismal results of the legal reforms of the 1790s. The enthusiastic construction of prisons matched with a more humane schedule of laws seemed at best to have done nothing—and at worst to have contributed to the propagation of criminals. The prison was characterized frequently in newspapers and handbills as a breeding ground for criminals. Writing anonymously on the need for a larger police department, New York magistrate Charles Christian spoke directly about the dangers posed by the state prison to his city: "The discharge in this city of the state prison convicts is productive of bad consequences to its inhabitants." And one outspoken New York lawyer declared flatly: "Our favorite scheme of substituting a state prison for the gallows is a prolific mother of crime. . . . Our state prisons, as at present constituted, are grand demoralizers of our people." The New York Society for the Prevention of Pauperism charged that the state prison "operates with alarming efficacy to increase, diffuse, and extend the love of vice, and a knowledge of the arts and practices of criminality."[14]

Charles Christian, in offering his treatise on the New York police, included a survey of the city's criminals and the institutions upon which they thrived. Thieves, sharpers, gamblers, pawnbrokers (dealing presumably in stolen property), and drunks were all on his list, but none were more important than the prostitutes and streetwalkers:

> Of the vast number of loose women that infest the streets of this city, a great proportion are so utterly depraved by all manner of low debaucheries, especially by the use of ardent liquors, so totally bereft of shame that they are to all appearance beyond the possibility of reform.[15]

Criminal women always seem to have drawn the special wrath of moralists and constables. Certainly in the New York of the early nineteenth century the anticrime crusaders were merciless to streetwalkers and other women of "easy virtue." The French traveler Alexis de Tocqueville was told by prison officials that "the reformation of girls who have contracted bad morals is a chimera which it is useless to pursue."[11]* Women were taken to be creatures of the senses (as men

* In his preface to the French traveler's report, translator Francis Lieber unleashes full fury on women criminals: "The influence of women, as wives and mothers upon their family, and also, if they stand single in society, upon those who are in some connexion with them, is, generally speaking, greater than that of men, as husbands, fathers, or

were supposedly governed by reason and therefore more tractable), and thus the loss of a woman's virtue was tantamount to the loss of her soul. In the literature and mores of the period, sex without marriage "brought a rotting, a decomposition of human virtue and dignity. If a girl had natural warmth and passion, even a single sexual experience made her capable of any crime."[16]

Virtuous agents of law and order considered these fallen women unredeemable, evil sluts who should be locked up and forgotten. Until the mid-1820s only about five female convicts a year were sent to the new penitentiary at Auburn, New York, where they were segregated in a single dark area cordoned off from the male inmates by sealed windows and double-locked doors. Apparently the barriers were not impenetrable, for in the spring of 1825, Rachel Welch, a young Irish immigrant, was discovered to be pregnant. Prison records described her as a violent, surly woman—a description that may have resulted from her strong-minded resistance to the advances of male guards. In any event, she was flogged in late July 1825 by the prison's assistant keeper in violation of a New York law against whipping women. Soon she developed serious medical problems, including several near miscarriages. Her baby was born in early December, but Welch died by the first of the year—provoking huge outcries from prison reformers.[17]

Most of these reformers were committed to the new "invention"—the penitentiary. Debates between proponents of the New York and Pennsylvania "systems" ran on until the Civil War, the Pennsylvanians insisting on total solitary confinement for the prisoner's entire term while New Yorkers supported the Auburn plan in which prisoners were brought together to work in silence during the day. But in both places the underlying object was to create an environment of iron

---

single, upon the morals of those who surround or are connected with them. . . . A woman given to intemperance, and, what is generally connected with it, to violence and immoral conduct in most other respects, is sure to bring up as many vagabonds and prostitutes as she has male and female children; and I believe I am right in stating, that the injury done to society by a criminal woman, is in most cases much greater than that suffered from a male criminal. . . . To all this must be added the fact, known to all criminalists, that a woman once renouncing honesty and virtue, passes over to the most hideous crimes which women commit, with greater ease than a man proceeds from his first offence to the blackest crimes committed by his sex. There is a shorter distance between a theft committed by a woman and her readiness to commit murder by poison, or arson, from jealousy or hatred, than between forgery or theft committed by a man, and murder or piracy."

discipline whereby the inmate would be schooled as he or she should have been during childhood. This theory is especially clear in the treatment of women prisoners.[18]

Prisons for women in today's America are most often run on the principle that "bad" women are the creation of weak mothers and an unhealthy family life. The inmates are really only naughty daughters grown up bad. By implication, the fallen woman is the product of the fallen mother, another bad woman who probably had a criminal heart but who, thanks to good luck, was never caught breaking the law. Even worse, since the mother is the pillar of the family, it is upon the female that the ultimate blame for crime must rest. Prison, the theory goes, must reduce the female felon to a naughty daughter, and it can do this by restricting the clothes she can wear, by controlling the way she walks, talks, and eats, the way she behaves with her "girl friends," and most importantly by the way she behaves toward her "elders." In prison her elders are the wardens, the keeps, the guards. If she is good, she is rewarded—with perfume or lipstick. If she is bad, she is punished by being deprived of cosmetics or frivolous treats. Such is the core of female criminal treatment today, and so was it desired by the prison reformers of the 1820s and 1830s.[19]

For this, however, women convicts needed new prisons, away from both male criminals and male guards. Thus new installations were proposed for both Auburn and Sing Sing prisons as well as for a third independent women's penitentiary at Albany. Mostly due to financial consideration, a single, distinct women's prison was eventually built at Sing Sing in 1839. It was constructed of marble, "after the model of a Greek temple with massive columns in a conspicuous place behind but above all the other buildings."[20]

Women at Sing Sing were ruled by a matron and two female assistants plus an internal police force. Although the "imposing structure" had been intended to eliminate contact with men and to suppress communication among the women themselves, it failed both objectives. A "continual hum of conversation" was reported by visiting inspectors, and since the architect had forgotten to design a kitchen, meals were brought by male inmates from their own prison. Almost immediately the prison was overcrowded. The delivery room for women who were pregnant before sentencing was so dark and devoid of ventilation that newborn babies died regularly. Having found eight women and five babies crammed into a single small room, inspectors, in the summer of 1844, reported that "innocent children perish gradually but certainly."[21]

Punishments for women who disobeyed the rules touched on the medieval. They were hung by their wrists with toes just touching the ground, and they were manacled in handcuffs and chains. They were gagged, their hair was cut short, and they were given small rations. Resistance among the prisoners reached such a peak one day in 1843 that a riot broke out. "Ten or twelve other women joined in. They swore and cursed, and broke benches, spoons, beds, everything they could lay their hands on. The guard was called in but the women would not obey and seized things to strike the guard. The whole guard was called in, or as many as could be spared from other duties."[22]

By 1844, official recommendations were issued for the construction of a new prison that would follow the stringent Pennsylvania system requiring continuous solitary confinement for all inmates. The "hazard of stultifying the mind" through long-term isolation, the reformers decided, was less tedious than "the certainty in our prison of corrupting the heart and destroying the moral sense."[23]

Auburn was completed in 1823, Sing Sing in 1825 and the two penitentiaries at Pittsburgh and Philadelphia were ready in 1826 and 1829 respectively. Connecticut, Massachusetts, Maryland, New Jersey, Ohio, and Michigan each completed their own copies during the 1830s, as did Indiana, Wisconsin, and Minnesota in the 1840s. Abroad, America's experiment with penitentiaries created intense excitement and interest. France, England, Prussia, even Hungary, dispatched investigators to bring back firsthand reports on how well these institutions worked.

Nominally, the penitentiary had been created to render punishment on the convicted criminal for his offense against society. The prisons of the 1790s had divorced the prisoner from the "corrupt" surroundings in which he had committed his crime, but they did not separate him from the corrupting influence of other inmates. That was meant to be the task of these larger penitentiaries. "Each individual will necessarily be made the instrument of his own punishment; his conscience will be the avenger of society," wrote a Philadelphia proponent of solitary confinement. Even the architecture of the penitentiary was calculated to reinforce prisoner obedience. In one of its annual reports, the philanthropic Boston Prison Discipline Society explained that the penitentiary was "a grand theatre, for the trial of all new plans in hygiene and education, in physical and moral reform" where the criminal "surrendered body and soul, to be experimented upon." Said one prison chaplain: "Could we all be put on prison fare, for the space of two or three generations, the world would ultimately be the better for it. Indeed, should society change places with the prisoners, so far as habits are concerned, taking to itself the regularity, and temperance, and sobriety of a good prison," then the true benefit would be to the public at large. And in Philadelphia, in 1831, Tocqueville and his companion Gustave de Beaumont concluded that it was "incontestable that this perfect isolation secures the prisoner from all fatal contamination."[24]

These penitentiaries, ostensibly designed to reduce grown men and women to dependent children, in fact acted as a new kind of state church to an increasingly secular society. To maintain the social order, colonial America had relied upon the Puritan church, through its web of paternal responsibility and its promise of damnation to the immoral. Public order had been inseparable from church discipline, and the church elders, who often doubled as magistrates, saw that both were carefully upheld. But with the removal of the church from public authority, a new institution was needed to impose moral discipline upon the unruly lower classes—thus the penitentiary. The new Republic found no other way of dealing with its great injustice, poverty.

Chapter 9

Gangs, Goons, and Ward Healers

As the biggest ports in the new Republic, New York and Philadelphia attracted the most immigrants. Insecure, underemployed or unemployed, rootless, exploited, these new Americans, wooed as they were by the new rich who needed their manpower, were also hated by the very same rich who called them rabble and feared their restlessness. Since it was the rich who controlled the criminal justice system, it was no accident that it was New York and Pennsylvania that produced the original penitentiaries.

New York was the more notorious. The heart of the city's criminal underclass was at Five Points, now the site of the Tombs prison and the county courthouse to the east of lower Broadway. The square, about an acre in size, had been an intersection of five streets converging on a public pond called The Collect. By the beginning of the nineteenth century, The Collect had become a public gathering place for sailors, day workers, and newly arrived immigrants who went there to fish and draw water for the tenement apartments built on the swampy lands of the pond's spillway. Throughout the early years of the century, the streets around The Collect had grown squalid and rundown. Frequent proposals were advanced to fill in the pond and thereby eliminate the loitering grounds of the area's suspect residents. When jobless sailors led a demonstration through the streets of lower Manhattan to The Collect in the winter of 1808, city authorities panicked. They directed that the pond be drained, and as soon as warm weather came, the hills along both sides of Broadway were leveled and the earth used to fill the dug hole. As the newly recovered land was thrown open to builders, New York City embarked on the nation's first urban renewal, crime control project.[1]

Predictably, the city failed. Reconstruction did little more than provide temporary jobs in the midst of a minor depression. The new buildings were dark, cheap, unplumbed tenements that soon housed Irish, Italian, and Jewish immigrants. Brothels and bars opened up on the lower floors. Bunker Hill, a knoll a few blocks north of Five Points and named in commemoration of the triumphant revolutionary war battleground, became a fenced area for bull-baiting in which a "live bull [was] chained to a swivel ring and tormented by dogs." Bets were placed on how many dogs would be gored before the bull was torn to death. On the side of the hill, a crypt housing the bones of a wealthy colonial family became the home of a Five Points hermit who was eventually murdered—probably by the gangs that unleashed the turf wars of the 1820s and 1830s.

But until then, Five Points remained a gay, lusty, ribald district, in the words of one writer, the original Coney Island of New York. Dance halls, lit with candles or whale-oil lamps and open until three in the morning, were scattered through the streets, and the only admission ticket was the occasional purchase of a mug of beer. On the sidewalks, day and night, vendors sold sausages, strawberries, yams, apples, or pears. So-called hot-corn girls walked the streets bearing heavy wooden buckets filled with roasted corn ears, and according to lore, hawked their treats in an almost musical voice:

> Hot Corn! Hot Corn!
> Here's your lily white corn.
> All you that's got money—
> Poor me that's got none—
> Come buy my lily hot corn
> And let me go home.[2]

After the panic of 1819, which again left the poor without jobs and food, a deeper decay began to hit Five Points, just as it did the slums of

Boston and Philadelphia. More crowded than ever with the nonstop stream of immigrants, the streets and alleys filled with garbage. The filth was said to be so deep it covered the tops of high-button shoes. People died regularly of malaria and other diseases. A few years later, Charles Dickens arrived on the scene and described what he saw in *American Notes:*

> Let us go again, and plunge into the Five Points. This is the place; these narrow ways diverging to the right and left, and reeking everywhere with dirt and filth. Such lives as are led here, bear the same fruit here as elsewhere. The coarse and bloated faces at the doors have counterparts at home and all the world over. Debauchery has made the very houses prematurely old. See how rotten beams are tumbling down, and how the patched and broken windows seem to scowl dimly, like eyes that have been hurt in drunken frays. . . .
>
> Open the door of one of these cramped hutches full of sleeping Negroes. Bah! They have a charcoal fire within, there is a smell of singeing clothes or flesh, so close they gather round the brazier; and vapors issue forth that blind and suffocate. From every corner, as you glance about you in these dark streets, some figure crawls half-awakened, as if the judgment hour were near at hand, and every obscure grave were giving up its dead. Where dogs would howl to lie, men and women and boys slink off to sleep, forcing the dislodged rats to move away in quest of better lodgings. Here, too, are lanes and alleys paved with mud knee-deep . . . ruined houses, open to the street . . . hideous tenements which take their names from robbery and murder; all that is loathsome, drooping and decayed is here.[3]

To the genteel entrepreneurs who lived uptown (above what is now Canal Street), the poor of Five Points were not just an embarrassment, they were a threat. Indeed, so frightened were property holders that occasionally they forced the city to try to keep the poor "in their place." This was sometimes accomplished by making a show of punishment as when, in honor of Lafayette during his much publicized tour of the United States in 1824–25, twenty highwaymen were hanged from the tall elm at the northwest corner of Washington Park. The "Hanging Elm" still stands today.[4]

"They love to clan together in some out-of-the-way place, are content to live in filth and disorder with a bare subsistance, provided they can drink, and smoke, and gossip, and enjoy their balls, and wakes, and frolics, without molestation," declared Robert Hartley, founder of the New York Association for Improving the Condition of the Poor. The missionary Josiah Strong denounced the people of the tenements as "a commingled mass of venomous filth and seething sin, of lust and drunkenness, of pauperism and crime of every sort." Treated as such, the poor had no choice but to organize—and fight back.[5]

From the 1830s onward, the muggers and thieves of lower New York were less often the wanton, the beguiling, the desperate, the footloose entrepreneurs of traditional crime. Instead, the new criminals ran in gangs. They were professional. They went through periods of training, apprenticeship, and maturation. There were territories over which they fought for control. They relied on patrons at city hall who gave them protection and to whom they provided votes and political support. And they each possessed their own distinctive mystique.

The Dead Rabbits, the Plug Uglies, the Roach Guards—their members were nearly always Irish, and, like the gangs of Spanish Harlem and South Bronx today, they carried bludgeons, bats, pistols, and chains. The Plug Uglies were supposed to have taken their names from the great tall hats they wore, stuffed full of leather and wool and pulled down over their ears during battle. The Shirt Tails were so named because they wore their shirts hanging outside their pants. A "rabbit" in contemporary slang was a rowdy, and a "dead rabbit" a real bruiser; the leader of that gang carried a real dead rabbit atop a spear into every battle.[6]

To the north of Five Points were the Bowery gangs, the best known of which were the Bowery Boys. The lore of the gang exploits and their territorial scraps is mostly that—glorified fables of prowess and terror drawn from the pages of sensational newspaper accounts or recorded through the legends of the streets. That they existed and controlled street crime in their own districts is incontestable. Most gangs also had their own bosses. The most notorious gang boss of the pre–Civil War era was a man known only as Mose, leader of the Bowery Boys. Described as "the Samson, the Achilles, the Paul Bunyan of the Bowery," Mose reigned over his territory with his constant companion, a little man called Syksey whose job it was to make sure a junior gang member was always present to hold the boss's used cigar butts. According to legend, Mose was eight feet tall, had hands "as large as the hams of a Virginia hog," and shoes "the soles of which were copper plates studded with nails an inch long." For bludgeons he would uproot lampposts, and for a knife he used a butcher's cleaver. "Once when the Dead Rabbits overwhelmed his gang and rushed ferociously up the Bowery to wreck the Boys' headquarters," according to one accounting of the legend, "the great Mose wrenched an oak tree out of the earth, and holding it by the upper branches, employed it as a flail, smiting the Dead Rabbits even as Samson smote the Phillistines. The Five Points thugs broke and fled before him, but he pursued them into their lairs around Paradise Square and wrecked two tenements before his rage cooled."[7]

Fearsome in their reputed exploits, the gangs did not necessarily strike terror in the hearts of New York's ordinary working people. To some extent, the Five Points and Bowery gangs were entertaining roustabouts who brought a measure of order amidst thieves into their neighborhoods. Sometimes their allies were Irish workingmen whose meager wages kept them just on the proper side of respectability.

From Five Points to the Bowery lay New York's original Sixth Ward, a strip that ran roughly up the center of lower Manhattan. But the Fourth Ward, which ran south down to the waterfront, developed its own criminal subculture by the 1840s. On elegant Cherry Street, where once the mansions of George Washington and John Hancock looked out over the East River, was Gotham Court, a double-row of ramshackle barracks that stood several stories high and ran 130 feet wide. More than a thousand people—mostly Irish and Italian immigrants and blacks who had escaped from the South—packed the Gotham Court, a first stop on their journey toward jobs and "American opportunity."

The real opportunity at Gotham Court, however, was for the thieves and pickpockets who hid out there, carefully scanning new arrivals. These gangs, among them the Daybreak Boys, the Swamp Angels, and the Slaughter Housers, either mugged their victims along the alleyways or waited for them to pass beneath specified windows where female gang members would dump a bucket of ashes on their heads, blinding them temporarily. The muggers would strip them of their clothes and money.

Most gangs were headquartered in bars run by their own lieutenants. Often as not these lieutenants were women who had the brains and brawn to hold their own in any fight that might break out. One hangout, the Hole-in-the-Wall, was run by Kate Flannery and Gallus

Mag, top members of a gang run by One-armed Charley Monell. Gallus Mag stood over six feet, held her skirt up with suspenders (or galluses), and always carried both a pistol and a bludgeon. Victims who protested their treatment at her place were knocked down and rolled on the floor; she would then bite the customer's ear, drag him into the street by her teeth, and if he resisted, rip the ear off and deposit it in a jar of alcohol she kept as a trophy case.[8]

Typical of the "marks" who passed through Gallus Mag's door was a German immigrant fresh off the boat. Followed out of the bar, he was clubbed unconscious while walking down by the Battery, robbed of the twelve cents he was carrying, and then thrown into the river, where he drowned. The two thieves, Slobbery Jim and Patsy the Barber, were members of the Daybreak Boys. On their return to Gallus Mag's, a quarrel erupted as to who deserved the larger cut of their twelve-cent loot. The quarrel became a fistfight until Jim slashed the Barber's throat, and while he was down, "stamped him to death with his hobnailed boots."[9]

The Daybreak Boys did most of their work at the time suggested by their name—in the quiet hours before dawn. Police claimed each member was a cold and vicious professional killer; during two years, 1850 through 1852, the gang was credited with twenty murders and the theft of $100,000 in property. By the middle of 1853, however, the two leaders of the Daybreak Boys had been convicted of murder and hanged. Slobbery Jim fled the city to avoid prosecution. Later that summer Bill Lowrie, the last of the gang's leaders, was captured during a dock robbery and sent to the penitentiary for fifteen years. At that point the gang collapsed.[10]

But that was only one such gang, albeit the most famous. Between four hundred and five hundred river pirates, organized among fifty gangs, roamed the Fourth Ward, according to an 1850s New York police report. The figures, however, may have been inflated since the report's purpose was to secure an expansion of the harbor police force. "The river pirates pursue their nefarious operations with the most systematic perserverance, and manifest a shrewdness and adroitness which can only be attained by long practice," wrote Police Chief George Matsell. "Nothing comes amiss to them. In their boats, under cover at night, they prowl around the wharves and vessels in a stream, and dexterously snatch up every piece of loose property left for a moment unguarded."[11]

By the time Chief Matsell issued his report of 1850, the gangs had become a normal part of everyday life in New York. South from what is now Houston Street, no quarter of the city was free of them. Matsell's peculiar concentration on riverfront pirates to the exclusion of Irish gangs is revealing; for it illustrates the second major transformation in big-city crime during the Age of Jackson: the politicizing of the criminal subculture.

The penitentiary, combined with the proliferation of police, and the determination of reformer-philanthropists to keep the poor under carefully controlled observation, left the would-be criminal only one alternative if he were to survive: He would have to become a professional, working consciously with other criminals according to a disciplined set of rules. Once organized, however, the gangs of New York were forced to recognize an extraordinary irony about themselves. Their power could no longer be measured merely by the breadth of their leader's shoulders. In a city of competing ethnic and economic interests, they could not stand aside from politics, or from the politicians who represented or appealed to these ethnic and economic interests. Conversely, Tammany Hall ward healers were acutely aware of the value of commanding "goon squads" on election day, and hence, in the early 1830s, began to buy titles to the bars, speakeasies, and hangouts used by the Bowery and Five Points gangs.[12]

The year 1834 provided the first hard test of gang clout in New York politics. That spring, the first direct election of the city's mayor took place. As election day approached, Tammany Hall politicos worked overtime building effective machinery that took advantage of gangster skills in and around polling booths. The election itself lasted three days. Pitted against Tammany Democrats and their Irish gangs were the Whigs and a new incipient movement of "native Americans" (meaning English descendants), animated by the threat they felt from the flood of lower-class Irish immigrants. Police in the Sixth Ward tried to quell the fighting between the "goon squads" from each side; but by the third day it was necessary for the city to call out the militia to suppress the riots. By then, however, the Tammany apparatus had claimed victory.[13]

The victors had hardly taken their seats of office when a second set of riots flared up on July 7, caused by Irish gangs marching on the home of the wealthy and outspoken abolitionist Lewis Tappan. Under attack from the native Americans, the Irish immigrants turned their own wrath on blacks and their supporters. The northward trek of escaped or freed slaves had seemed to squeeze the struggling Irish workers between two hostile forces. Symbol of the blueblood, the do-gooder radical Tappan was an easy target for the release of their anger. Led by gangs, rioters seized his home, carried furniture, paintings and personal memorabilia into the street and set them afire. From Tappan's house rioters moved into adjacent streets, looting houses and businesses alike. The fighting lasted two days. Among the dozen buildings sacked was a black church. Individual blacks were dragged from their homes, tortured and murdered. When the rioting ended on July 10, it was again due to the repressive forces of more than two thousand uniform militia and special police who had been called to duty.[14]

Anti-Irish sentiment created another riot in the summer of 1835, when one of the old Bowery gangs, the American Guards, joined the native Americans and a massive brawl erupted at Grand and Crosby streets on the Lower East Side and spread west to Five Points. Six months later, after the great fire of December 1835, the militia was once again called to suppress the worst looting the city ever experienced. The booty was eventually found in the tenements of Five Points and the Bowery.[15]

Throughout the depression years following the panic of 1837, ties between Tammany Hall and the Sixth Ward gangs grew stronger. Under ward boss Captain Isaiah Rynders, gang members were carefully shielded from prosecution and prison. Rynders, a United States marshall, ran his operation from a bar on Ann Street and counted among his deputies Edward Z. C. Judson, known more familiarly as Ned Buntline. For twenty-five years Rynders and his boys made the Sixth Ward an invincible Tammany stronghold and won for themselves a very special position in the criminal underworld. Although their actions were never publicly condoned by city hall, and in spite of the fact that their existence was often cited as an excuse for enlarging and professionalizing the police force, the Irish gangs and the Irish police developed a certain peaceful coexistence. The real crackdowns were waged against dangerous thieves and murderers on the waterfront, criminals who, like the Daybreak Boys, had failed to learn that crime without political organization did not pay.[16]

The port of New York, which became the nation's leading immigration center, gave the city a cultural diversity denied Boston, Philadelphia, or Baltimore. New York also superseded those cities as a financial and trading center. And when the Erie Canal linked the

Hudson-Mohawk river complex to the Great Lakes, New York took a commanding position in the commerce of westward expansion. Yet the upsurge of crime and public violence in New York during the Age of Jackson was not unique.

The 1830s and 1840s were noted for rioting in all the large coastal cities. Even Chicago and New Orleans, then comparatively small cities, were relatively violent. Sixteen riots broke out across the country in 1834 and thirty-seven in 1835, with a death toll of sixty-one people. "The horrible fact is staring us in the face, that, whenever the fury or the cupidity of the mob is excited, they can gratify their lawless appetites almost with impunity," warned the Philadelphia *National Gazette* in August 1835. Rioting continued until the outbreak of the Civil War, culminating with the bloodiest of them all, the New York draft riots, in which over a thousand people died. The causes of the riots were remarkably consistent: economic panic and unemployment; Protestant nativist animosity toward Catholic and Irish immigrants; Irish working-class attacks on wealthy abolitionists and freed blacks who, they feared, would steal the industrial jobs; and early labor strikes—in one word, poverty.[17]

Public rioting and crime were not, of course, synonymous—although one of the crucial contributions of nineteenth-century law enforcement was to denounce all political violence as indistinguishable from criminal assault. Since riots usually resulted in personal injury and attacks on private property, they were treated as important crimes by the courts. Yet the memory of the Revolution remained fresh enough to temper such judgment in the general public. How to distinguish crime from insurrection, therefore, required utmost care.

While Jackson dispatched federal troops on three occasions in order to suppress riots, his administration hesitated to denounce them outright. One Jacksonian aide went so far as to excuse rioting as "not properly speaking an opposition to the established laws of the country [but] a supplement to them—as a species of *common law.*" Such a policy, however, was not part of Jackson's so-called popular democratic commitment, as historical myth would have it. As we shall see, Jackson was often quite willing to disregard both the law and the courts. Nor was Jackson free of corruption. In exchange for total control of New York Democratic politics, for example, Jackson allowed his collector Samuel Swartwout to embezzle $1,250,000 and take it with him when he escaped to Europe in 1836 with the city's district attorney (who made only $60,000 on the deal). Jesse Hoyt, whom Jackson appointed as Swartwout's successor, rendered the Democratic president the same service in exchange for the same privileges, but his rake-off was only $201,580. In any case, Jackson never worried much about either crime or riots. He moved against either only when they threatened his political or economic self-interest.[18]

The Baltimore bank riot of August 1835, in the midst of the summer's explosive antiabolitionist demonstrations, tapped much of the country's general discontent. The Baltimore riot grew directly from the anger of the Bank of Maryland's depositors who waited a year and a half to get their money back after the bank had collapsed. Why the depositors chose the weekend of August 9 and 10 to act is unclear. Certainly it had been a "long hot summer" of street fighting up and down the coast. A drop in land prices resulting from Jackson's curtailment of land speculator's paper notes had already begun to spread some financial anxiety. Locally, the depositors had grown disgruntled with the slow legal maneuvering of the bank's trustees and "secret partners." During the preceding week anonymous "inflammatory" hand bills had been posted in the city encouraging citizens to protect their own self-interest by taking direct action.[19]

On Friday afternoon a worried Mayor Jesse Hunt addressed a still peaceful crowd, urging calm and requesting the bank to open its books to the public. The crowd grumbled but remained quiet overnight. On Saturday the bank's trustees answered that their books were being impounded by the county court. Immediately Mayor Hunt organized a citizen's guard armed with wooden sticks. Saturday night the guards stood watch over the home of attorney Reverdy Johnson, the bank's principal partner and the object of the rioters' wrath. At one point the guards demanded guns, got them, and in an ensuing melee, five people died. Sunday morning the guards were withdrawn; the mayor apologized and denied responsibility for the shootings. By Monday morning the homes and businesses of the four bank partners and the mayor had been sacked or burned. However, the rioters took scrupulous care to protect other people's property from damage. On Monday afternoon a voluntary citizens' patrol formed, and the city was quieted.

Although the bank's partners had not broken any laws, they had used the law to delay repaying depositors as long as possible, a maneuver which, according to a leading newspaper, brought fantastic profits to the partners and wrought severe hardship on the "widows and orphans, small dealers and thrifty persons, mechanics and others" who had deposited their money at the bank. The case of the depositors against the bankers had been eloquently argued in the handbills distributed before the riot:

> Arm! Arm! . . .—my Countrymen—Citizens of this Republic . . . and of this City, will you suffer your firesides to be molested—will you suffer your beds to be polluted—will you suffer your pockets to be rifled and your wives and children beggared. . . . Have not the whole Bar and the judges linked in a combination together, and brow-beaten these very people out of their just rights, with a full determination to swindle and rob the industrious and poor part of the community out of their hard earnings. . . . Gracious God!—is this our fair famed Baltimore—is our moral city come to this. . . . Let the warhoop be given. . . . Liberty, Equality, Justice or Death!!![20]

Despite popular sentiment twenty-two people were tried on riot charges and twelve were convicted. Of those indicted or implicated in the trial testimony, over three-quarters were carpenters or skilled mechanical workers. Only one was identified as a day laborer. One was a farmer and one a merchant. Few of the rioters displayed remorse. They saw themselves instead as heroes and were undoubtedly taken as such by most of Baltimore's working-class Catholics. Indeed as the banker's elegant houses were being ransacked, bands had played, and a merry crowd of several thousand had cheered.[21]

People identified as rioters suffered no particular stigma. Leon Dyer, an indicted leader of the riot, was in fact so popular that he was appointed acting mayor two years later, following the 1837 bread riot. The rioters had drained the wine cellars of two bankers, damning it as they drank it as "American blood." They had expressed glee in smashing the mayor's fine imported china. Most significantly—and symbolically—banker Reverdy Johnson's law library had been totally burned. "Here nothing stands between the individual citizen and *his* sovereign—the majority of the people—but the majesty of the law and the independence of the courts," a scholarly apologist for Jacksonian democracy had written. That majestic system of law, perceived as the thoroughly partial tool of the aristocratic class, was on the other hand exactly what the rioters of the period had grown to despise. The law, lawyers, and the legal system appeared to the populists and the Irish immigrants as a massive, sticky web, a barrier to the very idea of individual opportunity that had drawn them to America.[22]

The sentiment was best expressed in a book by ex-lawyer P. W. Grayson called *Vice Unmasked.* Grayson, who had allied himself with the New York workingmen's movement, denounced the expansion of the legal system both as repressive to the individual and as a corruptor of the "moral essence of man." The great edifice of law, he said, did more than anything else in America to undermine one's sense of personal integrity and social responsibility, reducing men to squirming connivers who would use the law only for the basest purposes.[23]

Grayson's proof was the court's attack on unions. From 1820, in industrial towns and cities, skilled craftsmen had begun the campaign for unionization. They were encouraged by the writings of the early utopian socialists, especially Robert Owen and Fanny Wright. Union advocates had maintained a steadily expanding momentum through the 1820s and early 1830s, culminating in a national convention in New York in August 1834, from which was born the National Trades' Union. However, within a year, the NTU split between unionists committed to Andrew Jackson's party and the more militant organizers, who viewed capitalism as fundamentally oppressive.[24]

"Workeys" and "workeyism," as the militants and their movement were called, had begun to spread alarm throughout the establishment. They had even threatened to displace the entrenched leadership of Tammany Hall in New York. The establishment reacted by charging that trade associations were antidemocratic, atheistic, dominated by foreigners—and illegal. Workers, according to one widely distributed pamphlet, were erecting an "oppressive and flagrant and unrighteous aristocracy."[25]

By the mid-1830s the courts had chosen to side openly with the employers. A decision made by the New York State Supreme Court in 1835 confirmed the conspiracy conviction of an entire shop of shoemakers in Geneva; the shoemakers had struck when a nonunion journeyman had been hired at less than union rates. Probably the most famous case came a few months later, in early 1836, when the Society of Journeyman Tailors struck to maintain a recently won wage increase. Relying on the recent supreme court judgment, authorities arrested twenty tailors for criminal conspiracy. The arrests were taken as a full-fledged attack on the workingmen's movement.[26]

When the tailors were convicted and fined $1,150, the workingmen and their supporters were outraged. Some twenty-five thousand people took to the streets for a mass demonstration on June 13. Most outspoken of all was William Cullen Bryant, then editor of the *New York Evening Post:*

> If this is not SLAVERY, we have forgotten its definition. Strike the right of associating for the sale of labour from the privileges of a freeman, and you may as well at once bind him to a master. . . . If it be not in the colour of his skin, and in the poor franchise of naming his own terms in a contract for work, what advantage has the labourer of the north over the bondman of the south?[27]

Several other strikes followed during the summer of 1836, but they were almost all outlawed by the courts. Organizers were fined, then imprisoned with highwaymen, thieves, and muggers as enemies of the Republic.

American historians are fond of labeling the years from 1830 to 1850 the great Age of Jacksonian Democracy. Andrew Jackson, the heroic southern populist, is still portrayed as the little man's president, the enemy of wealth and vested interests, a knight ever vigilant against the abuses of concentrated power. Andrew Jackson was indeed a man of independent mind. The years during and after his presidency were marked by strikes, violent upheavals of popular sentiment on the pressing problems of unemployment, slavery, rising poverty, race, religion, and immigration. Their cause was the steadily worsening conditions faced by working people in the cities. Though President Jackson was in fact rarely on the side of the little man, democratic forces did win power during the 1830s and 1840s to a limited degree. Transforming street gangs and volunteer fire companies into a tight netword of ward healers, the swelling masses of lower-class Irish immigrants in Boston, New York, and Baltimore formed tough political organizations that kept them in or close to city hall for most of the rest of the century.[28]

As a consequence, the threat of the immigrants and an angry, frequently violent, lower class spread fear among local authorities and within the federal government itself. In Maryland, one of the prominent Jacksonian loyalists fumed over the rebellious Democrats who applauded the Baltimore bank riot. Roger Taney, Jackson's attorney general and later chief justice of the Supreme Court, declared that armed guards should have fired on the demonstrators at once. Between the 1830s and the mid-1840s Democratic politicians launched serious campaigns for strong professional police and fire departments in Boston, New York, and Philadelphia. The famous 1835 mob attack on abolitionist agitator William Lloyd Garrison and his paper, the *Liberator,* provoked calls in the Boston press for better police protection, as had the burning of a Catholic convent a year earlier.[29]

Still the Boston City Council hesitated to make any changes. A third riot in June 1837, between volunteer firemen and an Irish funeral procession, drew fifteen thousand people into the streets and was suppressed only after the mayor called in a cavalry unit of eight hundred horsemen. This time the mayor argued successfully to the council that the city could no longer do without a "preventive" force of professional police. Rebuking those who had long opposed a standing force as a threat to civil liberties, he attacked "the incendiary" and "the lawlessly violent" as "guilty of treason against the constitution of his country."[30]

New Yorkers proved more resistant to the movement for professionalism, even though their city was far more violent than the others. The city was then patrolled by about five hundred night watchmen, responsible to the city council, the police, the justices, and the mayor. Another one hundred armed marshals were appointed by the mayor. Both were considered highly corrupt and susceptible to the whims of ward politics. Probably none of them had the force or effectiveness of the gangs run by Sixth Ward boss Isaiah Rynders. Still, the continuation of mass demonstrations and riots along with such sensational cases as the drowning murder of Mary Cecelia Rogers kept up the pressure for tougher police action.[31]

In 1842, Edgar Allan Poe published a gruesome story of a handsome young woman whose bloated, disfigured body was found on the banks of the Seine, the probable victim of a sadistic suitor. Poe's tale, "The Mystery of Marie Roget," was set in Paris but it fanned the flames of outrage in New York City, for it was a carefully drawn fictional account of one of the most sensational unsolved murder cases New Yorkers had known.

The real "Marie Roget," Mary Cecelia Rogers, left her mother's rooming house in midmorning July 25, 1841, and was found drowned, three days later, near Hoboken. The city's newspapers asked: Had she been seduced, kidnapped, raped, and strangled by some "dark-complexioned" sailor? Some writers even suggested that she might have died at the sloppy hand of a backroom abortionist. The wilder the speculation, the poorer was the performance of the police. "Not a step will be taken without a reward," charged the editorialists of the *New York Herald,* ". . . and even if they possess a clue to the mystery, still they would keep the secret intact, like a capital in trade, 'till public indignation has raised a sum sufficient, as a reward for bringing the facts to the light of day."[32]

Poe brought immortality to Mary Rogers, but the facts of her case were not unique to the New York of the 1840s. Lootings, muggings, and murders were as much a part of city life then as they are today, and so upset was the board of aldermen, that the members wailed in 1842:

> The property of the citizen is pilfered, almost before his eyes. Dwellings and warehouses are entered with an ease and apparent coolness and carelessness of detection which shows that none are safe. Thronged as our city is, men are robbed in the streets. Thousands, that are arrested, go unpunished, and the defenseless and the beautiful are ravished and murdered in the day time, and no trace of the criminals is found. The man of business, in his lawful calling, at the most public corner of our city, is slaughtered in the sunshine and packed up and sent away.[33]

These "men of business" naturally blamed the police, and Jackson's Democrats obediently did the same. All through the 1840s they introduced bills before the common council to abolish the existing force, complete with its patronage system, and replace it with a "London-style" constabulatory. Opponents of an armed professional force, among them the *Sun,* warned that such proposals would bring about "an absolute police despotism." Native Americans correctly foresaw an even more dangerous and corrupt police force than that which already existed; for by adding a layer of bureaucracy to the system, more power would go to such semirespectable political bosses as Captain Rynders than to the immigrant constituents themselves.[34]

Nonetheless, in 1845, after a decade of electoral wrangling, the

Democrats triumphed. A force of eight hundred police was sworn in and directed to bring order to the nation's largest city. Thanks to Jacksonian Democrats, crime and its management entered a new phase of development. Gangs of loosely organized, self-trained hoodlums evolved into a tighter network of professional craftsmen. There emerged a unique criminal class of men and women who required special knowledge and skills to succeed at their work, who lived in specified districts, who invented their own internal power structure, who established their own representatives to the authorities who would mediate with their antagonists, the police. This police, in turn, became dependent upon continued criminal success to justify their own existence. The professionalization of the police force thus turned crime into an exclusive occupation of those willing to work within the emerging system.[35]

Rioting diminished under New York's new system. For one thing, an upturn in the economy marked by more jobs and a cap on inflation improved living conditions somewhat. But more important, the Democrats managed to diffuse the explosive movements of the 1830s. The most outspoken radical Democrats were isolated as Jackson ignored them in favor of such law-and-order advocates as Roger Taney. Those radicals who allied themselves with the unions were frustrated by the courts which outlawed serious labor organizing. As for the disgruntled mass of lower-class Irish party members—those who had formed the "loco-foco" faction and fueled the gang riots against the abolitionists—they were thoroughly co-opted by the professionalization of the police. For just as the Protestant nativists had predicted, professionalism brought with it the most systematic police corruption New York had yet known.[36]

Police appointments were controlled directly by the aldermen of each ward. When Democrats won the ward elections, Democratic policemen were appointed—and the same was true for the Whigs. In the city's First Ward, only two of twenty-eight Democratic police were reappointed after the Whig victory there in 1848. In the Second Ward, twenty-eight of thirty Democratic police kept their jobs after the Democratic victory. Arrest of gang members became directly dependent upon their connection to important ward healers. Issuance of licenses to saloon owners and prosecution of barkeepers who opened their doors on Sunday was totally up to the whim of the reigning aldermen. Most police made no attempt to enforce either liquor or gambling laws.

Harassment of streetwalkers served only to drive prostitution into established brothels.[37]

Only when they were offered rewards, it seemed, did the police make any effort at recovering stolen property. One of the most notorious "reward" claimers, Robert Bowyer, made $1,640 between 1845 and 1847. In fact, the rewards were little more than fees charged by the police for the use of their contacts with the city's thieves and fences. By the mid-1850s, Bowyer's rewards began to run into the $1,000-a-year bracket, topping out at $4,700 for the eighteen months between January 1, 1855, and April 30, 1857. If ever a police force profited from crime, it was under the new uniformed professionalized system of the Democratic regime.

Probably the most corrupt policeman in New York was its chief, George Matsell, a Democratic stalwart who complained constantly that the city's growing crime problem was due to lenient judges who let crooks run free. (Since the police judges were an integral part of the ward structure, he was largely correct; the justices were notorious for releasing the friends of the district bosses.) Matsell, a blubberous man of some three hundred pounds, was a master of rhetoric and bombast; he saw his job more as that of a lobbyist than as a tough commander. He was also an astute politician, realizing that he could best keep the loyalty of his men by delegating nearly all operational authority to the precinct captains and pursuing a public image as champion of the "beat" patrolman.[38]

Matsell was immensely popular in Irish New York—a popularity enhanced no doubt by his enthusiasm for the fugitive slave law of 1850, pushed through Congress by Democratic politicians. The slave act, which authorized the police in the north to detain blacks suspected of having escaped from southern plantations, was a major blow both to the famed underground railroad and to the abolitionist cause. Capitalizing on Irish fear of black competition for jobs, Matsell launched a campaign to recover the southern slaveholder's "stolen property," a campaign so successful that the *New York Tribune* denounced him as a crass "slave catcher."

Chief Matsell's Democratic allegiance finally provoked an investigation by city aldermen. His opponents charged him with taking payoffs from gamblers, brothels, abortionists, and thieves and added that the entire department received kickbacks from lawyers whose clients had been sent to them by the police. When the aldermen requested information on how many police were Irish-born, Matsell stalled, then underreported the number by at least four hundred men. His critics, mostly Protestant nativists, then claimed to have proof that Matsell was himself foreign-born. "He is the source of the bloody strife at primary and legal elections," the investigators railed, "and continues, through brute force, and his own police satellites, to elect nearly all the heads of departments, judiciary, etc., who, in return, are his abject slaves." George Matsell weathered the storm and retained his job as chief. His inquisitors were simply unable to marshal enough detailed proof of corruption. Not until 1856, five years later, was it revealed that on a modest "public servant's" salary, Matsell had accumulated enough wealth to build a twenty-room mansion on a three-thousand-acre estate in Viola, Iowa.[39]

Corruption in New York was not simply a police problem. The city government was also on the take and encouraged its employees to play along. In the mayoral election of 1856, for example, all city civil servants were told to support the Democratic candidate, Fernando Wood, a man who had accumulated a wide reputation as New York's most underhanded and unethical merchant. Precint captains were instructed to contribute $15 to $25 each to the campaign, and every beat patrolman was told to donate something. Those who refused lost their jobs. Within a single week the department collected over $8,500—the modern equivalent of a quarter of a million dollars.[40]

As corruption ran wild through the city government, New York's crime problems exploded. Mass violence posed little threat, but personal attacks and theft were at an all-time high. New York's immigrants, most of them hungry and dwelling in hovels, made up half the population in 1855. The police themselves estimated that at least three thousand vagrant children roamed the streets. If they were to survive, it was by virtue of their wits, their fast fingers, and their physical strength. Pickpockets swarmed along the wharves and shopping districts. Crimes against individuals outnumbered larcenies by three to one. Arrests for murder were far more numerous in New York than in London. In the words of one English traveler of the mid-1850s, "probably in no city in the civilised world is life so fearfully insecure."[41]

By 1857 the reputation of the police had fallen so low—and the fortunes of the Democratic party had slipped so badly—that Mayor Wood proved unable to forestall a state legislative investigation into public corruption. Although the state house and the legislature were under the control of the newly formed Republican party, the cleanup campaign even won support from some dissatisfied Democrats. Intrigue swirled around the mayor's office throughout 1856. Eventually the legislature voted to remove police power from the city and establish a special metropolitan police to cover all the boroughs and Westchester County. At first Wood refused to honor the state orders, claiming they were an illegal invasion of local powers. For a while, in the spring of 1857, two separate forces patrolled the city. Once the metropolitan forces were ordered to storm the city police headquarters, but were driven back by the larger local forces. Finally, under ruling of the Court of Appeals on July 2, 1857, the mayor conceded defeat and all police authority was transferred to the state.[42]

Twenty-five years of Democratic leadership in the nation's preeminent city had demonstrated that public crime and government corruption were inseparable and endemic to urban life in America. Among the lower classes, crime was often seen as perhaps the only means of survival in a society that judged private property more sacrosanct than human life. But crime was also one of the most dependable means of advancement for the "upwardly mobile" members of the lower middle class. Together, the penitentiary movement, which often brought about a new cohesiveness among urban hooligans, and the movement toward police professionalism contributed significantly to the evolving ethos of American crime. Crime had taken its place as one of the many avenues of individual opportunity, and city hall became just another money-making enterprise.

Chapter 10

Desperation on the Borderlands

"If some of our cities are not like Birmingham and Manchester, it is owing not to legislation, but to the happy accident of our possessing the West." So wrote one of the leading Jacksonian radicals in the fall of 1834. Rough as life was for the lower classes in New York or Philadelphia, it was better than in industrial England, where authorities had felt compelled to organize a standing police force as early as 1829. Nothing in America, argued the Americans, could equal the human degradation of English factory life. The reason for this happy circumstance, they maintained, was "the abundance of vacant land [that] operates as the safety salve of our system." When hardships became too severe for the honest immigrant family, all they had to do, it was said, was move westward where free land offered the opportunity of a new life. By the same logic, those who refused the opportunity, who languished behind in the slums, constituted the true criminal underclass.[1]

The myth of the frontier was worldwide. That myth, even more than promise of high wages, was the magnet that, throughout the nineteenth century, drew German and English artisans to the United States. The frontier was a second chance where man, locked in combat with nature, could triumph and realize the dream of personal prosperity. What the immigrants found instead was an austere, treacherous, lonely place where failure and death lay behind vistas of incomparable beauty.

As Tocqueville wandered across what was then the frontier—western New York and Pennsylvania, Ohio and the whole Northwest Territory—he was impressed by the transient quality of the frontier settlements. "In the United States a man builds a house in which to spend his old age, and he sells it before the roof is on; he plants a garden and lets it just as the trees are coming into bearing; he brings a field into tillage and leaves other men to gather the crops; he embraces a profession and gives it up; he settles in a place, which he soon afterwards leaves to carry his changeable longings elsewhere." Indeed, Tocqueville did not exaggerate much: To live on the frontier was to accept a continuous state of flux, not only to be in danger of attack from the hostile, dispossessed Indian tribes, but also to be surrounded by an unending caravan of strangers, more properly migrants than immigrants.[2]

Two such migrants may illustrate the point. Born in different locales—one in Rhode Island, the other in New Jersey—and in different decades, they were both swept westward with the tide of migrant opportunity and compelled to survive on the edge of American civilization.

Daniel Drake left home when he was fifteen years old to study as an apprentice in a doctor's office in Fort Washington, Ohio. The year was 1800. Among the earliest settlers in Kentucky, his family had left New Jersey when he was an infant. Although he did not grow up in abject poverty, Drake's parents apparently lacked the money to send him back east to study in one of the leading medical colleges. A clever lad, Drake eagerly learned everything his master could teach him and before long outshone him. The young doctor prospered, as did his city, incorporated as Cincinnati in 1802. He opened the city's first drugstore. He introduced new types of treatment and medicine, among them man-made mineral water. He established Ohio's first medical college.

Daniel Drake did not restrict his interests to medicine alone. He became one of the city's most prominent businessmen. He brought national and even international recognition to the city with a book entitled *Picture of Cincinnati in 1815,* a promotional tract describing, and praising, everything from the area's archaeological past to its commercial advantages as a doorway to southern agriculture. He planned and built a teachers' college, an insane asylum, canals, even a municipal railroad. Daniel Drake was, to use historian Daniel Boorstin's term, the complete "booster," one of the models of frontier success.[3]

Stephen Arnold was also fortunate—at first. The son of a prosperous farm family, fourteen years younger than Daniel Drake, he was a quiet, inhibited, slightly nervous boy who by his early teens presented a predicament to his parents. He was bright but unable to work easily with the hired men on the family farm. Arrogance combined with a repressed moralism set him apart. He was a "boss's son" and he lacked either the humor or the self-confidence to handle the role without antagonizing his fellow workers. Attempting to solve the problem, his parents sent him to an academy where he proved to be an exceptional student. He was so successful he was appointed assistant to the headmaster at age eighteen.[4]

Midway through his academic training, Stephen Arnold had to return to the farm when his father fell seriously ill. Again, the gangly, bucktoothed young man had to work the fields with his "vicious," "dissipated" hired hands. Fortunately, his father recovered, and again Stephen left—this time to study medicine. He quit after five months, a victim of eyestrain. He returned home, and there stayed for two years. Incapable of managing the farm, he became dependent upon the declining resources of his aging parents. Rural Rhode Island, like most of agricultural New England, offered no opportunities.

A growing percentage of the Arnold neighbors had already given up eking out a living from Rhode Island's rocky soil. Some went to central and some to western Pennsylvania, some to the river valleys of northern Virginia, and a few, including one of Stephen's uncles, moved to Cooperstown in New York's Butternut Valley. Twenty-three years old, Stephen Arnold moved to a village outside Cooperstown in 1794. "There was no occasion of my going far to seek for business," he wrote. "At this early settlement of the country, there was business in plenty for people of every description; villages and towns were in plenty for people were in want of Physicians, School Masters, etc., and Merchants and Land Speculators in want of clerks."[5]

After two years as a clerk, Stephen Arnold was approached by a committee of citizens from Burlington Village who needed a schoolmaster. Bored and somewhat contemptuous of his common neighbors, he took the job, convinced that as a teacher he could bring a measure of civilization and moral uplift to this community of rough-cut farmers. Frontier school teaching was, however, a hardy profession. If children learned how to read, write, and make simple calculations, their parents were pleased. Most serious training took place on the farm, where children were a critical part of the work force for at least six months of the year. As a lot, teachers were as transient as the migrant farmers. Generally they were strangers on the move. Villagers expected to keep the teacher a year, maybe two. A teacher's prestige in the community, and even more in the classroom, stemmed from his success as a disciplinarian. A well-educated schoolmaster, especially one who took pride in his ability to read Greek and Latin, was doomed to frustration. One teacher in a neighboring town had found the job so exasperating he ended each class day in drunken prayer, "a bottle in one hand and a horsewhip in the other."[6]

Stephen Arnold could not have been expected to embrace his circumstance with joy or satisfaction. Nor did he. Twice he tried to quit. Twice he was persuaded to stay on. Seven winters passed. He married. He had no children, but he took in his wife's niece, Betsy, to raise as his own.

As the years passed, his exasperation grew. Time was slipping away—even by 1850, the normal male life expectancy was only 38.3—and he had realized few if any of his youthful dreams. His personal limitations, aggravated by the severity of frontier life, left Stephen Arnold an embittered man of small patience. On January 10, 1805, midway through a long dreary winter, his patience gave out. That day, he later wrote, he had been "provoked even to madness, through the ill behavior of my pupils."

The occasion came after dinner as Arnold sat down to tutor Betsy with her spelling. Her book open before her, she was told to pronounce the words she read. As her finger moved down the column, she came to the word "gig," a word she had already learned several nights before. But this time she stumbled: "Jig," she said, looking hopefully to her uncle for approval. Stephen Arnold interpreted the glance to be cocky insolence. He took the child outdoors into the snow, pulled her pinafore above her head and slowly beat her with a stick, then returned to try the lesson again. But the girl had been so traumatized by her uncle's furious outburst that she repeated her mistake. His fury intensified. Again they went out into the snow. By the end of the evening she had been beaten six times, and her back and legs had been reduced to shreds of raw flesh. Four days later the child died.[7]

Arnold disappeared into the snow-covered forest, and for two and a half months wandered through Pennsylvania by foot. Reports placed him all the way from Pittsburgh to Philadelphia. Posters went up throughout New York State for the "barbarian" child-murderer. Rewards were offered for any information leading to his capture. A "savage ruffian," a "monster," a "tiger in human shape," the newspapers called him. In the spring of 1805 Stephen Arnold had become the most wanted criminal in the state.[8]

Arnold was taken quietly in a Pittsburgh tavern the afternoon of March 28. He was spotted by a bounty hunter from upstate New York who had tracked him over three hundred miles to Pittsburgh. As his captor led him outdoors, Arnold pulled a pistol from beneath his coat, struggling to shoot himself in the head. A bystander foiled the suicide attempt. Taken to jail, Arnold was transferred to New York and ordered to stand trial in early June. He pleaded not guilty, but he offered virtually no defense. Not surprisingly, on June 4, he was convicted. He was ordered to be hanged six weeks later.[9]

There is no explanation as to why sentencing was delayed so long, but its consequence was profound. Within days, the wrath of Arnold's Burlington neighbors subsided. Arnold himself became totally withdrawn, consumed with "melancholy." By July 7, community sentiment had so changed that a petition for stay of execution was circulated and gathered about two hundred signatures. Just forty-eight hours before the hour of execution, the townsmen reached the governor and obtained the stay. To reach Cooperstown in time they had to recross the Hudson River and the Catskill Mountains—all by horseback.[10]

From dawn on July 19, the streets of Cooperstown were jammed. Hangings then were as entertaining as they were cathartic. For suspense this hanging was unsurpassed. At twelve o'clock, Stephen Arnold had been taken from the jail, placed in a wagon next to his coffin, and led in procession to the Susquehanna River Bridge at the edge of town. Following the wagon were two militia companies, the drummers of the funeral dirge, and no less than twelve thousand spectators. "The display of about six hundred umbrellas of various colors, the undulating hues, the vibration of thousands of fans in playful fancy, the elevated background of the landscape interspersed with carriages of various constructions and filled with people, the roofs of the buildings . . . covered with spectators, the windows crowded with faces . . . afforded whenever the mind was detached from the occasion, real satisfaction to the contemplative mind," wrote the editor of the local *Otsego Herald.* Finally, the funeral wagon reached the gallows, erected on a flat spot in the riverbank beside the bridge. Three prayers were offered. Arnold, shaken, sat for a moment on his coffin and spoke his final words. Then he turned to his executioner.[11]

"The Sheriff had adjusted the fatal cord, except for fastening it to the beam of the gallows, the prisoner remained apparently absorbed in solumn meditation," the *Herald* reported. "The thousands of spectators were waiting in silent and gloomy suspense for the fatal catastrophe, when the Sheriff, after a few concise and pertinent remarks to the prisoner, produced a letter from his Excellency Governor Morgan Lewis" containing the reprieve. Stephen Arnold collapsed. For a moment the crowd seemed caught in a silent panic. The sheriff himself seemed uncertain over what to do next. Gradually the crowd turned, some with angry muttering, and followed Arnold in his funeral wagon back to jail. Almost two years later, in the spring of 1807, Stephen Arnold's sentence was converted by the state legislature to life imprisonment.[12]

Daniel Drake and Stephen Arnold appear as prototypical characters of the American frontier, men who stood apart from the ordinary farmers and craftsmen. Most histories include the lives of the Daniel Drakes, tough individuals who thrived on self-reliance and naked opportunity, but few recount the alienated underside of the unsettled frontier, where such tales of human pathos as Stephen Arnold's were also everyday occurrences.

To many New England intellectuals, Stephen Arnold's crime would have posed no surprise. He, like most frontier settlers, had made a journey that was not only physically dangerous but spiritually perilous as well. He had gone to dwell in nature. For the orthodox Puritan mind, that trip was tantamount to visiting the kingdom of the devil. As old Cotton Mather would have described it, Arnold, plainly lacking inner grace, had wandered off from the security of God's well-ordered community and his soul had been seized by demons. Nature was the territory of writhing, lustful, depraved, savage spirits; nature could only become Eden through the emplacement of godly order.[13]

By 1800 Cotton Mather had lain in his grave for over sixty years.

Puritan hegemony had disappeared. But its mysticism, its influence over the imagination, had not died. Sublimated and reformed through the doctrine of Manifest Destiny, Puritan precepts survived throughout the nineteenth century, and nowhere so well as on the frontier, where white survival became synonymous with the struggle of order against savage chaos. If in the cities human beings had been corrupted into the life of crime, on the frontier, the fragility of Christian civilization had permitted the weak to fall slave to criminal passion. As he stood on the gallows, facing the multitudes for what he thought would be his final message, Stephen Arnold had said as much: It was his passions, he said, that had overcome him, for he had never intended to murder his niece. "It appears to me," he declared, "that if you will not take warning from this affecting scene you would not be warned though one should rise from the dead."[14]

Writers, moralists, and historians of the early nineteenth century were perennially fascinated by such frontier episodes. At a time when literature was valued for its symbolic, even its allegorical, content, the tales were chosen for their instructive power and soon they took on the character of myth. Stephen Arnold's story would probably have disappeared totally had it happened thirty years later in Cooperstown, New York. Had it taken place thirty years later on the banks of the Missouri, however, chances are it would have survived with much the same power and public drama. For it was a story of place, and the fascination it carried for contemporary newspaper readers as well as for historians was the drama of white civilization struggling with human nature.

The myths of the ferocious outlaw, which would so dominate the American West after the Civil War, found their antecedents in these earlier Manichean struggles. Take for example, the saga of Daniel Boone, hero, explorer, Indian fighter, champion of white civilization. Probably no human being was so subjected to literary scrutiny during the first thirty years after the founding of the Republic. New accounts were published every few years, each reflecting some peculiar twist on frontier mythology. And, as one student of American mythology has shown, the variation in the Boone narratives also reflect the sectional, cultural, and political interests of the storytellers. To the New England writers, Boone represented the uncivilized degeneracy of the riffraff who were being expelled to the frontiers, men and women who, because they lived in the land of the "savage" redman, had taken on his debased way of life. (Boone had actually lived with an Indian tribe as a captive.) Westerners saw him as the entrepreneurial hero, the man whose courage and integrity enabled him to forge a path to the opportunities of the New Eden. To southerners, he stood as the reflective, even philosophical, aristocrat who had left the comfort of the manor for the sublime solace of nature and natural order.[15]

Ultimately the shape of the mythology was controlled by northeasterners, and for a simple reason—they controlled the presses. Except for a few fledgling printers in Cincinnati, nearly all the pre–Civil War publishers were in New York and Philadelphia. Those writers who could claim more than a small regional following were, as a rule, comfortable members of the northeastern intellectual elite. Their principal subject was the taming of the savage continent through individual enterprise, a theme drawn from the dual heritage of Quaker commerce and Puritan industry. Unfortunately, the engine of enterprise also created outcasts, men who were not needed by the factories, whose agrarian sensibilities were unsuited to the industrial system or who were driven from their farms in one of the recurring financial panics. Bitter and vengeful at the fates their families suffered, more than a few of them struck back with a violent passion, enlisting in outlaw gangs that offered both personal freedom and the chance to act out the feelings of revenge they held inside. Among the deranged, the savage, and the fanatic, the prototypical western outlaw was a man striking back at the merciless, avaricious society he believed had done him wrong.

Of the early western outlaws, the most notorious were the Harpe brothers, whose vicious exploits were chronicled from the Ohio Valley to the Natchez Trace. The two brothers, Micjah (called Big Harpe) and Wiley (called Little Harpe), reached adulthood just before 1800 when the first river settlements were being built along the Ohio, Kentucky, and Tennessee rivers. It was the time of the river pirates depicted so romantically in the exploits of the courageous Mike Fink. "In describing the American backwoodsmen, a class of men peculiar to our country," wrote an Illinois judge in 1825, "I have thought it proper to introduce among other authentic anecdotes the story of the Harpes. My object was to display as well as the extraordinary sufferings to which the earliest emigrants to the western country were exposed, the courage with which they met and repelled those hardships." In the preface to his account of the crimes the judge remarked: "Neither avarice nor want nor any of the usual inducements to the commission of crime, seemed to govern their conduct. A savage thirst for blood—a deep-rooted enmity against human nature, could alone be discovered in their actions." Indeed, though they were thieves, the Harpes seemed not to have been especially greedy, taking usually either food or horses to serve their immediate needs. In most cases their crime was murder—without motive.[16]

Fragmented details of the Harpe brothers' childhood reveals only that their father had been a British sympathizer living in North Carolina during the Revolution. As such, they had been ostracized and reviled as children. According to one historian, Big Harpe, just before his death, explained his murderous career as retribution for the personal torment he always experienced from his neighbors. The historian, repeating one of the lingering fears of nearly all southern intellectuals, went on to note that "their tawny appearance and dark curly hair betrayed a tinge of African blood coursing through their veins." The Harpes were said to have crossed the mountains into Tennessee, taken common-law wives, and with their women joined those Creek and Cherokee Indians who were still resisting white encroachment, sleeping beneath the sky and wearing leather shirts and moccasins.[17]

The Harpes' first crime was robbing a man outside Knoxville in 1779, a robbery that would probably have gone unrecorded except that the victim claimed to be a preacher, producing a Bible with the name of George Washington written in it. "That is a brave and good man, but a mighty rebel against the King," Big Harpe told the preacher. And then, without explanation, the brothers returned the preacher's belongings, remounted, and as they disappeared into the forest, shouted, "We are the Harpes!"

The brothers' exploits continued for two more years. Thievery combined with murder was normal for them, we are told. Occasionally they bashed infants into trees until their skulls were cracked open. Meanwhile they kept moving, eventually to western Kentucky where they made their final assault. The time was mid-August, 1799; the place, the Green River in Henderson County.[18]

Having failed to find food in the first house where they stopped, the brothers moved on to the home of one Squire Silas McBee, a justice of the peace celebrated for his raids on outlaws, and therefore, one supposes, an apt target. But McBee kept a half a dozen hunting dogs who attacked the two men and drove them off. As night had fallen by then, they moved on to the house of Moses Stegall, whose wife they had known secretly in Knoxville. She invited them to stay the night, adding that her husband was gone and that a surveyor was also spending the night in her one spare bed, where all three guests would have to sleep. Before long they all retired. But once the surveyor had fallen asleep, one of the Harpes pulled a small ax from his belt and quietly bashed his brains out. Next morning they came down from the loft as though nothing had happened. Mrs. Stegall fixed breakfast; they took a butcher knife, slashed her infant's throat "from ear to ear," and then stabbed the mother to death. To cover up the murders, they set fire to the house. As the Harpes rode away, they were stopped by two neighbors and were forced to kill them as well.[19]

Within a day a posse had been mounted, led by Justice Silas McBee, Moses Stegall, and five other "daring backwoodsmen." After another day's ride, the posse caught up with the Harpes, first captured their wives, then shot Big Harpe while his younger brother escaped. As Big Harpe lay dying on the ground, a bullet lodged against his spine, McBee at first intended to shoot him to get it over, but then relented under the pressure of his fellow vigilantes. Stegall pulled a knife, explaining to Harpe he was about to cut his head off. For an hour, the men stood about Harpe, taunting him. Then Moses Stegall stepped up to him and pointed his rifle at Harpe's head. Harpe lurched from side to side in terror. "Very well, I believe I will not upon reflection shoot him in the head," Stegall said, "for I want to preserve *that* as a trophy." So he shot him in the heart, bent down, and with the knife he had earlier flashed, hacked off Harpe's head. He took it to a crossroads not far away, mounted it prominently on a tree, and left it to decay.[20]

Lone outlaws often wandered through the hills and river valleys of the frontier. A few, however, had begun to work in gangs daring to overrun entire towns. That was the plight of Bellvue, Iowa, a Mississippi River town where William W. Brown settled in 1837.

Brown came to Bellvue from Michigan. He was tall, dark, apparently rich, and considered altogether charming. He bought a house, converted it to a hotel, then opened a general store and meat market. Customers without money were given credit, and in the idle winter months he hired woodcutters to supply fuel to passing steamboats. Soon he became one of the most popular men in the county. The wages he offered even began to draw in new settlers. It was only after the arrival of the newcomers that the townspeople started to question Brown's intentions.

It was just then that counterfeit notes began surfacing, followed by an increase in petty thievery. Cattle and horses started disappearing. Circumstantial evidence pointed to the men who worked for Brown and boarded at his hotel. When one man was charged with passing bad bills, Brown acted as his counsel. Confronted with his neighbors' suspicions, Brown sent his men across the river on a woodcutting job. But still the robberies continued. Finally, in January 1839, the man Brown had defended in court attacked the niece of a leading townsman, James Mitchell. A gunfight ensued, and Mitchell shot the attacker through the heart. The fact that Brown and his men arrived with their guns drawn a few minutes later seemed ample proof that he was really the boss of an outlaw gang that had come to take over the town of Bellvue.

A few days later several of his men tried but failed to blow up the house where Mitchell was being held. One of the conspirators was caught and confessed. A warrant was issued for the arrest of Brown and most of his gang, but no townsman dared to carry it out. Triumphant, Brown returned to his business, and the robberies continued.

Not until spring, when the sheriff went for help to veteran army Indian fighter Thomas Cox, could a posse be raised to confront the gang. The showdown in Bellvue came on April 1. Inside Brown's hotel, most of the Irish gang members milled about. Outside hung a red flag with the words "Victory or Death" embroidered on it. Up and down the street, gang members marched, jeering and taunting Cox's posse, which lay back about a block away.

Late in the morning the sheriff came into the hotel. Brown asked him what he intended to do. "Arrest them all as I am commanded," the sheriff said.

"That is, if you can," Brown answered.

"There is no if about it," the sheriff said. "I have a sufficient force to take you all, if force is necessary, but we prefer a surrender without force."

The sheriff left, promising Brown that his men would receive fair trials. Just after noon Brown called Cox and the sheriff back to announce that a surrender might be arranged. Brown was lowering the muzzle of his rifle toward the floor when it accidentally discharged. Instantly the posse and Brown's men opened fire on each other. Brown fell to the floor with two bullets through his head. The two sides fought hand to hand with guns, knives, and pitchforks as the posse drove Brown's men up the stairs and set fire to the hotel.

Seven of the gang died. A lynch mob formed as soon as the other thirteen were caught, but the sheriff persuaded them to go home. The next morning Cox told the sheriff he had been relieved of his duty. The people would make their own justice by voting on whether the thirteen should be hanged or whipped and banished, Cox explained.

Two men walked through the crowd. One, carrying a box of red and white beans, repeated, "White beans for hanging, colored beans for whipping." Each of the eighty townsmen chose a bean and placed it in the empty box held by the second man. Cox counted the beans, then paused and asked if everyone agreed to abide by the vote. Reassured, he announced that there were three more colored beans than white. The thirteen men were taken to the post, whipped and placed in open boats on the Mississippi River with three days' supply of rations.[21]

The saga of such outlaws won immortality in the frontier lore. Harpes Head Road, for example, still exists in Henderson County, Kentucky. Probably most of the Harpe stories are true, or partially true, though when they were first printed in the 1820s some newspapers questioned the authenticity of the gorier details. But accurate or not, such stories were widely published during the early years of the Jacksonian upsurge for a "restructuration" of society. For, as the eastern cities were beginning to feel threatened by a criminal underclass in the 1820s, so their hegemony in national politics was being challenged by the emerging political forces in the West and the South, by those same down-home farmers and pioneers who looked to Old Hickory as the champion of the little man.

Until the 1820s, the settlements beyond the Appalachians, the towns of the Ohio Valley, the small farmers of Alabama and Mississippi who weren't quite part of the plantation system, the hunters, trappers and explorers of the Rockies, carried no political weight. National politics had remained the pastime of the southern gentry and the northern commercial–intellectual axis. To the old insiders, these frontier Jacobins appeared barely civilized, and with their rhetoric of rebellion against "concentrated power" they hardly seemed fit to take a hand in governing the nation. Little wonder then that the genteel reading public of Boston and Philadelphia was supplied these lurid tales of such "white Indians"—savages in disguise who talked of seizing the very foundations of the Republic. Little wonder too that in their clamor for political power the outsiders should champion a hero like General Andrew Jackson, who was not only able to rout the redcoats from New Orleans but who had also vanquished the miscegenated criminal heathen on the Florida frontier to establish order and respectability.[22]

At least since the Louisiana Purchase in 1803, the existence of Spanish Florida had been a thorn in the foot of the American South. In the logic of continental conquest, Florida made no sense. It was in the way of trade and presented a risk to national security. Increasingly, it had become a haven for recalcitrant Indians and runaway slaves. By the conclusion of the British War of 1812, almost the entire Creek Nation had been subdued, restricted to a small corner of southwest Georgia, and prepared for the inevitable removal to the Great Plains. Those Creeks who were in Florida—the Seminoles—had fared rather better under the Spanish missions, retaining control of their hunting rights and maintaining their own political integrity. They, as well as the Spanish, had also allowed, if not encouraged, the settlement of runaway slaves from Georgia; by 1818 there existed in Florida large communities of free blacks. Both the blacks and the Indians were armed and frequently raided the towns and plantations of south Georgia, stealing food, arms, general supplies, and encouraging slaves to rebel or run away.[23]

On July 30, 1812, Lieutenant Colonel Thomas Smith wrote his superior that recent attacks by Indians (who would soon ally themselves with the British), plus the escape of some eighty slaves, weakened the Georgia frontier. He continued: "They have, I am informed, several hundred fugitive slaves from the Carolinas and Georgia at present in their Towns and unless they are checked soon, they will be so strengthened by desertion from Georgia and Florida that it will be found troublesome to reduce them." Three weeks later Smith added: "The Blacks assisted by the Indians have become very daring." Had the War of 1812 lasted a little longer, General Andrew Jackson would happily have taken his campaign east into Florida. As it was, his subordinates had launched punitive attacks against the Spanish at Pensacola for alleged violation of neutrality in aiding Indians friendly to the British. But that was all. Still, Jackson's opportunity would come.[24]

"A Negro Fort erected during our late war with Britain . . . has been strengthened since that period and is now occupied by upwards of two hundred and fifty Negroes, many of whom have been enticed away from the services of their masters—citizens of the United States: all of whom are well clothed and disciplined," Jackson told the Spanish commandant at Penascola in spring 1816. By their daring raids, these escaped slaves had exacerbated the Indian threat and brought encouragement to other enclaves of rebellious runaways in the Carolinas and Virginia. He warned the Spanish that if the stealing and criminal raids by blacks continued, he would not hesitate to invade.[25]

The first attack on the black stronghold came at 5:00 A.M., July 15, 1816. Situated on a steep bluff above the shallow Apalachicola River, their earthen-walled fort withstood the initial shots. Moreover, the blacks were well armed; among their artillery were a thirty-pound cannon, three twenty-four-pounders, several smaller cannons, and a five-and-a-half-inch howitzer. They might have easily repulsed the assault had the white invaders not been lucky enough to land a red-hot ball in the fort's powder magazine. That fluke shot set off the whole magazine—some seven hundred barrels of powder left behind by the British. The explosion destroyed the fort, killing 302 men, women, and children. Of the 32 survivors, all black leaders were executed. In a move calculated to win the Seminoles to the army's side, the Indians were given the fort's small arms, on condition they help return the blacks to their slave owners in the United States.[26]

The Seminoles took the arms, but they made no effort to return any runaways. And the border raids continued. "Your Seminoles are very bad people," the American military commander warned the Indian chiefs, leveling charges of arson, cattle theft, and murder. He ordered them to give up the criminals within their land, adding at the end, "You harbor a great many of my Black people among you at Sahwahnee. If you give me leave to go by you against them, I shall not hurt anything belonging to you." King Hatchy, the Seminole chief, retorted by charging the Americans with theft, burning, and murder, and he promised to repulse any attack. Border skirmishes continued.[27]

Finally, in December 1817, Secretary of War John C. Calhoun told commanding general Edmund P. Gaines: "Should the Seminole Indians still refuse to make reparations for their outrages . . . it is the wish of the President that you consider yourself at liberty to march across the Florida line and to attack them within its limits." A few days later Calhoun directed Andrew Jackson to march his troops south from

Tennessee to take over the operation. Jackson answered: "Let it be signified to me through any channel . . . that the possession of the Floridas would be desirable to the United States, and in sixty days it will be accomplished."[28]

It took Jackson more than sixty days to keep his pledge. But within six months he succeeded. Florida became United States territory. Although Jackson was formally rebuked in Washington—he had, after all, waged an undeclared war against Spain—he was the greatest hero alive in the South and the West. Moreover, whatever the details of the censure movements against him, Jackson's campaign was fully consistent with his president's policies. In 1817, Monroe had written him directly: "The hunter or savage state requires a greater extent of territory to sustain it, than is compatible with the progress and just claims of civilized life, and must yield to it." Jackson, executing Monroe's dictum, had suppressed the Indians and routed the runaway slaves, the two symbols of the criminal instinct that so possessed the frontier mind. He—and those Democrats who followed him for the next thirty years—was in a position to make good on the promise he had made to the nation. "We are going to fight," Jackson swore, "for the reestablishment of our national character." But the Jacksonians' vision of that character was one that hated and wished to dominate every being who was not white.[29]

Jackson's campaign through Florida was a critical move, both for his personal career and in its effect on the southern frontier. Owner of more than a hundred slaves himself, Jackson brought reassurance to those southerners who had always worried about the North's superior economic and political power. Jackson was a man whom they could depend upon to fight for southern values. At the same time, he was a self-made man, a merchant, a lawyer, and a land speculator whose parents had been poor Appalachian farmers. He had even fought briefly in the revolutionary war. He was a symbol of hope to the little man, the small farmers of Tennessee or Mississippi who worked in the fields with the handful of slaves they owned.[30]

Once he had become president, Andrew Jackson seemed to speak for these "real people," as he called them, but his attack on the banks, for example, was really only a southern move against northern financial hegemony. In fact, Jackson showed little concern for the "real people." He talked about decentralization, but concentrated more power into the presidency than had any of his predecessors. He opposed unions. He forthrightly supported not only the existence of slavery but also the strategic expansion of slavery into the western territories. Even his opposition to the annexation of Sam Houston's Texas republic of 1836 was a tactic to delay and diffuse northern opposition to additional slave states until the South could be in a better political position. So committed was he to southern institutions that he hardly hesitated to break the law himself when he violated an order of the Supreme Court by driving the Cherokees out of the Blue Ridge Mountains. As demonstrated in his personal war on the Indians and runaway blacks of Spanish Florida, it was Jackson's attitude toward the law that left an indelible mark on the southern frontier. As he viewed it, the law was always subject to popular approval; without that local public approval the law could always be circumvented. Ultimately, Jackson's genius as a leader lay in his ability to evaluate his own popular support and measured it against his enemies' power.[31]

Chapter 11

The Crimes of Slave Power

Since the Stono rebellion of 1739, the white population of South Carolina had lived in panic at the possibility of being collectively beheaded by recalcitrant slaves. The more they feared black rebellions, the more they found them—in rumors, children's fantasies, and ordinary brawls. Each time, they reacted with vicious brutality, killing over the years hundreds of hapless blacks who happened to fit some imaginary description or who accidentally wandered into the wrong place at the wrong time. The harsher the repression, the more slaves ran away or dreamed of revolt. But precisely because the repression was so complete, actual uprisings were few.

Some did take place, in Louisiana in 1811, for example. Others were plotted, like the one in Frederick, Maryland, in 1814. One that might have had devastating consequences almost exploded in Charleston in 1822. It was to be led by Denmark Vesey, a freed slave who could go where he pleased, within the limits set by the color of his skin. A skilled carpenter respected by whites, Vesey owned $8,000 worth of property and lived only two blocks away from the governor of South Carolina. At fifty-five, he was the envy of the blacks who knew him.

But Vesey was married, and his wife was a slave. So, therefore, were his children. To visit them, Vesey was forced to beg permission from their master. Nor did the servility of his peers make his freedom more palatable. A calm, cool-headed, methodical, studious man with a charismatic demeanor and an uncommonly eloquent tongue, Vesey was convinced that only by seizing power would all black men in Carolina ever be respected and free. But he also knew, as Frantz Fanon would say a century and a half later, that in order to rebel, blacks first had to have faith in their own capacity to win.

For three years, Vesey patiently taught his followers to have that faith. Using both the Bible and myths from their African past, he educated, cultivated, harangued, cajoled, and trained scores of blacks to become aggressive but iron-disciplined lieutenants in the future army of liberation. He chose his top aides well: tough, smart slaves who knew their way around in both white territory and black compounds. Two of his immediate adjutants, for example, were trusted personal slaves of the governor himself; one had access to the white militia barracks; others were blacksmiths and silversmiths who knew how to fashion weapons; more still were handy with horses and boats. One was an expert at camouflage and produced wigs, mustaches, sideburns, whole noses, and chins meant to turn made-up blacks into convincing whites. All learned to use firearms. None were squeamish about pain, or killing. Reportedly, scores if not hundreds of blacks, both in Charleston and on the plantations, were ready for Vesey's word to launch America's truly social revolution.

But the word never came. Betrayed by one of the conspirator's sons, an entire secondary network was arrested in June 1822, a month before the revolt was to have begun. Beaten and tortured, most held out long enough for the vast majority of the conspirators to escape. Vesey and his top lieutenants were caught and tried. They denied to the end that they were engaged in anything more serious than periodic study or, in modern terms, consciousness-raising sessions. So firm were they in their affirmation of innocence that some historians have even claimed that no conspiracy existed, except in the imaginations of panicky whites. In any case, Vesey and his friends were found guilty in a secret trial and were all hanged.

The reason for the secrecy was given as "the need for guaranteeing the 'infected' rebels to prevent their insurrectionary germs from spreading to uncontaminated slaves." The truth is that Carolina officials were afraid to panic its white population. But by word of mouth, everyone knew of the alleged conspiracy, and panic they did.[1]

All through the South, whites organized vigilante groups to watch the blacks and kill them before they began killing. Whatever authorities existed in the South were either unable or unwilling or both to curtail vigilante action. Furthermore, the official who had most encouraged vigilantes by being one himself, Andrew Jackson, soon became president, giving vigilantes an added boost in their conviction that theirs was the true law because it was popular.

The aborted rebellion by Denmark Vesey, and other planned or squashed revolts by slaves in the South, also had an impact on antislavery whites. They too began to organize—and take the law into their own hands. They organized volunteers to go south to free slaves, an underground railroad to whisk runaway slaves to the north, and support groups to finance both operations and help the blacks survive in the north.

Abolitionist activities intensified, especially after the well-publicized rebellion in Virginia led by Nat Turner, which put an end to all manumissions in the South. Antislavery newspapers and pamphlets condemning the decadence of southern culture began to surface in small-town post offices throughout the South. Travelers with Yankee accents were found distributing leaflets. Abolitionist documents were discovered describing supposed networks of northern agitators who were prepared to lead an insurrectionary movement among the slaves. The memory of Nat Turner's bloody revolt was propagated everywhere, and rumors of lesser uprisings multiplied by the month. The South was afire with paranoia.[2]

To defend their threatened culture, the aroused southerners quickly perfected their vigilance committees made up usually of the leading citizens in each town. Travelers were stopped, their luggage searched. Northerners who could provide no suitable explanation of their business were held for questioning. Men and women caught with abolitionist tracts were whipped, tarred and feathered, or, upon occasion, hanged. Each vigilance committee, whose members dispensed justice on the spot, became in effect the central committee for general mob law.

In Virginia, just outside Washington, D.C., vigilance committees were appointed in each militia district and directed "to detect and to bring to speedy punishment all emissaries who may be found within the borders of our county, giving circulation to the papers or pamphlets put forth by the abolitionist associations of the North, agitating the question of slavery, and therefore endangering the peace and tranquillity of our land." In Virginia, Tennessee, Washington, Kentucky, and Alabama, suspected agitators were reported, seized by mobs, jailed, and their papers burned. But nowhere was the vigilante action so flagrant as among Andrew Jackson's longtime backers in central Mississippi.[3]

No riot, no rebellion, no insurrection, no demonstration of any kind ever took place in or near Madison County, Mississippi, during the year 1835. Yet by the middle of that summer more than a dozen white men and an unknown number of black slaves—probably several dozen—had been murdered in a wave of vigilante hysteria that engulfed the Yazoo River Valley. The story of these Yazoo Valley crimes had begun nearly two decades before and had encompassed a broad panorama of wartime heroics, Indian expulsions, white insecurity, land speculation, party politics, and river piracy.

The Yazoo River runs southwest into the Mississippi River about a third of the way up the western edge of the state. Toward its headwaters in the north had been the lands of the Chickasaw. In the center of the state, east of the Yazoo, had been the Choctaw. Both tribes had believed their territories safe from white expansion. That was only one of many illusions shattered in the succeeding decades.

So great had been the Mississippi sympathy for General Jackson's Florida adventure that the state legislature passed a special resolution in 1819 declaring that his victory "merits the approbation of his country." A year later the Mississippians followed their praise with a plea to Jackson that he negotiate the first expropriation treaty with the Choctaw. Jackson accepted, new land was opened for white settlement, and the governor wrote the hero of New Orleans that he would "live in our affections to the latest period of time." As a token of their affection, the newly selected site of the state capital was named Jackson.

When Jackson became president, he did not forget the Choctaw, with whom he had negotiated a treaty. Now he wanted them out of Mississippi altogether and into Oklahoma. Secretary of War John Eaton said to the Choctaw: "Your great father approaches and tells you to go, for your happiness depends upon it." Within two more years, in October 1832, the Chickasaws were forced to cede their land as well. As a result, some two-thirds of the land in Mississippi was held by the federal government and ready for settlement—or, more properly, for rampant speculation.[4]

Speaking at a dinner celebrating the new treaty, Jackson's lieutenant, Robert J. Walker, rhapsodized about the new flood of settlers who would soon bring unparalleled prosperity to Mississippi. Walker, described by one observer as a zealot in the Jacksonian cause comparable only to a crusader "upon his pilgrimage to the Holy Land," might have more honestly spoken about the promise of his own prosperity. Before the public lands went on sale, Walker and several confederates surveyed the new territory, and on the first day of sale bought up vast acreages which they later resold in smaller lots to individual farmers.[5]

Before the opening of the former Indian lands and the advent of the so-called flush times of the land speculation, Mississippi had stood somewhat apart from other states of the Deep South in her attitude toward slavery. All through the 1820s the state legislature had debated the merits of the South's "peculiar institution." Bills had been introduced to ban slave sales and slave imports from other states. Some old landholders, fearing competition and a drop in land values if the plantation system were extended to the newly opening territories, urged partial curtailment. Yet the fears of the old gentry could not hold back the designs of the upwardly bound newcomers.

Partly as a result of the speculator's work, and partly because of economic fluctuations surrounding Jackson's closure of the National Bank, the plantation system expanded and flourished. Central and northern Mississippi was settled not by thousands of hardy yeomen, cast in the Jeffersonian mold, but by a rash of hustling parvenus and downstate gentry. By the end of the 1830s, the vastly expanded plantation system had established itself so firmly that it would last until the second half of the twentieth century. And so the state, whose governor had denounced slavery in 1826 as "an evil at best," had so changed by 1836 that its legislature did "look upon the institution of slavery . . . not as a curse, but as a blessing, as the legitimate condition of the African race, as authorized by the laws of God and the dictates of reason and philanthropy."[6]

In this newly carved frontier, however, new problems arose. There had come a new breed of outlaw, more threatening perhaps than all the early cutthroats—the slave thieves, men who lured slaves away from their masters on the promise of smuggling them to freedom but instead resold them in the slave markets. Slave theft doubtless existed in the Old South; punishment for it was in most states a stiff prison sentence.

But the widespread anxiety about the crime seemed to parallel the rising hysteria about abolitionist agitators. Among incensed Mississippi editorialists of the 1830s, a strong suspicion existed that the whole antislavery movement was simply a subterfuge for the criminal plots of northern adventurers.[7]

Such fears of a criminal plot seemed to converge on a single individual in the winter of 1834–35. His name was John A. Murrell. Little is known of him. A gambler, probably a horse thief, certainly a highway bandit, he seemed to be a combination outlaw and riverboat dandy. He had been successful enough to buy a large farm on which he held many slaves. He was tall, dark, stylishly dressed, and because he spoke little of his past or of his frequent business trips, his neighbors in the old Choctaw country regarded him with suspicion. Then came a young soldier of fortune named Virgil Stewart, who, when he discovered that several of a friend's slaves had been stolen, allegedly by Murrell, vowed to catch the thief in the act. How much he really learned about Murrell in January of 1834 is unclear; the only record is Stewart's own rather self-glorifying account of how he infiltrated Murrell's gang and in so doing persuaded the villain to share his secrets. Always the clever spy, Stewart recounted how he deluded the vain Murrell, escaped to alert authorities and thereby succeeded in having the slave thief condemned to a long sentence in the penitentiary.[8]

Stewart published the account of his exploits in the spring of 1835, including in it a new and explosive charge: In addition to a lifetime of murder and mayhem, Murrell had been carefully planning a statewide slave insurrection. He and the blacks, said Stewart, were to take over Natchez on Christmas Day, 1835. They would move from town to town, murdering the plantation owners and their dumpy wives—though of course saving one pretty white woman for each freed Black—until they had conquered enough territory to establish their own villainous state, a base from which marauders could launch their attacks against the entire western frontier. The whole apparatus was known among its members as the Clan. There were secret codes of initiation and a peculiar handshake among members to acknowledge recognition. What was more, claimed Stewart, the danger was not past. Murrell was in prison, but the Clan was moving ahead without him. The result of Stewart's account: Mississippi went wild with witch-hunts. Within weeks, the gallows grew weary with the bodies of black slaves and white infidels.[9]

No sooner had the witch-hunts subsided than there came a frightening story from the wife of a wealthy planter named Latham, near Beattie's Bluff in Madison County. Gathering her skirts to step out for a promenade on the north veranda of her mansion, she claimed to have overheard an agrument between one of the house slaves and a field hand. The house girl was cradling one of her mistress's babies in her arms as she protested: "But this here is such a pretty baby! You all ought to know I never could kill that child!"

"When that day comes you-all got to, gal," the burly black man was supposed to have answered. "Won't be no never-could about it. Us got to kill them all!"

"Go on kill all you-all wants," was her answer. "Won't nobody touch this lamb here. I won't let them touch him!"[10]

Mrs. Latham went straight to her husband, and immediately the nursemaid was ordered to confess what she knew. The frightened girl apparently satisfied her master's worst fears, for within an hour he was off on his horse to warn his white neighbors of an impending black uprising. The planters had indeed much to fear, for in their enthusiasm to expand the slave system, so many blacks had been imported that the whites had become a tiny minority. In the words of the Jacksonian *Mississippian,* there was "so sparse a white population, as to preclude the possibility of building up any thing like an interesting state of society. Many of the owners of those large plantations reside in the older settled parts of the State, and not a few of them in other States—leaving on a plantation . . . no white person except the overseer."[11]

The day after Latham's alarm, blacks were being dragged in for questioning throughout Madison County. Any slave who claimed ignorance or refused to talk was summarily whipped. No court proceedings were necessary. As the planters saw it, they were confronted with a simple war of survival. Justice would surface quickest through the language of the lash, and no limits existed for the length of a flogging. And so the blacks began to confess. A blacksmith named Joe broke first: "He said that the negroes were going to rise and kill all the whites on the Fourth of July, a few days away, and that they had a number of white men at their head." Joe told all the names he knew, of a prominent white farmer nearby who was to enlist his own slaves in the rebellion, of two "steam doctors" who were part of the Clan, and of several slaves who would be "captains under these white men." Slowly more slaves buckled under to their tormenters and began to tell stories similar to Joe's, pointing to whites as organizers of the conspiracy. But the coerced confessions did not save the confessed. On July 2, both they and the suspects were taken out to a cottonwood grove near the Big Black River and hanged.[12]

The first of the whites brought in was one of the two steam doctors, Joshua Cotton. A newcomer whose wife was not with him, Cotton's greatest liability was probably his New England accent. He steadfastly protested his innocence to a newly formed white citizens committee until one of the planters whipped one of his slaves into talking. Cotton, the slave "confessed," was the same white man who first approached him with talk of rebellion. Perhaps he was guilty of working in Murrell's slave-stealing ring, luring the slaves into their trap with promises of freedom. Or perhaps Cotton saw an appropriate confession as his only hope for survival. In either case, he too began to talk: "Our object in undertaking to excite the negroes to rebellion, was not for the purpose of liberating them, but for plunder." Cotton gave a long statement implicating William Saunders and thirteen other white collaborators named by his accusers, including some in adjacent Hinds and Warren counties. Then he added that the conspiracy "embraced the whole slave region from Maryland to Louisiana, and contemplated the total destruction of the white population of all the Slave States." The next morning, the two doctors, Cotton and Saunders, were taken to jail. Accompanying them were several men who, "fastening a rope to the grating of a window in the upper story of the jail, and leaning a couple of rails against the wall, assisted the culprits upon the rails; then adjusting the other end of the rope around their necks, removed the rails."

Panic grew to fury over the next week. No one believed himself safe from slave attack. No one was safe from vigilante condemnation. In nearby Vicksburg, a brawl erupted between several gamblers and certain respectable citizens; five gamblers were taken straight to the gallows. But as in Salem a century and a half earlier, the accusations began to move up the ladder of social prominence. With that, a counterattack was unleashed. "It is acknowledged on all hands that the danger of an insurrection is over," two planters stated in a letter to the governor. "No person that we can learn stands in further fear of negroes. But the lawless pashions [sic] of man seem to have broke loose, and unless there is a stop put to the shedding of blood—confusion and revolution must shortly [reign] over the land." Another landowner urged "peace and moderation, and submission to the Civil Powers."

At first the governor rejected these pleas, offering instead to furnish the Madison County citizens committee the arms needed to suppress the threatened insurrection. But in mid-July he issued a proclamation calling on the citizens to turn over their suspects to "proper authorities."[13]

As the lynching subsided and some measure of calm began to return to central Mississippi, word of the failed "insurrection" spread eastward through the slave states. Cotton's statement, after all, had warned of a war against the whole white population of the South. Abolitionist propaganda continued to flow southward. In nearby Tennessee, the *Nashville Banner* screamed: "Behold, ye 'Liberators,' 'Emancipators,' 'Abolitionists,' the fruits of your extravagance and folly, your recklessness, and your criminal plots against the lives of your fellow men!"

"We know, sir," wrote several Mississippi planters in an open letter to the New York publisher of the antislavery paper *Human Rights,* "that the true object of all this is not to liberate the slaves which you know is wholly impracticable, but it is plunder!" In bitter rage, they promised speedy justice to the high-minded abolitionists: "Why send your dirty falsehoods and pitiful caricatures on inanimate paper? Why not send your Tappans, your Coxes, your Garrisons, or any of your chief apostles of iniquity, and enlighten and humanize the benighted and inhuman South? . . . Send them, sir—our sister state of Kentucky annually supplies us with the article of *hemp,* and it shall be at the service of your emissaries who are apt to be seized with the *group* on entering into our State!"[14]

In August, Robert Hayne, the former governor of South Carolina, led a seething mob into the Charleston, South Carolina, post office in search of abolitionist papers. By the time they left they had burned several bags of mail. A special committee was appointed immediately to search incoming ships for the hated abolitionist propaganda. A few days later the Carolinians won outright endorsement from Washington when Postmaster General Amos Kendall personally approved the destruction of the mail. "We owe an obligation to the laws," he wrote, "but a higher one to the communities in which we live, and if the *former* be perverted to destroy the *latter,* it is patriotism to disregard them." To give final sanctification of the Carolina vigilantes, President Jackson made a point of personally supporting Kendall and then in December asked Congress for authority to ban inflammatory literature from the mails.[15]

Jackson's support of the vigilantes was more than a passing detail

The years 1835 and 1836 were probably the high point of the abolitionist campaign in the South. Congressman and former president John Quincy Adams led the abolitionist campaign in Congress, and during the 1835–36 session, he presented petitions signed by thirty-four thousand people demanding an end to slavery in the District of Columbia. In May 1835 alone, the American Anti-Slavery Society distributed 175,000 pamphlets and newspapers. The people of America were becoming too polarized for the presidency to ignore the consequences. But Jackson, the slave owner, standard-bearer of democracy, not only ingored them. He exacerbated them by siding solidly with the racists and murderers.[16]

President Jackson temporarily saved slavery in the South by supporting its vigilantes. In so doing, he also guaranteed that the enacters of the lynch law would have to resort to bullets at Fort Sumter.

Chapter 12

The Crimes of Crime Prevention

President Andrew Jackson's message to his fellow Americans was crystal clear: If you disagree with the law and have the power to disobey it, do so. He certainly did—over the questions of slavery, vigilantism, Indian rights. He had the power to get away with it.

From the end of Jackson's presidency until the Civil War, which such a policy made inevitable, America was indeed ruled by the sword. Under Jackson's leadership, the American government came to see itself as a latter-day Jesuit company bearing forth the sword and the cross. America's sword was its army; its cross was "American democracy." The Puritan ethic became transformed into a social Darwinist philosophy of domination by the fittest and into a Protestant duty to conquer. It justified America's role as international gendarme. As John L. O'Sullivan, editor of the influential *Democratic Review,* said in 1840: "We have been placed in the forefront of the battle in the cause of Man against the powers of evil." The leading men of the country agreed. "The march of the Anglo-Saxon race is onward," proclaimed the *Washington Union.* Stephen A. Douglas, the Illinois politician later defeated by Abraham Lincoln, insisted that "our federal system is admirably adapted to the whole continent." Pennsylvania senator James Buchanan—later secretary of state, then president—gloated: "Providence has given to the American people a great and important mission, and that mission they were destined to fulfill—to spread the blessings of Christian liberty and laws from one end to the other of this immense continent." And the *New York Morning News* affirmed that it was "our manifest destiny to occupy and to possess the whole continent."[1]

Under the aegis of Manifest Destiny, Americans violated international law in Mexico, the Carribbean, and Central America, welched on treaties with Indians and the foreigners who had settled territories coveted by the United States, stole property, killed dissidents, hanged innocents. All their actions were justified, in the words of Ohio congressman Alexander Duncan, because nonwhites are "unfit." Lewis Cass, who had been President Jackson's secretary of war and later became Buchanan's secretary of state, explained in 1847, after the United States had stolen half of Mexico's best land, "We do not want the people of Mexico either as citizens or subjects. All we want is a portion of territory." And Buchanan, then secretary of state, added that we didn't want them in California because they were a "mongrel race." The *Democratic Review* simply called for "annihilating them as a race," and the powerful *American Review* called for "exterminating her [Mexico's] weaker blood."[2]

Manifest Destiny had one major aim: wealth for the wealthy. Mexico was conquered, Central America was coveted, Indians were murdered for land, minerals, trade monopolies, or strategic points for further expansion. The American public was manipulated, hoodwinked, cajoled, or lied to by the media of the time—led by the *Democratic Review,* the *American Review,* the *New York Evening Post,* the *Washington Union,* and the like—so that it would not oppose government giveaways to railroad entrepreneurs or the establishment of private business monopolies in foreign lands. In fact, so pervasive was the propaganda in those days that the average white American remained pro-imperialist even when the government tried to pretend it was not. The case of William Walker brings out the point.[3]

Born in Nashville in 1824, Walker was a qualified doctor, lawyer, and journalist by the age of twenty-four but practiced none of these professions. A frail-looking, 120-pound, tight-lipped, restless, egocentric ascetic and puritan, he wandered about for a couple of years, then showed up in San Francisco, raised a private army and, in 1853–54, invaded lower California to annex it to the United States. Defeated in battle, he escaped home to raise a new army, this time financed by a group of Boston corporations, including what would become United Fruit, and invaded Nicaragua. He captured Granada, declared himself "elected" president, proclaimed English to be the official language, and appealed to President Franklin Pierce to admit Nicaragua into the Union as a slave state even though Nicaragua had long before outlawed slavery. Pierce toyed with the idea, but before he could act, Walker canceled Cornelius Vanderbilt's transportation "concessions" (meaning monopoly), whereupon the millionaire entrepreneur financed and armed another private army to unseat Walker. Defeated at the battle of Santa Rosa, Walker was brought back to New Orleans where he was tried for violating U.S. neutrality laws. Though Walker never denied the charges, he defended himself by asking the white jury members whether they honestly could doubt that Nicaragua would not be better off as a slave state in the Union than as a free country outside it. The jury not only found Walker not guilty but applauded him enthusiastically. In 1860, Walker again invaded Nicaragua as well as El Salvador and Honduras with a private army, again declared himself president, again "legalized" slavery, and was again defeated, this time by the British, who handed him to Honduras, where he was summarily executed by a firing squad.[4]

Walker and the other privateers—filibusterers, as they were called—who abounded during the pre–Civil War era were neither colorful swashbuckling patriots nor venal continental bandits. They reflected the policies and tempo of the times. After all, President James Polk deliberately lied to Congress to persuade its members to vote the Mexican war. A few years later half of Washington supported a filibuster expedition, organized by the governor of Mississippi, to conquer Cuba; the invaders were caught and executed by the Spanish. After his election in 1852, President Pierce repeatedly plotted to annex Cuba. In 1854, U.S. minister to England James Buchanan was one of the authors of a secret memorandum, known as the Ostend Manifesto, which called for an outright invasion of the island, and in his campaign for the presidency in 1856, Buchanan made Cuba's annexation one of his promises.[5]

Though not all Americans were expansionists—President Zachary Taylor, for one, had not been—most whites certainly were. And they supported expansion not only against Mexico, but also against Indians and anyone else who was not Anglo-Saxon. Thus, for example, while most of the people in California, Oregon, and Kansas opposed slavery, they were equally adamant against allowing free blacks to enter their states or territories. And until Lincoln's victory, most of the nation's great leaders were fundamentally racist. Henry Clay, Daniel Webster, the old John Calhoun, the young Stephen Douglas, all looked upon blacks as inherently inferior and saw nothing wrong with using them as property.

Nor were they reluctant to violate the law if the needs of their constituents were at stake. Indeed, President Pierce did not view himself as unlawful when he encouraged election frauds in Kansas in 1854 to turn that territory into a slave state. And two years later, Buchanan, campaigning on a proslavery platform against a Republican crusade against slavery and polygamy as the "twin relics of barbarism," was equally corrupt. Thus it was very much within the mood of the nation when Supreme Court chief justice Roger Taney declared, in the infamous Dred Scott decision of 1857, that blacks had been regarded "so far inferior, that they had no rights which the white man was bound to respect; and that the negro might justly and lawfully be reduced to slavery for his benefit." Even Lincoln, during his famous debates with Douglas, rejected the nation of "perfect social and political equality with the negro."[6]

If proslavery leaders were willing to disobey national law to uphold the rights of their states to rule themselves, antislavery advocates were equally willing to defy the law to impose their view of morality on others. For the abolitionists, no matter how courageous and ethical history may judge them today, also saw themselves propelled by a "higher justice" to violate the law. Armed and financed by northern entrepreneurs bent on crushing, or at least curtailing, the South's economic might, the abolitionists stole, assaulted, and killed in the name of its principles. John Brown's murderous raid at Pottawatomie Creek in 1856, for example, was no more legal than Walker's burning of Granada. Yet to both, their justification was the greater glory of the Union.

Brown's raid was meant to be an act of retaliation for the Kansas massacre of 1856. The trouble had begun when groups of "border ruffians," organized by Missouri proslavery senator David Atchison, repeatedly clashed with free-state settlers, financed by the New England Emigrant Aid Society—"that vast moneyed corporation," according to Stephen Douglas. The proslavery goons, backed by Missouri lawmen, then sacked Lawrence, the free-soil center of Kansas. John Brown, a mystical abolitionist from Connecticut who had failed at business ventures in Ohio, Pennsylvania, Massachusetts, and New York before setting up a "freedom colony" on the Osawatomie River in Kansas, reacted by raiding a proslavery farm on the Pottawatomie and killing five men. Before he was hanged for his 1859 raid on Harpers Ferry, Virginia, Brown exclaimed: "If I had done what I have for the white men, or the rich, no man would have blamed me."[7]

Thus, by 1860, both sides were so committed to the Jacksonian principle of popular justice that both sides were ready to use the gun to impose it. Slavery was outlawed in the District of Columbia, but power there rested in the proslavery camps; slaves were held and traded in Washington almost as openly as in North Carolina. According to the fugitive slave law, one of the most viciously repressive acts ever passed by a U.S. Congress which deprived blacks of jury trials and the right to testify in their own defense, all escaped slaves were to be sent back to their masters. In Massachusetts, where law enforcers followed the dictates of the venerable abolitionist Senator Charles Sumner and his political henchmen, few escaped slaves were deported. In both cases might did make right.

In neither case was right truly right—and the people knew it. Those who defended individual freedom and states' rights against a "tyrannical" federal bureaucracy also espoused slavery for profit, humanity's greatest outrage. Those who proposed equality under the law and universal morality also sought total economic control of the nation and vast profits for a very few at the expense of the others, who would be forced to live in economic conditions not much superior to those of the slaves they wanted to free. With some notable exceptions, leaders of both sides really cared little about equality. They had few hesitations, for example, about cheating, exploiting, or even exterminating the Indians for their own profit.

Outrages against Indians were perpetrated throughout American history in almost every state and territory, and the expropriations of the Plains is only one, albeit typical, example. It began in the early 1840s when the trek to the Pacific Northwest became serious. By 1849, thousands of Mormons had crossed the Plains on their way to Utah. Thousands more had headed to Oregon. Now some fifty thousand gold hunters were on route to California. They moved in large wagon trains, passed by an old trading post at the junction of the Laramie and North Platte rivers, devastated the lands, decimated the bison herds, and brought cholera to the Indians.

To Indian agent Thomas Fitzpatrick—known as Broken Hand to the Teton Dakota (Sioux), Cheyenne, and Arapaho who populated the area—it was only a matter of time before the Indians' resentment would lead to conflict. To avert it, he requested that the tribes be given compensation. Instead, the government turned the trading post into Fort Laramie, then asked Fitzpatrick to bring the Plains leaders together there so that they might cede the route used by the wagon trains for a proposed railway, the Union Pacific Railroad.

Agent Fitzpatrick succeeded: chiefs from the Crow, Cheyenne, Arapaho, Shoshones, and the various Teton Dakotas agreed to give up large chunks of their land in exchange for government protection, sovereignty, and self-determination on their territory and $50,000 per year for fifty-five years.

No sooner had the treaty been signed, however, than Congress, in its ratification, cut the payment schedule to ten years and the U.S. Army invaded a Brule Dakota camp. The excuse was that a lame cow, owned by a Mormon wagon group, had strayed into the camp and had been shot. Lieutenant John L. Grattan, with thirty soldiers and two wagon guns, demanded that the culprit be brought to justice in Fort Laramie—in violation of Dakota sovereignty. Conquering Bear, the Brule Dakota chief, offered five horses for the dead cow. Lieutenant Grattan refused and ordered his men to open fire. Conquering Bear, his brother, and the other braves in the conference were killed, but other warriors, hidden around the army detachment, responded and killed Grattan and all his soldiers. The army thereupon dispatched a punitive force to wipe out the camp. The Dakotas retaliated and a full war ensued.

By September 1855, every Brule Dakota male, female, and child that could be found was "executed" on direct orders of the U.S. Army. Dakota lands, whether belonging to the Brule or other tribes, were seized, bison herds were exterminated, and the Indians who escaped the massacres were reduced to wandering gatherers. By 1858 what were to be the Union Central and Pacific railroads had been given, free of charge, the choicest sections of the Plains, and had sold most of what they did not need to miners, prospectors, and to the government, which had obtained the land in the first place so that it could be distributed later under the Homestead Acts. Neither the U.S. Army nor white settlers respected the Laramie or any subsequent treaty, and all Dakota tribes were considered as enemy. The war, which two decades later led to General Custer's death, could no longer be stopped.* [8]

Whenever the army was not around, justice on the Plains was taken over by the white settlers. And their form of justice was vicious. Based on defense committees that amounted to no more than marauding gangs, white justice meant the plunder of Indian settlements and the wanton killing and lynching of any Indian who got in the way of white settler schemes. It was vigilante justice at its Jacksonian best.

But by then, vigilantism had become as American as corn bread. In Kansas, the Anti-Horse Thief Association lynched anyone caught with a horse not his own. In Attakapas, Louisiana, French regulators shot all "desperadoes," which included wife-seducers. In southern Illinois, regulators killed more than twenty supposed outlaws without trial from 1846 to 1849. In Texas, after a series of mysterious fires of barns and buildings in Dallas, Denton, and other towns in 1860, vigilantes, fearing slave revolts, lynched three innocent blacks in Dallas and three antislavery whites in Fort Worth.[9]

In New Jersey, farmers organized vigilance committees to catch and hang horse thieves as early as 1788 in what is now Passaic. Such groups flourished before the Civil War in counties now called Somerset, Hunterdon, Bergen, Burlington, Mercer, Warren, Monmouth, Camden, Middlesex (begun in 1797), and Sussex. Inevitably all these committees were set up to protect property—their leaders were the localities' wealthiest men, who either controlled or ignored the established law-enforcement agency. And inevitably, they were immune from prosecution, even when it became known that in an excess of zeal they had hanged or shot innocent men. For these committees were, after all, America's only really effective law-enforcement body at the local level—even if they were in fact illegal.[10]

Among the most efficient of such "popular justice" groups was the Committee of Vigilance of San Francisco, organized in 1851 to cope with impoverished miners, squatters and farmers, and with the Hounds, another vigilante group. It all started, naturally enough, with the gold rush. At first, as thousands streaked in from the east, the hills around Coloma, near Sutter's Fort, where gold had been discovered, became a massive camp of freebooters, speculators, and miners who quickly ruined John Sutter's property, killed his cattle, and settled

*The authors would like to thank Professor J. Jorgensen of the University of California (Irvine) for his research on the Plains Indians.

accounts among themselves in free-for-all fashion as best they could. Sutter, who had gained the land around what became Sacramento as a grant from the Spanish governor, tried to keep order, but failed.

Those who had bought Sutter's land or who claimed legitimate title to it then organized themselves into defense groups. But by the winter of 1849, too many disappointed landless wanderers were squatting on the land, and the landowners resorted to force of arms to drive them out. The squatters, led by a doctor named Charles Robinson from Fitchburg, Massachusetts, who later became governor of Kansas, responded by setting up a regular system of land occupation and a resistance movement against the landowners and speculators bent on throwing them out. In the ensuing battle, on August 14, 1850, one of the squatter leaders was killed and Dr. Robinson was wounded. The squatters reacted by gunning down the sheriff, who had helped the landowners, and three of the toughest owners. The San Francisco militia was then dispatched and the squatters were evicted, many filtering down the hills to San Francisco itself, where, jobless and penniless, they resorted to crime. San Francisco became known as the most violent of American cities.[11]

It was not the former Sacramento squatters who were responsible for that violence. It was the Hounds. Originally members of the New York Volunteers in the Mexican war, the Hounds had come to California with the first gold seekers, failed to make a strike, then started raiding stores, restaurants, and saloons in San Francisco. Organizing themselves as a military unit, they enacted rules for conduct, elected their officers, and set up headquarters in a tent known as Tammany Hall. They paraded in the streets with music and banners and, changing their name to the San Francisco Society of Regulators, acted as a vigilante law-enforcement group, sometimes even carrying out the wishes of Alcalde (mayor) Leavenworth. Their main occupation, however, was to harass the Mexicans, Peruvians, and Chileans who lived in San Francisco.

One balmy July day in 1849, the Hounds went too far. After robbing a score of Latinos, they shot one Chilean and, on horseback, pursued a dozen more through the city and up Telegraph Hill, shooting wildly as they rode. The next day a group of alarmed wealthy citizens met at the corner of Kearny and Washington streets and organized a committee to stop the Hounds. Almost a hundred strong, the new vigilante group quickly rounded up nineteen Hounds, including their top leaders, tried them with great care, found eight guilty of conspiracy to murder, and banished them from the city, warning them that they would be hanged if they returned. That was the end of the Hounds, and the beginning of the San Francisco Committee of Vigilance.[12]

Formally organized in 1851, the San Francisco committee basically ruled the Bay city for two years, carrying out the justice its members—and indeed many of San Francisco's ordinary citizens—felt was being ridiculed by the city and state's corrupt courts. Most of the vigilante members had high stakes to protect, and the committee was meant to protect them. Sam Brennan, the committee's first president, for example, who launched the city's first newspaper, the *California Star,* was a rich land speculator and banker. Isaac Bluxom Jr., the committee secretary, owned a huge ranch in Sonoma County. Garrett W. Ryckman, second vice-president, was a successful brewer and businessman. James King of William, California, owned his own bank and launched the *Evening Bulletin.* James T. Tuan controlled much of the lumber moving out of Humboldt County. James F. Curtis, who later became San Francisco's chief of police, was a wealthy entrepreneur. James C. L. Wadsworth was a banker. William D.M. Howard, a merchandiser, was estimated at the time to be worth $375,000.[13]

These vigilante leaders not only controlled the criminal justice system, they controlled the lives of most ordinary folk in San Francisco. They lynched relatively few people and showed restraint in using the power they wielded, which is one reason why historians tend to describe them as honorable men. Some were Democrats, others Republicans, but most, as entrepreneurs, bankers, and merchants, opposed slavery. Thus they helped push California to the side of the North. Crime did abate during their heyday. After they disbanded in 1853, crime rose again, causing some of the committee leaders to try to reorganize in 1856. But by then, popular sentiment, though not the press, which the committeemen owned by and large, was opposed to lynch law. So instead, the committee set up the People's party, which later fused with the Republicans, and, as one historian put it, "practically controlled the government of San Francisco for more than ten years." But the fact remains that the committee's justice was rich man's justice. One of the outlaws prosecuted by the committee even tried to defend himself by pointing this out.[14]

The outlaw was Sam Whittaker, a member of the James Stuart gang. An ex-convict from Sydney, Australia, Stuart had escaped from a

Marysville, California, jail after being apprehended for stealing $5,000 from Dodge and Company in October 1850. In December he robbed and shot a storeowner, then stole horses around Sacramento, and finally settled in San Francisco. When some of his friends were arrested in Monterey for cleaning out a customs house of $14,000, Stuart organized their jail break. One of the friends was Whittaker, who was later caught by the vigilantes. At his trial, as the committee's papers reveal, "he blamed society for his downfall; he gave instances of injustice to show that a thief had a better chance than an honest man; he sneered at his own service on a jury which sentenced a prisoner to a term of imprisonment for the theft of a pistol, while greater offenders, skillfully defended, went scot-free; he showed how his successful efforts to corrupt officials caused him to despise the authorities he defied; and he boasted of his influence as a politician and of the dozen ex-convicts whom he led to the polls when called upon to assist in the election of Malachi Fallon, marshal of the city."[15]

Whittaker's defense did not succeed. He was eventually hanged. So was Stuart. But Whittaker's characterization of justice in San Francisco was fair enough, not only for San Francisco but also for every town and city in America where "popular justice" had led to rule by the gun.

Chapter 13

The Price and Profit of War

Every war encourages violence, corruption, and profiteering. Unless a population is soundly committed to the cause, it is difficult for people constantly to remember the difference between killing and exploiting the enemy and doing the same to a fellow countryman. Because of the fluidity of the structure of society in time of war, because of combatants' dire need for supplies, because of the intensity of life under threat of death, and, in general, because of the overall breakdown in traditional modes of behavior, morality is too often sacrificed to expediency. That was certainly the case in America during the Civil War.

But not immediately. At first, both Northerners and Southerners rushed to be part of the great crusade, so much so that Leroy P. Walker, the first Confederate secretary of war, and Simon Cameron, the Union counterpart, had to turn down thousands of volunteers because neither side could arm or equip them. But as the war prolonged itself, enthusiasm waned. It became harder and harder for either side to enlist new soldiers, and those who had joined up early now sought to get out. Defections and desertions became more and more common, though more so in the North, and both sides became more and more repressive, first threatening, then carrying out executions of those who refused to fight. People became increasingly restless, and crime skyrocketed.

The Union capitol, Washington, was perhaps the worst hit. There the crime rate soared so much that a special police force had to be created. In 1862, that force made 22,207 arrests, mostly for disorderly conduct, petty larceny, and prostitution. Politicians and city officials inevitably blamed blacks, but the fact is that far more Irish were arrested than blacks. Nor were the police able to curtail street crimes. By 1864, the number of arrests had risen to 23,545, of which 2,271 were suspected deserters who were turned over to the military, and unsolved crimes had almost tripled.[1]

If a rise in street crimes was to be expected during the Civil War, corruption in President Lincoln's administration was not. Yet it flourished. The worst culprits, according to a House investigating committee headed by Massachusetts Republican Henry L. Dawes, were Gideon Welles, Lincoln's secretary of the navy, and Simon Cameron, his secretary of war. Welles was accused only of appointing his brother-in-law, George D. Morgan, as exclusive purchasing agent of all Union naval vessels and letting him skip the country to Europe with $95,000 in kickbacks. But Cameron, who made private deals with friends for 1,092,000 Springfield-type muskets at $22.00 each while the government-owned Springfield armory was making them for $13.50, was accused of passing out 1,836,900 unadvertised private contracts out of a total government contract load of 1,903,800. Both Welles and Cameron survived the House's official "disapprobation," the former retaining his post (and efficiently developing the Union's navy, including the ironclads), the latter, though fired by Lincoln, eventually cashing in on his favors to capture control of the Republican party of his home state of Pennsylvania.

Another survivor of the Dawes committee investigation was Major General John C. Frémont, the explorer, former California senator, and commander of the Department of the West, who was charged with "favoritism, corruption and widespread speculation in contracts." Fired by Lincoln, Frémont eventually gained enough support from Republican dissenters to try to oppose him in 1864, and in 1878 became governor of the territory of Arizona.[2]

Frémont was not the only general accused of corruption during the Civil War. Another was General Neal Dow, a fanatical prohibitionist from Maine who, when he commanded the nonwar zone along the Gulf

Coast in 1862–63, was so determined to punish rebels that he emancipated slaves before Lincoln's proclamation, imprisoned slave owners, and "confiscated," as he called it, their property in violation of orders from his superiors. Sued for theft by a Mississippi plantation owner, Dow fought the case to the Supreme Court, which ruled in his favor in 1880. But while General Dow apparently genuinely believed he was helping the Union cause, the hundreds of Union government agents sent into the South to buy, confiscate, steal, or destroy cotton, the Confederacy's main cash crop, had no such motivation. Their unauthorized traffic in the crop cost both the U.S. Treasury and Southern growers millions and enriched the agents. Proceeds from such dealings deposited in just one Alabama bank, Jay Cook and Company, amounted to more than $20,000,000.[3]

Another type of government agent who could easily enrich himself while carrying out his duty was the sutler, the man officially sanctioned by Washington to dispense food, clothes, drugs and medicine, tobacco, and sundries at army camps in the field. Charging whatever price they thought the market would bear, Civil War sutlers were universally hated by the soldiers, but all government attempts to control the sutlers' profiteering failed. The sutlers got their price and reaped small fortunes.[4]

Larger fortunes were made in New Orleans during the war by both Union officers and civilian manipulators. Trouble began when Major General Benjamin F. Butler, who had taken New Orleans for the North on May 1, 1862, decided to ban the use of all Confederate notes and replace them with gold, silver or U.S. Treasury paper. But since no one was empowered to issue notes worth less than one dollar, the people of New Orleans started using railroad tickets as currency. Immediately, counterfeiters flooded the city with bogus railroad tickets. By the time the company decided to refuse to redeem them, so many were in use, hence so many poor people dependent on them, that the military was forced to countermand the railroad and force it to redeem them at face value, subsidizing its losses until counterfeit-proof coins could be introduced.[5]

No sooner had that scandal passed than another exploded, this time in the federal courts set up by the Union military. Judges were found to be on the take almost at all levels of the judiciary. Next, the Louisiana Republican party, organized by both local Unionists and Northern radicals supported by the military, was exposed in its fraudulent electoral practices. And finally, the military Command was itself accused of massive corruption, so much so that General Ulysses S. Grant assigned his friend and fellow West Point graduate Colonel James Stokes to investigate.

Stokes found the whole quartermaster's department corrupt to the core. Confiscated rebel property had been sold to pay the department's officers and aides "commutation" or living expenses. Local railroad fares had been pocketed by the military overseers. Funds for black recruits had disappeared. Money collected in rent on seized housing had vanished. Stokes even found that a stable of horses belonging to William G. Minor, who had been loyal to the Union all along, had been seized and sold at ridiculously low prices to New Orleans Unionists by quartermaster officers who kept the money. Indeed, so much did Stokes uncover, so many officers did he implicate in his reports, that he gained powerful enemies who could plot his downfall. Accused of corruption himself, Stokes was transferred before his charges could be aired in court. Though Grant believed in him, and appointed tough-minded, ruthlessly honest Major General William F. ("Baldy") Smith to follow up his leads, the war ended before the investigation was completed, and Stokes was never vindicated. He was mustered out of the army in 1865, went blind ten years later, applied for and was refused a pension. He died in 1890, bitter and impoverished. Not one of the officers he accused of making illicit fortunes during the war was ever brought to trial.[6]

The biggest wartime fortunes, however, were made by the railroad men. These fortunes were technically legal, but in fact were built by one of the greatest swindles in American history. The use of railroads by the Union forces, who were often outfought by Southern soldiers, was greatly responsible for hiding from the general public the vast corruption involved in building them. Indeed, Union armies were often saved by swift reinforcements shipped in by rail. But the fact remains that the railroads were built on public money for the profit of private individuals. The main railroad, the Union Pacific, was chartered under the Pacific Railroad Act to run west from the 100th meridian, to be joined by four branches along the Missouri River. The governing body of the road was to be 158 commissioners from twenty-five states and territories and 5 representing the federal government. Given the land free of charge, the railroad was to open subscription books for the $100,000,000 in capital stock to be offered to the public.

But less than a year after gaining its charter, the railroad was set up as an independent company without government supervision by a group of large stockholders, and the government did not disapprove. Among the stockholders were August Belmont, the U.S. agent of the Rothschilds; Erastus Corning, president of the New York Central; Thomas A. Scott, one of the heads of the Pennsylvania Railroad; Leonard W. Jerome, millionaire stockbroker and grandfather of Winston Churchill; William E. Dodge, the copper tycoon; Samuel Sloan, president of the Hudson River Railroad; Thurlow Weed, boss of the New York Republican party. Behind the cabal was Thomas C. Durant, one of the largest Union Pacific stockholders, who became the railroad's vice-president and general manager. For president, they chose Major General John A. Dix, a partner of Russell Sage, who had worked for Lincoln in the 1860 campaign.

The conspirators were convinced that Lincoln would not oppose their takeover of the railroad; after all, "Honest Abe" had been the lawyer for the Illinois Central Railroad, and most of these wealthy stockholders had helped finance his campaign. What's more, Lincoln's secretary of the interior, John P. Usher, who as assistant secretary had arranged for Samuel J. Tilden to be one of the railroad's federal commissioners and had gotten Tilden, on the very next day, to deposit funds into his account at a brokerage house specializing in railroad securities, now appointed the government's directors on the Union Pacific board. When he resigned from the cabinet in 1865, Usher was appointed the railroad's general counsel.

The scheme worked. Union Pacific was given a federal subsidy of up to $48,000 per mile. A dummy corporation, eventually known as Crédit Mobilier of America, was set up by the railroad to cash in on the construction contracts, and to dispense bribes to influential politicians, without attracting attention to the Union Pacific itself. In 1864, the line's federal subsidy was doubled.

While the rich got very much richer during the Civil War, ordinary folks suffered more and more. In the South, inflation and vast food shortages brought many people to the edge of starvation. In the North, higher and higher taxes on almost every conceivable product hurt mostly the poor, and while prices rose, wages fell; in real income, a worker earned 35 percent less in 1865 than in 1861. Even the government cut wages; at the government-owned armory, a seamstress who had been paid 17 cents for making a shirt in 1861 got only 15 cents in 1864 when prices had quadrupled. By that time she was getting only 8 cents from private contractors. Both the North and the South printed so much paper money to cover war costs that the dollar, worth 99.86 cents in the North and 82.7 cents in the South in 1862, was down to 50.3 cents and 1.7 cents respectively by early 1865.

Nor did people want to fight anymore. Thus both governments resorted to forms of conscription, which both populations resented, especially since the draft system worked on quotas imposed on localities, allowing the rich of both North and South to buy substitutes. Draft riots broke out in Wisconsin, Kentucky, Pennsylvania, New Jersey, and New York that had often to be put down by federal troops. Both governments then realized that one solution was to enlist the blacks. The South, however, feared that arming the slaves might be counterproductive. Instead, the Confederate government paid slave owners $30 a month to use their slaves not as soldiers but as logistical support of the Confederate army. In the North, Lincoln, who, in 1861, had promised "to make no attack, direct or indirect, upon the institution or property of any State," meaning that he would not abolish slavery where it already existed legally, changed his tune in 1862 and on January 1, 1863, issued the Emancipation Proclamation. By war's end, 178,895 blacks had served in the Union Army.[7]

The recruitment of blacks did not come fast enough to stop the draftable whites from being drafted. They had been so opposed to emancipation anyway that many had turned against Lincoln in 1862 when he had threatened to proclaim it; indeed in that year's congressional elections New York, Pennsylvania, Ohio, Indiana, and Illinois, which had all gone Republican in 1860, went Democratic. Most Northern whites hated blacks as much as did Southerners, and the emancipation, which Lincoln proclaimed out of expediency, made them blame the blacks for the war even more than before. Thus antidraft demonstrations usually turned into antiblack riots. The worst such riot hit New York City in July 1863.

It began on July 13 when a mob of mostly Irish workers sacked the drafting office. Next they turned against the rich, plundering their homes and stores. Then they attacked the Colored Orphan Asylum on Fifth Avenue and Forty-third–Forty-fifth streets, stealing all of the possessions of the children, who had, fortunately, been evacuated through a rear exit. After smashing the furniture, they set the building on fire, beat up the firemen who arrived to extinguish it, then rampaged through the streets for three days, beating up and killing every black person they could find. Sometimes they paused to rejoice; at one point the mob danced and shouted in imitation of Indian war chants around the stripped body of an elderly black they had clubbed to death on Seventh Avenue and Twenty-third Street. They raided black boardinghouses on Sullivan Street, killed the occupants, burned the buildings. They robbed the store of a German who sold goods to blacks, then beat him to death. They chased young black children all the way to the East River and let them drown.

At the house of William Nichols, at 147 East Twenty-eighth Street, the mob tossed a three-day-old infant out of the upper window. They hanged shoemaker James Costello of 97 West Thirty-third Street, then burned his body. They beat to death Peter Heuston, a dark-skin Mohawk Indian who had fought with distinction in the Mexican war as a member of the New York Volunteers. They castrated Jeremiah Robinson, then tossed him into the East River where he drowned. They pistol-whipped Joseph Reed, seven years old, until he died. They pounded another young black, caught at the corner of LeRoy and Washington, with rocks until he too died. By the time Union troops from the Gettysburg campaign arrived and quelled the riot, some three thousand people had died and $3 million worth of property was ruined.[9]

But the draft continued. Since each district was given a quota, one solution that was immediately applied by the rich was to offer a bounty to anyone enlisting. This system encouraged many young men to enlist, collect their bounty, desert, and enlist again. Worse, it also created the bounty brokers, professionals who would "arrange" the enlistment process. Paid a fee by their districts, these brokers advertised that they could pay volunteers more than any other. Or they filled their quotas by kidnapping, drugging, or otherwise shanghaiing innocent young men into the army. Some towns, such as Waterford, New York, hired just one broker to fill their whole quotas. Others, like New York City, which offered $300 per recruit, used any broker who could deliver. Bribery, forgery, assault became common, and no one of draftable age was safe.

In Elmira, New York, in January 1865 a combat veteran on leave was drugged at the railroad station by a bounty broker. He was taken to Syracuse, sold as a substitute, and sent to his new regiment while still dazed. When he realized what had happened, the veteran tried to get back to his old regiment legally, was foiled, decided to go anyway, and there was shot and jailed for desertion. Also in Syracuse in February 1865 an officer was drugged, enlisted, and sent as a private to the 192nd Regiment.

Usually, however, force was quicker than drugs. In August 1863, one Rochester broker raided an immigrant ship, carried off a batch of "raw Irishmen" at gunpoint, and sold them each for $325. In the fall of 1863, Ferdinand Schaffer, a medical graduate of the University of Breslau, Germany, came to the United States to be a doctor. His German-speaking landlady took him to the Brooklyn recruiting office, explaining it was a hospital office, and convinced him to sign the enlistment papers on the grounds it was a work contract. Hauled off by soldiers to Riker's Island, Schaffer was stricken with an inflammation of the lungs, skin, and testicles and started having epileptic fits, but four weeks later, and sicker than ever, he was sent on a eight-day boat trip to South Carolina, assigned to the Forty-first New York Regiment and thrown into battle. Daniel Lawrence, a merchant seaman having a beer in a Hester Street saloon one night during the same period, was ordered to enlist by a gang of brokers; he refused, so they stabbed him seventeen times. The result of the bounty brokers efforts: New York State paid out $86,000,000 in bounty fees to fill its quota, and produced one of the worst Union fighting forces in the war.[9]

But if most New Yorkers tried to avoid the war they hated—except those who profited from it—other Americans reveled in it. Most of the people of Kansas, for example, were totally dedicated to it, and on the Union side. Northern in origin, Republican in politics, and abolitionist in sentiment, Kansas sent more young men into the Union army than any other state, proportional to population. The state legislature, remembering the outrages perpetrated by Missouri border ruffians in 1850, declared all "rebel sympathizers" outside the protection of the law.[10]

Such sympathizers were called Copperheads, and they were severely persecuted. In Jefferson County, they lost their jobs and often their property. At Junction City and Fort Scott, neutralist newspapers were sacked. In Atchison and Shawnee Mission, Southern Methodist churches were wrecked. In Leavenworth, the anti-South atmosphere allowed Daniel R. Anthony, a Republican publisher who shot and killed his rival, R.C. Saterlee, editor of the Democratic *Herald,* in June 1861, to be acquitted. The following year, on June 15, the *Daily Inquirer,* which criticized Lincoln, was suppressed and its editor arrested for "giving aid and comfort to the Confederacy." On February 7, 1863, a mob led by Anthony broke up a Democratic convention. Two days later, Anthony led more Jayhawkers into smashing the *Inquirer*'s offices and running its editor out of town.

The Jayhawkers were not just armed members of an anti-South, antislavery mob. They were irregular soldiers, guerrillas. Their stated purpose was to clean Kansas of all Southern sympathizers. Some were certainly just that, dedicated unionists. But most were plain outlaws, or they became such after spending months, then years, fighting Missouri ruffians, irregulars, and Confederate raiders. Marshall Cleveland is an example. Tall and dashing, he belonged to a group of abolitionists who raided Missouri ruffian towns, stole horses and wagons, freed slaves, and was eventually made a captain in the Seventh Kansas Cavalry. He deserted because of a quarrel with Anthony, who was then a lieutenant colonel in that regiment, organized his own band of Jayhawkers, and continued to raid Missouri towns, gaining notoriety especially after robbing two banks in Kansas City, Missouri. Declared an outlaw by Kansas authorities, Cleveland and his band then robbed banks on both sides of the border until Kansas troops finally gunned him down outside of Osawattomie.

One of the most famous of the Jayhawker leaders was General James Lane, an adventurer who had fought in the Mexican war, had organized Kansas's Free-Soil (later Republican) party, and had worked for Northern abolitionists before the war began. In September 1861, he led a group of Kansas irregulars into Missouri in pursuit of General Sterling Price and his men, who had raided the pro-Union city of Lexington. Setting the tactic that was later copied by William C. Quantrill, the Missouri horse thief and murderer turned guerrilla leader, Lane punished all those along the route he thought had helped Price. All homes were robbed, scores of people shot. At Osceola, for example, nine people were killed, and all but three buildings set afire. It was probably in retaliation for Lane's march through Missouri that Quantrill raided Lawrence on August 21, 1863, sacked the town and murdered almost two hundred citizens, one of the most vicious acts of the entire war.

Lane survived the war, becoming Kansas's first senator; he committed suicide in 1866. But few Jayhawkers did survive. By the end of 1863, with the population fed up, vigilante groups sprang up throughout the state. Many Jayhawkers were killed, sometimes in fierce battles supported tactically but illegally by the Union forces stations in Kansas. Others joined the army or headed west. Some went into hiding, constantly pursued by the vigilantes who never hesitated to carry out justice in the field. No one bothered about the innocent wanderers, impoverished cowboys, or lost Civil War soldiers who were hanged or shot in the process.[11]

The term Jayhawkers applied only to the Kansas irregulars. But similar groups existed in almost every border area. In Hunt County, Texas, one Martin Hart gathered a group of embittered plantation workers in 1861. He got them all legalized by the county's chief justice, J.G. Stevens, on the grounds they were going to attack unionists in northern Arkansas, then obtained commissions in the Union army in Springfield, Missouri, by claiming to be an anti-Confederate group. For the next eighteen months, Hart's volunteers raided Confederate supply trains and stragglers, killing and plundering indiscriminately. In January 1863, they attacked Charleston, Arkansas, where rich landowners had sided with the South, gunned down as many of them as they could find, shot and killed a money-lender, then executed a Confederate colonel. Hart's group was eventually surrounded and wiped out by a Confederate regiment, and Hart himself, convicted of murder, was hanged.[12]

In most cases, however, the war's irregulars were eventually controlled if not crushed by vigilante groups. Indeed, vigilantism flourished during the Civil War. Perhaps the most fanatical of such groups were in Montana, in and around the mining town of Virginia City. Organized in 1863, the Montana Committee of Vigilance was supported by the local judges who felt that it could cope with crime, as one said, "more cheaply, more quickly and better than it could be done by the courts." During just one year, 1863–64, the Montana vigilantes executed more than a hundred real and supposed outlaws, including the Plummer gang and the notorious Joseph ("Jack") Slade.

Henry Plummer had begun his outlaw career in Nevada City, California, in the late 1850s, robbing stages and killing the husband of the woman he was wooing. Charming and dashing in appearance, and with solid political contacts, he avoided one hanging by getting a pardon from the state's governor and another by escaping from jail. After rampaging through the goldfields of Washington Territory, Plummer and his gang moved on to Lewiston, Idaho, where, by offering personally to pay the salary of all lawmen, Plummer gained control of the town. By 1861, Lewiston had been plundered dry by the gang, and local residents had decided to create their own vigilante law enforcers. Plummer then headed to Bannock, Montana, where he got himself elected sheriff and organized the systematic pillage of the town until the vigilantes of nearby Virginia City hanged Plummer and the members of his gang.[13]

Jack Slade was not a gang leader. "So friendly and so gentlespoken that I warmed to him in spite of his awful history," as Mark Twain wrote of him in 1861, Slade had been a good soldier during the Mexican war and a loyal freighter and wagon-train boss in Colorado after the war. Shot five times at close range by a fellow employee whom he was investigating for corruption on his boss's orders, Slade was bedridden for a whole year before he completely recuperated. Then he went gunning for his assailant. He caught him, tied him up, drank himself into a stupor, and shot him in the legs and arms. Finally, saying "To hell with it," Slade placed the barrel of his pistol in the culprits mouth and blew out the back of his head. Legend had it that he then whipped out a knife and sliced off the dead man's ears, keeping one as a watch fob and selling the other to buy booze.

There was nothing violent about Slade when he was sober. When drunk, however, he became a vicious cutthroat. As he wandered the hills and towns from Colorado to Virginia City, Slade drank his way into brawls and inevitably shot his way out, leaving his antagonists and any hapless bystander dead behind him. In July 1864, the Montana vigilantes caught him sober. Slade begged for his life, sobbing desperately and pleading for mercy. But the tough miners of Montana would not be moved. Slade was hanged from a sturdy beam holding up the sign of the Virginia City saloon. Popular justice had triumphed once again.

And so did it a few months later for John Wilkes Booth and his confederates when, on April 14, 1865, he shot and killed President Lincoln. To many Southerners—indeed, perhaps to some highly placed Northerners, if the assassination was part of a Northern conspiracy, as some firmly believe—Booth's crime was in perfect keeping with the Jacksonian—and now American—definition of people's justice. From that view, Booth's murder of Lincoln as an act of retribution for the conquered South was no more illegal or immoral than Slade's lynching.

Americans had become so pragmatic that morality and expediency had become synonymous. In the decades to follow, expediency would turn America into the greatest power on earth—but only at the price of the institutionalization of racism, corrupt government, and mass murder.[15]

PART III

Crime in the Expanding Nation

Law! What do I care about Law!
Hain't I got the power?

—Cornelius Vanderbilt, 1865

I can hire one half the working class to kill the other half.

—Jay Gould, 1886

I owe the public nothing.

—J. P. Morgan, 1901

Chapter 14

White Terror and "Honest Graft"

The post–Civil War period was probably the most corrupt in American history. Civil servants, judges, congressmen, senators, even the White House, were involved in frauds, kickbacks, swindles, and conspiracies. So extensive was the corruption that, as one historian put it, "it is high time that we cease to think" of it as accidental, "as regrettable lapses into moral frailty, arising in an age of transition, of emotional release after war. We must turn rather to examine the systematic, rational, organized nature of the plundering which was carried on."[1]

The systematic, organized nature of crime in post–Civil War America was due in great part precisely to the pragmatic might-makes-right notion of justice fostered by its entrepreneurs, its elite, and its success-oriented heroes. It is the inescapable corollary of the Manifest Destiny, the logical consequence both of the Puritans' self-righteousness and of the individualistic, achievement-heralding destruction of the Puritans' belief in a collective. Such individual pragmatism was never an exclusive feature of Americans. It is what made most great nations great. But the other such nations were also reined in by at least one powerful countervailing force—tradition.

Populated by immigrants from all walks of life, with differing ethnic, social, religious and experiential backgrounds, America allowed no room for tradition. Because of its vastness, the richness of its resources, the lure of its opportunities, it could not help but become a living, thriving experiment in social Darwinism that crushed every tempering tradition on its rapid road to expansion, consolidation, and continental, eventually global, hegemony. In this process, the poor, the oustiders, whoever tried to maintain their inherited culture and tradition, such as the Indians, had to be crushed. The result was that few of the ambitious could avoid callousness and crime, and few of those doomed to be crushed could survive without resorting to crime.

This became especially clear after the Civil War. Most traditional historians have dubbed the Reconstruction Era vindictive. Even encyclopedias use precisely that term. They feel that the Republican majority that controlled the Congress for most of the next two decades basically wanted to punish the South for its rebellion. They point to all the laws enacted by Congress to change the South into the Union image. Indeed, the lawmakers did enact the Thirteenth and Fourteenth amendments giving blacks the vote and protecting them from discrimination at the polls. General W.T. Sherman did distribute parcels of up to forty acres from South Carolina's Sea Islands to blacks and gave them "possessory titles." But none of these laws or measures fundamentally changed the South. As a result, racism and exploitation became so institutionalized that literally thousands of black, red-skinned, Chinese, and Mexican Americans were murdered in the ensuing century, and millions were kept in slave-like economic conditions.[2]

The fact is that Reconstruction was surprisingly tolerant toward the South. Both Lincoln and his former slave-owning Democratic successor, Andrew Johnson, expected Southern whites to establish new governments loyal to the Union. Johnson appointed provisional governors under direction to convene state constitutional conventions that were expected to adopt the Thirteenth Amendment ending slavery, repeal the acts of secession, and repudiate their war debts. When the Southern states did just that, Johnson considered Reconstruction ended. No Confederate officer was prosecuted for war crimes except Major Henry Wirtz, the commandant of the infamous Andersonville prison camp, who was hanged, and Jefferson Davis, who was jailed for two years under indictment for treason but never brought to trial. No Southern property was confiscated after the war, no plantation was divided. As Harvard historian David Herbert Donald admits: "Southern society was transformed only to a quite limited degree."[3]

Nor was Northern society significantly altered. Veterans were not helped to find jobs, get housing, obtain an education. The free 3 million blacks were either totally ignored by the government in Washington or told to get back in line. Union commander General N.P. Banks, head of Louisiana Reconstruction, insisted that blacks go back to the plantation where "they belong." General Oliver O. Howard, a dedicated abolitionist made head of the Freedmen's Bureau in March 1865, was ordered by Johnson in October to remove the blacks to whom Sherman had given land on the Sea Islands. Johnson further pardoned every Southern white rebel and ordered his "restoration of all rights of property." Union commanders then tried to force blacks to accept work contracts, which, after they were promised separate cabins and integrity of the family unit, most did on the grounds they could get nothing better. The sharecropper system was launched, a form of exploitation not much better than slavery itself.[4]

When some radical Republicans, notably Senator Charles Sumner of Massachusetts and Representative Thaddeus Stevens of Pennsylvania, objected—the latter introducing a bill to confiscate and distribute to blacks all plantations of two hundred acres or more owned by Southern rebels—they were roundly chastised as un-American. The *New York Times* shrieked: "An attempt to justify the confiscation of Southern land under the pretense of doing justice to the freedmen strikes at the root of all property rights in both sections. It concerns Massachusetts quite as much as Mississippi."[5]

The Republican Congress did pass some laws that, it hoped, would help the freedmen. One was the Southern Homestead Act of June 1866 which was meant to distribute the 800,000 acres owned by the government. Had this act been carried out, only one out of every forty black families could have profited. But through fraud, forgeries, and intimidation, it was the whites who ended up getting the land. Congress, through the Military Reconstruction Act of 1867, which gave overseeing power to Union military commanders, did try to make sure that blacks were allowed to vote. Where they could, blacks did. But of all the states where Northern settlers (called carpetbaggers by Southerners), antislavery Southerners (called scalawags by racists), and blacks had together dominant electoral strength, only South Carolina gained a black majority in the legislature. In the whole South, no black was elected governor, two won seats as senators and fifteen were elected to the House.[6]

By refusing to break the South's white power structure, Congress and the various Republican administrations that governed America after Johnson did little after 1868 for the freedmen, and the North in general relinquished all hope of establishing justice for the blacks. The South quickly took advantage of this. Its legislatures passed laws prohibiting blacks from buying or carrying arms, from assembling after dark, from being idle. Mississippi prohibited blacks from owning land, South Carolina from practicing any "art, trade or business" except husbandry or "that of a servant." Before the Fourteenth Amendment was ratified, Maine, New Hampshire, Vermont, Massachusetts, and Rhode Island (and later Iowa) gave blacks full voting rights. New York refused to eliminate its property-holding qualification. The reason was simple enough: As President Johnson himself put it, as Harvard University social scientists carefully explained, and as even radical Republican Ohio Senator Benjamin F. Wade agreed, blacks were not considered equal but rather to "have shown an instant tendency to relapse into barbarism." The whole power structure, and most whites, looked upon "the freedmen, in the main," as Wisconsin radical Republican Senator Timothy O. Howe declared, "as so much animal life." Thus, even when the black codes were repealed, Southern whites prevented blacks from voting by enacting the poll tax, then by the secret ballot (which stopped illiterate blacks from asking for help), finally by literacy prerequisites. And the North followed suit.[7]

When freed blacks still tried to vote, which they did in increasing numbers from 1868 to 1880 (from 20 to 50 percent of eligible voters which, however, as late as 1900 ranged only from 61 percent in Florida to 39 in Louisiana), whites resorted to terror. In Memphis in 1866, whites sacked the black neighborhoods, raping women, burning ninety houses, four churches and twelve schools, and indiscriminately killing 44 black men, women, and children. In one incident at about the same time in Arkansas, 29 blacks were killed. In another in South Carolina, the toll was 24. Four months later, a mob of whites, aided by the police, attacked a black political rally held in the Mechanics' Institute in New Orleans. Firing wildly, the police and former Confederate soldiers refused to recognize the blacks' white flags. At one point, one of the black conventionists, a Reverend Dr. Horton, waving a white handkerchief, begged the police from a window, "I beseech you to stop firing: We are noncombatants. If you want to arrest us, make any arrest you please, we are not prepared to defend ourselves." The police reportedly answered: "We don't want any prisoners; you have all got to die." Horton, three white radical Republicans, and 34 other blacks did die. The military eventually stopped the massacre, arresting 261 blacks, but not a single policeman.[8]

After that, armed white bands roamed Louisiana, whipping, beating, and killing blacks almost at will. In the next decade more than thirty-five hundred blacks died in massacres at Bossier, Cadlo, St. Landry, and Grant parishes, according to Brigadier General Philip Sheridan, who was military governor of the area before 1868 and again in 1875. In 1873, white leagues, paramilitary units which eventually gained as many as twenty-five thousand members headed by the large property holders, began to harass the Republican state government until, in September 1874, they seized New Orleans's city hall and the telegraph office. Next day, the leagues attacked the Republican militia, defeated it in a bloody battle, and set up a new regime. President Grant, who had been tipped off, ordered federal troops under General Sheridan to put down the insurrection, but when a similar rebellion took place in 1876, Washington this time did not intervene. White terror had won.[9]

White terror spread throughout the South. Already by 1867, General Howard, head of the Freedmen's Bureau, reported that he had the impression that the South was engaged in a deliberate policy of extermination of blacks. In Vicksburg, Mississippi, in 1874, white mobs forced a black Republican sheriff to resign at gunpoint, killed nine of the protesting local blacks, then roamed the countryside killing some thirty blacks at random and put out a wire over the Associated Press line that they had put down an insurrection. In Laurens, South Carolina, in 1870, whites gunned down thirteen blacks. In Colfax, Louisiana, in 1873, white leaguers stopped black election victors from taking office by murdering almost two hundred blacks and three white Republicans. In Meridan, Mississippi, in 1871, some thirty blacks were lynched. In Yazoo, four years later, eighty blacks were killed.[10]

In Florida, the terror perpetrated by the upper-class members of the statewide Young Men's Democratic Clubs affected every county. In Columbia County, seven blacks were killed to prevent them from voting in 1868; Dr. John Dreminger, a physician who had fought with the Union army and was trying to help blacks, was murdered. In Alachua County at the same period, 19 blacks were lynched; five of the murderers were identified, arrested, tried by a white jury, and acquitted. In Suwannee County, a thirty-seven-year old freedman who had managed to buy seven acres and was successfully farming them with his wife and children, was beaten for hours. He was, likewise, forced to watch the whipping inflicted on his wife and four children, then ordered to go back to work for his former master for only food and clothing or face execution. In Madison County, between 1868 and 1871, 29 blacks were murdered. In Clay County, Samuel Tutson, a black farmer who had benefited from the Southern Homestead Act, was dragged out of his house by a bunch of whites, stripped, beaten until unconscious. After his young child was tossed to the floor, permanently injuring its hip, his wife was whipped with a leather belt, buckle affixed, for the whole night; the deputy sheriff tried to rape her while she was tied to a tree and inflicted a permanent genital injury. The assailants also destroyed Tutson's house, but at their trial, after Tutson identified them, they were all found not guilty, while Tutson and his wife were jailed for perjury. In Jackson County, 153 blacks were murdered. By 1871, few blacks dared to vote, and the Democrats had consolidated their power.[11]

By far, the worst terror in the post–Civil War South was perpetrated by the Ku Klux Klan. Organized in Pulaski, Tennessee, in May 1866, by former Confederate soldiers who promptly elected one of their celebrated generals, Nathan B. Forrest, as their leader or Grand Wizard, the KKK was a secret sect of fanatical white racists bent on purging first the South, then the whole continent, of all nonwhite elements. Their method was terror and murder of any individual or groups who disagreed, and they did not hesitate to kill even the highest of unionist officials, such as North Carolina Republican state senator John W. Stevens, who was investigating them. In Georgia, where Klansmen operated with almost total impunity in every single county, they assassinated the white Richmond County sheriff because he opposed terror, they murdered white Wilkinson County sheriff Mat Deason because he had had sexual relations with a black woman, and they lynched white state senator Joseph Adkins for testifying in Washington about conditions in Georgia.[12]

When they did not kill, the Klansmen were especially vicious in their physical torment of blacks, whipping and castrating the men and whipping and raping the women. In Warren County, Georgia, the Klan systematically destroyed the crops of black sharecroppers, burned every black school, and killed or tried to kill black would-be voters who did not agree to vote against Grant. One such man was Perry Jeffers, who, with his sons, worked on a plantation four miles from Warrenton, the county seat. But in this case, Jeffers fought back. When the KKK night riders raided his house on November 1, 1868, Jeffers and his sons opened fire, killing one Klansman and wounding three. Four nights later, a hundred hooded men returned. Jeffers and four of his five sons had hidden in the woods. The fifth, a cripple, was in bed, nursed by Jeffers's wife. The Klansmen dragged the crippled son out into the yard and shot him eleven times. They then piled all of the houses' belongings and furniture, put the dead body atop, and burned the lot, forcing the mother to watch, then clumsily hanged her from the nearest tree. She survived, with a twisted neck.

Accompanied by the local Freedmen's Bureau agent whom they sought out for protection, Jeffers and his remaining sons tried to get to Augusta by daytime train, with scores of witnesses around. That did not stop the Klansmen. Boarding the train, they forced the Jeffers off at Dearing, marched them into the woods and executed the father and three sons, the fourth having chosen well the moment to make a dash into a dense section of the forest. The bureau agent reported the whole incident to the federally appointed governor who appealed to General George G. Meade, commander of the district. Meade refused to send troops, and the Klansmen continued their terror, killing more blacks and an anti-Klan doctor, G.W. Darden, in March 1869. Shortly thereafter, troops were finally dispatched to the area but did little to control the Klan, even after a group of Klansmen shot up a military detail. Some arrests were made, but not one Klansman was convicted of a crime.[13]

That was fairly typical. Though the Klan struck everywhere throughout the South, killing thousands of blacks and hundreds of white Republicans, federal forces did almost nothing to prevent the terror. President Grant did get Congress to pass a series of enforcement acts (1870–71) under which he proclaimed martial law in nine South Carolina counties where the Klan was especially ferocious, and he did order federal marshals to arrest various Klansmen throughout the South. But nowhere was the white racist economic superstructure crushed, a restraint applauded by most Northern as well as Southern historians, who claim to find in the North's tolerance a proof of pluralistic America's maturity. As a consequence, by 1877, the old Southerners, who called themselves redeemers, had seized total political as well as economic control of the South. For almost the whole of the next century, these redeemers, their descendants, and even the antimonopoly progressives and populists, who defeated the old Bourbon elite at the turn of the century, continued to violate the economic, social, political, and human rights of their black constituents, allowing or actually fomenting thousands of lynchings (twenty-five hundred reported deaths from 1884 to 1900 alone), and got away with hardly a protest from the Northern ruling elite until the 1955 boycott of segregated buses in Montgomery, Alabama.[14]

That too was no accident: the captains of American industry were so concerned about keeping government out of their affairs that they would permit murder, rape, arson, and torture to go unpunished rather than risk the precedent of federal interference. So avidly and staunchly did they defend the doctrine of laissez-faire that they consciously blinded themselves to all national outrages. Though they were perfectly willing to have the government protect their industries through tariffs and enrich them through land grants to railroads, they feared and hated the possibility of government inspection, regulation, and control of their financial activities. Once the government got into the habit of guaranteeing human life, they reasoned, it might decide to guarantee human livelihood, and that represented the greatest of all possible sins, for it attacked the principle of private property. As historian David Herbert Donald put it, "No violation of economic laws was deemed more heinous than interference with the right of private property—the right of an individual or group to purchase, own, use, and dispose of property without any interference from governmental authorities."

No one valued private property more than the industrial magnates who were stealing it.[15]

The biggest thieves were the railroad men, the steel, coal, and oil tycoons, and the bankers who financed the lot. Among the worst was Cornelius ("Commodore") Vanderbilt, a Hudson River steamboat captain who blackmailed the government-subsidized Pacific Mail Steamship Company into giving him $56,000 not to compete. During the Civil War, Vanderbilt, an opinionated, arrogant, secretive, superstitious egomaniac who kept a retinue of female mediums, spiritualists, and clairvoyants in his stark Washington Square mansion, sold rotten and ill-equipped ships to the Union at exorbitant prices. Never prosecuted, though denounced by Iowa senator James Grimes as "the most censurable" of the war profiteers, Vanderbilt retorted: "Law! What do I care about law? Hain't I got the power?" Turning his profits into railroad stocks, he gained control of the Hudson River Railroad. He forced the New York Central to sell out to him by refusing to allow a connection in Albany, requiring passengers to slosh through two miles of mud or snow. Then he watered down the combined stocks to net himself a $26 million profit. He went on to control the Lake Shore and Michigan Southern, Michigan Central, and Canada Southern railways, thus owning the connection between New York and Chicago, and compelled shippers to pay him such inflated rates and kickbacks that they would have to sell out to him, whereupon he lowered his rates and resold the firms at huge profits.[16]

Another of the great robber barons was Jay Gould, who bought and sold railroads as easily as he bought and sold state and government officials. Born in New York's dairy, Delaware County, Gould was educated in a local seminary where he wrote his senior essay on the theme "Honesty Is the Best Policy" and self-trained as a land surveyor. Small, frail-looking, and soft-spoken, he started his career setting up a leather goods firm with two partners whom he promptly swindled. Gould then printed and sold counterfeit shares in the Erie Railroad, skipped to New York with his partner James Fisk with $6 million in cash and the line's financial records. Having bought the support of New York political boss and Tammany Hall chief William Marcy Tweed, and through him New York legislators, Gould and Fisk defeated Vanderbilt's attempt to take over the Erie, then cornered the gold market, which caused the panic of Black Friday in 1869. A swashbuckling financier and stockbroker who made his first fortune during the Civil War by selling Confederate stocks in England and capturing Southern cotton for Northern dealers, Fisk was shot and killed in 1872 by a rival for the attention of Josie Mansfield, a famed New York actress. Gould went on to buy and sell railroads by manipulating stocks, waging rate wars, falsifying profit records, merging solvent with bankrupt lines, and intimidating rivals, sometimes by using gangs, such as Tommy Lynch and his Hell's Kitchen Mob which beat up Vanderbilt's allies on the Erie. When he died in 1892, Gould left a personal fortune of over $100 million.[17]

Gould lost only a few battles. One was to John Pierpont Morgan, who took his Albany and Susquehanna Railroad. Stern and impervious to public criticism, Morgan, the son of a British financier, was the most successful crook of his generation. During the Civil War he bought defective rifles from the government for $17.50 each, and sold them back to the Union at $110.00. After the war, Morgan began packaging loans and stock sales to finance railroads. In 1873, he used his contacts in Congress to stop the government's loan privileges offered to Jay Cooke, an ambitious financier who had reaped a huge profit during the Civil War by raising Union bonds and had now overextended himself to the tune of $100 million to develop the Northern Pacific Railroad. Without government backing, Jay Cooke defaulted, creating a panic that became the general depression of 1873–77. Morgan then used his power to generate a series of mergers of small railroads and, with the weight of his First National Bank of New York, to weld industries, mills, railroads, and other financial institutions into huge trusts. He drove independents out of business by price wars, dumping, and, mostly, by controlling transportation which stopped competitors from reaching markets. Morgan's greatest achievement was the $1.4 billion United States Steel Trust (1901), which combined some two hundred manufacturing and transportation firms, a thousand miles of railroad, 112 blast furnaces, employed 170,000 workers and controlled 60 percent of America's steel capacities. By 1912, together with the Rockefeller National City Bank, the House of Morgan controlled 112 corporations worth $22 billion.[18]

John D. Rockefeller, the secretive, conspiratorial clerk who started his first refinery in 1862 on the $4,000 he had embezzled in a produce business on the Cleveland docks, launched the first modern trust in 1882, the Standard Oil Company. Investing and reinvesting as fast as he could, Rockefeller gained so much of the oil market so quickly that he could force the railroads to accept his terms, directing them not to transport his competitors' product until they sold out to him. In the Pennsylvania town of Titusville in 1875, for example, Rockefeller agents told the owners of the twenty-seven refineries then functioning that Standard wanted to buy them out at low take-it-or-leave-it fixed prices. When the twenty-seven refused, Standard arranged for all transportation to the town to stop. By 1879, twenty-five of the twenty-seven had sold out at the price offered. The same tactic was used in Pittsburgh between 1874 and 1879. There, some of the refiners tried to use barges to move their oil, but the railroads refused to take the oil from the barges at their destination. Other refiners tried to build a pipeline, but there was no way to avoid crossing land owned by the Pennsylvania Railroad, which refused right-of-way. By 1904, Rockefeller's Standard Oil supplied 84 percent of America's oil. Its net profits exceeded $60 million per year. It held controlling interests in the copper, smelters, and tobacco trusts. Rockefeller also controlled various banks besides National City, Equitable and Mutual insurance companies, and was closely allied to the Morgan, Harriman, and Gould groups. Meanwhile, the poor of New York had to pay forty cents for a gallon of kerosene, when its delivered cost was less than dime.[19]

The trusts, bankers, and financiers may have helped America; they certainly did not help Americans, or at least not most of them. In the 1880s the average American worked 14 to 18 hours a day for subsistence pay. In New York City, bakers put in at least 84-hour weeks and 120 hours was not uncommon. And while the trusts consolidated their power, 5,183 businesses worth over $200 million failed. Almost 2 million people lost their jobs. In 1874, the Freedman's Savings Bank, run by white New York bankers, went bankrupt; 61,144 depositors lost their meager savings. William H. Cushman, who developed mines and utilities in Georgetown, Colorado, embezzled from the bank he set up from 1867 until it folded in 1877. Caught in 1880, indicted in 1881, the case was dropped in 1883, but his depositors were not refunded. Everywhere, the poor suffered. Their wages were cut 25 percent in 1877, but the prices of necessities skyrocketed. Between 1873 and 1886, coal mining corporations, transporters, and dealers, their operating costs lower each year as improved machinery and more efficient rail service (from 30,000 miles in 1861 to more than 200,000 in 1911) became standard, increased the price of coal to consumers by 100 percent while their profits, said Congress in 1893, were $200 million above a fair-market net. In New York City, 700,000 blacks, packed into slum tenements without toilets or electricity, stopped buying coal for heat altogether, burning instead whatever scraps of wood they could find. So did Jewish immigrants, whose young women, sewing on piecework in the garment industry, averaged eight cents an hour. Even skilled Slavic steel workers in Pittsburgh in 1910 had to put in a harsh 60-hour week to earn only $12.50, when an average two-room apartment cost $10.00 in rent weekly.[20]

While workers starved or died on the job (in 1900, 2,550 railroad workers were killed and 39,643 were so badly injured they could not resume their duties; they were not covered by insurance), the rich of the Gilded Age, as it was called, enjoyed their wealth as never before. Diamonds were set into teeth. Black pearls were placed into the oysters of dinner guests. At one function, after-dinner cigars were wrapped in $100 bills. At another, young women swimming in the host's pond were offered as gold fish, to be kept by whatever guest caught them. The collars on dogs were made of gold or diamonds, worth as much as $15,000. One plutocrat kept a private carriage and personal valet for a pet monkey who was driven about town every afternoon. Jay Cooke spent $1 million for his summer home. An opera buff spent $75,000 for a pair of opera glasses.[21]

Little of this would have been possible without corrupt governments, both state and federal. True, most politicians of the time did not view themselves as such. They simply saw their mission as that of stimulating America's great expansion and, convinced that only private business could accomplish it, they thought it normal to benefit from their efforts to help big business. "Politics is as much a regular business as the grocery or dry goods or the drug business," explained Tammany Hall's Democratic boss George Washington Plunkitt. Republican William Seward, the New York governor and senator who stayed on as secretary of state after Lincoln's assassination, agreed. The political party, he said, was "a joint stock association, in which those who contribute most direct the action and management of the concern." As a consequence of this attitude, congressmen gave huge land grants, subsidies, and loans to railroad promoters—and bought their stocks at preferred prices or accepted gifts outright. They passed a National Banking Act (1863) which killed local banks, allowed the major financiers to promote railroads and big industries, and in return got handouts from Jay Cooke, Morgan, and the rest. They saddled foreign goods with huge tariffs to protect U.S. manufacturers and keep prices high, and got paid off by the manufacturers. In 1876 they repealed all restrictions on the sale of public federal land in the South, ordering it sold to private interests as soon as possible—and got huge shares of it as the silent partners of the timber speculators who bought it. It was all what Plunkitt openly called "honest graft."[22]

Obviously, the reverse was inevitable: the railroad promoters, financiers, and big manufacturers exerted powerful influence on Congress. During the impeachment of Andrew Johnson, Jay Cooke and other prominent bankers, worried that the president would be replaced by House Speaker Benjamin Wade, the radical Republican from Ohio who wanted to distribute lands to blacks and give the vote to women, distributed thousands of dollars to block impeachment, and convinced enough Republican senators to save Johnson by one vote. These elected officials, known later as the railway congressmen, gave away, from

1865 to 1869, more than 32 million acres to railroads owned by Gould, Collis, Huntington, and other barons, and by Oakes Ames. A wealthy Massachusetts plow manufacturer, co-owner of the Union Pacific, Ames was a Republican member of the House from 1862 to 1873 and had direct influence on the committee granting his line a federal charter. In Congress generally, as Navy Secretary Gideon Welles put it, there was "little statesmanship in the body, but a vast amount of party depravity. The granting of acts of incorporation, bounties, special privileges, favors, and profligate legislation of every description is shocking."[23]

Until the era of Watergate, no government was as corrupt as that under the two administrations of Ulysses Grant. The president himself received a fully furnished mansion in Philadelphia, a $100,000 gift to pay off his Washington home mortgage, and a $75,000 library, though he rarely read a book—all paid for by businessmen, stockbrokers, bankers, and "fifty solid men of Boston." The Republican National Committee was for sale. Governor Edwin Morgan of New York, Republican Elihu Washburne of Illinois and cabinetman William Chandler of New Hampshire, who was committee secretary, ordered such Wall Street potentates as William B. Astor, Hamilton Fish, A.T. Stewart, William E. Dodge, and such railroaders as Vanderbilt and Huntington to hand over $5,000 to $10,000 each if they expected "a good contract." Chandler then distributed $3,000 to $3,5000 a month to newspaper reporters to guarantee them all a good press.[24]

The list of corrupt officials seemed interminable. Treasury Secretary George S. Boutwell of Massachusetts was hooked to financier Jay Cooke. Merchant Zachariah Chandler, who had been mayor of Detroit and senator from Michigan before becoming secretary of the interior, sold every state and federal office under his jurisdiction, as did Illinois senator John Alexander ("Black Jack") Logan, who was nominated for the vice-presidency in 1884. In New York, the whole Republican machine controlled by Senator Roscoe Conkling was on the take. Through his lieutenants and New York port commissioners Cornell, who later became governor, and Chester Arthur, who later moved up to the presidency when Garfield was assassinated, Conkling stole hundreds of thousands of dollars in tax revenue, "moieties," and counsel "fees" due the government. In Pennsylvania, Republican czar Simon Cameron did the same through control of the post offices.[25]

Back at the White House, General John Rawlins, Grant's secretary of war, got $28,000 from Cuban rebels to push the United States to annex the island. Rawlins's successor, General William W. Belknap, took bribes from Indian agents and sold appointments to lucrative army posts. Abel Corbin, Grant's brother-in-law, who often lived with the Grant family; Colonel Orville Babcock, Grant's personal secretary; and General Daniel Butterfield, the assistant treasurer recommended by Babcock, were all part of Gould's Erie Ring and profited by his Black Friday cornering of the gold market. Babcock, Zachariah Chandler, Columbus Delano, whom Grant had just made interior secretary, and General Benjamin Butler, who was then a Massachusetts representative, teamed up with the Cooke banking firm to take over the District of Columbia Board of Public Works and swindled the capital of some $17 million. Even James Garfield, then a congressman, was caught in the district ring for a mere $5,000 fee. "The connection is complete," Jay Cooke's agent wired him in jubilation. "I can hardly realize that we have General Garfield with us. It is a rare success and very gratifying, as all the appropriations for the District must come through him." No wonder that in 1872 Jay Cooke insisted that the reelection of Grant and the stalwart Republicans, all Grant faithfuls, for which he donated tens of thousands of dollars, was "a matter of life and death."[26]

Few were the government or elected officials who were punished for such wrongdoings. Indeed, it was usually the rare honest one who was penalized, such as Interior Secretary Jacob Cox, who tried to put an end to the corrupt practices of the Indian Service and corrupt land claims and railroad grants. The Republican chieftains, especially Butler and Zach Chandler, were furious, and Grant fixed Cox. The Crédit Mobilier scandal did, however, shake a few crooked politicians. Set up as the construction company of the Union Pacific, the Crédit Mobilier charged the railway exorbitant prices. The scheme was meant to keep Union Pacific, whose stocks were sold on the open market, from enriching anyone, while Crédit Mobilier, a closed corporation owned by Union Pacific's top directors, would reap all the profits. And it certainly did—100 percent dividend on its very first year. To avoid problems with Congress, Crédit Mobilier distributed a few hundred shares to leading congressmen. When the scandal finally broke in 1873 (because one top stockholder, Henry S. McComb, who had made his fortune through fraudulent Civil War contracts, blew the whistle when he was refused 650 "juice" stocks to distribute to his friends), almost all the railway congressmen were implicated. They had all bought Crédit Mobilier stocks cheap or received them free. Among them were three vice-presidents—Grant's first running mate, Schuyler Colfax; current vice-president, Henry Wilson; and Levi Morton, who would get elected with Benjamin Harrison. Among the senators in the scheme were "Black Jack" Logan, James Patterson of New Hampshire, and Iowa's William Allison, and among the representatives were Speaker of the House James Blaine, whose thereby tarnished reputation led to his defeat for the presidency in 1884; Henry Dawes; Garfield; James Brooks of New York; and, naturally, Oakes Ames. Together with the Crédit Mobilier's board, these men had pocketed $44 million, yet only two were censured—Brooks and Ames.[27]

The greatest scandal of the Grant administration was the Whisky Ring affair, which hit the public in 1875. Put into operation in 1870 by General John A. McDonald, with the alliance of Grant's personal secretary, Orville Babcock, and the chief clerk of the Internal Revenue Department in Washington, William Avery, the ring comprised all the major distillers in Milwaukee, Chicago, Peoria, Indianapolis, and St. Louis. McDonald "organized" his distillers and agent-officers into military "units," and purchased the *St. Louis Globe* through which he laundered much of the take. He ran such an efficient racket, overprinting whisky tax stamps, and collecting company kickbacks, that he netted $4 million in only four years. Of this, 40 percent went to high government officials, from Babcock and Avery to Senator Logan, who directed the ring in Illinois, and other Grant stalwarts in Wisconsin, Missouri, and Indiana, where Senator Oliver Morton reigned supreme. In 1874, Treasury Secretary Benjamin Bristow, sensing that his whole department might be in cahoots with the ring, hired special investigators from outside the government and broke the ring. "Let no guilty man escape," boomed President Grant. But when he found out that the investigation was leading directly to the White House, he started to undercut his secretary. And when it became clear that Grant's brother Orville and Interior Secretary Zach Chandler, who had lost his Senate seat, and even Grant himself might be exposed, he ordered his attorney general to stop. But it was too late. McDonald, Avery, and their lieutenants were tried, convicted, and sent to prison. Nor could Colonel Babcock avoid trial. But Grant rescinded every offer of immunity made by Bristow, refused to allow White House documents to be introduced in court and, as the coup de grace to Bristow's case, sent a deposition, sworn to before the chief justice, in Babcock's favor.

Babcock was acquitted in February 1876, and Bristow was forced to resign shortly thereafter. Many Republicans then tried to get Bristow nominated for the presidency, but Grant stopped that too, choosing instead the conservative Ohio governor Rutherford Hayes, "a third-rate nonentity," as Henry Adams wrote.[28]

Governor Hayes was not crooked. But his party had become, as Senator James Grimes, Ohio's scrupulously honest radical Republican, put it, "the most corrupt and debauched political party that has ever existed." Hayes's Democratic opponent was also considered honest, but he certainly was not. New York governor Samuel Tilden was really an old thief from way back, the railroad lawyer who had amassed a fortune from stock manipulation, the adviser of Gould and Fisk, the Tammany Hall politician once known as the Great Forecloser who had then turned against his old crooked pals. It was thus inevitable that the 1876 Hayes-Tilden campaign would be corrupt.[29]

It was probably the most corrupt in American history. Black voters were intimidated throughout the South. Ballots were falsified in Oregon, South Carolina, Florida, Louisiana, and Georgia by the boxfuls. In Florida, the Central Railroad gave its employees numbered Democratic ballots and, keeping a checklist with recipients' names, warned that the ballots better show up or the workers would be fired. Trains carrying ballot boxes were raided and the boxes stolen; in Florida, the Democrats actually wrecked one such train on its way to Tallahassee. In Washington, Senator Stephen Dorsey, a Republican carpetbagger from Arkansas, and Thomas Brady, the second assistant postmaster general, set up a Post Office Ring to steal vast sums to finance Hayes's campaign, bribe key political bosses, and buy votes. In New York, Chester Arthur, the customs house collector, did the same. When the voting ended on November 7, it seemed that Tilden, with 184 electoral votes, had defeated Hayes. The next day, counting South Carolina, which had been occupied by thirty-three army companies on Grant's orders, and Louisiana as Republican victories, Hayes's total would be up to 181. If Florida could remain Republican, Hayes would have 185, the victor by one. Out went the Republican orders to those three states' commanders: "Can you hold your state? Answer immediately!"

In South Carolina and Florida, where the army was under General Sherman, where the funds were controlled by Postmaster Brady, and where Department of Justice "investigators" answered to stalwart

Republican committee secretary and paymaster William E. Chandler, "holding" was easy. Enough votes were invalidated to swing those states out of the Tilden count and into Hayes's. But in Louisiana, the task was harder; at least 9,000 votes had to swing. Undaunted, the Republican overseers, backed by federal troops, took the word of every thief and prostitute the marshals could round up, and to the Democrats' wild protests, discounted 13,350 Democratic votes to give Hayes a 4,000-vote plurality. Republican negotiators offered Louisiana and Florida back to Tilden for $200,000 each, about "standard," said Tilden, but the Democrats bargained too long. Eventually an electoral commission in Washington voted eight (all Republicans) to seven (all Democrats) to give Hayes the election. In exchange, the Republicans promised to end Reconstruction by withdrawing all federal troops from the South, which they did. Thus a man who had originally lost the election became president of the United States, a fitting symbol of the corruption of the Gilded Age.[30]

Chapter 15

Law vs. Justice

If the gloss and glitter of the gilded age were to be maintained, the captains of industry knew that they had to keep their profit margins high—higher, indeed, than they had ever been before. That could only be accomplished if wages were kept low—dirt low—and one way to keep them low was to keep workers in constant competition for the jobs available. Thus an obliging Congress passed legislation in 1864 allowing industries to import foreign workers who would be legally tied to their jobs on meager salaries until they had totally paid off their fares. It was also the economic rationale for the South's terror against blacks: as long as the freedmen were too intimidated to demand better working conditions, white laborers, afraid of being replaced by blacks, would also hesitate to try to better their lot. Another system used by companies, the states and the federal government to keep workingmen powerless was prisoner leasing. Operating throughout the United States, but mostly in the South, the prisoner-leasing system provided mine owners, canal builders, and railroad companies with almost free labor. In North Carolina, for example, black prisoners laid almost all of the 3,582 miles of railroad track put down between 1876 and 1894. Since contractors did pay a fee, no matter how minimal, to the authorities, many prisons actually became prosperous.[1]

So lucrative did the prisoner-leasing system become in some areas that judges were pressured to hand out stiffer and stiffer sentences so that prison wardens could supply the laborers on at least six-month or year-long contracts. In Houston, Texas, in 1874, the hapless thief of no more than twenty-five cents faced a year as a convict laborer on the railroads or clearing forests. Constantly watched, working eighteen hours a day, the convicts were kept in "dens unfit for the habitation of wild beasts," as the governor himself admitted. Many died on the job. They were reported as "killed while trying to escape." In Minnesota, convict labor made many small enterprises wealthy. The practice began there in 1854 when John B. Stevens of Stillwater contracted prisoners to manufacture shingles and blinds, paying the prison $100 a year and an additional seventy-five cents per day for convicts who could be leased for a year. By 1880 the system was widespread. Seymour, Sabin and Company netted $135,000 from convicts building tubs, barrels and buckets in 1871, and $300,000 ten years later.[2]

Often the convicts were used as strikebreakers. In Briceville, Tennessee, in 1891, prisoners were sent to the Tennessee Coal Company to work the mines when they were shut down by the owners. The miners reacted by physically trying to stop the convicts, causing the legislature to empower the governor to use the state militia to suppress the miners' "insurrection." The miners stormed the stockade where the convicts were held, freed 163 of them, and burned down the stockade. That evening, striking miners at the Knoxville Iron Mine did the same, freeing 120 convicts and setting two guardhouses and the stockade office aflame. Two days later, striking miners on horseback stormed the nearby Cumberland Mine and freed 200 prisoners. Neither the convicts nor the attacking miners were apprehended, but within a month more convicts were shipped in from Nashville and the three-mine area was surrounded by the state militia. Miners and soliders fought pitched battles all summer long, in 1892, until two of the mines began rehiring the strikers, refusing to use convicts.

In August, however, the Grundy pit bosses of the Tennessee Coal and Iron Railroad Company, having cut the miners to half time, put 360 convicts to work full time. The miners overpowered the guards, seized the stockade and burned it down, freeing its prisoners. The miners then stormed the mines in the area until they were stopped by militia bullets at the Oliver Springs stockade in Anderson County. That brought out miners from the whole region. They charged the local garrison, captured its guns, and attacked Fort Anderson. The state was nearing rebellion when the main force of the militia arrived, dispersed and pursued the miners, arresting hundreds. Some 300 were sent to jail for conspiracy to murder, but most were quickly released once the prisoner-leasing system was reinstated and all the stockades rebuilt. The governor then signed a penitentiary bill in April 1893 that legally ended the lease system, though it actually continued until the new prison, accommodating 1,500, was finished in 1896.[3]

Such victories for miners were extremely rare, and in most confrontations the cost in workingmen's lives was very high. One of the biggest battles raged for years in Schuylkill County, Pennsylvania. Before the sixties, strife in the anthracite mines was relatively mild and centered mostly on those owners who paid the miners in chits redeemable only in the company-owned stores, which charged exorbitant prices. By 1871, however, the Reading Railroad had moved in and made working conditions intolerable. The Reading takeover was the work of its president, Franklin Benjamin Gowen, a second-generation Irish-American with thin lips, even features, and a flair for florid phrases. Educated at the elite John Beck's Academy, trained as a lawyer in a Pottsville firm specializing in coal mining, and as Schuylkill's Democratic district attorney, Gowen joined the Reading's legal department and at thirty beat the Pennsylvania Railroad in a major court jurisdictional dispute. Made Reading's president at thirty-three, he immediately set out to corner the coalfields in Schuylkill. Between 1870 and 1874 he purchased 100,000 acres through a front company and on credit. To recoup fast, he cut the wages of anthracite workers in January 1871 by one-third, and forced the independent mineowners to do the same or pay four dollars a ton on his freight line instead of the standard two dollars. The miners struck and appealed to the courts, but Gowen won the day by claiming that strikers had beaten the families of strikebreakers. He then got the other owners and railroads to consolidate and regulate all operations, thus forcing the miners to face a solid front.[4]

There was little the miners could do. The tens of thousands who lived and labored in Schuylkill and neighboring counties were totally hooked to the mining companies. They owned the stores, the land, the streets, even most of the tiny makeshift houses. Troublemakers were not only fired from their jobs but also immediately evicted from their houses by the company police. The work was long, arduous, and extremely dangerous; hundreds were killed and injured in Schuylkill every year. Children ages seven to sixteen earned less than three dollars a week for separating the coal, and adults were paid according to the cubic yard or ton they mined, giving the company endless opportunity to cheat them. The miners' union, the Workingmen's Benevolent Association, was helpless to challenge these conditions, short of striking, and the miners were too poor and too indebted to the company stores to risk many strikes. Thus the only justice possible was left to those who would secretly carry out revenge on the companies' foremen, police chiefs, or superintendants—the Molly Maguires.[5]

An offshoot of Ireland's secret Ancient Order of Hibernians, which traditionally had always defended the rights of common folk, the Molly Maguires first appeared, in legend at least, in Schuylkill in 1857, supposedly to avenge any Irish person unfairly treated. Indeed, whenever a mysterious murder took place, people blamed it on "the Mollies." As a consequence of Ireland's great famine of 1846–54, some 1,200,000 Irish had come to America, and the Irish constituted the largest ethnic group among the miners. Reading president Gowen claimed the Mollies were "guilty of a majority of all the murders and other deeds of outrage which, for many years, have been committed in the neighborhood." He wanted them wiped out, especially during the depression of 1873, when he increased the price of coal and cut the miners wages once again, thereby stimulating many acts of sabotage and night raids on his armed goons by "persons unknown." Thus, Gowen decided to hire the best detective available—Allan Pinkerton—to ferret out the Mollies and destroy them.[6]

Born in Scotland in 1819, Pinkerton at first had no intention of following in the footsteps of his father, a policeman. When he came to America in 1842 he worked as a cooper in Dundee, Illinois. By chance one day he caught a group of counterfeiters and became a deputy sheriff in Kane, then Cook, counties. In 1850, he opened his private detective agency, admitting that "the detective has to act his part, and in order to do so, he has, at times, to depart from the strict line of truth, and to resort to deception, so as to carry his assumed character through." Specializing in services for industrialists, Pinkerton quickly developed a stable of disciplined, efficient strikebreakers, plant and warehouse guards, and bounty hunters. Freely resorting to deception, he became an expert at framing labor agitators. His price for Gowen to wipe out the Mollies: $100,000.[7]

By then, work conditions in Schuylkill had deteriorated so much that the miners were ready to strike despite total lack of savings or provisions. Their wages constantly cut (from $18.20 a week in 1869 to $9.20 in 1877), totally indebted to the companies, which, after deducting the price of tools, food, and rent, usually handed out "bobtailed checks" (meaning statements showing a negative tally), the miners began to agitate for a statewide walkout. The strike began against Gowen's Philadelphia and Reading Railroad and its subsidiary, the Philadelphia and Reading Coal and Iron Company. But Gowen was ready. He had twenty-six miners arrested for conspiracy and jailed for one year. He cut wages again for those who continued to work, and forced the rest of the mines to do the same. And he had the courts declare the miners' union illegal. In a later report to stockholders, he admitted he spent $4 million to break the strike. The miners fought back as best they could, sabotaging production lines, setting fires to shafts, stores, telegraph offices, and derailing trains. Gowen used these incidents to get the state militia to intervene and patrol the area. Under cover of the militia, goons broke up union meetings with gunshots, and mine agents—Pinkerton's or Gowen's—murdered three union leaders. The miners, boasted Gowen, "left a long trail of blood behind them."[8]

It was at this point that James McParlan arrived in Schuylkill. Born in Ireland in 1844, McParlan had worked in a linen factory before coming to New York in 1867. After a stint in a grocery store, he went to Chicago, got a job as a "preventative policeman," as private detectives were called, then joined Pinkerton's agency. Under the name of James McKenna, he headed for the Schuylkill coalfields in October 1873. Charming and funny, shrewd and tough, with "eyes that were as cold as a cobra's," McParlan was paid twelve dollars a week, plus expenses, to work in the pits, pose as a counterfeiter and murderer "on the lam," infiltrate and spy on the Mollies. Inventing either the whole Molly Maguire story on orders of Gowen, as some historians claim, or just the part needed to convict them in court, McParlan eventually named 347 Mollies. Their trials lasted two years. The press condemned them in gory stories. The jury included members of anti-Irish and antilabor vigilante committees. The judge, grossly partial to the prosecution, allowed prominers to be threatened, told the jury that the Ancient Order of Hibernians was well known for its murderers, and allowed Gowen to make a summation speech, in addition to the three made by the prosecution. The outcome was that 20 miners were hanged and scores of others served a total of 124 years.[9]

The death and imprisonment of so many miners broke the union's drive for better working conditions. Gowen cut wages again in 1877, and this time the miners did not even protest. But such callousness did not save Gowen. Overextended and unable to raise enough funds to cover its debts, constantly plagued by strikes by the harassed railroad workers, the Reading went into receivership in 1880 and Gowen lost the presidency in 1881. By 1886 it was again solvent, and Gowen tried to regain his post. He failed. In 1889, he shot himself.[10]

Meanwhile strikes on the railroads had spread from coast to coast. Resistance had begun in a small town in West Virginia called Martinsburg in 1877 when the Baltimore and Ohio announced a 10 percent wage cut, the second in eight months, reducing the weekly pay package to five or six dollars. The workers stopped the line immediately, demanding not only that the cut be rescinded but also that they be given better hours and free passes from their destination back to their homes. The owners reacted by asking for help from the militia, but the troops fraternized with the workers, and farmers, fed up with falling prices but higher freight charges, offered the troops free food. The governor then appealed to President Hayes, who dispatched three hundred federal troops, the first time that such troops were used to crush labor violently in peacetime. In 1834, President Andrew Jackson had sent federal troops to suppress a strike on the Chesapeake and Ohio Canal, but fighting did not ensue. From 1877 to 1898, the army was used to put down more than three hundred strikes. This led to a redefinition of the role of the U.S. Army as, in the words of Major General George B. McClellan, a force for "quelling rebellion at home; putting down riots in our cities, or any other disturbances not sufficiently extensive or formidable to place them in the category of rebellions, but too serious to be disposed of by the ordinary police force of the localities where they occur."[11]

But the strike spread to the Pennsylvania Railroad. When the militia was ordered to break it in Pittsburgh, the local troops joined the strikers, forcing six hundred more troops to be sent in. These soldiers did fire into the pickets, killing twenty and wounding hundreds. Thousands of strikers, farmers, and other workers then attacked the soldiers, forcing them to retreat into the roundhouse, which the workingmen burned, along with 104 locomotives, 2,000-odd railroad cars, and all the railroad buildings in the area. Across the Allegheny River, other workers seized the local armory and used the arms to take over the telegraph office, sending messages up and down the line asking for support. When the Reading men struck, the National Guard tried to force them back to work by firing into their ranks, killing eleven. Instead, the enraged strikers tore up the tracks and gained the support of workers in steel mills, construction, stockyards, packing houses, and foundries. More troops intervened. In St. Louis, federal troops quashed a general strike. In Pennsylvania, three thousand soldiers rushed from one embattled zone to another. In Chicago, the authorities had been ready and waiting for an outbreak of popular discontent since January 1874 when the New York police had brutally smashed a march and rally at Tompkins Square by seven thousand unemployed workers. The Tompkins Square rally had been officially permitted, but New York police commissioner Oliver Gardner told the leader of the unemployed that he would stop the assembly. By what statute? he was asked. Retorted Gardner: "Never mind the law." Now, during a two-day orgy of wanton shooting and beating by ten thousand special deputies, soldiers, and police, Chicago's law enforcers killed almost fifty workers and maimed over a hundred more.[12]

Pinkerton attributed all the strikes and strife of 1877 to communists. "Every act of lawlessness that was done was committed by them," he said flatly. He also claimed that "tramps, who had nothing to lose in their philosophical way, entered upon the rioting and plunder because it seemed to be the order of the day." Every unemployed person was lazy, said Pinkerton; they were "a class of human hyenas, and all are thieves. Hundred upon hundred became demoralized by the lazy habits of camp life [during the Civil War] and were suddenly turned loose upon society without any employment, or desire of any. . . . It is easy to see how such a person shortly becomes a vagabond. From this stage it is but a step to a bullying mendicant; and from that condition to one of becoming a criminal in a small way is all easy and natural."[13]

The *Chicago Tribune* agreed with Pinkerton. Its editor prescribed "a little strychnine or arsenic" for every tramp. Other journals suggested "a stout rope thrown over the limb of a tree." Yet these armies of tramps, which did indeed roam the countryside in 1877, were the former hardworking employees of the railroads, mills, factories, and mines fired by the owners during the depression. Officially 1 million, from a total population of 45 million, were unemployed and unemployable. Actually, the figure was closer to 3 million. In New York, one-fourth of the labor force was out of work, and 30,000 were homeless. For each announced job opening, ten supposed tramps applied at once, no matter how bad the working conditions and how low the pay. In Connecticut the tramps did steal, but conspicuously, so as to get arrested during the wintertime in order to spend the cold in jail. In the spring, they set forth looking for work, swarming over the countryside of upstate New York and on to Ohio and Illinois. Everywhere they were beaten and shoved on by vigilante groups organized by the wealthy, such as Alexander Cassatt, vice-president of the Pennsylvania Railroad, who financed a phalanx of mounted police to clear his state of the rabble.[14]

In Scranton, Pennsylvania, most of the businessmen, storeowners, and active professionals banded together into the Scranton Citizens' Corps, led by the mayor and W.W. Scranton himself, who was then general manager of the Lackawanna Iron and Coal Company, and obtained guns from the railroads and mineowners in the region. After boosting the prices in all area stores, forcing the strikers and unemployed to raid the Stowers' Packing House, where they made off with a ton of meat, and the Lackawanna depot, where they stole sacks of potatoes, the Citizen's Corps attacked the strikers, firing wildly. In the ensuing battles, in which scores of workers were hit, the mayor was killed, forcing federal troops to intervene. Upon investigation, it was shown that the corps had caused the riot; fifty-three members were arrested, including Scranton. Judged by their businessmen peers, all fifty-three were found not guilty.[15]

Nowhere else, however, did the troops show any fairness in dealing with workers. In Schuylkill County, the National Guard division under command of Major General J.K. Siegfried not only supported the businessmen-vigilantes, but intervened as an occupation force, shooting unarmed or fleeing strikers. Though many individual soldiers sympathized with the strikers, and often actually helped them, the guard as a whole was especially brutal. On July 19, 1877, the troops tried to break the pickets at the Pennsylvania Railroad's Pittsburgh center, leading to fifteen deaths on the twenty-first. The next day, General Siegried ordered strikers attacked at various points, including Altoona, Lancaster, Columbia, and Harrisburg. By the time they finished their rampage, though hundreds of soldiers defected to the workers side, the troops had killed over a hundred in Pennsylvania alone. "General Siegfried practically acted as governor of Pennsylvania for some six or eight days," reported one contemporary witness. The strike there, as elsewhere in America, was broken. Wages were cut and hours lengthened. "Double-header" trains (running two trains together but with only one crew), one of the causes for the strike, became standard practice on all railroad lines for years thereafter.[16]

Bitter, angry, and frustrated, labor continued to protest, to organize, and to strike whenever a union was strong enough to resist the clubs of the Pinkerton men or other goon squads and the bullets of state or federal soldiers. In 1881, there were 471 strikes at 2,928 firms involving 129,521 workers. By 1885, the numbers had jumped to 645 strikes by 242,705 workers. Some were surprisingly effective, considering the fact that it was illegal to strike. In 1885, for example, strikers forced Jay Gould's railways—the Wabash, Missouri Pacific, and Missouri, Kansas and Texas—to restore a 15 percent wage cut. In March 1886, workers began to walk off their jobs across the country demanding an end to the ten- and twelve-hour day. By May 1, 340,000 workers had closed down 12,000 establishments. On that day, the demands for an eight-hour day were to be heralded from rallies in all major cities, but especially in Chicago, where 80,000 workers were striking.[17]

On the morning of May 1, a bright balmy Saturday, the *Chicago Mail* asked for blood. "There are two dangerous ruffians at large in this city; two skulking cowards who are trying to create trouble," the paper editorialized. "Mark them. . . . Make an example of them." One was Albert Parsons, thirty-eight, whose solid middle-class Yankee family had moved to Montgomery, Alabama. He had fought with the Confederacy, had been radicalized by the depression of 1873, and had become a socialist during the police riot of 1877 when he had been warned by the police chief to leave town or be hanged "to a Camp-post." The other "ruffian" was August Spies, thirty-one, a German-born socialist, newspaper editor, and labor leader. Throughout the day Pinkertons and militia men, armed with rifles, were stationed on rooftops, and 1,350 National Guardsmen in full battle gear and equipped with Gatling guns were waiting in the armory ready to attack. But the rally for an eight-hour-day, led by Parsons and Spies, was peaceful, and the *Mail* did not reap its blood. Two days later, after Spies finished addressing six thousand strikers near the McCormick Harvester Works, where fourteen hundred workers had been locked out for joining a union, a scuffle developed when scabs headed into the plant. Almost immediately two hundred Chicago policemen surged out of side streets and began beating and shooting the strikers, killing four and wounding scores. Spies responded by calling for a mass protest rally for the next day, to meet at Haymarket Square. The big press in America has rarely been on the side of the workingmen, and even more rarely on the side of justice, but this time it indulged in overkill, describing the labor leaders as mad anarchists and the crowd as "liquor-crazed."[18]

May 4, 1886, was an ugly day in Chicago. No sooner had Parsons, Spies, and other labor leaders spoken to the three thousand workers assembled at Haymarket Square than it started to rain. As most people began to leave, Captain John ("Clubber") Bonfield showed up with 180 policemen and ordered them to hurry up. At that moment a bomb exploded in the front ranks of the police. The cops then went mad, clubbing and shooting. Some of the strikers fired back, but the crowd dispersed fast. It was all over in a flash. Yet that began the real Haymarket affair, for, though some strikers were dead and hundreds wounded, what mattered was that one policeman had been killed on the spot and seven more died from wounds later. The *New York Times* cried murder and demanded vengeance. All further rallies and demonstrations were forbidden—except, of course, in support of the police. Hundreds of radicals and labor leaders were arrested as state's attorney Julius S. Grinnell told his law enforcers: "Make raids first and look up the law afterwards." Finally, on June 21, Parsons, Spies and six other radicals were charged with conspiracy and being accessories to murder—punishable by death.[19]

The Haymarket trial represents one of the most disgusting episodes in the American system of justice. Even Illinois governor John Peter Altgeld, risking his political career, said so publicly in 1893, accusing Judge Joseph E. Gary of flagrant prejudice. Indeed, of the twelve jurors not one was a worker, four said they hated radicals, and every single one admitted having formed an opinion about the guilt of the defendants before the trial—yet the judge, the defense having exhausted its preemptory challenges, disqualified none. "Much of the evidence given in the trial was pure fabrication," Governor Altgeld said later, adding that testimony was gained from "terrorized, ignorant men" whom police had threatened "with torture if they refused to swear to anything desired." Seven of the eight were condemned to hang, the eighth getting fifteen years. Lucy Parsons and the two Parsons children were arrested and jailed for trying to see Parsons before his execution. Appeals for clemency or pardons were denied.

The Supreme Court refused to hear the case. Spies, Parsons, and two others were hanged on November 11, 1887. A fifth had committed suicide in jail. The two others had their sentences commuted to life imprisonment. The *New York Times* was jubilant. Six years later, Governor Altgeld refused an "act of mercy." Either the men were innocent or they were guilty, he said. For five months he studied the record. On June 26, 1893, describing the trial as a complete sham and condemning Judge Gary as a bigot, he freed the last three defendants. America's press condemned him. In Chicago, New York, Philadelphia, Detroit, he was called unfit for the governor's chair. Everywhere big business donated funds to defeat him in 1896. He lost the election, and the workers lost their eight-hour day.[20]

Labor lost many important battles in those days when the law was almost universally on the side of the industrialists. The Carnegie steel strike at Homestead, Pennsylvania, a small town of twelve thousand people seven miles east of Pittsburgh is an example. In 1889, the Amalgamated Association of Iron and Steel Workers, affiliated with the newly formed American Federation of Labor, had gotten Andrew Carnegie to sign a truce on wage cutting for three years. But in January 1892, the "contract" having ended, Henry Clay Frick, who was running the plant while Carnegie was vacationing in Italy, ordered an 18 percent cut. The steelworkers struck, but Frick was ready. He had contracted Pinkerton to send 300 armed goons by barge to fight the strikers, while workers hired for other mills would be sealed into wagon trains and transported to Homestead as strikebreakers. In the ensuing battles, 9 strikers and 7 Pinkerton men were killed. The law attacked only the strikers: 167 were arrested, 34 charged with murder, and 27, on direct orders of State Supreme Court Justice Edward Paxson, who held no investigation, were indicted for "treason" against the state of Pennsylvania. Though none were ever tried, the arrests broke the back of the strike, and on November 20, 1892, the workers voted to accept the wage cut and return to their jobs. When Carnegie, whose company had already earned $100 million ($270,000 at Homestead alone), heard of Frick's victory, he wired him: "Congratulations all around—life worth living again—how pretty Italia." In the next nine years, reducing the number of his employees by 25 percent, Carnegie netted $106 million at the Homestead plant.[21]

That same year in and around Coeur d'Alene, Idaho, well-organized miners resisted wage cuts, lockouts, and the private armies of the owners so well for seven months that in July the governor, declaring a state of insurrection, asked President Benjamin Harrison to send troops. Major General J.M. Schofield, who commanded the fifteen hundred U.S. Army and National Guard soldiers sent to the area, thereupon instituted a reign of terror. He locked up six hundred union members in bullpens without warrants. He ordered mineowners to fire every union member and threatened those who didn't with confiscation. He locked up thirty union leaders on federal charges of criminal conspiracy. And, once the strike and unions were broken, he forced all miners returning to work to foreswear all future union activity. When the miners did organize and strike again in 1899, President William McKinley, who was dominated by the mine-owning banker-speculator Marcus Hanna, sent new troops to the area. They proceeded to repeat Schofield's tactics and smashed the union by sending one of its leaders to jail for seventeen years for murder and eight others for two years for interfering with U.S. mails, again on phony evidence.[22]

In Cripple Creek, Colorado, during the depression year of 1894, the miners did win a victory, thanks to the unprecedented neutrality of the governor. Trouble started in January when the gold mine owners decided to increase work time to ten hours a day and lower payments by fifty cents a day. Well organized and disciplined, most miners struck, while those who continued to work donated 10 percent of their salaries to keep the strikers going. They also got help from the miners of Butte, Montana, and the San Juan district of Colorado. When the managers got together to fund a private army, to be trained by the local sheriff, the miners started raiding hardware stores for arms and ammunition for the inevitable battle. One miner, Junius J. Johnson, who had spent three years at West Point, welded the strikers into tight, mobile squads. Other union leaders set up temporary housing away from family areas and a commissary to feed the popular army. When the battle began between the 125 deputized gunmen and the miners, some of Johnson's squads hit the shaft house and mine boiler room, sending them both three hundred feet into the air with dynamite. The sheriff armed more deputies. The miners got 200 reinforcements from Leadville and 100 armed diggers from Rico, a hundred miles away. Colorado's governor put the state militia on the alert, ordered both armies to disband and come to terms. Eventually, an agreement was reached: the eight-hour day remained and salaries went up to three dollars a day—a rare victory in those days for labor.[23]

The big event in that year of 1894 was, of course, the Pullman strike. It began on May 10 in the town of Pullman, Illinois, where everything was owned and controlled by George Pullman—the foundries making the railroad cars, the employees' homes, stores, even the lampposts. Workers were forced to buy at the company stores and rent was deducted from paychecks. A new labor organization, the American Railway Union (ARU), had spread quickly in Pullman since the failure of a ten-day strike in 1886. It was headed by Eugene V. Debs, a self-trained writer and editor from Terre Haute, Indiana, who had worked on trains from the time he was fourteen years old until he was elected to the Indiana state legislature in 1884. Launched in 1893 in the hope of uniting all the small independent railway unions, the ARU had led a successful strike that same year against the Great Northern Railroad and had established 465 lodges with fifteen thousand members by 1894. It was opposed by the General Managers Association (GMA), formed in 1886 by the owners of all twenty-six lines having terminals in Chicago.

At first the ARU tried to arbitrate the Pullman strike. When the GMA refused, the ARU asked its members to boycott Pullman cars. The switchmen who did were immediately fired. The strike then spread to St. Louis and Ludlow, Kentucky, where Pullman had other plants, and ARU asked for a national boycott by all railway workers, unionized or not, of Pullman wagons. Within two days, 18,000 workers were heeding the boycott; within three, the number was 40,000. On the fourth day, 125,000 railroadmen were refusing to service Pullman. As firings continued, so did strikes. By June 27, some 5,000 workers had stopped fifteen lines from moving in or out of Chicago. On the twenty-eighth, all twenty-six lines were idle as 18,000 workers were on strike. The GMA set up offices in Pittsburgh, Cleveland, Philadelphia, New York, and Buffalo to recruit strikebreakers, appealed for troops for the showdown and began collecting injunctions against the strikers. Union leaders were arrested in Indiana and Missouri. The Illinois militia was sent to protect the Illinois Central in Cairo. Thomas Milchrist, the federal district attorney in Chicago, wired Washington that strikers had stopped mail trains, which was untrue, and with that allegation got U.S. marshals the power to hire as many deputies as needed.

Still, the strike spread, so overworked, underpaid, and mistreated were all railroad employees across the country: some 260,000 had joined the walkout by the end of June. At that point, President Grover Cleveland's attorney general, Richard Olney, a corporation lawyer specializing in railroads who had at one time directed the Burlington and the Boston and Main lines and who owned a great deal of railroad stock, used the excuse of maintaining the flow of mail trains to grant all U.S. attorneys a free hand in smashing the strike. In Chicago alone, 5,000 federal marshals were deputized. Olney allowed the railroads to recruit two-thirds of the deputies and pick their own captains. He hired Edwin Walker, a GMA member and general counsel for one of the struck railroads, as "special federal attorney in Chicago," and got a nationwide injunction against the strike. As the federal troops arrived in Chicago, which had been peaceful until then, the strikers responded by throwing switches, toppling cars, blocking tracks. On July 6, an official of the Illinois Central cold-bloodedly aimed a pistol and shot two strikers. Angered, the crowd burned the line's yards and seven hundred cars. The 14,000 troops dispersed the rioters, killing 13 and wounding 53.

Using the Sherman Anti-Trust Act of 1890 against the unions, the two federal district attorneys, Milchrist and Walker, working with Judge William A. Woods, who was a protégé of Pullman and enjoyed free travel passes on all railroads, issued a series of injunctions which forbade ARU leaders from sending telegrams, speaking publicly, participating in any assembly, answering any question relating to the strike, indeed of exercising any of their constitutional rights. On July 10, Debs and three other union leaders were indicted for sending telegrams, then charged with criminal conspiracy to obstruct the mails, to interfere with interstate commerce, and to intimidate citizens in the exercise of their rights. Federal deputies then raided ARU's headquarters and illegally confiscated all of Debs's private papers, mail, and books. On July 12, Samuel Gompers called together the AFL's executive council and issued a statement of nonsupport for Debs and the ARU on the grounds that "a general strike at this time is inexpedient, unwise, and contrary to the best interest of working people." That was the crowning blow. The strike was over. Prosecuted by Milchrist and Walker, Debs and his three compatriots were convicted of contempt on September 5. Though the government dropped the conspiracy and other charges when defense attorney

Clarence Darrow stated his intention to subpoena Pullman and other GMA heads to prove that the conspiracy was their doing, labor had lost its biggest battle.[24]

After that it was easy for so-called law-enforcement officers to gun down unarmed workers. One of the worst massacres took place in the little village of Lattimer, in the heart of Pennsylvania's anthracite fields, in 1897. Protesting dollar-a-day wages and bondage to the company store, some four hundred unarmed miners, mostly Slavs who could barely speak English, carrying two American flags and no anarchist or socialist posters or materials, were peacefully marching toward the Pardee Company's mine when they were stopped by the local sheriff and a posse in the pay of the mineowners. Whether or not the sheriff ordered his men to fire above the strikers, as he claimed, is unclear, but the posse unleashed a salvo directly into the miners. Nineteen were killed, thirty-nine wounded, many shot in the back as the goon squad pursued the fleeing protesters and kept firing with obvious relish. Although the Austro-Hungarian government issued a protest, and sent an emissary to witness the subsequent trial of the eighty-seven posse members, the judge was so partial to the coal company, the defense attorneys so openly bigoted against the foreigners, and the district attorney so visibly sympathetic to the men he was prosecuting, that the twelve jurymen, each one an Anglo-Saxon Protestant Republican, had no hesitation in finding the murderers not guilty.[25]

So flagrantly was the law abused to defend big business and prevent workers from gaining a decent livelihood during this period, from the Civil War to World War I, that it would not be unfair to characterize it as a dictatorship of the rich. True, many reformers did denounce some of the worst outrages. Populists and progressives repeatedly tried to put an end to the alliance between government and Wall Street financiers, especially when they conspired to sell government bonds for gold on terms that would allow the banking houses to manipulate exchange rates for their benefit. In 1896, such reformers even mounted a formidable campaign to capture the presidency, putting up as their Populist-Democratic candidate William Jennings Bryan, a Nebraska congressman whose attack on the oligarchs was as sincere as his fundamentalist faith. Supporting free silver against Wall Street's controlled gold, Bryan traveled eighteen thousand miles, made six hundred speeches in his attempt to remoralize America—a personal crusade for a return to Puritan ideals. But with well-financed Democrats like Marcus Hanna against him, organizing America's entrepreneurial wealth behind McKinley, Bryan was defeated 7,104,779 to 6,502,925.

Other reformers were more successful, on smaller scales. Illinois governor Altgeld, who had pardoned the Haymarket framed, was not successful in stopping the president from sending troops to put down labor protesters. But Robert ("Battling Bob") LaFollette did stop the troops after 1900 when he captured the Wisconsin governorship. He then regulated railroads, created a more equitable state tax structure, put controls on banks, and enacted labor legislation that somewhat bettered workers' conditions. In New York, Governor Charles Evans Hughes tried, less successfully. to do the same. After McKinley's assassination in 1901, President Theodore Roosevelt also tried to control trusts to prevent them from fixing prices and manipulating markets. He helped the United Mine Workers get a 10 percent raise and the meat packers to win their strike in 1906. But he refused to support closed shops, to break up the efficient trusts, or even to suggest measures that might profoundly alter the life or hopes of the common people—one reason why he was defeated in 1912 by Woodrow Wilson.

As New Jersey's reformer-governor, Wilson had gotten his state to pass a direct primary law, railroad controls, workmen's compensation, and a corrupt practices act; in this he had been supported by Bryan and his Populists as well as by urban progressives. In his first eighteen months in the White House, Wilson did as he had promised, enacting reforms "so that the next generation of youngsters, as they come along, will not have to become the protégés of benevolent trusts, but will be free to go about making their own lives what they will." But then, obsessed with moral values and the integrity of his New Freedom, he refused to use the government against the trusts, which continued to beat, frame, even kill the workers, using the law to deprive them of justice. Louis Brandeis, who had fashioned the New Freedom, spoke out against this "financial oligarchy" which would surely turn into "political despotism," but Wilson ignored the pleas of Brandeis and others, instead becoming more and more an academician. "All the country needs is a new and sincere body of thought in politics, coherently, distinctly and boldly uttered by men who are sure of their ground," Wilson coherently uttered. He spoke boldly but did not act boldly. In 1913 alone, twenty-five thousand workers were killed on the job and another three-quarters of a million were seriously injured. During that same period, trusts doubled their net profits six times.[26]

Thus, labor had no choice but to get tougher. The toughest group of them all was the Industrial Workers of the World, the IWW or, as its members quickly became known, the Wobblies. It was launched in June 1905 by William ("Big Bill") Haywood, secretary-general of the Western Federation of Miners; Eugene Debs; Lucy Parsons, the widow of the Haymarket martyr; "Mother" Mary Jones, who was still a formidable mine workers' organizer at seventy-five; Charles Moyer, president of the WFM; Daniel de Leon, the intellectual mastermind of the Socialist party; Father Thomas J. Hagerty, a Catholic priest become socialist who now edited the American Labor Union's *Voice of Labor;* and various representatives from metal, machine, and brewery workers' unions. "The working class and the employing class have nothing in common," flatly stated the preamble to the IWW's constitution. The Wobblies recognized the fact that there was a class war in America, and they meant to win it.[27]

The first few months were slow for the IWW, which represented only fifty-two thousand workers. But things changed in February 1906 when Haywood, Moyer, and a third Wobbly were indicted for the murder of the governor of Idaho on the trumped-up evidence concocted by James McParlan, the Pinkerton spy in the Molly Maguires case who was now head of the detective agency's Denver office. Kidnapped during a Saturday night raid ordered by Colorado's governor, the three Wobblies were deported illegally to Idaho, causing millions of workers all over America to express their sympathy. Even conservative AFL leaders felt obliged to support them. Hundreds of fund-raising rallies were staged across the land, and there were some even in Europe. At the trial in July 1907, defense attorney Clarence Darrow so masterfully broke down one supposed witness and got the only other one to contradict himself so thoroughly that the Wobblies were freed. Haywood became a workingman's hero.[28]

Though some of the original founders quit the IWW, including de Leon, the whole of the WFM, and eventually even Debs, the union's uncompromising tactics and the total dedication of its remaining leaders and staffers won new converts quickly, some 100,000 by the end of 1912. In 1908, Wobblies organized the whole town of Goldfield, Nevada, from miners to dishwashers and newsboys, and forced management to raise salaries across the board—until the AFL joined management to break the IWW stranglehold. The Wobblies organized America's first sit-down strike in the GE plant at Schenectady, New York. In Portland, Oregon, they used mass pickets to sign up members, as well as close down shops. In New York, Spokane, and Missoula, Montana, they organized the unemployed, then used them as pickets. When they were ordered by an injunction not to speak in Spokane in 1909, they spoke one after another, forcing authorities to lock up five hundred crusaders for "free speech." When construction workers struck two railroads in 1912, they put up a "thousand-mile picket line" along the tracks from San Francisco to Minneapolis to watch for scabs.[29]

The Wobblies' biggest victory was in Lawrence, Massachusetts, in 1912. Known as "the worsted center of the world," Lawrence, a one-industry textile town of eighty-six thousand people thirty miles north of Boston, was controlled by Morgan's American Woolen Company, which had thirty-four plants worth $60 million spread throughout New England. Wages were shockingly low, even for 1912: $8.76 maximum for a fifty-six-hour week. Most of the workers earned $7.00 a week, and paid $5.00 of it for rent. One-third of the mill workers died by age twenty-five, and 172 infants out of every 1,000 died in their first year The strike began spontaneously on January 11, when a group of Polish weavers noticed that their pay had been cut thirty-two cents. The Italians then saw that their salaries had also been shortened and went on a rampage, smashing machines and breaking windows. When the AFL skilled workers refused to join the strikers, they appealed to the IWW. Moving in immediately, the Wobblies set up committees for each ethnic group, got them to elect their leaders, organized pickets, relief stations, soup kitchens, brought in doctors and replacements as one leader after another got arrested. Though 2,500 troops, plus scores of Pinkertons and police, harassed the pickets, arresting 355, sending 54 to jail, and routinely beat up the strikers—including women and children—the strike spread. Within two weeks, 23,000 workers, including the skilled workers who were disobeying AFL orders, had walked out. Management also tried to frame the IWW leaders by planting dynamite in known Wobbly centers. Though the New York police fingered the mill agent who had done the deed (found guilty, he was fined $500), two Wobbly organizers were charged with conspiracy to blow up mill property and to commit murder. Support rallies were held across America and in Europe, and in March, the millowners gave in, granting pay raises of up to 21 percent. Massachusetts authorities then arrested Haywood and seven other Wobbly leaders, charging them with conspiracy to intimidate workers. But in September, after 12,000 textile workers staged a one-day strike protesting the trials of their leaders, all the Wobbly leaders, including the two facing the dynamite charge, were freed.[30]

After Lawrence, and a few successful but minor organizing efforts, the IWW began to go downhill. Lacking money to maintain permanent offices, too militant to gain support from even the most progressive reformers in Congress, always attacked by the press, the AFL and other craft unions, and constantly pursued, arrested on trumped up charges, beaten and occasionally murdered by law-enforcement officers, the Wobblies began to disintegrate. Though they usually advocated peaceful pickets—in Lawrence, Haywood and the other IWW leaders kept repeating that any blood spilled would always be workers' blood—the Wobblies were so consistently characterized as dynamiters by the press that the epithet began to stick. John and James McNamara, the leaders of the iron workers who dynamited the viciously antilabor Los Angeles *Times* in October 1910, were members of the AFL, not of the IWW. But they were immediately dubbed Wobblies.[31]

In the following decades, the Wobblies were hounded American style—by lynch law. IWW poet Joe Hill, convicted of murder in a highly suspect Utah trial, was executed by a firing squad after he said his last words to his comrades: "Don't waste time mourning. Organize." After Haywood, the IWW's most dynamic leader was Frank Little, a half-Indian who served on the IWW's executive board. Little was a tireless organizer of metal miners in Arizona and Montana, a dedicated foe of Anaconda, whose work conditions were so poor that in just one 1917 incident 190 diggers had been killed. Little never complained of the endless hours required by the executive board, or of the endless beatings he received from goons. On August 1, 1917, Anaconda company guards raided his hotel room, beat him up, dragged him down to their car, tied him to the fender, dragged him several miles to a railroad trestle and hanged him. Wesley Everest was just an ordinary lumberjack who, though a member of the IWW, had fought in France. On Armistice Day 1919, the Centralia, Washington, chapter of the American Legion charged the IWW hall, guns blazing. Everest, dressed in full uniform, fired back, killing the legion head, and was eventually jailed. That night, the legionnaires raided the prison. As

Everest shouted to his fellow inmates, "Tell the boys I died for my class," he was strapped to a car, castrated, driven to a bridge, hanged, and riddled with bullets. While none of Everest's murderers were apprehended, hundreds of Wobblies were charged with the deaths of the legionnaires who had assaulted the hall. Eleven were tried before a judge who had given the legionnaire's funeral oration. When the jury returned a mixed verdict, the judge ruled it unacceptable. This time the jury came back with a verdict of guilty of second-degree murder. The Wobblies were sentenced to twenty-five to forty years in prison. Four years later, nine of the jurors, six of them under oath, admitted they had been pressured by the lumber trust owners. Defense witnesses who said that the legionnaires had fired first were jailed for perjury. The Wobblies served fifteen years in Walla Walla penitentiary.[32]

The events in Washington State were not unusual. Throughout America, Wobblies were arrested, tried for bombings or conspiracy on fake evidence, and jailed. In July 1917, members of the Bisbee Loyalty League, in Arizona, rounded up 1,200 supposed Wobblies (351 were AFL members), sealed them into a cattle train, shipped them under guard into the New Mexico desert where they were kept without food or water for thirty-six hours, then beat them up before locking them up in a federal stockade where they were held without charges for three months. In Butte, Montana, Wobblies and socialists kept winning elections between 1911 and 1921, so martial law was declared; the elected officials, union leaders, and all known Wobblies were arrested and jailed without trial. In Wichita, Kansas, 34 Wobblies were jailed during an oil strike in 1917, tried twenty-two months later, and 27 were sentenced to nine years for draft resistance. In California, 46 Wobblies were arrested when the governor's house was bombed by police provocateurs; so bad were the jail's conditions that 5 died; then 22 were sent to prison for ten years, the rest for up to five. Finally, President Wilson joined the campaign against the Wobblies, and at his instigation, 165 top IWW leaders, including Haywood and the whole general executive board, were arrested on September 28, 1917, and charged with various counts of sedition and conspiracy. "It is the IWW which is on trial here," declared the prosecutor when the trial of 101 of the Wobblies finally opened in Chicago on April 1, 1918. Though the defendants' constitutional rights of free speech, assembly, advocacy, and privacy were all flagrantly violated by the government, the U.S.

Supreme Court let stand two counts—enough to validate the twenty-year terms handed down to Haywood and 14 others and the lesser terms to all the rest.

Since the Chicago trial of the IWW proved that the law could openly be used to suppress and repress anyone opposed to big business, Wilson's attorney general, A. Mitchell Palmer, decided that he would not even bother with the law to crush dissenters. Thus, in a series of raids begun on November 7, 1919, he had some ten thousand foreign-born radicals, union leaders, and organizers arrested in seventy cities. Nearly two hundred and fifty were summarily deported. The rest, including members of the Amalgamated Clothing Workers, the International Ladies' Garment Workers, and the IWW, were jailed. Even Palmer's assistant, J. Edgar Hoover, recognized that the raids were unconstitutional. But even as a young man, Hoover was not one to worry over constitutional subtleties.[34]

The IWW trials and lynchings, the continual vigilante attacks, the Palmer raids, the Red Scare, the interventions by federal troops, the deliberate frame-ups, lies and conspiracies used to smash labor in America had their effect: most of the union leaders genuinely dedicated to the working masses either gave up, fled, were imprisoned, or were killed. Those who remained learned their lesson. They could either play ball with big business or they could make deals, for their own protection, with the only force strong enough to oppose the authorities in America—organized crime.

Chapter 16

Family Feuds, Cattle Wars, and Gunslingers

After the Civil War, crime along the frontier, in the territories and the sparsely populated states, was violent, often brutal, and usually committed as much by lawmen as by desperadoes. In fact, many of the lawmen *were* desperadoes, gunslingers who murdered for hire whether or not they were wearing a badge. Some of these killers had ridden with Quantrill's irregulars during the war, and many more claimed they had, when it became fashionable to say so, thanks to the outlandish stories published in the eastern press.

William Clarke Quantrill was a vicious, paranoiac horse thief and cutthroat. Born in Ohio in 1837, he came from a long line of scofflaws: His father had been an embezzler, his uncle a counterfeiter, his grandfather a horse thief, his great-uncle a pirate. Moving to Kansas in 1857, Quantrill tried teaching school and farming, failed at both, and settled near the Missouri border not too far from Lawrence with a bunch of white and Indian horse thieves. Indicted for murder and theft, he escaped, pretended to be an abolitionist, led five Northern raiders into a Missouri ambush, returned to Kansas, was caught, escaped from jail and finally turned his group of ruffians into Confederate irregulars when the war began. Given the rank of captain after his troops captured Independence, Missouri, in 1862, Quantrill then led his bushwackers into raids across the Missouri-Kansas free-soil areas, stealing everything of value and killing all prisoners. In August 1863 with 450 men, he sacked Lawrence, burning most of the houses and killing some 180 or 200 people. Frank James and Cole Younger supposedly rode with Quantrill in that raid. Jesse James and Jim Younger rode with Quantrill's top lieutenant, "Bloody Bill" Anderson, when he raided Centralia, Kansas, later that year, executing 200 Union prisoners. Jesse, who was then seventeen, was given credit for killing the Union commander, Major H. J. Johnson. Early in 1865, Quantrill and 33 men drove through western Kentucky, pillaging towns and killing noncombatants. In May, the group was caught by surprise by Union irregulars near Taylorsville. Quantrill was badly wounded and died a month later in Louisville.[1]

After the war, many of Quantrill's men headed south, ending up in Texas, which became one of the country's most violent states. Much of the lawlessness had existed before the war, fostered mainly by the fifty-two railroad companies that had bribed the legislature to pass fifty-two bills for their relief and special privilege. After the war, the Ku Klux Klan and the Knights of the Rising Sun terrorized blacks and new settlers, forcing the federal government to occupy the state until 1870 with forty-five hundred troops. Republican governor Edmund J. Davis, who won the 1869 election thanks to these troops, established a mostly black state police, which was ordered not only to fight the marauders but also to make sure that blacks were allowed to vote, thus gaining the animosity of most of the press. Though Davis allowed prison wardens to lease convicts to private developers and did not veto a bill granting the Southern Pacific a $16-per-mile subsidy, he did stop an added $6 million subsidy and a bill meant to divert land-grant territory from new settlers to the railroad. Thus he provoked additional condemnation from the press, which was then controlled by the railways. The press hit Davis mostly for his state police, whose adjutant general, James Davidson, fled Texas with $37,434.67 in state funds. That allowed the Democratic legislature of 1873 to abolish the police. After Davis was defeated for a second term in a fraudulent election which he resisted but which stood when President Grant refused to send federal troops, the new governor recreated the Texas Rangers, this time as an all-white but generally efficient force of professionals.[2]

One Texas outlaw that the rangers hunted for years was John Wesley Hardin. Born in Bonham, Texas, in 1853, Hardin killed his first man, a black who had whipped him in a wrestling match, at fifteen. He escaped to Navarro County, started gambling to earn a living, killed a circus performer the next year for $100, then a total stranger, and a deputy who caught him in 1871. The next month he gunned down two Mexicans during a game of monte. That year he shot an Indian who tried to charge Hardin a dime to cross his territory on the way to Abilene, then killed five Mexicans in a saloon fight. Once in Abilene he befriended Wild Bill Hickok, who was sheriff. Hickok let Hardin get away with killing a stranger who badmouthed Texas. In August of 1871, Hardin and a friend were back in Gonzales, Texas, where they spotted a black state police trooper. Enraged, Hardin shot and killed him. "A posse of Negroes from Austin came down after me," Hardin wrote proudly in his autobiography. "I met them prepared and killed three of them." Soon after that he was caught in a showdown, was shot four times before he surrendered, survived, and in September 1872, sawed his way out of the Gonzales jail. Arrested again in 1874 he escaped again by killing a deputy sheriff, got caught once more three years later by a ranger lieutenant who made sure he remained secure through his trial, sentencing, and shipment to the pen. In prison he wrote his autobiography, arrogantly listing all his crimes, but he also studied law and was pardoned in 1884. Settling down in El Paso, he practiced his new profession for a decade. But the lure of the gun was too strong. He resumed running horses, gambling, and killing along the Texas border until a local sheriff, not willing to risk confronting the fastest gun in Texas, shot him in the back in 1895.[3]

After his 1872 escape Hardin had hidden out in De Witt County and there joined the Taylor faction in Texas's longest, bloodiest feud. No one is quite sure how the feud started. Some say that it was out of racism, the general hostility that white Texans felt toward the federal troops, who used black policemen to patrol the area. There was talk in those days that since a lot of cattle were being rustled, since blacks were unemployed, and since, therefore, the blacks had to be the rustlers, the troops were protecting the rustlers. Others claimed that the feud started when the Taylors killed a white officer, forcing white deputies working for the Union to come after the Taylors. In any case, the feud lasted thirty years, continuing long after the principals were gone or dead.

Those principals included, on one side, the five cattle- and land-owning Taylor brothers—Pitkin, Creed, Josiah, William, and

Ruckus—their wives, in-laws, friends, and, as years passed, all their offspring. The other side was headed by Billy Sutton, a twenty-two-year-old landless six-footer who, in 1868, was eking out a living by occasionally working as a local peace officer, that is, helping the Yankee authorities. In the spring of 1869, a small group of bounty hunters under the command of Jack Helm, a vain and arrogant killer who would later become captain in the state police, and C.S. Bell, a writer and soldier of fortune from the North, showed up in De Witt County with a federal mandate to raise a posse to track down the killers of the Union officer, believed to be the Taylors. Bell and Helm deputized fifty men, among them Bill Sutton, armed them and set out on a rampage, killing twenty-one people, including two Taylor offspring and a dozen of their friends. When Helm became a state police captain in 1870 he made Sutton a permanent deputy, and together they tracked down more Taylor men, killing Henry and William Kelly, who had married Pitkin Taylor's daughters. Sutton's men then raided Pitkin's house and shot him. The Taylor clan swore revenge and De Witt County became engulfed in war. In 1873, Sutton was shot by William and his son, Jim Taylor, but survived. It is at this point that John Wesley Hardin showed up and joined the Taylor clan to fight Jack Helm, who had been fired from the state police but was now sheriff of De Witt. Helped by Hardin, the Taylors bushwacked two Sutton men in neighboring Gonzales County, then tracked down Helm himself. Jim Taylor killed him.

Both sides now recruited heavily. In May, with Sutton, who took over Helm's post, commanding fifty men and the Taylors backed up by seventy, a truce was reached. Peace returned to De Witt until December, when the Sutton faction killed a Taylor man. The ensuing confrontation led to several deaths on both sides, but the battle was a standoff, so another peace was agreed upon. On March 11, 1874, Hardin went to visit his father in Comanche and on his way spotted Sutton, who, fearful that he would get waylaid sooner or later, had decided to flee to New Orleans. Hardin tipped off the Taylors, and Bill, Jim, and six more gunmen rushed down to get him. They did. Bill was caught by Cuero's new city marshal, tried and sentenced to ten years, but the court of appeals eventually overturned the decision on a technicality. The marshal rearrested him in September 1875 for another murder and brought him to Indianola for trial. But Bill escaped, and on November 17, the marshal was ambushed by five masked men and killed. The following month, a Cuero vigilante posse, fed up with all the killing, caught Jim Taylor and two other Taylor clansmen and shot them. Bill thereupon moved to Oklahoma, became a peace officer, and was killed trying to stop another gunslinger. That quieted De Witt for a while.

But not for too long. During the night of September 19–20, 1876, ten Taylor clansmen with handkerchiefs over their faces surrounded the home of Dr. Phillip Brassell, a Georgia constitutionalist who had settled in Texas to cure his tuberculosis and had voiced sympathy but offered no help for the Sutton pro-Union faction. They took him and his three sons out into the woods and started firing. The doctor and his oldest son were killed, the two younger sons, having made a dash for cover into the woods, escaped. They identified some of the killers, and a warrant was issued for them the next day. Turning themselves in to the court at Clinton, the Taylor clan so intimidated the local townsmen that all of them swore the killers were seen elsewhere during the time of the murders, and they went free. The judge appealed directly to the governor for ranger help. After investigating the whole town, Ranger Lieutenant Lee Hall took sixteen of his men on the night of December 22 and surrounded the house where one of the killers was celebrating his wedding. Hall, his carbine at the ready, walked into the house. The fiddler stopped. The dancers froze. Then the newlywed asked: "Do you want anybody here, Hall?"

"I do," thundered Hall. "I want seven men for murder. I want you . . ." and he called out the names.

One of the killers yelled: "How many men have you got?"

"Seventeen, counting myself."

"Well," retorted the killer, "we've got over seventy, and we'll fight it out."

"Now that's what I like to hear," Hall boomed. "Move out your women and children and be quick about it. We don't want to kill them, but we came down here for a fight and we want it." Hall's audacity stopped the killer. He pressed his point. "Get ready, men!" he shouted to his rangers outside. "They're going to move out the women and children and then we'll have it. Sweep the porches with those shotguns when I give the word, and shoot to kill!"

All seventy men hesitated. "We don't want to kill you all," said the killer meekly.

"Then give me that gun—quick," snapped Hall, and took it. He called in two of his men and within minutes the whole crowd was disarmed.

"You might let us finish our dance out," said the newlywed. "I've just been married."

"All right," Hall agreed. "But if any man tries to get away, we'll kill him. We'll take you all to town at daylight."

The party continued. The rangers kept guard all night, coming into the house two at a time to partake of the wedding meal. At dawn the seven killers and one more rounded up elsewhere on the way were brought into Clinton and jailed. The rangers guarded the jail and the court. The judge, despite Taylor clan threats, refused bail. The trials continued for years. There were numerous changes of venue, hung juries, overturned decisions, appeals, and finally pardons on the grounds that the accused had been good Confederate soldiers. The final decision in the last case came down in October 1899—thirty years after the feud had begun. Not one of Dr. Brassell's murderers spent a day in the penitentiary. But the killings had finally stopped in De Witt County.[4]

Meanwhile another feud in which scores were killed had erupted to the northwest of De Witt, in Mason County. It had started during the summer of 1874 over cattle rustling. Most of the thefts were carried out by outlaws, and their victims were usually the new settlers, mainly German-born farmers who had not supported the Confederacy during the war. Honest and hardworking, these settlers were also competing for land with the big cattle ranchers who aided the outlaws. By early spring 1875, the depletion of the herds had become serious. Then in March, Sheriff John Clark arrested five men on cattle-rustling complaints made out by the big ranchers. There was no evidence against them, but he brought them in and locked them up pending a hearing in the Mason jail. As soon as he left, a mob surrounded the jail and got Deputy John Worley to hand over the five. Informed at the last minute, Sheriff Clark and Ranger Lieutenant Dan Roberts, who happened to be in town buying grain, rushed to the lynching, their guns blazing. They managed to save two of the five, one of whom later gunned down a lyncher, then disappeared.

Two months later, Tim Williamson, a reputable stockman in charge of Charles Lemburg's herds, was arrested by Deputy Worley for supposedly stealing one cow owned by a major rancher. Lemburg offered to pay the cow's cost and put up Williamson's bond on the spot, but Worley refused. On the way into town they spotted a group of marked and masked men riding toward them. Sensing what was about to happen, Williamson begged the deputy to let him go. Instead, Worley shot his horse. Two minutes later, Williamson lay dying next to it. Scott Cooley, a former Texas Ranger who had been farming nearby and was a friend of Williamson's, heard about the lynching, went to Mason and found out the killers' names, got four more Williamson friends—John Ringgold, George Gladden, and John and Mose Beard—and rode for vengeance. In July they got one, a big cattleman. Next they tracked down Deputy Worley, and Scott Cooley shot him through the heart. In August, Cooley's men gunned down another. By then, Sheriff Clark was aware of Cooley's gang. He followed them until he caught them at Keller's Store near Cold Springs. In the shootout, Mose Beard was killed and George Gladden was shot nine times but survived. Cooley retaliated by killing the man who had betrayed them to Clark.

Major John Jones arrived with fifty rangers later that day. By then another of the lynchers had been killed in Mason itself. Jones learned that the rest of the lynchers, and some of their friends, had formed their own gang and were also roaming the hills hoping to kill Cooley and his riders before they killed them. Jones then dispatched his rangers to bring Cooley in, but none did, though rumor had it that they kept seeing him. Assembling his troops, Jones reminded them of their oath. He understood their sympathy for Cooley, he said, and offered an honorable discharge to any ranger who could not in all conscience carry out his orders. Cooley was now an outlaw, he said, and had to be stopped. Three rangers took the discharge; twelve asked and were granted transfers. The rest did their job. They caught Gladden, who had recovered and killed another lyncher, and sent him to jail. John Ringgold was also jailed but escaped and left the state, as did John Beard. Sheriff Clark resigned and left the country. Cooley returned to his bailiwick where friends hid him out until he died a few years later.[5]

Texas was full of bloody feuds in those days. In Lampasas County northwest of Austin, early in 1873, a local vigilante group, known as Minutemen, which had been organized to keep Indians, Mexicans, and blacks off good grazing land, was unable to curtail the rash of cattle rustling. The rustlers were led by five Harrell brothers and included their families and a dozen hangers-on. "I'm going to clean out those damned Harrell boys," boasted Captain Thomas Williams of the state police as he and his seven men stopped to have a drink on the way to

Lampasas town. As soon as he got there the shooting began. Captain Williams and three of his men were killed almost at once, while only one Harrell, Mart, was wounded. After taking Mart to convalesce at his mother's, the rest of the Harrell gang went into hiding, so that when a new state police detachment arrived, only Mart and three innocent friends got arrested. Once Mart had recuperated, the Harrells returned, battered down the jail door with sledgehammers and Winchesters, freed all the prisoners, and headed for New Mexico.

Settling down to raise—and steal—cattle in Lincoln County, the Harrell clan were soon in trouble. On December 1, 1873, they shot up the town, killing the Mexican sheriff but losing three men, including Ben Harrell, and returned three weeks later to avenge their dead clansmen by gunning down four Mexicans at a local dance. That provoked the governor to appeal for troops, and when President Grant responded by sending a detachment from Fort Stanton, the Harrells left Lincoln to return to Texas. On the way, they raided the farm of a white settler married to a Mexican, and got bushwacked in revenge by her family, losing one clansman. The Harrells then killed five hapless Mexicans they chanced upon on their way. Back in Lampasas, the Harrell clan continued to rob and steal until the last day of February 1874 when the sheriff with a posse of fifty surrounded them and brought them to jail. By October 1876, all twenty of those indicted were free, either acquitted or released on change-of-venue bonds. But the violence seemed to stop.

Then, in January 1877, a neighbor of the Harrells named John Pinckney ("Pink") Higgins accused the youngest of the Harrell brothers, Merritt, of stealing his cattle. The Harrells laughed him off. A few days later Pink strutted into the saloon where Merritt was guzzling and shot him four times. Tom and Mart were then bushwacked but only wounded in March. In April Pink Higgins was arrested by rangers, but in June all the files were stolen from the courthouse, freeing Pink from indictment. Three days later, the Harrells shot it out with Higgins and his friends, though only one man died. Finally, in July, a ranger detachment sent by Major Jones brought in both clans and forced them to sign a peace treaty. But in May 1878 the feud started again when the Harrells murdered a storeowner during a robbery. Mart and Tom Harrell were arrested by the rangers, indicted, and jailed at Meridian. One cold Sunday in December, more than a hundred masked horsemen invaded Meridian, kept all the people attending church services at bay, smashed into the jail and pumped hundreds of bullets into the two Harrell brothers. Later that day Pink Higgins, who had meanwhile sold his ranch, moved to New Mexico. The feud was finally over.[6]

The bloody confrontation that took place in that same period in the extreme western part of the state was not really a feud. It was a small war and is known as such—the El Paso Salt War. Caused primarily by the difference in concepts of law between Mexicans and gringos, it vividly illustrates how America's obsession with private property led to misery and murder. The first problem was the border. For generations, Mexicans had waded or walked during the dry seasons across the Rio Grande without incident. Then Texas became American and suddenly the river was meant to be an international boundary, with those on one side being Mexicans and those on the other Americans. Obviously, this political boundary had little meaning to the Mexicans whose family members lived on both sides. More important, land was not private to Mexicans; it belonged to the *pueblo,* literally, to the people, or the community, and was portioned out to each family by the *alcalde,* or mayor, according to need. Some Mexicans grew rich, though most of course remained poor. But the system worked well enough and the feuds that occurred had to do with honor, broken marriage promises, or personal insults, not with property. When the river dried up and the valley around El Paso grew sterile, there was one other way to survive: The tough *hombres* of the area would trudge up the two long roads to Guadalupe Peak, a hundred miles to the east, collect its high-quality salt, and sell it on both sides of the border.

But then the Anglos moved in. No one had actually claimed the land legally, so in 1865 one man grabbed the best part. Before that led to a showdown, it was discovered that better salt, or at least more of it, existed outside his land. But then, in 1868, a group of whites, who became known as the Salt Ring, grabbed the rest. For a while, Mexicans continued to mine the salt without much problem as the Salt Ring members broke up into two factions and fought it out among themselves. Finally in 1872, Charles Howard, a Democrat lawyer from Missouri who had fought well in the Confederate cavalry and was an excellent shot and a smooth politician, started taking over the salt lands. It took him five years (and at least one murder) to consolidate his hold, but by 1877 he ran the area politically, legally (he had become district judge), and financially. With that, he posted the land and warned that he would "prosecute anybody who raids my property."

Outraged, the Mexicans banded together and took the salt by force of arms. The confrontation became so bloody that the governor sent the rangers. Leaders of the Mexicans rallied their people: Two hundred volunteered to do battle. More rangers, white vigilantes, and two sheriffs' posses arrived. The Mexicans increased their armed combatants to five hundred, and surrounded the ranger station, where Howard and his top aides had holed up. After four days of shooting, Lieutenant John B. Tays, the ranger in command, surrendered—the only ranger officer ever to have done so. The Mexicans took Howard and his aides and executed them by firing squad. By January 1878, more rangers had reestablished Anglo control, though permission to haul out the rock salt from the Guadalupe mountain was wisely granted back to the Mexicans. In March, a grand jury of whites indicted the six leaders of El Paso's Mexican army. The governor then offered fat rewards for their capture. Not one Mexican ever tried to collect, and the six were never caught.[7]

The really big wars, in Texas and throughout the West and Southwest, were about land and livestock. And they were usually fomented, or started directly, by the land barons. Many of them got their land by cheating the settlers: first they claimed the 160 acres allowed all homesteaders, then they had their relatives, their bankers, and their cowhands claim the land adjacent, legally combining it all within a few years by showing sale records. Historians estimate that less than one out of every ten acres actually went to homesteaders. The rest was grabbed up by the barons, who operated in syndicates. Between 1880 and 1884, such trusts, organized mostly in New York and Boston, seized almost 50 million acres.

These cattle barons ganged up on the small settler in various ways. First of all, they organized armies of rustlers to harass and ruin the independent stockman. From 1862 to 1864, raiders from Kansas stole more than 3 million head of cattle belonging to Indians, who had already lost their buffalo herds, and to northern Texans. The barons often had the small ranchers framed as rustlers and got the sheriffs, who were always in the barons' pay, and local vigilantes, whom they also paid and led, to track down and often kill independents. Next they got their state legislatures, which they controlled, especially in Texas and Kansas, to create boards of livestock commissioners. The boards hired inspectors and detectives, usually local gunslingers, to supervise roundups and handle the sale of mavericks. All animals with "unacceptable" brands, meaning not owned by cattlemen association members, were confiscated and sold by the board to the members. In 1884 in Texas that amounted to sixteen thousand head of cattle worth a market value of $35 to $45 each, sold to members at $3. The board then used its cut to pay the wages of the "inspectors." The big cattlemen also used blacklists to stop new settlers: Any cowboy who owned land, bought cattle, or accepted payment in stock was prohibited from working on the members' ranches. Since the small ranchers could rarely afford to hire help, the blacklist was most effective in keeping ambitious cowboys from starting ranches of their own.

Many of the settlers could not afford cattle. But they could start a sheep herd. Propagating the theory that sheep destroy cattle grazing land, the cattle barons sparked a sheep war which, on and off, continued until World War I. They ordered their cowhands to don masks and raid the sheepmen. The sheep were poisoned, clubbed, shot, dynamited, burned, and stampeded over cliffs. Charles Hanna, who first brought sheep into Brown County, Texas, in 1869, decided not to argue with the false propaganda about the danger to grazing land; he kept his sheep corralled. One morning when he went out to turn them loose onto his walled-in range, he found every one of his 300 sheep with its throat cut. In 1883, sheepherders were ordered at gunpoint to leave Texas. In 1894, raiding parties in Garfield County, Wyoming, stampeded 3,800 sheep over a bluff into Parachute Creek. In Piñon Mesa in the same county in 1902, two-thirds of a flock of 1,000 Angora goats were stabbed by fourteen masked cowmen. In 1906, raiders shot 200 sheep grazing in Dominguez Canyon. In Garfield, again in 1909, 1,500 sheep were clubbed and knifed during the night. Most cattle ranchers, big or small, believed the propaganda about sheep and goats. They even believed it when, after sheep farms were fenced in, the cattle barons said that sheep ruin grazing lands even when they don't graze in them. For the cattle barons, it was simple economics: If lamb wasn't available, beef prices would soar. By 1880, America had 40 million head of cattle, one-third of them in the Great Plains and territories.[8]

Another tool used by the big cattlemen to ruin the small and independent rancher was wire fencing. Most of the barons, and syndicates operating through dummy ranchers, owned the best land, meaning land where water was available. By fencing such land they cut off water from the small ranchers' cattle, which would soon die, forcing the ranchers to sell out. In 1874, the amount of barbed wire installed on the range was 10,000 pounds. Two years later, the figure had jumped to 2,840,000. By 1880, the number was 80,500,000. Nor could homesteaders afford barbed wire. In 1974 the cost was $20.00 per 100-pound roll. After that the price dropped steadily to $3.45 in 1890, but it was still too expensive for the small rancher. Of course, if he did fence his land, the cattle barons organized fence-cutting raids. But usually it was the small rancher, seeing financial ruin, who would cut fence.

After sending thousands of petitions to state legislatures and then to the interior secretary complaining that the fences prevented their cattle from reaching the water holes on public lands, to which all citizens were guaranteed access, and getting no response, the small ranchers organized themselves into groups of night raiders and cut fences. The big cattlemen, who spent fortunes fencing their lands, were furious. The Frying Pan Ranch in the Texas panhandle, for example, had spent $39,000 for wire and posts to fence its 250,000 acre pasture. What's more, the barons fenced everything—roads, towns, other peoples' farms. In Archer County, the county seat was totally blocked off. When drought hit Texas in 1883, the small ranchers went berserk and started cutting everywhere. The nine miles of fence around Abel H. Pierce's ranch on the coastal plain was cut between each post. On a Tehuacana Creek ranch, south of Waco, not only were the wires around the 700 acres snipped, but the fields were set aflame. In Tom Green County, cutters must have labored long hours to snap the wire between each post in a ranch nineteen miles long. In all Texas between the years 1880 and 1885, some $20 million worth of wire was destroyed. As a result, the Texas legislature in 1884 made fence cutting a felony, punishable by five years in jail, and ordered the rangers to pursue the cutters. Putting up an illegal fence, however, was deemed a misdemeanor, even if it was done knowingly. The legislature gave such ranchers six months to tear them down or, if they blocked public roads, to install gates. The dice were loaded in favor of the cattle barons. They won the fence war.[9]

Not all the feuds of the times were of such proportions. The fifteen-year battle between the Hatfields and McCoys apparently started over a sow and some pigs. Living on opposite sides of a stream dividing West Virginia from Kentucky, the Hatfields and McCoys were also divided ideologically. William Anderson ("Devil Anse") Hatfield had been a

Confederate captain, while Randolph McCoy had fought as a Union irregular. They did have one trade in common—moonshine—but that didn't seem to bind them any closer. By 1888, when the feud ended, a whole slew of Hatfields and McCoys had been killed.

Another such feud took place during ten years in Williamson County, Illinois, a bloody place originally settled by hardy and hospitable but prejudiced and superstitious mountain folk from Tennessee, the Carolinas, and Virginia. One historian counted no fewer than 495 assaults with a deadly weapon and 285 murders there between the years 1839 and 1876. The biggest feud, begun in 1868 over a crop of oats, involved four families: the Hendersons and the Sisneys on one side, the Bulliners and the Crains on the other. By the time it ended, "Old George" Bulliner and two of his sons; Marshall Crain; James Henderson; George Sisney; and a couple of dozen of their friends and relatives were dead, and six more were in jail. Between 1890 and 1906, strikes at the local mines, which exploited diggers as harshly as anywhere else in America, led to the deaths of another score of folks, but it was the Henderson-Bulliner feud that gave the county the name Bloody Williamson.[10]

But for the most part the killings were over land desired by the railroads, the cattle barons, or the timber trusts. In 1880, in the fertile valley around Mussel Slough, in what is now Kings County just south of Fresno, California, the killer was the Central Pacific Railroad owned by Leland Stanford, California's former governor and future senator. Led by one John J. Doyle, who had carefully studied the land-grants provisions and concluded that the valley could not be claimed by the railroads, a bunch of settlers had begun farming the area in 1871. So successful had they become by 1874, that Doyle petitioned Washington for title for himself and his neighbors. He was ignored. He tried again. After three hundred appeals, the farmers set up a Settlers' Land League, raised money among themselves, and sent Doyle to Washington in 1875. He managed to talk some representatives into introducing a bill for relief of the settlers, but it was defeated by the stalwart railroad congressmen. Still, the farmers kept at it, investing time, money, and effort to make the valley bloom. In 1879, Doyle went back to Washington, but failed again. Later that year, after the farmers had jointly completed a vast irrigation project to benefit them all, a federal court ruled that the land belonged to the railroad if it wanted it. Doyle then appealed to Stanford himself and invited him to come see the valley, which he did in April 1880. Stanford looked impressed, and agreed to discuss possible settlements.

Instead, a month later, a United States marshal and deputies showed up with a dispossession order. But they did not present it. A barbecue for the whole region was in progress, so the marshal asked to talk to Doyle. The two men and some of Doyle's friends went off into a nearby tent. While they talked, some of the other farmers approached the deputies. Two of the farmers were armed, but their weapons were down. One of the deputies, whose name was Crow, had been a farmer in the valley. The men taunted him a bit. Then, suddenly another deputy fired, hitting no one. One of the armed farmers replied, hitting the deputy in the groin. Crow aimed his shotgun at the farmer and killed him. Then he aimed at another farmer, unarmed, who was just sitting dazed on his horse. Crow's shot catapulted him into the air, dead. Crow reloaded his shotgun and killed another unarmed farmer. He walked a hundred feet up to a rancher who seemed paralyzed with fright and put two bullets from his pistol through the man's chest. At that point the only other armed farmer, trembling with rage, fired at Crow but missed. Crow killed him too. Then he left the scene and started to walk to his house a mile and a half away. He never got there; some farmer bushwacked him on the way and killed him. When the wounded deputy died, the toll became six.

Seventeen farmers, including Doyle, who had been with the marshal and had not yet seen or been told about the dispossession order when the shooting started, were indicted for resisting arrest and sent to jail. As for the rest, they were given a choice: get off the railroad lands or pay $25.00 to $30.00 per acre (the going price was then $2.50 an acre). News of the massacre spread throughout California. No less than forty-seven thousand people signed a petition on behalf of Doyle and the other sixteen in jail and sent it to President Hayes. Neither Hayes nor any other official responded. A few years later, a rash of armed robberies began to plague Leland Stanford's Southern Pacific Railroad. When one of the bandits was caught, he identified himself proudly as a farmer from Mussell Slough.[11]

Farmers weren't the only folks cheated in California. Lumberjacks saw whole northern forests, and those of Oregon and Washington, whipped out from under their feet by the great land speculators who resold them to eastern timber trusts. No sooner did Congress pass the Timber and Stone Act in June 1878, which was meant to give 160 acres to each person who worked the land, than the speculators, using dummy names, fraudulent affidavits, and wide-scale bribery, laid claims to the choicest sections. Whenever some homesteader managed to outfox them, they simply had him killed. Stephen Douglas Puter, known as the king of the Oregon land fraud, was later caught and confessed all in a book. He told how he and his partners used to round up sailors from the ships that stopped along the coast, or the poor folk in the various cities' rooming houses, offer them $100 a piece to sign and register the land-grant forms they had already filled out, then sell the combined package to eastern syndicates. Sometimes an investigation was initiated by the General Land Office. On such occasions, Puter said, he would merely bribe the investigators. In one case which got challenged in Washington, Puter bribed every official up the line, from Eureka, the Humboldt County Seat, and Portland, Oregon, all the way to Washington. He got the commissioner of the General Land Office for $500, and the key senator, John H. Mitchell, for $2,000.[12]

Though scores of lumberjacks got bushwacked during these frauds, few of them led to wholesale slaughters. Along the plains and cattle trails, however, massacres were rather common. There, the West was certainly wild. In great part, the reason was that so many former soldiers, trained to ride well and kill quickly during the Civil War, were now unemployed. They had flocked west to find land. Instead they discovered that corruption had become standard not only among the cattle barons but also among the lawmen, the state officials and even the government agents and U.S. Army commanders. Most of the unemployed veterans could find neither land, which was practically monopolized by the barons, nor jobs. Some started robbing stagecoaches and, after 1868 when the railroadmen teamed up with the big ranchers to take over the land of the small settlers, the railroads. Since communications were so poor, such robberies were relatively easy and, contrary to myth, involved very little violence. Between 1870 and 1884, Wells, Fargo and Company reported that 313 of its stages had been hit, yet only four passengers, four drivers and two guards were killed. Of the robbers, eleven were gunned down and seven were hanged.

Most of the veterans who went west ended up as paid employees of the cattle barons, and it was these respectable ranchers who turned them into rustlers as they ordered them to steal the cattle of their competitors or, more often, of the smaller ranchers. In fact, one careful historian has estimated that more than half of the western outlaws were hired hands, at least at the beginning of their gunslinging careers.[13]

Such gunslingers were all over Lincoln County, New Mexico, after the Civil War. Established as a territorial county in 1869, Lincoln was made up of hundreds of thousands of acres along the fertile Pecos River Valley in the southeastern sector of the state, the home of the Mescalero Apaches. The Indians were driven off, the buffaloes and antelopes were butchered, and the best part of the range was fenced off for the ninety thousand head of cattle driven up from Texas in 1872. Agricultural, mostly grain, farms were also set up. Huge fortunes began to be made on these lands of the public domain. And the rivalries inevitably led to wars.

Since New Mexico did not become a state until 1912, all top officials were appointed by Washington. The Santa Fe Ring, as these officials became known, were all corrupt, including Governor Samuel B. Axtell; Attorney General Thomas B. Catron; the government agent for Indian affairs; the district attorney for Lincoln; the sheriff; the commander of Fort Stanton, which was the biggest army base in the area; and various of their underlings. The ring, headed by Catron, who was also a banker, land speculator, and financier, at first worked closely with Lawrence G. Murphy. Murphy was an Irish immigrant who had fought with the Union forces, then had become a sutler at Fort Stanton, and in 1869 had established a general merchandising and livestock company in Lincoln. Another Irish-born Union veteran, James J. Dolan, who had worked for Murphy and took over the firm when Murphy died in 1878, expanded the livestock operation. That consisted of stealing cattle and selling them to the government for the Indians. For this operation, Dolan not only made Catron an actual though silent partner but also hooked Governor Axtell by lending him money. He and his partners also needed a great many gunmen. They got them by hiring Jesse Evans, a vicious Texas-born murderer who put together a formidable gang of some fifty gunslingers, some of them Union veterans, others homeless Confederates, others still former Quantrill raiders on the lam, and a few cowpoke drifters. The Catron-Dolan-Evans syndicate, backed by lawmen, the courts, and the local military, ruled Lincoln County almost unchallenged until the nineties.

The syndicate did have one powerful enemy, however, a Tennessee-born Scotsman named John S. Chisum, who had started amassing cattle in Texas in 1854 and in 1863 drove 10,000 head up the Pecos to sell them to the Navajos and Mescaleros. Settling in the unclaimed, unsurveyed land in the public domain along the Pecos, and keeping out all competitors by friendly persuasion if possible but by the gun if not, Chisum soon owned the largest herd in America and probably the world—100,000 cattle, much of which his cowboys had rustled from Indians and small ranchers. But Chisum was not pleased with the Dolan monopoly on grain and dealings with the Indians. So he teamed up with one Alexander A. McSween, a Presbyterian minister turned lawyer, and John H. Tunstall, a refined English adventurer who expected to survive by never carrying a gun, and financed them into launching first a merchandising company that soon outflanked Dolan's by contracting all the independent farmers and then a bank which panicked the Santa Fe Ring. The ensuing war between the two factions led to the death of more than a hundred cowboys—and made William H. Bonney world famous.

Born in a slum tenement in New York City in 1859, Billy is said to have killed his first man at twelve or fourteen. His family had moved to Kansas and from 1862 to 1875 when he arrived in Lincoln, he is supposed to have gambled and killed occasionally to survive. What is known for sure is that he was hungry and unemployed when Dolan spotted him, saw his skill with a six-shooter and hired him as a cowhand. His job was rustling cattle, mainly from Chisum's Jinglebob Ranch. Billy did as he was told for a while but when he met Tunstall in town one day, he was so impressed by the Englishman's suave, polite, patronizing manner, which Billy interpreted as care and interest, that he switched sides. Tunstall was then murdered in cold blood by a posse deputized by the Dolan-appointed sheriff and led by Evans. Billy swore revenge. Within a month he had killed several members of the posse, including the sheriff (but not Evans, who was always too fast with the gun or with a getaway horse). One day, a group of fifty Dolan men managed to surround Chisum's troop at McSween's ranch house. The gunfight lasted three days (some say five) before one of Evans's gunslingers sneaked through the barrage to set the house aflame. McSween was killed as he rushed out, and Billy shot the assailing deputy through the head as he escaped. That made him the most wanted man in New Mexico, and when Pat Garrett was made sheriff in 1880, he declared that getting Billy would be his top priority.

A brutal, sadistic gunman, Garrett tracked Billy for months. In July 1881, he caught him unawares in an old ranch house and shot him in the back. Billy the Kid was then twenty-one—and was reputed to have killed twenty-one men. As for Garrett, who as a loyal Dolan henchman was judged to have committed "justifiable homicide," he was himself gunned down in 1908 by one of the tenants on his farm, whom he had long and mercilessly exploited. Garrett's killer was acquitted on grounds of self-defense.

President Hayes replaced Governor Axtell and sent federal troops to Lincoln. That brought the war to a close. Only the pawns and a few secondary money-men had died; the principals, as usual, survived. Chisum retained both his fortune and his title as cattle king. Catron became head of New Mexico's Republican party and enjoyed his millions until his death in 1921. Evans, who was tried for murdering a Texas Ranger and escaped in 1882, was never recaptured. Dolan retired to wealth and splendor.[14]

The rich also triumphed in Johnson County, Wyoming, where a similar war raged on and off from 1879 to 1892. The antagonists there were more clear-cut. On one side were all the small settlers, homesteaders, and independents who came after the Civil War and tried to eke a living from the land. On the other were the big cattlemen, many of whom had made their fortunes and grabbed the best land during the Civil War. The cattle barons viewed all small ranchers who managed to survive as rustlers and inevitably hanged them. It was in fact after the hanging of the popular Ella Watson, known as Cattle Kate, and her lover Jim Averill, who were both described as rustlers but were actually small homesteaders, that a full war broke out.

In 1891, the cattle barons decided to do away with the settlers once and for all. They had organized themselves into the Wyoming Stock Growers' Association and had decreed that any cattle found in possession of any nonmember would be considered stolen unless the rancher could produce a bill of sale from the association itself. Thus armed with a self-proclaimed legal edict, they went after the independents. But the small settlers and ranchers, who quickly bound together into a self-defense association, fought back with surprising success. So, in 1892, the stock growers started recruiting a vast army of gunfighters from Montana, Idaho, Colorado, and mainly Texas. Armed with brand-new weapons given them by Wyoming's governor, the growers' army invaded settler territory. The Texas contingent came up by Pullman cars on a train chartered in Denver. They all met in Casper, on the Powder River, and started shooting at the homesteaders, killing the very best of Wyoming's pioneering settlers. Federal troops eventually arrived on the scene and arrested forty-five of the killers. They were then all given bail, which the wealthy cattlemen easily raised, and released. The gunslingers from Texas quickly disappeared. Only the indicted Wyoming cattlemen showed up for their trials in 1893. The prosecution called not a single witness. The case was dropped.[15]

No wonder there were so many killers in the Wild West. The rich and the greedy, killers themselves, had too often proved that the way to get ahead was to steal and to murder. And the law was nearly always on their side. Thus, the gunslingers of the West were sometimes lawmen, sometimes outlaws, sometimes both. In any case, none of them were anything like the men celebrated by myth and television. They rarely got into *mano a mano* showdowns, rarely risked death for honor's sake. Usually they shot their victims in the back. Black Bart (real name Charles E. Bolton), for example, has often been described as a robber who never used a gun. In fact, he held up twenty-seven stagecoaches, most of which were carrying mail, and always at gunpoint. The myth about him was probably generated by raconteurs who liked his verse. In one Wells Fargo strongbox he had lifted off a stage, emptied, then abandoned, he left this ditty:

> I've labored long and hard for bred,
> For honor and for riches,
> But on my corns too long you've tred,
> You fine-haired sons of bitches.[16]

Sam Bass, a train robber born in Indiana, first used the gun as a deputy sheriff of Denton County, Texas, then stole horses from the Choctaws in Indian Territory. He double-crossed friends and kept their loot, but got crossed himself at twenty-seven and was killed by rangers during a bank robbery in 1878.

Robert Dalton was a deputy marshal in 1888 in Indian Territory and used that post to plan railroad robberies with his brothers. The Dalton gang went on to rob banks and eventually got wiped out (three dead, one captured and sent to the pen) when they tried to hit two banks simultaneously in their hometown of Coffeyville, Kansas.

Tom Horn was deputy sheriff of Yavapai County, Arizona, in 1888 when he brought in the Apache Kid and was probably one of those paid off in the plot that sprung the Kid. From 1890 to 1894, he worked for

James McParlan, the old Pinkerton union buster, then probably hired his gun to the Powder River invaders in the Johnson County War, but was eventually tried and convicted of murdering sheepherders and was hanged in 1903.[17]

Contrary to myth, Jesse James never rode with Quantrill. Jim Younger, who rode with Jesse in Missouri, was a deputy sheriff in Texas. William P. Longley supposedly outdrew thirty-two men; in fact, he shot them in the back. Most of his victims were unarmed blacks. Henry Plummer, whose gang of a hundred or more highwaymen robbed everyone around Bannack, Montana, was sheriff and mayor of the town.[18]

The most famous gunfighters of the West, who were both lawless and lawmen, were, of course, Wyatt Earp and Bat Masterson. Both were basically professional gamblers and crooked faro dealers. Both were brawlers, though Masterson pretended not to carry weapons in order to avoid gunfights. Both desperately sought badges to give them cover for their illicit activities and allow them to carry weapons legally in the frontier towns that banned them, such as Dodge, Wichita and Tombstone. Earp and his alcoholic and sadistic sidekick, John ("Doc") Holliday, a Georgia-born racist, tubercular dentist who had fled west after killing a series of unarmed blacks, both liked to beat up women. Holliday was also a notorious pimp and professional gambler. The whole group, deputy sheriffs or not, were repeatedly run out of western towns, and they all landed in Tombstone in 1881, where Virgil Earp, Wyatt's brother, was marshal. Masterson missed the famous gunfight at O.K. Corral, which really took place in a street nearby, because he had to rush back to Dodge City when his younger brother, Jim, the marshal there, became involved in a feud and was afraid to do his own shooting. The O.K. Corral gunfight itself has long been a bone of contention among historians. At the inquest, Virgil Earp and his brothers, as well as Holliday, whom Earp had deputized, were found innocent of murdering the three Clanton clansmen. But the folk of Tombstone thought otherwise, and they ran the lot out of town. Masterson was also chased out of Dodge. For a while they all ended up in Denver, gambling. Wyatt Earp managed to avoid an extradition warrant from Arizona and went on to California where he died in his bed in 1929, a fading legend. Masterson, hustled out of Denver, took a train for New York in 1902, fleeced a Mormon elder of $16,000 at faro, got arrested upon arrival but was saved by Big Tim Sullivan who then ran Tammany Hall. Though constantly in trouble, and arrested again for carrying a concealed weapon, Masterson's bogus legend led President Theodore Roosevelt to appoint him deputy marshal for southern New York. He ended his career as a sports writer for the *Morning Telegraph,* and died at his desk in 1921.[19]

A legend has also been created around the outlaws known as the Wild Bunch, especially since Hollywood romanticized two of them in the film *Butch Cassidy and the Sundance Kid.* Though they often rode with the Ketchum gang, a group of nasty killers, the Wild Bunch was a far more engaging troop of thieves to romanticize. For they had become outlaws in response to the actions of railroadmen and cattle barons, who either stole their lands, causing them to become drifters, or ruined them by placing strangleholds on irrigated grazing lands and markets. The Bunch included, among others, its leader, Butch Cassidy, born George Leroy Parker in Circleville, Utah, in 1867; and Harvey Logan, a part Cherokee Kentuckian who was run out of his Wyoming homestead by big cattlemen. Logan changed his name to Curry and tried homesteading again near Landusky, Montana, but was harassed by Pike Landusky, the deputy marshal who had founded the mining town. This led to a showdown in which Landusky drew first but was killed. Other members were Ben Kilpatrick and Bill Carver, poor cowboys from Concho County, Texas, who were charged with murder when they defended themselves against the cattle barons and killed one; and Harry Longabaugh, a Texas trail herdman who rustled the cattle of the barons around Sundance, Wyoming, but was not known as the Sundance Kid.

By the time Butch Cassidy welded these and scores of other cowboys—at one point the Wild Bunch could roster up to a hundred riders—into a disciplined, professional gang, all had been hardened criminals in their own right. But none had robbed the poor. They were easygoing, fun-loving, generous, expert horsemen who rustled the cattle from the great spreads, helped out the small homesteader at roundup, and were reputed never to have welched on a debt or squealed on a friend. From Mexico to Canada their reputation was golden, and thus all along the difficult trails they easily found friends or strangers to hide them out, furnish fresh horses, and cover up their tracks, usually by taking the holdup horses, cleaning them, and putting them into their own herds. The Bunch would then flee on fresh horses or disguised as merchants or farmers in slow-moving wagons.

By the turn of the century, the Wild Bunch was known all over the West, indeed perhaps throughout America, Mexico, and Canada. It was then that they staged their most spectacular robberies, such as the bank heist at Winnemucca, Nevada, on September 19, 1900 which netted $32,000 and the raid on the Great Northern Railroad express at Wagner, Montana, on July 3, 1901. A few months later the Bunch broke up. Logan (Curry) was caught but escaped from a Tennessee penitentiary in 1903; he made his way back to Colorado, realized he could never go straight, and shot himself on June 4, 1904. Bill Carver had been recognized in Sonora, Texas, in 1901, and was shot getting off his horse. Ben Kilpatrick was killed in Texas in 1912. Cassidy, Longabaugh and his lover, Etta Place, made it to New York, took a freighter to Buenos Aires, bought a ranch in central Argentina, then started rustling the European potentates who set up vast ranches and were exploiting the poor mestizo peons. It took a whole provincial army to surround them. At that point Cassidy shot Harry Longabaugh and then himself.[20]

To the literally thousands of railroad cops, Pinkertons, federal marshals, and assorted lawmen who had tried to catch the Wild Bunch, that was the end of the greatest outlaws of the West. The governors of Colorado, Utah, and Wyoming had once even held a special conference in Salt Lake City just for the purpose of coping with the Wild Bunch. But to the armies of poor settlers, handicapped homesteaders, and exploited cowboys up and down the trails from Texas to Montana, the Wild Bunch were much more than outlaws. They were avengers, rebels against the tyrannical railroads and cattle trusts which made the West so lawless by legally pillaging the public domain.

Chapter 17

Red, Yellow, Black

In its four thousand years of recorded history the world has witnessed a number of holocausts in which an entire race was systematically exterminated. Genocide is the term of international law for such exterminations. Usually it is carried out as a matter of legal, state policy, as when Nazi Germany attempted its "final solution," the total obliteration of the Jewish people in Europe. Sometimes it is justified under a contrived pretext, as when the Turks under Abdul Hamid II massacred the Armenians on the grounds that they were subverting his empire. When white Americans tried to exterminate the Indians, they relied on neither policy nor pretext. They did it out of greed, and without benefit of law. They simply wanted the Indians' land and the resources that lay beneath it. The resulting record of white lawlessness is of course notorious: Indian tribes were forced to sign 370 treaties with the federal government, each one of which was violated until they had lost almost 2 billion acres of land. By World War I, more than a million Indian people had been killed.[1]

Land was certainly the principal attraction in the westward expansion. But there were other, lesser profits to be made by the petty exploiters who joined in the extermination game. The most grizzly enterprise was the traffic in human scalps. In Denver in the 1870s,

Indian scalps were worth $10 each. In Central City the price was $25, in Deadwood, South Dakota, $200. Naturally, the killers were proud of their bloody prizes. Kit Carson, who "pacified" the Navajos in New Mexico in 1862–63 for the Indian-hating military commander, General James H. Carlton, bragged how he destroyed everything in the Indian villages, not just people but also "more than two million pounds of Navajo grain." The Navajos who were taken prisoner and interned in the forts of Canby and Wingate didn't fare much better. In a single week in 1864 at Fort Canby, 126 died of dysentery and exposure. Congress then allotted $100,000 for relief of the Navajo prisoners. The Bureau of Indian Affairs channeled most of that sum into the pockets of its own corrupt agents or supplier friends, paying, for example, $18.50 for army blankets that retailed at $5.85. Only about $30,000 worth of goods ever reached the Navajos; by May 1868, more than two thousand of the near ten thousand prisoners were dead.[2]

Fearing similar treatment, the Cheyenne and Arapaho decided to sign a peace treaty. The federal government promised to give them supplies for the winter if they stayed on their reservation, which they did. Then, early one morning in November 1864, when most of the camp was still asleep, the Colorado Volunteers under Colonel John M. Chivington attacked them without warning at Sand Creek, killing 450 men, women, and children. Chivington's men systematically raped the young women before scalping them, cut off the dead braves' genitals and placed both on display when they returned to Denver. Congress demanded an investigation of the massacre, which was carried out in 1865, but nothing came of it except a 500-page report two years later detailing the corruption of Colorado Indian agents and the miserable conditions of the tribes.[3]

As more whites poured into the Plains, the government wanted to extend the Powder River Road from Laramie to the goldfields of Bozeman, Montana, through the territory of the Dakota Indians. Ignoring the treaty, which forbade it, federal troops went ahead and built forts along the trail. In January 1865, incensed over the Sand Creek massacre, a thousand Cheyennes and Dakotas attacked the stockade at Julesburg, killing eighteen whites and stealing all the provisions. They also attacked the cavalry near Horse Creek, and when they found scalps from Sand Creek in the wagons, chopped up the soldiers. Led by Crazy Horse, they hit outposts all along the road. A detachment of soldiers commanded by Captain Fetterman, who boasted that he could seize all the Dakota nation with fifty men, went in hot pursuit. Crazy Horse fled until Fetterman was well into the icy waters of the Peno River, then turned around and hit him from all sides. Every soldier in Fetterman's eighty-man detachment was killed. Crazy Horse lost thirteen of his own. But it was only a temporary victory. More soldiers came, then more, and still more. Finally Red Cloud signed another treaty, which Crazy Horse honored—until Congress broke it by passing a rider to the budget that denied the rights of Indians to sign treaties.[4]

Obviously jealous of Chivington's Sand Creek massacre, General George Custer brought his troops up onto the Washita River in Oklahoma on Thanksgiving Day 1868. He waited until the Indians in a small village across the bend were fast asleep, then, violating the Treaty of Medicine Lodge, attacked in force, killing all its occupants—103 men and an unknown number of women and children, whom Custer didn't think were worth adding up. At Camp Grant, Arizona, in 1871, a detachment from Tucson attacked 300 women, old men, and children working the field under firm protection of the U.S. Army, killed 118 women, 8 men, and sold 30 children into slavery in Mexico. President Grant, in this case, was furious. He demanded a trial of the murderers. He got one, but the judge told the all-white jury that killing Indians who might be a menace was not murder. The defendants were acquitted. The local Denver newspaper remarked: "We congratulate them on the fact that permanent peace arrangements have been made with so many and we only regret that the number was not double. Camp Grant is the last of those victories for civilization and progress which have made Sand Creek, Washita . . . and other similar occurrences famous in western history."[5]

In the summer of 1872, the Northern Pacific Railroad, protected by four hundred federal soldiers, broke another treaty and came right into Oglala, Dakota Territory, laying tracks. Crazy Horse led his warriors into various skirmishes but avoided full battle. Now commanded by Custer, the cavalry sought out the Dakota Sioux, but Crazy Horse stayed mobile. In 1875, miners invaded the Black Hills, sacred ground of all the Sioux tribes; Crazy Horse, joined by Sitting Bull, harassed the invaders. Red Cloud again negotiated with the whites, agreeing to let them into the hills for $6 million worth of provisions per year for seven generations and a white promise to respect the sacred lands. But there was gold in those hills, and the whites violated the treaty once again.

Crazy Horse and Sitting Bull attacked. Custer pursued and pursued and pursued—to the Little Big Horn and his own death. More troops came. Finally in May 1877, Crazy Horse realized it was useless. He agreed to parley. Instead he was jailed by Little Big Man, his former ally, under orders of Red Cloud, who had become nothing more than a paid federal agent. Crazy Horse drew his knife. Held by Little Big Man and another Indian renegade, Swift Bear, Crazy Horse was run through from behind by a bayonet, on orders of Red Cloud. The final act of exterminating the Indians was underway.[6]

The white man got the Indian lands, which the Indians had never considered private property, for, as the chief of the Nez Percé Indians once said, "No man owns any part of the earth. No man can sell what he does not own." The white man didn't own it, but he sold it, or stole it and then sold it. But it wasn't ordinary people who got it, at least not much of it. As the railroads and the cattle and timber men reaped millions, the ordinary settler paid more and more to ship his farm products to market and received less and less for them. The homesteader-rancher was fenced off from water. The workers' wages were repeatedly cut. From suffering and frustration came anger. But anger against whom? If the common laborer attacked the railroad president, the mineowner, the distributor, the landlord, he would soon be jobless, beaten, perhaps even killed. So he attacked the foreigner, the one who looked different or thought differently, the one who worked for lower wages.[7]

The blacks, of course, were the hardest hit by such racism. But they weren't the only ones. In the West the victims were Chinese. They were brought to America to do tough menial jobs. As contract laborers, they built the railroads, worked in mines, built bridges, wrapped cigars. They were paid less than whites and were charged a special tax which whites were not. But they lived together in large families and in tight little neighborhoods soon described as Chinatowns. Isolated by language, custom, and strict family hierarchy, they developed a tradition of frugality and saving that enabled them quietly to accumulate small parcels of property. Not surprisingly, their relative financial gains only exacerbated the already existing hostility of the white workmen. Before the Civil War there were fifty thousand Chinese in California alone and in 1861 they paid some $14 million to the state and communities in special taxes and licenses. In 1864, there were a thousand whites and three thousand Chinese working on Leland Stanford's Central Pacific

Railroad, which paid the Chinese one-third the wages of whites. Between 1865 and 1869, there were still a thousand whites but the number of Chinese had grown to nine thousand.[8]

Then, in 1869, the railroad was finished and suddenly the nine thousand were on the job market competing against whites. Competition led to confrontation, and anti-Chinese riots. Egged on by the *San Francisco Chronicle,* founded by three de Young brothers in 1865 as the *Daily Dramatic Chronicle,* the Bay Area's whites constantly harassed, often stoned, and occasionally killed the Chinese. The de Youngs called themselves antimonopoly reformers and protectors of the working class. But they protected whites only and their real interest was power, which they intended to get by crusading against the installed politicians and backing a slate that could overthrow them. For that role the de Youngs chose a white workingman's party organized by a bigoted Irish immigrant named Denis Kearney who campaigned under the slogan "The Chinese Must Go."[9]

Meanwhile, the Chinese were having an even tougher time outside San Francisco. Even before the end of the Civil War, Chinese miners had been driven out of the Nevada silver mines by angry whites. In one incident at French Corral all the Chinese cabins were destroyed and scores of Chinese were severely beaten. One white was arrested and found guilty of provoking the riot and was fined $100. Then, in 1867, anti-Chinese agitation became worse in all the mining camps. In California, they were forbidden to testify in the courts, and no white seemed to care much what happened to them. In Mariposa, since no white man ever came forward to testify against fellow whites who attacked Chinese, prosecutions came to a standstill. Chinese were robbed, beaten, and killed, and women were raped. The justification was that all Chinese women were prostitutes, and this was based on the fact that there were so few women living in the Chinese community. Indeed in 1870, only 7.1 percent of the total Chinese population were women, and of these many were prostitutes, since they could get no other jobs. In a census taken in six mining communities in California in 1870, out of the 444 women whose average age was 27.6, the number of prostitutes was 232. Almost all the 8,141 Chinese males worked in the mines at one-third of the whites' wages; the women were not allowed to cook or be waitresses in local bars or clean mine offices. They could not afford to sit idle in their shacks, so many sold their bodies.[10]

Not all of them had made the choice freely. Many of the Chinese women were forced into prostitution by white masters, for in California, Chinese slavery was quite common. In the early sixties, young Chinese, usually between the ages of twelve and sixteen, were shanghaied in one locality in China and sold, according to age, strength, health, and appearance, for $50 to $100 each. By 1868, the trade grew to such proportions that the slaves were sold openly in auctions in California. Opium was legal in California until 1909 and very cheap; that was the main source of distraction and escape for the Chinese. One writer on the subject has claimed that four out of every ten Chinese adult males smoked it, and that there were opium dens in every Chinese neighborhood, two hundred within nine San Francisco city blocks in 1876.[11]

The first major massacre of Chinese which attracted the attention of law officers—and indeed was caused by them—took place in Los Angeles on October 24, 1871. Los Angeles then only had about six thousand people, many of them Mexicans, a few hundred Chinese, and only six policemen. The Mexicans and Chinese got along without problems; they both lived near a street called Calle de los Negros, which was the so-called sin street of gambling and boisterous bars. The Chinese population was divided into tight but peaceful clans, called tongs, which did not interrelate, or weren't supposed to. But when Ah Choy of one tong married a woman from another tong and refused to pay for her (Chinese tongs owned their women), a minor tong war broke out. Ah Choy and another man were arrested for attempted murder, but Choy was bailed out when his tong put up $6,000 in gold. That set the whites of Los Angeles to fuming about how rich the Chinese were. Then, one night, Ah Choy was waylaid and shot. A mounted policeman, Jesus Bilderrain, saw the murderer dash into the Coronel block, an L-shaped building where most of the bride's tong members lived. Bilderrain shot at the fleeting figure and ran up to the block house. He was shot and wounded. Soon, a crowd of white men had arrived and were emptying their pistols and rifles into the building. Since no one fired back, a local rancher went up to the door, received two bullets in his chest and died. With that, Marshal Francis Baker, who had just arrived, deputized every white man present and told them to shoot to kill.

The first victim was an unfortunate Chinese bystander who tried to get out of the way. He was caught and hanged from a post in a nearby lumberyard. Next, some whites climbed up onto the building's roof, chopped out a hole with hatchets, and poured bullets through it. Two unarmed Chinese ran out of the house and were quickly riddled with gunfire. The marshal and an aide then went into the building, found three dead Chinese and a dozen or so more crouching terrified in corners. They were dragged out by the mob, kicked, beaten, robbed, and finally hanged—including a fourteen-year-old boy. The whole house was looted and destroyed; twenty Chinese were killed. Eventually, of the six hundred whites who had participated in the looting and killing, ten were indicted and convicted of murdering one of the victims, Dr. Chin Lee Tong. But the state supreme court reversed the sentence on the grounds that the indictment did not actually say that the doctor had been murdered, only that the ten had murdered him: "Admitting that the defendants did all these things, still, it does not follow by necessary legal conclusion that, after all, any person was actually murdered."[12]

So vociferously anti-Chinese did California's white working class become during the 1893 depression that by 1874, both the Democratic and Republican parties were openly espousing anti-Chinese measures in their campaign programs. In 1876, a joint special committee of the state's legislature recommended anti-Chinese legislation. Then in July 1877, sparked by speeches by the demagogue Kearney, whom San Franciscans still honor as a "great reformer," ten thousand Bay Area whites went on the rampage, sacking San Francisco's Chinatown, looting stores, beating Chinese, burning twenty-five laundries and dozens of houses. That got the politicians moving in Washington. President Hayes felt queasy about violating the 1868 Burlingame Treaty with China, which guaranteed some rights to the Chinese in America, but once Garfield was president Congress finally passed the Chinese Exclusion Act, which stopped all Chinese immigration for ten years and prevented naturalization of those in America who were not already citizens. The act, passed in 1882, was extended in 1892.[13]

But that didn't take care of the Chinese who were still working in America. In February 1885, there erupted a series of riots provoked by the accidental shooting of a white council man in Eureka, in Humboldt County, where the Chinese were used as cheap lumber labor. All Chinese were given twenty-four hours to get out of town. They were then expelled from the whole county, most of them ending up in San Francisco. The Chinese sued Eureka in the courts, but the law didn't apply to minorities and they lost in 1886. In September 1885, armed whites invaded the Union Pacific coal mines in Rock Springs, Wyoming, and drove the Chinese out, murdering twenty-two and destroying fifty houses. The company, which owned the houses, got the army to quell the riots, but the sporadic sniping attacks on the Chinese finally drove them away. Similar outrages were perpetrated throughout the Northwest; the toll was twenty-eight Chinese killed, fifteen wounded and $150,000 worth of their property destroyed or stolen. In all these cases, there were many trials, but no one was ever convicted.[14]

Massacres carried out by angry workers were not limited to the West and South, nor to people of different colors. In New York City in 1870 and 1871, Irish Catholics attacked Irish Protestants in such massive riots that thirty-eight people died, hundreds were wounded, and several regiments had to be called in to help the police. In sectors of Utah where Mormons were not the dominant force, they were often subjected to attacks and pillage, especially after the Edmunds Act of 1882 defined polygamy as a federal crime. Catholics were beaten and some killed in riots in mining towns and in Butte, Montana, and in Kansas City, Missouri, in 1894. In the late eighties, Jewish businessmen were assaulted and their stores sacked in various parts of America, especially in the South. In a New Jersey mill town in 1891, some five hundred workers in the glass works attacked the Jewish neighborhood when the company hired fourteen young immigrant Jews from Russia; after three days of riots, the whole Jewish community left town. In several poor parishes of Louisiana in 1893, debt-ridden farmers stormed into the various small towns and wrecked stores owned by Jews. In southern Mississippi that year, night riders burned dozens of farmhouses belonging to Jewish landlords.[15]

But of all the whites in America, it was the Italians who suffered the most persecution and the most casualties. One reason for Anglo hatred of Italians, especially in the South, was that Italians were not inflexible toward blacks. They were willing to work and deal with them. In the little town of Tallulah, Louisiana, for example, five immigrant Sicilians set up shop and sold their goods to blacks, treating them squarely; within a few years, all five Italians were lynched. In the Colorado coalfields in 1895, striking miners executed six Italians who were thought to have killed an Anglo saloon owner. In New Orleans, where corruption among the police, the politicians, the judges, the coroners—even the press—had been notorious since the 1880s, unemployed

Italians tended to band together into gangs hired to intimidate voters, control wards, and generally carry out the interests of the politicos. Some of them, especially those known as the wharf rats because they lived in shanties under the wharves, naturally became hardened criminals. This antagonism toward the Italians was fawned by the city's yellow press, generating public paranoia by implying that a mysterious and omnipotent mafia had taken control of the city. It was in this atmosphere that one of the worst anti-Italian incidents was unleashed in 1891.[16]

It began the previous year when David C. Hennessy, the Italian-hating police superintendent for New Orleans's French quarter, was blasted by shotguns by five men. Hennessy had managed to shoot back before he collapsed, and as he lay dying he supposedly told a friend, Bill O'Connor, who had rushed up, that his murderers were "dagos." O'Connor also hated Italians, and no one else heard the policeman's last words, yet on the strength of this tale, hundreds of Italians were rounded up. Within three hours of the shooting five Italians were charged with the murder. Encouraged by the anti-Italian mayor, Joseph A. Shakespeare, more men were brought in. As the raids continued throughout Little Palermo, the Italian quarter, and guns were found in the homes, the city began to say that every Italian was a member of the mafia. Finally, the select Committee of Fifty, hand-picked by the mayor, indicted an additional fourteen Italian men, charging Joseph P. Macheca as being the ringleader. The suave, prestigious leader of New Orleans's Italians, which made up a little less than 10 percent of the city's population, Macheca was their most influential politician and the richest. And that was the key.

In New Orleans in those days, Italians got along well with blacks, and many of both communities voted. The poor Italians worked in the sugar cane mills and fields, in the lumber mills, and on the docks for the fish and oyster firms. The rich owned stores, some of the port's operations, and were partners with Anglos in some of the city's casinos and whorehouses. Mayor Shakespeare was a reformer of sorts; at least he wanted to close down the casinos, to the great consternation of the other politicians, the gambling-house owners, and the police. Shakespeare, his chief of police, Hennessy, and the latter's cousin, Michael, who worked with him, were opposed in their reforms by the police board, whose members were all part of the gambling ring. Over the mayor's vote, the police board hired an anti-Shakespeare chief of detectives. The Hennessy cousins killed him. That had all been a decade earlier. In 1882, convinced he could not win reelection, Shakespeare did not run. But he ran in 1888, won, and promptly rehired Hennessy, giving many gambling ring members plenty of motives for the killing. But neither the police nor the press even hinted at such a possibility.

Instead, on February 28, 1891, the first nine of the accused nineteen went on trial. It lasted two weeks. There were no Italians on the jury. Mysterious witnesses, sixty-seven in all, popped out of nowhere to identify the accused as Hennessy's murderers. Nevertheless, the case was shaky, full of contradictions and obvious lies. On the day the defense was to present its case, one of its lawyers was arrested for possessing a gun, and the press hinted that he was trying to bribe the jury. When the verdict came in, six of the accused, including Macheca, were found not guilty; regarding the others the jury was hung. The crowd was outraged. Next morning, March 14, 1891, the press headlined the call for a mass rally to "take steps to remedy the failure of Justice in the Hennessy case," asking people to "come prepared for action." Somewhere between twelve thousand and twenty thousand showed up in Congo (now Beauregard) Square.

The "action" was obvious. Ten prison guards stationed outside the gates disappeared. Warden Lemuel Davis understood. He tried to reach the mayor, the chief of police, then the governor and the attorney general. None could be contacted. The crowd surrounded the prison hollering for the prisoners, who still included the six found not guilty but not yet freed. Some one hundred fifty armed men threatened to shoot. The warden told the nineteen that he could not hold the gates. He set them all free and wished them luck in finding hiding places inside the jail. When the mob finally broke in, six of the nineteen were trapped in the women's section of the jail. A hundred rifles mowed them down. Another of the nineteen was thrown out alive, tossed from one end of the crowd to the lamppost on the other, and hanged. In all eleven were killed, including Macheca. Their bodies were leaned against a wall and put on display. Thousands, including twenty-five hundred mothers holding their children, came to gape at the dead. Eight had miraculously survived in the dungeons of the prison. Said the New Orleans *Times-Democrat* the next day: "We are sure to have plenty of censure and vituperation heaped upon us by outside communities for our yesterday's proceeding but the censure and vituperation will not hurt, emanating either from ignorance or from malice."

The *Times-Democrat* could not have been more wrong: America applauded the lynchings. The great champion of justice, the *New York Times,* congratulated the lynch mob because the Italians' death made "life and property safer" in New Orleans. The *Washington Post* said that the lynching broke the "reign of terror" imposed by Italians. The *St. Louis Globe-Democrat* claimed that the lynchers were merely exercising their "rights [of] popular sovereignty." The *San Francisco Chronicle* repeated as if it were fact a rumor that the jury had been bribed. Even the *London Times* approved in an editorial which the *Times-Democrat* promptly reprinted. The Italian government demanded a federal investigation. President Harrison refused and the two countries withdrew their respective ambassadors. Future President Theodore Roosevelt, who didn't like "dago diplomats," as he said publicly, called the lynching "a rather good thing."

A grand jury investigating the lynchers started hearings on March 17. The members of the trial jury swore under oath that they were never influenced, by pressure, intimidation, or money, to make their decision, which was based strictly on the evidence. Nevertheless the grand jury concluded that the Italians had bribed their jury, hence that the lynchings were justified. President Harrison knew otherwise: His special investigator had reported to him that the jury was fair and that the evidence proved the nineteen Italians were not guilty. Meanwhile, the jury members were fired from their jobs, boycotted, and run out of town. America's press accused Italy of sending its hoods to America. Rumors spread that the Italian fleet was going to attack American harbors. The *Illustrated American* dedicated a whole issue to war with Italy. The secretary of war ordered a strengthening of harbor defenses. Thousands of men volunteered to fight Italy. Pushed by Secretary of State Blaine and Navy Secretary Benjamin Franklin Tracy, President Harrison took this opportunity to ask Congress to enact measures and devise a budget to enlarge and modernize the U.S. Navy with twenty new battleships and sixty fast cruisers. These ships had nothing to do with coastal defenses, but only later did it become clear why the president had requested them: Blaine and the other expansionists in the cabinet and Congress wanted a war with Spain in order to seize Cuba, Puerto Rico, the Philippines and other Spanish possessions and they used the uproar over the lynchings to get the ships they would need later on.

Meanwhile more Italians were lynched in Louisiana, six in 1896, and no one protested. Only in 1955 did the truth come out when a member of the "execution squad," which had been organized on March 13, 1891, by the Committee of Fifty, died in Tampa, Florida. He left a letter admitting that the whole trial, the lynching, and the aftermath had been a conspiracy organized by the Committee of Fifty. Most of the members of that committee were Anglo businessmen who competed against such Italian entrepreneurs as Joseph Macheca. Probably because he had been lynched on March 14, the eight who survived, including five who had not yet been on trial, were released, with all charges dropped.[17]

With presidents, judges, and congressmen supporting the lynch law, usually to the benefit of the rich, it is not surprising that so many Americans died unjustly in the years before the New Deal. In New Jersey, the vigilante societies were given police power and could "apprehend and arrest" anyone without warrant. Nor did excesses tarnish the vigilantes' moral posture. In Rawlins, Wyoming, bandit George ("Big Nose") Parrott was caught by vigilantes and hanged. Next day, he was skinned. The skin was then tanned and turned into a medical instrument bag, razor straps, a pair of lady's shoes, and a tobacco pouch. The shoes were exhibited for years at the Rawlins National Bank. Occasionally vigilantes did support the poor; in Kentucky and Tennessee in 1906, night-riding tobacco farmers attacked representatives of the great tobacco companies. Usually, however, though the vigilantes themselves may have been poor, they struck at their own class or indeed at those who were even worse off than they. The solid middle- or upper-class organizers of the vigilantes used them to defend property in general, meaning their own property. From 1882 to 1903, over a hundred blacks were reported lynched every single year. The number lynched far exceeded those executed legally. And that does not include those killed during the race riots, which continued periodically into the twentieth century.[18]

One of the worse riots took place in Springfield Illinois, once the city of Abraham Lincoln, then one of the most corrupt in the Midwest. Along Washington Street, scores of brothels, gambling saloons, drug dens flourished, protected by politicians and the police. Mostly unemployed or terrorized by the police into carrying out the dirtiest work of the crime syndicate, the blacks of the area were often used as strikebreakers. From 1870 to 1905, twenty-five had been killed by whites. Juries rarely convicted a white man for killing a black man. Then one day in 1908, two black men were jailed for supposedly raping white women. Springfield's whites went mad. They sacked the black neighborhood, destroyed all black stores and those of whites whose clientele was black. They killed an old black barber, Scott Burton, then tore into the home of eighty-four-year-old cobbler William Donegan, because he had been married for thirty years to a white woman. He was sleeping at the time, but the mob yanked him up, dragged him to a tree one block from the state house, hanged him, then slashed his throat and hacked him with knives. Some three thousand blacks sought refuge with the National Guard. They were warned by the mob leader to get out of town. "All niggers are warned out of town by Monday, 12 M. sharp," read posters all over Springfield. They were signed: "Buffalo Sharp Shooters." Most blacks left, by train or foot. One baby died of exposure near Pittsfield, the seventh to die as a result of the riot.[19]

On Feburary 12, 1909, Lincoln's centennial, a group of reformers met in Springfield, chosen precisely because of the 1908 riot, to discuss racism in America. The group included social workers, W.E.B. Dubois, jurists, religious leaders, the philosopher John Dewey. Out of their discussion was born the National Association for the Advancement of Colored People, incorporated in 1910. But the NAACP could do little to stop the riots that spread across the land. From then until 1916, more than five hundred blacks were killed, including sixty-two mulattoes, in Georgia, Louisiana, and Texas. Since most of these sixty-two were axed during the night in black neighborhoods, it was thought that the killer or killers were blacks. Indeed one informant inside the Church of Sacrifice, which blossomed in those areas for a while, claimed that the church leaders approved of these murders, quoting the Bible: "Every tree that bringeth not forth good fruit is hewn down, and cast into the fire." The speculation was that blacks, perhaps members of this church, wanting to fight back but unable to strike at whites, went after the next best possibility, people of mixed blood.[20]

After World War I, the number of lynchings increased. Even the reformers of the New Deal could not stop them. From 1936 to 1966, no less than twenty-eight hundred blacks were put to death illegally.[21]

Chapter 18

Shady Ladies

If she didn't want to stay home waiting for a man to marry her and beget children, there wasn't much an urban woman could do before World War I. Most, of course, had to find some kind of work since their fathers or husbands were paid too little by the railroads, the mines, the mills, or the manufacturers to support a family. Some slaved away in the city sweatshops, toiled long miserable hours on piecework in the mills, washed clothes, served as maids to the rich; a few thousand clerked in offices. Getting such office jobs wasn't easy: The women had to be young, attractive and flirtatious. They were then immediately "surrounded by men who seek [their] moral destruction," as one observer reported at the time. No wonder that relatively many women, whether forced to do so out of poverty or a desire to be independent, became prostitutes and criminals. For, to most men, the working woman was a whore and was treated as such.

In Washington when Dr. John B. Ellis was writing *The Sights and Secrets of the National City*, published in Chicago in 1869, there were "about 600 female clerks in the service of the Government," mostly in the Treasury, Post Office, and Interior departments. They earned $600 to $900 a year, "sums notoriously insufficient to support the woman decently." Thus they were prey to their employers, as one

Printing Bureau division superintendent knew quite well. He took one of his clerks aside and, as reported by Ellis, "deliberately told the said girl that if she would go with him to a certain hotel in that city, and submit to his wishes, he would raise her salary to $75 per month." Should the woman have refused, he would "threaten her with dismissal from the place in which she earns her bread." In general, for a woman to get work in Washington, Ellis complained, "it is said that a woman's virtue is made the price of such an appointment, which price is paid to the party through whose influence the place is obtained; and it is asserted that public men provide for their mistresses by placing them in the Government offices."[1]

It wasn't only Washington's officialdom that viewed independent women as whores. Most men across the land thought the same. In Idaho, for example, the most popular argument against giving women the vote was that it would lead to their loss of "modesty," which would naturally turn them all into sluts. Women were not allowed to own property, and when they tried to vote in Pennsylvania in 1871 under the Fourteenth Amendment, the courts ruled that the word "freeman" in the Constitution obviously applied only to men. So low was the status of women that the law could not protect them from physical assault. In Nevada in 1877, the state legislature finally reacted to the huge number of protests against wife-beating by passing a law that any male so convicted must be tied to a post in the center of the county square and wear a sign saying "wife or woman beater" for ten hours. Lawyers then argued that such public humiliation was cruel and unusual punishment, and though that argument was overruled, men were never so punished.[2]

With neither decent work nor help, and prejudged as whores anyway, many immigrant women did choose the only profession readily available to them. And for all the clamor against prostitution, few cities or towns really cracked down hard; in fact, prostitution was a source of revenue for most small towns. Fines varied from place to place, but Wichita before the turn of the century was fairly typical: Prostitutes were fined $8 a month plus $2 for court costs; brothel keepers paid $18 plus $2. Many of the immigrant women were actually brought to America as prostitutes. The worst such case was in San Francisco, where, by 1850, Chinese women, shanghaied and drugged in their homeland by American entrepreneurs or their Chinese agents, were bought and sold like cattle. In the seventies and eighties, in response to numerous complaints of slavery, the trade was actually regulated by contracts which read:

> For the consideration of (fill in sum of money), paid into my hands this day, I (name of girl), promise to prostitute my body for the term of (number) years. If, in that time I am sick one day, two weeks shall be added to my time, and if more than one day, my terms of prostitution shall continue an additional month. But if I run away, or escape from the custody of my keeper, then I am to be held as a slave for life.

The Chinese women forced to sign such contracts, which were considered valid, could not read or understand the words. Naturally they were rarely paid the sum specified.[3]

Many of the Chinese slave-prostitutes were sent to the Comstock Lode, where huge silver deposits transformed the northwestern Nevada mining camps of Virginia City and Gold Hill into thriving towns, until the mines were depleted in the seventies and abandoned in 1898. In 1860, both were shanty towns with a combined population of less than three thousand people. By 1873, they had schools, churches, hotels, theaters, long rows of pleasant brick buildings, and thirty thousand people tightly segregated into Mexican, Latino, black, Chinese, and white sectors. Each had its own restaurants, saloons, and brothels. By then, too, the freewheeling rowdy atmosphere generated by adventurers, prospectors, and gamblers was over. The area was now ruled by the mineowners who controlled the whole lode in a tight monopoly. There were to be no more of the happy rags-to-riches stories that had lured so many fortune hunters in the sixties.

During the 1864 depression, the Bank of California, which had lent the small mine and mill owners money to operate, foreclosed and combined its assets into a subsidiary called Union Mining and Drilling Company. The bank went on to control the Virginia and Truckee Railroad, which shipped the ore, the Tahoe Basin, which was needed to timber the mines, and the water supply. Eventually it lost its holdings to another trust, whose hold on the area's opportunity for big money was just as rigid. Thus, the entrepreneurs had nowhere to focus except on entertainment—vice. For example, John Piper, who owned the Comstock's opera house, served as a Virginia City alderman and was chairman of the 1877 state assembly committee on public morals, was one of the biggest landlords in the city's red-light district. Chicago University's Marion Goldman, who has carefully researched the whole area, reports that, thus protected by the town's brothel-owning elite, prostitution became a major industry and "by far the largest occupational category for all women working outside the home."[4]

The first of the great brothel madams of Virginia City was Julia Bulette, a British-born adventuress who came to Nevada in 1860 by way of a seven-year stint as a high-class whore in New Orleans. Her rococo establishment, known as Julia's Palace, became a cultural center where fine wines and food were served and roughhousing strictly forbidden. Julia was much appreciated by the city's elite; she donated considerable sums to charity, served as a nurse when an epidemic hit town, and catered to so many politicians that the local temperance and morals squad of middle-class women could never influence their husbands into closing down her palace. When she was murdered during a robbery one night, it was middle-class married men who formed the posse that tracked down and hanged the killer.[5]

There were many famous madams throughout the West in those days. One was Mattie Silks, who participated in the only pistol duel ever recorded between two women. A blonde, blue-eyed replica of Lillie Langtry, the stunningly beautiful actress of the time, Mattie was a successful brothel owner at nineteen in Springfield, Illinois, but moved on to run houses in Kansas and Texas before settling down in Denver. Claiming to have been taught how to shoot by Wild Bill Hickok, she always carried an ivory-handled pistol in the pocket of her frock. She supported her gambler boyfriend, and it was over him that she fought the duel. The boyfriend, a handsome Texan who had ridden with Quantrill, was her second. She fired first but missed. The other lady also missed, hitting the Texan in the hand. Mattie finally married her Texan, and when he died in 1900 of ptomaine poisoning, she adopted his daughter by his first marriage. Mattie ran her plush operation until 1915 and also worked for the St. Louis Railroad as a lobbyist. Until the closing of the Silks Hotel, as her main establishment was called, Mattie made and spent millions. She remarried in her late sixties, "to have somebody to care for me when I'm old," and aged gracefully, dying in 1929 at the age of eighty-three.[6]

One of Mattie's toughest competitors in Denver was Jennie Rogers, a tough, shrewd operator from St. Louis who purchased her first house from Mattie for $4,600. According to her friends, she then went into some form of partnership with a client, St. Louis's chief of police. This cop had blackmailed a local millionaire, whose wife had disappeared, by planting the skull of an old Indian in the millionaire's yard and digging it up in front of two other witnesses who were part of the conspiracy. The millionaire knew of course that it was a frame, but since he had political ambitions, he coughed up $17,780—the price for building a luxurious new brothel in Denver. Jennie ran it without problems until, in 1889, she caught her bartender-husband in bed with one of her girls and shot him. He was only wounded and quickly disappeared, but business was not so good after that. She married a Chicago politician in 1904 and died in 1909, at which point her competitor Mattie Silks bought her house for $14,000 and became the unquestioned queen of the madams.[7]

Another "quality" madam, Rosa May, who set up shop in the mining camp of Brodie, California, was born in France. Dark-eyed, curly-headed, and petite, Rosa was very cute, and adoring miners lavished upon her much of the gold they dug up. She was also pursued by one Ernest Marks, owner of Brodie's Laurel Palace Saloon, and she let him court her for years without conclusion. After saving her first million, she went off to France for two months, returning with fifteen trunks of gifts, mostly gold match boxes, cuff links and the like for Marks, whom she decided was indeed her man. She was very nice to miners, allowing them credit, even giving them loans when the mines began to dry up, and nursing them when they started coming down with pneumonia. Then she too contracted the disease and died at the turn of the century.[8]

One of the most beautiful of the West's big-time madams was Fannie Keenan, known as Dora Hand, who ran a series of houses in Dodge City. Twelve men were said to have died fighting over her. The thirteenth then came gunning for the fourteenth, fired two shots—and killed Dora by mistake. Not all the shady ladies of the West, as historian Ronald Miller calls them, were just brothel keepers. Some were gamblers as well, others outright outlaws. Belle Siddons, sometimes known as Madame Vestal, was a Confederate spy during the war, then a sharp and very crooked professional gambler who married one of Quantrill's riders. After he was hanged by a posse in 1878, she began to drink heavily, became addicted to opium, finally did open up whorehouses first in Cheyenne, then in Las Vegas, New Mexico, finally in Tombstone, Arizona, but couldn't run them well. She reverted to gambling, was arrested in San Francisco in 1881, and died in jail.[9]

The famous Calamity Jane, born Martha Jane Cannary in Missouri in 1852, tried to pass herself off as a man in a man's world. Wearing pants, smoking and drinking, her hair short, she managed for a while to be a mule skinner, army scout, and pony-express rider. She was certainly a good shot and a close friend of Wild Bill Hickok, probably his mistress for a while, and some say his wife just before he was murdered in 1876 by Jack McCall. She then earned her living as a prostitute, procuress, and mule skinner. In 1885 she married Clinton Burke in El Paso and together they ran a whorehouse in Boulder, Colorado. Eventually they separated and she ended up drunk in Deadwood in 1899. A year later friends found her in a black house of prostitution suffering from rheumatism and delirium tremens. She died destitute in 1903.[10]

Belle Star, born Myra Belle Shirley in Carthage, Missouri, near the Kansas border in 1858, was not as myth has depicted her. She was certainly not the gorgeous "bandit queen" of subsequent Hollywood movies. She was wild but not daring, cruel but not courageous. Her family moved to Texas during the Civil War and she became a cheap prostitute until the James-Younger gang showed up on the lam from their great robbery of the Liberty, Missouri bank. She became Cole Younger's mistress and had a daughter by him. After he left, she worked as an entertainer-prostitute in a saloon, then started dealing poker and faro. She married outlaw Jim Reed and gave birth to a son, married Sam Starr when Reed was gunned down, and spent the next decade rustling horses and cattle from small homesteaders in Oklahoma. When Sam Starr was killed in a gunfight with a deputy sheriff in 1886, Belle returned to prostitution, married another outlaw, Jim July, in 1889, and was bushwacked near her ranch three months later. Some said the killer was one of her many discarded lovers. Others thought the murderer was her son, Ed Reed, with whom she had been having a sado-masochistic incestuous relationship and who had become jealous of Jim July.[11]

One prostitute who made millions and never returned to her profession was Cassie Chadwick, a destitute Toronto wench who was working in a rundown Cleveland bordello in the 1880s when she met a gullible doctor named Leroy Chadwick. No sooner had he married her and bought her a few refined frocks than she zipped off to New York City, registered at the plush Holland House, "accidentally" bumped into a wealthy Cleveland lawyer, asked him to be good enough to take her briefly to the home of her father, and, to the lawyer's total shock, strutted into Andrew Carnegie's Fifth Avenue mansion. On the pretext of checking up on a servant she managed to stay inside for half an hour talking to Carnegie's housekeepers, and waved good-bye to the butler, whom the lawyer waiting outside assumed to be Carnegie. As she climbed up into the carriage she dropped a piece of paper, which the lawyer retrieved for her. It was a promissory note for $2 million signed by Carnegie. Asking the lawyer to swear secrecy, she confided that she was Carnegie's illegitimate daughter and had another such note, for $7 million at home, but after all would soon inherit bachelor Carnegie's $400 million.

Naturally, the lawyer told everyone, and for the next decade Cassie borrowed $1 million a year from bankers, who never dared ask Carnegie to confirm her story but were happy to charge illegally exorbitant interest rates while waiting for the steel tycoon to die. Cassie spent every penny she made in the most lavish existence then known (one dinner party alone cost her $100,000). Finally, one New England banker decided to check. Carnegie issued a formal denial. The bankers panicked. One bank in Oberlin, Ohio, which had lent Cassie $800,000, never survived a depositer's rush. She was finally tried, convicted, sent to prison for ten years and died in jail in 1907, regretting not one of those fabulous years.[12]

More successful, as far as the law was concerned, was Belle Gunness, a widow with three children in Laporle, Indiana, who advertised for suitors in various newspapers, enticed at least fourteen to her home, killed them, chopped them up into pieces, buried them in her pig pen, and stole their money. In 1908, her house burned to the ground killing her three children and a woman whose head was never found. Because Belle's false teeth were in the ashes, she was listed as the headless woman. But her handyman, who admitted being her lover, later said the woman was a derelict that Belle had enticed into the house and killed. Jilted by Belle, the handyman, who also confessed to being her accomplice after the fourteen bodies had been dug up, was convicted for burning down her house. In prison he said he was supposed to rejoin her and that the fire was meant as a cover-up. Belle Gunness was never captured.[13]

New York City's shrewdest woman criminal prior to World War I was Fredericka Mandelbaum, known as Marm, or Mother, Mandelbaum. Born in New York in 1818, she married young and was a bored housewife and mother of two daughters and one son until the age of forty-one. A large, 250-pound woman with heavy black brows, Marm Mandelbaum then started fencing stolen goods for thrills as much as money. She bought a three-story building at 79 Clinton Street, at the corner of Rivington, just before the Civil War and by 1862 was said to have fenced $4 million in stolen goods. Her apartment was lavishly decorated with the furniture, drapes, and knickknacks lifted from the homes of New York and Long Island aristocrats. Protected by Boss Tweed's Tammany Hall, she enjoyed entertaining famous criminals, police officials, and politicians, sometimes with sumptuous dinners, sometimes with elegant balls. Among the criminals who often attended was George Leonidas Leslie, one of America's greatest bank robbers (estimated total: $12 million), whose biggest single hit was the Manhattan Savings Institution ($2,747,000) but who was murdered in 1884 by his own gang members. Another regular was Mark Shinburn, a suave, gentle, sophisticated burglar and safecracker who operated alone because he hated crooks and did so well that he retired in style in Monaco as "Baron Shindell."

Marm Mandelbaum had a real soft spot in her heart for female outlaws. She trained many of them to ply their trades—eventually opening up a school for criminals on Grand Street—and fenced their take. Among them were Black Lena Kleinschmidt, Old Mother Hubbard, and Kid Glove Rosey, all accomplished pickpockets who had been born poor. Another was Sophie Lyons, New York's most notorious confidence woman, who fleeced scores of gullible males traveling in Pullman cars. In 1884, when neither her political contacts nor her high-powered lawyers could stop reformers from indicting her for grand larceny and receiving stolen property, Marm Mandelbaum fled to Canada with her family, her furnishings and some $10 million, returning to New York occasionally thereafter in disguise to visit and encourage her pupils and friends. She is believed to have died three years later.[14]

New York was not the most sinful city in America in those days, nor was San Francisco. That honor went to New Orleans, and it was there that most of the country's shady ladies flourished. They were involved in almost every illicit activity, from accessory to murder as gun molls, stake-outers, and fingerers for the hard-drinking, fast-brawling Live Oak Boys gang to voodoo frauds and white slavery. Indeed, those who arranged for the kidnapping or purchasing of young white girls, preferably virgins, to be set up as concubines or locked up as prostitutes were often women. One was Mary Thompson, who ran a cigar store on Royal Street as a front for her real business. Another was Spanish Agnes, who operated a beauty shop. There was even a respected schoolteacher named Louisa Murphy, whose main income was derived from trading in female flesh.[15]

Most of the vice was centered in the French quarter, called the Sewer, where police rarely ventured except in force. The quarter was full of "concert-saloons," forerunners of the modern nightclubs, where enticing young waitresses called beer-jerkers served beer and food and offered themselves as dance partners. Paid no salary but a commission on drinks, plus tips, the girls were allowed to contract customers for later services. The floor show in these joints, rather mild by today's standards, but wild for those times, consisted of a cancanlike dance called *clodoche,* performed by women who competed with the beer-jerkers for after-hour rendezvous, and "art poses by living models," put on by similar women dressed in ankle-length body tights. Occasionally, when the law was safely bribed, the beer-jerkers would strip completely while dancing, encouraging their male clients to do the same.

Whatever did happen there, the concert-saloons were not brothels. Those existed next door, and up the street, and on the next—in fact, everywhere both in and out of the French quarter. In 1870, when the city population was less than 200,000, no less than 100 brothels were operating, from the ten-dollar elegant house to the fifteen-cent stalls, called cribs, in black neighborhoods. Almost every politician and police official was part of the system and they often actually owned the houses as silent partners. They were certainly steady customers in the fancier "palaces." One such mansion, owned and operated by Kate Townsend, was moved into fashionable Basin Street in 1866 and no outcry from "Suffering Property Holders," as the *Times* put it, could shut it down. "Minnie Haha," a black beauty who claimed descendency from Hiawatha, opened another such plush bordello on Basin Street nearby two years later. She had a huge granite hitching post equipped with gilded iron rings and her name chiseled into it erected at the curb for the gentlemen's horses, offered the horses apples and the men champagne, and if they stayed overnight, their clothes would be pressed and their shoes shined by morning. At another palace, proprietress Kitty Johnson offered a lavish dinner to the winner of a duel that two of her suitors were determined to hold right out in front. Kitty and her staff watched while the two men shot it out. One man was killed and the other ate the meal her chef had prepared.[16]

Kate Townsend, born Katherine Cunningham in Liverpool, England, in 1839, began her career as a hustler along Liverpool's notorious Paradise Street. She arrived in New Orleans in 1857, joined Clara Fisher's brothel in Philippa Street (now Dryades), saved her money, and opened her own place on Customhouse Street, where she prospered and made influential friends. She then opened her three-story marble Basin Street house, the most luxurious bordello in America at the time. But as the years wore on, she became very fat and very bitter, beating and humiliating her "fancy man" Treville Sykes, until one night in November 1883, he slashed her to death with a bowie knife. Sykes won his trial, thereupon producing Kate's last will, in which she left him her entire fortune. But by the time every official stole his cut, including $33,142.65 for the state treasury and $30,000 for his own lawyers, Sykes ended up with exactly $34—a fitting revenge for Kate Townsend.[17]

In the 1880s and 1890s, brothel owners diversified into the equally lucrative white-slave trade. Louisa Murphy, the teacher who sold young virgins for $800 each, was no longer operating. One of Mary Thompson's girls had escaped and warned the police, who told Mary to stop. Spanish Agnes, however, was still in business, as she admitted in an interview with the New Orleans *Mascot* November 22, 1890:

> I frequently receive orders from the keepers of fashionable places. These ladies ask me to send them girls, or women for that matter. I always prefer to have experienced women than virtuous girls, because there is less fear of trouble. I am in correspondence with women like Molly Waters and Abbie Allen of Galveston; these people write me for girls. . . . Not a very long time ago a mother brought me her three daughters and offered them for sale. Two, she said, were bad, and the youngest still unacquainted with vice and the wickedness of the world. She demanded $25 for the girls and expressed her belief that she ought to get more for the guileless maiden.[18]

In May 1892, the *Mascot* investigated New Orleans's vice practices.

It found that brothels were paying little or no tax and that slavery was amazingly common in the thousands of brothels that laced the city. One *Mascot* reporter was even offered a fifteen-year-old at a bargain price by a top procuress, Emma Johnson. When he refused, she blurted: "You're a fool! The girl's a virgin! You'll never get another chance like this in New Orleans."[19]

Maybe the reporter didn't, but others did, by the dozens. Brothels continued to prosper, as did bawdy bars, concert-saloons, gambling clubs, opium dens, and the traffic in young girls. A certain Miss Carol, who procured girls for brothels and rich individuals, also started dealing in young boys for homosexuals and was so successful that she financed a new kind of brothel, one exclusively populated with males. Opened in the nineties, the gay brothel, on Lafayette Street near Baroma, featuring Lady Richard, Lady Beulah Toto, Lady Fresh, and Chicago Belle, who were all young males, was an instant hit. But for the city blue bloods, it was a bit much. They finally prevailed upon the city council to pass an ordinance which, while continuing to make prostitution illegal, set aside two areas where all brothels had to be located, one in the French quarter and one above Canal Street in the Anglo zone—thirty square blocks totally occupied by brothels, bars, and cabarets.[20]

Since the ordinance had been sponsored by an alderman named Sidney Story, the red-light district was dubbed Storyville, and it soon became the most celebrated and profitable tourist attraction in America. Tours were organized, always beginning with the Arlington Annex, a bar located at the corner of Customhouse and North Basin streets, which was known as the town hall of Storyville. Arlington Annex was owned by Thomas C. Anderson, the area's political boss, a member of the legislature until 1908, who also owned various saloons, cabarets, and a whole string of whorehouses. He became richer and richer, invested in oil, and in 1928 married one Gertrude Hoffmire, alias Gertrude Dix, the madam of a brothel he owned at 209 North Basin Street. When he died in 1931, he left Gertrude his fortune, but Irene Delsa challenged the will on the grounds that she was his daughter. The charge was verified and the two women split the estate. Irene Delsa's husband turned out to be the manager of one of Anderson's bawdy bars. Thus the fortune remained, if not exactly in the family, at least in the same profession.

In 1899, when New Orleans had 285,000 people, Storyville offered

230 brothels, 30 houses of assignation and more than 2,000 prostitutes. By 1910, with the population up to 339,075, the number of whorehouses, including cribs, was down to 175, employing only 800. Most sociologists explain the sudden drop to a change in middle-class sexual mores, especially regarding premarital sex. That was certainly the viewpoint of Countess Willie V. Piazza, a notorious madam, who wailed that "The country club girls are ruining my business!" More probable is the fact that by World War I many new industries, offices, and legitimate services were hiring female employees. Independent-minded and poor women now had new chances to earn a living. In the America of 1892, the destitute mother who sold her three daughters into prostitution-slavery could take comfort from one fact that all the moralists who would have condemned her would probably have overlooked: Her three daughters would survive in the whorehouses. They might not have at home.[21]

Chapter 19

The Big Apple

By the end of the nineteenth century, New York City was the entrepreneurial Gotham of America, the gateway to the thousands of immigrants who poured into the country in search of fortune and happiness, the launching center for continental if not international conspiracies, truly the big apple. It was therefore the irresistible magnet to America's greatest robbers, swindlers, confidence men, corruptors—and reformers.

New York was a tough place to live during those years after the Civil War when William Marcy Tweed ran the city. Of the nearly one million people who were packed into the two miles surrounding Union Square at Fourteenth Street, then the city's epicenter, no less than 44 percent were foreign born, 21 percent in Ireland, 16 percent in the German states. Most were very poor; some 250,000 or 300,000 people were crammed into a one-mile square East Side district of tenements with faulty or nonexistent toilet facilities, poor heating, leaky roofs, and no fire protection. The streets were full of trash and sludge. The death rate was incredibly high and unemployment increased constantly, first because of the thousands of returning and abandoned veterans, then because New York had begun its transformation from a manufacturing to a financial city. Many of these unemployed had no choice but to roam the streets, begging and stealing. When they banded into gangs, New York became America's most terrifying metropolis.[1]

The most violent of New York's gangs were the Whyos, who evolved from the old Five Points Gang, made their headquarters at the Mulberry Bend but roamed throughout the city, raiding homes and shops in Greenwich Village and fighting other gangs as far uptown as Hell's Kitchen, above thirty-fifth Street. The Whyos' favorite drinking spa was the Morgue, on the Bowery, whose owner claimed that his liquor was as good for embalming corpses as it was to drink. During their heyday, the Whyos, who numbered five hundred criminals, would accept no new member unless he had killed at least once. They even advertised their services in handbills passed out openly from Chatham Square to Broadway. The price list, as found in the pocket of Whyo leader Pike Ryan when he was arrested in 1884:

• Punching	$ 2.
• Both eyes blacked	4.
• Nose and jaw broke	10.
• Jacked out (blackjacked)	15.
• Ear chawed off	15.
• Leg or arm broke	19.
• Shot in leg	25.
• Stab	25.
• Doing the big job (murder)	100. and up.

The top Whyos were Danny Lyons and Danny Driscoll, who controlled street operations jointly and efficiently until they had a falling out in 1887. That led to a series of murders, which, in turn, led them both to the gallows in 1888. Another street boss was Dandy Johnny Dolan, who won the respect of his mates by inventing a copper eye-gouging apparatus which he hooked onto his thumb. Dolan used it to remove the eye of James H. Noe, whom he killed, when the latter spotted him stealing goods from his brush factory at 275 Greenwich Street; Dolan was eventually caught and hanged because, it is said, he kept the eye as a trophy and flashed it occasionally.

The Whyos were rarely bothered by the police. They paid off regularly, and they all volunteered during elections to vote dozens of times for Tammany Hall candidates. Without such political protection, some of the other major gangs fared less well. Among them were the

Gas House Gang; the Hartley Mob; the Molasses Gang; Bowery's Rag Gang; the Little Dead Rabbits and the Forty Little Thieves, who kept youngsters as apprentices; the Baxter Street Dudes and the Nineteenth Street Gang, both composed of teenagers; and the Daybreak Boys, who were all under twelve years old and did their stealing along the docks. The Gas House Gang, which controlled the East Side above thirtieth Street, was destroyed by Police Captain Alexander ("Clubber") S. Williams, who ordered his cops to club any and all gang members "with or without provocation" when they saw them.[2]

Clubber Williams was not typical. Usually, New York's policemen clubbed only those who had neither bribed them nor gained official protection. In both cases, of course, they acted against the law. Clubber Williams was even proud of it: "There is more law in the end of a policeman's nightstick than in a decision of the Supreme Court," he said. And he was right: Innocent citizens formally complained about his brutality eighteen times, but he was always acquitted by the board of police commissioners. Some of these same commissioners allowed William Sharkey, a notorious gambler, burglar, and head of a gang called the Sharkey Guards, to escape from New York's Tombs prison in 1873. Sharkey was a Tammany Hall "heeler," that is, a fixer during the reign of Boss Tweed.[3]

But the only sure way of making lots of money in those days was to be corrupt. Gould stole stocks. Cooke manipulated bonds. Congressmen accepted bribes. Customs agents received illicit gifts. Judges sold verdicts. Manufacturers produced dangerous goods. There was even one large factory in Brooklyn that made tea out of wood shavings. Boiled with old leaves, dried and then dyed, the end product tasted like tea but was a slow though deadly poison. No wonder that those who were enterprising stole. And some thieves were amazingly daring. One lone thief, dressed as a clerk, walked into one of Wall Street's biggest brokerage houses with papers in his hands, mingled with the other clerks for a while, then strutted up to the safe, which was being guarded by the banker-broker himself. "Will you please to move, sir, so I can get at the safe?" he asked politely. The banker did and the thief calmly took out $100,000 worth of U.S. bonds and ambled off. By 1871, there were thirty thousand professional thieves in New York, two thousand gambling dens and three thousand saloons where violence among customers was standard fare. It was not a time of great respect for law.[4]

If there was a general clamor to bring some kind of order into this mess, no one with power quite agreed on what to do. Some straitlaced shopkeepers and parlor society reformers suggested stopping immigration. But the country's major manufacturers, millowners, and railroadmen were firmly opposed to such a drastic measure, fearing the loss of cheap immigrant labor. On the other hand, they also sought to establish a clearly delineated aristocracy of refined, revered gentlemen who would set the city's cultural tone, control its press, embellish its avenues and parks, and turn its opera houses and concert halls into formidable and fashionable attractions to the gentry of the world. To achieve their objectives, however, they needed more than money; they needed political power. That required marshaling the votes, in particular the votes of New York's ill-fed, ill-housed, ill-paid, and ill-treated teeming masses who had no reason to favor the elegant amusements of the uppercrust. Thus the would-be aristocrats faced a troublesome dilemma.

The haughty, patrician editorialists of the *New York Times* suggested, none too subtly, that it would be preferable if the masses would relinquish the vote and trust to the wisdom of their betters. But the nation's populist heritage was far too strong for that. Too many ambitious entrepreneurs had climbed upward on the backs of voters for too long for them suddenly to allow suffrage to be limited. The Civil War had been fought, theoretically at least, to give blacks the vote everywhere. No veteran was about to give it up, even if all he did with his vote was sell it. Besides, the spoils of electoral patronage, established under Jacksonian Democracy, provided the glue that held together the city's police department.

Like all aristocratic-minded Americans, the worried owners and editorialists of the *Times* simply did not know how to handle a heterogeneous population, alienated and miserable, rootless and restless, but politically free. The aristocrats had a grand vision of America, based partially on the rigid class distinctions of England. But, unwilling to cater to the needs of the rabble, whom they considered crass and uncouth, they could not turn that vision into reality. Educated mostly at Harvard or Yale, New York's aristocrats were fundamentally un-American: they believed in propriety, visible gentility, tradition, Old World manners, and the quiet rule of "the better families." Eventually they learned how to perpetuate their power from the rear of the hall, choosing to rule through demagogic frontmen who had the common touch and knew how to fight dirty.

One of those commoners who learned the technique early was Boss

Tweed. Born in New York City to a Scottish father who made chairs for a living, Tweed was anything but an aristocrat. He was yanked out of public school at eleven and sent to learn a trade. At fifteen, he was taught bookkeeping for half a year, then put to work first in an office, then in the brush factory his father had bought. At twenty-one, he married the daughter of the factory's biggest shareholder and eventually had eight children. At twenty-seven, he organized a volunteer fire engine company, made himself foreman, and had the head of a tiger painted on the engine—the same tiger that was the symbol of Tammany Hall. Thus Tweed understood street politics. He made his contacts with firemen, cops, street hustlers, and, by delivering the votes, moved up the ladder of the Democratic party machine. He became an alderman in 1851 and was elected to Congress in 1852. Five years later he was a power in Tammany Hall, the Democratic organization that had elected and reelected Fernando Wood mayor. Wood was now considered a renegade because he opposed the Civil War, gave patronage posts to nonparty faithfuls and had allied himself to the bluebloods. Tweed decided to get Wood.

Tweed needed allies. He chose them well. The most important was Peter Barr Sweeny, who had waited on tables in his father's saloon while training to become a lawyer. Tweed did not like him, but he recognized his "brains," as he used to say. He had backed him for district attorney in 1857 and now made him his chief of operations. Another Tweed ally was Abraham Okey Hall, a lawyer and journalist who was born poor but of old English stock, dressed with care (he was known as "the elegant") and posed as a blue blood. Hall was first an assistant, then a regular district attorney. Richard ("Slippery Dick") Connolly, leader of the Twenty-first Ward, county clerk in 1851 and state senator in 1859, was an Irish immigrant and was loved by New York's Irish. He was a wizard with figures and extremely valuable to Tweed. Another loyal cohort at that time was George G. Barnard, whom Tweed supported for county recorder in 1857 and who made Tweed a lawyer when he became a judge in 1860. In 1861, led by Tweed, this team was instrumental in defeating Mayor Wood. After that Tweed gained unchallenged control of Tammany Hall. He made Sweeny city chamberlain in 1866, Hall mayor in 1868, and himself school commissioner, assistant street commissioner, president of the board of city supervisors, New York County Democratic chairman, and a state senator. John Hoffman, a Tweed ally and former mayor, won the governorship that year, and Slippery Dick Connolly took over the city's finances as comptroller. Their hold on New York was complete.

Naturally their first obligation was to repay their supporters. So they created twelve thousand new city jobs and gave them to their stalwarts. Known as the Shiny Hat Brigade, these beneficiaries of the patronage system took over every branch of the city government. Many were immigrants. But many others were given jobs by companies doing business with the city, on Tammany's threat to cancel the contracts. Tweed also arranged for the naturalization of thousands of immigrants (41,112 in 1868 alone), which, of course, gave him more votes. Added to the votes of the city's thugs and gang members, ward heelers and corrupt officials, many of whom voted as often as a dozen times in each election, the votes of the immigrants and Shiny Hat Brigademen were sufficient to guarantee Tammany Hall's victory repeatedly. Indeed Tweed ruled until 1871, when he was arrested and jailed, but that did not destroy the organization, which was in full control again by 1874. John Kelly governed New York from the hall until 1866, Richard Croker from then until 1901. Not until the impeachment of Governor William Sulzer in 1913 did Tammany Hall suffer a serious defeat, and then it made a strong comeback in the twenties.[5]

To finance these jobs, the cost of doing anything at city hall rose astronomically. For example, the net received from $100,000 worth of permits after salaries and other deductions were taken out, dropped to $23,077.72 in 1866 and $13,749.95 in 1870. It was estimated that to receive $194.00 in February 1871, the city paid out $2,840.66. A month later the cost for $145 was $2,843.70. By April, the city spent $2,842.64 to get exactly $6.00. In just four years, 1867–71, the municipal indebtedness went from $30 million to $90 million. Every company doing business with the city had to offer kickbacks. Tammany friends were encouraged to file claims against the city, which, thanks to the benevolent overseeing influence of Judge Barnard, were inevitably ruled in favor of the plaintiffs, who then paid back a fat "commission." Prostitution added another source of revenue. Within three miles of city hall were four hundred brothels employing four thousand whores and paying $600 a week for protection. The state legislature, controlled personally by Tweed after 1868, also contributed some $2,225,000 between 1869 and 1871.

But the biggest financial boondoggle from which the Tweed Ring gained its operating funds was New York's new county courthouse building. Begun in 1858 on a budget of $250,000, it had cost almost $13 million by 1871 and was still not finished. Among the itemized expenses were: $1,575,782.96 for furniture, including so many chairs at $5.00 apiece that were they to be put side by side, they would have extended seventeen miles; almost $3 million for plastering; $41,190.95 for "brooms, etc."; $7,500 for thermometers; $75,716.13 for "not defined" repairs; $5,691,144.26 for carpets and carpet repairs. The companies cashing in on these "expenses," all Tammany faithfuls, paid some of the money to the Tweed Ring, some to the hundreds of new employees, and pocketed huge profits. Just to maintain the heating apparatus, for example, the maintenance subcontractors had to hire thirty-two engineers, firemen, secretaries, clerks, messengers, and inspectors for a total wage package of $42,000 a year. In addition to the bills on the new courthouse the city government paid out another $15,750,000 in fraudulent bills by 1871. Raised through city and state taxes, Tweed's gigantic manipulation of funds was certainly fraud, but also one of the biggest conspiracies to redistribute the wealth ever attempted in America.[6]

How the Tweed Ring got away with it was, first, by bribing the state legislature (cost: $100,000) to pass the Tax Levy Bill, which gave the city comptroller the power to raise huge sums for public works through bond issues, and second, by getting a new city charter, which increased home rule, centralized authority, and consolidated departments. Under this new charter, the mayor appointed the comptroller and all heads of departments. The Street and Water departments were put under a new commissioner of public works. More importantly, the board of supervisors was replaced by a board of audit, which scrutinized all bills sent to the city and county. The board of audit was composed of Mayor Hall, comptroller Slippery Dick Connolly and the commissioner of public works—Tweed himself.[7]

In 1870, the Tweed Ring made a crucial mistake: it appropriated money for New York's parochial schools. The city's anti-Catholic blue bloods were outraged. The venerable *Harper's Weekly* had already begun a campaign to expose the ring. Now it was joined by the *New York Times,* which launched a massive investigation. It reported that Tweed had a Fifth Avenue mansion worth $350,000, a country house in Greenwich, Connecticut, where the stables alone must have cost some $122,000, and quipped: "It is better to be one of Mr. Tweed's horses than a poor taxpayer of this city."

In the years since, few historians have noted the significance of that *Times* statement. Of course, Tweed and his henchmen were crooks. Tweed and Sweeny had both been made officers of Gould's Erie Railroad. Tweed was paid $100,000 a year in "fees" for his "legal advice." Of the two printing houses that handled all of city hall's paper, Tweed owned one outright and was a major stockholder in the other. He bought the quarry in Massachusetts that furnished all the marble needed by the new county courthouse. Sweeny was a director of the Ninth National Bank, the Mutual Gas Company, the Dry Dock and Erie railroads. Hall, whose motto, inscribed on his stationery, read *Fortuna Juvat Audentes* ("Fortune Favors the Bold"), gave his law firm $204,500 worth of business in 1870 alone. Slippery Dick Connolly, who earned $3,600 in 1857, was worth $6 million in 1871. But the fact remains that those whom they fleeced were not "poor taxpayers," as the *Times* complained. There were no income taxes in those days. Tax was on property, and the thousands of Irish, German, Slavic, and Jewish immigrants who were unemployed or who slaved twelve to fourteen hours seven days a week did not own property. The Tweed Ring found many of them jobs, others better living conditions. While the ring members admittedly made a fortune, they literally saved thousands from starvation. Of course they were creating an electoral constituency which was terribly threatening to the *Times*'s nativist and anti-Catholic political allies.

In May 1871, Tweed's daughter was married at the Trinity Chapel. Later, at the reception in his mansion, guests brought $700,000 worth of gifts, which particularly perturbed the *Times*. Rarely a day passed that it failed to run an exposé of some Tweed Ring maneuver. The ring began to worry. It offered George Jones of the *Times* $500,000 to silence the paper's attacks, and $500,000 to Thomas Nast, whose vicious caricatures of Tweed adorned each issue of *Harper's Weekly*, to study art in Europe.

Finally in September 1871, a Committee of Seventy was formed to get the Tweed Ring. It was headed by Samuel J. Tilden, the railroad lawyer, stock manipulator, and former friend of both Gould and Tweed, without whose help Boss would not have become chairman of New York's Democratic party. One of the most contemptible politicians in the country, Tilden, who won the presidential elections of 1876 but got swindled out of the electoral college count, was the quintessential patrician, educated at Yale and New York University. He went after his former ally with a vengeance. He obtained documents indicating Tweed had fraudulently misappropriated more than $6 million from New York City's treasury and got a warrant for Tweed's arrest.

The Tweed Ring collapsed. Sweeny escaped to Canada. Hall defended himself through three trials and eventually won an acquittal. Connolly, arrested and released on $1 million bail, fled to Europe with $6 million and was never seen again. Barnard was impeached. Tweed was tried twice. The first jury, in January 1873, ended deadlocked. The second convicted him. The original sentence of twelve years and $12,750 fine was reduced in 1875 to one year and $250. But he then faced a civil suit in the name of the state for recovery of the $6 million. It was during this trial that he skipped, hiding first on a farm in New Jersey, then traveling to Florida, sailing to Cuba and finally to Spain. Recognized, it is said, through one of Thomas Nast's cartoons, he was nabbed and returned to New York in November 1876.

Stricken with heart trouble, diabetes, and bronchitis, William Tweed offered to turn state's evidence against the sixteen other Tweed Ring members under indictment and give up all his property for his freedom. The state accepted, so Tweed wrote out his confession. The attorney general read it and returned it. The deal was off. Why? Because Tweed's confession implicated Daniel Manning, later President Cleveland's secretary of the treasury; Peter Cooper and Robert B. Roosevelt, who were leaders of the anti-ring crusade; David Bennett Hill, who was to be governor in 1885; and a whole battery of legislators, congressmen, and six senators who had worked with or accepted bribes from the ring. Most important was the fact that Tweed's confession clearly implicated Tilden and the attorney general themselves. Thus, Tweed was double-crossed. The *Times,* which had lusted for the scalps of the entire ring, now reversed itself and said it was "totally at a loss" to find what good could be served by grilling Tweed "or any one else on that subject." The sixteen other indictments were dropped. Tweed died in jail in April 1878. The city had recovered a total of only $894,525.24. It had cost the city $257,848.34 to do it.[9]

Most of the ring's members died quickly, except Mayor Hall, who continued to wage battle for himself, the poor, and the dissenters until 1898. Before he died, the Harvard-educated Hall had the chance to stage one more great performance, the defense of Emma Goldman, the formidable anarchist and feminist leader. Goldman wrote about her own defense by Hall: "His client was an idealist, he declared; all the great things in our world have been promulgated by idealists. More violent speeches than Emma Goldman had ever made were never prosecuted in court. The moneyed classes of America were seeing red since Governor Altgeld had pardoned the three surviving anarchists of the group hanged in Chicago in 1887. . . . He closed his speech with an eloquent plea for the right of free expression." But Emma was convicted for inciting a riot and jailed for a year, and elegant Oakey Hall was soon forgotten.[10]

So have Tweed's lasting accomplishments been forgotten He widened Broadway from Thirty-fourth to Fifty-ninth streets. He built Columbus Circle and Riverside Drive. He diverted millions for orphanages, homes for the shelterless, and hospitals. He finished the Metropolitan Museum, the New York Stock Exchange, and the public library (then called Lenox). Most important, he championed the immigrant, helped him find a job, a home, a club which, undoubtedly often corrupt, nonetheless did acclimatize him to his new country and helped turn him into a proud citizen. That, above everything else, is why the nativists and the patricians hated him most.[11]

PART IV

Crime in the Superstate

There is no time to waste on hairsplitting over the infringement of liberty.

—*Washington Post,* 1919

All I ever did was to sell beer and whiskey to our best people. All I ever did was to supply a demand.

—Alphonse Capone, 1929

I'll tell you about a public standard of morality. In my humble opinion there is none in the United States. Individuals, and each one grows up with the standards of the household he was born in, the society he's permitted to live in, based upon his economic position in life.

—James Hoffa, 1963

Chapter 20

Chicago—No Quarter, Either Way

If at the turn of the century there was any one city that was unabashedly American, it was Chicago. Long before the trial of Boss Tweed, New York had become a place apart from the popular spirit of the country, an urban principality possessed of foreign customs and languages, envied and despised by the provincials who built factories and plowed fields along the plains and river valleys of the West. But Chicago was always central to the spirit of American enterprise. It was the railroad hub of the nation; its packinghouses fed the country's first and greatest population explosion. Its businessmen traded in truly American commodities—grain futures and sowbellies—not in the bonds and debentures over which international plutocrats haggled on Wall Street. Founded on a muddy, bug-infested swamp, Chicago was erected by wave upon wave of iron-willed immigrants who renounced the world of their parents to create the finest temple to industrial prosperity in the Western Hemisphere.

But of all the heartland images to be drawn from Abe Lincoln and Carl Sandburg, none fully captured the urban symbolism of Chicago for so many Americans. The secret of Chicago's endurance and its fascination for the country and the world rested in its boisterous embrace of political corruption—Chicago, "the gangster city." At the same time "Boss" Richard J. Daley, the bullet-headed Irish mayor who never moved away from the blue-collar neighborhood of his birth, could pound his fist and proclaim Chicago "the city that works." That dual epithet cut to the heart of Chicago's mystique, a mystique that thoroughly captivated the great muckraker and reformist Lincoln Steffens. "First in violence, deepest in dirt; loud, lawless, unlovely, ill-smelling, irreverent, new; an overgrown gawk of a village, the 'tough' among cities, a spectacle for the nation—I give Chicago no quarter and Chicago asks for none," Steffens wrote in a 1903 report on the reform movement entitled "Half Free and Fighting On." Confidently he declared there was "little doubt Chicago will be cleaned up." It was a prediction to which he did not, in the future, often refer.[1]

The particular reform movement that so inspired Steffens was only one of the city's frequent ritualistic exercises in psychic purification. Following the Civil War there had been a short-lived cleanup of police department graft. Some years later came an anticorruption city charter revision. By the late nineties, reformers targeted the public "boodlers," Samuel Insull and Daniel Yerkes, who together fleeced the city of millions by securing monopolies over the electrical utility and streetcar franchises. Yet despite all these purification drives, the city's fundamental political arrangements remained untouched, developing a steady refinement toward what is best called "the Chicago system."

The Chicago system relied on a simple device: the election of two aldermen from each of the city's thirty-six wards. Populated mostly by German and Irish immigrants, the wards each tended to have their own distinctive ethnic mix. The ward aldermen were the basic power brokers who could deliver whole voting blocks to the mayor and other city politicians. In turn, city hall granted them a virtual lock on distribution of public jobs and patronage in their wards, even including appointment of local police officials. In such a rough, unpolished town of newcomers, frontier businessmen, and main-chance speculators, it is hardly surprising that saloons should have provided the primary entertainment during the late nineteenth century. Nor is it surprising that a city only slightly removed from the real frontier should have a gambling hall in virtually every saloon, and that the leading saloons in each ward would become the forum where political alliances and deals were constructed. More than a few of the most prominent aldermen were first barkeepers and gamblers, just as many of the most powerful back-room political bosses were gamblers who made regular police payoffs, who controlled neighborhood gangs, and who could call on their clients and runners to man the armies of ward heelers needed on election day. Since the 1870s the system had been run by Big Mike McDonald.[2]

Michael Cassius McDonald, king of the Chicago gamblers, presided for twenty-five years over a city that had, temporarily, the atmosphere of a frontier town. The great Chicago fire of 1871, which began on Sunday October 8, leveled 2,024 acres of Chicago—more than seventy-three miles of city streets and eighteen thousand buildings for a total loss of $20 million. One of the buildings destroyed was the city jail. Turned loose, the thieves and robbers went on a rampage, cleaning out every business firm, store, and mansion they could find. After the rebuilding of Chicago had begun in November, every trainload of mechanics, carpenters, and bricklayers coming into Chicago also included scores of crooks bent on profiting from the city's lawless atmosphere. When Mayor Joseph Medill reacted by closing down some of the more notorious gambling dens and whorehouses, the underworld united to defeat him in his bid for reelection. On November 4, 1873, Harvey D. Colvin was elected mayor. His superintendent of police cooperated with the underworld and especially Big Mike McDonald.[3]

Once a candy vendor on trains servicing Chicago, McDonald built his real fortune with a gambling hall called the Store at Clark and Monroe streets, which became his political headquarters as well. With various partners, he bought the *Chicago Globe,* became treasurer of the Lake Street Elevated Railroad, which he readily bilked, and formed a bookmaking syndicate controlling betting at Chicago and Indiana racetracks; the syndicate cleared three-quarters of a million per year. In 1875, Mayor Colvin was voted out, and with him went the whole board of police commissioners which worked closely with McDonald. But in 1879, McDonald threw the weight of his political organizations, which included the People's party that he had launched in 1872, behind Carter H. Harrison. Elected, Harrison ordered McDonald's enterprises off limits to cops. Harrison's first superintendent of police, Simon O'Donnell, did raid McDonald's Store once; he was immediately demoted to captain. His successor, William J. McGarigle, was a detective handpicked by McDonald.[4]

Democrat Carter Harrison was elected five times. He and McDonald ran Chicago from 1879 to 1887 and again in 1893. He was also a landlord, owning the entire block on Harrison Street between Clark and

Pacific, which included a hotel, a gambling den, a saloon, and a whorehouse. For all his obvious corruption, however, Harrison was friendly to the poor and did much to find jobs for the many immigrants who flocked to the city and who voted for him when they became naturalized citizens. In the federal election of 1884 and in the mayoralty election of 1885, McDonald's candidates were not sure of winning, so his machine resorted to wide-scale fraud. In the first election, entire ballot boxes were switched. In the Second Precinct of the Eighteenth Ward, such a switch was spotted by McDonald's opponents and the tally sheet was proven to be a forgery, leading to a sensational trial at which Joseph C. ("Oyster Joe") Mackin, a close McDonald aide who also owned a saloon on Dearborn Street, was convicted and sent to the Illinois State Penitentiary at Joliet for five years. At the second election, although the thief of one ballot box was apprehended, enough fraudulent votes sneaked through to give Harrison victory by 375 votes out of a total of 86,329.[5]

McDonald's reign in Chicago did not stop with the election of John A. Roche, a Republican, in 1887. Nor did it end when Harrison, who had made a successful comeback, was assassinated by a dissatisfied city employee in 1893. Tax assessments that year, for example, were openly reduced for those who had contacts or handed out light bribes. Harrison's property was assessed at $300, that of John P. Hopkins, who succeeded him, at $150. The property of all sixty-eight aldermen was assessed at a total of $1,700. William Pinkerton, whose goons were now employed by railroads, banks, mines, and mills was declared worth only $400.[6]

In 1893, Chicago was seat of the World's Fair. For that, McDonald underlings, working with the police, the judges, and the city clerks, systematized the underworld. Pickpockets were assigned regular corners. Since some would be caught by the victims, fixers were chosen, jury panels were fixed, cops on the beat were bribed. As one top sly-fingers, Eddie Jackson, known as "the Immune," later told an interviewer: "The arrangement with the police was a 'regular take weekly' of $250. . . . The returns were good. It was a poor week without $1,500 for my end. In the summertime a Sunday alone would net us $500. . . . The favors done by the boss and organization were on the basis of friendship and in return for loyal service. This friendship extended within the faction from the national committeeman, a party boss, to the low criminal, loyal in the ranks. Since the development of the syndicate, which is on a more businesslike basis, the syndicate may continue in power despite the changes of factions or parties in power by contributing to both or all factions likely to win."[7]

Corrupt or not, the McDonald-Harrison-Yerkes ring worked for the common man better than Harrison's two successors ever did. Thus, in 1897, the people of Chicago voted in Harrison's son, Carter Jr., who was mayor until 1905 and again from 1911 through 1914. During Carter Jr.'s first reign, the new McDonald-Harrison-Yerkes combination of crime, politics and transportation fleeced the city of millions in revenues, and stole millions of tourists' wages or savings. But the city boomed. Population soared from a little over one million in 1890 to 2,185,283 in 1910, of which 184,884 foreign-born adults could not speak English and 75,580 white immigrants could neither read nor write in any language. Yet they managed to survive, partly because Big Mike McDonald had organized his syndicate in such a way that ward politicians were almost always accessible, with translators, to these foreigners.[8]

McDonald had raised boss politics to an artform, an effective system of public administration that for twenty-five years had spared him the periodic paroxysms of reform. When his machine did finally collapse, it was because he had been overcome by forces far greater than the electoral reformists at the Municipal Voters' League. The challenge came instead from the redistribution of the city's immigrant population, combined with the total restructuring of business and industry brought about by mass production. Together, these larger social transformations then sweeping the nation gave birth to a new "industrialized" underworld that an old-fashioned Irish boss like McDonald could not control. Instead, the three decades following 1900 demonstrated that the city's genius for innovation continued unblemished. Entrepreneurial Chicago reorganized neighborhood gang warfare into a streamlined system of business terrorism orchestrated by the city's biggest newspaper tycoons. It launched the first great beer wars and provided a model for the nationwide system of Prohibition racketeering. And it consolidated citywide gambling by seizing control of the national racing wires, a move that laid the basis for Las Vegas and the expansion of syndicate crime across the nation. The entrepreneurs of Chicago crime during these years did for the underworld what Henry Ford's assembly line did for the overworld of American business. They created a spirit and a system of industrial organization. In doing so they reminded the public of how thin was the veneer between the world of law and progress and the world of violence and corruption.

The first Chicago crime bosses of the twentieth century were James ("Big Jim") Colosimo and Mont Tennes. Colosimo ran the best brothels on the South Side of Chicago. Tennes ran a string of gambling houses on the North Side. Both men owed a deep debt to the recurrent good government campaigns and to the crooked First Ward politicians who had always insulated themselves from those reform movements.

Until the summer of 1907 Tennes had run one of many important bookmaking outfits, each more or less restricted to its own part of town, under the dominion of gambling boss Mike McDonald. But as McDonald grew older, his influence had begun to wane. Campaigns by the Municipal Voters' League against the boodlers had struck hard at the system of graft over which he presided just as a new generation of competitors was rising up around him. When his young wife was charged in February 1907 with murdering a handsome young fellow who had been her friend and probable lover, he was unable to buy off the indictment. His health failed and he fell into a prolonged state of shock. By August he was dead.[9]

"Mike McDonald is dying," the *Chicago News* had editorialized as he lay on his death bed. "When the city had a scant half million this man ruled it from his saloon and gambling house by virtue of his political power. . . . Bad government was accepted as a matter of course. Vice sat in the seats of power and patronized virtue with a large and kindly tolerance, asking only that it remain sufficiently humble and not too obtrusive. Gambling was a leading industry. . . . Elections were controlled by the sweep and simple methods of chasing away voters and stuffing ballot boxes." Now, the *News* proclaimed, the city would celebrate McDonald's wake with the triumph of clean government and the banishment of the corruptors.

But instead of reform, Chicago was plunged into a state of open warfare among the surviving gamblers—a leitmotif of city crime continuing even today. The battles, named by historians the Bombing War of 1907, had begun earlier in the summer but escalated sharply on August 14, when Second Ward gambling chief James O'Leary's den was bombed. Five days later, at about 10:00 P.M., a packet of dynamite exploded in Tennes's backyard. The windows of his house shattered, his wife and children were sent scrambling downstairs, and neighbors soon gathered out front to demand that Tennes hire special police to protect the street. By the end of September three more bombs had exploded, two at Tennes's offices and one at the home of the Cook County sheriff.[10]

To the *News* and *Tribune,* this was all proof that a new and uncontrollable crime wave was breaking over the city. Prosecutors were said to possess evidence that Tennes had already built an iron monopoly on hundreds of the city's bookies who depended upon his wire service for their daily racing reports. Earlier in the year he had bought exclusive Chicago distribution rights to the Payne News Agency, the only national racing wire in the country, then based in Cincinnati. Creation of a national racing wire gave gamblers what the chain store gave to the large manufacturers. Through Tennes's service, bookies could receive instantaneous reports on horses around the country. And through the wire service they could offer the smallest neighborhood bettor the chance to wager on horses thousands of miles away, a privilege previously available only to the rich. At the same time, they could "layoff," or balance, the local bets they were taking by placing private bets at other tracks. Naturally, business boomed.

Tennes paid the Payne service $300 a day for Chicago rights, and each bookie paid him 50 percent of his net receipts for the day. Included in the price was protection from police raids. Tennes's prices were apparently fair, for the police conducted no raids that fall despite a grand jury investigation. Amidst the bombing and mayhem, Police Chief George M. Shippy declared: "It looks as if there was a big gamblers' war on in Chicago. I still maintain, however, that there is no gambling worthy of the name in existence at the present time."

When one independent gambler-alderman was subpoenaed before the grand jury, his saloon was bombed. The bombings went on throughout that year and the next as Tennes quietly continued his expansion with the confidence displayed the night his own home was dynamited:

"Too bad, too bad, so they have attacked me again, have they?" he answered a questioner musingly.

"Do you suspect who the guilty persons are?"

"Yes, of course I do, but I'm not going to tell anyone about it, am I? That would be poor business."

By January 1909 Mont Tennes was the undisputed boss of gambling in Chicago.[11]

The waspish editors of the *News* and *Tribune* denounced Tennes and the complicity of the political-police machine that protected the gamblers. But for a great many others—the shopkeepers, entertainers, restaurateurs, and thousands of immigrants—gambling seemed a vital ingredient in the city's commerce. Chicago was known across the land as a wide-open town, a place where with hard work, imagination, and luck a man could turn the American dream into reality. Gambling brought in tourists. It provided jobs for the poor and the new arrivals who could not find work, and it offered cheap amusement with the possibility of profit. Most important of all, gambling provided the social cement that held the system of city politics in shape, regardless of which party filled the mayor's office. There was no better illustration of the marriage between vice and politics than in the careers of the two aldermen from the First Ward, Michael ("Hinky Dink") Kenna and "Bathhouse John" Coughlin.[12]

Bathhouse John ran a spa at 145 West Madison Street, patronized mostly by gamblers and trackmen. Hinky Dink ran a saloon not far away. Although both aldermen had been loyal protégés of Mike McDonald, they had once upset the old man by lagging in their endorsement of a machine-backed mayoral candidate. McDonald felt the two young aldermen should be taught a lesson. The morning after the election, he directed police to raid all the gambling houses in the First Ward, including Hinky Dink's saloon—a highly embarrassing raid since one of the alderman's duties was to provide security against such raids. The lesson was instructive all right; the two politicians then built a ward machine that would survive into the 1940s. The plan was Kenna's: together they would approach all the brothel and gambling hall owners, collect regular payments from each and establish a defense fund to put two lawyers on permanent retainer for the protection of any operator. It was the same tactic used by industrialists in 1895 to establish the National Association of Manufacturers and by Al Capone to keep the Prohibition beer halls in line.[13]

To hold power over Chicago's First Ward was, and is, a position of unparalleled influence. At its center is the Loop. State Street shops and restaurants were then equal to those along Fifth Avenue in New York. At the ward's northern edge were the mansions of businessmen and judges, one of whom, John Coverly, had begun his career as a lawyer in the Coughlin-Kenna protection apparatus. To the south were the tenements and flophouses where newly arrived Greeks, Poles, Italian, and Slavic immigrants worked as runners, hookers, dealers, enforcers, street sweepers, and election monitors. Hinky Dink and Bathhouse John were ideal bosses of the ward, models of urbanity who were as much at ease with bankers as they were with Black Hand extortionists. So broad was their reputation that New York Tammany Hall boss Richard Croker came to Chicago soliciting campaign support for his Democratic mayoralty candidate. The Cook County Democracy, as the Chicago organization was called, chartered a private train to New York, where they marched in a grand parade supporting the Tammany ticket. At the head of marchers were the glamorous twosome from the First Ward, strutting in full formal morning dress, silk hats, white gloves and trim, furled umbrellas swinging neatly at their sides.[14]

Through his first campaign in 1897 and each succeeding election, Carter Harrison, Jr., had relied on Hinky Dink and Bathhouse John as "the two rocks of Gibraltar." At each election they ran a virtual army of tramps, winos, and flophouse customers, policed by gambling hall underlings, and paid fifty cents a vote followed by a free beer at Hinky Dink's bar. In 1911, making a comeback after six years of retirement, Harrison gave unqualified credit where it was due: "On election day, as previously on primary day, my old-time friends of the First Ward, Hinky Dink and Bathhouse John, came through with flying colors."[15]

Chicago's 1911 summer was especially hot. Politically, it was near the boiling point. Whatever modest pressure the previous reform mayor, Fred Busse, had put on the criminal underworld, Harrison's election came as a signal to gamblers across the nation that Chicago was once again wide open. At the same time, however, anti-immigrant campaigns launched by a mostly blue-blood reform movement attacked the underworld. Caught between the gamblers and the reformers were the police department and the politicians threatened by Harrison's comeback.

First came a scathing report from the vice commission, a board of fifteen prominent businessmen, ministers, lawyers, and progressive social reformers appointed by Busse to clean up the city's whorehouses. Already aldermen Kenna and Coughlin had been forced to cancel their First Ward ball, the annual patronage celebration they held in the coliseum for the gamblers, hookers, and madams of their district. When former Mayor Busse appointed the vice commission in 1910, he had presented them with a practical question: "Should vice be segregated? If so, what would be the method of maintaining control of segregation districts?" It was a polite way for the Republican mayor to diffuse some of the reform fervor and to draw a truce with the invincible Democratic First Ward machine which could have exposed Busse's leniency toward Tennes and a protection racket run by a gangster who had been one of Busse's biggest backers. But by mid-1911, when the commission made its report, Busse was no longer mayor. Denied any direct clout in city hall, the commission's only alternative was to embarrass the Harrison team before it had fully resumed power. Profits from prostitution, they declared, exceeded $15 million a year. Over five thousand women worked the brothels and streets, more than half outside the red-light district of the First Ward. More houses were opening every day. Bar licenses, they charged, were issued as little more than a cover for the brothels and gambling halls. Hinky Dink and Bathhouse John escaped direct exposure in the commission report, although a damning reference was made to the old coliseum balls.[16]

In August 1911 two of Tennes's estranged partners and an independent gambler sued to break his monopoly over the racing wire syndicate, the General News Bureau. Already the Payne News Agency had complained that Tennes's operation was squeezing them out of business, that Tennes had moved beyond Chicago and was selling racing results to every major city in the country. One newspaper report claimed he had customers in twenty-one cities from Baltimore to San Francisco, from Detroit to San Antonio. Some seventy poolrooms in New York alone paid him an average of $4,000 a week. One of his angry partners claimed "that there were three hundred gambling rooms, from poolrooms to faro and roulette wheels, operating in Chicago; that the income amounted to more than half a million a day; that Mont Tennes was the operator of a gambling news service with Chicago as its center and radiating all over the United States; . . . that the Payne racetrack system and others were put out of business by dynamite bombs and the torch; . . . and that poolrooms in Chicago which failed to subscribe to the service were closed down by the police." Tennes, the suit alleged, had contributed $20,000 to Carter Harrison, Jr., in his successful mayoralty race.[17]

Other witnesses in the suits echoed the same charges, especially those concerning police protection. "I've got evidence," one of the litigants swore, "to go before the grand jury and secure the indictment of police officials for collecting eighty-five dollars weekly graft from three protected gambling houses."

In September, the Civil Service Commission opened its own investigation into police graft. Three gambling districts were identified, and this time Hinky Dink was named as the most prominent protector in the city with a fiefdom running from Madison Street in the Loop all the way to Sixty-Third Street. Prosecutions against low-ranking police began and were moving up through the inspectors. Bombs exploded—a desperate effort to scare off the prosecutors. The police chief continued his denials of corruption only to be undercut by an assistant chief who admitted that raids were regularly "tipped off." Finally the commission brought forward its star witness, gambler Harry Brolaski.

Brolaski testified that he had personally conspired with the chief (prior to his appointment) to pose as a converted reformer who would expose independent gamblers who had not entered Tennes's syndicate. Co-conspirators, he testified, included aldermen Coughlin and Kenna, two police inspectors, a lieutenant, the assistant chief, and Mont Tennes. But despite a few resignations from the police department, the commission failed to break the union between the gamblers, the police, and the Democratic machine. And before the year ended all three civil suits against Tennes had been dropped.[18]

Successful or not, the two investigations by the special Vice and Civil Service commissions proved embarrassing to Mayor Harrison. He had to make some public gesture. So it was that about 1:00 A.M., October 25, 1911, police under direct order from the mayor arrived quietly at the doors of the poshest brothel in Chicago, the famed Everleigh Club. There was no ruckus and virtually no arrests. Minna and Ada Everleigh, who had discreetly built a clientele of the finest gentlemen in the city, had decorated their parlors in flowing silks and gold brocades, hung tapestries and fine European paintings along the hallways, and even installed a gold-leaf piano in the central sitting room. The Everleigh sisters had run a tasteful establishment. And they had political tact. Once the police had left, they carefully draped the furniture and fixtures with dustclothes, and went off on a six-month European excursion. They had been assured by the First Ward's two vice lords, Ike Bloom and Big Jim Colosimo, that the whole incident would be forgotten by the time they returned.[19]

Ada and Minna Everleigh had not made many mistakes in amassing their fortunes. They noticed that Ike Bloom's operation, the Freiberg Dance Hall on Twenty-second Street between State and Wabash, had not been raided, and understood. Until then, Bloom had always played second fiddle to Big Jim Colosimo, the sisters' chief ally and perhaps the ward's third most powerful political broker behind Hinky Dink and Bathhouse John. A glowing moon-faced Italian with a thick, neatly trimmed mustache, jaunty checkered suits and a penchant for diamond rings, diamond tie pins, diamond studs and buttons, even loose diamonds he fondled in his pockets, Colosimo was one of Chicago's most engaging rogues.

"Diamond Jim" Colosimo was also a man who had paid his dues to the city's political machinery. Born in Italy, he had come to America as a child. He had worked as a news vendor, shoeshine boy, Black Hand terrorist, pimp and street sweeper, the last of which earned him a niche in the First Ward machine when he organized his coworkers as a voting block for Hinky Dink Kenna. He had married a successful madam, taken over management of her brothel, and, with a Frenchman, built a chain of bordellos that maintained exchange agreements with other prostitution rings in New York, Milwaukee, and St. Louis. He had even managed to turn the 1909 conviction of his French partner to his own advantage, for he not only escaped being charged personally, but also used the occasion to import a talented young nephew from New York as his new partner. That young man, as clever as he was tough, came ostensibly to protect his prosperous uncle against so-called Black Hand extortion threats he had received. In fact he became the organizational genius behind Colosimo's brothel business, expanding it to include a number of gambling halls. His name was John Torrio.[20]

When the Everleigh sisters returned to Chicago in the summer of 1912, their earlier assessment was reaffirmed. Anyone could have sensed the passion with which the newspapers bore down on the red-light districts. But the sisters had spotted a subtler set of maneuvers, borne out in a long list of indictments filed September 25 against several brothel owners. Included was the ward's Democratic precinct captain, the "right arm" of Hinky Dink Kenna, through whom Colosimo had climbed to power. A few days later the state's attorney joined the campaign and issued a warrant against Colosimo himself, among others. Bloom was not arrested. Instead he helped form a thinly disguised payoff fund known as the Friendly Friends and asked the Everleigh sisters to contribute $40,000, a request they declined.

By the end of 1912, one police inspector had been sent to the state penitentiary in Joliet for taking bribes, two others had been suspended, and evidence was steadily mounting against the police chief, who would be forced out of office by the end of 1913. Each day the newspapers reported new skirmishes among the vice kings, the state prosecutor, the city prosecutor, the mayor's office, and the city police. The mayor even went so far as to appoint one Major M.C.L. Funkhouser as a special deputy police commissioner to investigate vice independently. At another point the hookers staged a protest march through the streets. Dressed in plumes, furs, kimonos, and robes, they concluded their march, then dispersed and strode proudly up the walks of the stately downtown mansions to ask for a night's lodging. Bombings punctuated the sound of night traffic as the whole system of underworld business seemed threatened with upheaval.

Campaigns against Italian communities had also intensified after 1910 when 194 "Sicilians" were arrested one night following the murder of a probable police informer. Black Hand extortion threats stole front-page headlines as national magazine writers warned of Italian conspiracies to export secret criminal societies across the ocean. Calls for civic reform were again surfacing, but this time they became a convenient outlet for all sorts of nativist fears and frustrations that had begun to rekindle the Progressive movement.[21]

Unlike the trust-busting Progressives a decade earlier, these reformers relied on the new science of genetics to explain the flaws in society. Robber barons and monopolists remained important public enemies. But white middle-class nativists added a new target: the great waves of southern Italians, Polish and Jewish immigrants whose darker skins betrayed their supposedly inferior ancestry. In league with these "inferior" immigrants were the armies of prostitutes who were fouling the manhood of native American sons. These apparently evil intruders seemed to be subverting the very fabric of middle-class life, dragging down hardworking families and snatching from them the promise of progress and prosperity. Crooks, swarthy dagos, vile sluts, and shameless politicians became millionaires, the diatribes proclaimed, while honest men and women faced rising prices and scarce jobs. Nationwide attacks against "Papists" and dark immigrants like the Italians had the same hysterical tone prevalent during the witch trials of Salem. If the old dream of a new and better world seemed to be collapsing, then the cause was said to be the presence of bad and diabolical people: Quakers, witches, blasphemers, Jews, and Sicilians. Following unwritten tradition, the only solution appeared to be a purge of these people. All that was needed was an appropriate incident.

It came on June 15, 1914, when Detective Sergeant Stanley Birns of Major Funkhouser's morals squad was killed in the line of duty. Sergeant Birns was murdered, the *Tribune* declared, because the police department and the underworld had jointly fought the special morals division:

> It is the common suspicion of almost everyone who keeps in touch with civic affairs that the "Bath" [Coughlin] is the real man behind Freiberg's Dance Hall, although Ike Bloom is the ostensible proprietor and manager. It is Freiberg's that goes on undisturbed when raids are made all about the district. . . . Captain Michael Ryan of the Twenty-second Street Police Station . . . is the Chief of Police of the First Ward. The "Hink" put him there. The "Hink" and the "Bath" keep him there. He has been denounced as either notoriously corrupt or incompetent. But Funkhouser, Dannenberg, Gleason [the new police chief] and Hoyne [the new state's attorney], himself, cannot budge Ryan from that station. They have all tried and failed. . . . Ryan is the hub. His plain clothes policemen, his confidential men, are spokes, and sections of the rim are the "Big Four" or the "Big Five" as conditions happen to be at the time, the dive owners and keepers controlling strings of saloons and resorts that travel along without interruption.
>
> But more important than any or all of these parts—the one thing without which the wheel could not revolve—is the axle, and this axle is the "little fellow" to every denizen of the district, or "Hinky Dink."[22]

This blast from the *Tribune* was too much to ignore. Hoyne publicly named Colosimo and John Torrio as operators of the biggest vice ring on the South Side. Colosimo's former partner, Maurice Van Bener, and independent gambler Jakie Adler were picked up as key witnesses in the murder of Sergeant Birn and in a larger plot against the whole morals division. Colosimo himself was locked up for half a day. Even Minna Everleigh was persuaded to testify that she had paid over $100,000 to the bosses for protection. The smaller, independent whorehouses throughout the city were raided and closed. Ike Bloom's license was revoked. Captain Ryan was transferred. Coughlin and Kenna were said to be finished.

It was a powerful summer for reform. Except that no one was convicted. Nobody in fact did testify before the grand jury about Birn's killing. Ike Bloom got his license reissued within a few months, and he suffered only a loss of dignity when Captain Ryan's successor removed the picture of him that had been hanging in the Twenty-second Street police station for several years. Hinky Dink and Bathhouse John won by as big a margin as ever in the next city council elections. In the end, even Colosimo and Torrio emerged unscathed, securing dominion over vice in the First Ward.

Despite victories over both their competitors and the reformers, 1912 had been an expensive year for Colosimo and Torrio. Trials, especially those where witnesses chose not to testify, required a lot of money. Neither was the publicity generated by the trials helpful to business. As a solution to both problems, Torrio took a decisive step which would eventually prove critical to the gang's near monopoly over all Chicago rackets. Quietly, and without any help from Colosimo, he moved a major share of his personal operation to suburban Burnham, south of the city.

Alert to the new opportunities opened up by the mass production of the private automobile, Torrio saw that by dispersing their business, he could respond more flexibly to city hall's periodic reform rituals. Burnham, a small, working-class town, was hardly important enough to merit the attention of the newspapers or the Cook County reform element. Town officials, most of them part time or volunteer, charged a lower price in graft yet guaranteed a secure base from which to survive future cleanup campaigns. And for Torrio's respectable middle-class customers, the suburbs offered the sort of discreet anonymity not often found downtown. A professional man could drive out alone in his new Ford after work, unobserved by his friends, take a few spins on the roulette wheel, visit the upstairs brothel, and arrive home for late dinner with his wife and children.

The sort of resilient foresight that brought Torrio to Burnham was foreign to the old vice operators who had not survived the reform movement. As their businesses fell beneath the weight of repeated raids and escalating payoffs, more of the market opened to men like Torrio. Steadily he encouraged his "Uncle Jim" to spend more time minding his restaurant, the then famous Colosimo's Café on South Wabash. Meanwhile Torrio took over as operational manager, coordinating the First Ward houses with the suburban ones and opening betting parlors in the backrooms of downtown cigar stores. The modern businessman would say he was laying a "commercial infrastructure." A straightforward man, Torrio saw it as building an organization. During Prohibition, he and his gangster colleagues would rely on that organization to lay the foundations of modern organized crime.[23]

But neither Torrio nor any other gangster would have succeeded without help from the straight world. Politicians, gamblers, whores, and whoremongers seem always to demonstrate a certain affinity for one another in the annals of urban America. In prewar Chicago, however, a new element entered the equation—the press. If the gamblers and the vice lords were forced into professional organization by the changing face of politics, another set of young toughs won affluence and stature at the behest of big business, particularly the big businesses operated by Chicago's swashbuckling newspaper tycoons Medill McCormick and William Randolph Hearst.

Hearst roared into Chicago in 1900 to launch his newest paper, the *American.* His personal fortunes, like his empire, were at a peak that year. The Spanish-American War had just ended, a war that had been mounted largely in response to the jingoistic fabrications of his *New York Morning Journal.* He had also begun to believe that the presidency was within his reach, an ambition greatly advanced by the chain of popular, gossipy, sensational newspapers he was building. There was one more battle he had to win if he were to have enough influence to get his readers to send him to the White House: Hearst's newspapers had to top all others' circulation.

Although Hearst made few personal appearances at his Chicago newspapers, his key operative (and later the publisher of the papers), Andrew M. Lawrence, was a genius at infiltrating Chicago politics. The *American* immediately presented itself as the workingman's newspaper. It wailed against the privileges and the policies of the Republican "trust" papers, carping continuously about how they had leased public property from the city school board on which to locate their two buildings. The *American* hated the British Empire, championed the eight-hour workday and consumed entire forests lamenting the plight of widows and orphans. By 1905, the *American* had successfully placed its own man, Fred Dunne, in the mayor's office.

Dunne was perfect for the Hearst operations. Publicly identified with the reformers at the Municipal Voters' League, he had also struck a deal with Hinky Dink Kenna and thereby won the support of the First Ward's underworld troops. Andrew Lawrence, affectionately known as

"Long Green," had understood from the onset that he could not amass a giant circulation solely by printing the sensational heart wrenchers that had been so successful in New York. Chicago presented a practical problem. Newsboys had already taken every important street corner, and there were so many papers on their racks that no room was left for the *American* and its subsequent afternoon sister, the *Examiner*.

Lawrence hired Max Annenberg away from the *Tribune*'s circulation department, and Max brought along his youngest brother, Moe.* The brothers were sharp, aggressive hustlers, whose German immigrant parents ran a junk shop. As children, Max and Moe had helped their father peddle his wares, and as messengers, street sweepers, and paper boys, they had learned to be tough. When the young men went to work for Andrew Lawrence, they understood that it would take muscle to convince news vendors to display the papers. Within a few years, Max had become circulation manager of the *American* and Moe held the same job at the *Examiner*. Through brawn and guile, Hearst journalism had emerged as the voice of the downtrodden, just as it had in New York, Los Angeles, and San Francisco. It was now a question of using brawn and guile to capture the street corners.[24]

To protect those corners for the *Tribune*, McCormick in 1910 rehired Max Annenberg. As a counterplay, Andrew Lawrence also rounded up a gang of toughs. By October the first shots of the notorious Chicago circulation wars had been fired. Except for stories in the socialist press, it was a war that went largely uncovered, though it dragged on for two full years. Scores of men and boys were cut down by gunfire in the streets as the deadly brawling between the two circulation staffs escalated. "The circulation manager of the Chicago *Tribune* [Annenberg] furnished revolvers to some of these sluggers and the slugging crew of that paper rode around in a big black automobile truck," a reporter for the *Daily Socialist* wrote in October 1911. The following summer, after reporting on numerous ambushes, the *Daily Socialist* brought the whole affair before the Cook County grand jury, only to have the investigation quashed by state's attorneys Wayman and Hoyne, both of whom were loyal to the *Tribune*. "Why should not Mr. Wayman ascertain, and at least hold up to public reprobation," asked

* Moe Annenberg's son Walter must have learned well from his father and uncle, since he became a press czar himself (*TV Guide, Seventeen, The Daily Racing Forum*) before becoming President Nixon's ambassador to England.

the independent *Inter-Ocean,* "the men whose money nourished and sustained these bravos trained to swagger through the streets with automatic guns in $5,000 automobiles, wounding or killing whosoever their employers dislike? But Mr. Wayman will not. He dare not. Everybody knows that."[25]

When newsboy Charles Gallanty refused one August morning in 1911 to take an extra thirty *Tribunes,* one of Annenberg's men bloodied his face, threw him to the street, and continued kicking him in the head as the boy desperately held onto a fire hydrant to keep from being dragged into an alley. Not only newsboys were open to attack. Three Hearst thugs were killed the same summer, each shot to death as they stood drinking in neighborhood taverns. "Dutch" Gentleman, one of Hearst's men, stood in a bar on South State Street, bragging about his exploits, daring any man to challenge the deft accuracy of his trigger finger, when one "Mossy" Enright of the *Tribune* slipped quietly behind him. Dutch spun around just fast enough to have his abdomen slashed open by the force of six .44-caliber slugs. He died before he had a chance to draw, his intestines oozing onto the sawdust-covered floor.

By midsummer 1912, the circulation wars had brought far more terror to the streets than had the bombing campaigns of Mont Tennes. By then, however, it had also become a campaign to break the newspaper unions, a campaign that had been initiated nationally that spring by the American Newspaper Publishers' Association. Through a clever maneuver by Andrew Lawrence and the Chicago Publishers' Association, the city's major papers ceased to recognize the pressmen's union.* Hearst, the workingman's champion, locked arms with the so-called Republican trust papers and through their armed circulation gangs began to strongarm news vendors who continued carrying the two union papers, the *Daily World* and the *Daily Socialist.* Circulation for the latter soared to 300,000, but with bloody consequences. The *Daily Socialist* reported on May 6, 1912:

*Lawrence first notified the pressmen that the Hearst papers would void their own old contract in favor of the union's standard citywide newspaper contract, which the union accepted. Once done, Lawrence further notified the union he would control the number of men hired, a concession the pressmen also accepted. Since the union's acceptance of that provision was a technical violation of the citywide contract *in management's favor* the publishers' association declared all contracts void, denied recognition to the Chicago Web Pressmen's Union No. 7, and locked the doors against union members. Although the pressmen were locked out, the newspapers reported the incident as an illegal strike in violation of the union contract.

> Sluggers employed by the trust newspapers this morning beat up into unconsciousness Alexander Hickey, a news-driver, who was delivering the Chicago *Daily World,* and then kidnapped him in an automobile under the pretense of taking him to a hospital. The assault and kidnapping occurred in front of the elevated station at Wilson and Evanston Avenues. Guns were used by Max Annenberg, circulation manager of the *Tribune,* who was in charge of a squad of plug-uglies who rode to the station in an automobile.[26]

Hickey charged Annenberg with attempted murder, and several witnesses confirmed his account. Nonetheless, the charges were dropped, and instead Hickey was brought before the grand jury by Judge John R. Caverley. Annenberg, it turned out, had carried a private commission naming him a deputy sheriff.

On June 16 streetcar conductor Frank Witt was accidentally killed along with two other men when three Hearst circulation boys opened fire on a loaded trolley. Two of the three Hearst men had records for assault. On June 29, nineteen-year-old Earl Farrell was shot when a Hearst man, posing as a union striker, opened fire into a crowd that had gathered to buy union papers. On July 5, another Hearst employee killed a newsboy who had refused to sell the *Examiner* because it was not a union paper. And on July 29 yet another Hearst thug boarded a trolley and began spraying the ceiling with lead because the passengers were not reading Hearst's *American.* A report in the October 26 edition of the *Evening World* asked some of the critical questions raised by the Hearst and Annenberg gangs:

> Besides the Witt murder is the case of George Hehr, a teamster, who was shot on the corner of Adams and Desplaines Streets on the night of August 8 at 7 o'clock. *Seven Chicago American wagon drivers surrounded Hehr's wagon. Revolvers were drawn by the Hearst drivers. Hehr had no revolver. But Hehr was shot. He died before word could be sent to his young wife at home.*
>
> The seven Hearst drivers, all personally known to 'Long Green' Andy Lawrence, were named by the coroner's jury. . . .

More than two months have gone since the murder of George Hehr. It was just as *coarse, brutal and indefensible murder as that of Frank Witt.*

Three grand juries have been sitting since Frank Witt was shot to death. Two grand juries have been sitting since George Hehr was shot to death. . . . *'Who is back of the gunmen?'*

Question: Did 'Long Green' Andy Lawrence from his office in the Hearst Building reach for the telephone and give orders to the Democratic City Hall authorities to 'protect' the murderers?

Question: Did Victor Lawson, president of the Publishers' Association and editor and owner of the Daily News *reach for a telephone and send word to the Republican State's attorney to 'protect' the murderers?*[27]

The implication left by the *Evening World* and by Hearst biographer Ferdinand Lundberg is that the circulation wars ended as a conspiracy among the newspaper tycoons to break the unions by arming and organizing the city's gangsters. Lundberg even charges Hearst with "preparing to *inaugurate the system of gang warfare and racketeering which was to cost the City of Chicago and the nation billions of dollars and the death of thousands of citizens.*" In fact, many of the key men on both staffs in the circulation wars later became racketeers in Al Capone's gang and in the nationwide gambling syndicates.[28]

Hearst and his newspapers have come to symbolize the very worst in sensational yellow journalism, an unscrupulous pandering to public fear and bigotry combined with reactionary flag waving. Much of that indictment is true. Hearst's performance in fomenting the Spanish-American War, largely a gambit to build daily circulation, won him a well-deserved reputation as America's most opportunistic publisher. It also demonstrated how powerful, and how dangerous, his burgeoning empire could be. For more than any other publisher, and maybe more than any other politician, William Randolph Hearst could sense the temper of America's working millions. During four years in the U.S. Congress he built a sterling progressive record introducing tough legislation in support of the eight-hour day, limiting monopoly mergers, demanding the breakup of the coal-railroad combines, even calling for public ownership of utilities—all of it marked by the flamboyance reflected in a 1902 campaign banner reading, "IN THE MIDST OF

PROSPERITY WE ARE COAL-LESS, PORKLESS, AND PENNY-LESS." For a man hell-bent on winning the presidency, these early years of the century were of course opportune times to line up with the reformers and appear as the champion of the common man. Yet for all the millions of readers his papers and magazines could claim, he could never quite galvanize them behind his lavish campaigns. At best he succeeded in spreading panic through the country's financial and political leadership.[29]

It was an age of rising radicalism, and various leaders began to fear that these millions of common men might metamorphose into the armed masses of the coming revolution. Some even imagined that the people's army might find an ally in that unscrupulous demagogue William Randolph Hearst.* Within the ruling circles of business and government, campaigning against Hearst became popular, not because he was guilty of yellow journalism but because he was thought to be agitating the lower classes. Little wonder then that the McCormick family—newly arrived aristocrats, inventors who had made American agriculture a wonder to the world, and proud publishers of "the Greatest Newspaper in the World"—would feel duty bound to block the march of Hearst and his press.

There is little doubt that when McCormick repurchased the services of Max Annenberg and crew he knew he was hiring a flying wedge of the best gunmen in town to do the work they knew best. The *Tribune* dropped its daily sales price to a penny, and if most accounts are correct, Annenberg deployed the more effective squads of fighters. By July 1912—the month in which the Progressive party held its convention in Chicago and the Democrats their convention in Baltimore—the circulation wars were at their bloodiest. The Republicans nominated Taft, and the Progressives chose Roosevelt (neither of whom would win the election); the candidate backed by Hearst, Missouri

*As historian Gabriel Kolko has noted, the reinvigorated Progressive party's key problem was to appear as radical reformers while in fact shoring up the powers of big business, a sleight-of-hand they accomplished by pressing for federal business regulation in their 1912 platform: "We therefore demand a strong national regulation of interstate corporations. The corporation is an essential part of modern business. The concentration of modern business, in some degree, is both inevitable and necessary for national and international business efficiency. . . . Under such a system of constructive regulation, legitimate business, freed from confusion, uncertainty and fruitless litigation, will develop normally."

populist "Champ" Clark, never left the gate. He was wiped out at the Democratic nominating convention. And no sooner were the presidential campaigns completed than Annenberg began to draw in his boys and wind down the war.

Nationally, McCormick's Progressive allies suffered defeat. Locally in Chicago they carried the election and the *Tribune*'s circulation grew. The *Examiner*'s declined. And Long Green Andy Lawrence, the Hearst publisher, took most of the blame for having initiated the bloody circulation battles a decade earlier. In Chicago, the home of Hearst's most powerful newspapers, the Hearst organization was morally tarnished, politically shaken, and serviced by a few dozen gangsters peddling papers on the sidewalk.[30]

It was the gangsters, and indeed the gangster politicians of the corrupt First Ward, who would provide continuity to the political life of Chicago, access for the Hearst newspapers to the city government, and a mechanism for realigning festering ethnic antagonisms that could have provoked yet another war in the streets. Chicanery and double-crosses turned Chicago into a political brier patch, the details of which will probably never be untangled. A brief sampler of the characters and events from the opening of World War I in 1914 to the famous bootleg shootouts of the mid-twenties will illustrate the almost baroque intrigues of the era.

In 1915 William Hale Thompson won the mayoralty in the name of reform. Thompson, forty-five, came from the same respectable upper-crust background as the Municipal Voters' League members who had first sponsored him in aldermanic elections fifteen years earlier. He should have brought solace to the hearts of Progressives like the McCormicks. Instead the Hearst papers switched party loyalty and led the campaign for Thompson's victory. The champion of "America First" boosterism, Thompson proved to be much less interested in reform than in business, the unfettered pursuit of trade. Casting discretion to the winds, Thompson declared Chicago to be once again "a wide-open town" for gamblers. Nothing could have endeared the mayor better to gambling boss Mont Tennes, or to the expanding gambling-prostitution combine of Big Jim Colosimo and John Torrio.[31]

In 1916, a year after the election, the Civil Service Commission reported that a group called the Sportsmen's Club was distributing bushels of money to the city administration to protect the operation of slot machines in Chicago. The head of the Sportsmen's Club, James A.

Pugh, had managed Thompson's successful mayoral campaign. Mayor Thompson's name was displayed prominently on the club letterhead.* [32]

In 1917 a ruddy-cheeked twenty-five-year-old Irish tough named Dion O'Bannion was promoted to chief of circulation for the two Hearst newspapers. O'Bannion had run with the North Side Irish gangs since he was ten, had served time for burglary and assault by the time he reached eighteen, and then was hired to do his part in the circulation wars. He would leave the papers in 1922, the same year he was again indicted on robbery charges.[33]

In 1918, as in 1917, the pressure on Mont Tennes seemed to intensify as the city police made several raids on his gambling halls. A bookkeeper close to Tennes turned state's evidence against him. A leak in his wire service ciphering code was said to have cost him several thousand dollars.[34]

In 1919 Thompson was reelected mayor, the beneficiary of a bitter Democratic split which pitted the city's massive German population against an alliance of flag wavers reveling in postwar anti-German hysteria. Thompson's narrow plurality in the election heightened his sensitivity to the changing pattern of the city's ethnic votes. The two most dramatic changes in the old electoral alignments were the continuous flood of job-hungry blacks migrating from the South and the explosion in Chicago's Italian population.[35]

If William Hale Thompson, Jr., has earned any enduring epithet, it is as the most corrupt mayor in modern American history. His severest critics claim that by the end of his career he was nothing more than the plaything of "the Big Fellow," Al Capone. This may be true. But he was also a man who understood the profound social consequences of industrial prosperity. While the reformers dreamed neat and tidy dreams of progress toward middle-class respectability, Thompson saw that booming business had nearly trebled the city's volatile slum and tenement population, providing them with neither services nor repre-

*Other prominent members of the club were Mont Tennes (whose lawyer was also the club's lawyer); Herbert Mills, a slot-machine manufactuere; John J. Lynch, a gambler who would later become Tennes's partner and later still would jointly run the gambling wire service with Moe Annenberg, brother of the *Tribune*'s Max Annenberg; First Ward vice boss Big Jim Colosimo; James V. Mondi, later one of Al Capone's chieftains; Police Chief Charles C. Healey and Police Captain Morgan Collins. The police chief, among others, was indicted by state's attorney Malcolm Hoyne, a protégé of the *Tribune*'s, but as usual there were no convictions.

sentation. The proof was in the numbers: From 1910 to 1920 Chicago's black population jumped from 44,103 to 109,458. By 1930 there were 233,903 blacks in the city, an overall increase of over 400 percent. If they could provide Hearst with a major market for his newspapers, they could deliver Thompson a major block of votes at the polls.*

"As mayor of the city . . . he was hailed as 'Big Bill, the Builder,' Chicago's greatest booster, the defender of the weak, the champion of the people, while at the same time in certain newspapers [notably the *Tribune*] the word 'Thompsonism' came to be a symbol for spoils politics, police scandals, school-board scandals, padded payrolls, gangster alliances, betrayal of the public trust, bizarre campaign methods, and buffoonery in public office," as one historian has written. Thompson spoke out for Negro rights, and blacks gave him their votes. In turn he dealt out lucrative patronage positions in the primarily black Second Ward.

Under Thompson, the so-called black-belt wards secured enough support from city hall to put two black aldermen on the city council, elect two representatives and a senator to the state legislature and send a congressman to Washington. Not so surprisingly, black gamblers, bootleggers and vice lords were left alone to become some of the district's most successful businessmen. Speaking to a black audience in his 1915 campaign, Thompson could not have been plainer: "I'll give you people the best opportunities you've ever had if you elect me. I'll

*The Hearst papers constantly trumpeted themselves as the friend of Negro rights, a somewhat disingenuous claim since the papers had grown increasingly hostile to labor unions and many of the blacks had been brought north as unwitting strikebreakers. During the 1919 race riots, precipitated in part by antagonism between stockyard workers and black scabs, Hearst reporters alone entered into the ghettos. A former Hearst reporter recounted his venture into rioting black Chicago on the rear of a company motorcycle. "How about it?" he said to his driver. "Shall we go in there?"

"Sure," the driver said. He lifted the end of a banner with the paper's name on it, which was attached to the motorcycle, and said, "This will get us by. The paper's been giving the jigaboos all the best of it. They won't pop off at us."

In they rode, the reporter holding on in terror, when a shot went off, fired by the driver. Looking up, the reporter saw, atop a nearby roof, a black woman was struggling with a black man to keep him from aiming his rifle at the white intruders. "One side's enough to worry about!" the gun-waving driver shouted back to the reporter.

"Who was the driver of the motorcycle?" the reporter later asked rhetorically. "He was Dion O'Bannion, at the time employed as 'circulation slugger' for the newspaper." Within three years O'Bannion would become a Prohibition racketeering boss.

give your people jobs, and any of you want to shoot craps go ahead and do it."

Powerless in a hostile, white neighborhood, Chicago's blacks won influence by maneuvering within the existing Republican machine. Or, as historian Allen Spear put it, they came to dominate their districts "not by rebelling against the regular organization but by their leverage within it." It was the same technique being used by Big Jim Colosimo and his Italian comrades in the adjacent First Ward. Like the black migrants, the Italian immigrants too were proliferating. From 1910 to 1920 the Italian population rose from about 75,000 to 125,000.[36]

Despite their growing numbers, Chicago's Italians were dispersed in pockets throughout the city, none of which were large enough to exercise real power in city government. Only in the First Ward, ironically, where relatively few Italians lived, did they have a man whose clout in the mayor's office had been demonstrated. That man was Colosimo, and, increasingly, his second, John Torrio. Unlike the power of the neighborhood bosses in San Francisco, New York, and New Orleans, their power was based not on anything as ephemeral as ethnic loyalty but on the profits of their businesses and the payoffs they could make to city hall. By the end of 1919 those businesses stood on the threshold of success beyond Colosimo's wildest dreams. Then on October 28, 1919, Congress enacted that greatest of all reforms: Prohibition.

Hardly anyone now denies that Prohibition became the biggest boon to organized racketeering in American history. The general prosperity of the 1920s could not have been a worse time for enforcing a puritanical suppression of popular tastes. If anything, the transformation of liquor into a forbidden fruit stimulated consumption. The hypocrisy of the law was so obvious that millions received just as big a kick out of breaking the law as they got from drinking the alcohol itself. Yet Prohibition was only a catalyst for the proliferation of syndicate crime. The circumstances of its organization lay buried in the nation's social structure, just as the triumphs of Torrio and Capone ran deep into Chicago's social structure. A few vital events provide the outlines.[37]

At 4:00 P.M., May 11, 1920, Big Jim Colosimo sat in his café on South Wabash awaiting two truckloads of contraband whiskey. No whiskey ever arrived. But a hired killer, probably paid by John Torrio, did and ended the reign of Colosimo. Many of Chicago's most prominent politicians appeared for Colosimo's funeral. "Three judges, eight aldermen, an assistant state's attorney, a congressman, a state representative, and leading artists of the Chicago Opera Company [Enrico Caruso had been a regular at Colosimo's restaurant] are listed as honorary pallbearers, as well as gamblers, ex-gamblers, dive-keepers, and ex-dive-keepers," the *Tribune* reported. Alderman Hinky Dink Kenna and John Powers, the Irish boss of the Nineteenth Ward, were among the pallbearers. Bathhouse John Coughlin knelt grandly at the casket.

As heir to all Colosimo's brothels and gambling halls, Torrio became the city's most powerful and ingenious crime boss. His earlier reliance on suburban Burnham as a secure operations base began to pay dividends, and he expanded into a dozen other towns to the south and west, including Chicago Heights, Stickney, Forest View, Blue Island, and eventually Cicero. Carefully, he was building a network along Chicago's southern arc that would enable him to penetrate the city quickly and easily. The same year new attacks were made against Mont Tennes, raids so numerous that the *Daily News* reported: "Since the advent of the Thompson administration it has been freely whispered that Mont Tennes has been forced to surrender a large interest in the [General News Bureau] to politicians."[38]

The following year, Anthony D'Andrea, a defrocked priest and convicted counterfeiter, led a determined fight to topple John Powers as boss of the Nineteenth Ward, a position he had held for over twenty years. D'Andrea had a strong base in the unions and was president of the fraternal Unione Siciliana. Furthermore, the ward had slowly turned into a predominantly Italian colony. Not too surprisingly, election day left blood on the polls as goon squads for both sides hit the streets. By a tiny 321 vote margin, Powers prevailed. On May 11, three months after the election, D'Andrea was blasted in the chest by a sawed-off shotgun. By summer's end three more of his followers were murdered. As historian John Landesco pointed out several years later, Chicago politics permitted no alternative to the sort of showdown exemplified in the D'Andrea-Powers affair. "It is true," he wrote, "that D'Andrea used the same methods as Powers, but it is also true that only a D'Andrea, willing to use force without stint or limit, could rise to leadership in the situation against the use of fraud, the connivance and protection of politics, and the highly developed qualities of 'ward heeler' leadership which John Powers possessed along with the availability of protected, armed partisans. We use the term 'the struggle for self-determination'—it was nothing short of that. That is why the Italians made D'Andrea a national-group hero, as manifested in his royal funeral." In other words, the legitimate politicians had set up a system which no one but a gangster was powerful enough to challenge.[39]

In contrast to the Italian defeat in the Nineteenth Ward was Torrio's success in the First. During 1922 and 1923 he struck deals with a number of Chicago brewers to distribute their beer to his expanding chain of saloons and speakeasies. He became part owner (in fact, he was probably the full owner) of three breweries. He never attempted to displace his two genial aldermen, Kenna and Coughlin, but allowed them to continue in office with his support. He had contributed several tens of thousands of dollars to Mayor Thompson's successful campaign in 1919, and now Thompson responded by insulating him from raids. As a gesture to his Italian constituents he named one Carmen Vacco to the post of city sealer.* Most importantly, by keeping police pressure on Mont Tennes, the Thompson machine enabled Torrio and his top field marshal, Al Capone, to gradually assert control over most of the gambling bookies who had used Tennes's wire service. By late 1923, Tennes announced that he had sold a 40 percent interest in the General News Service to Jack Lynch, a Sportsmen's Club member who had been one of Mayor Thompson's earliest promoters. Tennes apparently "lost" a half million dollars that year on his race books—an amount that coincided, some reporters noticed, with the amount Al Capone later claimed to have won at the track.[40]

*When Mayor Thompson returned to office in 1927, he named another Italian, Daniel Seritella, city sealer. Not only was Seritella a close companion of Al Capone's, who may have been Thompson's most lavish financial backer, he was also an old Hearst circulation man who had got his start in the newsboys' union. According to James Ragen, Hearst circulation manager from 1922 to 1927, *Herald* and *Examiner* publisher Andrew Lawrence "picked up the phone and called the mayor and said, 'We'd like Seritella' and hung up. I told Dan, 'You have the job.'" After Ragen left Hearst, he was hired by the new proprietor of Tennes's old General News Bureau, Moe Annenberg. He remained its general manager until Annenberg's income tax evasion conviction in 1939, then became general manager of the successor Continental Press Service until his murder in Chicago in 1946. After his first boost from Hearst, Seritella went on to become a city alderman and state representative. He returned to the racing wire business in the forties and was widely suspected of having had a hand in Ragen's murder during the so-called national wire service war that produced killings of high-level racketeers in Las Vegas, Chicago, and Cleveland.

Torrio's genius in those years was the low-key diplomacy with which he assembled blocks of power. He even carried himself like a diplomat, his neatly trimmed hair graying at the temples, his clothes conservative and impeccably tailored, in stark contrast to his predecessor, flashy "Diamond Jim," and to the belligerent Anthony D'Andrea. A thoughtful businessman, he also took care to delegate responsibility; the gunplay, for example, he left to Capone. His motto was the "Union of Each for the Good of All." Through Torrio, even the tough, somewhat hotheaded Dion O'Bannion maintained cooperative agreements with the Italian Genna brothers in his district.

Torrio's system of fluid alliances would probably have continued for many years had the city's reform elements not succeeded finally in installing their own man as mayor. But when William E. Dever became mayor on April 3, 1923, Chicago virtually fell apart at the seams. Neither Torrio nor his aldermen retained any influence with the new administration or the new police chief. Raids could not be bought off nor speakeasies protected. The system of alliances through which lower-class Irish and Italians had gained some measure of political influence fell into chaos. Torrio's prestige as the compleat fixer plummeted.

The reformers' campaigns to clean up graft, corruption, and patronage and to run the hoodlums out of government also meant that the masses of immigrant working people lost the only identifiable (though admittedly crooked) power brokers they had ever had. The first result of this power vacuum was open warfare among all the old gangs. Before the election, reformers complained that Thompson permitted violent shootouts in the streets. Within six months of Dever's election, occasional gun battles had escalated into full-fledged guerrilla warfare. During the three years from September 1923 to October 1926 some 215 gangsters died as they battled for control of the beer business. Among the victims was Dion O'Bannion, murdered in his florist shop by the Genna brothers over an apparent beer concession dispute. (A contributing factor in O'Bannion's killing may have been the Gennas' onetime connection with Anthony D'Andrea, who had fallen prey to an Irish boss.) Torrio himself was wounded in January 1925 with a bullet in the neck. Shortly thereafter he decided not to contest a minor bootlegging conviction. After serving nine months in prison, he left Chicago permanently and returned to New York, where his business sense and talent for organization brought him even greater prominence.[41]

With O'Bannion's murder and Torrio's flight, the North Side concessions fell to Hymie Weiss (né Karl Wajciehowski), a wiley Pole who quickly cemented an alliance with Irish West Siders. To most outward appearances the gangs were divided, as an English journalist put it, into "Weiss guys" and "Capone guys." Soon enough, all but a few of the leaders were dead guys. First to go was Angelo Genna, president of the Unione Siciliana, which prior to Genna's tenure, had been a fairly respectable and influential Italian civic association. If Capone had a rival among the city's Italians, it was Genna. His life ended when three sawed-off shotguns broke through the window of his new $6,000 roadster and fired point-blank into his head and chest. The date: May 26, 1925.

Two weeks later another Genna brother was killed in a police shootout, and a third died in July. Six months later, an ally of Genna's who had succeeded to the presidency of the Unione had his head blown off in a barber's chair. Then, within two weeks of that killing, two Jewish subordinates of the Genna gang were slain. Three more Genna brothers survived, but they were careful not to get in the way: The fall of the underworld house of Genna was complete.

Among the beneficiaries was Alphonse Capone, who installed his own man as president of the Unione. Back and forth the bullets flew, an Irishman here, a Pole there, a Sicilian somewhere else. Chicago became enveloped in death. Capone's men apparently suffered greater casualties than the others simply because they had been the dominant gang and they provided easier targets to upstart competitors who had much to gain and little to lose. Eventually, of course, he succeeded in the warfare, picking off Weiss's top lieutenants and finally Weiss himself. On October 11, 1926, as Weiss stepped from his car to the sidewalk in front of Dion O'Bannion's old florist shop, a burst of machine-gun fire cut him to shreds. The worst of the beer war was over, at the very spot where the opening shots had been fired. It had lasted just one month short of two years.[42]

Capone denied killing Weiss, as he sat in robe and slippers at his room in the Hawthorne Hotel, pontificating. "There's enough business for all of us without us killing each other like animals in the streets. I don't want to end up in the gutter punctured with machine-gun slugs, so why should I kill Weiss?" Some days later he added: "Hymie Weiss is dead because he was bull-headed. Forty times I've tried to arrange things so that we'd have peace in Chicago and life would be worth living. Who wants to be tagged around night and day by guards? I don't, for one. There was, and there is, plenty of business for us all and competition needn't be a matter of murder, anyway. But Weiss couldn't be told anything. I suppose you couldn't have told him a week ago that he'd be dead today. There are some reasonable fellows in his outfit, and if they want peace I'm for it now, as I have always been."[43]

By the end of 1926 Chicago had had enough of reform. The following spring, with the backing of Capone, Mayor Thompson reclaimed his office. Capone was now the supreme underworld king in Chicago. He had learned well the lessons he had been taught in the service of respectable and respected big business.

As the quintessential example of free enterprise and opportunity, as the town whose industrial tentacles stretched across the continent to unite frontier destiny with Yankee ingenuity, or simply as the wide-open town of Mayors Harrison and Thompson, Chicago was the sort of city where men like Torrio and Capone were all but inevitable. Nor is it surprising that at a time when Americans were generating myths of their boundless potency and unlimited resourcefulness that a figure such as Capone would be seen as both a merciless cutthroat and a hero to the masses. To some he was the heir to the myths of Jesse James and Robin Hood, an outlaw who looked after his own people the best way he could. Soliciting memories of the bootleg era, Kenneth Allsop found only one among several dozen people who would flatly denounce Capone. A lawyer, whose father had been an Illinois attorney general, told Allsop, "Capone was relatively innocent compared with some of the men who dominated business and public life then—and I'm thinking particularly of Samuel Insull [one of Lincoln Steffen's boodlers, who fleeced the city of millions through monopolizing electric power distribution], who conducted his financial operations like a ruthless brigand."

Many of the respectable people Allsop interviewed simply restated Capone's own *apologia pro sua vita:* "All I ever did was to sell beer and whiskey to our best people. All I ever did was to supply a demand that was pretty popular." Because Prohibition transformed most ordinary adults into petty criminals, respect for law in general declined. However, one man who had hung around the Capone gang while he worked on a university study project offered a subtler explanation for Capone's complex public image:

> I couldn't look upon the gangs of the Prohibition period as criminals. The people of Chicago wanted booze, gambling, and women, and the Capone organization was a public utility supplying the customers with what they wanted. It couldn't have operated one hour without the public's consent. . . . One thing about the gangsters—they were integrated individuals. Among them there were fewer potential patients for the analyst's couch than I've met in any other group. They knew exactly what they were doing. They may have been wrong only about one thing. Capone and the others really believed that they were running the city, but I don't believe they were. They were the executives and the technicians. The city was being run by the politicians and by City Hall, and the big bosses weren't interested if the gangsters killed each other, providing they kept delivering the money. I had respect for Capone. In the Depression he did wonderful work. Before the New Deal got going they set up block restaurants for the unemployed, free food with the compliments of the Organization—and you didn't have to listen to any sermons or get up and confess. You sat down and they gave you a real meal with tablecloths on the tables, and no one rescued you. Even the union racketeering wasn't as bad as it's been painted. I knew one racketeer well who ran a hotel workers' union. He ran it with an iron hand, but he also provided a health clinic, a psychiatric department and picnics and social outings.[44]

Capone no doubt had his own motives. If he provided food and shelter for destitute South Siders, chances are that he saw charity as a way to promote his own "respectability," pay off political debts to friendly politicians, or perhaps solicit loyalty from a lucrative "territory." None of which diminishes the fact that hungry people were being fed. Instead it suggests that behind the romance of the mythic Scarface stood a very smart businessman, a man who in the classic sense of the phrase was "doing his job"—and doing it well. For beneath the complex and confusing aura of old-time Chicago gangsterism was the mundane business of men and women going to work. Crime then, as always, was for most people a way to earn a living.

Cops, police reporters, courthouse lawyers, and private investigators—the so-called respectable professionals whose work revolves around the world of crime—tell the same story. Burglars, killers, car thieves, pimps, and racketeers seldom pour out heart-wrenching tales of personal torment, psychological confusion, or endless remorse. In his seminal, and still unmatched, study of organized crime in predepression Chicago, John Landesco devoted an entire chapter to the life histories of several unnamed gangsters. One, an ex-con in his early thirties, had been a "gambler, pimp, shoplifter, burglar, and stickup man." His story is devoid of either justification or condemnation. The man grew up in an exclusively Italian neighborhood. His father worked at a factory and ran a corner newsstand on the side. His mother spoke no English, raised nine children and "carried bundles on her head"—the sewing she took in from commercial dress shops. Their house was a shanty by the railroad tracks. The parents were the very models of hardworking, thrifty American immigrants. Eventually, after the gangster son was grown, the parents managed to buy a house in a better neighborhood two miles to the west. Three of the four sons reared in the first house had criminal records. The younger children who grew up in the family's second house were all clean.

As Landesco extracts the convict's childhood history, the episodes constitute an urban version of Huck Finn and life on the Mississippi. Neighborhood kids are cutting school, shooting dice in the back alley, traipsing off in gangs (not unlike kids' gangs in 1950s television) to the nickel movie house to boo and cheer their heroes, stealing milk bottles off front porches for lunch and even outsmarting night elevator operators downtown in order to steal candy from cigar counters. The kids were creating a social life of their own, and they were doing it in the only logical place they could: on the stoops, streets, and alleys of slum Chicago. Since their parents had virtually no money to give them, they used their ingenuity to find their own. Financially and culturally, they lived in a world apart from their parents, and, as Landesco noted, "without the gang, life would have been grim and barren for these children."

If the gang was play, it was also vocational training. "Out of the gang at the school came the fast friends and the acquaintances of later life who have made their mark in the criminal underworld. This man can recall famous forgers, leading gamblers, burglars, labor racketeers, and many notorious criminals in every form of criminality, who were neighborhood boys in his own gang." As Landesco's subject talked about his childhood friends who had gone into the rackets, he made no moral distinction between them and others who had found ordinary jobs. They had chosen their work on a purely practical basis. "He takes as his pattern the men in the neighborhood who have achieved success. His father, although virtuous . . ., does not present as alluring an example to him as do some of the neighborhood gangsters. The men who frequent the neighborhood gambling houses are good-natured, well-dressed, adorned and sophisticated, and above all, they are American, in the eyes of the gang boy."

Landesco makes his point even clearer with the case history of a twenty-five-year-old con just released from Joliet state prison and returned to his old neighborhood to find that bootlegging had made it prosperous. "Every wop has got a car in front of his home," he said. When he looked up his old buddies, he discovered that one was managing a gambling house, some were driving beer trucks, and another was a petty politician who also fenced stolen property. At first he talked with them about finding a legitimate job to satisfy his parole conditions.

"Do you really have a yen for being a poor working sap?" one old friend finally asked.

"Yes, my father worked as a laborer for twenty-seven years. He is all worked out now and his boss is going to pin a medal on him," he answered with an ironic smirk.[45]

Another interview, with a gambler and confidence man, shows that careers in crime seemed not only lucrative but also challenging and attractive. "The men of the underworld are the brainiest men in the world. They have to be, because they live by their wits. They are always planning something, a 'stick-up,' a burglary, or some new 'racket.' They are constantly in danger. They have to think quicker and sharper than the other fellow. They have to 'size up' every man they meet, and figure out what 'line' to use on him. The leading men of the underworld can move in every circle of society. They are at home in Chinatown, along the 'main stem,' in gambling dives or in the best hotels and the 'Gold Coast.' When they have a lucky 'break' they can live like millionaires; when their money is spent they plan new schemes."[46]

By the mid-1920s the Chicago Crime Commission estimated that there were ten thousand professional criminals working in the city. By comparison there were some fifty thousand workers in the meat-packing and stockyard "jungle." Measured by the amount of money handled and the number of people employed, the "criminal trades" stood as a small but important industry in Chicago. To suppose that all or even most of the working criminals were deviants, the products of warped childhoods and evil influences, would certainly have struck Capone or O'Bannion or Weiss—or any immigrant kid raised in America's ghettos—as absurd. A life in crime, especially when the crime to be committed involved little more than providing amusement to the middle and upper classes, was simply a better deal than the spiritual dyspepsia and physical degradation promised in the stockyards and the factories. For some, especially the Sicilian Italians, crime provided an entry into respectable society that neither politics nor industry could offer.

Politics, and the accompanying patronage positions, remained in the tight grasp of the Irish and WASPs until well into the Depression. Industrial jobs were dominated first by native whites, then by the Germans and other northern European immigrants. Even within the Italian colonies, it was the immigrants from the northern provinces who owned most shops and controlled the labor banks through which most jobs were dispensed. Colosimo, Torrio, and Capone had been virtually the only Italians to win prominence in city life. That their methods were illegal seemed to bother no one but a few rich blue-blood reformists. Indeed law in itself seemed incidental to the everyday workings of city life, useful chiefly for settling disputes between competing interests—be it over newspaper sales, streetcar franchises, gambling wires, or chains of speakeasies.

Working criminals were not so much concerned with breaking the law as with ignoring it. Under such circumstances the Sicilians who worked for Torrio and Capone were ideal employees. Steeped in a centuries-old tradition of anarchic antagonism to authority, they had no historic reason to consider law as a tool of personal or social progress. Besides, the dreariness and low pay of the factory wage system were alien and unappealing to them. Whatever risks he ran—and life-and-death risks were hardly new—the man who worked the rackets knew that his survival and success would depend on the trust and personal loyalty he shared with other men.

Left to his own devices Big Jim Colosimo was a two-bit hoodlum and political subordinate of the First Ward bosses. Yet by establishing a system of loyal friends for whom he did favors and who returned them in full, he built a small business and earned limited local respect. Then came John Torrio, who entered the Chicago system not as a peasant but as a technician, a specialist, a professional, and who reached his prime as a manager of "public services." The citizens of Chicago demanded to drink, to whore, and to gamble, and with as little embarrassment as possible. So long as he succeeded in maintaining publicly peaceful management, he held uncontested power over the rackets. When his management system collapsed, he reconsidered his career and moved back to New York City to work within the powerful and exclusively Italian gangs of Little Italy. Capone, like Torrio, entered Chicago as the boss's number-one man and became operations manager for the beer delivery system. But unlike Torrio he combined military skill with organization and demonstrated the power—firepower—to become an independent force in city politics. He did what none of his predecessors had ever done. With the reelection of Mayor Thompson in 1927, he brought an old ally, Daniel Seritella, to one of the highest appointive jobs in the city, the post of city sealer.

Because of Seritella's appointment, because of Thompson's open proliquor stance, and because he had heavily bankrolled the Thompson campaign, some have called Capone the unofficial mayor of Chicago from 1927 to 1931. It is a credit that probably exaggerates Capone's role in the city. Hearst publisher Andy Lawrence, after all, made the actual telephone call that gave Seritella his job, a sign of cooperation between the publisher and the gangster also reflected when two ex-Hearst circulation managers, Annenberg and Ragen, took over the national racing wire that serviced Capone's gambling houses. Yet as Hearst and McCormick and Thompson exercised power, so did Capone. To achieve that position on his own terms, with his own organization, in less than a decade, was nothing less than an American success story. Even more amazing, his organization survived him and became a cornerstone of the industry he had helped create. For a swarthy little fat boy with a disputed birthplace, Alphonse Capone had done well for himself. As the Irish might have said, he had become one of the Quality.[47]

Chapter 21

1919

> When they return home what will our war veterans think of the American who babbles about some vague new order, while dabbling in the sand of shoal water? From his weak folly they who lived through the spectacle will recall the vast new No Man's Land of Europe reeking with murder and the lust of rapine, aflame with the fires of revolution.
>
> —John Dos Passos, *1919*

The ordeal of World War I, the Great War, was so wrenching to so many Americans that the nation itself seemed unrecognizable after it was over. It was not just the savagery of this first fully modern war, though the memory of the rotting corpses in Flanders fields would linger on for half a century. It was not just the phobic patriotism in the war's wake that unleashed political convulsions across the land. Nor was it the jingoistic braggadocio of the veteran doughboys, boasting that they had brought the United States to manhood. All of these had a share in the postwar spirit. But there was a brooding undercurrent that, in spite of all the heroism, the war itself had been a fraud. It had not been the war to end all wars. A growing minority now saw it as a conflict among the mighty and the powerful for control of an emerging industrial order. That sense of betrayal was by no means limited to the pacifists and the radical agitators. It had slipped into the hearts of common folk as well as into the heads of New England aristocrats. A rising generation of popular writers, Fitzgerald, Hemingway, Dos Passos, began to tell stories of a nation at war with itself, where the old virtues of simple honesty and fair play seemed no longer to apply, and where the best young men were cast adrift, exiled to foreign places because their homeland seemed infected by avarice and duplicity.[1]

In that first year after the war the signs of dissolution were everywhere:

San Francisco: Tom Mooney

As Tom Mooney sat in prison through the spring of 1919, his name was already lighting the fires of passion throughout the nation. Three years earlier he had been arrested, tried, and convicted of murdering nine people and maiming forty others when a bomb exploded during a war-preparedness parade in the heart of San Francisco. Mooney was an Irish labor agitator who had taken on the operators of San Francisco's street railways. He and his wife had tried to organize the United Railroads Carmen. The union drive failed, but Mooney's personal standing grew dramatically. He was young. He was handsome. He was a magnetic public speaker. And he had begun to command enormous influence in San Francisco's large Irish neighborhoods. He and his fellow radical unionists were just dangerous enough that the railroad operators, who had formed the Law and Order Committee of the San Francisco Chamber of Commerce and had organized the preparedness-day march, were determined, as one said, to "show the sons of bitches where to get off."

Five days after the bomb exploded, Mooney, his wife, Warren Billings, and two others were arrested. If the district attorney had any hard evidence against Mooney, it has never been discovered. In the middle of his trial, his lawyer produced a photograph of Mooney and his wife taken during the parade. The face of a clock which also appeared in the photograph proved that Mooney was a mile from the explosion just eight minutes before it went off. The prosecution's investigator was a private detective previously employed by one of the biggest union busters on the West Coast, Pacific Gas and Electric Company. Only a few months earlier, he had offered two of Mooney's current codefendants a "reward" to testify against him, an offer they bluntly rejected. The prosecutor's star witness was an out-of-work waiter who testified that he had seen Billings place a suitcase against the wall of a saloon where the bomb exploded and then walk over to Mooney for a brief conversation. The waiter swore first that the suitcase incident happened at 1:50 P.M. When the photograph showed Mooney to be a mile away at 1:58 P.M., the waiter recanted his testimony, moving the incident up almost half an hour.

Mooney's conviction provoked such a scandal that his name became a battle cry for union organizers and political radicals across the country. So great was the campaign on his and Billings's behalfs, that President Wilson personally intervened, asking the California governor to commute their sentences or offer them a new trial. As a result the two had their sentence reduced from death to life in prison. The campaign for their freedom continued.[2]

Spring 1919 brought new energy to that campaign. The end of World War I had released a torrent of excitement and pent-up anxiety. For some three years unionists had agreed to curtail their demands in the interest of national preparedness. War's end brought with it a burst of inflation and mounting wage demands from workers. Suddenly, on the first breezes of spring, industrial strikes began to break out in city after city: 175 strikes in March; 248 in April; 388 in May. Amidst it all, the persecution of Tom Mooney transformed him into a national symbol. Tom Mooney's sentence suddenly became the veiled threat facing every workingman and workingwoman in America. No free unionist could count on justice as long as Tom Mooney was denied it.

Union locals, mostly from the West Coast, pressed for a new crusade that spread panic among the open-shop business leaders, the district attorneys and even the Justice Department prosecutors in Washington. Starting on Independence Day, 1919, there would be a nationwide general strike which would not end until Tom Mooney and Warren Billings were freed. To the old-line nineteenth-century industrialists a general strike meant certain anarchy. To the heads of government, still reeling from the success of the Bolsheviks in Russia, the Mooney strike sounded the call of revolution here at home. Police in every major city were put on special alert. Public buildings were under guard as July 4 approached. National Guardsmen were deployed. Two companies of the army's Fourteenth Infantry were stationed in downtown Chicago as a thousand new volunteers were added to the police force. In Oakland, known radicals were rounded up and jailed as extra "insurance." New York placed eleven thousand police on twenty-four-hour duty on the eve of Independence Day. And the newspapers screamed. "REIGN OF TERROR PLANNED," bellowed the San Francisco paper of labor's great friend, William Randolph Hearst, while the *Cincinnati Enquirer* warned its readers of "PLANS FOR WIDESPREAD VIOLENCE AND MURDER."[3]

But on July 4, 1919, the sun rose and the sun set; Independence Day passed much as usual. Tom Mooney passed the day quietly in San Quentin. The loudest explosions were the cracks of ordinary firecrackers and Roman candles popping off at patriotic lawn picnics. Even in San Francisco, the great Mooney strike failed to produce a single anarchist soapbox speaker. Murder, mayhem, and mass hysteria had existed only in the imaginations of newspaper editors and zealous law-and-order agitators. Had the union organizers been half so clever in their campaign for Mooney's freedom as the "100 percent Americans" had been in campaigning against the union "terrorists," Tom Mooney might well have walked from jail a free man. Instead the true-blue patriots, the American Legionnaires and the dedicated enemies of Irish popery drove home a tough message: Lock up the agitators and call out the cops; even Bolshevik terror can be contained. As for Tom Mooney, let him be labor's bleeding symbol, not of justice denied but of a troublemaker contained. A Tom Mooney in "the pen" was surely better than the memory of a Tom Mooney in the electric chair.[4]

Tom Mooney remained in prison for twenty more years. The boom and flash and the bathtub gin of the twenties, the crash of '29, the bread lines of '32, the sit-down strikes of '36, where the hired goons of Henry Ford broke the heads of Flint autoworkers, all passed before Tom Mooney was finally vindicated. Yet as early as 1920, it became known that many of the prosecution's witnesses had perjured themselves, with the knowledge of the D.A., and that the case against Mooney had been a travesty. A Labor Department investigation of the D.A.'s behavior confirmed that he had deliberately compromised himself. Two witnesses confessed to perjury. Between 1918 and 1929 a long list of prominent citizens joined in the petition for Mooney's pardon, including: the police captain who had been in charge of the preparedness-day parade and who had first investigated the crime; the district attorney who came to office after Mooney's conviction; and nine of the ten trial jurors still living. Even the assistant D.A. who had prosecuted Billings wrote in 1926 that in his "opinion, under all the circumstances, that the public interest would be best subserved by granting pardons to both Billings and Mooney."

That same year the governor of California wrote: "I believe no person that permits himself to analyze the situation entertains any doubt that Mooney and Billings were convicted on false testimony," adding that "if a new trial were granted there would be no possibility of convicting Mooney or Billings." The governor, Friend W. Richardson, nonetheless refused to pardon the two men. Year after year appeals were made to the California judiciary, and time after time the appellate judges found technical justifications for failing to rule or denying the two men's motions. At one hearing the waiter who had testified against Mooney for the prosecution admitted lying on the witness stand. Describing that witness, the state supreme court justice wrote "that a more abject spectacle of debased and degenerated manhood was never before presented to a body of judicial or quasi-judicial investigators." But, they added, perhaps he had been a responsible man in 1916, at the time of the trial.[5]

At last, in December 1939, a new California governor acknowledged the actual crimes that had been committed by the state prosecutors against Mooney and Billings. He pardoned Warren Billings in November. The next month Tom Mooney walked freely through the gates of San Quentin and into blustery San Francisco. He was fifty-eight. He died less than three years later.

Cincinnati: Arnold Rothstein

The way William Maharg told the story, he was at home in Philadelphia when a Western Union boy rang the doorbell with a telegram. The message was from Bill Burns, an ex-baseball player who had grown rich in the oil industry and had become an insatiable gambler. It read: ARNOLD R. HAS GONE THROUGH WITH EVERY-

THING. GOT EIGHT IN. LEAVING FOR CINCINNATI AT 4:30. BILL BURNS.[6]

That cryptic wire from a onetime ball player to Maharg, an ex-boxer and small-time gambler, became a centerpiece on one of the strangest and most damning criminal scandals of twentieth-century America. No one was killed. There was no fleecing of the public treasury. Neither violence nor espionage played the slightest role. Yet the alleged perpetrator considered the charges so despicable that he publicly volunteered to face a grand jury and explain everything he knew about the crime. Not "under any circumstances," he swore, would he have considered joining such a conspiracy. The whole affair, he told reporters, constituted a frontal assault on the most cherished tenets of the American system.

This crime against the nation was the "fixing" of the 1919 World Series. The "fixer" was Arnold Rothstein, a short dapper Broadway bon vivant, son of a prosperous clothing wholesaler, and the top financial wizard of the national gambling underworld. The men who threw the game were eight star players for the great Chicago White Sox, who gave the case its final epithet, "the Black Sox Scandal of 1919."

The tale began sometime in July of that year, in the middle of the baseball season, when the players made a joint demand for higher pay. Some were paid as little as $2,500 a year and several others earned under $4,500. The team's owner refused any raises despite the team's extraordinary win record. Slowly but steadily the players' anger and frustration turned to bitterness, even as they sewed up the pennant several weeks before the season ended.

It was during a series of east coast games that sealed the American League title that White Sox pitcher Eddie Cicotte and first baseman Chick Gandil decided to turn bitterness into action. If they couldn't make a decent wage playing straight, then there were other ways to make it. Since more money was wagered on the World Series than on any other event of the year and since no one believed that the Cincinnati Reds had a prayer of beating the White Sox, serious gamblers with inside information could win several fortunes if the Sox lost. All it would take for the Sox to lose was some consideration, say $10,000 to each player in on the scheme—in round figures, $100,000.

At the end of World War I, when entire office buildings were being erected in New York City for well under a million, $100,000 was a lot of money. John Torrio or Al Capone might spend that much on tight bootleg operations, but to put up that amount of cash on something as loose as the World Series, where a double cross could blow the deal halfway through, was a risk only a few men could take. Cicotte and Gandil knew no such gamblers. The first man they tried was a Bostonian said to be the biggest gambler in New England. Although he couldn't raise the money, he told the players, he knew someone who had it. "I'll talk to A.R.," he promised. But that was the last the players heard from him.

Discouraged, Cicotte tried once more. He looked up Bill Burns and the ex-boxer. The gambit fascinated Burns. But again, it was way beyond his reach. And again, he said the best bet for a bankroll was the mysterious and debonair A.R. To reach Rothstein, Burns said he would have to go through yet another man in the heady world of high-life gambling, one William Maharg of Philadelphia. Soon the cast of the conspiracy would involve more than a dozen people, so many that it became mired in confusion and angry claims of betrayal and double cross. When Maharg visited Rothstein in New York, the great gambler declined to get involved. At that point the whole scheme seemed dead. No wonder then that Maharg was baffled when back in Philadelphia he received Burns's telegram reporting that Rothstein had reconsidered his initial decision and had instead "gone through with everything." The record of what happened next comes from Maharg, who testified in the trial one year later.

"I went to Cincinnati the next day [after receiving Burns's telegram] and joined Burns. He said that after I had left New York he ran into Abe Attell, the fighter, who had gone to Rothstein and fixed things. Burns added that Rothstein had 'laid off' us because he didn't know us, but was very willing to talk turkey with Attell, whom he knew.

"Attell was in Cincinnati, quartered in a large suite in the Sinton Hotel. He had a gang of about twenty-five gamblers with him. He said they were all working for Rothstein.

"Their work was very raw. They stood in the lobby of the Sinton and buttonholed everybody who came in. They accepted bets right and left and it was nothing to see $1,000 wagered.

"I had my first suspicion on the morning of the first game when Burns and I visited Attell. We asked for the $100,000 to turn over to the White Sox players for this part of the deal. Attell refused to turn over the $100,000, saying that they needed the money to make bets. He made a counterproposition that $20,000 would be handed the players at the end of each losing game. [At that time a team had to win five games to take the series.] Burns went to the Sox players and told them and they seemed satisfied with the new arrangements."

If Maharg's account is true, that is the last satisfaction the players found. After they lost the first game, Attell changed the rules again and refused to pay anything until the series was over. If they didn't like it, they should go see Rothstein in New York. "I went to New York and called on Rothstein," Maharg began to testify when the judge in the 1920 trial stopped him, ruling that conversations with Rothstein were "irrelevant."

The Chicago White Sox lost the World Series as their fans booed in disbelief. No one in baseball believed that either fate or the players' talent could have turned so bad so fast. Nor could the millions of fans so easily accept the losses they were taking with neighborhood bookies. If the players had felt cheated by their paltry wages, the crowds and the public at large felt they had been cheated by the national pasttime. The game that embodied the very idea of the fair deal, as native to America as Yankee Doodle, had been sullied. The wave of anger and disbelief was captured in a little boy's supposed plea to White Sox fielder, Joe Jackson, "Say it ain't so, Joe. Say it ain't so."

The president of the American League was the first to charge openly that the Sox had fixed the series. "The man behind the fixing of the series," he stated flatly, "was Arnold Rothstein." Those charges came in September 1920, a year after the series. Immediately the state's attorney in Chicago began bringing witnesses before a grand jury. The players, the managers, the middle-men gamblers, all marched forward to bare their souls. And in each case, one sinister name overshadowed all others. Arnold Rothstein was the man responsible, they said. Arnold Rothstein gave the orders. Arnold Rothstein controlled the money. Arnold Rothstein ran the double cross. Arnold Rothstein was the star, the director, and the producer of the whole scheme.

Arnold Rothstein denied lifting a finger to make the fix. "The world knows I was asked in on the deal and my friends know how I turned it down flat," he told reporters. "I wasn't in on it, wouldn't have gone into it under any circumstances and didn't bet a cent on the series after I found out what was under way. My idea was that whatever way things turned out, it would be a crooked series anyhow and that only a sucker would bet on it." And with that, the Chicago state's attorney, a Republican reformer known mostly for his failures, made a remarkable public statement: "I don't think Rothstein was involved in it."

Arnold Rothstein may have fixed the Black Sox series. Or he may not have. Two New York journalists, examining the remnants of his personal papers at his death, claimed they found the proof.

During the year between the grand jury proceedings and the trial, all the minutes of the hearings conveniently disappeared, along with three signed confessions. The trial was hardly underway when the whole case was dismissed. Rothstein's biographer has written that the great gambler hovered on the brink of going into the fix up until twenty-four hours before the series opened but then backed off. But he noted, correctly, that the series could not have been fixed without Rothstein. The reason is that without Rothstein there could have been no payoff. Without the prospect of big money, the star players could not have justified betraying their careers and their reputations, and they could not have sold the scheme to the five other players involved. Worse perhaps, without the great and sinister hand of such a godfather, the whole affair would have seemed a petty heist, devoid of the grandeur that comes from selling the nation's greatest public diversion to the nation's most notorious public enemy.[7]

Between the playing of the Black Sox series and Rothstein's public appearance a year later, Prohibition wiped the bars and saloons clean of legal whiskey. It was an event that would soon so inflate Rothstein's fortunes that gambling dwindled to little more than an amusement for him. Within a couple of years he had become the biggest bootlegger in America, importing entire shiploads of Scotch from Britain, deploying his own fleet of small boats to meet the ships out beyond U.S. waters and to bring the whiskey safely through customs along the New Jersey and Long Island coasts. A year or two later he had taken over most of the unions in New York's garment industry, sometimes selling his strong-arm services to the employers, sometimes selling them to the radical unionists. By the late twenties, just before he was murdered, he launched an entirely new racket, a sideline to bootlegging that would long outlast Prohibition and that made him the financier of all the New York underworld. The new line was narcotics, specifically heroin.[8]

Despite his power and his wealth as the first great businessman of American crime, Rothstein is not remembered for his racketeering or financing. The crime that ensured his legend is the one he may never have committed, an event which, like the savage war that had just ended, violated a dream.

Washington: A. Mitchell Palmer

Short, with a face like a ripe round smiling tomato, A. Mitchell Palmer liked to dress with elegance. His political skills, like his oratory, were almost brilliant. But his ideas were pedestrian. His personal fears, matched by insecurity about his small-town Pennsylvania background, always undercut his judgment and left him prey to the manipulations of more clever politicians. He began his adult life as something of a crusader, a reformer who jousted at the weaker flanks of the great trusts, a friend of the unions and the workingman and a rather aphoristic devotee to the cause of civil liberties. As a state politician, congressman, and federal bureaucrat, he was more than a minor national figure and less than a major one. His college roommate, later a Republican governor of Pennsylvania, described him aptly on their graduation day. He said, "Mitch, you are a worthy gentleman—young and handsome, and well endowed with talent. You can orate, elocute, write for print, sing, and, on rare occasions, you have been known to study, but no one ever knew you to run any danger of overexertion." Mitch Palmer was a middle-brow man, one who seemed surely destined to find some position of national importance. Yet few if any of his college friends and professors would have predicted the notorious fame he eventually achieved when as attorney general for Woodrow Wilson he gave his name to the most fanatical red-baiting witch-hunt of the twentieth century, the Palmer raids of 1919 and 1920.[9]

Palmer's name did not become one of America's household words until 1919, the year he was appointed attorney general. At the beginning of his term, he was openly antagonistic to the rising calls for government action against syndicalists, reds, aliens, and agitators. It took several months of continuous barrages from business leaders and newspaper editors before he began to act. Two events had a major influence in pushing him toward the leadership of the hysterical campaign. The first came on May Day, 1919.

On that morning newspapers all over the country ran banner headlines and bloodcurdling stories describing a vast conspiracy to murder many of the nation's highest officials. Thirty-six bombs had been mailed from New York to cabinet members, including Palmer, several senators, Supreme Court Justice Oliver Wendell Holmes, and a variety of business tycoons, among them John D. Rockefeller and J.P. Morgan. The bombs had been timed to explode May 1. Only one did, blowing off the hands of a maid in Georgia senator Thomas Hardwich's Atlanta home. Most of the remaining bomb packages were discovered by a postal clerk in the central Manhattan post office.[10]

The second event exploded with a sharp crack on the night of June 2, at exactly 11:15 P.M., just as Palmer turned out the lights in his Dupont Circle town house. Seconds later came another explosion so severe it shattered the windows of the house across the street where lived young Franklin and Eleanor Roosevelt. The Roosevelts had returned home moments earlier. Their cook was reported so frightened by the blast that she screamed, "The world is coming to an end!" Roosevelt checked on the safety of his son, then ran to Palmer's house. He found the doors and windows destroyed. As he and Palmer examined the wreckage, they realized that had Palmer been downstairs, he might have been killed. A few minutes later the two men discovered that at least one person had died in the explosion. Bits of bone, flesh, and clothing were scattered among the pieces of wood, glass, and paper that covered the floor, the front yard and several neighbors' lawns. About fifty copies of an anarchist pamphlet were found nearby, undamaged. Entitled "Plain Words," the pamphlet described impending class war, acknowledging, "There will have to be murder; we will kill . . . there will have to be destruction."

Palmer retained his public composure after the bombing, but it had shaken him to learn that radicals could successfully assault a high government officer. "I remember," he later told a Senate committee, "the morning after my house was blown up, I stood in the middle of the wreckage of my library with congressmen and senators, and without a dissenting voice they called upon me in strong terms to exercise all the power that was possible . . . to run to earth the criminals who were behind that kind of outrage."[11]

Throughout the summer the antiradical campaigns intensified. Police worked hand in hand with private vigilante squads and strikebusters. Mounted police in Chicago, Detroit, Boston, Seattle, and New York were deployed against any large meeting of unionists and radicals. Army tanks were used in Cleveland in an assault on twenty thousand people peacefully gathered at a public square to hear political speeches. By early fall almost every major newspaper in America demanded severe police action against the agtators, despite the fact that nearly all the mass violence that had taken place was initiated by police and mobs, not the nonviolent agitators.

Although Palmer had continued to refrain from any overt crackdown, he had taken one critical step. On August 1, he appointed a young Justice Department lawyer to manage a new agency to be called the General Intelligence Division, or GID. That lawyer was J. Edgar Hoover, and his job was to amass as much information as he could on radicals and provide it to the Bureau of Investigation. Quickly the twenty-four-year-old Hoover set up files on more than two hundred thousand radicals across the country. He, more than any other man in the government, interpreted the goals and tactics of radicals in America and advised the attorney general on how dissident people and organizations should be treated.

Hoover's reports, supposedly based in part on a thorough reading of Marx, Engels, Lenin, and Trotsky as well as the anarchists, brought a new direction to official thinking about radicalism. Communists, labor organizers, and radicals of every stripe had been active in the industrial cities since the era of Andrew Jackson. State and federal agents had often suppressed them with force and considerable violence. U.S. Army troops had been pressed into duty to maintain order during the strikes of 1877. Agitators had been killed in battle and mob lynchings and occasionally been tried and hanged. But for the most part the government treated them straightforwardly as political adversaries. They may have been regarded as heinous enemies of the state, as were Chicago's Haymarket anarchists, but even bomb-throwing radicals had merited at least a disparaging respect. Hoover, however, took another tack. Radicals, he reported, were not principled political adversaries. They were simply criminals, he said, "a gang of cutthroat aliens who have come to this country to overthrow the government by force."[12]

The newspapers echoed Hoover's rhetoric. Patriotic societies demanded that Attorney General Palmer kick out the "Bolsheviks" and "alien reds." The government was being "especially tender in its treatment of disloyal elements," one said. Pacific northwesterners declared they had "about reached the end of the road of patience." A U.S. senator from Washington, fuming over the successes of IWW organizers, warned that there was a "real danger that the government will fall." The anti-immigrant, nativist *New York Times* attacked Palmer directly, complaining that he had "ancient and outworn views on immigration; views which, coming from the head of the Department of Justice, are not pleasant to hear when all over the country, alien or foreign-born agitators are carrying on in many languages, in five hundred or more papers and magazines, the Bolshevist and I.W.W. propaganda for the overthrow of the government." Focusing on Palmer personally, the *Times* went on: "Some of these enthusiasts of destruction tried to kill Mr. Palmer himself. The sound of their bombs is still in our ears. From Seattle to Gary and New York, their campaign of murder reaches."

When Boston's city policemen went on strike in September, riots broke out. Two men were killed by sporadic machine-gun fire. Businessmen and bankers panicked. They stayed open all night, hiring armed guards to protect their property and their money. Again the newspapers screamed with fury. "POLICE STRIKE: RIOTS IN BOSTON—Gangs Range Boston Street, Women are Attacked, Stores are Robbed, Shots are Fired," a headline in Hearst's *San Francisco Examiner* reported. Some papers wrote of an encroaching "Sovietism." Others warned of terror and chaos. The *Wall Street Journal* announced that "Lenin and Trotsky are on their way." A cartoon in the *Los Angeles Times* depicted a paunchy cop leaning happily against a lightpole while the Maid of Boston was being clubbed by a vicious rapist.[13]

If he were to survive as a public figure, Palmer knew that he had to act decisively. For the time being, however, he lay low, whether because he preferred to stay behind the scenes while encouraging men like Hoover and William J. Flynn, head of the Bureau of Investigation, to flood the papers with propaganda, or whether because he was genuinely reluctant to unleash a federal witch-hunt, one can only conjecture. However undecided Palmer may have been, he was made well aware of the feelings of the public. "I say that I was shouted at from every editorial sanctum in America from sea to sea," he later explained about November 1919. "I was preached upon from every pulpit; I was urged—I could feel it dinned into my ears—throughout the country to do something and do it now, and do it quick."[14]

On November 7, he acted. Alerted in advance, the *New York Times* reported what happened: "Choosing the second anniversary of the Bolshevist revolution in Russia, as the psychological moment to strike, the federal government, aided by municipal police in New York and several other large cities, last night dealt the most serious and sweeping blow it has yet aimed at criminal anarchists. Armed with warrants for dangerous agitators whom federal agents have trailed for months, the raiders swarmed into the Russian People's House in New York and into similar gathering places of alleged 'Reds' in Philadelphia, Newark,

Detroit, Jackson, Mich., Ansonia, Conn., and other cities, broke up meetings, seized tons of literature and herded the gangs of foreign men and women into various offices for examination, whence most of those who proved to be the most sought after of radicals found their way into cells."[15]

The raid in New York, the first of the Palmer raids, was on the Russian People's House, a cultural center where two rooms were rented by the radical Union of Russian Workers. Other occupants in the building included a steamship company, a dockworkers school, and a random smattering of small businesses. The Bureau of Investigation held warrants for twenty-seven people when it opened the raid. Some two hundred were beaten, corralled, and pushed into waiting patrol trucks which had completely encircled the building. Passersby on the street were questioned and a few who admitted being Russian were jailed. Other raids were under way throughout the city. Altogether over six hundred people were jailed that night in New York City alone—almost all of whom eventually were released. The same pattern held as Palmer's men moved against radicals in other cities. Holding warrants for thirty-six people in Newark, agents arrested a hundred and fifty.

The *Times* made passing reference to the agents' brutal tactics, but only subsequent affidavits revealed the unprecedented viciousness of the assault. Pitch dark, unventilated "punishment rooms" in the Hartford jail, four feet three inches by eight feet ten inches with concrete floors and no furniture, held ten to fifteen people each for between thirty-six and sixty hours. Prisoners were threatened with summary lynching or gassing. In New York a Russian language teacher told a poignant and representative story:

> I wear eye-glasses and the agent of the Department of Justice ordered me to take them off. Then without any provocation, struck me on the head and simultaneously two others struck and beat me brutally. After I was beaten and without strength to stand on my feet, I was thrown down stairs and while I rolled down, other men, I presume other agents of the Department of Justice, beat me with sticks of wood which I later found were obtained by breaking the banisters. I sustained a fracture of my head, left shoulder, left foot, and right side. . . . I was examined by various people and released about 12:00 midnight.[16]

By day's end, November 8, A. Mitchell Palmer may well have been the most popular man in the United States. As Pershing had led his troops first in Mexico and later against the Huns of Germany, Palmer had led the administration of a sick and failing president into a new war in the defense of Christianity and patriotism. The press applauded and the courts approved. Indeed the whole operation, like the Palmer raids to come on January 2, had been a marvel of legal ingenuity. Since Bolshevism, anarchism, communism and other kinds of radical agitation were not illegal in themselves, Palmer turned to the Department of Labor, which had the administrative authority to deport undesirable aliens.

Palmer reasoned correctly that the great majority of radical organizers were aliens. By working jointly with the Labor Department, he could unleash Hoover and the Bureau of Investigation to bombard the press with warnings of the criminal threat posed by foreign subversives, a strategy supported by such antilabor industrialists as Henry Ford and Judge Albert H. Gary of U.S. Steel. Labor Department agents tagged along on the raids and undertook the technicalities of actually deporting the aliens. Credit for the scheme went to Palmer. Newspaper cartoonists and editorialists portrayed Palmer as "lion-hearted" and "A Strong Man of Peace," a man who had brought "joy to every American." He was, in the vision of a New Orleans cartoonist, the strong arm of Justice grasping the wrist of a swarthy, hook-nosed Red Heathen who was about to pour poison into "the chalice of state."[17]

So great was Palmer's triumph that by the January 2 raids he felt free to move against any radical organization, demanding that every member furnish proof of citizenship. People arrested were to be denied permission to talk to any person outside the jails without the express permission of Hoover, Flynn, or Palmer. The agents were well trained and ready when the day came. Within one twenty-four-hour period over four thousand radicals were arrested. Agents broke into homes, restaurants, social clubs, bowling alleys, even pool halls, splitting apart families, taking parents from their children. Standard rights of due process, including police search warrants and defendants' right to counsel, were categorically denied. Aliens were held for deportation proceedings and citizens were turned over to local authorities to be prosecuted on the flurry of new criminal syndicalism laws then being enacted. Aliens seized in New England were taken to Boston, forced to hobble in chains from the immigrant station to the docks, and shipped to Deer Island in Boston harbor, where they were detained in a building without heat. On the island, one man fell five stories to his death. One went insane. Two died of pneumonia. In New York City 400 were arrested. Over 100 were arrested in Philadelphia, and 115 were taken in Pittsburgh; 800 were arrested in Detroit, 400 in Chicago, and 100 in Kansas City.[18]

There are probably no two days in the history of the nation when agents of the federal government committed more illegal acts than on November 7, 1919, and January 2, 1920. Palmer, the country's highest law-enforcement official, had violated the law to redefine political activity as criminal activity. Indeed, his greatest legacy may have been the rapid proliferation of state laws banning political radicalism. By 1920, no less than thirty-five states had passed laws making such activity criminal. Few people regarded the government's actions as scandalous. The *Washington Post,* for example, defended the illegality of the Palmer raids: "There is no time to waste on hairsplitting over infringement of liberty." Millions of Protestant Americans felt that raids were justified against Jews, Catholics, and heathens who had mounted a silent competition with pure native workers. The raids represented the kind of patriotic stand for which the Great War had just been fought, a stand against "the inferior races," whose natural products were crime and communism. It was a theme Palmer himself repeated in describing the vile people he had caught: "Out of the sly and crafty eyes of many of them leap cupidity, cruelty, insanity, and crime; from their lopsided faces, sloping brows and misshapen features may be recognized the unmistakable criminal type."[19]

Like the witch-hunt at Salem, Massachusetts, almost two and a half centuries earlier, the inquisitor's triumph was short-lived. In January 1920, Palmer might have gotten himself elected president for life. But seven months later, when he was campaigning hard for the presidency, he failed even to win the Democratic nomination. Psychopolitical analysts explain his late mercurial brush with fame as the consequence of a nation venting itself of its wartime passions and hatreds. It is an argument with some merit. More telling, however, are the sources of Palmer's strength: the press, a few ultraconservative industrialists who were the last holdouts against unionism, and an unorganized mass of citizens united only by their fear of foreigners—all volatile elements in a postwar America whose political shape was undergoing tremendous transformation. Ultimately the men who were Palmer's friends, those who wanted to cut off the flow of dangerous immigrants, would be outmaneuvered by the political moderates and unionized industrialists who realized how vital cheap immigrant workers were to the growth of business and commerce. The radical ranks in the unions had of course been decimated, so much so that by spring 1920 there was little left of the agitation over which Palmer continued to rant. Conservative union leaders led by Samuel Gompers had mounted a serious counterattack. Several prominent businessmen even organized something called the Inter-Racial Council, a propaganda outlet in defense of foreign-born workers. Among its members were such magnates as Cleveland H. Dodge, E.G. Grace, and Thomas Lamont, and it was chaired by none other than T. Coleman du Pont, who blithely dismissed the previous year's excesses as "sheer Red hysteria, nothing more."[20]

Defeated, Palmer retired to his home in Stroudsburg, Pennsylvania, concerned himself with the family's bank, suffered a series of debilitating heart attacks, and offered occasional advice and ghostwriting to his friend Franklin Roosevelt until his final attack in May 1936.

New York: Robert P. Brindell

CONTRACTOR IN TERROR OF LABOR BOSS . . . SPECIAL JURY ASKED ON BUILDING . . . LABOR LEADER DESCRIBED AS 'ABSOLUTE BOSS' IN THIS CITY

These and similar headlines told New Yorkers of a dark, sinister postwar conspiracy, a plot conceived by a few dozen grafters and bosses to sap the lifeblood of their city, denying scarce housing to thousands of eager, work-hungry veterans, propelling rents into a fantastic price spiral. The scandal, the headlines, and the dramatic legislative hearings chaired by state assemblyman Charles Lockwood, broke during the fall of 1920. But the events which provoked the scandal, events which formed one of the original textbook cases of business and labor racketeering, belonged to the year 1919. Although the scheme lasted only a year before it was exposed, schemes like it would recur repeatedly during the century.[21]

Racketeering had been one of the scare words attached to labor organizers since the end of the Civil War. It was a word that connoted the demimonde of dirty business: muscle men, goons, extortion artists, and fixers, men whose tentacles bound the hands of hardworking laborers and energetic businessmen. By the end of World War I, though, it was a term that had begun to slip into disuse, replaced by the Red Menace, the Bolshevist threat, and the Wobblie bombers. The substitution of Reds for racketeers as a focus for national hysteria was a pathetic irony of the war years and their aftermath. For by 1919 the Reds—communists, socialists, anarchists, Wobblies, and any other agitators stammering on the fringes—may have numbered 140,000 people, while in the industrial power centers of New York, Chicago, Detroit, and Cleveland, brutal business and labor combines were remaking the face of urban life.[22]

In New York it was a brilliant semiliterate named Robert P. Brindell who saw and snatched the opportunity to take control of the city's construction industry. And though the newspapers portrayed him as a diabolical thug dedicated to terrorizing the city's private builders, it was only through the secret connivance of the construction magnates themselves that he built his corrupt empire.

Brindell had come to New York from Canada. He found work first as a clerk, then as a longshoreman, and eventually as a dock builder's helper in 1905, the job which made him a union member. Clever and forceful, he was adept enough at politics to be named business agent for the Independent Dock Union seven years later. After 1912 his power in the unions blossomed. Six years of harsh internecine maneuvers among the Carpenters Union, the iron workers, and two dockworkers unions gave Samuel Gompers the chance to bring all the New York building trade unions under his control in the American Federation of Labor. Locals were recognized and derecognized, officers elected by the locals were summarily fired from above, and at one point sixty-three locals were suspended for disagreeing with the citywide District Council of Carpenters. Brindell, who had learned the value of a well-aimed billy club in local elections, grew more powerful at every turn. With an approving nod from the city's contractors, the district council awarded him control of the New York building trade unions at the 1918 convention. Within a year Robert P. Brindell made himself the highest-paid union boss in America.[23]

In October 1919, Brindell brought the business agents of nearly all the builders' unions in New York into a Building Trades Council. Business agents were the top officers in each union; naturally, Brindell made himself the permanent president of the council. His salary was $14,000 a year. In addition, he ran his own local, number 1456, and collected fifty cents per month from each of its five thousand members. Only the top brass from each local could run for the council, and they of course could always be suspended for any reason by the international. Only one copy of the council's minutes was made, and it was never distributed. Rent on the council's offices was paid to none other than Mrs. Robert P. Brindell, owner of the building, at the rate of $1,000 per month.

Some 115,000 men were represented by the sixty unions under Brindell's control. Unions that resisted him did not survive long. One, composed of highly skilled house-wreckers, was called the Zaranko Union, after its president. Though independent, it was recognized by the AFL. But it refused to join Brindell's council. To force Zaranko into line, Brindell stopped all other builders' unions from working on the same site with Zaranko's. Brindell called strikes against any contractor who hired Zaranko, demanding that his own newly fabricated wreckers' union be used instead. Contractors who used Zaranko's men found that no unions would work for them on subsequent jobs until they had paid a "tribute fee" as penance for past behavior.[24]

Once he had brought the unions under his control, Brindell's tactics were direct and unchangeable. A few examples documented by Lockwood's investigators are illustrative:

In the fall of 1919 the Starboard Realty Corporation started work on an office building at Seventh Avenue and Thirtieth Street. A few months later, a hundred and fifty men walked off the job charging the company with hiring nonunion workers. The job supervisor called Brindell and asked him to end the strike. "About a week thereafter," legislative investigators reported, "two delegates of Brindell demanded $60,000 to call off the strike and finally agreed to take $25,000." A few days later, after negotiation by intermediaries, Starboard's president drew $25,000 in cash from his bank, handed it to the supervisor, who turned the money over to the two Brindell "delegates." Instantly the strike ended, and the nonunion men were rehired without a whimper from any corner.[25]

In February 1920 two of Brindell's delegates warned Anthony Paterno that he would have trouble with his workers unless he paid $6,000 strike insurance. The workers on the job were full AFL members but they were not part of Brindell's council. Paterno bartered the price down to $3,000 and had no further trouble.[26]

In May 1920 workmen threatened a strike against Albert Hershkovitz on the grounds he was using nonunion steel workers to erect a loft building in the garment district. Hershkovitz visited Brindell at home on May 20, the day the strike was threatened. Brindell demanded $25,000 in cash. Hershkovitz paid it. The strike threat vanished, and Hershkovitz wrote off the money as a construction cost.[27]

In May 1920 George Atwell was preparing for a demolition job at Fifty-seventh Street and Broadway. He advised Brindell he would pay $10,000 to the wreckers, but Brindell offered to get the job done for $5,000. All Atwell had to do was pay Brindell the other $5,000, which he did by the end of the month. Atwell paid a similar bribe to Brindell that month to get a cheap demolition contract on other buildings on the Upper West Side. The two continued their financial relationship throughout the summer.[28]

While Brindell was extorting city builders in exchange for labor peace, he was also demanding money from other contractors just to get workmen for their jobs. In one case during August 1920 Brindell insisted that a contractor enter a peculiar partnership before beginning work on an extension of the Plaza Hotel. Not only did he have to take Brindell's friend as a partner, he also had to pay Brindell $3,000 off the top. Earlier that year the mighty Cunard steamship line acquiesced to Brindell's "suggestion" that it obtain strike insurance before it began a $35 to $40 million dock construction project. Cunard paid $32,000 before the Lockwood investigation exposed the extortion.[29]

Racketeering threats from Brindell's delegates—sometimes called members of the Grafters Union—counted for only half the plot. The other half came from the cooperative contractors who were members of the Building Trades Employers Association, or its subunits. The ringleader for the employers was attorney John T. Hettrick. The three associations he ran directly were the plumbers, the steam fitters and the cut-stone contractors. For his work he took between 1 and 3 percent of each contract. That work, stated simply, was rigging the bids made by city builders. He did it the same way gangsters cheated on their taxes. He kept a double set of books, or rather a dual set of multicolored cards. When a contractor entered one of Hettrick's associations, he was given a book of cards on which to enter job bids. Each association had its own color codes. So, when a steam-fitting contractor wanted to bid on installing a heating system for a new hotel, for example, he would file his estimate on a yellow card and mail the card to Hettrick. When Hettrick had received all the yellow card bids, he would mail back a second card, perhaps orange, to the steam fitters advising each one what his bid should be. With Hettrick's "advice" in hand, each contractor would file a final bid, not with the builder but directly with Hettrick. Sometimes Hettrick even made the necessary final adjustments to assure a steady flow of jobs to each contractor as his turn came up. Bids that were "too low to permit the particular member to take the job allotted to him, were increased so that this member became the lowest bidder. His estimates were frequently increased but the others were increased proportionately so that he would get the job," investigators reported.[30]

Hettrick proved particularly adept at fleecing the city on repairs for public schools. Five bids entered for limestone work on PS 43 in Brooklyn were typical. In order to make the bidding appear especially hot, Hettrick added a sixth phony "accommodation bid." "Before the bids were put into the city," the investigators reported, "the members filed in Hettrick's office the following estimates for the job: $4,405; $3,996; $3,987; $2,583 and $3,767.50. Again Hettrick's magic pencil boosted the first to $4,705; the second figure to $4,925; the third figure to $5,150; the fourth figure to $4,283; the fifth figure to $4,980. Hettrick inserted an 'accommodation bid' in the name of one of his members for $5,260. The job went to the member who had bid to the city $4,283 on Hettrick's suggestion, although the same member had been willing to do the job for $2,583."[31]

The biggest grab Hettrick contrived was for a masonry contract on a proposed new courthouse. Representing nine members of the so-called limestone ring, he persuaded the city to change building material specifications from granite to limestone facing. The nine "limestone conspirators" then met in Hettrick's office and agreed that only one of them would enter a bid while the rest would subcontract to him. When the city awarded its contract, it agreed to pay $9.00 per cubic foot for the limestone—even though private builders then were paying no more than $4.50 to $5.00 per cubic foot. By the time the job was over, New York City had been swindled out of about $800,000. Hettrick was paid $52,000 for his services.[32]

The circle of graft had been completed in June 1919 when a thousand contractors and builders joined to form the Building Trades Employers Association in which Hettrick and his clients were the toughest operators. The Lockwood committee found that, "The Employers Association and the constituent associations entering into its membership are more largely than any other single factor responsible for the acts that have done so much to cripple building operations in the City of New York. . . . It was largely through the assistance and encouragement of this Association by reason of its contracts with the Council and with other labor Unions that these constituent associations were able to force unwilling members into their fold and to impose upon them unlawful restraints upon competition." Not only were relations between labor czar Brindell and the employers described as "intimate." The committee also found that Brindell wielded almost as much power in the Employers Association as he did in the council—a power great enough to write clauses into the association's bylaws pressuring members to hire only union men covered by Brindell's council. When those clauses weren't enough, the Employers Association hired Brindell's men to force maverick contractors to join up under threat of strikes.[33]

When his inquiry was completed, Charles Lockwood seemed overwhelmed. "Throughout the length and breadth of the country," he reported, "there are combinations between the manufacturers and the dealers; between producers and manufacturers; between dealers and the unions of workingmen, so that the whole industrial and commercial system in the industries connected with building construction is riveted in an interwoven and interlocking criss-cross of combination and obligatory arrangement."[34]

Lockwood's dramatic relevations sent Brindell and many of his cohorts to Sing Sing. For a while the newspapers excerpted his hearings and plastered them across their front pages. There was nominal reorganization in the Building Trades Council. Brindell's union competitors enforced his banishment from the council after he was paroled. And a certain air of reform wafted through the Employers Association. But no one seemed to have his heart in it, least of all in city hall, where Mayor John Hylan was a friend of Brindell's and the secretary of Tammany Hall was an official of the council. Brindell had been banished, but the reliability of his system made it the unofficial code for the future.

* * *

Omaha: William Brown

On September 28, 1919, a mob of several thousand people stormed and set fire to the $1 million county courthouse in Omaha, attempted to hang the mayor, then dragged a black prisoner from the jail, lynched him on a trolley pole and burned his corpse beyond recognition. Fifty policemen were beaten. One member of the mob was killed.[35]

The man they lynched in Omaha was William Brown. He had been arrested and charged with the rape of a white girl, Agnes Loebeck, a few days earlier. When he was picked up earlier that day, he was found to be living with a white woman. He was taken directly to the county jail. In the previous ten days, forty other "undesirable" black men had been driven out of town by the police. Since the previous winter, local newspapers had been filling their front pages with lurid tales of black desperadoes run amuck against the white population. White unionmen seemed to be growing more resentful each day about the use of blacks as strikebreakers against the teamsters and the meat cutters. Fearful that a bloody pogrom was being planned against them, blacks began both to arm themselves and to hold public meetings. At one such meeting in April they condemned the police chief for having said, "If the better class Negroes did not get together and ferret out the criminals of the race there would be a repetition of the East St. Louis riots." Such inflammatory remarks, combined with the papers' consistent coverage of blacks as criminals, seemed sure to provoke a bloodbath, they warned. But blacks continued to be portrayed, and charged, as the perpetrators of a growing crime wave. During late summer twenty white women claimed to have been assaulted or raped—all allegedly by blacks.[36]

Then came the rape of Agnes Leobeck. A dozen or more black suspects had been questioned and each of them had been threatened with a potential lynch mob. When William Brown was formally charged and jailed, the white men and women of Omaha were ready to wait no longer. At about 2:00 P.M., a crowd of some five hundred people formed in front of the stone Greek Revival courthouse. Their anger grew as their numbers mounted. At least a thousand were there by four o'clock, their chants and catcalls echoing against the courthouse wall as they demanded that the sheriff turn Brown over to them. Then a dozen armed men, none older than twenty, began pushing against the building's gates. When they held firm, one of the armed men secured a rope to a second-story window ledge, shinnied up to it, and helped station a ladder over which the rest scrambled in. Once inside, they opened fire on the police.

The men failed to take the building, but their daring led the crowd to a frenzy. As night fell, thousands joined the assault, many of them armed. Nearly all the jail windows were shot out. The sheriff's attempt to break up the mob by turning interior fire hoses against them only compounded their rage. Just past seven o'clock a small group entered the county treasurer's office, doused the files and furniture with kerosene, and set the building ablaze. When the fire department arrived, the mob axed their hoses. Gradually they were forcing the officials higher and higher into the building until the sheriff led everyone, including the prisoners, to the roof, where they were exposed to a rain of ricocheting bullets.

Mayor Smith came out of the courthouse to make a personal plea that the people go home and leave Brown to stand trial. He walked down the long stone steps into the crowd urging them to move away from the building. As he talked several men began to close in around him, pushing him toward a trolley pole.

"Give us the key to the jail!" one shouted.

"If we can't get the nigger, we'll lynch you!" another warned.

"He's no better than the nigger!" others taunted, as they pressed in tighter.

Then one yelled, "Get that rope!" And a rope was thrown over the pole. "Throw it over the pole and string the mayor up," a dozen more commanded. They fitted the noose around his neck and slowly began to pull until the sixty-year-old man's feet were off the ground. Two policemen, otherwise helpless, managed to cut the rope. But another rope was found, tied to the mayor's neck, and again he was pulled from the ground, blood dripping from his mouth. Again the police managed to cut him down, this time pushing him into a ready car which sped him off to a hospital.

Meanwhile, story by story, flames were engulfing the courthouse. Only the silhouettes of the sheriff or his deputies flickered past the windows as the prisoners begged, prayed, and demanded that Brown be thrown to the mob. According to all the newspaper accounts, Brown remained totally calm throughout the ordeal. By eight o'clock, when the sheriff had retreated to the roof, the mob had reached the fourth floor, just beneath the jail, which was one floor below. The mob leader warned the sheriff that he, his deputies, and the prisoners would burn if Brown were not handed over.

Brown walked over to the sheriff.

"I am ready to go down," he said.

"You know what they will do? They will tear you to pieces," the sheriff said.

"I am ready to go down the steps," Brown repeated.

The sheriff refused to give him up, even after the other prisoners continued pleading. He had begun to walk down the stairway to address the mob, whose leaders were at the same time pushing their way up. The deputies and the prisoners stood above and behind him.

"Give us the nigger or we will kill every mother's son of you," the mob shouted.

As the sheriff was trying to force them back down, several prisoners pushed through the line of deputies with Brown locked passively in their arms. A few seconds later Brown was handed over. He did not resist or complain. A reporter for the *New York World* described what followed:

"The mob, dragging Brown, rushed downstairs. Reports say that the few policemen and county officials who were scattered through the building offered no resistance to the mob.

"The mob started with Brown to the main floor of the building. Before they got to the ground floor he had been beaten unconscious and every vestige of clothing torn from his body.

"'Here he is!' yelled the captors.

"Thousands of persons who were standing around the building rushed around to the south door, where the negro was.

"'String him up and let us fill his body full of bullets,' they shouted.

"Brown was dragged through the crowd, bruised and bleeding at the end of a rope, while the crowd shouted. A fusillade of shots was poured into the body as it lay for less than a minute on the pavement. An agile boy climbed a telephone pole on the corner of 18th and Harney Streets. Somebody threw him the rope and threw it over the brace near the top of the pole. The crowd pulled it and the negro's body swayed in the air. More than a hundred shots were fired at the corpse.

"'He certainly displayed nerve at the end,' said Sheriff Clark."

The next day in Omaha, people were bragging to one another how they had stayed up all night watching Brown's corpse roast on a bed of logs until the head, the arms and the legs had been burned off.

Chapter 22

The Fruits of Temperance

To the casual observer, America in the twenties was awash in crime. To some extent, that observation was correct. Statistical evidence did suggest that thefts, muggings, and common assaults increased immediately after the war. But the evidence is scant, the statistics generally unreliable, and whatever trend did exist seems to have disappeared by the early twenties. Popular pundits and newspaper editorialists cited the Senate's flamboyant investigation into the Teapot Dome scandal as evidence that the moral bonds had so disintegrated that President Harding and his Ohio gang had turned the White House into a brothel that serviced Sinclair and other western oil oligarchs. Yet the Teapot Dome scandal, soon accompanied by the revelation of open graft in the Veterans' Administration, did not greatly distinguish Harding's administration from Grant's or those of the Gilded Age when the railroad robber barons were buying corporate favors by the gross. Corruption, be it at the White House, on Capitol Hill, or among the boys in the mayor's offices, was nothing new.[1]

If the twenties seemed to be the decade of crime, it was not because the middle class was suddenly in danger of criminal assault. Objectively, crime was probably no greater a threat to most people than at any time during the previous century. What was new about crime in the decades between the two world wars was that it became a thing apart from daily life, an independent, identifiable, palpable force in the affairs of the nation. It ceased to be merely the handiwork of the masses, men either demented, evil, or desperate. Suddenly criminals could be rich, debonair, articulate, and capable of administering large organizations. Crime, like the manufacture of the automobile, had become a mass-production industry for the New Era.

Mass-produced crime is not just another term for the old rackets organized by neighborhood gangs. It was made possible by the new economic order that evolved out of World War I. By the time the war was over the American economy no longer revolved around the corner groceries and neighborhood shops where most household items had been crafted and sold. Just as the steel, oil, and rubber magnates had already forged an industrial system based on "efficient" production for the nation as a whole, so too the war had mobilized the nation's economy to streamline the production of consumer goods. Never before had industry realized it could produce so much for so many. Never before had the federal government claimed such broad powers of regulation and control over industry. What had been a nation of regional economies was now consolidated into a unified economic system, which would soon wipe out most of the personalized, community factories and businesses that had characterized the America of Whitman and Twain. Everywhere corporate mergers were becoming the order of the day. The consolidations of the twenties brought about such giant food, soap and automobile combines as Maxwell House, Colgate-Palmolive, and Chrysler. Greatest of the new conglomerates were the chain stores, an entirely new invention for retail marketing. Their success was phenomenal, a growth from some 29,000 units in 1918 to 160,000 units in 1929. In just twenty years—1912 to 1932—the A&P supermarket chain mushroomed from 400 stores to 15,500 stores and captured a full 10 percent of America's retail food market.[2]

Smart men like John Torrio, Arnold Rothstein, and eventually Charlie ("Lucky") Luciano were as alert as anyone to the profits available from mass-production efficiency. Torrio was the first of the old-style gang leaders to realize that the chaotic arrangement of turf-bound neighborhood rackets hampered the business opportunities that Prohibition bootlegging offered. There were too many people negotiating with too many smugglers and warehousemen, each of whom had their own payoff schedules with local precinct captains. Crime, like most retail business, had been organized on the principle of local self-sufficiency. Bookies, prostitutes, grifters, and thieves tended to work within a single neighborhood, dominated by individual gang leaders. Torrio understood that the clever entrepreneur could make far more money by organizing his business along product lines: a single operation for running brothels. One building might house all three operations, but each racket should be managed independently on a citywide basis and judged according to the profits it reaped. Torrio, Capone, or one of their top deputies took care of "administration"—bribery and payoffs to city officials and negotiation with dissident gangs (which usually simply meant their elimination).[3]

The building of the criminal underworld did not always follow the Chicago pattern. When Torrio fled the shower of lead along Lake Michigan for the security of New York City, he found a fundamentally different situation. At least 1 million Italians lived in New York, most of them concentrated in Little Italy and the Lower East Side between the Jewish tenements and Chinatown. The district remained largely Italian-speaking. It possessed its own strongmen. Jobs were controlled by labor brokers who also had control of most of the city's fresh-produce supplies. The Italians had very little influence with Irish-dominated Tammany Hall. Their position with the city's gambling and bootlegging rackets was subordinate both to the Irish and to the Jews. They were largely controlled by the "Mustachio Petes" who had recently come over from the old country and who were fully satisfied to work within their own communities, putting down the individual Black Hand extortion artists who flourished in the early years of the century. Thus, even as late as the 1920s, New York's Italian gangsters were still almost "pre-American" in that they had not yet insinuated themselves into the city's normal social and political life. As historian Humbert Nelli has deftly argued, it would take the bloody "family" wars of the late twenties and early thirties to Americanize the Italian mobs and bring them into an integrated criminal system.[4]

New York was by no means placid during Prohibition. Rum runners and bootleggers were shooting each other all over town, competing for control within their own territories, and occasionally fighting for new turf. At least a thousand gangsters were killed in the warfare. "Bootleggers and their molls were pinioned with wire and dropped alive into the East River," wrote the authors of one particularly graphic account. "They were encased in cement and tossed overboard from rum boats in the harbor. Life was cheap and murder was easy in the bootleg industry, and those men of ambition who fought their way to the top were endowed with savagery, shrewdness and luck."[5]

Ironically, it was through Arnold Rothstein, the son of a Jewish clothier, that a new generation of Italian gang leaders came to control the New York underworld. For it was Rothstein who did more than anyone else to Americanize the gangs and bring them into the melting pot of modern business. "Rothstein's main function was organization," his biographer wrote. "He provided money and manpower and protection. He arranged corruption—for a price. And, if things went wrong, Rothstein was ready to provide bail and attorneys." Rothstein developed working relationships with gamblers and bootleggers in other cities. He was the virtual founder of the narcotics traffic. He sent his men into the thoroughly chaotic garment industry, which until then had been dominated by hundreds of small entrepreneurs and Jewish tailors who had almost no understanding of efficient mass-production and marketing techniques. As the garment workers began to organize unions, Rothstein offered his men for hire as strikebreakers. On other occasions, when union workers were being beaten on the picket lines, he sent in his toughs to fight off the company goons. Either way, he exacted rich tribute from his clients and secured a place for his gangs in the booming garment industry.[6]

Not surprisingly, Rothstein was more interested in talent than heritage when he chose men to run his operations. The result: His gangs numbered as many Italians as Jews. Young Italians who had grown up in America were especially attracted to Rothstein. Not only were Dutch Schultz and Louis ("Lepke") Buchalter starters for Rothstein, but so were Frank Costello, Albert Anastasia, and Lucky Luciano. When Rothstein was murdered in 1928, it was John Torrio, the consummate diplomat, who succeeded him as fixer, financier, and broker for the increasingly streamlined bootleg underworld.

These were the circumstances that led up to the events that most crime writers describe as the birth rites of the modern syndicate underworld. Briefly, it was a struggle between the followers of Joseph Masseria, who had organized loose bands of robbers and extortionists into the city's most powerful Italian gang. He was called Joe the Boss. His chief competitor was a relative newcomer, Salvatore Maranzano. His followers were also recent arrivals, refugees from Mussolini's campaign against Italy's own underworld outlaws. Certain that a violent showdown was approaching, Luciano made a tactical decision to join Masseria, whom he believed was the weaker of the two and therefore the more vulnerable. The first killing came at lunch on April 15, 1931. Luciano left Masseria alone in a Brooklyn restaurant while he went to the men's room. While Luciano was washing his hands, unknown gunmen appeared and killed Masseria. Though Luciano was universally credited with having arranged the murder, he succeeded to the leadership of Masseria's organization. A few days later he and Maranzano met in Chicago under Al Capone's auspices to seal a peace agreement.

That agreement lasted six months. Maranzano declared himself the "Boss of Bosses of all the Mafias in the United States," and demanded unquestioned allegiance from what was little more than a loose alliance of Italian crime organizations in a half dozen cities across the country. A brittle and paranoid man who had come to the United States as an adult, Maranzano's only experience was with other Italians. Outside the Italian communities he had to rely exclusively on Luciano. It was an impossible arrangement Luciano never intended to endure. It ended just after lunchtime on September 10, 1931, when four men describing themselves as federal agents entered Maranzano's office suite, lined up the secretary and nine men against the wall, then quietly walked into the boss's office and shot him. Reflecting Capone's national stature, Chicago was chosen as the location for a new meeting, and a new alliance of crime organizations was founded at Luciano's behest. What had previously been a cooperative among territorial bosses was replaced by a businessmen's board representing diverse professional interests: narcotics, gambling, liquor, and so on. Luciano, Capone, and the cult of efficient management had made major inroads against what had been hardly more than a feudal system of territorial control.[7]*

The firepower of the American underworld was an item of continual fascination, both at home and abroad. Rothstein, Masseria, Dutch Schultz, and Torrio were at once gangsters and celebrities, well-known to reporters and their readers. (One reporter in Chicago had grown so

*The six members of the board were Luciano, Vincent Mangano, Joseph Profaci, Joseph Bonanos, all of whom were New Yorkers, plus Al Capone and Frank Milano, the head of the Mafia in Cleveland who worked in close alliance with Moe Dalitz in liquor operations. Thus, though business organization and profits became key, the three most important geographical areas of criminal racketeering continued to have representation.

close to Capone's world that he ran a side deal with one of the gambling operations, got in over his head, tried a double cross, and ended up as just another gory victim.) With the rise of the huge newspaper chains run by Hearst and Scripps-Howard, the graphic stories of hoodlum life in New York and Chicago became front-page fare across the country. Readers in Seattle, San Antonio, and Milwaukee were suddenly made privy to the latest shootout in Brooklyn or Cicero. Racketeers who had only begun to imagine building national crime syndicates, bootleggers who had been little more than importers to their colleagues in the hinterland, were transformed into men of national stature. Thanks to the giants of the yellow press, gangsters could command respect anywhere they went.

Because they were characterized as simultaneously glamorous and brutal, the criminal lords gained a respect that ordinary tycoons could never have: They were Faustian heroes who had achieved the American dream through an explicit compact with the devil. Even if that compact required a daily routine of murder and mutilation, most Americans were not terribly upset. That was simply the price one had to pay to keep liquor flowing. The fact that anyone who took a drink—and that included tens of millions—was also a kind of criminal produced a real if vicarious bond between the public and the gangsters. By 1929 the Prohibition Bureau had actually arrested over half a million people for violating the Volstead Act.[8]

Ruminating over the American situation in 1931, England's *Manchester Guardian* concluded that "all the machinery of law exists in America, but the thing does not work properly." The *Guardian* attributed America's crime complex to the failure of "the public conscience" to "function as it should." Walter Lippmann took the problem of the public conscience a step further, reminding his readers that the rackets performed two very useful duties for American society: First, they enabled blue-blood reformers and jingoistic populists to perpetuate the hypocrisy that America was still a Protestant utopia officially free of drinking, gambling, fornication, and dirty books even though all of those things were widely available. What could be more fitting than that Jews and Catholics were the providers of the forbidden fruit? Second, Lippmann pointed out that racketeering served to bring the small labor-intensive family industries into the mass-production economy. Thus racketeering constituted "a perverse effort to overcome the insecurity of highly competitive capitalism." Added Lippmann:

"The point of all this is that we are all so much addicted to lawbreaking that the existence of a great underworld which lives on lawbreaking is not wholly alien and antagonistic to the working assumptions of our lives. Because of their own strong addiction to lawlessness, Americans as a whole are by no means clear in their own minds as to the moral grounds on which they could challenge the underworld and go to war against it."[9]

Prohibition was such a farce that by the election of 1932, politicians had begun to call for a change. The production of corn sugar, an essential ingredient used by the illicit distilleries, had leapt from 152 million pounds in 1921 to 960 million pounds in 1929. Prohibition had not only organized the underworld, it had also trebled the production of domestic whiskey. New York's Alfred E. Smith, identified with the "wet" forces, had been defeated in 1928, but even "dry" Herbert Hoover felt compelled to appoint a high-level commission to examine the failure of Prohibition enforcement. It was called the Commission of Law Enforcement and Observance, or simply the Wickersham Commission, after its chairman, George Wickersham. Almost two years passed before the commission issued its report, and its conclusions were as contradictory as the public spirit. Conceding that Prohibition did not work, that it had bred wanton disrespect for the law, that it had corrupted mayors and police forces everywhere, and that it generated phenomenal profits for underworld enterprises, the commission nonetheless recommended continuation of "the noble experiment." Its final report was satirically summarized by a verse columnist for the *New York World:*

Prohibition is an awful flop.
    We like it.
It can't stop what it's meant to stop.
    We like it.
It's left a trail of graft and slime,
It's filled our land with vice and crime,
It don't prohibit worth a dime,
    Nevertheless we're for it.[10]

"There is as much chance of repealing the Eighteenth Amendment as there is for a hummingbird to fly to the planet Mars with the Washington Monument tied to its tail," declared a Texas senator who was one of Prohibition's staunchest defenders. That was in the spring of 1931. Two and a half years later Prohibition was repealed. Its death came at the hands of liberal reformers like Walter Lippmann and Franklin Roosevelt's New Deal allies in Congress. Liquor, like the glittering silver screen, would become an essential avenue of escape for millions of desperate people whose dreams had been dashed by the Depression.

For Torrio, Capone, Luciano, and their compatriots neither repeal nor the Depression brought on hard times. Bootlegging had transformed them into skilled business managers. It had provided them with the necessary capital to diversify. Capone's liquor operations in a single year of the late twenties grossed a minimum of $60 million. He and the others were accumulating cash so fast they had to make new investments. Little wonder then that they were astute enough to foresee repeal and to negotiate exclusive distribution contracts with distilleries for the time when legal whiskey would again flow freely. Who, after all, knew the business better?[11]

The two most notorious gangsters to get an early lock on legal liquor were Torrio and Frank Costello, who was also a top gambling boss. In December 1933, the month repeal was ratified, Torrio paid $62,000 for the newly organized import firm of Prendergast and Davies Co. Ltd. According to the Internal Revenue Service that firm was "the biggest corporation of its kind in New York City . . . until well into the middle of 1935." Apparently Torrio did as well with his "legitimate" business as he did with the bootleggers, for by the time the IRS decided to launch an investigation, it claimed the company was grossing several million dollars each month.[12]

December 1933 was also the month that Costello and his partner Phil Kastel became agents for Alliance Distributors, Inc., a New York importer and distributor of Scotch and Canadian whiskeys. A few years later, in 1938, Costello fronted the cash for Kastel to buy the British holding company of a large distillery that had used Alliance as its American distributor. Costello then became a "personal agent" for the British firm and was directed "to promote the interests of the company in the United States by personal contact with the wholesale and retail merchants . . . by frequenting first-class hotels and restaurants, and asking to be supplied with the company's brands marketed in the United States." Frank Costello was a hard man to refuse.[13]

Were modern liberal economists to characterize late Prohibition, they might describe it as the "takeoff" period between poverty and development. Technology, opportunity, and the accumulation of cash enabled a poor, static, oppressed, and underdeveloped domestic colony to enter America's pluralistic "developed" society. Never mind, of course, that only a few aggressive entrepreneurs became really powerful while the rest remained poor and isolated; the same is true of the "less-developed countries." Besides the whiskey business, the underworld entrepreneurs took off in a number of other directions during the late twenties and the thirties. Included were:

Bars and restaurants. When Prohibition was enacted, the Hotel and Restaurant Employees Union had sixty-five thousand members. By 1923 that number had dropped to thirty-seven thousand as workers eagerly sought jobs in underworld speakeasies. Repeal brought a predictable reinfusion of members into the HRE, but as organizers complained in both Chicago and New York, many of the new recruits were mob-controlled functionaries. Capone called the shots in Chicago. In New York, Dutch Schultz, the bootleg magnate, took over. In the 1932 elections for control of HRE Local 16, three of Schultz's ex-employees "won" the top union jobs. They began an immediate campaign to drive out the independent left-wing unions that had grown up in the city during Prohibition. As union workers complained of extortion, rigged strikes, and autocratic rule, Schultz and company swiftly organized some 90 percent of New York restaurateurs into the Metropolitan Restaurant and Cafeteria Owners Association. Charges to the owners included a $250 initiation fee, $5 per week dues, and other special assessments to avoid strikes. New York State special prosecutor Thomas Dewey later claimed that over $1 million had been extorted from the restaurant industry—15 percent of which may have gone to the union locals. Schultz had resurrected the union, but as historian Matthew Josephson has written, "Workers employed in such places found that nothing resembling a union shop was established; that conditions remained as intolerable as before; and that when workers protested they were beaten up by hoodlums, discharged, and placed on an employers' association blacklist."[14]

The garment industry. Two men, "Charlie the Gurrah" Shapiro and Louis ("Lepke") Buchalter were direct heirs to Arnold Rothstein's extortion racket in the garment industry. They controlled both employers and unions, a circumstance whose roots were acknowledged even by the Republican crime-busting prosecutor, Governor Thomas

Dewey: "The Amalgamated [Clothing Workers of America] still in its organizational phase, would send delegates to an open shop to recruit for the union. The employer would buy protection from the Jewish Mob. Amalgamated delegates would be beaten up, employers who showed an interest in the union terrorized . . . [so the] union began to do business on its own with the Jewish Mob." At the International Ladies' Garment Workers Union, racketeers used the same strategy and with such demonstrable strength that Communist party officials attempted to guarantee protection for their organizers by negotiating directly with Rothstein and his successors. Despite a temporary respite from attack, the Communist officers in the union were soon ousted altogether by the gangsters and their allies, who were paid off by the shopowners. In the words of one union historian, "The Right met gangsters with gangsters."

Buchalter and Shapiro were amazingly clever and subtle as they maneuvered through the chaotic maze of the garment industry. According to New York district attorney Frank Hogan, their annual take ranged from $5 million to $10 million a year from the industry while they maintained an army of some 250 enforcers and collectors. Only in the fur trades were they outmaneuvered by the left-wing Needle Trade Workers Industrial Union. Former NTWIU officials acknowledged they had hired the gangsters for protection during the twenties, but the secret of their resistance to a gangster takeover seemed to lie in a long socialist tradition among the membership combined with a willingness to keep their own internal squads of enforcers, who on occasion paid off the police to arrest the strike-breakers.[15]

The waterfront. General corruption had proliferated along the waterfronts of Brooklyn and New York since the teens under the gangs run by boxer Paul Vacarelli (who took the name Paul Kelly in that Irish-dominated city). Joseph Ryan, president of the International Longshoremen's Association and a power in Tammany Hall, brought order and protection to the union's shakedown operations. But it would take Albert Anastasia—working in concert with Vincent Mangano, an Italian "family" head and gambling boss, and Joe Adonis, the payoff man for Brooklyn police and politicians—to lock up the docks for the Italian underworld. Shippers paid to guarantee that their cargo would be loaded. Workers paid kickbacks to "hiring bosses" who picked them from each day's "shape-up" at the dock. Loansharking, estimated at

$200,000 a year, was built into the system as new employees were advised to borrow from syndicate men in the union. By 1937 Anastasia claimed direct control of six ILA locals in Brooklyn. One insurgent who dared to challenge his men disappeared in 1939 only to be discovered a year later in an Ohio lime pit. Beyond that, Anastasia was the reputed boss of Murder, Inc., the so-called mob enforcement agency.[16]

The movies. One of the Capone organization's smart moves during the Depression had been to open a series of soup kitchens throughout Chicago. People could see that Big Al's boys had hearts of gold. When Capone operative William Bioff joined George Browne in running Local 2 of the International Alliance of Theatrical and State Employees, the union began ladling out free soup for unemployed actors. Soon they ladled money into their pockets as well, though they waged a genuine fight for the union's members. When in 1929 they demanded that the owner of a large Chicago movie house circuit restore 20 percent paycuts levied against employees, Browne and Bioff did sell out for a $20,000 payoff. But most of the money went to the soup kitchen. Their success drew the attention of Frank Nitti, who had succeeded Capone when he was convicted of tax violations in 1931. Nitti told Browne to run for the IATSE presidency at the union's 1934 convention. Among those who would be supporting him at the convention were representatives from Luciano, Buchalter, and Al Palizzi, a top boss in Cleveland. The price they extracted for delivering the presidency to him was a 50 percent cut, later hiked to 75 percent, of all IATSE extortion money.

Browne and his new personal representative, Bioff, lost no time collecting. To avert a movie projectionists' strike in New York, they demanded $150,000; in Chicago the figure was $100,000. Movie chains that refused to cooperate were stink bombed. Bioff explained the situation bluntly to the head of Loew's, Inc., in 1936: "I want you to know I elected Browne president and I am his boss. He is to do whatever I want him to do. Now your industry is a prosperous industry and I must get $2 million out of it." Browne finally settled for $50,000 a year from each of the big four distributors, Twentieth Century-Fox, MGM, Loew's, and Paramount. A fifth anted $25,000 into the deal. A day after the negotiations were completed the presidents of Fox and Loew's came together to Browne and Bioff's hotel suite in Hollywood and placed $75,000 in cash on the bed. Corrupt or not, the two union leaders also won major concessions for their members, so much so that they received hearty cheers at the 1938 convention. Then they made their mistake by ordering a 2 percent tax on all IATSE members' earnings, an assessment that brought them about $60,000 a month. Union dissidents had already hired the progressive writer-attorney Carey McWilliams to file disclosure suits against Browne and Bioff. From 1938 to 1939 rancor grew until some members began to testify before a federal grand jury. Browne and Bioff were convicted of extortion in 1941 and given long sentences. Then they too testified, and on March 18, 1943, indictments were slapped on Nitti and several of his top men in Chicago. On March 19, Nitti committed suicide.[17]

Narcotics and gambling. The end of Prohibition provided the occasion for a reassessment of underworld vice operations. For while entrepreneurial criminals were eager to extract money from susceptible industries, they remained aware of the enormous profits still to be made from the nation's moral and legal hypocrisies. Narcotics syndicates were widely scattered and not nearly so dependent on New York and Chicago. Kansas City housed one of the biggest midwestern networks, while New Orleans and San Francisco were key import and distribution centers. All the rackets leaders in New York seem to have had some interest in the narcotics traffic. According to the Federal Bureau of Narcotics, Lepke ran one of the largest rings, smuggling in $10 million worth of drugs. Much of his supply apparently was cradled across the Atlantic aboard such plush oceanliners as the *Queen Mary* and the *Aquitania*. Luciano, who had been arrested twice on narcotics charges in 1916 and 1923, denied any continuing involvement with drugs. Critical crime writers, however, doubted his protestations of innocence. In 1933 he sent his most trusted lieutenant, Vito Genovese, to Italy to set up a drug-smuggling operation. When Genovese was forced to flee the U.S. in 1937, he returned to Italy, where he managed the eastern end of the network he had already established. Another Luciano associate, Nicola Gentile, was arrested in 1937 on charges of helping to run a nationwide "dope syndicate" that handled between $5 million and $25 million a year.[18]

As horse racing enjoyed a resurgence in the early thirties, gambling became an important source of cash for most syndicates. The cozy arrangements between Moe Annenberg and the Capone-Nitti organization had their ups and downs as Annenberg's general manager Jimmy Ragen tried to negotiate with Cleveland mobsters. But Annenberg was eventually indicted for evading income taxes, and Ragen died of severe shotgun wounds during a business trip to Chicago after World War II.

In the end, one of the most important gambling entrepreneurs during the Depression, Frank Costello, took over control of much of the racetrack operations as well. He and partner Phil Kastel also secured New York distribution rights for slot machines manufactured by the Mills Novelty Company of Chicago. During their first year of business, in 1931, they placed 5,186 slot machines in cigar stores, candy shops, and speakeasies, grossing between $18 and $36 million. Costello's expenses were heav. Said his biographer: "Half the police department and all of Tammany Hall was on the payroll." After reformer Fiorello La Guardia successfully banned the slots from New York City, Costello took his business elsewhere—to New Orleans, where, he said, Senator Huey Long had issued him a personal invitation. Although Long was assassinated midway during the transfer, some 8,100 of Costello's machines were placed in New Orleans shops "unmolested by the police." The machines cost almost $1 million. Over the next ten years, 1935 to 1945, they paid him some $33 million—obviously a good investment.[19]

Numerous other rackets flourished alongside these standard enterprises. Organizers for the Teamsters Union turned to the gangsters of Cleveland and Detroit for muscle to fight off antiunion goons hired by industrial shippers and cargo companies. In New Jersey, underworld figures were invited into the trucking business by Henry Ford. Loansharking, one of the privileges of rich men with cash, permeated all underworld rackets. New York sharks lent five dollars on Monday and collected six on Friday, bargain rates for small-time bettors. A Russell Sage Foundation report issued in the mid-thirties estimated that loan sharks grossed $10 million a year. Prostitution also remained a lucrative corporate enterprise in some cities, particularly New York. Though it may have been his least important interest, organized prostitution proved to be the racket that finally sent Luciano to the penitentiary.[20]

Luciano's conviction was special prosecutor Thomas Dewey's first big victory in his war on the underworld. Starting with the hookers themselves, he found witnesses to describe a grand hierarchical system through which "Little Davie" Betillo, a Luciano assistant, had systematized collections and protection for two hundred whorehouses employing some one thousand women. It was, Dewey claimed, a $12 million annual business. Testimony from several of the "bookers" who made collections at the houses identified Luciano as the sovereign genius of the racket. Corroboration came from hotel maids who had seen the ring's leaders in Luciano's rooms. Since he lacked evidence of Luciano's direct role in running the prostitution operations, Dewey went to the New York State Assembly to get a special state conspiracy law enacted specifically for this case. Drawing on the voluminous trial testimony, a New York newspaper summarized the case with this graphic account of an alleged Luciano meeting:

> In a dingy basement of a restaurant in New York's Chinatown, three men and a woman sat at a table. The woman was Cokey Flo. She conducted a house of prostitution. Beside her sat a huge, swarthy man with slicked hair and the neck and shoulders of a stevedore. . . . Cokey Flo was his mistress. The second man at the table, Little Davie Betillo, had sharp features and a face as dead white as a dead fish's belly.
>
> The third man was the most striking-looking of any of them. Low off his forehead, curly brown hair started, falling back in thick waves. His swarthy face bore scars like pockmarks. His lips were a cruel, straight line. Incongruously, he had dimples. His eyes, set under bushy dark eyebrows, were the most arresting feature of a face that was definitely sinister. One was wide open, alert. The other, his right eye, drooped, giving him a singular appearance of sleepiness.
>
> He was known in the underworld as "The Boss."
>
> His lips twisted open as he spoke. "I don't like the racket," he said. "What the hell. There's not enough dough in it for the risk we take."
>
> The man with the dead-white face spoke pleadingly: "Try it a little while longer. We can make it go. There's big money in it if we handle it right."
>
> The Boss shook his head: "Maybe we'll only be sticking our necks out. This Dewey investigation is coming on. That may make it tough."
>
> The other man said, "What's that to be afraid of? You know how these things go. He'll grab a bunch of prossies and a couple of bondsmen. And that'll be all."
>
> The Boss considered this silently, then nodded. "All right,

Davie. Let it go for a couple of months. Let's see what happens. But you haven't got the racket up well enough to make it worth while. Here's what we'll do. We'll put all the madams on salary. No more fifty percent stuff. We'll syndicate every house in New York. We'll run them like chain stores."[21]

And so Lucky Luciano was sentenced to thirty to fifty years in Dannemora prison. He would stay there until 1942 when U.S. Navy intelligence officers asked that he be moved closer to New York to assist them in their waterfront operations. After the war, he was deported to Italy.[22]

Dewey's second big case during the Depression was the trial of James J. Hines, the last powerful Irishman in Tammany Hall. It was an anticlimactic affair, more the death knell to an ancient system of politics than the exposure of a new scandal. Born a blacksmith's son in 1877, he had risen to power through the streets and mastered the art of precinct patronage. As far as he knew, patronage was the definition of politics, the direct representation and protection of the people who had brought him to power. A liberal of sorts, he was a man whose picture could always be found in the *Daily News* at Thanksgiving, dispensing turkeys. For his support of Franklin Roosevelt in the 1932 Democratic National Convention, he became the new president's primary patronage dispenser in New York City. That he was also the political bagman for most of the city's gamblers and gangsters was hardly an embarrassment to him. If anything he took it as a mark of modern flexibility that he could switch from the old Irish bosses to such newcomers as Frank Costello and Dutch Schultz.[23]

Yet Hines knew well that the system was ending. In the old days the neighborhood gangs feared Tammany and needed its protection. So they paid. By the thirties Tammany's old base had evaporated. It no longer had the troops to control elections. A new city had arisen where Irish power had been replaced by Jews, Italians, and middle-class white professionals, where blue-blood reformers and a sensationalist press had repeatedly tried to shut off the patronage troughs. To keep his men in power at all, Hines needed new allies. Even the police were no longer reliable, as evidenced in a brief exchange between Hines and former police commissioner Edward Mulrooney. Hines needed a favor for an underworld friend. The commissioner refused.

"Jim, why do you bother with that type?" Mulrooney asked. "They are no damn good."

"Ed, you know we need those fellows on election day and we can't forget them between elections."[24]

The fellow on whom Hines depended the most was Dutch Schultz, whose numbers racket in Harlem was worth millions. The most precise estimate was $20 million per year, less expenses to employees and friends like Hines. Schultz did not live to see Hines indicted. His hot-headed individualism and paranoia over Dewey seemed dangerous to Luciano and Costello. Schultz had even bragged that he would have Dewey assassinated, clearly a reckless notion to other underworld leaders. So while he was dining in Newark in October 1935, Dutch Schultz was shot. His businesses were distributed to loyal Luciano underlings. The numbers racket went to one of his top assistants, "Trigger Mike" Cappola.[25]

Less than three years later, on May 25, 1938, James J. Hines, once the most powerful Democrat in New York State, was arrested as "a coconspirator and part of the Dutch Schultz mob." According to the prosecution, Hines paid off judges, police, even the district attorney. It took two trials for Dewey to nail him. The first ended in a mistrial. But the second brought a conviction on February 25, 1939. Asked by a reporter how he felt, Hines answered simply: "How would you feel if you were kicked in the belly?"[26] He was only sixty-three. But in a world where crime could no longer operate through street politics, protection, extortion, and favors, he was much older. The system that had made him so powerful was no longer viable. No one individual could continue to control crime or politics, at least not in New York. That control was now passing to the corporations.

Chapter 23

The Boondock Underworld

General Benjamin G. McKenzie, gentleman, raconteur, lawyer, and local prosecutor of the infamous Scopes monkey trial in Dayton, Tennessee, spoke plainly to his audience about the evolutionist carpetbaggers from the North: "They had better go back to their homes, the seats of thugs, thieves, and Haymarket rioters, and educate their criminals than to try to proselyte here in the South."

General McKenzie was not a general any more than "Colonel" Darrow, the famed defense lawyer, Clarence Darrow, was a colonel. But these sobriquets of southern manners were the least of the illusions and confusions surrounding the case that one writer dubbed "The World's Most Famous Court Trial." For a while it certainly was. Newspapers from all over the world sent reporters to Dayton. Western Union brought in twenty-two operators to handle the daily dispatches. The *Chicago Tribune*'s radio station, WON, broadcast the proceedings live. For the eleven days in July 1925 that the trial lasted, transatlantic cable companies reported a fantastic boom in transmissions. Japanese, Russian, German, Italian, and English papers were hounding the international news agencies for any copy they could get. Regardless of their own ideology or religion, the readers of the world sat at the edge of their seats to witness the outcome of what had been promoted as the sparring match of the millennium between God and Science.[1]

Few contemporary commentators seriously regarded the trial of John T. Scopes as an important criminal case. His offense, after all, was only that he had taught the theory of evolution in a high school biology class. No one in Dayton considered him a criminal. He was a lanky, good-natured, red-haired twenty-four-year-old who coached the school football team. Even the complaint against him was a put-up job by a local American Civil Liberties Union sympathizer who wanted the state's new antievolution law tested in court. The reporters from outside Tennessee, most of them northerners who came to examine the peculiar mores of this quaint southern town, certainly did not consider Scopes a dangerous man. Not even Austin Peay, the Tennessee governor who signed the original law, believed it a serious criminal statute. "Probably the law will never be applied," he had said. "It may not be sufficiently definite to admit of any specific application or enforcement. Nobody believes that it is going to be an active statute."[2]

When the Dayton grand jury indicted John Scopes, Governor Peay was as upset as any northern liberal. He had signed the law as a political gesture to the fundamentalist Baptists and Methodists who made up the majority of his constituents. Though it may have seemed a meaningless law, it was one that he could not veto. Now, the prospect of a trial with Clarence Darrow and the ACLU leading the defense threatened to dredge up all manner of political rancor. While local Daytonians might expect to have their town put "on the map," Peay, the president of the state university and the state board of education—both of which depended on the favor of the legislature for their programs—knew that the trial would make Tennessee famous, and ridiculous, as the monkey trial state.

And yet the Scopes trial, even if it was no more than a final futile struggle by fundamentalists against the tides of modernism, was nevertheless one of the most vital cases in the annals of American crime. Like many of the great Puritan prosecutions two centuries earlier, it raised fundamental questions about the meaning of crime in America. The case and the law were trivial to the progress of jurisprudence. The case established no precedent. The law produced no further prosecutions. But the issues of authority, ethics, and personal alienation were vital to America's future view on the course of crime.

John Washington Butler, a mildly prosperous Tennessee farmer, wrote the law in 1924. Early in 1925 it passed both houses of the legislature with overwhelming majorities. Already the teaching of evolution had been banned in Oklahoma and Florida. Similar campaigns were under way in California, Oregon, Kentucky, South Carolina, and several midwestern states. Governor Cameron Morrison of North Carolina seemed to take personal offense at Darwin's theories as he yanked a biology text from the schools, declaring: "I don't want my daughter or anybody else's daughter to have to study a book that prints pictures of a monkey and a man on the same page." For many of the prominent politicians, fighting evolution may have been pure political expediency. For men like Tennessee's John Butler, however, the doctrine of evolution seemed a sacrilegious assault upon the fundamental precepts by which they lived their lives. Like the witches who seemed to be the diabolical front men for the progressive merchants of Salem, the evolutionists seemed to be the agents of a cold, godless world ruled by criminal profiteers.[3]

"In the first place," Butler wrote in defense of his law, "the Bible is the foundation upon which our American Government is built. . . . The evolutionist who denies the Biblical story of creation as well as other Biblical accounts, cannot be a Christian. . . . It goes hand in hand with Modernism, makes Jesus Christ a faker, robs the Christian of his hope and undermines the foundation of our government." By Butler's standards, the government had long ago lost its foundation. That was the issue of the terrible persecutions at Salem and of the recurring revival movements up until the Revolution. Yet even before the Revolution, Americans had opted for a secular state where man's behavior would not be subject to God's authority. The separation of church and state meant quite simply that men had only to answer to themselves for the authority of their laws.

By 1925 that was hardly a radical idea. Little wonder then that an acerbic if sometimes shallow wit like H.L. Mencken should come to Dayton and believe himself to have fallen through the lookinglass. Writing for the *Baltimore Sun,* he reported: "In brief this is a strictly Christian community, and such is its notion of fairness, justice and due process of law. . . . Its people are simply unable to imagine a man who rejects the literal authority of the Bible. The most they can conjure up, straining until they are red in the face, is a man who is in error about the meaning of this or that text. Thus one accused of heresy among them is like one accused of boiling his grandmother to make soap in Maryland." At first Mencken was fascinated with these strange people, but after a day or two temper displaced curiosity. The people of Dayton were "morons," for whom "nine churches are scarcely enough." As for books, there was nothing but "melodrama and cheap amour." The town fathers knew "nothing that is not in Genesis." H.L. Mencken and the literate elite of the Northeast were discovering America. They were revolted, and they ridiculed their discovery.[4]

Dayton, Tennessee, however, was not an aberration. The Tennesseans' attack on the evolutionists, like those launched in their sister states, was an attempt to use the law as a kind of weapon in spiritual warfare. Historian Ray Ginger, who has written the most incisive study of the Scopes affair, called the law a form of "prayer emerging from an overwhelming but vague anxiety." To know that anxiety and what produced it was to know something about the turmoil that infused the violent life of the frontier and the rural countryside. It was to know something of the inarticulated frustrations that had earlier motivated the rebel bankrobber Jesse James and would help to lionize the modern bankrobbers of the late twenties and thirties.

Much of that anxiety, perhaps the core of it, was the old complaint from southern farmers about the soullessness of the industrial North. Karl Marx could never match the vitriolic diatribes written by antebellum southerners about the human degredation of the capitalist wage system. The entire reason for the Civil War, the southerners always argued, was to satisfy the profit-hungry industrialists. By the 1920s those predictions had become reality. Sherman's march to the sea was nothing compared to the industrial invasion that was sweeping the South, wooing thousands from the farm to the factory. The South was being integrated not racially but economically into the nation. As the stories of Tennessee Williams and William Faulkner showed so clearly, the old way of life was disappearing. "Newly arrived in the growing cities, men found themselves faced with an aching solitude and alienation, and they sought an emotional haven in religion," Ray Ginger wrote. Throughout the South church membership jumped 50 percent between 1906 and 1926. The population of Memphis, for example, rose 23 percent in those years while church membership increased 62 percent. God, the alienated people of the South hoped, would bring solace from a cruel, inhuman world.[5]

To the uprooted southern farmers in the cities—and to the ones who still held on during a period of falling farm prices—the government of the United States posed a special dilemma. Fervently patriotic and well represented in the Congress, they could nonetheless see that the leaders of the obviously corrupt and polyglot cities of the North were steadily tightening their control over the entire nation. Populist heroes from the South and West—men like Tom Watson or even the Wisconsin LaFolettes—had had their hour and were now on their way out. The country people had successfully voted in Prohibition as an act of Christian fidelity, but if they were to have any real impact, they would have to confront the frail structure of government itself. Their delusion was the desperate belief that through law they could reformulate the basis of government. The Scopes trial became the theater piece through which they would press their case. When the famed populist orator William Jennings Bryan offered to argue for the prosecution, they were guaranteed that the issues would be carried to the nation.

However much he many have misunderstood the frustrations of the locals in Tennessee, Mencken's assessment of Bryan was apt and succinct: "Bryan is no longer thought of as a mere politician and jobseeker in these Godly regions, but has become converted into a great sacerdotal figure, half man and half archangel—in brief, a sort of fundamentalist pope." Dayton would be his drilling ground for a new crusade against a society of darkness and depravity. His argument was a strange stew of Jacksonian Democracy and medieval theology. As a democrat and a populist he had long railed against the bankers, the oligarchs and the robber barons who had profited from the labor of the common worker. All men, he believed, stood equally before God. Darwinism, and the fashionable social Darwinists, on the other hand, presupposed an elitist view of mankind in which only a few were adequately "evolved" to hold the reins of power.

Thus the Darwinists not only denied God credit for creating man and enacting the laws of morality. The Darwinists also arrogated to themselves a godlike authority based on the survival of the strongest. Their politics therefore denied democratic rights to the majority of working people. Their morality was the morality of the jungle. Their godless society was the terrain of the vicious, of the corrupt—of the criminal. Witness the gangland underworld of Chicago and New York. As one apostolic minister from Zion City, Illinois, wrote during the trial, Darwin had completed what Copernicus had begun. The ancient astronomer had denied that God was the center of the universe and man his steward. Now Darwin and the evolutionist denied man's connection to God, indeed denied an organized purpose to life. Without purpose, "the millennium will be at hand." Without God, man was lost and alone in the universe. Science, the religion of the rich, dictated that all values were relative. Each person would live and die with nothing to validate the justice of his works. Bryan and the dirt farmers were confronting the great theological and philosophical issue of the century: Is God dead? If so, they said from the pit of their suffering, life can have no ultimate meanings.[6]

Speaking to his courtroom audience in Dayton, where as many as ten thousand people were gathered on the lawn beneath loudspeakers, Bryan held up a copy of the biology text Scopes had used in his classroom. There were 518,000 species listed on a diagram: 8,000 protozoa, 360,000 insects, 13,000 fish, 3,500 reptiles, 13,000 birds. He listed them all. "And then we have mammals, 3,500," he said, "and there is a little circle and man is in the circle. Find him. Find him," he demanded. "Talk about putting Daniel in the lion's den. How dared those scientists put man in a little ring like that with lions and tigers and everything that is bad!" Playing on counselor Darrow's well-known agnosticism, he asked the jury, "How could anyone find pleasure in taking from a human heart a living faith and substituting therefore the cold and cheerless doctrine, 'I do not know?'"[7]

Scope's conviction was of course a foregone conclusion. So for that matter was the dismissal of the case by the Tennessee appellate court, which was far less interested in the quandries of life down on the farm than it was in ending the degrading display Tennessee had suffered. The Scopes trial was also Bryan's final public battle. Seventy years old, he had taken the stand himself and allowed Darrow to make a fool of him. Even the courtroom audience laughed at his simpleminded explanations of biblical myth. It had been his last chance to resurrect a populist campaign against the corrupt and the powerful symbolized by Teapot Dome, Tammany Hall, and the rule of Big Bill Thompson. Less than a week after the trial ended, Bryan was dead.

Bryan's pyrrhic victory was a metaphor for the collapse of the whole fundamentalist movement that had engulfed much of the Midwest and West. Articulated in a variety of ways—antievolutionism, race hatred, anti-Catholicism, anti-Semitism—the underlying complaint was that the little people in America had gotten a bad deal. They were demanding not only religious fundamentalism but a return to political fundamentalism across the board. It was that old American refrain dredged out by the poor and middle-class farmers who saw themselves being pushed aside by the money changers in the city. Echoing the lost dream of the Puritan fathers, they called again for the creation of a city of God, or as John Winthrop had proclaimed it, a "citty upon a Hill." Dedicated to the rediscovery of that purified Eden, they had tried to create a law that would preserve their dream.

At the same time the most militant fundamentalists took the law into their own hands, launching the vigilante raids of the Ku Klux Klan. But by 1925 the organized violence of the Klan—the murders, the floggings, the castrations, and the brief seizures of governorships and statehouses in Texas, Alabama, Oklahoma, and Indiana—had also begun to fall apart. The Klan had constituted the armed forces of the fundamentalist movement. Klan leaders were often country preachers. David Chalmers, author of an intensive study of Klan behavior in the 1920s, has written that "the real lure of the Klan was its anti-Catholicism and its promise to fulfill the puritan creed. The Klan, in short, appeared to be doing what the Church talked about. It promised to bring Christian righteousness to society, to make it dry and moral. Here were the good folk of a minister's congregation asking only that he join them and make the community as it ought to be. . . . Those who formed the Klan, in the early days of its success in particular, were the better citizens as well as the law enforcement officers of their community."

Because of the Klan's ability to organize, it had achieved tremendous political clout which protected it from criminal prosecutions for several years. As a result, the Klan, responsible for at least as many murders as New York's Mafia families in the early twenties, was not characterized as a criminal organization. But as the states began to crack down on it in the late twenties, its membership dropped from over 3 million to a few hundred thousand between 1924 and 1928.[8]

Why extreme fundamentalism disappeared remains one of the enigmas still dividing American historians. Rising general prosperity may have deflated the movement's anger. The governors and mayors may have feared that the Klan would unleash real anarchy unless suppressed. The passions and hatreds let loose by the war and inflamed by Palmer's Red raids may finally have cooled. Likeliest of all the explanations is that the farmers and the preachers knew they were beaten. Political control of the nation had already shifted to the cities. The rebellion of the Klan, the symbolic persecution of the heathen culture, were the death struggles of a defeated people.

The anger and the spirit of rebellion, however, lived on, particularly in the Midwest and the Plains states. Illinois, Iowa, Kansas, Missouri, all harbored bands of disgruntled farmers who continued to speak out against the bosses and the bankers of the East. The Grange and the Farmers Union remained militant critics of the government. Their members continued to believe that American cities were in the "death chambers of American civilization." They were places of decadence, administered by crooked politicians for the profit of the indolent rich. An angry southern Illinois editor spoke the spirit of the region when he wrote, "There are between the City Hall in New York and the Battery Wall—a distance that can be walked in ten minutes—thousands of high binders in the world of speculation who have never done an honest day's work in their lives, but who make often in a day and frequently in a week as much if not more than the average farmer makes in a year."[9] Worse, the schemes of the industrialists and the bankers seemed to be impinging directly on rural life. Farm prices had collapsed at the beginning of the twenties, and they never fully recovered. Succumbing to pressure from the mushrooming cities, the states were hiking property taxes. The immigrant tide had begun to move out of the cities and into the countryside. In Indiana, Illinois, and Iowa preachers and newspaper editors inveighed against the proliferation of Jews and Italians in their communities. Unlike their fundamentalist cousins in the South, the grain farmers turned to modern biology for a defense of their culture. One prominent biologist-lecturer, Edward Wiggam, warned:

> On an average one child is born to every three of the graduates of our leading women's colleges. But one low-class, broad-backed, flat-chested, stout-legged, high-necked, stupid, ugly immigrant woman will in the same time produce three. By this process the average American woman is rapidly becoming ugly. With a decline in beauty, there

> always comes a decline in intelligence. Every decline in intelligence brings a decline in morals. The crime wave is no mystery to biologists.

Within a tangle of racism and Christian fundamentalism, the orators and the editors were etching a desperate vision of their own decline and disintegration. The fecundity of urban corruption, so obvious in nearby Chicago, seemed to be creeping out across the cornfields as though it were some insidious, malignant growth, multiplying and destroying all the virtue of life on the land.[10]*

By the terrible, early years of the Depression, the farm people had been defeated in their political drives and aspirations. The frantic vigilantism of the Klan had been crushed. And dust-bowl droughts and mortgage foreclosures spread relentless disasters. In the industrial cities unemployed workers were turning again to radicalism and unions. But on the prairie the tradition of political organization was fragile at best, and recent experience had shown nothing but failure. Taught by the elements to survive alone on the plains, the farmers' real tradition had always been to fight each battle man to man. Nowhere else in America was the cult of individualism so deep or so strong. In an era when rural people saw themselves as the victims of a commercial and financial elite, it is hardly surprising that they should have begun to grant a certain perverse glory to the outlaws who attacked that elite. For half a century politicians and writers had been ambivalent about the crimes of even the most brutal outlaws. Describing the shooting holdup of a county fair in the 1870s, a Kansas City reporter had written that the robbery was "so diabolically daring and so utterly in contempt of fear that we are bound to admire it and revere its perpetrators." The bandit raids of the twenties and thirties were not quite so common as they had been in the Old West. The institutions of law and order were

*The nightmare had its roots in the economic decline of farming during the 1920s. Don S. Kirschner has shown the devastating effect of the collapse in farm prices during the early twenties. From an all-time high of $1 billion in 1919, Iowa farm income dropped to $336 million in 1921. In 1917 the average farm family earned $3,000 a year; four years later they had to get by on half as much. Farmers across the Corn Belt were also faced with rising property taxes. As the cities cried for more and more tax dollars, farmers urged passage of state income taxes, arguing that property taxes worked unfair hardships on people whose only asset was land. Merchants and bankers fought them, and in almost every case farmers were forced to pay higher land taxes at the same time that their incomes were falling.

not as weak. Nor could the bankrobbers claim the same political-economic justification offered by such former Confederate rebels as Jesse James and the Younger brothers. Yet the temper and the anxiety of rural life extended a certain appreciation to the bankrobbers as the enemy of the farmers' enemy. That anxiety is what helped to elevate such gunmen as John Dillinger, Pretty Boy Floyd, and Bonnie and Clyde to a special status as the dark heroes of the Depression.[11]

Even in his hometown John Dillinger never quite managed to project himself as a Robin Hood of the New West. He held up banks because he was an angry man and he wanted money. Nor was he precisely a victim of poverty and desperation. His father was a "prosperous grocer" in a suburb of Indianapolis. His mother died when he was three. In his early teens, he had moved with his father, sister, and stepmother to Mooresville, a town twenty miles southwest of Indianapolis. He was an obstreperous boy, and his father believed the farm would be a healthy antidote to the godlessness of city life. It was a belief shared by thousands of Indianans who were turning to the church and to the Klan between 1915 and 1923.

But it didn't seem to have much effect on young Dillinger. Had he had faith in the organized rebelliousness of the Klan riders, he might have joined them. Instead, he saw a gray world wherever he turned. He quit school at sixteen and took a succession of jobs: at a veneer mill, as an errand boy, at a machine shop. He was called "sober" and "industrious" by his employers, but they complained that "he would not stay long." When he began to develop a serious relationship with his uncle's stepdaughter, the uncle broke it off, for he had a richer suitor in mind.

Angry and depressed, John Dillinger struck out on his first bold move. It was the evening of July 21, 1923. Oliver Macy and his wife had driven their new car to the Friends Church for an evening service. John Dillinger sometimes went too, but on this night he chose to wait outside on the street. When the service began, he opened the door to the Macy car, cranked up the engine and left Mooresville for the thrill of the city. When Dillinger and the car were found in Indianapolis a day or so later, Macy refused to press charges. Even so Dillinger panicked and, giving a false St. Louis home address, enlisted in the Navy.

After four months Dillinger went AWOL and returned briefly to Mooresville. But the car theft, combined with his Navy experience, had changed him, had broken the bonds that tied him to the suffocating life of a Hoosier farm town. Six months after his return he and a buddy from the local pool hall held up a grocer they had known since childhood, striking him with a heavy iron bolt. Apparently Dillinger didn't even try to avoid capture, for two days later he was arrested at his father's farm and brought before the grocer for identification. "Why, John, you wouldn't hurt me, would you?" the grocer asked reluctantly. Indicted only for the holdup, Dillinger pleaded guilty and was sentenced to ten to twenty-one years. His partner, who pleaded not guilty, was given two to fourteen years. Long afterward Dillinger's father blamed his son's fantastic criminal career on the "raw deal" the courts had given his boy.[12]

The rest of Dillinger's life—not quite ten years—became the stuff of Hollywood movies and cheap gangster stories. Nine of those years were spent in prison, until his parole in 1933. In prison he matured, met real bankrobbers and hoodlums, and established contacts that would enable him to turn his one year of freedom into an orgy of revenge against authority. In fourteen months he robbed a dozen banks. He smuggled guns to his former fellow inmates at the prison in Michigan City, Indiana. He attacked police stations and city hall offices. He kept beautiful women and vacationed on Miami beach. He made dazzling escapes from lawmen who were proud to be pictured next to him. He even dared return to his father's farm for a family reunion where he posed before a photographer, holding a machine gun and the wooden pistol he had once used to break out of jail. Through it all he swore that he had killed only one man, though there were probably more.

Had there been a "man of the year" award for 1934, Dillinger would probably have won it. Next to Clark Gable, he was the most romanticized man in the country. As Al Capone was the symbol of smart success for Chicago's lower-class immigrants, so Dillinger became the handsome bad boy for small-town America. Mayors, police chiefs, and bankers denounced him in their demands for law and order. But a great many common people cheered enthusiastically as he thumbed his nose at the judges and the prisons and the proliferating army of agents commanded by that tough little bulldog at the FBI, J. Edgar Hoover. The citizens of Mooresville, Indiana, even raised a petition for his pardon in 1934, recalling how a similar amnesty had been granted to Frank James. His father began to receive requests that he join the vaudeville circuit as a speaker. The old man displayed a certain backhanded affection for his son when Dillinger came home for the family reunion. "Oh, yes." the old man told a reporter, "John came down here to look in on me. He was hurt in the leg a little, but not much. I don't aim to tell no lies, even to keep things like that quiet. I didn't tell the police because they didn't ask me. John's not in Indiana now." A writer visiting Mooresville wrote that he asked the local people how they felt about Dillinger. "I like him fine," a gas station boy told him. A Mooresville banker even admitted he had seen Dillinger "visiting around with his old friends."

"You mean to say that the most wanted criminal in America could stroll around here in his home town, eighteen miles from Indianapolis, without anybody turning him in?" the writer asked.

"Nobody ever did," the banker said flatly.[13]

Dillinger had his enemies in Mooresville, including the town board and the *Mooresville Times.* Most respectable citizens, the paper editorialized, were anxious to have Dillinger behind bars. But, it protested: "The failure is not at Mooresville nor among the people as a whole. It is with public officials or with the system of nominating and electing public officials who cannot match the ingenuity and recklessness of desperate criminals." Bad as he was, the paper seemed to be saying, Dillinger was not as bad as the incompetent masters of government who could only waste money.[14]

Such sentiments were naturally disturbing to officials of the new administration in Washington. Public Enemy No. 1 had repeatedly slipped through the fingers of the most powerful government in history and had won winking credit for doing so. And it wasn't just Dillinger. There was Pretty Boy Floyd, the onetime Missouri booze runner who had machine-gunned a small phalanx of agents and police in the Kansas City train station while attempting to free another famous outlaw, Frank Nash. In Oklahoma City, Texas oilman Charles Urschel was kidnapped by George ("Machine Gun") Kelly. Bonnie Parker and Clyde Barrow were holding up banks all along the Mississippi Valley. And Ma Barker's gang was allegedly blowing banks and kidnapping rich businessmen from the Great Plains to the Florida peninsula.

To J. Edgar Hoover, who had cut his teeth rounding up radicals during the Palmer raids, these bandits posed a threat to the stability of the nation. What with Communists making trouble in the cities, clamoring for the overthrow of all capitalists and bankers, and with subversive troubadours like Woody Guthrie playing to homeless dust-bowl Okies, these heroic bankrobbers could undermine all respect for authority. To do his job, to force the nation to respect authority, Hoover insisted that he had to have more authority. If anarchy were to be avoided, the FBI would have to be granted new powers.

Until 1934, FBI agents were seriously restricted. Their jurisdiction covered interstate prostitution (the Mann Act), attacks on federal banks (which did not cover most small-town banks), interstate kidnapping (thanks to the kidnapping of aviator Charles Lindbergh's baby), interstate auto thefts, and "crimes against the United States." However, agents could not carry guns and they could not make their own arrests. They could only enter kidnap cases when invited by local authorities or by federal marshals. Taking his campaign for expanded powers to the public, Attorney General Homer Cummings declared, "We are now engaged in a war that threatenes the safety of our country—a war with the organized forces of crime."[15]

On May 18, 1934, Hoover and Cummings won from Congress the power they demanded. In a single day and without recording the vote, both houses passed six new laws. A month later three more laws were passed at the bureau's behest. Among the results of the new legislation, it now became a federal crime to cross state lines to avoid prosecution; to kill or assault a federal agent; to hold a kidnap victim for more than seven days regardless of crossing state lines; to extort money via telephone or any other means covered by interstate regulation; to rob any bank that was a member of the Federal Reserve System or to transport stolen property worth $5,000 or more across state lines; to assist as a federal prison employee in any kind of prisoner escape. Perhaps most importantly, FBI agents would henceforth be armed and authorized to make their own arrests.

Bureau agents had, of course, used weapons before they won authorization. In April 1934, for example, officials at Rhinelander, Wisconsin, were tipped that Dillinger, Baby Face Nelson, Pretty Boy Floyd, and several others were staying at a motel and roadhouse called Little Bohemia. Hoover was alerted in Washington, and agents descended on the town by air, train, and bus. Just after suppertime, Saturday May 1, a convoy of agents pulled into sight of Little Bohemia. As they came to a stop, three men—members of a nearby Civilian Conservation Corps camp who had stopped for supper—walked out of the building toward their car. Lest any badmen should escape, the FBI agents opened fire with submachine guns. The outlaws inside returned the fire as Floyd and Dillinger escaped out the back. Two of the CCC men were injured. One was killed.

The new laws won congressional approval with virtually no opposition voiced. Only William H. King, a Utah Democrat, spoke strongly against it. Acknowledging the dangers posed by "gangsters and racketeers," he warned that the new laws were a gross violation of states' rights. "I shall vote against it," he said, "because I believe it will be abused in its adminstration . . . and I have not any doubt on earth that in the hysteria now existing, and that which may follow, persons will be imposed upon, will be arrested and prosecuted under the Federal law, where the facts and circumstances will not warrant it. . . . We are challenging the competency of the States to govern their own affairs. We are substituting a Federal criminal code for the criminal codes of the States."[16]

Armed with both guns and a congressional mandate, Hoover's men went to work. First on the list was Public Enemy No. 1. Tipped off by Dillinger's current girl friend, a former madam from Gary, Indiana, Bureau agents learned that he planned to see a late afternoon showing of *Manhattan Melodrama* at a Chicago movie house. At about 6:00 P.M. on July 22 twenty agents gathered at the entrance to the theater. They had decided to wait until the film was over before moving. Dillinger (or, according to some investigators, someone who looked like him) was just coming out onto the street when he noticed that his girl had dropped behind. According to two eyewitness accounts, Dillinger never pulled a gun until he was shot. A mechanic who was standing outside a garage across the street swore that he had a clear view of the killing. "Suddenly I saw a tall man fire two shots in quick succession. He seemed to be standing almost beside the man who was shot. The wounded man fell to the alley without uttering a sound." A woman watching from her second-story parlor confirmed the account, adding, "I thought at first that it was a holdup and the victim was killed." A coroner's inquest ruled Dillinger's death as justifiable homicide and declared the agents were to be "highly commended." For some, however, the agent's action was not so clear-cut. Dillinger's father said bluntly: "They shot him down in cold blood." Some reporters regarded the inquest as hasty, if not incomplete. Even the staid Associated Press was somewhat incredulous over the nature of the coroner's hearing: "The man who ran him down was not present; the man whose bullet killed him was not named, and the informant who led him to his death was not mentioned."[17]

The killing of John Dillinger eliminated the first Public Enemy No. 1 named by the FBI. The continuous generation of new public enemies reflected Hoover's genius for promotion. As one gangster succeeded another in the No. 1 slot, Hoover was able to propagate the notion that America was filled with a never ending supply of vicious criminals. By adding fuel to the popular mythology of a monolithic crime cult, he glorified both the gangsters and his own invincible G-men, the nickname given FBI agents by none other than the Texas outlaw Machine Gun Kelly.

Thus with Dillinger gone Hoover anointed Lester Gillis, known as Pretty Boy Floyd, the new Public Enemy No. 1. Floyd was apparently gratified, having coveted Dillinger's glamorous status. Although he never had a single flamboyant year comparable to Dillinger's 1933–34 record, Floyd had been holding up banks and businessmen since the late twenties when he was paroled from a three-year prison sentence. Like Dillinger, Floyd had developed a sense of craft and a network of contacts in prison that would serve him well on the outside. Back at work in 1928, he reportedly boasted to his banker victims: "You can say to your friends that you were robbed by Pretty Boy Floyd." And like Dillinger, he commanded a certain level of admiration from the press and the public.

"Floyd's methods have been ultramodern," an AP dispatch said. "Eastern Oklahoma officers say they have fired at him point-blank and that he only laughed and fled unscathed. They believe he habitually has worn a bulletproof vest and a steel skullcap. Submachine guns have been standard equipment in his bank raids, and usually he has kidnapped the cashier or bank president after scooping up his loot, releasing his hostage unharmed after pursuers were distanced."[18]

Floyd's end came in a shoot-out with FBI agents near Clarkson, Ohio, after he had made a trip east from his usual haunts in the Cookson Hills of Oklahoma. The date was October 22, 1934, exactly three months after the agents had shot Dillinger. In the words of one writer sympathetic to Hoover, Floyd was overcome because he failed to realize how the FBI had been "geared into a fighting machine against gangland and crime on a nationwide basis."[19]

One month later, in November, George ("Baby Face") Nelson fell before the guns of the Bureau. In January 1935 a massive sunrise assault with tear gas, machine guns, and high-powered rifles on a lone south Florida cottage killed Ma Barker and her son, Fred. Given the hour of the day and the surprise of the attack, there is no indication the Barkers even went for their guns. Fred Barker was one of two leaders in the Karpis-Barker gang. According to Alvin Karpis, Ma Barker had no role in the gang, although Hoover claimed she was the mastermind. Karpis, who was in New Jersey at the time of the Florida attack, barely escaped a gun battle at his Atlantic City Hotel. In May 1936 he was surrounded by FBI agents in New Orleans when he walked out of his house unarmed and unwarned. Hoover, who had named him the new Public Enemy No. 1, had come to New Orleans to bring Karpis in personally. When the director later described his success in capturing the last of the western "hoodlums," Karpis was offended. "I'm no hoodlum. I'm a thief," he said proudly.[20]

Chapter 24

The Guns of Dearborn

Dillinger dead. Capone and Luciano in prison. By the end of the 1930s the epic figures of the new American underworld had been eliminated. A cocky J. Edgar Hoover could swear that "not one" criminal syndicate was operating anywhere in America. Nothing could have been further from the truth.

For a while the public seemed to believe it. The swashbuckling highwayman, the dashing bank robber, the lone, vengeful enemy of the state was gone. The armed might of Hoover, buttressed by the new sophisticated tools of police technology, had ended one of the oldest traditions in lawlessness, the great American outlaw. Although he had had nothing to do with locking up the Italian gangsters, Hoover had so stolen the show with his publicity campaigns against the bankrobbers that he could claim credit for having decimated the entire underworld. Moreover, he could use the imprisonment of the old bootleg mobsters as evidence that the syndicates were no longer an important threat.[1]

The government's violent assault on notorious outlaws had an added importance during the depression. At a time when millions of middle class people—doctors, lawyers, merchants, local public officials—were fearful that the nation itself might not survive its economic collapse, a successful campaign against individual, well-known outlaws vividly demonstrated the government's strength. Hoover's cleverness in devising the revolving public enemy file was undeniable: men who rob banks are not just enemies of the bankers; they are enemies of the people and of America herself. Men who catch the men who rob banks are therefore the protectors of the people. The corollary to the argument was obvious: Anyone on the bureau's list of enemies was by definition an enemy of America. Thus Hoover was able to use his public-enemy campaign to bolster his more important attacks on radicals and labor agitators. They more than anyone, he believed, were the real menace to America. The result was that Hoover and his men were able to define the meaning of crime in America, to use it as a weapon of political purpose, and to focus public concern on a specific kind of crime. Not only did Hoover deflect attention from other more common offenses, but in the process he also encouraged the proliferation of corporate vigilantism on a scale never before imagined.

The cases of corporate crime, especially against labor unions, are legion. But none match the notoriety of Henry Ford and his right hand man, Harry Herbert Bennett.[2]

Nominally director of personnel for the Ford Motor Company, throughout the thirties, Bennett was second in importance only to "Mr. Henry." He was a short, tough, muscular man who had worked as bodyguard for Ford's children. He then became chief watchman at the company's River Rouge plant in Dearborn, outside Detroit. Bennett's real power, however, came from his administration of the Ford Service Department, the massive security force employed to keep order in the plants. Ford Service had existed before Bennett came to power, but he was the man who transformed it into what the *New York Times* called the biggest private quasi-military force in the world.[3]

Bennett staffed Ford Service with ex-fighters, University of Michigan football players, parolees from Jackson State Prison, and a broad cut of the Detroit underworld. Ex-cons were particularly high on Bennett's list, both for the Service Department and for regular assembly-line jobs. Indeed, Ford claimed credit as a social crusader for his company's policy of hiring released prisoners. In 1934 Bennett told a Detroit reporter that he had some eight thousand former inmates on his payroll. But Bennett's hiring instincts stemmed not from a bleeding conscience but from his need to maintain an army of toughs who could man the front lines in the company's repeated clashes with labor organizers. He also knew that there were considerable advantages to keeping close contact with the city's organized underworld, particularly its leaders. As early as 1927 Ford had entered into an arrangement with the boss of Detroit's Sicilian bootleggers, Chester LaMare.[4]

Federal agents described LaMare as Detroit's version of Al Capone. His gang controlled bootlegging and other rackets in the "down river" waterfront strip on the city's south side. By 1928, when he was working for Ford, Prohibition agents claimed that his men dominated a $215 million bootlegging business, making it the state's second largest industry. His lieutenants were not above subjecting their enemies to cool winter plunges beneath the ice of the Detroit River. Repeatedly arrested on one charge or another, LaMare was eventually convicted on a Prohibition violation in 1927. He would have gone to prison then—and perhaps lost power to either the Jewish Purple Gang or to his Italian rivals, the Licavoli brothers—had Harry Bennett not stepped in with an offer of occupational rehabilitation. Mr. LaMare, he told the judge, could better serve society under the tutelage of that great American folk hero and builder of moral virtue, Mr. Henry Ford. Soon Chet LaMare was a partner in a Ford sales agency called the Crescent Motor Sales Company. Better yet, he was given a concession to sell fruit to the lunch-hour food wagons at Ford's River Rouge plant; that concession alone is reported to have brought him $100,000 a year.

After several embarrassing press reports, Ford did finally announce somewhat obliquely that LaMare was not working for Bennett. The following year, when LaMare seemed to be losing ground to rival gangs, Ford canceled his fruit concession. But that was not the end of Ford's or Bennett's underworld connection. When LaMare was assassinated in 1931, Emil Colombo, brother and partner of Ford's chief counsel Louis J. Colombo, Jr., represented his widow and provided some apparent protection. Another regular at Bennett's office—though he may not have been technically an employee—was Joseph Tocco, a west side bootlegger who was involved in gang wars throughout the Depression years. When a Tocco ally, Leonard ("Black Leo") Cellura, stood trial for murder in 1937, the judge reported that he had been pressured to go easy on the defendant. The judge told Cellura that "efforts have been made by misguided persons even in the precincts of this court building to interfere with the ordinary course of a trial for murder and have not ceased with your conviction. If these efforts are continued I may find it necessary to expose the persons making them."

The judge did not "expose" Cellura's backers, but at least two of them were Bennett allies. John Gillespie, a former Republican boss who had become an insurance broker for Ford, regularly visited Cellura in his jail cell. Then, after the prosecutor had called Cellura a dangerous "killer" during the trial, Gillespie reportedly cornered him outside the courtroom and in a loud, threatening voice, shouted, "You can't call my friend a 'killer' and live in this town." With only slightly more subtlety, meanwhile, Ford Serviceman Sam Cuva kept showing up armed and sat at the trial in the front row of the spectators' gallery glowering at witnesses. Cuva later was convicted on a charge of assault to commit murder. It even turned out that while Black Leo was free on bail, Ford was generous enough to provide him a car registered in his own name, "in care of the Ford Motor Co., Dearborn." Eventually Ford entered into business arrangements with no less a crime czar than Joe Adonis, one of the Brooklyn bosses of Murder, Inc.[5]

Harry Bennett's fondness for gangsters was not a schoolboy adoration of comic-book tough guys. Bennett's arrangements had a point. The combination of his underworld alliances with the spying and enforcement squads of his Service Department made him the best-informed man in Detroit. At a time when the police seemed powerless to stop the depravations of the criminals and the agitation of the anarchists, Bennett was promoting himself as a private gangbuster, a kind of Junior J. Edgar Hoover of Michigan. Nicknamed the "Little Fellow"—in contrast to "Big Fellow," Al Capone—Bennett became a heroic figure in the pages of the *Detroit News* and *Free Press.*

Although his own underworld connections were acknowledged, Bennett nonetheless came to be seen as the cop of last resort. When two couples were murdered in Ypsilanti in the "torching" of a car, Ford Servicemen found the murderers. In a famous kidnapping case in 1929, Bennett's men secured the release of the child from his abductors. Later it turned out that Bennett had gone to one of Chester LaMare's cohorts who ordered the child released and the ransom money returned to the child's parents. After Henry Ford was personally involved in an automobile accident in 1927, Bennett "reassured" the public that his boss had not been the target of an assassination attempt. "Our connections with the Detroit underworld are such," he announced proudly, "that within twenty-four hours after the hatching of such a plot we would know of it."* Late in his life Bennett recalled that LaMare had once told him: "I am the king. You deal with me and nobody gets killed."[6]

By plying his connections to solve celebrated crimes, Bennett could promote the heroic image of Henry Ford and his motor company. Moreover, since his underworld connections were often assumed to be doing nothing worse than supplying speakeasies with booze, Bennett could be forgiven for his unsavory methods. That at least was the way Bennett's newspaper friends looked at it. For the auto workers in the plants, Bennett's exploits with the underworld conveyed another message. Not only could they be roughed up on the job by agents of the Service Department, but if they should dare undertake serious union organizing, they might also have to defend themselves against a reserve army of gangsters.

Historian Keith Sward has detailed the Servicemen's routine manhandling of line workers in the plants. Any man called to the office would be pushed and shoved as he walked down the aisles and made to feel as though he were a convict in a prison shop. Night workers would have lights flashed in their eyes and be subjected to demeaning questions. Once they were off the open floor, workers would be flogged by Servicemen if they dared complain about working conditions. One of Bennett's top hirelings, Ralph Rimar, quit Ford and sold his story of company brutality to the New York newspaper *PM*. Rimar had supervised a squad of spies and toughs for Bennett between 1933 and 1935. They worked both inside the plant and on the streets of Dearborn, providing intelligence reports to Ford allies in the town hall. "My own agents reported back to me conversations in grocery stores, meat markets and restaurants, gambling joints, beer gardens, social groups, boys' clubs and even churches. Women waiting in markets buying something might discuss their husbands' jobs and activities; if they did, I soon heard what they said." So intense was the Ford

*The circumstances of the "accident" held their own intrigue. Henry Ford had been called to testify in a libel suit brought against him by Aaron Sapiro. A rich developer of farm marketing coops, Sapiro had been accused of fleecing his clients in Ford's blatantly anti-Semitic *Dearborn Independent*. There is considerable evidence that Ford's accident and subsequent hospitalization may have been a convenient ruse enabling him to avoid testifying. Ford Servicemen had already tried to physically prevent a court from serving him with a subpoena. "No, no no; take it away," the old man exclaimed as he let the subpoena fall between his knees, and the process server fled.

company's harassment, so determined was it to prevent any incipient union activity, that in 1928 even the staid *New York Times* characterized Ford as "an industrial fascist—the Mussolini of Detroit." A few years later worker resentment had built to such a point that even *Fortune* magazine warned of an impending explosion at the River Rouge plant: "The atmosphere is loaded with tension. You feel that if someone fired a cap pistol, 35,000 hearts would burst."[7]

By spring 1937 the cap pistol had gone off. The previous winter had been the bloodiest in the history of the automobile industry. United Automobile Workers organizers had withstood assaults by thugs, local police, National Guardsmen and KKKers in Flint as they staged sit-down strikes against General Motors. There was even some evidence that Flint's city manager had plotted with vigilante groups to murder Roy Reuther, brother of Walter, and two other UAW organizers. But by the first days of spring, the union had won a major victory. GM workers were finally organized. Ford then became the major holdout. He was also the most bitterly antiunion of all the automakers.[8]

The UAW officials knew that to organize Ford, they would have to endure brutal assaults from Bennett, his several thousand Servicemen and his underworld allies. Their biggest confrontation came on May 26, 1937, at Gate 4 of the huge River Rouge plant, known among the workers as the Sweat Shop or the Butcher House. Hundreds of UAW volunteers had prepared to distribute leaflets at the afternoon shift change. The leaflets included quotations from the Wagner Act on the right to organize and exhortations to join the UAW. Gate 4 was the main plant entrance. It gave on to an overpass crossing Miller Road to an electric railway station on the other side. Although Ford had built the footbridge, it had been leased to the Detroit Railway Commission for public use. Walter Reuther, then president of a west side local, described what happened as the UAW volunteers began their leafletting:

> I got out of the car on the public highway, Miller Road, near Gate 4. Dick Frankensteen [another UAW officer] and I walked together to the stairs. I got up the stairs and walked over near the center of the bridge. I was there a couple of minutes and then all of a sudden about 35 or 40 men surrounded us and started to beat us up. I didn't fight back. I merely tried to guard my face. The men . . . picked me up

> about eight different times and threw me down on my back on the concrete and while I was on the ground, they kicked me in the face, head and other parts of my body. After they kicked me for a while, one fellow would yell, "All right, let him go now." Then they would raise me up, hold my arms behind me and begin to hit me some more. . . . Finally they got me next to Dick who was lying on the bridge and with both of us together they kicked me again and then picked me up and threw me down the first flight of stairs. I lay there and they picked me up and began to kick me down the total flight of steps. . . .
>
> There were about 150 men standing around. . . . I should say about 20 were doing the actual beating. . . . They started to hit me again at the bottom of the stairs and slugging me, driving me before them, but never letting me get away. . . . The more we tried to leave, the worse it was for us. . . . They drove me to the outside of the fence, almost a block of slugging and beating and hurling me before them. . . . While I was being driven down I had glimpses of women being kicked and other men being kicked. . . . All the time I had the permit to distribute the leaflets in my pocket, but no one would look at that. I might add, the police standing around did nothing to prevent the slugging.[9]

Walter Reuther's account was corroborated in testimony before hearings at the National Labor Relations Board later in July 1937. Ministers, newsmen, and other union people recounted the same story. A few minutes before the attack, a United Press photographer had spotted "about twenty-five carloads of men parked under the overpass." When he attempted to take their pictures, he was surrounded and driven out. Later he returned, and his pictures became some of the most vital documents in American labor history. At least three of the assailants were identified as Ford men. One, Sam Taylor, was a foreman and president of the ultra-right-wing Knights of Dearborn. The other two were Wilford Comment (who carried handcuffs hanging from his rear pocket) and Ted Greiss, who was a wrestling referee. Both worked for Bennett as Ford Servicemen. They and three other Servicemen, Everett Moore, Charles Goodman, and Warshon Sarkisian, were later charged with assault. Testifying before the NLRB,

Joseph P. Barnick, a Ford Serviceman from April to June, admitted that he had been instructed to "beat up" anyone he saw passing out leaflets.[10]

Ford tried other tactics to crush the UAW. That same spring, four other "unions" sprung up overnight, all under the aegis of top men in the Ford Service Department. One, the Ford Brotherhood of America, Inc., was outlawed by the NLRB as a company union created to intimidate workers from joining the UAW. Mack Cinzori, whose membership in the UAW was unknown to the company, testified at NLRB hearings about a "vigilante group" organized by Ford executives. "Last January," he testified,

> my foreman, Mr. Bleau, along with the general foreman, asked me if I wanted to work at Ford's. I said I did. They asked me if I wanted to work there long. I said sure I did. They said: "I suppose you have heard of sit-downs. We want you to watch for agitators or anybody that wants to sit down and let us know and nobody will know anything about it. . . ."
>
> Sometime in June, Bleau called me over and takes me to a man named Slim, a star man [salaried employee]. Slim told me they was going to form a vigilante group and they don't believe in no kind of organization. He says workers is liable to shut off the power plant and we are liable to be off for six months.
>
> He says to me if there is trouble I am supposed to pick up a lead pipe and start swinging and get to the place where the trouble is. In the gang there is supposed to be three of us and the minute trouble starts we are to hit on the head of anybody that gets in the way no matter who it is and get to where the trouble is.
>
> Last month we had a sort of drill. We was called to Slim's main desk. There was seven from our department and three from another department. An assistant to the star man said he tried to get us together in five minutes but it took eight minutes and we were late.[11]

The July hearings before the NLRB proved devastating to Ford's antiunion policies. Company hooliganism, designed to terrorize the workers into rejecting the union, backfired. Bennett's men were no longer characterized in the press as heroes but as the thugs they were. Although Bennett had denied any company responsibility for the "battle of the overpass," a reporter for the *Detroit Times* recognized one of the thugs as a man who had been questioned in police headquarters about a recent holdup. He told the *Times* reporter before the fight: "We were hired, as far as I know, temporary, to take care of these union men that are to distribute pamphlets." He also added that he had been hired by the Service Department and that four thugs had been assigned to each union person.[12]

Bennett continued his war with the UAW for another year. Then, in the summer of 1938, he took a new tack, approaching UAW president Homer Martin directly. Martin, the union's first president, had been an inept administrator, a hater of radicals and a breeder of internal factionalism. He also knew that he could not survive as president. For these and other reasons he began to negotiate a private peace with Bennett which, had it succeeded, would have left the union with no bargaining power at all. The intricacies of Martin's maneuvers and the response of the other union officials were infinitely complex. Suffice it to say that when word of the discussions leaked out, Martin was isolated from the other UAW leaders. By January 1939 he had been suspended by the UAW's parent organization, the Congress of Industrial Organizations (CIO). Bennett of course reacted firmly to the charges of a deal. "That's a cockeyed lie," he bellowed. "I never conspired with him."[13]

After Martin was expelled, he tried to organize his own union and take it into the AFL. It was a feeble effort at best, lasting only a few months and was backed by no more than a few thousand members nationally. In his memoirs Bennett acknowledged supporting Martin's rump union and after its failure providing Martin with a furnished home and financial support. He did not, however, outline certain other details of his relationship with Martin.[14]

According to Harry Elder, formerly a vice-president of a UAW local in St. Louis and then personal bodyguard to Martin, Bennett financed much of Martin's work. In a sworn affidavit Elder said that shortly after he arrived in Detroit, Martin asked him to "take some 'boys' and some guns and make a raid on the Communist party headquarters" in Detroit. Two men he was instructed to "get"—but not kill—were Walter Reuther and Emil Mazey, another UAW leader. He said he was then given $250 to return to St. Louis "to get some boys to help out and to get some guns." Elder said he had often stood guard at public telephone booths while Martin called Harry Bennett to discuss business arrangements.[15]

In May 1939 Elder went with Martin to Ford headquarters for a meeting with Bennett. It was the first time Elder had met the Little Fellow and he was treated to quite a show. Bennett called a judge of the Wayne County Circuit Court to ask a favor for his friend Homer Martin. When the call was completed, Bennett reportedly told Martin, in a rather grand manner, that "the case was 'in the bag.'" According to Elder, Bennett said that "Ford had promised to 'go along' with [Martin] and to give him financial help." At another meeting in Bennett's office Martin reportedly asked Bennett for $3,500 and was assured that the money would soon be forthcoming. The next day John Gillespie, the Republican politician and Ford confidant, came to Martin's hotel room while Elder stood guard outside. "I can sure use this," Elder heard Martin say after some talk about money. A half hour later Martin and Elder went down the street to catch a cab. "When we were outside of the hotel, Martin banged one fist against another, stating, 'Boy, I got it! Got it! Got it!' He seemed very pleased. He showed me a pack of bills. The bills were unfolded, flat, and were about two inches high. They were in packages with paper strips around them such as are used by banks. They were new bills. Those that I saw were of twenty-dollar denominations. He put these bills in his inside coat pocket where they bulged out quite noticeably."

After describing the bulge in Martin's pocket, Elder made some careful statements. The two men took the cab to the office of a man named Jerry Aldred in the same building where Martin kept his own offices, but Aldred was gone. The following morning they returned and, "Martin tossed some bills on Aldred's desk." Elder said he was unable to hear what Martin and Aldred discussed. Then he added, "The night of the day that Martin turned this money over to Jerry Aldred, Joseph Green shot [a Martin foe named] Ferris. I saw Green the morning after the shooting in Homer Martin's room. I heard Green tell Martin that he, Green, had shot Ferris. Martin said to me, 'Now you see, that's the way these guys mess up things. I want you to go to St. Louis and get some boys who know how it should be done.' Martin told Green to hide out until Martin could find out what the lawyers would have to say. Since I was going to St. Louis on that day to get some men, it was agreed that Green would hide out in my room."

Through Bennett, Martin was introduced to many of Detroit's top corporate executives. The door was even opened to an exclusive union contract with the Eaton Manufacturing Company in Cleveland. Each time Martin and Elder came to visit Bennett, they were chauffeured back to Detroit from Dearborn in a fresh new company car. In the end it was all for naught. Martin became known as one of Bennett's collaborators, and eventually even his bodyguard left him. By the winter of 1940, he had faded from public attention, a broken man. It was then that "Mr. Henry" was said to have taken pity on him and to have asked Bennett to help him out. On June 28, 1940, the *Detroit News* ran a short item announcing that John Gillespie, the once powerful politician and labor negotiator, and Homer Martin, the once powerful union leader, had formed a partnership to sell autoparts.[16]

About the time Martin and Gillespie were setting up business, a far more startling revelation came to light about Ford's underworld allies. A six-part series on the crime empire of Joe Adonis in the *New York Post* revealed that the gangster held a monopoly on the delivery of Ford cars on the East Coast. "Adonis Firm Gets 3 Million From Ford," the *Post* headline declared. The firm, Automotive Conveying Company, held an exclusive contract with Ford's mammoth assembly plant at Edgewater, New Jersey. From there automotive trailer trucks delivered new cars to dealers in New Jersey, New York, Rhode Island, Massachusetts, Connecticut, Pennsylvania, Delaware, the District of Columbia, Virginia, and Vermont. Although the *Post* found no evidence of any illegal transactions between Ford and Adonis (whose real name was Joseph Doto), the gangster's control of the delivery company came about through a back door. Until the Edgewater plant was completed in 1931, new cars had been individually chauffeured to each dealership. The drivers worked for a small-business man, one T. Kramer. Then Ford decided new cars had to be trucked to dealers. To handle the new arrangement, Kramer entered into partnership with a Buffalo hauler and began to order a fleet of expensive trucks. When that partnership fell apart after a few months, Kramer was desperate for cash to pay off his orders. Unable to raise money from friends and relatives, he turned to the large Ford dealers, dealers who were well known and carefully scrutinized by Harry Bennett and his Service Department watchdogs. At White Auto Sales Company in Brooklyn, T. Kramer found a friend. He was told to come back in a few days, and when he did, he was introduced to Joe Adonis, who seemed patient and sympathetic. After the usual formalities, he invited Kramer across the street to discuss the deal over drinks in his own speakeasy.

"Adonis agreed to put up whatever money we needed to keep the business going," Kramer said. "I gave him 49 percent of the stock as collateral. If I couldn't hold up my end, I was to turn over the business to Joe, but if it worked out he could either stay in or pull out and I was to pay off at a regular rate of interest. One of the terms of the agreement was that I was to give Paul Bonadio, a relative of his [still connected with the business in 1940], a job. Neither Joe nor I was to sell or give away stock without the approval of the other." Adonis's initial investment, Kramer said, was at least $100,000. Bonadio was made bookkeeper. Four months later, Kramer got out. It was only after his withdrawal that Ford gave the company its exclusive contract for Edgewater plant deliveries.

Confronted with the *Post*'s revelations, Ford corporately denied any knowledge of Adonis's interest in the conveying company or in the White Auto Sales, where he was also a partner. "Nowhere in any of our records do we find the name Adonis," its statement said. Ford's disingenuous statement was hardly convincing, but lacking hard evidence of corruption, there was little that public officials could do. Because of minor misstatements in its filing papers, White Auto Sales did lose its license later in the year. Adonis was also indicted on a multitude of charges late in 1940, including kidnapping, assault, and extortion. But all the charges were dismissed.[17]

Despite the fanfare, Ford suffered little damage. The car business was booming, and once the United States began preparing for World War II, the assembly lines geared to full capacity. Bennett could be scolded by the press for the gangster acquaintances he kept, but no official agency ever investigated the reasons why a security guard needed underworld connections. Thus no one ever discovered how much Ford money had been channeled into the coffers of underworld organizations, what Ford got in exchange, or how the deals enabled criminal entrepreneurs to enter the world of legitimate business. On the eve of Pearl Harbor, underworld exploits had become passé. Moreover, as the old Jewish and Italian gangsters were dying or retiring to the penitentiaries, their heirs were not so interested in publicity. Fully American, they had learned to listen to lawyers and accountants so that they could become regular partners with men like Mr. Bennett and Mr. Ford.

The Ford Motor Company's connivance with gangsters symbolized both an end and a beginning for the routine involvement of corporations in crime. Manufacturers had been hiring goon squads to keep their workers in order for over a century. Harry Bennett's Servicemen did nothing that Jay Gould and Leland Stanford had not invented fifty years ealier. Henry Ford, however, was a man caught between times. He was at once the great American folk hero, the inventor of the modern, efficient assembly-line industry, the man who railed against the financial autocracy of Wall Street, the friend and sometime defender of Adolf Hitler, the egotistical, rigid tyrant who scandalized his fellow carmakers by offering his workers five dollars a day and who impressed his very identity into every automobile he made.

Yet Ford's real legacy was the creation of the modern, streamlined, impersonal corporation administered by cool managerial bureaucrats for whom personal egotism was anathema and the cult of efficiency was all. His corporate involvement in crime was part of a great transition in American industry. It is not enough to say that he hired thugs to do his dirty work: It was his system of blending them into his corporation that made all the difference. He, or more particularly Harry Bennett, recognized that criminal entrepreneurs had advanced beyond the stage of working as personal errand boys for great masters. Their interest was in doing business, with a regular systematic cash flow, monitored by bookkeepers and protected by lawyers. To pay off Chester LaMare or Joe Adonis for peace-keeping services out of the president's hip pocket was messy. To incorporate them into the supply and production of a company division was to acknowledge and measure their value as a legitimate part of the business of making and selling automobiles.

Chapter 25

Corporations and Conspiracies

Forty years after Harry Bennett hired his thugs to beat up union organizers, Ford Motor Company officials were summoned to court in two important criminal investigations. In the fall of 1978 prosecutors in Elkhart, Indiana, charged the corporation with homicide after three people were burned alive in Ford Pintos. The evidence, compiled by journalists and emanating from civil suits, tended to show that company executives had knowingly allowed the Pinto to be sold with a faulty gas tank which would explode in rear-end collisions. It was the first case in American legal history that a corporation had been indicted for murder. At about the same time top Ford staffers were hauled before a federal grand jury in Washington, D.C., on charges that the company had paid a $1 million bribe to an Indonesian general in order to obtain a $30 million contract for the construction of a satellite communications system. These cases of the late 1970s, set alongside the company's early history of hooliganism, raise profound questions about American corporations' increasing involvement in routine illegal behavior.[1]

To the men of Henry Ford I's generation, corporate crime was one of the embarrassing necessities of running a business, a private hypocrisy of the industrial estate. But in the decades following World War II, word of the hypocrisy began to slip out to the public. While radicals and agitators of the thirties were always charging industrialists with lawbreaking, it was not until the late fifties that Americans in the mainstream began to acknowledge the problem. A breaking point came in 1959 when the nation's two largest electrical manufacturers, General Electric and Westinghouse, were exposed for having conspired to build the biggest illegal cartel since the passage of the Sherman Anti-Trust Act. Altogether, twenty-nine corporations and forty-five top executives were prosecuted on a price-fixing scheme covering sales of \$1.75 billion. The great electrical equipment scandal was the biggest white-collar crime story of the postwar era, and it helped stimulate a series of congressional investigations throughout the sixties and seventies. One result was the eventual acknowledgment that no other crime wave—not dope, auto theft, welfare fraud, muggings or burglaries—could equal the toll taken by white-collar criminals. By 1976 the Joint Economic Committee of Congress fixed the cost of white-collar crime at \$44 billion per year—as against \$4 billion for such common property crimes as robbery and burglary.[2]

Criminologist Edwin Sutherland, who coined the phrase white-collar crime in the 1940s, examined seventy of the largest corporations in the United States and found that they had all been charged with at least one illegal act. Forty-one were convicted on outright criminal charges. The combined offenses committed by the seventy firms totaled 980 violations of law including: 307 restraints of trade; 222 infringement of patent rights; 158 unfair labor practices; 97 phony advertising claims; and 66 illegal rebates (usually kickbacks). White-collar crime also includes the work of well-dressed con artists, embezzlers, and undifferentiated company thiefs. A 1977 study undertaken by the American Management Association estimated that such crimes against business run from \$30 to \$40 billion a year. But for its impact on American life, both symbolically and concretely, nothing begins to equal the record of the giant banks and private corporations.[3]

A complete history of corporations involved in crime would amount to nothing less than an encyclopedia of modern business development. Files on the payments of bribes to foreign officials in the first half of the 1970s fill several shelves at the Securities and Exchange Commission in

Washington. The *New York Times* computerized survey of major American newspapers and magazines lists over four hundred entries under the heading "corporate crime" between 1970 and 1978. The sheer volume of material, combined with the intricacies of multinational finance, make it technically difficult to mount comprehensive investigations of corporate crime. Whereas prosecuting a car thief may require one assistant district attorney, a standard police file, and part of an investigator's time, the prosecution of a company involved in overseas bribery, securities manipulation, consumer fraud, or price fixing can require a dozen attorneys and several years of work. The price fixing conspiracy put together by G.E. and the other top electrical manufacturers is an apt example of the sophisticated schemes being used two decades ago.[4]

"This is a shocking indictment of a vast section of our economy, for what is really at stake here is the survival of the kind of economy under which this country has grown great, the free-enterprise system," U.S. district judge J. Cullen Ganery said solemnly before he began sentencing of the individual defendants in the case. Ganery had heard witness after witness testify about the friendly meetings among competitors, which had evolved into a series of precise agreements by the end of the decade. One of the first of the conspiracies had begun in the switchgear division of General Electric, the section of G.E. that made giant industrial circuit breakers and accounted for 25 percent of corporate sales. Switchgear accounted for some $75 million in business a year from 1951 through 1958. Between $15 and $18 million of that went to public agencies on a sealed-bid basis and the rest was open bid in contracts to private utilities.

Nothing seemed terribly illegal about what the executives were doing, at least not at the time. They did not believe they were consciously gouging the public with inflated prices. They had simply agreed to bring a little stability to the industry by rotating the business on a fixed percentage basis to the top four electrical manufacturers: G.E. would get 45 percent, Westinghouse 35, Allis-Chalmers 10, and Federal Pacific 10. Every two weeks or so the executives met to decide whose turn it was to submit the lowest bid. A similar scheme involving general managers and vice-presidents apportioned contracts among the top four on the much more valuable private utility jobs. These meetings were held each week, and a single executive was appointed each month to notify the rest about upcoming jobs, to keep track of equipment prices, and to assign the bids each company would file. A reporter for *Fortune* magazine recounted the story in terms that might have applied to Arnold Rothstein's rum-running system or to the construction rackets of Robert Brindell's day:

> Their conspiracies had their own lingo and their own standard operating procedures. The attendance list was known as the "Christmas card list," meetings as "choir practice." Companies had code numbers—G.E. 1, Westinghouse 2, Allis-Chalmers 3, Federal Pacific 7—which were used in conjunction with first names when calling a conspirator at home for price information ("This is Bob, what is 7's bid?"). At the hotel meeting it was S.O.P. not to list one's employer when registering and not to have breakfast with fellow conspirators in the dining room. The G.E. men observed two additional precautions: never to be the ones who kept the records and never to tell G.E.'s lawyers anything.

As the years went by, similar cartels involved nearly every division of General Electric. During periods of falling orders in the mid-fifties, the pressure to keep sales volume high was so great that all the companies began offering cutthroat discounts, underselling their own price-fixing agreements. New cartels were established on the ashes of their burned-out predecessors. When the seven leading switchgear manufacturers conceived a new cartel in the late fifties, they devised a much more sophisticated arrangement that came to be known as the "phases of the moon" formula. But when federal prosecutors began to subpoena corporate records, they were baffled. They even hired cryptographers in hopes of discerning a pattern in company bids. They, too, were stumped. Finally, a sales manager for one of the medium-size companies turned over his private records at meetings held among the cartel executives. At first the prosecutors remained perplexed. All they had were a half dozen columns of numbers on plain sheets of paper. Then the sales manager explained: One column listed the seven companies by code numbers, each of which "phased" into top position every two weeks. The second column showed how much each company was to adjust its bid from the formal "book price." Thus, every company would enter a different bid but still allow the priority company to offer the lowest one and get the business. As *Fortune* reported, "if it were No. 1's [G.E.'s] turn to be low bidder at a certain number of dollars off book, then all Westinghouse (No. 2), or Allis-Chalmers (No. 3), had to do was look for their code number in the second group of columns to find how many dollars they were to bid *above* No. 1. These bids would then be fuzzed up by having a little added to them or taken away by companies 2, 3, etc."

When the trials ended in 1961, seven industry executives were sentenced to short terms in a federal prison. Fines against individuals and corporations came to just under $2 million. Several careers were destroyed. But as *Fortune* discovered while interviewing most of the principals, the pervasive attitude was that such conspiracies were simply "a way of life" in the upper reaches of American business. Said an executive: "One thing I've learned out of all this is to talk to only one other person, not to go to meetings where there are lots of other people."

Discretion, indeed, may have been the principal lesson of the electrical price-fixing scandal. For over the next fifteen years corporate executives graduated to far more sophisticated forms of chicanery, utilizing multinational currency speculation, computerized fund transfers, and elaborate offshore banking arrangements to avoid paying taxes. Notorious con men like Texan Billy Sol Estes—who soaked investors of $20 million by selling shares in empty fertilizer tanks—captured headlines in the sixties. Riding the boom years of the late sixties, when prices were artificially fueled by government war spending, blue-sky financial wizards put together fantastic mutual funds, land companies and octopuslike conglomerates only to have them collapse as soon as the economy took a downward pitch in the early seventies.

One of the biggest conglomerates was the glamour queen of Wall Street, Equity Funding, Inc. Between 1964 and 1972 Equity Funding gathered together dozens of apparently promising companies—savings and loan associations, insurance trusts, oil, gas and land development ventures. The bright boys who ran the show dazzled investors with the outfit's obvious success. The evidence was its unparalleled growth. Annual reports told of $20 million in bonds invested with a midwestern bank and other millions loaned to mutual funds. What the reports did not disclose were the fabricated figures they had been using since 1964.

When the whole house collapsed in 1972–73, the real reports showed that Equity Funding owned no bonds, had made no loans to mutual funds, and operated insurance companies in which 60 percent of the policies were phony. [5]

These were the high-class flimflam men, the sort of quick-cash operators who always appear when times are good and money plentiful. The granddaddy of them all was Robert Vesco, who with help from underworld friends fleeced Investors Overseas Services of some $200 million. But con men and boomer boys can be easily explained and easily dismissed as exceptional rogues in the army of honest men. W. Michael Blumenthal, the former president of Bendix Corporation, said as much before he was named secretary of the treasury. Responding to the considerable publicity surrounding corporate political bribery abroad, he claimed that "if the misbehavior of a large corporation makes news, that is because the majority of large corporations do not misbehave."

Several surveys of corporate behavior in the 1970s suggest that the reverse is true. One, undertaken by Ralph Nader's Congress Watch, tabulated cases of corporate illegality committed.by firms represented on the elite Business Roundtable. Of the 157 Roundtable corporations, 58 percent admitted making illegal or improper payments or had been sued by the federal government for consumer and antitrust violations during the five years between January 1, 1973 and January 1, 1978. During the same period, 400 corporations—including over a third of *Fortune*'s 500 industrial leaders—admitted making illegal or improper payoffs totaling more than $750 million. In a 1976 report, the U.S. Securities and Exchange Commission said flatly that it was "unable to conclude that instances of illegal payments are either isolated or aberrations limited to a few unscrupulous individuals."[6]

These criminal conspiracies cut across all varieties of big corporations, from American Home Products Corporation, which spent $6.4 million in overseas political payments, to Trans World Airlines, which engaged in rate fixing and illegal fare cutting, to United States Steel, which was cited for consumer safety violations and deceptive advertising. Roundtable companies were involved most often in three large categories of illegal behavior. Twenty-two corporations (14 percent of the represented firms) were cited for consumer safety hazards or deceptive advertising. Thirty-nine (24.2 percent) faced Justice Department suits and indictments for price fixing and other antitrust violations. Sixty-one (38.8 percent) made illegal or improper political payments (see table).

Table of Top U.S. Corporations' Illegal or Improper Payments, Foreign or Domestic*

Company	*Date*	*Amount*	*Nature of payments*
Alcoa	1972–74	$400,000	foreign, from secret fund
American Home Products	1971–75	$6,462,000	foreign political contributions
Boeing Co.	1970–75	$70,000,000	foreign commissions
Carrier Corp.	1972–75	$2,614,000	foreign commissions
Chrysler	1971–76	$2,438,000	secret funds abroad
Cities Service Corp.	1971–75	$1,049,400	foreign
Dresser Industries	1971–75	$24,000	to foreign officials
Exxon	1963–75	$56,771,000	foreign political contributions
FMC	1973–75	$200,000	foreign, to secure sales
Ford Motor Co.	1973–74	$60,000	to foreign political parties
General Tire & Rubber	1950s–75	$1,349,000	foreign and domestic political payments
B.F. Goodrich Co.	1971–75	$124,000	foreign commissions
Goodyear Tire & Rubber	1970–75	$846,000	to foreign officials
Gulf Oil Corp.	1960–73	$6,900,000	foreign political contributions

*Source: Congress Watch, Feb. 4, 1979, based on: *Report of the Securities and Exchange Commission to the U.S. Senate Committee on Banking, Housing and Urban Affairs,* May 1976; *Corruption in Business* (New York: Facts on File, 1977); *The Invisible Hand: Questionable Corporate Payments Overseas* (New York: Council on Economic Priorities, 1976); Forms filed with SEC on date indicated.

Company	*Date*	*Amount*	*Nature of payments*
Ingersoll-Rand Co.	1971–75	$797,000	acknowledged but not described
Koppers Co.	1971–75	$1,500,000	foreign
Kraftco Corp.	1969–75	$699,500	foreign
	1972–76	$550	domestic campaign contributions
3M Co.	1963–72	$545,799	secret fund for domestic political campaign contributions
	1975	$52,000	foreign
Reynolds Metal Co.	since 1970	N.A.	undisclosed amounts to foreign political parties
R.J. Reynolds Inc.	1968–73	$190,000	to presidential and congressional candidates disguised by diverting royalties
	since 1968	$5,500,000	to foreign officials and governments, disguised on books as commissions
	1971–75	$19,000,000	foreign rebates to shippers by Sea-Land, a subsidiary
Rockwell Int'l Corp.	1971–75	$676,300	foreign, to secure sales
Standard Oil Co. of Ind.	1970–75	$1,359,400	foreign
Tenneco, Inc.	N.A.	$865,480	foreign
AMAX, Inc.	1972–76	$64,877	foreign
Armco Steel Corp.	1971–75	$18,060,000	foreign
Atlantic Ritchfield Co.	1969–76	$262,000	foreign
Boise Cascade Corp.	1971–76	$340,100	foreign
Champion International	1971–75	$537,000	foreign

Company	*Date*	*Amount*	*Nature of payments*
Clark Equipment Co.	1971–76	$95,000	foreign
Coca-Cola	N.A.	$300,000	foreign
Dart Industries, Inc.	1971–76	$126,000	foreign
Dow Chemical Co.	N.A.	$2,500	foreign
Firestone Tire & Rubber	1970–76	$97,000	foreign
GAF Industries	N.A.	N.A.	
General Electric Co.	1972–75	$550,000	foreign
General Foods, Inc.	1971–76	$162,751	foreign
H.J. Heinz Co.	1971–76	N.A.	foreign
Hercules, Inc.	1971–75	$597,000	foreign
Marcor, Inc. (Mobil)	1971–76	$635,517	foreign
Mobil Oil Co.	1970–73	$2,000,000	foreign contributions to Italian political parties
Monsanto Co.	1971–76	$533,300	foreign
J.C. Penney	1971–75	$373,000	foreign
Ralston Purina Co.	1970–76	$154,000	foreign
Scott Paper Co.	1971–76	$229,000	foreign
Shell Oil Co.	1969–73	$6,600,000	to Italian political parties
Stauffer Chemical Co.	1975–76	$7,500	foreign
Weyerhaeuser Co.	1971–76	$1,180,000	foreign
White Motor Co.	1971–76	$1,016,000	foreign
Xerox Corporation	1971–75	$100,000	foreign
United Aircraft Corp.	1973–75	$2,040,000	sales fees to foreign government employees or officials
Westinghouse Electric	N.A.	$223,000	foreign

Company	*Date*	*Amount*	*Nature of payments*
Greyhound	1973–76	$155,000	foreign, to secure sales
Eaton	1972–77	$117,000	foreign
Deere	1971–76	$28,850	foreign
Burlington Industries	1971–76	$300,000	foreign
Norton	1972–76	$300,000	foreign
Libbey Owens	1973–76	$226,000	foreign, to secure sales
International Harvester	1972–75	$273,500	improper political contributions
Kaiser Industries	1975	$85,440	foreign
PPG	1972–75	$115,000	foreign facilitating payments to officials and agents
Olin	1971–76	$31,000	secret slush funds and payments to foreign officials

Plainly, the most significant drift in corporate crime has been to political bribery. A closer look at the Nader survey shows that of the ninety-one corporations involved in some illegal maneuver during the 1973–78 period, sixty-one, or 67 percent, acknowledged making political payoffs. In the pecking order of big-time crime, bribery is king.[7]

Two of the most infamous bribery scandals of the seventies revolved around elaborate payment schemes by Lockheed Aircraft and Gulf Oil. Between 1970 and 1975 Lockheed paid $38 million in foreign bribes, most of them designed to win overseas contracts after the collapse of domestic U.S. aircraft sales in the late sixties. Some $12.6 million had been paid to Japanese government officials to win favor for the troubled corporation, and Japanese premier Kakuel Tanaka was charged with personally accepting $1.6 million. The $12.5 million in payoffs made by Gulf Oil—one of the world's seven leading oil giants, founded by

Andrew Mellon—provided a still more revealing glimpse into the seamy side of multinational finance.[8]

Gulf's system of "Black Funds," "Gray Funds," and special Bahamian bank accounts may not have paid out as much money as other corporate bribers, but its intricacy and sophistication made it a model of how political slush funds operate around the globe without regard for local or national laws. As the corporation's own court-ordered confession puts it, the setup operated by Gulf executives was "shot through with illegality." Gulf's off-the-books political funds were discovered by the special Watergate prosecutors in 1973 as they were probing a string of illegal corporate contributions to Richard Nixon's 1972 presidential campaign fund. Gulf had given $100,000 to the Nixon campaign. By then the corporation had operated its political funds successfully for fourteen years. Money had been fed to politicians wherever Gulf had the slightest financial interest. A thousand dollars was sent to Kentucky to buy tickets for a banquet in honor of Governor Louis B. Nunn. Some $35,000 had been spent on the heated campaign for the Allegheny county commissioner, where Gulf's Pittsburgh headquarters are located. The vice-president of a Gulf subsidiary delivered envelopes stuffed with cash to Senator Howard Baker and to Congressmen Hale Boggs, Melvin Price, Joe L. Evins, Craig Hosmer, and Chet Holifield. Millions more were paid to public officials in South Korea and Italy. A general in Bolivia was given his own helicopter. And a bureaucrat in the Turkish government was paid a meager $1,000 to persuade the Turkish Petroleum Authority to release certain impounded Gulf funds.[9]

Small or large, almost all the payments came from a series of accounts held in the Bank of Nova Scotia in Nassau. The management of the political funds, and the choice to locate them offshore in the Bahamas, was undertaken at the direct, personal behest of one of Gulf's most dynamic and aggressive executives, W. K. Whiteford, who until 1965 was chief executive officer and chairman of the board. Whiteford was a tough, crusty boss, the same sort of imaginative arm-twister as the top men at General Electric who demanded both unwavering loyalty and unmatched productivity. He was a man who wanted results by any means necessary.

In 1959 Whiteford had been troubled. Domestic appetite for oil was insatiable, but long-range supplies of crude oil were not inexhaustible. And the State Department seemed unwilling to support Gulf in the kind of expansion program necessary to develop supplies of crude. That was why, according to one of Whiteford's most trusted subordinates, he "decided to create a fund out of which political contributions or payments could be made, presumably to help Gulf maintain a political atmosphere conducive to its foreign expansion plans." Whiteford ordered that an old and largely defunct Gulf subsidiary, Bahamas Exploration Company, Ltd., of Nassau, become the administrative unit for generating large bundles of cash that trusted couriers would deliver to Gulf's friends around the world.

By early January 1960 agreements among the Bank of Nova Scotia, the Bahamian Controller of Exchange, and the head of the financial office in Pittsburgh were set. On January 15, Horace R. Moorhead, the Gulf treasurer, sent signature cards to the bank in the name of Bahamas Ex. and enclosed a check for $250,000. Any officer of Bahamas Ex. was given blanket permission to withdraw up to $25,000 cash per month from the account. For the next thirteen years a tiny handful of Gulf's most powerful executives continued the system, transferring around $440,000 a year in corporate funds from Pittsburgh to Nassau. Two checks for about $200,000 each were sent twice a year, once in January or February and again in July. To square the books, the money was charged off at a predetermined rate of about $33,000 per month in deferred expenses owed by Bahamas Ex. Conveniently, Chairman Whiteford was also a director of the Bank of Nova Scotia. When one W. C. Harris was named to the largely honorary position of vice-president at the bank, Whiteford sent him a wry note of congratulations: "This is good news, especially to me, as the next time I have to make a confidential arrangement to secure political funds I can put the blame on the bank should this great institution and W.C. Harris, vice-president, fail to protect my anonymity." Eventually, Whiteford lost his anonymity, but by then he was dead. For the thirteen years during which his political fund operated, it processed approximately $9.6 million. Some $4,530,000 was carried back into the United States to swell the wallets of American politicians. Another $3 million was spent in similar schemes elsewhere.[10]

Gulf's "confession" of its own misdeeds was one of several such reports issued by multinational giants once the Justice Department and the SEC began their investigations of political slush funds. In his initial discussions about setting up the Bahamian accounts, Gulf's Whiteford told the other executives that he had talked to top management at the other oil companies and they had all set up such arrangements for political payoffs. A report from General Tire and Rubber Company acknowledged that it had spent tens of millions of dollars in questionable and "outright illegal" payments between 1964 and 1975. General Tire funneled $3.3 million through a Lichtenstein bank account to government officials and fixers in Chile and Rumania, where it did business. "At least $239,000 is known to have flowed through" a Mexican subsidiary, much of it to win governmental approval for a price increase on General tires. The company's international division kept secret accounts in Morocco, Chile, Portugal, Angola, and Spain. "From at least the 1960s until 1975, General Tire International systematically overbilled . . . foreign affiliates and other foreign companies. . . . During the fiscal years 1974 and 1975 alone, direct overbillings credited to GTI income accounts totaled more than $1 million. Rebates received from 1964 through 1975 and credited to income exceeded $4 million," the report said. A similar but smaller operation existed at Firestone Tire and Rubber. Secret slush fund accounts there amounted to slightly more than $1 million, $333,000 of which went to domestic U.S. political campaigns. [11]

Stanley Sporkin, who was appointed chief of the Enforcement Division at the Securities and Exchange Commission in the mid-1970s, won a reputation as a tough "bribe buster" for his probes into these multinational payoffs. He said that before he entered the government, businessmen continually came to his Washington law firm, pushing closer and closer toward the perimeter of the law "until they had one leg over the line between right and wrong. We'd tell a client that something was *wrong,* and then he'd ask, *'But is it legal?'"* Powerful and respected businessmen complain that it is their job to operate on the outer boundaries of the law, that indeed they are acting irresponsibly if they do not pursue every advantage available to them in earning the best return on their investors' dollars. When Congress passed the Corrupt Practices Act of 1977 forbidding foreign bribes, many argued that the government was actually subverting large corporations' abilities to do business on the world market. "Our hands are tied," an executive for an international construction firm told a journalist. "The lion's share of the construction jobs in the Persian Gulf, for instance, is now going to Korean and European companies and payoffs have to be a major factor" [12]

Political bribery is not the only kind of payoff undertaken by conglomerate businesses in recent years. Virtually every major firm in the U.S. liquor industry was discovered offering kickbacks in the mid-seventies to bars, restaurants, and distributors to win preferred treatment for their products. Joseph Schlitz, Anheuser-Busch, Miller Brewing Company, C. Schmidt and Sons and Foremost-McKesson, Inc. (a dairy-pharmaceutical combine that is also probably the largest U.S. liquor distributor), were all charged by the Bureau of Alcohol, Tobacco and Firearms (BATF) with giving illegal kickbacks to retailers. "Price rigging and payment of illegal inducements are carried on in the beer industry to such a scale that they have become a way of life," a BATF investigator said. One direct result of the kickbacks was to further consolidate control over the beer industry. "Through illegal acts," one former SEC lawyer explained, "a handful of giants has destroyed hundreds of smaller brewing companies to the detriment of the public and the business community in this country."[13]

A case that may prove to become the most outlandish bribery and price-rigging scheme of the century sprung from the aftermath of the 1973 Arab oil boycott. Though a panic swept the country over warnings of a predicted long-time oil shortage, the crisis dissipated in a matter of months as the oil industry "discovered" untold billions of barrels of new reserves in Mexico, Alaska, off the Atlantic coast and in the shale of the Rocky Mountains. So great was the actual oil supply that the industry began to complain of an oil glut by the summer of 1978. Nonetheless, in 1973 the government was besieged by the oil companies to allow prices on new domestic crude oil to rise in line with imported oil prices. The ins and outs of the pricing schemes may be extremely intricate but, as Justice Department and congressional investigators reported several years later, the company executives were not at all confused.

Concocting a vast conspiracy of kickbacks, bribes, and payoffs, dozens of companies, led by the major international firms, fraudulently arranged to certify old cheaper pre-1973 crude stocks as new more expensive oil, thereby overcharging buyers by up to six to eight dollars per barrel. Each transaction involving the relabeled oil could net companies a $1 million profit, and the higher prices were passed straight to American consumers, whose gasoline and home fuel bills promptly soared. According to a confidential congressional memorandum, Department of Energy (DOE) officials knew about the fraud and "allowed these schemes to continue and proliferate, creating a government-condoned new class of white-collar criminals—overnight 'DOE Millionaires.'" At its peak, the scheme was soaking consumers of almost $2 million a day in overcharges, amounting to almost $2 billion after four years. It was, as one DOE attorney said, "possibly the largest criminal conspiracy in U.S. history."[14]*

Bribery of foreign heads of state, oil company price gouging, and kickbacks to local beer hall operators may appear to be crimes of vastly different scope and meaning. Often, in fact, such acts may not be technically "criminal," even though they are illegal violations of federal regulations. Corporations caught making these under-the-table deals are usually sued by federal agencies in civil court and settled by offering "consent decrees" and payment of a fine. The same sort of actions undertaken by an individual, however, would be patently criminal and would usually elicit a criminal prosecution. The most obvious difference, of course, is that no individual has the power, manifested in huge legal staffs with limitless budgets, possessed by large corporations.

Equally important is that most crimes committed by corporations involve such economic technicality that their victims are unseen. A 1971 Nader task force called it the Invisible Bilk in which everyone, from monopoly orange juice processors to the auto manufacturers, was gouging consumers, a total of $48 to $60 billion a year through price fixing, low productivity, and unwillingness to pursue technological innovation. Thus the steady concentration of private business into fewer and fewer hands has had a dual effect. As it promotes political corruption abroad, it foments economic corruption at home. Or, as Judge Ganery said angrily when he sentenced the G.E. executives in 1961, their conspiracy constituted a subversive attack on "the free enterprise system" itself.[15]

Responding to Judge Ganery after the trial, one of the electrical company executives said flatly: "No one attending the price-fixing gathering was so stupid he didn't know the meetings were in violation of the law. But it is the only way a business can be run. It is free enterprise." In fact, both the judge and the executive-convict were

*A similar conspiracy flared in 1979 when, under the excuse of a cut in Iran oil exports, the public was led to believe that there was a huge oil shortage. In fact, there was such an oil glut that the U.S. was trying to dump its Alaskan yield in Japan so as to relieve pressure on over-supplied California. Nevertheless, the Carter administration talked about rationing, the big oil companies cried about "shortages," and the cost of gasoline soared again.

confused. Each cited "free enterprise" as the justification for his actions, for enforcing the law and for breaking the law. Yet the electrical industry in 1961 bore no more resemblance to the ancient, romanticized memory of competitive free enterprise than does a modern laser beam to Thomas Edison's first incandescent light bulb. And the conviction of almost four dozen electrical industry executives did nothing to curtail the control of a few huge monopolies.

The trial of G.E., Westinghouse, and the others was instead a kind of public ritual—as the Scopes trial had been a ritual—in which the heroes of old-fashioned democratic fair play were given a chance to joust with the giants of a new era. The democrats may have won convictions, but over the coming two decades the corporations would win their case as more and more independent businesses came to be consolidated into relatively few conglomerate empires. Whether or not such concentration and connivance is inimical to the laws and economic foundations of the country had become irrelevant.[16]

No less a man than Henry Ford II has averred that the modern corporation should not be concerned with the nation's laws, politics, or social traditions. "I do not agree," he said not long after the electrical scandals, "that the time has come, or is likely ever to come, when a corporation should assume social or other nonbusiness roles. I believe business corporations will continue to serve society best as individual companies vie to achieve long-range profitability consistent with the public interest." Plainly stated, law and public responsibility have nothing to do with business. It is an argument, one suspects, that might be lost on the several dozen men, women, and children who were burned alive in Ford Pintos that company executives knew in advance were defective. In itself Henry Ford II's pronouncement is little more than a genteel rendering of Cornelius Vanderbilt's remark, "Law! What do I care about law? Hain't I got the power?" However, the 1970s are not a simple replay of the Gilded Age in which businessmen, bureaucrats, congressmen, senators, and presidents sparred for the spoils of an expanding nation. The corporate domain of the 1970s is one that looks beyond nations, and thus beyond the laws of nations.[17]

The idea of sovereignty itself is likely to become an anachronism in these days when industrial and banking houses operate without respect for the laws of a single nation. Describing how the world's second largest bank, First National City of New York, used offices on three continents to speculate against the U.S. dollar, *Business Week* magazine reported that we are at the dawn of a new epoch, the era of "stateless money." For Citibank, which derives half its revenues from foreign continents, neither the laws nor the economy of the United States were as important as aggrandizing its position as an independent global institution outside the authority of nations.

To act outside the authority of government laws is to become an outlaw, no matter how respectable appearances may seem. When the power of the outlaw grows greater than the power of the state, then the very idea of law is undermined, and the commitment to the fundamental social contract is revoked. Lawlessness at the top becomes both a mirror and a model for the jungle that lies at the bottom.

Chapter 26

The Crime Regulators

On May 20, 1975, Merle Baumgart, a lobbyist for the American Bankers Association, was found dead. His body was discovered floating face down in the Potomac River a mile or so north of downtown Washington, D.C. His scalp had been ripped loose from his head, and much of his skull was crushed. His jacket was soaked with blood, and his loafers were still on his feet.

Merle Baumgart's death was ruled accidental. His car had left the George Washington Memorial Parkway on the Virginia side of the Potomac. It had apparently gone out of control and plunged into the river, police said. Yet two years later, in the summer of 1977, Baumgart's death became the focus of a major government inquiry, which would reveal how a tightly regulated American industry controlled by a single federal agency had become intimately intertwined with daily lawbreaking and underworld gangsterism. The government agency is the Interstate Commerce Commission. The business is the interstate trucking industry.[1]

The death of Baumgart, the ensuing Justice Department investigation, the personal relations among a cabal of Baumgart's high society friends, a lobbying campaign by a friend of Baumgart's on behalf of a New York Mafia boss, and the eventual assassination of an elegant Capitol Hill restaurant maître d' who was one of the last to see Baumgart alive—these are some of the elements in a shrouded tale that describes how the federal government has done more to regulate crime than to eliminate it. It is a story whose roots are sunk in the depths of the Depression, when the ICC brought all interstate trucking under its jurisdiction. And it is a story that provides the background for the near guerrilla warfare that broke out on the nation's interstate highway during the 1970s among independent truckers, Teamster drivers, and the owners of large-scale trucking fleets.

When they found Merle Baumgart's body, the national park police had no reason to suspect any of the Byzantine intrigues that would eventually unfold in the case. They knew only that he had been a moderately successful lobbyist of middle age who had earlier worked for Representative Peter Rodino, chairman of the House Judiciary Committee. Most park policemen do what their name suggests. They monitor automobile and foot traffic in the city's endless public grounds, handing out speeding tickets and watching for teenage vandals. Murder is not their métier. Except for an alert young detective on the force, Baumgart's death might have slipped quietly into oblivion. Three details, however, caught the detective's attention. Since there was no water in Baumgart's lungs, he had apparently died before he reached the river. No more than one minute could have elapsed between the time the car left the parkway and the time it hit the water. His shoes remained on his feet even though he had been thrown clear of the car. Accident victims almost always lose their shoes in violent auto crashes. Baumgart's jacket was matted with blood, an unlikely condition for someone who was almost immediately plunged into the water.

Each of these anomalies might normally have caused police to initiate a murder investigation, except that in this case there was an eyewitness, the driver of the car. A Washington sales clerk, she had accompanied Baumgart to several bars and restaurants that evening. She explained that the car had run off the road and into the river, that she had miraculously escaped unhurt, climbed the steep bank up to the parkway, flagged down a passing car, and persuaded its driver to take her several miles to a friend's home. It was not until she reached her friend's house, changed clothes, and took a cup of tea that she recovered from shock enough to remember that Baumgart had been a passenger in the car. Then she called the park police.[2]

Although Baumgart's death was ruled accidental, the perspicacious young detective decided to forward his questions to an organized-crime detective on the metropolitan police force, and from there it percolated upward to the Justice Department's own organized-crime strike force. Soon there were more strange developments in the case. According to the Washington *Star,* early on the morning of May 20, before the news had been publicly reported, another lobbyist telephoned a Washington lawyer to tell him that their friend Baumgart was dead. The lobbyist was Daryl Fleming, once a Washington representative for Kellogg and an intimate of many Democratic politicians. The lawyer was Martin R. Martino, Washington counsel for two trucking companies owned by the sons of the late Mafia boss Carlo Gambino. As soon as Martino learned of Baumgart's death, he picked up his telephone and dialed a third man, Alexei Goodarzi, the maître d' of the most elegant restaurant on Capitol Hill, the Rotunda, where Merle Baumgart was last seen alive. Addressing him on a first-name basis, Martin told Goodarzi to "hold" Baumgart's tab from the previous evening. Goodarzi apparently agreed, for the sake of discretion. Tips from Baumgart's friends also revealed a bizarre late-night episode just ten days earlier at the exact spot where his car seemed to run off the road. Baumgart had been driving alone when another car forced him to stop and two men ran toward him and began smashing the windshield with baseball bats. He escaped by jamming his car into reverse, then speeding off along the shoulder.[3]

In itself, Baumgart's death appeared to lead into a blind alley. Debt and mid-career professional problems had plagued him, but there seemed to be no obvious motive for murder. Yet the probe into his personal affairs led into the glittering demimonde of private clubs, expensive entertainment, political favors, and sexual diversions. It was the same world that had destroyed two of Washington's most powerful kingpins, Congressmen Wilbur Mills and Wayne Hayes, when they were discovered courting or supporting go-go girls and auxiliary playmates. It was also the same world of exclusive parties, chic dinners, and cash payoffs that had enabled Korean rice dealer Tongsun Park to buy the support of dozens of U.S. congressmen. Merle Baumgart, Daryl Fleming, and Martin Martino lived at the center of that social world, and their clients' money covered much of the tab for it. One young woman who worked in Congress and was part of the scene described it bluntly: "We called it going from the Hill to the valley to the swamp."[4]

Once federal investigators began to probe "the swamp," the tangled trails seemed to wander all over Capitol Hill as well as into the key government agencies of the Department of Housing and Urban Development (HUD) and the Interstate Commerce Commission. A top labor relations official at HUD was found to have held meetings with the Mafia boss Carlo Gambino. Rumors began to surface of "mob-related activity" in federally financed home building and insurance. Lobbyist Fleming, it turned out, had provided several bathroom fixtures—a sink, a toilet, and a bathtub— to Congressman Fred Rooney, free of charge. Investigators began to look at Martino's involvement with a series of prepaid health-care plans for Teamster Union members. Fleming was also named as an unindicted coconspirator in a bribery-conspiracy case involving a former aide to Congressman Daniel Flood. The former aide had personally sponsored Alexei Goodarzi when he emigrated from Iran to the United States and became maître d' at the Rotunda. It was there that Goodarzi developed special friendships with Martino, Baumgart, Fleming, and dozens of influential lobbyists and politicians. It may also have been at the Rotunda, or its parking lot, that three .32-caliber slugs were fired neatly into the back of Goodarzi's head on May 12, 1977—two years after Baumgart's death and well after the government's general investigation had begun.

On the night before his murder, two days before he planned to leave the country, Goodarzi met with an investigator for the House Ethics Committee, which was looking into Capitol Hill payoffs. Goodarzi had offered services to patrons of the Rotunda, regularly placing bets for legislators and supplying female companions for congressmen at the expense of certain lobbyists. The morning after his murder, police found about two dozen autographed pictures of congressmen and a notebook containing the private numbers of a hundred congressmen, aides, lobbyists, and women.[5]

One man who often patronized the Rotunda, who had known both Goodarzi and Baumgart and who had worked with Fleming and Martino, was Robert Oswald, a seasoned federal bureaucrat with intimate knowledge of the commercial trucking industry. Robert Oswald was then ICC secretary and its chief congressional liaison officer. Possibly the most powerful professional employee at ICC, his job included screening applications of trucking companies for new routes and corporate mergers. According to one of his colleagues, Oswald maintained an "open door" to Martino, regarded as a "friend of the staff who had free-flowing access" to Oswald's office.[6]

The more federal prosecutors learned about the relationships existing among Oswald, Martino, Fleming, and Baumgart, the more they concentrated their investigation on influence peddling within the ICC by trucking companies and alleged organized-crime racketeers. Martino had represented Oswald in a divorce proceeding, and as an independent lobbyist, Baumgart had reportedly agreed to intercede with Oswald on behalf of a New Jersey trucking firm. Fleming and Martino had also shared offices. Among other cases, investigators focused on a petition by Thomas and Joseph Gambino, sons of the Mafia boss, to merge two trucking companies into a single firm. That petition was denied in 1970. But in 1973, the Gambino brothers won approval for their petition on a three-year "probationary" status. Only about six months passed, however, before the probationary clause was removed from the Gambinos' operating certificate. No formal hearing had been held. Approval for their new authority had been granted by the administrative bureaucracy that Oswald headed. The lawyer and chief advocate for the Gambinos was Oswald's "open-door" friend Martin Martino.[7]

By mid-1978 Robert Oswald had been indicted for bribery. "One of the suspicions," a prosecution source told one newspaper reporter, "is that influence was brought to bear within the commission" through current ICC officials. Investigators believed that a variety of deals had taken place including one where ICC officials had enabled a gangster-owned New York trucking company to merge with a second company which already had ICC authorization to ship between the Northeast and the Gulf Coast. Thus the result was that the first company acquired an extremely profitable long-haul shipping route which had previously been denied it on direct application.[8]

Specifically Oswald was charged with accepting $2,000 from a man named Tony Grande, who was an associate of Thomas Gambino's, owner of Consolidated Carrier Corporation, and another $2,000 from Edward Lubrano, an associate of Grande's. Other counts included accepting free junkets, helping Gambino's attorney, Martin Martino, prepare a brief that was to be submitted to the ICC, and attempting to obstruct the subsequent Justice Department investigation of the case.

Most of the evidence against Oswald came from Lubrano and Oswald's old friend, lobbyist Daryl Fleming. Both swore that Oswald had been paid $4,000 for his cooperation in getting the Gambino's ICC certificate approved. Fleming and Lubrano, who were granted immunity in the case, were held in protective custody and were providing the government with other information about organized-crime infiltration of congressional offices and HUD. Lubrano had been previously convicted of labor extortion, conspiracy to commit murder, and possession of a gun silencer. Oswald, in the words of the prosecutor, had been nothing less than a "private lobbyist" for the Gambino company.[9]

In a dramatic courtroom session, Oswald repeatedly denied the accusations. He did admit having dined with Gambino twice and having had a role in the ICC's decision. The twist in the case came when New York congressman John Murphy testified that he was the person who had introduced Oswald to Gambino. Murphy said he and Gambino had been friends since the two were in school together, and that because of that friendship he had made the introduction to help Gambino win ICC approval for his company's request. Oswald swore that he had only followed Murphy's request "to keep on top of the case." Despite the testimony of the government's two witnesses, Oswald was acquitted.[10]

The alleged bribery of Robert Oswald, which formed the core of the case against the company and ICC officials, was a classic example of the corrupt milieu that often ensnares Washington regulatory agencies. Because this particular case involved a senior bureaucrat, a flashy lawyer with alleged ties to organized-crime figures, and the probable murder of a prominent lobbyist, it attracted the sustained interest of the Washington press. Yet while news stories focused on the probe into organized crime's influence on Capitol Hill, little attention went to the background of how the ICC had structured corruption into the trucking industry. The presence of the Gambino family may have brought spice to the porridge, but such high-rolling pressure for large companies to obtain scarce shipping licenses was hardly unusual. Nor was it unusual to find those same companies using all their muscle to squeeze the small independent operators completely out of business. In fact, it is because of the ICC that trucking has become one of the most thoroughly rigged industries in America.

The problem began in 1935 when the major trucking companies and the Teamsters Union jointly pressed the federal government to regulate their industry in the same way that the railroads were regulated. Until then there was no restriction on the tariffs and rates that trucking companies could charge their freight customers. Trucking was one of the most competitive and decentralized businesses in the nation. It was so competitive that the owners were eager for the government to stabilize prices so that small independent haulers could not offer cut-rate tariffs. Regulation would also establish minimum wages for the drivers. When the ICC took over, it began issuing certificates to so-called common carrier companies to haul commodities over certain routes between specific cities. There was no charge for the certificates. Within a few years, authorized, certified trucking companies had criss-crossed the country providing regulated freight service. Soon there were no more certificates to be issued because all the routes had been taken. Technically the ICC continued to issue new certificates but the great majority of them were modifications to already existing routes conforming to the construction of new highways and shifting population pockets.[11]

Not so surprisingly, the price of entering the trucking business went up. Since the ICC would not issue a new certificate for a route already covered by another "certificated" company, the newcomer was forced to buy rights from a company that already had one—if, of course, the old company wanted to sell. Once again competition entered the trucking industry, but this time it was a competition not for the customers but for the right to have customers. By the mid-1960s prices for hauling certificates were skyrocketing. The American Trucking Associations estimated that between 1962 and 1972 certificates quadrupled in value. When one large company went bankrupt in 1975, it was able to sell its rights for $20 million, even though the rights had originally been granted free.

An internal ICC study showed that during the four years between 1973 and 1977 trucking companies spent over $80 million for federal certificates. The certificates themselves—not including real estate, trucks, or mechanical equipment—became major investments. For several years the ICC failed to release an internal study documenting the enormous profits that companies made buying and selling certificates. Clinton Trucking Company, for example, bought an ICC certificate for $29,376 in 1969. Suffering financial troubles, Clinton sold the certificates one year later for $151,627—a profit of 416 percent. In another case, when Georgia Highway Express decided it wanted to enter the Cincinnati market, it struck a deal with Ohio-

Kentucky Express, Inc., which had rights to deliver most commodities in the greater Cincinnati area. Georgia paid Kentucky-Ohio $15,000 for its local rights, which the seller had purchased only a year earlier for $3,000.[12]

Traffic in trucking certificates is thoroughly legal. As far as the ICC is concerned, the money spent to get into business is a private matter and not subject to regulation. The consequences of the agency's position, however, are often extremely expensive, highly illegal, and dangerous. Ostensibly the ICC decided to regulate trucking in order to guarantee the public a cheap reliable freight service. The traffic in certificates alone has increased the costs of regulated trucking. It has reduced the number of companies in the industry—from about 200,000 in the mid-thirties to slightly over 16,000 in the mid-seventies. It also costs more for regulated companies to ship their goods than it does for the nonregulated or exempt carriers, which are usually permitted to carry only agricultural produce. One economist found that costs for regulated general freight carriers were more than twice those of exempt carriers. Such dismal financial details provide the basic reason why violence is always simmering just beneath the surface of the trucking industry—all the way from shoot-outs on the highway to murders in the capital.[13]

Take for example, the case of Dayton Air Freight, a small trucking company in southern Ohio. Sometime before dawn on September 5, 1978, someone slipped into the yard, placed several bombs in key locations, and within a few minutes the office, the garage, and a huge truck had been destroyed. The company's owners had no known enemies or hostile competitors. Their mistake had been made a few weeks earlier when they chose to go before a Senate committee in Washington to testify in favor of deregulating the trucking industry.[14] Deregulation of the trucking industry would accomplish two things. It would collapse profiteering in the trucking-certificate traffic, leaving the major companies with hundreds of millions of dollars in worthless investments. One company alone, for example, Transcom Lines, valued its thirty-one ICC certificates in 1977 at $12.5 million. Investments of that size are worth fighting for. But removing ICC restrictions would have a second and even more devastating effect. It would throw the door wide open for hundreds, perhaps thousands, of independent owner-operators, the so-called cowboys of the highways. They are the tough ones, the wild, colorful, restless independents who have inspired country singers, B-grade movies and the citizens band radio craze. They are the truckers who carry high-velocity rifles behind their seats, who wake up in the morning to find their rigs firebombed, and who regard the ICC as their principal enemy.[15]

If the independent truckers have a wide and sympathetic following in America, it may indeed be because of the enemies they have chosen. First is the government, second is the national trucking cartel represented by the American Trucking Associations, and third is the Teamsters Union. Anybody who can withstand the firepower of those three has to be tough. Mike Parkhurst, the president of the Independent Truckers Association, has been one of the toughest. He once described the independent trucker as nothing more than a modern sharecropper, a few steps removed from the cotton pickers of plantation days. It was an apt characterization. The reason stems from the fact that the ICC bars independents from hauling anything except raw or frozen produce.

"Let's say you go down to get some potatoes," Parkhurst explained to a magazine interviewer. "You start hauling them in April, when they start coming out of Florida, to Boise, Idaho. Now you're twenty-two hundred miles away from home. What do you get in Boise, Idaho? There aren't many things you can legally haul out of Boise, Idaho, and if you can't find a load of something like apples or potatoes, you can go. . . . There might be an air-conditioning manufacturer in Boise who had a load of air conditioners going back to Florida. You can't haul them. Even though they want you to, even though they say, 'Harry, we want you to put these on your truck.' If they put those air conditioners on your truck and you agree to haul them for a thousand dollars, you're breaking the law. You have to lease your truck to a company that's not in the business of hauling anything. They just own the license. They'll say, 'We'll let you haul the air conditioners, but you have to give us thirty percent for the privilege of hauling them.'"[16]

To avoid the financial uncertainties of hauling produce, many independents accept that cut and contract directly to the giants. "You know Mayflower, North American, all those big companies? Those tractors are owned by the guys who are driving them. Because they have to lease their tractors back to the companies and the companies in turn take thirty to fifty percent off the top." Besides paying the sharecropper's cut for leasing rights, the small independent truckers have been faced with blatant harassment from the ICC itself. A congressional investigating committee headed by Representative John Moss reported in 1976 that the ICC consistently discriminated against "small carriers, and against those carriers who keep good records." The ICC conducted its harassment through its compliance program, whose officers are stationed randomly along interstate highways. Their job is to check the contents of each load and the accuracy of shipping reports. Field inspectors file reports of violations with the ICC that can either exact civil fines from the trucker or press a criminal prosecution against him.[17]

To determine how the ICC regulations were being enforced, the Moss committee examined how the violations were handled—which ones were dropped, which drew civil fines, and which were prosecuted in the criminal courts. After months of plowing through internal ICC files and violations dockets, the Moss committee unearthed an extraordinary report that had been collecting cobwebs since 1972. That report corroborated the complaints from hundreds of independent truckers that the government was out to get the little guys while it let the big operators off easy. In 94 percent of the cases examined, if the violator had gross annual revenues *exceeding* $250,000, the prosecution was dropped. But for violators whose revenues were *under* $250,000, cases were dropped only 4 percent of the time. Even worse, three-quarters of all the violators were in the higher revenue category. Another report by the Government Accounting Office reached the same conclusion. The ICC's practices, it said, "resulted in all motor carrier violators being treated alike—which tended to favor the more serious violator. . . . In one extreme situation two motor carriers were each fined $1,500, although field agents had discovered 17 violations by one and 2,000 violations by the other."[18]

The statistical evidence that the Moss committee cited was compiled in the early seventies. As the decade ground on, the ICC's hostility to small operators only intensified. As late as 1977, a year after Moss released his findings, the ICC's new enforcement director announced publicly and vehemently that he intended to wage war on produce haulers who contracted with agricultural co-ops. "In the last seven years there have been 83 ICC actions against co-ops, but I promise you that in the next 18 months we will initiate hundreds of actions. . . . It will be hard for them to open up after we successfully prosecute them because it is difficult to run a company from jail."[19]

Agricultural cooperatives are the bridge to survival for thousands of independent truckers. Drivers can contract with them directly and guarantee themselves several months of steady work. Since they are exempt from ICC certificate regulations, they provide scarce shelter for the independent. Under that exemption, co-op drivers are also permitted to transport a limited amount of regulated nonagricultural freight as backhaul. The limit is 15 percent of their annual tonnage. Thus co-ops give the drivers a break on the expensive dead-head trip back home.

The ICC's attack on co-op drivers was not totally capricious. The miniboom in the numbers of independent truckers during the 1960s brought about the establishment of scores of "co-ops" that were little more than protective shells for the drivers. The ICC's stated aim was to weed out the "sham" co-ops from those really run by farmers. There lay the rub. The only get-tough policy it had announced in decades was directed at the weakest and most fragile sector of the entire trucking industry. Suddenly it had discovered that America's highways were being taken over by thousands of criminals, malefactors of a sinister nationwide combine—the cauliflower and diesel underworld. The victims in this newfound combine were everywhere. But they were not the usual victims of crime in America. The victims were not the farmers whose "exempt" status guaranteed them trump bargaining power with the truckers. Nor were consumers the victims, since the exempted haulers provide the cheapest freight rates in the country. The real "victims" that the ICC would protect with its law-and-order campaign were the old-time enemies of the independent owner-operators, the national trucking corporations and their bedmates, the Teamsters Union.[20]

Just as the ICC has overwhelmingly directed its criminal and civil sanctions against small-scale violators—while almost always dropping its prosecutions against the major national operators—so its selective attack on the co-ops reveals how criminal law becomes the tool of special interests. As one driver argued in 1977 after he was charged with a violation of ICC rules, the government has embarked on "a deliberate and intentional policy to annihilate agricultural cooperatives by felony prosecutions." The government's allegiance is all the more obvious given its failure to use the criminal laws against the more blatant and notorious offenses of the trucking industry: pension violations by the Teamsters Union, continuous concentration of the industry into what is regularly described as a corporate cartel of a few companies, constant overloading of trucks, which has made automobile driving on many midwestern freeways deadly dangerous, and of course the lack of any comparable campaign against the large operators which the ICC's own records show to be the most frequent violators of its shipping rules.[21]

That is the context in which such flamboyant trials as the bribery prosecution of Robert Oswald must be taken. It is easy for the American press to seek out allegedly iniquitous characters who have sold out the public trust. And it is a hallowed tradition for editors and reporters to salivate and clamor for reform if those nefarious characters spring from an underworld of foreign names and sinister organizations. Robert Oswald admitted that he had twice eaten lunch with Thomas Gambino and that he had taken a special interest in the Gambinos' petitions with the ICC. Other actions that Oswald took seemed to suggest questionable judgment. But once the jury had heard all the evidence, it decided that it did not believe the government's witnesses, that Oswald had done only what his superiors at the ICC had expected of him, that he had simply responded to the needs of a large American trucking company whose involvement with the underworld was unknown. As he told the court, all he had done was to follow a congressman's request to help the company "get a fair shake."[22]

It is the kind of fair shake reserved for companies like that of the Gambino brothers—large outfits with direct access to congressmen, lobbyists and federal bureaucrats. Meanwhile it is for the small-time operator, the independent entrepreneur who starts out with all the rules written against him, that the criminal courts are reserved.

Chapter 27

Organized but also Institutionalized

Throughout the 1960s there was a particularly worrisome story passed along among the top echelon of the U.S. Department of Justice. It involved the attorney general's office and the "mob"—the rackets, the syndicate, the underworld. Every two or three years the story would slip into Washington's exclusive gossip circles. It concerned the year 1962 when Robert F. Kennedy was making his tough-guy reputation by authorizing wiretaps on leading gangsters all over America. He and a tiny coterie of trusted associates then had their eyes on a man who had frequently been described as Washington's absentee "godfather," one Charlie ("The Blade") Tourine, a New York–based impressario of narcotics, pornography, numbers betting, and back-room gambling. After months of surveillance, they decided they had Tourine cold and could raid one of his operations within three days. Final plans were set in action in New York and Washington. Then at the last moment a set of wiretaps run on Tourine by the New York district attorney's office revealed that Kennedy's men had been "made," their cover blown. The

New Yorkers called Washington to say that Tourine had just been tipped off by phone about his impending bust.

Downcast, the men at the Justice Department thanked the New York D.A. and began anew, this time restricting access to the plans for Tourine's bust to only top officials. Two weeks passed. The new raid was set for a Saturday. On Thursday the New York D.A. called again. Once more their tap on Tourine's Manhattan apartment revealed he had been tipped off. "What's going on here anyhow?" one assistant attorney general demanded. "Nobody but the top brass knew about it this time." Officially, Kennedy's assistants said the leaks had to have happened in a field office of the Justice Department. But their real concern was that the underworld of organized crime had a spy or spies in the highest reaches of the attorney general's office.

Paranoia—perhaps justified—over the underworld's ubiquitous power has been one of the pervasive undertones to political life in the United States since the end of World War II. Comfortable in the belief that Hoover's FBI had eradicated the old depression-era racketeers, postwar Americans were awakened in the early fifties to confront two sinister forces said to be undermining the foundation of the nation. One, a foreign enemy with domestic footsoldiers, was the Communist monolith. In the Hiss and Remington perjury, the Rosenberg spy, and the Communist Ten Smith Act trials, as well as during Senator Joseph McCarthy's witchhunt hearings into Communist penetration of movies, labor unions, and government, the full force of the law was applied to rout it out. The other sinister threat, made famous by the hearings of Senator Estes Kefauver, was the fantastically successful penetration by a new generation of gangsters into almost every facet of the U.S. economy. The hearings brought notoriety to those new "syndicates," and in a few cities ordinary people with Italian names were subjected to McCarthylike persecutions. But not until the 1960s, during the three years Robert Kennedy was attorney general, would the federal government prosecute the racketeers with the same fervor it had used on political "subversives." The reason, simply stated, is that after the war, syndicate crime found a vital and highly valued place for itself in the structure of American society.

Senator Kefauver's committee issued a long report which has been the starting place for investigations into organized crime every since. The report asserted flatly: "There is a nationwide crime syndicate known as the Mafia. . . . Its leaders are usually found in control of the most lucrative rackets in their cities. There are indications of a centralized direction and control of these rackets." The existence or nonexistence of the Mafia is itself an issue which has brought good friends to fisticuffs. Until Robert F. Kennedy became attorney general, J. Edgar Hoover denied there was any such thing. Then, as Kennedy's crusade gained notoriety, Hoover revealed the existence of something called La Cosa Nostra, also a nationwide Italian crime syndicate that found its roots in the heyday of the Prohibition gangsters.[1]

Mafia is a term that is inherently confusing. Historically it refers to secret societies of bandits in Sicily during the eighteenth and nineteenth centuries. It became a fashionable term among police and crime writers after the New Orleans lynchings in the 1890s and off and on during Prohibition. Student activists in the 1960s who were from Italian families even spoke occasionally of relatives who were in the Mafia or of the power wielded by the Mafia in their parents' neighborhoods. The size, geographical extent, and structure of the Mafia, however, always seemed to be elusive in any of the characterizations.

By concentrating on the Italian character of the syndicates, the Kefauver investigators and Hoover managed to ignore the man who was probably the most important financial genius the underworld has ever known—Meyer Lansky. They also left no place for James Hoffa, the Teamster boss whose life became a metaphor for labor racketeering. Moreover, most of the accounts provided in public hearings relied on unnamed, confidential sources whose reliability could never be checked. Those who did testify publicly were usually low-level hoodlums who worked in a single syndicate, usually in a single city, and who were almost never privy to the decision-making councils of "the bosses." The most famous of these was Joseph Valachi, who worked in the Vito Genovese crime family which was originally organized by Lucky Luciano. Valachi's testimony before Senator Joseph McClellan's Permanent Subcommittee on Investigations provided the basic outline of the underworld's development since the twenties.[2]

But it was Valachi, a very young man in 1931, who gave out the grossly erroneous account of the so-called Castellammare Wars following the assassination of Salvatore Maranzano. Based on Valachi's recollections, serious journalists and sociologists described these "wars" as a nationwide "mass extermination" orchestrated by Luciano in which forty mobsters allegedly died. When historian Humbert Nelli investigated the list of supposed murders by combing the newspapers of twelve large cities for the three months following Maranzano's murder, he found not mass murder but at most one killing (in Denver) that might have been related to the demise of the old "Boss of Bosses." Valachi's version of gangster history after World War II was less shrouded in myth and mystery but it is a speculative account at best, a story of a progressively monolithic conspiracy, drawn from fragmentary flecks of information.[3]

There have been about a dozen "histories" of organized crime in America written since the end of World War II. They range from Kennedy's *The Enemy Within* to *The Valachi Papers* (written with Peter Maas) to the probing journalism of Hank Messick that explores the power of the Jewish-dominated "Cleveland syndicate" uniting Meyer Lansky and the Las Vegas casino owners with the executive officers of the International Brotherhood of Teamsters. Gangsters are not noted for opening their books to investigative reporters, so most writers on organized crime have had to depend upon raw police files. There is, therefore, a shadowy quality to all the accounts, not unlike Plato's allegory of the cave, in which we can only surmise what the actors are doing because we are only permitted to face the wall watching the movement of their shadows. Are the two figures whose shadows briefly merge merely passing one another from an oblique angle, or have they met to discuss an agreement? As bosses rise and fall before each other's knives and bullets, as family organizations prosper and wither in their struggle for new territories, as unions and insurance funds and gambling combines and hotel chains conspire and collapse, there remain always the questions of who is in control, for how long, and why American society has been uniquely supportive of such large-scale racketeering.[4]

The characters, organizations, "wars," and "families" of these syndicates have been described at length in the crime histories. Briefly there are two traditions out of which the modern syndicates have grown. One is the Jewish gangsters, who trace their roots to Rothstein, Lepke, Gurrah, and an old Cleveland bootleg ring called the Mayfield Road Gang where Moe Dalitz rose to power. The Jewish mobsters diversified quickly into labor racketeering and invested their money in gambling resorts, legal and illegal. The Italian gangsters, also rooted in bootlegging, remained much more closely tied to their own neighborhoods, to the industries where their people could get jobs (trucking and dock work) and to the corrupt political machines of old northern cities. While they too developed financial sophistication after the late thirties, they followed in much the same path as the Irish before them: they used their control of vice—back-room gambling, prostitution, pornography, narcotics—and the payoffs that went with it to lay the foundation for control of city political machines. Frank Costello's position in the 1940s as the *eminence gris* behind a resurrected Tammany Hall in New York is the clearest example.[5]

Before he was convicted of taking payoffs from the Dutch Schultz mob, New York's old Tammany boss Jimmy Hines had admitted that the hall couldn't stay in business without the boys from the syndicate. La Guardia's cleanup campaigns, combined with the loss of federal patronage under President Franklin D. Roosevelt, left the city's old political system in a shambles. It was not until the war years, when little attention was given to domestic, urban politics that Tammany began to rebuild itself, and it did so under the direction of Frank Costello. By then the Irish no longer ran the city, and they had long since lost control over the vice dens. Costello, who had succeeded John Torrio as the master businessman of the vice rackets, thus was able to name almost all the Tammany district leaders. A seasoned *New York Times* political reporter who later worked for Mayor Robert Wagner said that "Costello gunmen actually policed the meetings, and cooperative, or else frightened, captains elected Costello's henchmen as district leaders."[6]

Costello's apartment on Central Park West became a gathering place for the most prominent judges and Democratic politicians in the city, including Bill O'Dwyer, who was elected mayor in 1945. On the one hand he sponsored charity benefits and was appointed vice-chairman of the Salvation Army's annual fund-raising drive. On the other hand, he was thoroughly acknowledged as the senior statesman of the underworld, where payoffs to the police were so well organized that a top Brooklyn bookie began his scale at $2 for beat cops running up to $6,500 a month for the chief inspector's office. The Costello regime operated with such confidence in the late forties that according to writer Nick Pileggi, "gamblers were making book from the tableside phones at Champ Segal's midtown restaurant, across from Lindy's, and detectives, in $200 suits, wolfed down free steaks and acted as bodyguards and messengers." In 1949 the Manhattan borough president admitted freely that "If Frank Costello wanted me, he would send for me." A year later, as he faced the accusations of Senator Kefauver's committee in Washington, Costello himself stomped out of the hearing room drawing a contempt citation rather than endure what he considered insults to his reputation. Before he left, however, he was asked about his relations with New York City political leaders. "I know them, know them well, and maybe they got a little confidence in me," he answered with pride.[7]

The pride Costello took in bringing Italians into the top ranks of New York's political leadership was short-lived. By the end of the Kefauver hearings, he was driven back to the shadowy world of the rackets, the status and respectability he had so craved snatched away. He remained a gangland boss, a member of the twenty-four-seat "national commission" of Italian syndicate leaders which police and crime writers described as the "board of directors of the Mafia." He had accomplished in New York what Capone had achieved two decades earlier in Chicago. But his fall was more than the fall of a single gangster at the hands of a new reform movement. After Costello's political demise, Tammany really was finished. Postwar America brought the dissolution of machine politics in every important city except Chicago.

The promise of wholesome Americanism gave city life a bad name as tens of millions fled to the suburbs. Except for the black ghettos, poor and ethnic neighborhoods fell before the blade of the bulldozer. Massive superhighway systems redistributed the population and political power blocks were thrown into disarray. The real pluralism of New York, where polyglot ethnics had always bought their own representation in city hall, gave way to a system of professional "urban management" that was recasting Manhattan as a national financial center to be populated by middle-class professionals and public service workers. Frank Costello, like Brooklyner Albert Anastasia, the rival chief of Murder, Inc., was closing out a political era in America. By 1957 Anastasia would be murdered and Costello "deposed" in a power struggle that also symbolized the end of an era in syndicated crime.

The events following the old men's removal as nationally ranked Italian gangsters proceeded with Byzantine complexity. There was the famous 1957 meeting of sixty-five gangsters at Apalachin, New York, supposedly called by a member of the old national commission of the twenty-four families to close membership in the Italian crime families and to reach an agreement over national leadership. Proof that any illegal conspiracies took place there is hard to find. Law-enforcement professionals and most congressional investigators have believed that the Apalachin meeting was called to centralize control over all underworld rackets throughout the nation. Others believe the meeting was little more than a superconvention of businessmen (who happened to be criminal entrepreneurs with a great deal in common and many shared "contracts") called to discuss mutual problems brought about by the 1957 Senate hearings into labor racketeering—hearings in which Bobby Kennedy was chief counsel.[8]

About the same time Jimmy Hoffa and his allies from the Cleveland syndicate were taking control of the Teamsters Union and of its multimillion-dollar pension funds. The heirs to the Capone gang, who were both Jewish and Italian, had seized the national racing wire after Jimmy Ragen's murder in 1946, and with the help of Bugsy Siegel and the Clevelanders, they were turning Las Vegas into the most lucrative gambling spa in the world. Meyer Lansky, with the help of the Clevelanders, was doing the same thing in Havana while one Santo Trafficante, an independent racketeer in Tampa, Florida, was also working with Lansky to develop Caribbean gambling. The intricacies of the relationships, which confound the imagination, frequently led to bloody warfare between one aggrieved party or another. The details are important and readily available. What is to be emphasized here is that these competitive businessmen of the underworld saw and seized the opportunities that the postwar boom offered them. Just as Torrio and Rothstein and Capone had capitalized on the chain-store system of marketing vice in a single well-organized city, so the crime entrepreneurs of the fifties were able to spot an indispensable niche for themselves in the mass-consumption economy of postwar America.[9]

After spending two years as chief counsel for Senator John McClellan's labor rackets committee, Kennedy declared that racketeers had achieved unparalleled powers over business and political life: "In some communities in the United States local law enforcement is completely under the control of gangsters. . . . Gangsters have taken complete control of a number of industries to obtain a monopoly, often with the help of dishonest union officials." Despite the fact that such dramatic pronouncements were politically useful (Robert Kennedy was then running his brother John's presidential campaign), the statement was accurate. And it pinpointed the primary advance made by the new generation of underworld gangsters.

While they had to maintain alliances with corrupt police officials for protection, criminal entrepreneurs concentrated more and more attention on business opportunities as an end in themselves. To do that they depended increasingly on the technicians of modern business: lawyers and accountants. They were also among the first to realize that the U.S. economy was becoming less and less an industrial economy and more and more a "service" economy.

Writing in the early 1950s, sociologist Daniel Bell criticized the cop mentality of the Kefauver hearings, arguing that the old industrial racketeers were being replaced by syndicates concentrating on leisure and service industries. "*Like American capitalism itself, crime shifted its emphasis from production to consumption.* The focus of crime became the direct exploitation of the citizen as consumer, largely through gambling. And while the protection of these huge revenues was inextricably linked to politics, the relation between gambling and 'the mobs' became more complicated." Newspaper reporters still continued to cover the feuds and fights among New York's Italian crime "families" for control of territory, reinforcing old-fashioned notions of slow-witted, feudalistic Mafia hoodlums. The killing of Joey Gallo, the shooting of Joseph Columbo, the kidnapping of Joseph Bonnano, suggested that nothing much was new. And indeed the strong bonds of family tradition in Italian neighborhoods, like those in Chinese communities, show up in the organizations of criminal businessmen. But even Francis Ford Coppola's *Godfather* portrays a "mob" where blood was less important than understanding modern money management. The ability to take advantage of the changing economic conditions is most clearly demonstrated in the meteoric rise of the Teamsters.[10]

The power and the corruption of the Teamsters was made possible thanks only to the postwar upheavals in American industry. First came the decline of the railroads, which had always been the backbone of heavy industry and a major guarantor of prosperity in the nation's steel mills. Concommittantly, the federal government decided to create an entirely new interstate highways system which, when it was completed, enabled trucking companies easily to undersell their railroad competitors. No particular skill was needed to drive a truck, so labor was plentiful. Moreover, the kinds and amounts of goods being shipped throughout the country expanded phenomenally. The general trend toward corporate concentration meant that consumer items—television sets, automobiles, kitchen appliances, furniture, clothing, to name a few—increasingly would be manufactured in a few huge plants to be shipped nationwide as local and regional manufacturers went out of business. The archaic system of national rail lines could not possibly handle the increasing load and routing complexity that resulted. Entire towns had grown up in a few years where only trucks could offer service. By the mid-1950s, just a decade after the war, trucks had so dominated American transportation that the Teamsters had become the largest union in the country (1.6 million members), so large that a national strike would mean instant national paralysis. Add to that power the fact that ICC regulations had forced the industry into a national network of local cartels, and it is hard to see how anything except rigging and racketeering could have resulted.[11]

Although the most notorious connections between Teamster officials and gangsters have been the investments and loans of union pension funds in Las Vegas casinos controlled by organized crime syndicates, the most obvious merger of union and racketeering figures had been in New Jersey. Reporters who have tried to follow the labryinthine trails uniting trucking companies, Teamster local officials, and syndicate bosses have usually been stymied. Bergen County, across the Hudson River from Manhattan, is the domain of Anthony ("Tony Pro") Provenzano, one of the most powerful gangsters on the East Coast. During the mid-fifties he worked in the crime family of Eugene Genovese, who, by most accounts, was the leading Italian racketeer in the country after 1957. By the early sixties Provenzano was described by federal investigators as a "captain" in the Genovese family. He was also one of Teamster president Jimmy Hoffa's closest East Coast allies. Earlier in his career Hoffa had certified a number of phony "paper" union locals to Provenzano in exchange for political support at the national conventions. Provenzano allegedly used the locals to make money through loansharking, extorting money from contractors and trucking companies, and raiding union pension funds. It was one of the many arrangements of convenience Hoffa had made in each section of the country. Eventually Justice Department investigators would believe that Hoffa's arrangement with Tony Pro brought about his murder.[12]

In June 1978 Tony Provenzano was sentenced to life imprisonment for having murdered a union rival in 1961. Police investigators believe he is responsible for the permanent disappearance of two other New Jersey men who dared to cross him—not counting Jimmy Hoffa. Six months after his murder conviction, Provenzano still held control over the three biggest Teamster locals in the New York area, numbers 560 in Union City, 84 in Fort Lee, and 522 in Queens and Elizabeth, according to a long, detailed report in the *Bergen Record*. Rotating the offices of those three unions among himself and his two brothers, Sam and Nunzio, Provenzano has run the three locals at least since the early 1960s. Sam Provenzano is president of Teamster Joint Council 73, a regional union organization governing forty-three locals in New Jersey and a dozen more in New York, Pennsylvania, and Connecticut. Sam also replaced Tony as an international vice-president of the union. The Provenzanos like to keep Teamster affairs in the family.[13]

An example of how the Bergen County Teamster officials use their cozy relationships to undercut their members is the case of Local 863. Local 863 provides drivers to the huge twenty-four hour discount supermarket chain, Pathmark. Because supermarket shoppers tend to arrive in bunches—Saturday is a heavy day, Tuesday a light one, and peak sales come at the beginning of the month after paychecks are distributed—Pathmark needs a varying schedule of deliveries from its warehouses. Rather than pay drivers overtime for peak days, or keep drivers idle on light days, Pathmark came to terms with Joseph Pecora, who runs Local 863. Pathmark decided to hire the minimum number of drivers it needs and to avoid expensive ($20 per hour) overtime wages by hiring "casual" drivers who work for one of three "leasing firms." These drivers may be paid as much as $3 less per hour and they receive no fringe or pension benefits. One of these leasing firms, Decana Labor Supply, is paid about $9 per hour in labor costs, roughly the same as union scale, and about $2 per hour service fee. The drivers who work for Decana, however, say they earn only $6 an hour. Thus Decana makes $5 per hour on each driver it supplies, $5 that does not go to Teamster members. Where it does go is to Thomas Pecora, the owner of Decana, who is the son of Joseph Pecora, the president of Local 863. Since Joseph Pecora holds the post of vice-president in Joint Council 73 under Sam Provenzano, it is an arrangement that obviously has the approval of the New Jersey Teamster hierarchy. Like the Provenzanos, the Pecoras shuffle their family members through the three Teamster locals they control and they do it at a lucrative rate. Joseph and his son, Joseph Jr., for example, were paid a total of $105,813 in salary in 1977. Joseph Sr. is also a convicted shakedown artist, and he plus two of his brothers were identified by Senator McClellan's investigators as members of the Genovese crime organization.[14]

Such a deal to enrich Teamster officers at the expense of member drivers is only one of the scams New Jersey syndicate bosses have used. Once a union local, or district council, has been integrated into a larger criminal enterprise, it becomes an extremely valuable platform from which to run any number of moneymaking rackets, from organizing sports gambling books to fencing stolen merchandise. "Gambling and loansharking are epidemic in some truck terminals," the *Bergen Record* reported. "Theft of cargo is so common that some dockmen are called shoppers; they work from lists of models and sizes 'ordered' by co-workers. Household appliances, designer clothes, liquor, and weapons disappear by the truckload."[15]

More sophisticated operations include rigged bankruptcies, in which trucking companies are bled of all their cash, and raids on bank mortgages and insurance funds are made. In 1977, a lawyer, an accountant, and six others pleaded guilty to contriving the sham bankruptcy of Translease Systems, Inc., a Manhattan truck leasing company. The racketeers for whom the lawyer worked used strong-arm tactics to take over three other leasing companies and a parts supplier. Then they submitted false bills for service and leased equipment to Translease, kept the receipts, and through a complicated maneuver devised by the lawyer and the accountant took control of twenty-six semitrailer trucks. Gino Gallina, a lawyer for a Jersey City trucking company and a former Manhattan assistant D.A., told a wire service reporter that he had turned state's evidence in the Translease case and that prosecutors saw it as part of a larger conspiracy of a certain Mr. Big to drive several trucking companies into bankruptcy. Within hours of his statement Gallina was blasted in the face and neck with seven bullets as he walked down a Greenwich Village street. According to the *Bergen Record,* the so-called Mr. Big behind the bankruptcies was Anthony Provenzano.[16]

The evidence of such Teamster-based racketeering has reached voluminous proportions. Trial testimony, Senate hearings, an occasional investigation by the Department of Labor, and a number of devastating books have shown how the union's locals are used in every major city by underworld racketeers. Apologists for the Teamsters argue that for all its faults, the union has done a magnificent job in raising wages and securing benefits for its men. Hoffa, who was at once one of the most brilliant and one of the most corrupt union leaders in American history, was always eager to answer critics who condemned

Teamster hooliganism. Not surprisingly he often began by talking about Bobby Kennedy, the attorney general who had sent him to prison for jury tampering. For in Kennedy's obsessive war with the Teamsters Hoffa saw a certain kind of patrician bigotry which has been the hallmark of wealthy reformers since the holy crusade of Samuel Tilden and the *New York Times* against Boss Tweed.

"I was reading a story about Bobby Kennedy which talked about the fact that Bobby was born to the silk and I was born to the burlap," Hoffa once told an interviewer, "and the author wondered what the difference would have been if I had been born to the silk and Kennedy to the burlap. Well you can't change life very easily and you can't go back, but I would venture to say that, knowing what I have did [sic] to get where I am at now and what it took to be a part of building this union, that Bobby Kennedy would have found out that it is one thing to *make* people do things and another thing to get people to do things *without* making them. He would have found out that you do not always have a choice of who you deal with, who you associate with or what you do and the way you do it to be able to get a project completed successfully." Then he added, "I'll tell you about a public standard of morality. In my humble opinion there is none in the United States. Individuals, and each one grows up with the standards of the household he was born in, the society he's permitted to live in, based upon his economic position in life."[17]

Hoffa's disgust with Bobby Kennedy was more than personal bitterness. By 1963 Kennedy had brought successful indictments against almost a hundred Teamster members and officials. The war between the two men had become a war between two immensely powerful organizations—and the "economic position in life"—they represented. They stood before the public as the latter-day knights of darkness and light, in which the workingman appeared ensnared by the darkness of the underworld, and justice became the avenging tool of privilege. Reflecting on his youth in Detroit, Hoffa spoke of the desperate struggle to survive: "The depression in Detroit, it was knock down, drag out, starving people; it was murder, murder. . . . In the early days every strike was a fight. . . . I was in a lot of fights, got my head broke, got banged around. My brother got shot. We had a business agent killed by a strikebreaker. . . . Our cars were bombed out. . . . They hired thugs who were out to get us, and Brother, your life was in your hands every day. There was only one way to survive—

fight back. And we used to slug it out on the streets." He saw too how the Purple Gang's Moe Dalitz had organized the Detroit laundry workers (and shaken down the laundry operators), and the lesson left an indelible mark: trust nothing but the threat of brute strength. It was not so much that he only respected the law of the jungle, but rather that his experience told him that in America nothing exists but the jungle. Men who lived by the jungle law—notably mobsters—fought not for elusive principles but for cold, hard cash. Murray Kempton, the journalist, once pressed Hoffa about his penchant for bringing so many convicts into the union. He answered, "If a guy has a record, he can't double-cross you. Who else would hire him?" Kempton saw Hoffa as possessed of both a proletarian consciousness and an odd perverse integrity that elevated gangsters into working-class heroes. "In Hoffa there had been placed and misplaced the germ of radical pessimism—that intuition of the ubiquity of evil—that had nowhere to live except in consort with the criminal class."[18]

The guy with a record, or several guys with records, seem to have double-crossed Jimmy Hoffa after all. The reason is that gangsters, like most businessmen, are very practical people. The rackets they had built with Hoffa's cooperation continued on without him, and his oft-repeated threats to expose the corruption of his union enemies could well have proven very expensive. Especially embarrassing would have been the secrets he could have told about Teamster influence in the federal government and the rising importance of syndicate influence in Washington. That influence covered far more than the trucking industry's influence with the ICC.

The fantastic expansion of the federal bureaucracy, the power of its myriad regulatory agencies, and the massive amounts of money spent on public contracts have made Washington the second most important financial center in the United States. The enormity of the federal largess—be it in the high salaries paid to professional employees, the billions spent on construction of new buildings, or the hundreds of millions approved for consulting firms—place it at the fountainhead of the service sector where money is most easily diverted to illegal purposes. Federal and congressional investigators have reported that important national gangsters have begun to show a rising interest in Washington, especially since the late 1960s. New Jersey labor racketeers became increasingly frequent visitors on Capitol Hill and at the Department of Housing and Urban Development (HUD). Newspaper reports in 1977 alleged that emissaries from the late Carlo Gambino, at that time the most powerful underworld figure in New York, had been paid at least $1 million for their representation in Washington.[19]

Traditionally, Washington has been described as free of the usual big-city rackets. That has been true in part because Washington is such a peculiar city. It has no industry, no harbors, no garment district, no true ethnic ghettos like Chinatown or Little Italy, no warehouse and trucking center, none of the usual focal points of syndicate activity. Moreover the District is mostly black, a fact that has kept the old big-time gangsters mainly on the white perimeter. It has two papers of varying fortune and presentation: They see sending investigative criminal reporters into the District rather as Queen Victoria saw sending explorers into the Congo. As late as 1976, three-quarters of the *Washington Post*'s organized-crime file was being cribbed from New York papers. When the *Washington Star* bought the *Washington Daily News,* the only paper that tried to cover crime, it sent all the *Daily News* clips to the dump. The periodic stories that do emerge are mostly about black bookies and junkies, admittedly important people making millions of dollars a year. A very good story may even note that virtually every black corner grocery in the District picks up numbers on a more regular schedule than it gets fresh produce.

But few reporters are sent out to examine reports of hidden Teamster investments in construction near Crystal City, or the way the rackets penetrated some of Washington's best restaurants, or the regular presence of the city's gambling lords in singles' hangouts off Connecticut Avenue below Dupont Circle, or how from 1972 to 1975 ownership of the sex theaters and book stores underwent a surprising upheaval and ushered into the city one Mickey Zaffarano, identified by the FBI and the *New York Times* as one of the three largest mob porno kings in the country. Largely as a result of the dailies' myopic attitudes, the top police department officials brusquely deflect any serious inquiry.

"Where do you find the mob?" Phil Manuel, an investigator for the Senate Permanent Subcommittee on Investigations, asked rhetorically. "Where there's money and growth. Over the last fifteen to twenty years government payrolls have expanded geometrically. That means construction and entertainment have had to expand right along." A big piece of those payrolls has gone to the mostly single, mostly white young professionals who are guaranteed notably higher salaries than their counterparts earn elsewhere in America. Transient and freed of long-term debts, they have unusually high quantities of disposable income. They are the people who can afford several nights a week at the smart bars, who can afford to drop $50 to $100 a week for football bets on the Washington Redskins.[20]

A secondary attraction in Washington, some organized-crime analysts have claimed, has been the realization by racketeers of how much excess there is in the government contracting business—especially in health programs and defense plant construction. If bureaucrats and corporations can grow rich on the government waste, why shouldn't the racketeers hire accountants to do the same thing? In 1975 alone, there were six major national exposés of racketeering in the medicare payment programs.[21]

Most of the growth in Greater Washington has come during the last fifteen years. But there have been underworld organizations in Washington far longer, ready and able to take advantage of any opportunities that appeared. Among those organizations, the best-known patron has been Joseph Francis Nesline. Federal and New York law-enforcement agents have described him as a major underworld power on the East Coast. In recent years he has been a regular companion to Meyer Lansky. In the fifties and early sixties Nesline was described as the man who set the number for bookies throughout the Washington area. As late as 1963 he appeared as the principal in a series of back-room casinos scattered throughout the city and its suburbs.[22]

Until the middle of the sixties, the white mob's biggest syndicate business in Washington was running casinos, numbers, and sports bets. The police department in those days, some of whose officers were found to be on the take, refused to bother with the gambling operations. Nesline's subordinates kept up monthly payments to precinct houses, and kept as clients senators, representatives, and even high officers in the executive branch. Then the Manhattan district attorney opened surveillance on gambling boss Charlie Tourine, and the syndicate connection with Washington began to emerge. Tourine, described by Justice Department agents as a former "Enforcer" for a group of leading eastern racketeers including Meyer Lansky and "Trigger Mike" Coppola, is alleged to have held major interests in Cuban gambling casinos until he was driven out by Fidel Castro.[23]

The Manhattan D.A.'s men received regular information about several gambling clubs in the district, so much information that D.C.

police were forced to act. First the pressure came against the Amber Club and the Spartan-American Club, both in the District. The clubs offered blackjack, craps, and poker. Stakes ran in the low hundreds on bad nights to the low thousands on good ones. When police pressure intensified, the operators moved to suburban Maryland, where they opened a new casino called the Sportsman's Club. Testimony before a Maryland grand jury in late 1964 and early 1965 revealed that Nesline and half a dozen subordinates who had been in and out of prison on federal gambling charges were moving out to the clearer suburban air.

Probably nothing would have stopped the Sportsman's Club had it not been for a diligent St. Mary's deputy sheriff, Benjamin Burroughs, who learned about the new club and discovered how many politicians and law-enforcement officers were in on it. Deputy Burroughs first went to the FBI, then he spoke to the club owners. Two days after opening night, June 8, 1963, Burroughs received a phone call, advising him to come to a restaurant parking lot that night to talk about the Sportsman. It was during the phone call that he realized how big an operation the club was to be, for the two men he was to meet were Tourine and Nesline. They talked about "something they had going across the street," then added: "We'd like to give you a little money to tide you over."[24]

Three days later, the Maryland state police raided the Sportsman's Club. Tourine, who had moved to Washington temporarily from his Central Park South apartment in New York, was arrested on the spot and suffered a minor heart attack. Also arrested was Nesline, whom several witnesses identified as the owner and ultimate boss of the club.

Nesline and Tourine were convicted in St. Mary's County by the local magistrate's court. That led to a pecular twist, for the vagaries of Maryland law then guaranteed any defendant the right of a second trial, called an appeal, simply for the asking. Nesline and Tourine appealed and asked for a change of venue to nearby Howard County where the case was placed on the "inactive" list, thereby leaving the two master gamblers convicted but free of a sentence.[25]

Since June 1963, Tourine and Nesline have been more careful if no less active. In 1975, the two men tried to get a casino license in London. Working for Tourine and Lansky, Nesline also opened a casino in, of all places, Dubrovnik, Yugoslavia, in the late sixties. Regular junkets left from Dulles airport to Dubrovnik for about a year before Marshal Tito, fearing too big a take was being skimmed off the top, had the place closed down.[26]

Fragmentary descriptions from informants, acquaintances, and former girl friends portray Nesline as a man whose power grew from his technical expertise in setting up and running gambling casinos to controlling all the high-stake gambling operations in Washington, with a steady clientele of its upper cream. Among his friends was one Stanley Bender, head of the Blake Construction Company, builder of the new J. Edgar Hoover FBI Headquarters. Bender's wagers, along Nesline's circuit, were reported to run as high as six figures. One of the tenants in Bender's own building was the National Association for Justice, a so-called prisoner's rights organization founded by Jimmy Hoffa, and which involved Hoffa's pal, the same Nesline. Bender, who hired NAJ recruits, was also a steady participant in Nesline's elite poker games, where Bender admitted losing more than $100,000 in just one night.[27]

Few people interested in organized crime in Washington are concerned about private poker games. But these games and the men who run them are certainly not involved in penny-ante fun sessions. Until 1975, big games ran regularly after closing hours in the basement room of a restaurant a few blocks from the White House. According to a Drug Enforcement Administration (DEA) investigation, the maître d' of that restaurant was the "muscle man" collector of bad debts for the Nesline operation. One guest who showed up every four to six weeks for a card game called "$5,000 freeze-out" was Vince Promuto, then DEA director of public affairs. Another game, run by Nesline in the Watergate building, with stakes running into the thousands, included cabinet officers as well as senators and congressmen. The games became so notorious that Watergate resident and Republican minority leader Senator Hugh Scott tried to get them stopped. Scott, who has since retired, was apparently not successful. "There are a great deal of very big bettors here," a Justice Department official said in 1976, so many that the gambling rackets make up one of the biggest industries in Washington—all of it tax clear. That, however, is only part of the story. For the gambling rackets provide two other crucial benefits: access to political decision makers and ready cash for investments in drugs, porno operations, and prostitution.[28]

The call-girl business of Washington is controlled by the same underworld organization that runs the gambling. One Capitol Hill prostitution ring has been described as offering some of the classiest courtesans in North America, their minimum prices starting at $500. They are on call for party caucuses and conventions, and during the administration of President Nixon, they were flown regularly for retreats at Key Biscayne, Miami Beach, and Newport Beach, California. One woman who disappeared in 1969 and who had been very close to Nesline was known to have been the client of a vice-president on a regular basis. Investigators believed but could not prove that she was paid off with contract favors or administration consideration for her friends—which is precisely why men such as Nesline run such rings.[29]

Compared to "the malefactors of great wealth" who commanded American industry and paid off half of the U.S. Congress during the Gilded Age, the culture of underworld corruption in Washington may seem a rather lame affair. The bloody arts of persuasion utilized by Teamster gangsters in New Jersey appear hardly more terrible than the sacrificial killings orchestrated by the corrupt railroad robber barons. What links the two epochs together is not so much the particulars of the crimes committed in the name of commerce—murder is murder, whether delivered by a luger in the back of the head or by a shotgun blast in the chest—but rather their incidental quality. When Jimmy Hoffa denied the existence of a public morality in America, he was acknowledging a tradition of debasement that has recurred and flourished time and time again whenever the country entered a new era of economic growth. The rather well known argument by Daniel Bell that organized crime is merely another technique for the lower classes to achieve upward mobility—to capture their place in the marketplace and in the sun—was an astute observation in the 1950s when most public officials depicted racketeering as the work of a mysterious and nefarious army of bad people with foreign names.

The progress of organized criminal syndicates since the fifties, however, has revealed something that Bell did not notice. That is the emergence of organized crime as an enduring, systematized profession, one that has become institutionalized in national and local politics and which parallels the systematization and institutionalization of corporate crime. Be it the movement of racketeers into the land swindles of the Southwest, the laundering of money for political campaigns, or the corrupt brokerage of phony doctor bills to milk the medicare system, the underworld today uses the same complicated computer technology and international banking system services employed by the First National City Bank or the Gulf Oil Corporation. No longer do rackets offer the quick route to success for tough kids from the street. The real insight of onetime street toughs like Hoffa or Provenzano was they realized that to become kingpins they had to be master business technicians. The irony of their success is that the industry they built can no longer provide opportunity to people like themselves.

Chapter 28

The Law of the Streets—Dead End

On a rather brisk October morning in 1973, newspapers across America ran the same remarkable banner headline across the tops of their front pages: 'I AM NOT A CROOK'—NIXON. The president of the United States had felt so beleagured by the investigations into the Watergate scandal that he had gone to the public to swear before them that he was not a criminal.

No president, not even Grant or Harding, had ever suffered such humiliation before the public. Richard Nixon, the archconservative who had barged to victory largely by promising to wage war on criminals, seemed mortified at having to make such a desperate proclamation. The man who had promised to quit mollycoddling the crooks was being exposed to the world as the biggest petty crook of all, a man who had hired burglars to ensure his reelection, who had suborned perjury among his highest aides, who had laundered cash through shady offshore banks also used by the underworld, and who had even indulged in petty cheating on his income tax statements.[1]

On the surface, at least, it was an irony of cosmic proportions. Never mind that the Watergate scandal really concerned a grand and extraordinary political intrigue among a dozen of the most powerful agencies in the country. For the public, as for most of the press, the issue was crime, and the editorial cartoonists soon displayed the president sporting a bandit's mask, his aides slinking through back alleys with bags of burglar's tools and, eventually, his attorney general clad in the striped suit of a two-bit convict. Watergate seemed the apotheosis of the criminal society run wild, where even crime-stoppers turned out to be hoods.

To many European observers, the American compunction to treat Watergate as a cops-and-robbers caper seemed altogether baffling. What they failed to understand was the importance of crime, now and historically, as the one American issue before which all others pale. In a land where profound issues of class and ideology have always been dismissed as antique artifacts of the Old World, cases of serious political conflict are easily reduced to Manichean struggles between good guys and bad guys. Bad guys break laws and get caught; good guys send them to jail. If the good guys get caught breaking the law too, then the public assumption is, more often than not, that they—like their Puritan forebears—fell from grace and succumbed to greedy temptation. Thus, for the most part, Richard Nixon was portrayed not as a man who was sabotaged by his political enemies, but as one who failed his oath of office to uphold the law.

Americans' ability to reduce, and thereby diffuse, any social issue to a problem of crime is absolutely essential to understanding the formulation of almost any of the large problems that faced the nation in the 1960s and 1970s. Indeed, ever since Sacco and Vanzetti were legally executed in 1927 for a murder they probably did not commit rather than for the anarchist agitation they certainly maintained, virtually all major incidents of dissent in America have been treated as criminal. Thus, the Rosenbergs were executed as spies not as Communists; Alger Hiss was jailed as a perjurer not as a radical; the Black Panthers were gunned down for supposedly bearing arms and not for organizing the Oakland ghetto. J. Edgar Hoover maintained that all civil rights activists in the South were really only Communist-inspired looters who were blackmailing decent citizens through the threat of violence. Welfare mothers who stayed at home in their ghettos were viewed as lazy loafers who conspired to defraud the government. Antiwar demonstrators who marched the streets of Washington were vandals intent on fanning the flames of destruction. Reduced to the status of criminals, the political content of their actions erased, they could be lumped together with muggers, arsonists, and burglars.

In the same way important political leaders who lost their fights could be denied the martyrdom around which their supporters might rally. Therein lay a second and deeper irony in the demise of Richard Nixon and the other Watergate criminals. As the men who had worked hardest to neutralize political dissent by denouncing it as criminal, they became the victims of their own technique. They became a part of the growing crime wave they had always cited as justification for their tough campaigns for law and order. The menace of rising crime, a real problem rooted in deep, difficult issues of class and race, was impressed so forcefully and fearsomely on the public that it devoured anyone who was touched by it.

By the time Nixon had secured his landslide mandate for a second term, he had succeeded in defining crime—drug dealing, murder, assault, robbery, burglary, and so on—as the most dangerous domestic issue in America. Indeed the threat of crime seemed to be everywhere. In 1976, the FBI reported, ordinary American citizens were three times as likely to be the victims of murder, rape, assault, robbery, or car theft as they had been in 1960. By the 1970s Chicago police were reporting an average of almost two murders a day. Supposedly safe, new cities like Tucson and Phoenix began to edge out Boston and New York as centers of violence and theft. The insides of Detroit were abandoned to all but the most desperate black street gangs, and New York's South Bronx became the clichéd example of an inner-city "war zone" where nothing but the shells of burned-out buildings remained. Recalling the metaphors of disease that reformers had always used to describe the immigrant ghettos of the nineteenth century, journalists and sociologists began to speak of the blight, of the uncontrollable cancer that was squeezing the life out of the great cities of America. Once again the nation was captive of a massive crime wave, and no man, woman or child was safe from it.[2]

Despite the notorious unreliability of the FBI's crime statistics, and despite the eagerness of much of the press to capitalize on crime stories, the threat of street crime does seem to have worsened during the last two decades. In his masterful review of the proliferation of street crime, *Criminal Violence, Criminal Justice,* Charles Silberman provided a comprehensive sketch of America's criminal "society," an analysis of the changing makeup of the criminal population and several insights into reasons why the number of ordinary criminals has grown so rapidly. He noted, as have many other professional crime watchers, that the tremendous upsurge in street crime paralleled the maturing postwar "baby boom." Petty crime has always been the special product of the young, and by the late sixties fully half the population was under twenty-five. Yet even the population explosion was not enough to account for the size and intensity of the crime explosion. Silberman pointed out that a 40 or 50 percent jump in these crimes could have been predicted as a result of the demographic bulge, but instead the crimes increased by nearly 200 percent.[3]

Conservatives, including such men as Harvard's James Q. Wilson, who advised the Nixon administration, pointed to the old bugaboo of social permissiveness. The police and the courts, they said, have been hamstrung by rulings that enable criminals to escape punishment through technical loopholes in the law. Liberals, such as Silberman, surveyed the careers of common criminals and observed that the combination of poverty, unemployment, racial oppression, and the anomaly of life at the bottom leads teenagers to conclude that crime offers the best alternative for survival, and occasionally for escape. Both critiques are probably correct. A rigid, well-financed, and harsh criminal justice system might well eliminate much of the drug dealing, theft, and intrafamily killing that has made America the most violent of all modern nations. Draconian laws do seem to work when they are backed up by massive and arbitrary firepower. But aside from the repressive consequences of such an approach, in which as many as 5 percent of the country's population might have to be imprisoned, it ignores the role that street criminals play and have always played in American society. And it ignores the changing structure of American society as a whole, a society in which street crime is necessarily becoming a permanent and relatively cheap means of survival for as many as 10 to 20 million people who will probably never enter the regular economy.[4]

In recent years, an increasing number of social scientists, including economists, anthropologists, and folklorists, have begun to focus their attention on the so-called culture of crime. One of the best students of criminal life, Bruce Jackson, has recorded the life stories of several dozen killers, thieves, hookers, safecrackers, fences, and assorted crooks. These are straightforward accounts of life on the street and in prison from ordinary people who are not particularly glamorous and who often view their crimes as nothing more than the work they happened to do. There is in many of their stories an air of fatalism, as in the account of Slim, a thirty-seven-year-old black man from Arkansas who was sentenced to twenty years for robbery and had earlier served five years on a manslaughter charge. "See, just like I told you before, Bruce, life is handed to a man in two buckets," he said. "It's a bucket full of 'I haven't did that yet,' and then there's an empty bucket marked 'I ain't gonna do that no more.' Now you reach into this bucket of 'I haven't did that yet' and you come up with something. You try it. If you like it, you hold that, you know, you hold it to you. And you get another one of those 'I haven't did this yet.' But if it fucks up on you, the first thing you do is drop it over in this 'I ain't gonna do it no more' bucket. That's the way I feel about life, you know. That's one of those things that's in that 'I ain't gonna do it no more' bucket—like doing time in Arkansas. Don't do that no more. I got enough of that, and it didn't work out right, so I had to put it in that bucket." Crime, so far as Slim could see, was a label that had been put on some of the work he did to make a living. Sometimes a job paid. Sometimes it didn't.[5]

Slim, however, was something of a professional, a man who had developed skills that enabled him to survive as a criminal on the streets and as a prisoner in "the joint." Men and women who have survived as criminals into adulthood almost always develop such skills, and some—like safecrackers—consider their work a craft. The finest crafts probably involve burglary, grand larceny, and fencing, where a combination of guile and technical expertise is often essential. These professional criminals, who may work with the gangsters of organized crime as local subcontractors—for example, in the interstate marketing of stolen securities or stripped down auto parts—are the modern decendants of the prerevolutionary counterfeiters, of New York's original Five Points gangs or of the horse thieves and rustlers on the open frontier. Some are full-time criminals, but a much larger proportion apparently use crime as a supplement to low-paying legitimate jobs.

Most criminologists believe that the number of criminals who stay in crime drops dramatically after about age twenty to twenty-five. The reasons are fairly simple. The leading juvenile offenses—auto theft, burglary, and drug dealing—are high-risk crimes with a relatively low payoff. Skilled house burglars, a recent study by the Rand Corporation found, seem to move on to robbing savings and loan companies, jewelry stores, or other businesses where the take is much larger and the risk of violence and apprehension much lower. Moreover, there seems to be a period in the young adult's life when he has to "promote" himself in the criminal subculture—particularly at the bars and street corners where contacts are made, trusts established, and information exchanged—in order to form alliances with other street criminals that will lead to bigger jobs. Such "promotion" on the street is a delicate business since police and police informants also work the same territory. Not too surprisingly a certain weeding-out process develops in which clever thieves learn how to succeed and the rest are either scared off or wind up in jail. Thus for teenage kids who have started out as gang members who may even have dabbled in a wide range of petty rackets, the prospect of finding steady work in a burglary ring or in the numbers racket may be as elusive as finding a straight job on a construction crew.

Criminologist Julian Roebuck tells of a young man in an eastern city who had "applied" for a regular job with the local "numbers man" and each time was rejected. "He say, 'Man what you talking about? You just don't have the class for the numbers,'" Roebuck's informant recalled. "I say, 'Well, I can learn.' He say, 'Hell, man, you been arrested for every petty crime in the book. You been locked up too much. All the cops know you too good. You got jail fever.'" Steady work, straight or crooked, is hard to find when you start at the bottom.[6]

With the prospect of big success in crime so tenuous, the question remains, "Why the big boom in teenage crime?" It is not enough merely to point out that inner-city unemployment may run to 20 or 30 percent and as high as 50 or 80 percent for young black adults. Good criminal jobs are also scarce. The answer, to the extent that becoming a criminal involves a conscious choice, may be the same as to the question of why lower-class people are the biggest betters on such long-shot gambles as the numbers racket where the odds are usually 600-to-1 or worse: Failing any other alternative, they reckon, why not take the big risk? Jail, meaning the prospect of getting caught, is bad but certainly no worse than daily misery in a ghetto or starvation. Besides, the choice is not all that dramatic; the petty rackets are a regular part of daily life. As John Allen, himself an ex-felon, has written, criminal businesses—narcotics sales, gambling, fencing stolen property—are as central to lower-class neighborhoods as the laundries, corner markets, and liquor stores. "There's so many things that go on—it's a whole system that operates inside itself," he said in a recent book. "Say I was to take you by it. You want some junk, then I would take you to the dude that handles drugs. You want some clothes, I could take you somewhere that handles that. You want some liquor, I could take you someplace other than a liquor store. Of course, it's all outside the law." What some sociologists and economists have called the "irregular economy" is in fact integral to lower-class communities, so much so that one New York City official speculated that many an "honest" Harlem businessman was able to stay in business only because of the occasional loans and cut-rate deals available through the local numbers broker. Crime has become a way of "getting along" for people who live on the margins of American society.[7]

Historically, social workers and criminologists have labeled criminals and other "marginal" participants in American society as deviants or unfortunates who, because of social and economic deprivation, invested their time and energy unwisely. Since the ghetto riots of the 1960s, however, a number of economists have turned their attention to the lower-class sections of the nation's cities. Their technical and systematic studies of the "microeconomies" of particular neighborhoods and of the employment patterns at the bottom of our society suggest a way of life remarkably similar to John Allen's impressionistic description. Greatly simplified, their findings show that job opportunities in the United States fall more or less into two broad categories—the primary sector of steady, often unionized, better-paying jobs with long-term security and fringe benefits, and a secondary sector "marked by low-paying, unstable, and dead-end employment, with frequent layoffs and discharges." The jobs in the "secondary labor market" include a wide variety of low-skilled work—passing out advertising leaflets, janitorial and restaurant jobs, working in department stores and discount houses and filling the large number of mostly mechanical slots in the mushrooming electronics and data-processing industries. But because those jobs are both scarce and low paying, they contribute only a part of the income that supports people in lower-class and ghetto neighborhoods. The rest of the "ghetto economy" is provided by public welfare payments, government job-training and development programs, and criminal or "quasi-legal" work.

Only a few social researchers have begun to explore the complex of relations between crime-related income and the other sources of support that these secondary workers depend upon. Preliminary investigations at the Vera Institute of Justice in New York City have suggested that the boundaries between legitimate and illegal jobs may often be imaginary, that many people switch back and forth between low-paying jobs and petty rackets, mixing occasional day labor with sporadic burglaries, holdups and minor drug dealing. Then as the risks of violence and jail become more obvious and the promise of making big money disappears, the petty crooks tend to drift toward a combination of public support and occasional legitimate work. In that way street crime offers the first range of jobs that teenagers and young adults can easily find; at the same time it provides cheap merchandise (through fences) and cheap escape (through drugs and stolen liquor) for people who have left the street rackets but are still locked into the secondary economy with little chance of moving up into better-paying jobs. That is the "system" John Allen described, and given the general stagnation in the overall economy, it is a system that is likely to grow larger rather than smaller.[8]

Temporary or even supplementary job opportunities are not the only attractions of petty crime, especially for teenagers who are leaving school for the streets. The very fact of its riskiness seems to make the criminal life appear more alluring to the teenage kid on a dead-end track than does the prospect of shuffling through life as a janitor or carwash boy. If a fifteen-year-old kid in southside Chicago has a one-in-ten chance of making it as a car thief with a gang of ten friends, a job which guarantees excitement if not a certain future, then why not opt for excitement? Ex-burglar John Allen expressed the tremendous psychological attraction of the criminal alternative in a single sentence: "What I really missed was the excitement of sticking up and the planning and the getting away with it—whether it came out to a car chase or just a plain old-fashioned foot race outrunning the police—knowing all the little alleys and shortcuts to go through." The very act of pitting his life against the incredible odds that were stacked against him led Allen and untold numbers of other bright urban outlaws to choose crime as the most fulfilling option available to them.[9]

The dark side of that compulsion to find escape through excitement is the unrelenting threat of violence on the street. Allen may have gotten his kicks by outwitting his police pursuers. But the same frustration and anger may also build toward the violence of random assault, homicide, and rape. The drive to find quick thrills has probably always been a constant of street life. A Chicago delinquent of the 1920s explained that he was "always looking for thrills," that he "always wanted to be in the midst of any excitement, whether it was stealing, breaking windows, breaking in school houses and tearing up the furniture, or playing a ball game." Rising rates of homicide and rape between strangers—crimes which historically involved acquaintances—have suggested to some criminologists that young men are increasingly motivated by a desire to take vengeance on a legal and moral structure which they perceive as their enemy. Although this is obviously only part of the explanation, some women's movement activists have cited the sharp increase in reported rapes as a predictable result of a culture in which men are surrounded by the artifacts of material success—many of them illustrated by sexual symbolism—with no chance of achieving them. Rape, especially of strangers, then becomes a form of perverse self-assertion, and the subjugation of the victim becomes a moment of triumph over normal frustration.

Just as adult crime holds out the lure of fleeting psychological fulfillment, a similar promise attracts young gang members who are just beginning adolescence to enter the life of the street. In a remarkable interview with journalist Ianthe Thomas, a youngster who uses the name Nato spoke about his life in a gang called the Savage Nomads. He gave the interview in his mother's South Bronx apartment where there was no running water and the only toilet was a tin bucket that was periodically dumped out the bedroom window:

> I been raised in the gangs. Like my brothers were, only they're in jail now and one got on junk so my mother said he's dead. Gangs are families. Like brothers and sisters all together. We rumble cause you have to show blood. Blood is strength. In the Bronx there's a lot of blood.
>
> People say gangs is bad. Not to me. Gangs help each other, but we fight if there's static. This is just how we live. School don't mean nothing. They don't teach your head for jobs and for living. Eating too. Schools don't teach your head to eat.
>
> You ask me who I am. I am somebody. Down East 139th street they say, "No trouble in stores." Then they throw you

out. So maybe we burn them. Then they gone. We still here. We still somebody.

This is our country up here, like a whole world. Everybody took the money and went, but the gangs stay. We own all this land and all these buildings. If we got money like a country we could rule this place like kings.

They say gangs will die. They say gangs come and go. But the Savage Nomads is forever. Even people, like adults, tip their hats to us. 'Cause we are like polices.

Some people could leave but they don't 'cause people is real and they stick together. I know there's another world like the one on T.V. But this is a world, too.

If you write gang things people will think we just party and rumble. But mostly we make families with real weddings. Some girls get down with every dude, but really we believe in families.

My mother don't want me in no gang. But here you have to be. Everybody beat on you if you not a member. Gangs is protection. When I wear my colors I get respect. Since I been eleven I been in gangs. First just one small one named the Masked Marauders. Just four of us. We control Tiffany Street. We do crib jobs to make some change. Taking off old ladies and kids. But that's jive time and other gangs would take us off if we step out of our territory.

Up here everybody packs. I don't carry heavy hardware like a .45. Too much kick with that sucker. Too much like a rifle. I just carry a .32 automatic. I got my first piece when I was twelve. I stole it off a junkie. That's when my friend Frankie got hit over on Melrose Avenue. Two dudes just took him off. They said he stole their dog. It weren't true but they pumped him in the face.

I walked across the George Washington Bridge that day. This white toll man said get off the bridge. I shot at him twice. They never wrote down one word in the papers but I shot at him twice.

I wanted to get away that day. My mother told me my father lives in Jersey. I was going to see him. Maybe he had some money for me. I didn't find him so I just walked around in those big parks over there.

That's when I joined the Savage Nomads. Big Man took me in. He speaks like a law thinker does 'cause he done heavy time. He don't want the gangs to fight and he don't let no cliques fight. He says that white people want us to fight each other then they don't have to deal with us.

You talk with Big Man and he scares you like something bad. That's the prison eyes he has. He's a cool nigger with dead eyes like the devil. Even cops respect him 'cause they say he took off three guys at once.

Sometimes I think this is wrong. That's it. It's just wrong. Not for me 'cause I'm a man. But for little children growing up here. They see nothing and then they feel nothing. I know that some people have money and cars and food. Then you think "why can't I have that?" But what good does thinking do?

I been raised here from the time when buildings were more pretty and parks had trees. Now we don't have anything. But you get with your clique and you talk and party and get high. You can feel good. Like somebody.

"They give themselves names that speak of isolation, power, anarchy," journalist Thomas wrote. "Young Nomads, Tomahawks, Mortar Girls, Savage Nomads, Roman Kings, Black Stone Nations. The membership transcends age and sex. Young babies sit on mattresses next to automatic pistols, never crying for food because their inner timing dictates that stickups occur in the late afternoon and that's when the food comes."[10]

The odds are not good that Nato will long remain a "somebody." Most likely he will go to jail, as his brothers did. Or he will die. For just as teenage street crimes shot up wildly during the sixties and early seventies, so did teenage deaths. In a nine-year study of Chicago homicides that seems to parallel research in other cities, investigators found that the violent deaths of young black men (age fifteen to twenty-four) increased by over 300 percent from 1965 to 1973. The killing of young black women rose by 150 percent, as did the killing of blacks older than twenty-four. The number of young black offenders also increased, and by a similar proportion, from 72 in 1965 to 231 in 1973. Furthermore, these killings were somewhat less likely to take place between acquaintances than in the past. In a majority of the cases the killer and the victims did know each other somewhat, but personal familiarity between victim and assailant seemed to be less each year. And the number of cases in which the two did not know each other at all went from 95 to 307 during the nine-year period. All of which indicates that while public concern over assault against the middle-class whites may have been justified, the most frequent victims of crime are the people who live in lower-class communities where, as young Nato said, desperate people live by "blood" and die by blood with routine regularity. Beyond the grim statistics, there seems little reason to believe that many teenage gang members matriculate upwards either into the ranks of organized crime or into the semiprofessional world of independent criminal entrepreneurs.[11]

That is not to say that young street hoods are unacquainted with big-time organized crime. Those who by chance are born into the families of successful adult criminals, who have lucked into good contacts with neighborhood racketeers or who have the support of strong ethnic ties may make it into one of the large black, hispanic or Italian crime organizations. With luck and brains they may even be sent to college and fight their way into positions of power and status. But more likely their acquaintance with the organized rackets is as arbitrary as their acquaintance with the police. In their daily toil, they merely drift across the streets, selling nickel bags of smack, stripping down cars, collecting and selling information to whoever will buy it. They are the essential—but expendable—footsoldiers of the criminal system in lower-class America. And they are easily replaced by their younger brothers and sisters, who are always eager to play the odds of survival on the street.

A case in point is the way auto thievery has been transformed. Since the early 1970s the real money in car theft has not been in selling the actual automobile, but rather in selling its parts. As automobile prices skyrocketed, organized-crime entrepreneurs spotted a lush opportunity to supply junkyards and used-parts shops with stolen automobile components. In 1977, Senate investigators found syndicate-controlled shops operating in Chicago, Baltimore, Boston, New York, Miami, St. Louis, and a score of other cities, including even small towns in rural North Carolina. They estimated that one car is stolen in the United States about every thirty-two seconds. Within forty-eight hours of its theft, it will usually have been totally dismantled. Most of such work is handled by teenage gangs. One such Chicago gang was paid from $25 to $50 per car. Occasionally, an especially bright boy from the gangs might work his way into the larger organization, but that seems to be the exception more than the rule. From the racketeers' point of view the gangs are useful only as gangs—kids who live on the street and know the scene. The tight professional business organizations, which maintain interstate distribution systems, have little place for volatile, illiterate hoodlums.[12]

The racket that most viciously unites street hustlers, organized racketeers, and the police is the drug traffic. During the first Nixon administration, the "epidemic" of heroin use was frequently cited as a primary cause of the rising inner-city crime rates. Junkies were thought to be stealing the country blind in order to scratch up enough money to support their habits. Later studies have cast considerable doubt on how much burglary and assault can be blamed on insatiable drug users. A large percentage of heroin users, if not most of them, are not addicts but so-called chippers, people who take heroin once or twice a month and never develop a physiological dependence. There is no particularly good reason to suppose they spend most of their time stealing color televison sets to pay for their drug purchases. Yet despite the uncertainty over how much secondary property crime drug users commit, there are obvious victims to the drug trade: the individual users who do become addicts and to a larger extent the impoverished communities which are sapped of billions of dollars in cash each year and which also suffer the loss of the young men and women who might have been their most valuable assets. Harvard social scientist Mark Moore, who was a consultant to the U.S. Drug Enforcement Administration, estimated that in the early seventies retail heroin sales averaged $470 million a year in New York City alone. The hierarchy of that drug industry ranged from the eighteen thousand or so "jugglers" who sold just enough to pay for their own habits to the twenty-five major syndicate distributors who earned $500,000 net each a year and another twenty-five importers who cleared about $200,000 each.

More often than not those importers never saw the product of their profits—indicative of the distance between them and the street hustlers. For though South Bronx gang members like Nato's brothers might dream of reaching the good life by moving up the ladder of the dope industry, not one in a thousand ever succeeds. They are locked at the bottom of a class system within the world of crime whose internal barriers are every bit as forbidding as those in legitimate society. Indeed, until the 1960s, the hierarchy of the drug industry was so rigid that the principal consumers of hard drugs—poor blacks—held no position whatsoever in the traditional Italian syndicates that controlled distribution. Since then, the appearance of a supposed "black Mafia" has brought a handful of well-organized black criminal entrepreneurs into importing and distributing heroin in a few large cities—notably Washington, New York, Detroit, and Chicago. And as a result of federal crackdowns on Corsican and Italian smuggling connections, new drug routes opened up through Mexico and the Caribbean which, in turn, created opportunities for new Latino and Mexican syndicates within the United States.[13]

Occasional large crackdowns notwithstanding, drug trafficking has proven to be a variety of crime which law-enforcement agencies are least able to suppress. The exasperation over drug abuse that politicians and community activists began to express in the 1970s was reflective of the historic confusion out of which the drug problem grew. Like Prohibition, the drug laws passed before and immediately following World War I were part of a program to legislate morality and to enforce police control over a discontented and volatile lower class. Their passage was to a large degree the product of the nativist tirades against fiendish radicals and dull-witted immigrants, both of whom were supposed to be responsible for soiling native American purity with the nasty substances. A ferocious campaign to close medical drug treatment centers after 1918 was enthusiastically endorsed even by the American Medical Association, which labeled drug use the "vice that causes degeneration of the moral sense, and spreads through social contacts, readily infects the entire community, saps its moral fiber and contaminates the individual members, one after another, like the rotten apples in a barrel of sound ones."

Between 1914 and 1938, some twenty-five thousand doctors were arraigned for having treated drug users; three thousand served penitentiary sentences. As a New York Academy of Medicine report stated much later, in 1963, "the abandoned addicts, in order to satisfy their compulsive needs, were driven to the illicit traffic." Just as Prohibition had enabled bootleggers to erect their first national cartels, so the increasingly tough narcotics enforcement enabled the same syndicates to build an illegal cartel for the control of the drug traffic. As John Coffee, a congressman from Washington, noted in 1938, "through the operation of the law . . . there was developed also, as a counterpart to the smuggling racket, the racket of dope peddling; in a word, the whole gigantic structure of the illicit-drug racket, with direct annual turnover of upwards of a billion dollars."[14]

By the 1970s nothing much had changed from the scenario laid out by Congressman Coffee except that the market for drugs had multiplied many times over as the size of the nation's ghettos grew, as a new need for drugs among alienated middle-class youths appeared, and as a whole complex of federal, state, and local narcotics control agencies proliferated. An old familiar debate also recurred during the sixties and seventies. Drug use was not only criminal, but it became the subject of a new moral fervor. Cultural and political dissidents were lumped together as members of a "drug culture" that threatened the fundaments of the public tranquillity and the social order. Growing drug abuse, political conservatives and police officials argued, eroded respect for law. Proliferating drug abusers, by the fact of their existence, were deemed a direct challenge to authority. The prospect was frightening: the collapse of stable middle-class values combined with drug-related lawlessness in the lower-class ghettos might well prove explosive. Even worse, the apparent successes of radical leaders in both communities seemed to some a harbinger of pending anarchy. The old "victimless" crimes of drug abuse and drug trafficking created a kind of public discourse in which "the crime problem" was identified as central to the entire social and cultural fabric of the nation. And when the government attempted to intensify its antidrug policing efforts, matters worsened.

The creation of the federal Drug Enforcement Administration in 1973 drastically aggravated the problem. The core of the DEA drug control strategy was the buy-and-bust system whereby agents were sent into the streets with large rolls of cash to buy their way into the drug peddling rackets, theoretically working their way up to the syndicate kingpins who ran the industry. In fact, they barely got off the streets. For fiscal year 1976, the DEA budgeted over $9.9 million for the purchase of evidence and information. To begin a new case, an agent would buy a gram of heroin for around $150 (in 1975 prices) wholesale and make one or two more purchases at that quantity to build confidence with his supplier. For his fourth and fifth buys, he would escalate to four grams, pressing his contact to introduce him to a bigger dealer who would sell him an ounce at $4,000. By the time he made his final purchase, he would have already spent about $1,650. Should he then score his "big" bust, he would reclaim the money and use it again on new cases. But the net result of his six buys was that he had bought over $5,000 worth of heroin, even if in real hard cash he had used only his original $1,650.

As far as the wholesalers were concerned, the DEA agent had put into circulation upwards through the industry some $5,000. The only loser in the deal was the small wholesaler who was arrested for selling an ounce of heroin. Because the agent's $1,650 amounted to over $5,000 in purchasing power, some analysts estimated that DEA buy-and-bust gambits actually stimulated the drug trade. As one former DEA executive wrote in a critical review paper for the White House, "buying creates a market and stimulates production. . . . [It] is an input of money into the system and it generates a profit at all points beyond the point where enforcement action was taken." Like Nato's brothers in the South Bronx, most DEA agents never worked their way anywhere near the organized-crime bosses who controlled the system and made the most profit from it. All that most of the agents actually accomplished was to build up a network of informants on the street and to interject themselves as participants in the criminal system, hovering just on the legal side of formal entrapment. Thanks to them, they helped the system weed out the weak links and thus fortify itself.[15]

The long-term implication of the government's fifty-year-old drug control policy is clear and unmistakable: Drug traffic is an endemic part of lower-class American communities, especially the most alienated—the black and Latino. The role of the police is limited to regulating the volume and the geographical boundaries of the traffic. That, of course, has never been the stated position of any government authorities and indeed it may not even be the intent of the agencies and officials responsible for policing the traffic. To the people who live among the pushers and the police informants, it seems an inescapable conclusion—as indeed it was to Congressman Coffee over forty years ago. "Morphine," he argued in Congress, "which the peddler sells for a dollar a grain, could be supplied, of pure quality, for two or three cents a grain [1938 prices]. The peddler, unable to meet such a price, would go out of business—the illicit-narcotic-drug industry, the billion-dollar racket, would automatically cease to exist." Even more pointedly, he asked, "Why should persons in authority wish to keep the dope peddler in business and the illicit-drug racket in possession of its billion-dollar income? . . . If we, the representatives of the people, are to continue to let our narcotics authorities conduct themselves in a manner tantamount to upholding and in effect supporting the billion-dollar drug racket, we should at least be able to explain to our constituents why we do so." By acting as the ultimate guarantor of the narcotics syndicates, in much the same way that the ICC has been the guarantor for the interstate trucking cartel, the government police agencies have made themselves part of a three-way partnership with the rackets and with the criminal street culture that has grown at such alarming rates during the last two decades.[16]

Today a simple program of drug decriminalization might no longer suffice. The immense industry that Congressman Coffee predicted has become fact. It has so penetrated the complex world of petty street crime and united it to the hierarchy of syndicate crime that most medical and police alternatives cannot but fail. The huge effort to wean drug users away from heroin by providing methadone treatment centers has largely backfired. Frequently such centers only substituted one addiction for another, and corruption in the operation of the clinics became rampant within a year or two after their opening. Occasionally, the dependable supply of the daily methadone "fix" freed the petty street criminal from drug hustling and enabled him to concentrate more of his time on robberies and holdups.

The dilemmas of drug abuse and trafficking are, if anything, a paradigm for the larger issue of crime in the streets. The inability of the federal and local police to do any more than control or crudely regulate the drug traffic is symptomatic of their inability to eradicate any of the other petty crimes that produce violence and loss of property. For the police cannot eliminate an economic system that has evolved as a primary means of support for millions who already live at the margins of the "legitimate" society—any more than the police 150 years ago could eradicate the gangs of Irish immigrants who were then building the patronage system upon which the great cities of the East were to be governed. As Robert di Grazia, the former chief of police of Boston and St. Louis put it a few years ago: "We are not letting the public in on our era's dirty little secret." The secret, he said, "is that there is little the police can do."[17]

There is a bigger secret that Chief di Grazia did not mention. That secret, lost in the uproar over muggers, gangsters, and dope addicts, is that crime has become an inherent ingredient of the American system.

It is a means of making money, regulating business, supporting the poor. And, as the burglaries, fraud, frame-ups, illegal spying, and drug experimentations on unsuspecting victims by the FBI and the CIA made clear during the Watergate aftermath, it is often a way of running the government. According to a 1976 congressional study, street crime, the crisis issue that breeds fear and sells newspapers, costs society at most only one-tenth as much as does the respectable crimes of corporate price fixing, computer embezzlement, and tax fraud. Yet neither the politicians nor the press like to acknowledge such a fact. Instead, they focus on the street. Because it is visible and immediate, such crime is considered more real than all the rest. To individual Americans, it represents the triumph of brute force over law and civilization, and becomes a major cause of their fear and insecurity.

Postscript

Shortly after Independence Day, 1979, two violent killings were reported in the American press. One was the execution of Carmine Galante, the reputed mafia boss, as he sat at lunch on the patio of a Brooklyn restaurant. The other killing was an old murder in which new evidence had been found: the assassination of President John F. Kennedy, which, according to a special committee in the U.S. House of Representatives, now appeared to have involved the underworld of syndicate crime.

Though Galante seemed to be little more than the latest victim in a long history of syndicate power struggles and ritual rub outs, his death nonetheless proved to be a great occasion for selling newspapers. Seven years had passed since New York's last major gangland slaying; Galante's demise reassured the press that life amongst the hoodlum element continued as it always had. Mob murders at second-rate Italian restaurants have long ranked high among the abiding amusements of the yellow press. But the House Assassination Committee's revelation that Gulf Coast gangsters—some of whom may have worked with the Central Intelligence Agency on Cuban missions to eliminate Fidel Castro—probably had a hand in killing the president was given minimal attention in the newspapers or on television. To be sure, reports of the committee's conclusions had been partially leaked in prior months, and the committee's investigators had always been surrounded by controversy. Yet no major newspaper pursued the report in depth, and nowhere was a press campaign mounted to pursue these new leads in the most notorious murder of the century. The *New York Times,* in its role as the newspaper of record, might have been expected to excerpt the report; instead it chose to solicit from the former legal counsel to the Warren Commission a piece attacking the committee's findings.

Some social critics would suggest that the failure to follow up the sinister implications of an underworld involvement in the Kennedy assassination is evidence of a controlled press. Others have written that after fifteen years the public is simply tired of reading about the case. There may be merit to both positions. However, the differing treatment of the Galante and Kennedy cases raised a problem that reaches to the roots of American culture. To the extent that we perceive crime as an exotic, sometimes glamorous enterprise carried on by social deviants in a mysterious "underworld," we are setting it outside the mainstream of American tradition. Press coverage of the Galante killing—in which reporters spun fantastic tales of gangland conferences, complots, and dinners celebrating the "hit," stories relying on law-enforcement sources which prosecutors themselves discounted—perpetuated the notion of such a mysterious semi-American underworld whose members were only slightly removed from the "greaser" immigrants of the twenties and before.

Such formula journalism is an obvious reflection of the nativist and racial prejudices that ethnics have long suffered in the United States. But it also taps other traditions whose antecedents are found much earlier in the Anglo-American past, conventions as old as the original Puritan settlements of New England, where the existence of a criminal subculture took on a symbolic importance in maintaining public authority. To most Puritan Americans the offenders who paraded through the courts in small but steady numbers were a reminder that the devil was always at work, striving to corrupt men's souls and to spread chaos on earth. Theocratic authorities found it vital to remind the people constantly of the peril they faced if their godly defenses were let down even momentarily. Throughout the course of American history, the size, membership, and activities of the criminal population has changed, as we have shown, in response to the requirements of government authority, to the dictates of powerful individuals both public and private, to changing social mores, and even in response to the ebb and flow of some political movements. To the extent that criminal law is the public code which arbitrates between individual action and state authority, these events of our criminal history seem fairly predictable, be they as bizarre as the Salem and the Scopes trials, as brutal as the western range wars and the Dearborn union attacks, or as diabolically manipulative as the patriots who controlled the revolutionary mobs and the sundry conspirators who managed the Watergate scandals.

Yet beyond the immediate details of criminal activity at any given historical moment there exists a continuing rhetoric about crime which has become a hallmark of American politics. That rhetoric posits an ever present abyss on which we, as a nation, are forever tottering. The Puritans feared that they might fall from the New Jerusalem into the territory of the devil. Throughout much of the nineteenth century one feared that he might fall prey to nature's inherent savagery. Today, it is the threat of degeneration and mob rule—the rule of a savage and uncontrollable mob on the streets and of an insatiably greedy syndicate mob which would corrupt our most hallowed institutions. The rise of mob rule represents the ultimate challenge to the increasingly fragile social contract on which we have based our civilization. At the same time it serves as the justification for abuses of political authority which are an equally dangerous threat to the social contract. Thus, symbolically, the public perception of mob crime in America, complete with the diabolical aura surrounding it, has become part of the ongoing political debate about the decline of public order. Stated plainly: The underworld lurks everywhere within our system, ready to erupt at any moment, and our only protection is the force of law and order. So we read in ghastly detail of the death of Carmine Galante and of the savage scheming of his cohorts. Yet we learn little hard information about the actual power that Mr. Galante and his associates already exert on our institutions and some of our public authorities, and of their consequent ability to shape the destiny of our nation. Fragments of these stories percolate to the surface in occasional official hearings or special reports, but the bulk of the facts remains submerged, feeding our fears and speculations. The incomplete account of the killing of the president will probably remain forever incomplete as gangsters more important than Mr. Galante are killed off and official files are destroyed or sequestered in the interest of national security.

The implications of a Kennedy assassination conspiracy, as indicated by the House Committee's report, should be given prominence in the press, since they suggest that mob crime is endemic to the political process itself. Moreover, to probe the case fully, the public would necessarily be reminded of several myth-shattering facts: that Kennedy came from a family deeply implicated in Prohibition-era bootlegging and apparently involved with liquor syndicates of the twenties and thirties, some of whose members are still alive; that his brother, Attorney General Robert F. Kennedy, and probably John Kennedy as well, knew about—and may have approved—the CIA's use of syndicate killers to advance U.S. foreign policy objectives in Cuba; that a vast hemispheric network of right-wing terrorists grew from the nucleus of syndicate and anti-Castro Cuban vigilantes encouraged by the CIA during the Kennedy years and after; that cooperation between syndicate members and the largest labor union in America, the International Brotherhood of Teamsters, may have included the Kennedy assassination or its cover-up, just as the eventual murder of Teamster boss James Hoffa may have had its source in the Kennedy killing and may have compromised high officials in the administration of Richard Nixon. These and other volatile issues are raised in the House report, although none of them is fully resolved. The immensity of such an investigative task is itself forbidding, for it would require probing the inner workings of some of the most powerful public and private institutions in the United States. Moreover, the very act of investigating presupposes the ubiquity of institutional crime in America and would constitute a contemporary acknowledgment of that force which we have called the sixth estate, the criminal estate. That knowledge, suggesting the true dimensions of the criminal enterprise in the United States today, is the principal fruit of the assassination investigations that have already been undertaken. To pursue them to their conclusions would eliminate forever the sort of exotic mythmaking and journalistic exploitation which surrounded the shooting of Carmine Galante and other such hoodlums, and which disguises how thoroughly the story of crime is tied to the story of America.

Notes

Chapter 1: Harmony vs. Blasphemy

1. John Noble and John F. Cronin, eds., *Records of the Court of Assistants of the Massachusetts Bay Colony, 1630–1692,* vol. II, Boston: 1904, 78 (hereafter *Recs.).* James K. Hosmer, ed., "History of New England, 1630–1649," *Winthrop's Journal,* vol. I, New York: 1908, 282–83.
2. John Winthrop, "A Model of Christian Charity," in Perry Miller, ed., *The American Puritans: Their Prose and Poetry,* New York: 1956, 83.
3. Winthrop, "Speech to the General Court, July 3, 1645," *The American Puritans: Their Prose and Poetry,* New York: 1956, 90–93.
4. *Recs.*, vol. II, 121. Numbers of cases heard before the Court of Assistants are based upon the authors' own tabular analysis of the official records. All criminal cases recorded in the published court minutes for the periods 1630 to 1641 and 1661 to 1673 were divided into seven categories: those involving offenses against public authority, offenses against the church, killings, violence and assault, sexual behavior, property offenses, and miscellaneous.
5. Kai Erikson, *Wayward Puritans: A Study in the Sociology of Deviance,* New York: 1966, 114–37.
6. Erikson, 176–78. The actual number of church-related convictions ran as follows: 1651–56, 0; 1656–60, 86; 1661–65, 171; 1666–70, 101; 1671–75, 4; 1676–80, 2.

7. See *Recs.*, vol. II.
8. Erikson, 180–81.
9. Jules Zanger, "Crime and Punishment in Early Massachusetts," *William and Mary Quarterly* (hereafter *WMQ*), July 1965, 475.
10. *Winthrop's Journal,* vol. I, 52n. *Recs.*, vol. II, 6, 9; Zanger, 476.
11. *Recs.*, vol. II, 80. *Winthrop's Journal,* vol. I, 285–86.
12. *Recs.*, vol. II, 16. *Winthrop's Journal,* vol. I, 64.
13. *Recs.*, vol. II, 18, 21, 34, 41.
14. *Ibid.*, 65, 108, 109.
15. *Ibid.*, 161–63. *Winthrop's Journal,* vol. I, 139.

Chapter 2: Common Bawds and Praying Indians

1. Eric J. Hobsbawm, *Social Bandits and Primitive Rebels,* Glencoe, Ill.: 1959.
2. *Recs.*, vol. III, authors' tabulations.
3. Zachariah Chaffee, ed., "Records of the Suffolk County Court, 1671–80," *Publications of the Colonial Society of Massachusetts,* vol. XXIX, Boston: 1933, 82–83.
4. *Recs.*, vol. III, 226.
5. *Ibid.*, 83–84.
6. Bernard Bailyn, *New England Merchants of the Seventeenth Century,* Cambridge, Mass.: 1955, 86–87.
7. Quoted in Michael Kamen, *Empire and Interest,* New York: 1970, 38.
8. Abbot E. Smith, *Colonists in Bondage,* Gloucester, Mass.: 1965, 26–42.
9. Kammen, 21.
10. Smith, 285–306. Marcus W. Jernegan, *Laboring and Dependent Classes in Colonial America, 1607–1783,* Chicago: 1931, 45–56. Michael Kammen provides a useful discussion of the relation between political and ethnic pluralism and growing class stratification in *People of Paradox,* New York: 1974, chapter 3.
11. Paul Boyer and Stephen Nissenbaum, *Salem Possessed: The Social Origins of Witchcraft,* Cambridge, Mass.: 1974, 90. See also William MacLeod, "Aspects of the Earlier Development of Law and Punishment," *Journal of Criminal Law and Criminology,* vol. XXIII.

12. Francis Jennings, *The Invasion of America,* Chapel Hill, N.C.: 1975, chapter 14; see also 247–48, 250–51. Neal Salisbury, "Red Puritans: The 'Praying Indians' of Massachusetts Bay and John Eliot," *WMQ,* 3d ser., XXXI, 27–54.
13. Quoted in Jennings, 249.
14. Alden T. Vaughan, *New England Frontier: Puritans and Indians, 1620–1675,* Boston: 1965, 212. Vaughan, it should be noted, is very much an apologist for the colonists' viewpoint.
15. *Ibid.,* 234.
16. Wesley F. Craven, *Colonies in Transition,* New York: 1968, chapter 4. Douglas E. Leach, *Flintlock and Tomahawk: New England in King Philip's War,* New York: 1958, chapter 16.
17. John Winthrop, *Winthrop Papers,* Massachusetts Historical Society, vol. V, Boston: 1929, 39.
18. Jennings, 279–80, 285. Richard S. Dunn, "John Winthrop, Jr. and The Narragansett Country," *WMQ,* 3d ser., XII, 68–86. Dunn, *Puritans and Yankees: The Winthrop Dynasty of New England, 1630–1717,* Princeton, N.J.: 1962. George D. Langdon, Jr., *Pilgrim Colony: A History of Plymouth, 1620–1691,* New Haven: 1966, 161–62.
19. For this account and succeeding paragraphs, the authors have relied primarily on Jennings, chapter 16.
20. Jennings, 287. Salisbury, 41. John Easton, "A Relacion of the Indyan Warre," in Charles H. Lincoln, ed., *Narratives of the Indian War, 1675–99,* New York: 1913, 20. Samuel G. Drake, *Biography and History of the Indians of North America from Its First Discovery,* Boston: 1856, 109–10.
21. Leach, 30–31.
22. Jennings, 294–95; Samuel E. Morrison, *Harvard in the Seventeenth Century,* New York: 1936, 220–21, 352–53. John Mason, *A Brief History of the Pequot War,* March of America Facsimile Series, no. 23, Ann Arbor: 1966. Drake, 193–96.
23. Jennings, 295. Leach, *Ibid.* Easton, 7–8.
24. *Ibid.*
25. Jennings, 296.
26. Easton, 12.
27. Edward Ward, *Boston in 1682 and 1699: A Trip to New England,* New York: 1970, 5–9.

Chapter 3: Poor Witches, Prosperous Devils

1. The basic facts of the witchcraft cases are well known and widely available. General background can be found in George L. Kittredge, *Witchcraft in Old and New England,* Cambridge, Mass.: 1929, and Marion L. Starkey, *The Devil in Massachusetts,* New York: 1949. See here Samuel G. Drake, *The Witchcraft Delusion in New England,* vol. III, New York: 1970, 4–11.
2. *Ibid.,* 27–30.
3. *Ibid.,* 65. W. Elliot Woodward, *Records of Salem Witchcraft Copied from the Original Documents,* vol. II, New York: 1969, 115–16.
4. *Ibid.,* 118.
5. Robert Calef, *More Wonders of the Invisible World: Or, the Wonders of the Invisible World Displayed in Five Parts,* in George Lincoln Burr, ed., *Narratives of the Witchcraft Cases, 1648–1706,* New York: 1968, 372–73. Samuel Sewall, *Diary,* Massachusetts Historical Society, *Collections,* 5th ser., 5, Boston: 1878, 367–68.
6. The account here of wealth and status within Salem Village, and particularly of the relative positions of the Putnam and Porter families, relies on the research of Paul Boyer and Stephen Nissenbaum in *Salem Possessed: The Social Origins of Witchcraft,* Cambridge, Mass.: 1974.
7. *Ibid.,* 110–32.
8. *Ibid.*
9. *Ibid.,* 81–92.
10. *Ibid.,* 123–26.
11. *Ibid.,* 45–49. See also Charles W. Upham, *Salem Witchcraft,* vol. I, Salem, Mass.: 1924, 258–69.
12. Boyer and Nissenbaum, 136–43.
13. *Ibid.*
14. *Ibid.,* 35. Upham, map following xvii.
15. Boyer and Nissenbaum, 82–86.
16. *Ibid.,* 131–32; Bailyn, 144–45.
17. For background on executed witches, see Boyer and Nissenbaum, 54–56, 147–49, 192–206. Other accounts can be found under each witch's name in Upham and in Woodward.
18. Edward Ward, *Five Travel Scripts Commonly Attributed to Edward Ward,* New York: 1933, 3–9.

19. Perry Miller, *The Puritans,* vol. I, New York: 1963, 186–87.
20. Cotton Mather, *Memorable Providences, Relating to Witchcraft and Possessions,* Boston: 1689, 1–19; Boyer and Nissenbaum, 23–28.
21. Increase Mather, *Cases of Conscience Concerning Evil Spirits Persecuting Men,* Boston: 1693, 66.
22. Increase Mather, "A Discourse Shewing What Cause There Is to Fear that the Glory of the Lord, is Departing from New-England," 1702, in Ward, *Five Travel Scripts,* xvi–xvii.

Chapter 4: Pirates and Profiteers

1. Shirley H. Hughson, "The Carolina Pirates and Colonial Commerce, 1670–1740," *Johns Hopkins University Studies in History and Political Science,* vol. XII, 9–34. Alexander O. Exquemelin, *The Buccaneers of America,* New York: 1924, part I, 9–79. Lloyd H. Williams, *Pirates of Colonial Virginia,* Richmond, Va.: 1937, 24–26. Herbert L. Osgood, *The American Colonies in the Seventeenth Century,* vol. II, New York: 1904, 221–22. William B. Weeden, *Economic and Social History of New England,* vol. I, New York: 1963, chapter 9, 337–78.
2. Carl Bridenbaugh, *Cities in the Wilderness,* New York: 1938, 177–78, 203–4.
3. Hughson, 12–18.
4. Philip Gosse, *A History of Piracy,* New York: 1932, 141–75. Hughson, 12–18.
5. Exquemelin, 59–60.
6. Gosse, *A Pirate's Who's Who,* Boston: 1924, 293.
7. Hughson, 13–14.
8. For a general discussion of the effect of the Navigation Acts on the colonial economy, see Weeden, vol. I, 232–67. See also Hughson, 17–23; Bridenbaugh, 177; and Charles A. and Mary R. Beard, *The Rise of American Civilization,* New York: 1930.
9. Hughson, 44–49.
10. *Ibid.,* 57–60, 71–72. Osgood, vol. II, 428–31. Craven, 303.
11. Hughson, 59. Osgood, vol. I, chapter XVI, esp. 546–47. Alexander Spotswood, *The Official Letters of Alexander Spotswood, Lieutenant Governor of the Colony of Virginia, 1710–1722,* R.A. Brock, ed., vol. II, Richmond, Va.: 1882, 45.

12. Gosse, *History of Piracy,* 193. Osgood, vol. I, 549–50.
13. Captain Charles Johnson, *A General History of the Robberies and Murders of the Most Notorious Pirates,* New York: 1926, 130–41.
14. *Ibid.,* 205.
15. *Ibid.,* 203. Johnson, 141.
16. Gosse, *A Pirate's Who's Who,* 256, and *History of Piracy,* 203–5. Johnson, 135.
17. Robert E. Lee, *Blackbeard The Pirate: A Reappraisal of His Life and Times,* Winston-Salem, N.C.: 1976, 20–21. Gosse, *A Pirate's Who's Who,* 255–56. Williams, 83–85. Johnson, 5.
18. Gosse, *History of Piracy,* 193. Lee, 11–13. See also Cyrus H. Karraker, *Piracy Was a Business,* Rindge, N.H.: 1953, 134–64. Addison B.C. Whipple, *Private Rascals of the Spanish Main,* New York: 1957, 182–83.
19. Hughson, 70–72. Osgood, *The American Colonies in the Eighteenth Century,* vol. II, New York: 1924, 561–64.
20. Hughson, 74–75. Williams, 100–1. Osgood, *Eighteenth Century,* 548. Lee, 28–30.
21. Hughson, *Ibid.* Williams, 101–4.
22. Hughson, 76–78. Spotswood, 273. Lee, 56–57.
23. Spotswood, 274, 305, 318. Williams, 107–8. Hughson, 76–78. Leonidas Dodson, *Alexander Spotswood,* Philadelphia: 1932, 217–19. Lee, 99–105, 108–12.
24. Williams, 109–12. Lee, 113–26.
25. Lee, 123–25. Osgood, *Eighteenth Century,* 548–49. Hughson, 82–83.
26. Lee, 143–56. "Council Journals," *North Carolina Colonial Records,* vol. II, 343–44, 349, 359. Hughson, 82–83.
27. Osgood, *Eighteenth Century,* 225, 252. Dodson, 282. Lee, 94–97.
28. Weeden, 344–45. Osgood, *Eighteenth Century,* vol. I, 531–32. Edward B. O'Callaghan, ed., *Documents Relative to the Colonial History of the State of New York,* Albany: 1853–57, vol. IV, 307, 459, 480. (Hereafter, *N.Y. Docs.).*
29. *N.Y. Docs.,* 447. See also Thomas J. Archdeacon, "The Age of Leisler—New York City, 1689–1710," in Jacob Judd and Irwin H. Polishook, eds., *Aspects of Early New York Society and Politics,* Tarrytown, N.Y.: 1974.
30. *N.Y. Docs.,* 433–34. Craven, 280–81. For a discussion of class instability and the quest for legitimacy in America during the

Glorious Revolution, see Michael Kammen, *People of Paradox,* chapter 2. Osgood, *Eighteenth Century,* vol. I, chapter 7, especially 253–57.

31. *N.Y. Docs.,* 221. Osgood, *Eighteenth Century,* 228.
32. *N.Y.* Docs., 275.
33. *Ibid.,* 221–24.
34. *Ibid.*
35. *Ibid.,* 307, 447.
36. *Ibid.,* 323, 381, 397. For a general summary see Weeden, 346–48.
37. *N.Y. Docs.,* 389–403.
38. *Ibid.,* 390–91, 323–24.
39. *Ibid.,* 531–37.
40. Weeden, 349–52.
41. *Calendar of State Papers, Colonial Series, American and West Indies, 1700,* London: 1862–1939, 83.
42. Weeden, 366–78.
43. *N.Y. Docs.,* 532, 781–97.

Chapter 5: Counterfeiters and Regulators

1. Bridenbaugh, 220.
2. Samuel Sewell, *Diary,* Massachusetts Historical Society, *Collections,* 5th ser., 5, 93, 189. Bridenbaugh, 229.
3. Bridenbaugh, *Cities in Revolt: Urban Life in America, 1743–1776,* New York: 1955, 112.
4. For additional discussion, see Frederick B. Tolles, *Meeting House and Counting House: The Quaker Merchants of Colonial Philadelphia, 1682–1763,* Chapel Hill, N.C.: 1948, chapters 2 and 3. Gary B. Nash, *Quakers and Politics: Pennsylvania, 1681–1726,* Princeton, N.J.: 1968, Chapter 7, especially 336–43.
5. *Minutes of the Provincial Council of Pennsylvania,* Philadelphia: 1852–53, vol. I, 527, vol. III, 109. Lawrence Gipson, "Crime and Its Punishment in Provincial Pennsylvania," *Lehigh University Publications,* vol. IX, 6–8. Bridenbaugh, *Wilderness,* 221.
6. Gipson, 10–12, 14.
7. Douglas Greenberg, *Crime and Law Enforcement in the Colony of New York, 1691–1776,* Ithaca, N.Y.: 1974, 214–23.
8. *Ibid.,* 54, 223.

9. Bridenbaugh, *Revolt,* 113. Richard B. Morris, *The Encyclopedia of American History,* New York: 1976, 941.
10. Bridenbaugh, *Revolt,* 111.
11. Bridenbaugh, *Ibid.* Richard M. Brown, *The South Carolina Regulators,* Cambridge, Mass.: 1963, 29–32.
12. Kenneth Scott, *Counterfeiting in Colonial America,* New York: 1957, 10.
13. *Ibid.*, 7.
14. *Ibid.*, 219, 186–87.
15. *Ibid.*, 188. Bridenbaugh, *Revolt,* 111. Quoted in Scott, 10.
16. *Ibid.*, 195–96, 202.
17. *Ibid.*, 202–8. Owen Sullivan, "Narrative of the Wicked Life and Surprising Adventures of that Notorious Money Maker and Cheat, Owen Sullivan . . . Hanged in the City of New York May 10, 1756 . . .," *Early American Imprints, 1689–1800,* Worcester, Mass.: 1956, microprint no. 7796.
18. For a discussion of the social and economic background of colonial counterfeiting, see Brown, chapter 1.
19. Ernest Griffith, *History of American City Government: The Colonial Period,* New York: 1972, 389–91. *South Carolina Gazette,* January 25, 1772. *New York Weekly Journal,* August 23, 1736.
20. Brown, 30–35.
21. *Ibid.*, 10.
22. *Ibid.*, 11.
23. *Ibid.*, 27.
24. *Ibid.*, 29–30.
25. *Ibid.*, 31–33.
26. *Ibid.*, 38–39.
27. *Ibid.*, 46.
28. *Ibid.*, 49.
29. *Ibid.*, 52.

Chapter 6: Convicts, Concubines, and Corrupt Officials

1. Bridenbaugh, *Revolt,* 110. Evarts B. Greene and Virginia D. Harrington, *American Population Before the Federal Census of 1790,* Gloucester, Mass.: 1966, 22, 117–18.
2. Jernegan, 47–48.

3. Curtis P. Nettels, *The Roots of American Civilization,* New York: 1938, 398.
4. Jernegan, 48. James Boswell, *Boswell's Life of Johnson, Together with Boswell's Journal . . .,* vol. II, Oxford: 1934–50, 302.
5. Walter H. Blumenthal, *Brides from Brideswell: Female Felons Sent to Colonial America,* Rutland, Vt.: 1962, 17. Richard B. Morris, *Government and Labor in Early America,* New York: 1965, 326. Kammen, *Empire and Interest,* 21. Some other historians have made somewhat smaller estimates. Blumenthal places the figure at 35,000, one-third of whom were women. Fred Wellborn, in *The Growth of American Nationality,* New York: 1943, 67, says 40,000 transported convicts were scattered over Pennsylvania, Maryland, Virginia, and the West Indies.
6. Blumenthal, 19.
7. *Ibid.,* 42.
8. *Ibid.,* 15, 21. Greene and Harrington, 125.
9. Jean Buvat, *Journal de la Régence,* vol. I, Paris: 1865, 441. H.C. Semple, *Ursulines in New Orleans,* New York: 1925, 230.
10. Blumenthal, 58–59.
11. *Virginia Gazette,* May 24, 1751.
12. Smith, *Colonists in Bondage,* 129–33, 227, 265–70. Fairfax Harrison, "When the Criminals Came," *Virginia Magazine of History,* vol. XXX, 250–60. Louis H. Dielman, ed., "Transportation of Felons to the Colonies," *Maryland Historical Magazine,* vol. XXVII, 263–74. J.T. Scharf, *History of Maryland,* vol. II, Baltimore: 1879, 38.
13. Hugh Jones, *The Present State of Virginia,* New York: 1865, 114, 53.
14. Louis Wright, *The Dreams of Prosperity in Colonial America,* New York: 1965, 65.
15. Smith, 246–52, 41. Thomas J. Wertenbaker, *The Planters of Colonial Virginia,* Princeton, N.J.: 1922, 48.
16. Thomas J. Wertenbaker, *Virginia Under the Stuarts, 1607–1688,* Princeton, N.J.: 1958, 146. H.R. McIlwaine, ed., *Minutes of the Council and General Court of Colonial Virginia, 1622–1632, 1670–1676,* Richmond, Va.: 1924, 454–61.
17. Smith, 297–98. Wertenbaker, *Planters,* 80. Philip A. Bruce, *Institutional History of Virginia in the Seventeenth Century,* vol. I, New York: 1910, 424.

18. Bruce, *Institutional History,* vol. II, 360–61.
19. Nettels, 395–96. Wertenbaker, *Planters,* 129–30.
20. Wertenbaker, *Planters,* 129, 150–51.
21. David J. Mays, *Edmund Pendleton, 1721–1803: A Biography,* vol. I, Cambridge, Mass.: 1952, 174–83. The following paragraphs on the Robinson scandal rely on Mays's account.
22. *Ibid.,* 180.
23. *Ibid.,* 186; For further detail see Mays, appendix II, 358–69.
24. *Ibid.,* 175.
25. Quoted in *ibid.,* 178.
26. *Ibid.,* 68, 71–72. Percy Flippin, *The Royal Government in Virginia, 1624–1675,* New York: 1919, 82–83.
27. Forrest McDonald, *E Pluribus Unum: The Formation of the American Republic, 1776–1790,* New York: 1965, 65. See also Robert McColley, *Slavery and Jeffersonian Virginia,* Urbana, Ill.: 1964, 6, and his "Travelers' Impressions of Slavery in America from 1750 to 1800," *Journal of Negro History,* vol. I. Eugene D. Genovese, *Roll, Jordan, Roll,* New York: 1974, 54.
28. Genovese, 58. Peter H. Wood, *Black Majority: Negroes in Colonial South Carolina from 1670 through the Stono Rebellion,* New York: 1974, 240–68.
29. Gerald W. Mullin, *Flight and Rebellion: Slave Resistance in Eighteenth Century Virginia,* New York: 1972, 54–55.
30. *Ibid.,* 57.
31. *Ibid.,* 60–61. Genovese, 599.
32. Genovese, 588.
33. Mullin, 314–16.
34. *Ibid.,* 317, 323–26.

Chapter 7: Smugglers and Conspirators

1. Edmund S. and Helen M. Morgan, *The Stamp Act Crisis,* Chapel Hill, N.C.: 1953, 40–52.
2. Franklin Dexter, ed., *Extracts from the Itineraries and Other Miscellanies of Ezra Stiles,* New Haven: 1916, 204. See Gertrude S. Kimball, ed., *The Correspondence of the Colonial Governors of Rhode Island, 1723–1775,* vol. II, Boston: 1903, 376–81.
3. The episode of the smuggling aboard the *Polly,* similar in most

details to the account given by Morgan, *Stamp Act,* is taken from *Treasury Papers,* class I, bundle 442, Library of Congress transcripts, 211–21.

4. Francis Bernard to Lord Halifax, May 11, 1765, *Bernard Papers,* Harvard College Library, vol. III, 211–15. Morgan, 47.
5. Morgan, *ibid., The Representations of Governor Hutchinson and Others, Contained in Certain Letters Transmitted to England,* Boston: 1773, 53–54.
6. *Newport Mercury,* September 17, 1764, quoted in Morgan, 49. *Providence Gazette,* September 15, 1764. J.R. Bartlett, ed., *Records of the Colony of Rhode Island and Providence Plantations in New England,* vol. VI, Providence, R.I.: 1865, 414.
7. James Otis, *Brief Remarks on the Defense of the Halifax Libel,* Boston: 1765, 5. (On pamphleteering, see also Morgan, 51–52.)
8. The most complete profile of McIntosh is G.P. Anderson, "Ebeneezer McIntosh: Stamp Act Rioter and Patriot," The Colonial Society of Massachusetts, *Publications,* vol. XXVI, Transactions, 1924–26, Boston: 1927, 15–64. See also Dirk Hoerder, *Crowd Action in Revolutionary Massachusetts, 1765–80,* New York: 1977, chapter 4. John Rowe, *Letters and Diary of John Rowe, Boston Merchant, 1759–1762, 1764–1779,* Boston: 1969, especially February 7, 1765, 76.
9. Governor Thomas Hutchinson to Thomas Pownall, March 8, 1766, in "Letterbook," *Massachusetts Archives,* vol. XXVI, 207–14. Suffolk Court Files, Suffolk County (Boston), no. 86536. On the structure, membership, and influence of the Loyal Nine and the later Sons of Liberty, see George P. Anderson, "Pascal Paoli: An Inspiration to the Sons of Liberty," Colonial Society of Massachusetts, *Publications,* vol. XXVI, 180–210. John Adams, *Diary and Autobiography,* vol. I, Lyman H. Butterfield, ed., Cambridge, Mass.: 1961–66, 270–71, 294. See also William Gordon, *The History of the Rise, Progress, and Establishment of the Independence of the United States of America,* vol. I, London: 1788, 175. Morgan, 157–86.
10. Several accounts of the August 14 and 26 riots are available. The clearest and most accessible is Morgan, on which this account is based except for specific additions which are noted below. Samuel Mather to his son, August 17, 1765, in *Letters from the Rev. Samuel*

Mather to His Son, 1759–1785, vol. XVI, Massachusetts Historical Society, Boston Town Records, Boston: 1886 ff., 142.

11. Anderson, "Ebeneezer McIntosh," 29–32.
12. *Massachusetts Archives,* vol. XXVI, 146–47.
13. Thomas Hutchinson, *Diary and Letters,* vol. I, Peter O. Hutchinson, ed., London: 1883–86, 70–71. Hutchinson to Gage, *Bernard Papers,* vol. IV, 62–64.
14. Samuel G. Drake, *History and Antiquities of Boston,* Boston: 1856, 712.
15. Peter Oliver, *Peter Oliver's Origin and Progress of the American Rebellion: A Tory View,* Douglass Adair and John A. Schutz, eds., San Marino, Calif.: 1961, 54. Hutchinson to Pownall, *Massachusetts Archives,* 207–14.
16. For two basic accounts of the *Liberty* incident, see G.G. Wolkins, "Hancock's Sloop *Liberty,*" Massachusetts Historical Society, *Proceedings,* vol. LV, 239–84. W.T. Baxter, *The House of Hancock: Business in Boston, 1724–1775,* Cambridge, Mass.: 1945, 260–68. Also of interest is George Bancroft, *History of the United States,* vol. V, London: 1854, 109–12.
17. Massachusetts Historical Society, *Proceedings,* XLIV, 688–89. Ezra Stiles, "Stamp Act Notebook," *Stiles Papers,* Yale University Library, quoted in Morgan, 239. Henry Laurens to Joseph Brown, October 28, 1765, "Laurens Letter Book," *Historical Society of Pennsylvania.* General Gage to Secretary Comway, December 21, 1765, in Clarence E. Carter, ed., *The Correspondence of General Thomas Gage with the Secretaries of State, 1763–1775,* vol. I, New Haven: 1931, 79.
18. Quoted in Bernard Bailyn, *Pamphlets of the American Revolution, 1750–1776,* vol. I, Cambridge, Mass.: 1965, 86.
19. Quoted in *ibid.,* 85, n. 38.
20. Allan Nevins, *The American States During and After the Revolution, 1775–1789,* New York: 1924, 451–56. Page Smith, *A New Age Begins: A People's History of the American Revolution,* New York: 1976, 712–13.
21. See, for example, John D. Cushing, "The Judiciary and Public Opinion in Revolutionary Massachusetts," in George A. Billias, ed., *Law and Authority in Colonial America,* Barre, Mass.: 1965. Page Smith, 670.

22. "Letters of Jonathan Sewell," Massachusetts Historical Society, *Proceedings,* 2nd ser., vol. X, 414.
23. William H. Nelson, *The American Tory,* London: 1961, 148–49.
24. Hector St. John de Crèvecoeur, *Sketches of Eighteenth Century America,* New Haven: 1925, 178–79. Also see Merrill Jensen, "Historians and the Nature of the American Revolution," in Ray A. Billington, ed., *The Reinterpretation of Early American History,* San Marino, Calif.: 1966.

Chapter 8: Poverty, Property, and Prisons

1. See Robert H. Bremner, *From the Depths: The Discovery of Poverty in the United States,* New York: 1956.
2. William Bradford, *An Enquiry How far the Punishment of Death Is Necessary in Pennsylvania,* Philadelphia: 1793, 43. Cesare Beccaria, *On Crimes and Punishments,* Henry Paolucci, tr., Indianapolis: 1963, 43–45, 58–60.
3. See David Rothman, *The Discovery of the Asylum,* Boston: 1971, chapter 4. Orlando Lewis, *The Development of American Prisons,* Albany, N.Y.: 1922. David B. Davis, "The Movement to Abolish Capital Punishment in America, 1787–1861," *American Historical Review,* no. 63, 1957, 23–46.
4. Data relating to Middlesex drawn from William E. Nelson, "Emerging Notions of Modern Criminal Law in the Revolutionary Era: An Historical Perspective," *New York University Law Review,* vol. XLII, 450–82.
5. For a discussion of Federalist attitudes toward private property, see chapter 10, in Bernard Bailyn *et al., The Great Republic,* Boston: 1976.
6. For a rich account of the commercial free-for-all see McDonald, *E Pluribus Unum.*
7. Beard, *The Rise of American Civilization,* 321 and chapter 7 generally.
8. John Adams, *Diary and Autobiography of John Adams,* Cambridge, Mass.: 1961, 260.
9. Quoted in Edwin Powers, *Crime and Punishment in Early Massachusetts,* Boston: 1966, 192–93.
10. Quoted in Nelson, 477.

11. (No author), *The Record of Crimes in the United States,* Buffalo: 1833, 158–201.
12. Quoted in Bailyn *et al.*, 390–95.
13. Bremner, 3–4.
14. Rothman, 94. Charles Christian, *The Police of the City of New York,* New York: 1970, 8. W. David Lewis, *From Newgate to Dannemora,* Ithaca: 1965, 62.
15. Christian, 16.
16. Gustave de Beaumont and Alexis de Tocqueville, *On the Penitentiary System in the United States,* Carbondale, Ill.: 1964, 123. David B. Davis, *Homicide in American Fiction, 1798–1860,* Ithaca: 1957, 155–60, xiii–xv.
17. W. David Lewis, "The Female Criminal and the Prisons of New York, 1825–1845," *New York History,* vol. XLII, 1961, 215–36.
18. Rothman and Lewis offer useful discussions of the competition between the two systems.
19. For a contemporary treatment of modern women's prisons, see Katherine Burkhart, *Women in Prison,* New York: 1973.
20. Lewis, "The Female Criminal," 221–30. J. Thomas Scharf, *History of Westchester County, New York,* vol. II, Philadelphia: 1886, 349.
21. Lewis, "The Female Criminal," 229.
22. State of New York, *Assembly Documents,* 70th session, vol. III, no. 255, part 2, 58–61, quoted in *ibid.,* 231.
23. *Ibid.* Also State of New York, *Senate Documents,* 67th session, vol. I, no. 20, 34.
24. George W. Smith, *A Defense of the System of Solitary Confinement of Prisoners,* Philadelphia: 1833, 71. Boston Prison Discipline Society, 4th *Annual Report,* 54–55. James B. Finley, *Memorials of Prison Life,* Cincinnati: 1851, 41–42. Gershom Powers, *Letters of Gershom Powers, Esq.,* Albany, N.Y.: 1829, 14. Beaumont and Tocqueville, 23.

Chapter 9: Gangs, Goons, and Ward Heelers

1. Most of the description of Five Points life in lower New York follows the account of Herbert Ashbury, *The Gangs of New York,*

New York: 1927, chapters 1 and 2. See also James Richardson, *The New York Police,* New York: 1970, chapter 1.

2. Asbury, 6.
3. Charles Dickens, *American Notes,* London: 1842, quoted in *ibid.*
4. General R. Wolfe, New York: *A Guide to the Metropolis,* New York: 1975, 73.
5. Quoted in Bremner, 5–6.
6. Asbury, 28–37. Paul Dolan, "The Rise of Crime in the Period 1830–1860," *Journal of Criminal Law,* vol. XXX, 859–61.
7. *Ibid.*
8. *Ibid.*, 47–49.
9. *Ibid.*, 52.
10. *Ibid.*, 65–69.
11. *Ibid.*
12. Richardson, 28–30. David Grimsted, "Rioting in Its Jacksonian Setting," *American Historical Review,* vol. LXXVII, 361–77.
13. Richardson, 28–30.
14. *Ibid.*, Asbury, 39–40.
15. Asbury, 38. *Documents of the Board of Aldermen of the City of New York,* vol. I, no. 17, 145–50; vol. II, no. 1, 12–13.
16. Asbury, 43–44. Richardson, 36. *Proceedings and Documents of the Board of Assistant Aldermen of the City of New York,* vol. XIX, no. 56, 192–93. *Documents of the Board of Aldermen of the City of New York,* vol. X, part 1, no. 53, 793–94.
17. Grimsted, 363–64. Philadelphia *National Gazette,* August 11, 1835.
18. Quoted in Grimsted, 365. Francis Grund, *The Americans in Their Moral, Social and Political Relations,* Boston: 1837, 180.
19. Details presented here follow Grimsted, 376–82.
20. Quoted in Grimsted, 382.
21. *Ibid.*
22. Francis Bowen, "The Independence of the Judiciary," *North American Review,* October 1843, 420.
23. See P.W. Grayson, *Vice Unmasked, An Essay: Being a Consideration of the Influence of Law on the Moral Essence of Man,* New York: 1830, especially 165 ff.
24. See discussion in Arthur Schlesinger, Jr., *The Age of Jackson,* New York: 1945, chapter 15.

25. Francis Lieber, *Manual of Political Ethics,* vol. II, Boston: 1838, 348.
26. Schlesinger, 194–95.
27. *New York Evening Post,* June 13, 1836.
28. Andrew Neilly, "The Violent Volunteers: A History of the Volunteer Fire Department of Philadelphia, 1730–1831," Ph.D. dissertation, University of Pennsylvania, 1960.
29. Frank O. Gatell, "Roger B. Taney, the Bank of Maryland and a Whiff of Grapeshot," *Maryland Historical Magazine,* vol. LIX, 262–67.
30. Roger Lane, *Policing the City: Boston, 1822–1885,* Cambridge, Mass.: 1967, 26–38.
31. Richardson, 32–36.
32. *Ibid.,* 37–38. William K. Wimsatt, Jr., "Poe and the Mystery of Mary Rogers," *Publications of the Modern Language Association of America,* vol. LVI, 230–48. *New York Herald,* August 11, 12, 1841.
33. Quoted in Richardson, 26. *Proceedings and Documents of the Board of Assistant Aldermen of the City of New York,* vol. XIX, 188.
34. Richardson, 37–38.
35. *Ibid.*
36. See generally, Richardson, chapters 3 and 4.
37. *Ibid.,* 56–57, 62–63. "Quarterly Report of the Police Captain of the Tenth Patrol District, October 1, 1850," *New York Municipal Archives, Valentine's Manual,* New York: 1848, 69–71.
38. See Robert Ernst, "The One and Only Mike Walsh," *The New York Historical Society Quarterly,* vol. XXXVI, January 1952.
39. See summary of charges in Richardson, 69–72. See also *New York Tribune,* March 24, April 10, 1851.
40. *New York Times,* April 18, 1857.
41. Robert Ernst, *Immigrant Life in New York City, 1825–1863,* New York: 1949, 191–93. Charles Loring Brace, *The Dangerous Classes of New York,* New York: 1872. Richardson, 52–53.
42. Richardson, 100–7.

Chapter 10: Desperation on the Borderlands

1. Of the many modern works in Jacksonian history, the following

were the most useful in the preparation of this chapter: Marvin Meyers, *The Jacksonian Persuasion,* Stanford, Calif.: 1957. Edward Pessen, *Riches, Class and Power before the Civil War,* New York: 1973. Stephan Thernstrom, *Poverty and Progress,* New York: 1964. Rowland Berthoff, *An Unsettled People: Social Order and Disorder in American History,* New York: 1971.

2. Alexis de Tocqueville, *Democracy in America,* vol. II, New York: 1946, 136.
3. Daniel Boorstin, *The Americans: The National Experience,* New York: 1965, 119.
4. Louis C. Jones, "The Crime and Punishment of Stephen Arnold," *New York History,* July 1966, provides the basis for this account.
5. *Ibid.,* 251.
6. *Ibid.*
7. *Ibid.,* 252–54.
8. *Ibid.,* 257–59.
9. *Ibid.,* 261–62.
10. *Ibid.,* 263.
11. *Ibid.,* 265.
12. *Ibid.,* 268.
13. Consider, for example, the portrait of the Puritan attitude toward nature in the stories Nathaniel Hawthorne was writing during the romantic era, particularly his classic short story, "Young Goodman Brown."
14. Jones, 265.
15. Richard Slotkin, *Regeneration Through Violence: The Mythology of the American Frontier, 1600–1860,* Middletown, Conn.: 1973, 394–465.
16. Otto Rothert, *Outlaws of Cave-in-Rock,* Cleveland: 1924, 59–60.
17. *Ibid.,* 60–64.
18. *Ibid.*
19. *Ibid.,* 110–13.
20. *Ibid.*
21. John C. Parrish, "White Beans for Hanging," *Palimpsest,* vol. I, no. 1, 9–28.
22. See Meyers, *ibid.,* and Berthoff, chapter 4.
23. Edwin C. McReynolds, *The Seminoles,* Norman, Okla.: 1957, chapter 3.
24. Herbert Aptheker, "Maroons within the Present Limits of the

United States," *Journal of Negro History,* vol. XXIV, 167–84.

25. *Ibid.*
26. McReynolds, 79.
27. *Ibid.*, 81–82.
28. *Ibid.*
29. Bailyn *et al.*, 383.
30. Beard, *Rise of American Civilization,* chapter 12.
31. See Edwin A. Miles, *Jacksonian Democracy in Mississippi,* Chapel Hill, N.C.: 1960. Bailyn *et al.*, 598–99, 555, 630–32.

Chapter 11: The Crimes of Slave Power

1. John Lofton, *Insurrection in South Carolina: The Turbulent World of Denmark Vesey,* Yellow Springs, Ohio: 1964, 131–56. Genovese, 411, 494, 559, 588, 593–97. See also Robert S. Starobin, ed., *Denmark Vesey: The Slave Conspiracy of 1822,* New York: 1970. For the view that no conspiracy existed, see Richard Wade, "The Vesey Plot: A Reconsideration," *Journal of Southern History,* vol. XXX, 148–61.
2. See Clement Eaton, "Mob Violence in the Old South," *Mississippi Valley Historical Review,* vol. XXIX, 351–70. Miles, chapter 9; and "Mississippi Slave Insurrection Scare of 1835," *Journal of Negro History,* vol. XLII, 48–60. Herbert Aptheker, *American Negro Slave Revolts,* New York: 1943, chapter 13. H. R. Howard (comp.), *The History of Virgil A. Stewart,* Spartanburg, S.C.: 1976.
3. *Alexandria Gazette,* August 29, 1835. Eaton, 358–59.
4. Miles, *Jacksonian Democracy,* 5–6, 55–57. Natchez *Mississippi State Gazette,* June 2, 1819. Eaton to John Pitchlynn, August 5, 1830, *Andrew Jackson Papers,* Library of Congress, Washington, D.C.
5. Miles, *Jacksonian Democracy,* 87, 93.
6. *Ibid.*, 123–27.
7. *Ibid.* Natchez *Free Trader,* October 29, 1835. See Coates, especially parts 3 and 4, and Rothbert, 179–241. See, for example, the following newspapers during the summer of 1835: *Southern Argus* (Columbus), *The Mississippian* (Jackson, Miss.), *The Enquirer* (Richmond, Va.), and the *U.S. Telegraph* (Washington D.C.).
8. Coates, 175–78, 206–7.

9. Coates, 251–54, 257–71. Miles, "Mississippi Slave Isurrection Scare," 48–49. Howard, 116–26.
10. Quoted in Coates, 281.
11. Miles, *ibid. Mississippian,* March 14, 1834.
12. Coates, 282–83. Howard, 223–32.
13. Quoted in Miles, *ibid.*, 54–55.
14. See the Raleigh, N.C. *Register,* August 4, 1835. *U.S. Telegraph,* September 24, 1835.
15. Eaton, 358. Raleigh *Register,* August 25, 1835.
16. Eaton, 355–58.

Chapter 12: The Crimes of Crime Prevention

1. "The Progress of Society," *The United States Magazine and Democratic Review,* July 1840, 87. *Washington Union,* June 2, 1845. *Congressional Globe,* 28th Cong. 2nd Sess., 1844, appendix, 68, and 1st Sess., 1844, 380. *New York Morning News,* December 27, 1845. For the religious justification of Manifest Destiny, see Kenneth M. MacKenzie, *The Robe and the Sword: The Methodist Church and the Rise of American Imperialism,* Washington: 1961.
2. *Congressional Globe,* 28th Cong. 2nd Sess., 1845, appendix, 178, and 29th Cong., 2nd Sess., 1847, appendix, 215. Buchanan to General James Shields, April 23, 1847, "Buchanan Papers," Historical Society of Pennsylvania. *Democratic Review,* March 1847. *American Review,* March 1847.
3. See Norman Graebner, ed., *Manifest Destiny,* New York: 1968. Julius W. Pratt, "The Origins of Manifest Destiny," *American Historical Review,* July 1927, 795–98.
4. John Gerassi, *The Great Fear in Latin America,* New York: 1965, 228–29.
5. See David M. Potter, *The Impending Crisis, 1848–1861,* New York: 1976. J.H. Smith, *The War with Mexico,* vols. I and II, New York: 1919.
6. See Allan Nevins, *The Emergence of Lincoln,* vols. I and II, New York: 1950. Don E. Fehrenbacher, *The Dred Scott Case: Its Significance in American Law and Politics,* New York: 1978. Paul M. Angle, ed., *Created Equal? The Complete Lincoln-Douglas Debates of 1858,* Chicago: 1958.

7. See C. Vann Woodward, *The Burden of Southern History,* Baton Rouge, La.: 1960. Louis Ruchames, ed., *John Brown: The Making of a Revolutionary,* New York: 1964.
8. Mari Sandoz, *Crazy Horse,* New York: 1942, 5–6, 21–35, 45–127. Thomas Berger, *Little Big Man,* New York: 1964, 336–38. Grace Hebard, *Washakie,* Cleveland: 1930. Mari Sandoz, *The Battle of Little Big Horn,* New York: 1966. Douglas E. Branch, *The Hunting of the Buffalo,* Lincoln, Neb.: 1962, 130. Wayne Gard, *The Great Buffalo Hunt,* Lincoln, Neb. 1968, 390.
9. Joseph G. Rosa, *The Gunfighter: Man or Myth?,* Norman, Okla.: 1969, 19. Alexandre Barde, *Histoire des comités de vigilance aux Attakapas,* Saint-Jean-Baptiste, La.: 1861. Richard Maxwell Brown, "American Vigilante Tradition," in Hugh Davis Graham and Ted Robert Gurr, eds., *Violence in America,* New York: 1969, 218–26. T.R. Fehrenback, *Lone Star: A History of Texas and the Texans,* New York: 1968, 338.
10. Anthony S. Nicolisi, "The Rise and Fall of the New Jersey Vigilante Societies," *New Jersey History,* 1968, no. 86, 29–53.
11. Josiah Royce, *California,* New York: 1948, 368–77.
12. Mary Floyd Williams, *History of the San Francisco Committee of Vigilance of 1851,* Berkeley: 1921, 105–7. See also Alan C. Valentine, *Vigilante Justice,* New York: 1956.
13. Valentine, appendix, 441–53.
14. *Ibid.,* 403–5.
15. *Ibid.,* 291–92.

Chapter 13: The Price and Profit of War

1. Philip D. Jordan, "The Capital of Crime," *Civil War Times Illustrated,* vol. XIII, no. 10, 4–9, 44–47.
2. Fred Nicklason, "Civil War Contracts Committee," *Civil War History,* vol. XVII, No. 3, 232–44. See also Brooks M. Kelley, "Simon Cameron and the Senatorial Nomination of 1867," *Pennsylvania Magazine of History and Biography,* vol. XXCVII, no. 4, 375–92.
3. Frank L. Byrne, "A Terrible Machine: General Neal Dow's Military Government on the Gulf Coast," *Civil War History,* vol. XII, no. 1, 5–52. Richard W. Griffin, "Cotton Frauds and

Confiscations in Alabama, 1863–1866," *The Alabama Review,* vol. VII, no. 4, 265–76.

4. Donald P. Spear, "The Sutler in the Union Army," *Civil War History,* vol. XVI, no. 2, 121–38.
5. Elizabeth Joan Doyle, "Greenbacks, Car Tickets, and the Pot of Gold: The Effects of Wartime Occupation on the Business Life in New Orleans, 1861–65," *Civil War History,* vol. V, no. 4, 347–62.
6. Doyle, "New Orleans Courts under Military Occupation, 1861–65," *Mid-America,* vol. XLII, no. 3, 185–92. Philip D. Uzee, "The Beginnings of the Louisiana Republican Party," *Louisiana History,* vol. XII, no. 3, 197–211. Doyle, "Rottenness in Every Direction: The Stokes Investigation in Civil War New Orleans," *Civil War History,* vol. XVIII, no. 1, 24–41.
7. David Herbert Donald, "Uniting the Republic, 1860–1890," in Bailyn *et al.*, 659, 700–1, 704–5, 709.
8. Hon. J.T. Headley, *The Great Riots of New York, 1712 to 1873,* New York: 1873, reprinted Miami: 1969, 169–277. Irving J. Sloan, *Our Violent Past: An American Chronicle,* New York: 1970, 29–33. Headley claims that the death toll was 1,200. But Sloan, who puts it at 1,500 whites, points out that black deaths were not counted. Between 1860 and 1865, the black population in New York City dropped from 12,472 to 9,945. See also Adrian Cook, *Armies of the Street,* Lexington, Ky.: 1974.
9. Eugene C. Murdock, "New York Civil War Bounty Brokers," *Journal of American History,* vol. LIII, no. 2, 259–78. See also his *One Million Men: The Civil War Draft in the North,* Madison, Wisc.: 1971.
10. *The Laws of the State of Kansas,* 1863, 50.
11. Albert Cartel, "The Jayhawkers and Copperheads of Kansas," *Civil War History,* vol. V, no. 3, 283–93. Rosa, 37. John N. Edwards, *Noted Guerrillas: Warfare of the Border,* Dayton, Ohio: 1975, 37.
12. William E. Sawyer, "The Martin Hart Conspiracy," *Arkansas Historical Quarterly,* vol. XXIII, no. 2, 154–65.
13. Williams, 417–20.
14. Rosa, 51. Jay Robert Nash, *Bloodletters and Badmen,* New York: 1973, 506–8. Mark Twain, *Roughing It,* San Francisco and Hartford: 1872. T.J. Dimsdale, *The Vigilantes of Montana,* Virginia City, Mont.: 2nd ed., 1882.

15. See David Balsiger and Charles E. Sellier, Jr., *The Lincoln Conspiracy,* Los Angeles: 1977. David E. Herold, *The Conspiracy Trial for the Murder of the President,* New York: 1972. Louis J. Weichmann, *A True History of the Assassination of Abraham Lincoln,* New York: 1975.

Chapter 14: White Terror and "Honest Graft"

1. Matthew Josephson, *The Politicos, 1865–1896,* New York: 1963, 127.
2. See entry under "Summer, Charles" in *The Columbia Encyclopedia,* New York: 2nd ed., 1950, 1916.
3. Bailyn *et al.,* 735.
4. *Ibid.,* 738, 741.
5. *Ibid.,* 743.
6. Warren Hoffnagle, "The Southern Homestead Act: Its Origins and Operation," *The Historian,* vol. XXXII, no. 4, 612–29. Bailyn *et al.,* 763.
7. Bailyn *et al.,* 760–61, 811.
8. Joe M. Richardson, ed., "The Memphis Race Riot and Its Aftermath" (Report by a Northern missionary), *Tennessee Historical Quarterly,* vol. XXIV, no. 1, 63–64. John A. Carpenter, "Atrocities in Reconstruction Period," *Journal of Negro History,* vol. XLVII, no. 4, 242. "Reports on the Select Committee on the New Orleans Riots," *House Reports,* 39 Cong. 2nd Sess., no. 16. Donald E. Reynolds, "The New Orleans Riot of 1866 Reconsidered," *Louisiana History,* vol. V, no. 1, 5–27.
9. Jules Archer, *Riot! A History of Mob Action in the United States,* New York: 1974, 74. Richard Hofstadter and Michael Wallace, eds., *American Violence: A Documentary History,* New York: 1970, 101–08.
10. Carpenter, 245. Archer, 76. Hofstadter, 224, 223, 234.
11. U.S. Congress, Joint Select Committee on Condition of Affairs in the Late Insurrectionary States, *House Reports* 22, 42nd Cong. 2nd Sess., 13 vols, vol. XIII. Ralph L. Peek, "Lawlessness in Florida, 1868–71," *Florida Historical Quarterly,* vol. XL, no. 2, 164–85.
12. Thomas B. Alexander, "Kukluxism in Tennessee, 1865–1869," *Tennessee Historical Quarterly,* vol. VIII, no. 3, 195–219. Archer,

74–75. Stanley F. Horn, *Invisible Empire: The Story of the Ku Klux Klan,* Cos Cob, Conn.: 1969, 198–99. Allen W. Trelease, *White Terror: The Ku Klux Klan Conspiracy and Southern Reconstruction,* New York: 1971, 226–46.

13. Trelease, 229–30, 233–36, 240–41.
14. John H. Franklin, *From Slavery to Freedom,* New York: 1947, 431.
15. Bailyn *et al.*, 742–43.
16. Meade Minnigerode, *Certain Rich Men,* New York: 1927, 103–33. *Congressional Globe,* 37th Cong., Jan. 29, 1863. *Senate Report 75,* 37th Cong. 1863. Sidney Lens, *Labor Wars: From the Molly Maguires to the Sitdowns,* New York: 1973, 35.
17. Lens, 5. Minnigerode, 146. Richard O. Boyer and Cameron M. Herbert, *Labor's Untold Story,* New York: 1955, 72, 77, 39, 40–45, 77. Richard O'Connor, *Iron Wheels & Broken Men,* New York: 1973, 144–49, 183–88, 192–93, 282–86. See also his *Gould's Millions,* New York: 1962. Edwin P. Hoyt, *The Goulds: A Social History,* New York: 1962. Julius Grodinsky, *Jay Gould, 1867–1892,* Philadelphia: 1957.
18. "Government Contracts," *House Report, No. 2,* 37th Cong., 2nd Sess., 1862. Boyer, 73. Lens, 5. Henrietta M. Larson, *Jay Cooke, Private Banker,* Cambridge, Mass.: 1936, 85–86, 383–411. Harry Stack, *The Jay Cooke Story,* Sandusky, Ohio: 1948, 9–13. Ray Ginger, *Age of Excess: The United States from 1877 to 1914,* New York: 1975, 219–21, 225–27, 236–37.
19. Boyer, 73–75. Peter d'A. Jones, ed., *The Robber Barons Revisited,* Boston: 1968, 47–56. John Moody, *The Truth About the Trusts,* New York: 1904, 490–93. Ida M. Tarbell, *The History of Standard Oil Company,* New York: 1933, 158–61. Ginger, 31.
20. Boyer, 79. Jeremy Brecher, *Strike!,* San Francisco: 1972, xiv. Abby L. Gilbert, "The Comptroller of the Currency and the Freedman's Saving Bank," *Journal of Negro History,* vol. LVII, no. 2, 125–43. Cheryl Freeman, "Wanted: The Honorable William H. Cushman, *The Colorado Magazine,* vol. XLIX, no. 1, 35–54. Jones, xiv. Henry Demarest Lloyd, *Wealth Against Commonwealth,* New York: 1894, 11–15.
21. Jones, 109. Boyer, 76.
22. Bailyn *et al.*, 874, 872. Beard, 7. Paul Wallace Gates, "Federal Land Policy in the South, 1866–1888," *Journal of Southern History,* vol. VI, no. 3, 303–30. Brecher, xiii.
23. E.P. Oberholtzer, *Jay Cooke, Financier of the Civil War,* vol. II,

Philadelphia, Pa.: 1907, 28. Gideon Welles, *Diary,* Boston: 1911, vol. III, 425–26, 474, vol. II, 548–49.

24. B.P. Poore, *Perley's Reminiscences of Sixty Years in the National Metropolis,* Philadelphia: 1886–87, vol. II, 218. Elihu B. Washburne Papers, Library of Congress, "Chandler to Washburne," October 19, 1968. J.F. Rhodes, *History of the United States from the Compromise of 1850,* vol. IV, New York: 1893–1925, 533.
25. Josephson, 61–99.
26. Allan Nevins, *Hamilton Fish: The Inner History of the Great Administration,* New York: 1936, 184. *Congressional Record,* 44th Cong., 1st Sess., vol. IV, pt. 7, (Belknap Trial). Nevins, 285. Larson, 269. R.L. Caldwell, *James A. Garfield: Party Chieftain,* New York: 1931, 241. U.S. Congress, Senate, 43rd Cong., 1st Sess., *Report No. 453,* vol. II, 1075.
27. Nevins, 466. Lens, 37–38. O'Connor, 89–92. Caldwell, 221–30. Stephen E. Ambrose, "Blaine vs. Cleveland," *American History Illustrated,* vol. I, no. 6, 32–40.
28. John McDonald, *Secrets of the Great Whiskey Ring,* St. Louis: 1880, 47, 114–20, 35, 17–18, 51. Albert S. Bolles, *The Financial History of the United States, 1861–1885,* New York: 1886, 400–42. *Whisky Frauds Report,* U.S. Congress, House of Representatives, 44th Cong., 1st Sess., Doc. 186, 3, 6, 3, 11, 33, 353, 355, 369–72. W.B. Hesseltine, *Ulysses S. Grant: Politician,* New York: 1935, 208, 379–80, 337. *Whisky Frauds,* 5–6, 11, 30, 355, 369, 399. Ulysses S. Grant Papers and Letterbooks, Library of Congress, Grant to Pierrepont, July 17, 1875. Nevins, 797. Henry Adams, *Letters, 1858–1891,* W.C. Ford, ed., Boston: 1930, 288.
29. Horace White, *The Life of Lyman Trumbull,* Boston: 1913, 341. De A.S. Alexander, *A Political History of the State of New York,* vol. III, New York: 1906–23, 274–75, 340–41.
30. Alexander Clarence Flick, *Samuel Jones Tilden: A Study in The Hayes-Tilden Disputed Presidential Election of 1876,* Cleveland: 1906, 90–145. Jerrell H. Shofner, "Fraud and Intimidation in the Florida Election of 1876," *The Florida Historical Quarterly,* vol. XLII, no. 4, 321–30. C.R. Williams, *The Life of Rutherford Birchard Hayes,* vol. I, Boston: 1914, 481. John Bigelow, *The Life of Samuel J. Tilden,* vol. II, New York: 1895, 12, 13, 17, 95. U.S. Congress, House of Representatives, 44th Cong., 2nd Sess., *Miscellaneous Documents,* 138, 144–45.

Chapter 15: Law vs. Justice

1. *Eighth Annual Report of the North Carolina Bureau of Labor Statistics,* 1894, 257. Blake McKelvey, "The Prison Labor Problem," *Journal of Criminal Law and Criminology,* vol. XXV, no. 2, 254–70.
2. Edward King, *Texas 1874: An Eyewitness Account of the Conditions in Post-Reconstruction Texas,* Houston: 1974, 41, 46. James Taylor Dunn, "The Minnesota State Prison During the Stillwater Era, 1853–1914," *Minnesota History,* vol. XXXVII, no. 4, 137–51.
3. A.C. Hutson, "The Overthrow of the Convict Lease System in Tennessee," *The East Tennessee Historical Society's Publications,* 1936, no. 8, 82–102.
4. C.K. Yearly, Jr., *Enterprise and Anthracite: Economics and Democracy in Schuylkill County, 1820–1875,* Baltimore: 1961, 176–77. Lens, 19–21.
5. Lens, 14.
6. Wayne G. Broehl, Jr., *The Molly Trials,* Cambridge, Mass.: 1964, 122–23, 126–27, 75, 27–28, 86. Anthony Bimba, *The Molly Maguires,* New York: 1932, 10. Allan Pinkerton, *The Mollie Maguires and the Detectives,* New York: 1973, 13–16.
7. Broehl, 131–36. Pinkerton, 16. Lens, 22.
8. Bimba, 55–69. Marvin Wilson Schlegel, *Franklin B. Gowen: Ruler of the Reading, 1836–1889,* Harrisburg, Pa.: 1947, 65–70. Lens, 23–24.
9. Broehl, 146–49, 274–307, 340. Pinkerton, 24, 552. Lens, 23, 27–28. Boyer, 51. (Both Lens and Boyer say McParlan was born in 1847.) Schlegel, 84. J. Walter Coleman, *The Molly Maguire Riots,* New York: 1969, 119, 157. Bimba, 88, 101, 115, 124.
10. Broehl, 347. Schlegel, 286–87.
11. Boyer, 63. Brecher, 1–5. Lens, 31–33. Barton C. Hacker, "The United States Army as a National Police Force: The Federal Policing of Labor Disputes, 1877–1898," *Military Affairs,* vols. XXXII/XXXIII, 255–65. Richard B. Morris, "Andrew Jackson, Strikebreaker," *American Historical Review,* vol. LV, 54–68. John L. Blackman, Jr., *Presidential Seizure in Labor Disputes,* Cambridge, Mass.: 1967, 5–6, 315.
12. Brecher, 10–21. Lens, 33–34. Hofstadter, 345–47. Herbert G. Gutman, "The Tompkins Square 'Riot' in New York City on

January 13, 1874: A Re-Examination of Its Causes and Its Aftermath," *Labor History,* winter, 1965, 44–70.

13. Allan Pinkerton, *Strikes, Communists, Tramps and Detectives,* New York: 1969, 79, 95–96, 80, 47, 30.
14. Lens, 40. Robert V. Bruce, *1877, Year of Violence,* Indianapolis: 1959, 20–21.
15. Samuel Crothers Logan, *A City's Danger & Defense, or Issues & Results of the Strikes of 1877 Containing the Origin & History of the Scranton City Guard,* Scranton: Penn.: 1887, 55–103, 132–54.
16. George B. Stichter, "Documents and Eye-Witness Accounts," *The Schuylkill County Soldiery in the Industrial Disturbances in 1877, or the Railroad Riot War,* Schuylkill County Historical Society: 1907, 193–215.
17. Lens, 56–57. Brecher, 28, 31–32, 34, 39.
18. Lens, 59, 62. Boyer, 93–94. Corine J. Naden, *The Haymarket Affair—Chicago, 1886,* New York: 1968, 12–17.
19. Brecher, 46. Lens, 63–64. Boyer, 101–2. Naden, 18–19.
20. Naden, 29–50. Boyer, 102–3. Lens, 64–65.
21. *Ibid.,* 69–72. Brecher, 53–62. Boyer, 132. John K. Winkler, *Incredible Carnegie,* New York: 1931, 132, 144, 166, 18.
22. Lens, 113–15, 122. Brecher, 63–64.
23. Lens, 117–19.
24. Brecher, 80, 78, 81–93. Lens, 90, 80–83, 86, 92–109. Colston E. Warne, ed., *The Pullman Boycott of 1884: The Problem of Federal Intervention,* Boston: 1955, 26–28 63–72.
25. Victor R. Greene, *The Slavic Community on Strike: Immigrant Labor in Pennsylvania Anthracite,* South Bend, Ind.: 1968, 130–42. Michael Novack, *The Guns of Lattimer,* New York: 1978, 1–276.
26. Bailyn *et al.,* 945, 973, 975, 856, 860.
27. Lens, 151–52.
28. *Ibid.,* 153–54.
29. *Ibid.,* 155–68.
30. *Ibid.,* 169–86. Donald B. Cole, *Immigrant City: Lawrence, Massachusetts, 1845–1921,* Chapel Hill, N.C.: 1963, 178–88. Boyer, 175. Patrick Renshaw, *The Wobblies,* New York: 1967, 133–56.
31. Lens, 188.
32. Renshaw, 187–212.
33. *Ibid.,* 215–47.

34. *Ibid.*, 238–39. Stanley Coben, *A. Mitchell Palmer: Politician,* New York: 1963, 232–34.

Chapter 16: Family Feuds, Cattle Wars, and Gunslingers

1. Albert Castell, "The Bloodiest Man in American History," *American Heritage,* October 1960, 22–24, 97–99. W.E. Connelley, *Quantrill and the Border Wars,* Cedar Rapids: 1910, 43–44, 122–27. Robertus Love, *The Rise and Fall of Jesse James,* New York: 1926, 17–19, 22–24. Lawrence D. Bailey, *Quantrill's Raid on Lawrence,* pamphlet published by Bailey: 1887, reprinted by Kansas State Historical Society: 1899, 52 pages.
2. Robert W. Shook, "The Federal Military in Texas, 1865–1870," *Texas Military History,* spring 1967, 19–20. Otis A. Singletary, *Negro Militia and Reconstruction,* Austin: 1957, 9. *House Executive Documents,* 40th Cong., 2nd Sess., no. 1, 470–73. "Report of the Secretary of War, 1868–1869," *Report of the Committee on Affairs in the Late Insurrectionary States* (serial no. 1529), 42nd Cong., 2nd Sess., 18–19. W.E.B. Dubois, *Black Reconstruction,* New York: c. 1935, 560. Joseph G. Rosa and Robin May, *Gun Law: A Study of Violence in the Wild West,* New York: 1977, 59–60. W.C. Nunn, *Texas Under the Carpetbaggers,* Austin: 1962, 43, 48, 66–74. Charles W. Ramsdell, *Reconstruction in Texas,* New York: 1910, 316–17. William T. Field, Jr., "The Texas State Police, 1870–73," *Texas Military History,* fall 1965, 131–42.
3. John Wesley Hardin, *The Life of John Wesley Hardin As Written by Himself,* Norman, Okla.: 1961, 5–6, 12–24, 30–37, 42, 46–55, 58, 60–69, 71–77. Wayne Gard, *Frontier Justice,* Norman, Okla.: 1949, 227–28. Thomas Ripley, *They Died With Their Boots On,* New York: 1935, preface.
4. C.L. Sonnichsen, *I'll Die Before I'll Run: The Story of the Great Feuds of Texas,* New York: 1951, 19–20, 28–29, 32–46, 67–69, 71–87. Gard, 43. Hardin, 80, 85.
5. Gard, 52–57. Margaret Bierschwale, "Mason County, Texas, 1845–1870," *Southwest Historical Quarterly,* April 1949, 380. C.L. Douglas, *Famous Texas Feuds,* Dallas: 1936, 149–59. Stella Gipson Polk, *Mason and Mason County,* Austin: 1966, 53.
6. Maurice Garland Fulton, *History of the Lincoln County War,* Tucson: 1968, 19–23. Gard, 46–52. Sonnichsen, 97–105, 109, 116–17. Douglas, 134–35.

7. C.L. Sonnichsen, *The El Paso Salt War (1877),* Texas Western Press of the North: 1961, 3–20, 23–27, 29, 32–33, 36–45, 48–53, 56–61. Rex W. Strickland, "Six Who Came to El Paso," *Southwestern Studies,* vol. I, no. 3, 19–20.
8. John Upton Terrell, *Land Grab: The Truth About "The Winning of the West,"* New York: 1972, 182–236. Wayne Gard, *Rawhide Texas,* Norman, Okla.: 1965, 72–73. Gard, *Frontier,* 81–92.
9. Terrell, 243–44. Gard, *Frontier,* 105–11, 117–18. R.D. Holt, "The Saga of Barbed Wire in Tom Green County," *West Texas Historical Association Year Book,* Abilene, Texas: 1928, 32–34. Rosa, *Gunfighter,* 52. Henry D. McCallum, "Barbed Wire in Texas," *Southwestern Historical Quarterly,* vol. LXI, no. 2, 213–17.
10. Paul M. Angle, *Bloody Williamson: A Chapter in American Lawlessness,* New York: 1962, 72–116.
11. G.B. Glasscock, *Bandits and the Southern Pacific,* New York: 1929, 15–25.
12. Stephen A. Douglas Puter, *Looters of the Public Domain,* Portland: 1907, 17–21, 46–78, 442–47.
13. Oscar Osborn Winther, *The Transportation Frontier: Trans-Mississippi West—1865–1890,* New York: 1964, 141–43. See the annotated bibliography in Ramon Frederick Adams, *Six-Guns and Saddle Leather: A Bibliography of Books and Pamphlets on Western Outlaws and Gunmen,* Norman, Okla.: 1954.
14. Harry Sinclaire Drago, *The Great Range Wars,* New York: 1970, 78–79, 48, 50, 54–58, 121–22, 213–33. Fulton, 8, 17, 33, 43, 51–52, 121–22, 213, 225–26, 273–74, 74, 97, 112–14, 137, 146. Gard, *Rawhide,* 71–72. William Keleher, *Violence in Lincoln County, 1869–1881,* Albuquerque: 1957, viii–xiii, 113, 137, 142–49, 82–83, 117–18, 124, 142–44, 53–56, 213, 233, 247–48, 281, 107–8. Walter Pannell, "Civil War on the Range," *The Welcome News,* Los Angeles: 1943, 298–318. Philip Rasch, "Chaos in Lincoln County," *The Denver Westerners Brand Book,* vol. XVIII, 1963, 167. Philip Rasch, "Five Days of Battle, *Westerners Denver Possee Brand Book,* vol. XI, 1956. Rosa and May, 24–27. Victor Westphall, *Thomas Bender Catron and his Era,* Tucson: 1973, 78–80, 123–24. Lela and Rufus Waltrip, *Cowboys and Cattlemen,* New York: 1967, 33–45.
15. Gard, *Frontier,* 126–31. Rosa and May, 31–35. Ronald Dean Miller, *Shady Ladies of the West,* Los Angeles: 1964, 117–18. Struthers, Burt, *Powder River: Let 'er Buck,* New York: 1938, 291,

276–78, 292, 279, 282, 286. Drago, 280, 287, 267–71, 274–80. Oscar H. ("Jack") Flagg, *A Review of the Cattle Business in Johnson County, Wyoming, Since 1882: And the Causes that Led to the Recent Invasion,* Cheyenne: 1967, 8. A.S. Mercer, *The Banditti of the Plains,* Norman: 1954, 49, 42, 75–76, 117, 222, 127–28, 18, xxxviii, 19, 31, 22–23, 25–26, 35, 40. Rosa, *The Gunfighter,* 53. Rosa and May, 32–34. Helena Huntington Smith, *The War on Powder River,* New York: 1966, 199, 221, 225–26.

16. Winther, 141–42.
17. Charles Marin, *A Sketch of Sam Bass, the Bandit,* Norman, Okla.: 1956, 180. Rosa and May, 44. Eugene Cunningham, *Triggernometry: A Gallery of Gunfighters,* New York: 1934, 352–83.
18. Peter Lyon, "The Wild Wild West," *American Heritage,* August 1960, 32–34. Rosa and May, 48. Gard, *Frontier,* 169–79.
19. Lyon, 32–48. Hofstadter, 400–6. Rosa and May, 119–26.
20. Allan Swallow, ed., *The Wild Bunch,* Denver: 1966, 25–50, 83–85, 88–95, 126–27.

Chapter 17: Red, Yellow, Black

1. Joseph Jorgensen, "A Century of Political Economic Effects on American Indian Society, 1880–1980" (manuscript, 18, 20, 22), see *Journal of Ethnic Studies,* vol. VI.
2. Terrell, 48–56. Langdon Sully, "The Indian Agent: A Study in Corruption and Avarice," *American West,* vol. X, no. 2, 4–9. Edmund Danziger, Jr., "The Steck-Carleton Controversy in Civil War New Mexico," *Southwestern Historical Quarterly,* vol. LXXIV, no. 2, 189–203. New Mexico was no exception. Corruption was flagrant throughout the Indian Bureau. See, for example, Danziger's article "The Office of Indian Affairs and the Problem of Civil War Indian Refugees in Kansas," *Kansas Historical Quarterly,* vol. XXXV, no. 3, 257–75.
3. Terrell, 12–13. Jorgensen special research. Harry Kelsey, "The Doolittle Report of 1867: Its Preparation and Shortcomings," *Arizona and the West,* vol. XVII, no. 2, 107–20.
4. Jorgensen research. Sandoz, *Crazy Horse,* 152–224. D'Arcy McNickle, *They Came Here First: The Epic of the American Indian,* New York: 1975, 204–7.

5. Terrell, 11, 4–10.
6. Jorgensen research. Sandoz, 278–334. Berger, *Little Big Man,* 362–445.
7. Hervey Chalmers II, *The Last Stand of the Nez Perce: Destruction of a People,* New York: 1962, 20.
8. Milfred Wellborn, "The Events Leading to the Chinese Exclusion Acts," *Historical Society of Southern California,* vol. IX, 49–53.
9. Mark W. Hall, "The San Francisco 'Chronicle': Its Fight for the 1879 Constitution," *Journalism Quarterly,* vol. XLVI, no. 3, 505–10. Bailyn *et al.*, 758–59.
10. David V. DuFault, "The Chinese in the Mining Camps of California: 1848–1870," *Historical Society of Southern California,* vol. XLI, no. 2, 156–66.
11. Alexander McLeod, *Pigtails and Gold Dust,* Caldwell, Idaho: 1948, 156–60, 173–79.
12. William A. Heaps, *Riots USA: 1765–1965,* New York: 1966, 61–70. D.P. Dorland, "Chinese Massacre at Los Angeles in 1871," *Annual Publication of the Historical Society of Southern California,* vol. III, 22–26.
13. Wellborn, 54–77. Bailyn *et al.*, 758–59. Richard H. Dillon, *The Hatchet Men: The Story of the Tong Wars in San Francisco's Chinatown,* New York: 1962, 119–23. McLeod, 212.
14. Lynwood Carranco, "Chinese Expulsion from Humbolt County," *Pacific Historical Review,* vol. XXX, no. 4, 329–40. Issac Hill Bromley, *The Chinese Massacre at Rock Springs, Wyoming Territory,* Boston: 1886, 1–3, 91. Alexander Howard Meneely, *The Anti-Chinese Movement in the Northwest,* University of Washington M.A. thesis, 1922, 56. Hofstadter, 324–28.
15. Headley, *Riots,* 290–305. Kimbal Young, *Isn't One Wife Enough?*, New York: 1954, 352, 380–409. David Brion Davis, "Some Themes of Counter-Subversion: An Analysis of Anti-Masonic, Anti-Catholic & Anti-Mormon Literature," *Mississippi Valley Historical Review,* vol. XLVII, no. 2, 205–24. John Higham, *Strangers in the Land: Patterns of American Nativism, 1860–1925,* New York: 1966, 84, 92–93. Maury Reuben, *The Wars of the Godly,* New York: 1928, 206–11.
16. Higham, 90–169. Joy Jackson, "Crime and the Conscience of a City," *Louisiana History,* vol. IX, no. 3, 231–33.
17. Richard Gambino, *Vendetta,* New York: 1977, 1, 3–6, 8, 12–18,

44, 46, 49, 52, 58, 62–87, 95–111, 114, 117–27, 135, 150–51. John E. Coxe, "The New Orleans Mafia Incident," *Louisiana Historical Quarterly,* vol. XX, 1089–1090.

18. Nicolosi, "Rise and Fall," 43. Richard Maxwell Brown, "Legal and Behavioral Perspectives on American Vigilantism," *Perspectives in American History,* vol. V, 101–11. Fred M. Mazzulla, "Undue Process of Law—Here and There," *Westerners Denver Possee Brand Book,* vol. XX, 273–79.
19. James L. Crouthamel, "The Springfield, Illinois, Race Riot of 1908," in Joseph Boskin, ed., *Urban Racial Violence in the Twentieth Century,* Beverly Hills: 1969, 8–18.
20. *Ibid.*, 18–19. William Ivy Hair, "Inquisition for Blood: An Outbreak of Ritual Murder in Louisiana, Georgia and Texas, 1911–1912," *Louisiana Studies,* vol. XI, no. 3, 274–81.
21. William L. O'Neill, ed., *Echoes of Revolt: The Masses,* Chicago: 1966, 242.

Chapter 18: Shady Ladies

1. *New York Times,* June 14, 1976.
2. T.A. Larson, "Women's Rights in Idaho," *Idaho Yesterdays,* vol. XVI, no. 1, 3. Ira V. Brown, "The Women's Rights Movement in Pennsylvania, 1848–1873," *Pennsylvania History,* vol. XXXII, April 1965, 153, 163. Nevada Legislature, *Statutes of the State of Nevada Passed at the Eighth Session of the Legislature, 1876–1877,* Carson City: 1877, chapter 43. Marion Goldman, *Goldiggers & Silverminers Prostitution & the Legislation of Morality on the Mining Frontier,* University of Chicago Ph.D. dissertation, 1977, 337–38.
3. Egal Feldman, "Prostitution, the Alien Woman and the Progressive Imagination, 1910–1915," *American Quarterly,* vol. VIX, no. 2, 192–206. Rosa and May, 87. Miller, *Shady Ladies,* 59–60.
4. Goldman, 167, 169, 171–72, 176–79, 192–93, 196. Miller, 85–88.
5. Miller, 96–102.
6. *Ibid.*, 102–5.
7. *Ibid.*, 122–25.
8. *Ibid.*, 136–37, 134–35.
9. *Ibid.*, 112–16.
10. *Ibid.*, 108–12.

11. Nash, *Bloodletters,* 119–21
12. *Ibid.*, 235–38.
13. *Ibid.*, 360–61. Asbury, *The Gangs of New York,* 212–18. Inspector Thomas Byrnes, *1886—Professional Criminals of America,* New York: (reprint) 1969, 153, 194–96, 225, 115, 118, 145, 205–6, 252–56, 309–10, 326–27.
14. Herbert Asbury, *The French Quarter: An Informal History of the New Orleans Underworld,* New York: 1968, 330–36, 276–83. Ernest G. Vetter, *Fabulous Frenchtown,* Washington: 1955, 160.
15. Vetter, 150–65. Asbury, *French Quarter,* 336–45.
16. Asbury, *French Quarter,* 351–62.
17. *Ibid.*, 368–78.
18. *Ibid.*, 391–93.
19. *Ibid.*, 394.
20. *Ibid.*, 393, 430–33, 435–36.
21. *Ibid.*, 455.

Chapter 19: The Big Apple

1. Seymour J. Mandelbaum, *Boss Tweed's New York,* New York: 1965, 7–8, 12, 15.
2. Asbury, *Gangs of New York,* 225–46.
3. *Ibid.*, 235–37. Herbert Asbury, *All Around the Town,* New York: 1934, 180–82.
4. John H. Warren, Jr., *Thirty Years' Battle With Crime,* Poughkeepsie, N.Y.: 1874, 258–63. Matthew Hale Smith, *Bulls and Bears of New York, With the Crisis of 1873, and the Cause,* Hartford & Chicago: 1875, 317–20. Gustavus Myers, *The History of Tammany Hall,* New York: 1917, 225. Mandelbaum, 47.
5. Alexander B. Callow, Jr., *The Tweed Ring,* New York: 1965, 15–118. Alfred Connable and Edward Silberfarb, *Tigers of Tammany,* New York: 1967, 145–51. See also *Dictionary of American Biography* on Tweed Ring members. Denis Tilden Lynch, *"Boss" Tweed: The Story of a Grim Generation,* New York: 1927. Myers, especially 225.
6. Callow, 119–20, 142–63, 199–206. Mandelbaum, 77. Connable and Silberfarb, 154–55. "How New York Is Governed: Frauds of the Tammany Democrats," *New York Times Publication,* 1871, 5, 10, 13–15.

7. Connable and Silberfarb, 157–58.
8. Callow, 154, 236, 247–50, 31–46. *Harper's Weekly,* January 22, 1870.
9. Callow, 250, 259, 268, 282–99.
10. Croswell Bowen, *Elegant Oakey,* New York: 1956, 260–65. Emma Goldman, *Living My Life,* New York: 1931, 128–31.
11. Leo Hershkowitz, *Tweed's New York: Another Look,* New York: 1977, 139, 154–55.

Chapter 20: Chicago—No Quarter, Either Way

1. Joseph Lincoln Steffens, *The Shame of the Cities,* New York: 1968, 234.
2. Virgil W. Peterson, *Barbarians in Our Midst: A History of Chicago Crime and Politics,* Boston: 1952, chapter 4. Also see Lloyd Wendt and Herman Kogan, *Lords of the Levee,* Indianapolis: 1943.
3. Herbert Asbury, *Gem of the Prairie: An Informal History of the Chicago Underworld,* New York: 1940, 112, 140, 100–2. Peterson, 39–46.
4. Peterson, 45–47. John Joseph Flinn, *History of the Chicago Police,* Chicago: 1887, 211–13. Frederick Rex, *The Mayors of the City of Chicago from March 4, 1837 to April 13, 1933,* Chicago: 1945.
5. Asbury, *Gem,* 112.
6. *Ibid.,* 138.
7. As quoted in John Landesco, "The Criminal Underworld of Chicago in the '80s and '90s," *Journal of Criminal Law and Criminology,* vol. XXV, no. 3, 345, and "Chicago's Criminal Underworld of the '80s and '90s," *ibid.,* vol. XXV, no. 6, 929.
8. Peterson, appendix. Henry B. Leonard, "The Immigrants' Protective League of Chicago, 1908–1921," *Journal of the Illinois State Historical Society,* vol. XLVI, no. 3, 283.
9. Nowhere in American urban history is there anything comparable to the study of early organized crime and gang life that Landesco published as part 3 of the Chicago Crime Commission's *Illinois Crime Survey,* Chicago: 1929. This chapter relies heavily on Landesco's work.
10. *Chicago Daily News,* August 9, 1907. Peterson, 85–88.
11. Landesco, *Crime Survey,* 871.

12. Peterson, 85–88. See Wendt and Kogan, chapter 3, on Coughlin and McKenna.
13. Carter H. Harrison, *Stormy Years, The Autobiography of Carter H. Harrison,* Indianapolis: 1935, 75–84. Wendt and Kogan, 71–79. Peterson, 59–61.
14. Harrison, 129–133.
15. *Ibid.*, 294.
16. The Vice Commission of Chicago, *The Social Evil in Chicago,* Chicago: 1911, 32–34, 72–78, 119–30.
17. Landesco, *Crime Survey,* 881–87.
18. *Ibid.*
19. See Charles Washburn, *Come Into My Parlor,* New York: 1934. Peterson, 93–94.
20. Fred D. Pasley, *Al Capone: The Biography of a Self-Made Man,* Garden City, N.Y.: 1930, 13–17. Humbert Nelli, "Italians and Crime in Chicago: The Formative Years, 1890–1920," *American Journal of Sociology,* vol. LXXIV, January 1969, 385–87. Peterson, 106–7. Landesco, *Crime Survey,* 845–46.
21. Landesco, *Crime Survey,* 846–48. Peterson, 94–95. See Nelli, *The Business of Crime, Italians and Syndicate Crime in the United States,* New York: 1976, 87–100, for a summary of Black Hand activities and press response to them. On anti-Italian campaigns, see Nelli, "Italians and Crime in Chicago." Two useful articles exploring Progressivist antiprostitution campaigns are Roy Lubove, "The Progressives and the Prostitute," *The Historian,* vol. XXIV, May 1962, and Egal Feldman, "Prostitution, the Alien Woman and the Progressive Imagination, 1910–1915," *American Quarterly,* vol. XVIX, summer 1967.
22. *Chicago Tribune,* July 15, 1914.
23. Landesco, *Crime Survey,* 909–11. Nelli, *Business of Crime,* 122. Peterson, 107–10.
24. Ferdinand Lundberg, *Imperial Hearst, A Social Biography,* New York: 1936, 139–73.
25. *Chicago Inter-Ocean,* June 11, 1911. *Daily Socialist* quoted in Lundberg, 153–55.
26. Lundberg, 155–59, 167–69.
27. *Chicago Evening World,* October 26, 1912.
28. Lundberg, 153.
29. W.A. Swanberg, *Citizen Hearst,* New York: 1961, 250–51.

30. Gabriel Kolko, *The Triumph of Conservatism,* New York: 1963, 198–99. Higham, *Strangers in the Land,* 175–82. Swanberg, 327.
31. Peterson, 97–100. For background on Thompson's early years see William H. Stuart, *The Twenty Incredible Years,* Chicago: 1935.
32. Landesco, *Crime Survey,* 890–92.
33. Peterson, 125. Lundberg, 162–63. Landesco, *ibid.,* 916–17.
34. Landesco, *ibid.,* 892–98.
35. Lundberg, 163.
36. St. Clair Drake and Horace R. Cayton, *Black Metropolis: A Study of Negro Life in a Northern City,* New York: 1970, 348. Harold F. Gosnell, *Machine Politics: The Chicago Model,* Chicago: 1937. Allen H. Spear, *Black Chicago: The Making of a Northern Ghetto, 1890–1920,* Chicago: 1967, 187–90. Lundberg, 163.
37. The best general summary of Prohibition bootlegging in Chicago is Kenneth Allsop, *The Bootleggers and Their Era,* Garden City, N.Y.: 1961.
38. *Chicago Tribune,* May 15, 1920. *Chicago Daily News,* May 12, 1920.
39. Nelli, *Business of Crime,* 105–11.
40. Landesco, *Crime Survey,* 901. *Chicago Tribune,* June 26, 27, 1946.
41. Nelli, *Business of Crime,* 163–65. Landesco, *ibid.,* 923–31.
42. Allsop, 88, 92. Landesco, *ibid.,* 927–28. Peterson, 125–28.
43. Quoted in Allsop, 120, 122–23.
44. *Ibid.,* 250–51.
45. Landesco, *Crime Survey,* 1044–1046.
46. *Ibid.,* 1048–1049.
47. See Nelli, "Italians and Crime in Chicago."

Chapter 21: 1919

1. Quoted in William Leuchtenburg, *The Perils of Prosperity,* Chicago: 1958, 142.
2. The most complete accounts of the Mooney-Billings case are in Richard H. Frost, *The Mooney Case,* Stanford, Calif.: 1968, and Zachariah Chaffee, Jr., Walter H. Pollack, Carl S. Stern, *The Mooney Billings Report* in *Wickersham Reports,* vol. XV, Montclair, N.J.: 1968.
3. Robert K. Murray, *Red Scare: A Study in National Hysteria,*

Minneapolis: 1955, 111–17. *San Francisco Examiner, Cincinnati Enquirer,* and *New York Times,* July 4, 1919.

4. Murray K. Levin, *Political Hysteria in America,* New York: 1971, 34–38.
5. Chaffee *et al.,* 1–13.
6. The most complete account of the "Black Sox" scandal, on which this sketch relies, is in Leo Katcher, *The Big Bankroll: The Life and Times of Arnold Rothstein,* New York: 1959, 138–48.
7. Craig Thompson and Allen Raymond, *Gang Rule in New York: The Story of a Lawless Era,* New York: 1940, 53.
8. See Katcher, chapter 18.
9. Quoted in Coben, *A. Mitchell Palmer,* 4.
10. *New York Times,* May 1, 1919. "Attorney General A. Mitchell Palmer on Charges Made Against the Department of Justice by Louis F. Post and others," *Hearings,* Committee on Rules, U.S. House of Representatives, Washington: 1920, 157–58.
11. *Washington Post,* June 4, 5, 1919. *Washington Evening Star,* June 3, 1919. Coben, 205–6.
12. Coben, 207. Zachariah Chaffee, *Free Speech in the United States,* New York: 1920, 204–17. *New York Times,* April 25, 1919. On use of vigilante groups, see U.S. Senate, Committee on the Judiciary, "Charges of Illegal Practices of the Department of Justice," *Hearings Report,* 66th Cong., 3rd Sess., Washington: 1921.
13. Coben, 214. *New York Times,* October 17, 1919. *San Francisco Examiner,* September 10, 1919. *Wall Street Journal,* September 12, 1919. *Los Angeles Times,* September 12, 1919.
14. Senate Committee on Judiciary, "Charges of Illegal Practices," 580.
15. *New York Times,* November 8, 1919.
16. Murray, 206–09. Levin, 56–61.
17. Murray, 198.
18. *Ibid.,* 213–18. National Popular Government League, *Report of Illegal Practices of the United States Department of Justice,* Washington: 1920, 41–42. Senate Committee on Judiciary, "Charges of Illegal Practices," 381, 494.
19. Murray, 232–35. Chaffee, *Free Speech,* 575–80. *Washington Post,* January 4, 1920. *Literary Digest,* no. 64, January 17, 1920, 13.
20. Higham, *Strangers in the Land,* 232. The general material for this sketch is drawn from Coben.

21. *New York Times,* October 22, 23, 1920. Other sources besides newspaper reports for Brindell's activities in the construction industry include New York State Legislature, Joint Legislative Committee on Housing of New York State, *Intermediate Report,* Legislative Document no. 60, Albany, N.Y.: 1922. *Final Report,* Document no. 28: 1923. A vivid rendering of the case is found in Harold Seidman, *Labor Czars: A History of Labor Racketeering,* New York: 1938, chapter 6.
22. Gordon S. Watkins, "The Present Status of Socialism in the United States," *Atlantic Monthly,* December 1919, 821–30.
23. John Hutchinson, *The Imperfect Union: A History of Corruption in Trade Unions,* New York: 1972, 36–40.
24. *Intermediate Report,* 36–38.
25. *Ibid.*, 38–39.
26. *Ibid.*, 40.
27. *Ibid.*, 40–41.
28. *Ibid.*, 44–45.
29. *Ibid.*, 47–49.
30. *Ibid.*, 69.
31. *Ibid.*, 72–73.
32. *Ibid.*, 76–77.
33. *Ibid.*, 80–81.
34. *Ibid.*, 65.
35. *New York Tribune,* September 29, 30, 1919. *New York World,* September 30, 1919. *New York Times,* September 30, 1919. The following account is drawn largely from these newspapers. Further background can be found in Arthur Waskow, *From Race Riot to Sit-In,* New York: 1966, 110–20.
36. Quoted in Waskow, 110.

Chapter 22: The Fruits of Temperance

1. Betty B. Rosenbaum, "The Relationship Between War and Crime in the United States," *Journal of Criminal Law and Criminology,* vol. XXX, no. 1. The best brief summary of the scandals of the Harding administration is in Frederick Lewis Allen, *Only Yesterday,* New York: 1931 and 1959, chapter 6. An astute scholarly account is Burl Noggle's *Teapot Dome: Oil and Politics in the 1920s,*

Baton Rouge, La.: 1962, especially 177–215. See also Chicago Crime Commission, *The Illinois Crime Survey,* part 2, Chicago: 1929. Hank Messick, *Lansky,* New York: 1971. Thomas E. Dewey, *Twenty Against the Underworld,* New York: 1974. Landesco, *Crime Survey,* 969–97.

2. See particularly Kolko, and Robert H. Wiebe, *The Search for Order,* New York: 1967. See also Leuchtenburg, 192–93.
3. Landesco, *Crime Survey,* 909–17.
4. Nelli, *The Business of Crime,* 128–29, 197–203. Nicholas Gage, "The Mafia at War," part 1, *New York Magazine,* July 10, 1972.
5. Thompson and Raymond, 100.
6. See Katcher, *The Big Bankroll.*
7. Many versions of these killings have been published. Two of the most reliable are Messick, 50–58, and Nick Gentile, *Vito di Capomafia,* Rome: 1963, 112–19. For a more scholarly approach, see Nelli, *Business of Crime,* 203–7.
8. Charles Merz, *The Dry Decade,* Garden City, N.Y.: 1931, 65–71, 259.
9. Quoted in Walter Lippman, *Forum,* February 1931, 65–67, and January 1931, 3.
10. Merz, 260. Quoted in Allen, 182. See National Commission on Law Observance and Enforcement, *Prohibition,* vol. IV, Washington: 1931.
11. Merz, ix.
12. Investigative files of Internal Revenue Service, quoted in Nelli, *Business of Crime,* 222.
13. *Ibid.,* and Leonard Katz, *Uncle Frank: The Biography of Frank Costello,* New York: 1973, 83–92.
14. Hutchinson, 118–21. Matthew Josephson, *Union House—Union Bar,* New York: 1956, 212–18. Dewey, 279–82.
15. Benjamin Stolberg, *Tailor's Progress,* New York: 1944, 138–39. Hutchinson, 72. Benjamin Gitlow, *I Confess,* New York: 1939, chapter 10. *New York Times,* April 7, 1927. Philip Foner, *The Fur and Leather Workers Union,* Newark: 1950, 82–90.
16. Nelli, *Business of Crime,* 107–9. Hutchinson, 93–99. New York State Crime Commission, *Fourth Report,* Albany, N.Y.: 1953, 33–38.
17. Hutchinson, 130–38. Nelli, *Business of Crime,* 248–51. Carey McWilliams, "Racketeers and Movie Magnates," *New Republic,*

October 27, 1941. Seidman, 177–84.

18. Nelli, *ibid.*, 237–39. Dewey, 185–87, 227.
19. Nelli, *ibid.*, 223–25. Katz, *Uncle Frank,* 83–92. Thompson and Raymond, 378–90. T. Harry Williams, *Huey Long,* New York: 1969, 824–25.
20. Nelli, *ibid.*, 233. *New York Times,* December 4, 1935. Hickman Powell, *Ninety Times Guilty,* New York: 1939.
21. Quoted in Dewey, 191–92.
22. Dewey, chapter 10. See also Powell.
23. Dewey, chapter 18.
24. Quoted in Michele Pentaleone, *The Mafia and Politics,* London: 1966, 181–83.
25. Henry Chafetz, *Beat the Devil: A History of Gambling in the United States from 1492 to 1955,* New York: 1960, 380–88. Paul Sann, *Kill the Dutchman: The Story of Dutch Schultz,* New Rochelle, N.Y.: 1971, chapters 13 and 14. Nelli, *Business of Crime,* 228–29.
26. Dewey, 473.

Chapter 23: The Boondock Underworld

1. Ray Ginger, *Six Days or Forever,* Boston: 1958, 130. This account relies on narratives found in Arthur Garfield Hayes, *Let Freedom Ring,* New York: 1928, 25–89; Allen, *Only Yesterday,* 142–46; but particularly on Ginger.
2. Quoted in Ginger, *Six Days,* 7.
3. *Ibid.*, 64.
4. *Ibid.*, 34. H.L. Mencken, "The Monkey Trial: A Reporter's Account," in Jerry R. Tompkins, *D-Day at Dayton,* Baton Rouge, La.: 1965, 39.
5. Ginger, *Six Days,* 8, 13–14.
6. Mencken, 44. Ginger, 74.
7. Ginger, 133.
8. David M. Chalmers, *Hooded Americanism: The first Century of the Ku Klux Klan, 1865–1965,* New York: 1965, 290–99.
9. Don S. Kirschner, *City and Country: Rural Responses to the Urbanization in the 1920s,* Westport, Conn.: 1970, chapter 2, especially 2–3, 24, 37–38, 169–77.
10. *Ibid.*, 37–38, 169–77.

11. Joe B. Frantz, "The Frontier Tradition: An Invitation to Violence," in Hugh D. Graham and Ted R. Gurr, *Violence in America,* New York: 1962, 119.
12. Hank Messick, *Gangs and Gangsters,* New York: 1974, 121–25. Robert Crome and Joseph Pinkson, *Dillinger: A Short and Violent Life,* New York: 1962, 8–15.
13. Crome and Pinkston, 203, 198–99.
14. *Ibid.*, 206.
15. Sanford Ungar, *FBI,* Boston: 1975, 73.
16. *Ibid.*, 74–75.
17. Crome and Pinkston, 253–56. Messick, *Gangs and Gangsters,* 146.
18. Paul I. Wellman, *A Dynasty of Western Outlaws,* Garden City, N.Y.: 1961, 330.
19. *Ibid.*, 349.
20. Messick, *Gangs and Gangsters,* 181–84. Wellman, 343–44.

Chapter 24: The Guns of Dearborn

1. Jay Robert Nash, *Citizen Hoover: A Critical Study of the Life and Times of J. Edgar Hoover and His FBI,* Chicago: 1972, 82.
2. The primary critical reference on Harry Bennett's role at Ford is in Keith Sward, *The Legend of Henry Ford,* New York: 1948. Also useful is Harry H. Bennett, *We Never Called Him Henry,* New York: 1951.
3. Sward, 337–42. *New York Times,* June 26, 1937.
4. Sward, 293–301.
5. *Detroit News,* May 11, 1929, June 25 and December 16, 1937. Sward, 303.
6. *Detroit News,* September 26, and October 2, 1930. Sward, 331. *New York Times,* April 2, 1927. LaMare statement quoted in Victor Reuther, *The Brothers Reuther,* Boston: 1976, 204.
7. Sward, 306–7, 318–19. *New York Times,* January 8, 1928, *Fortune,* December, 1933.
8. See Reuther, chapter 13, 143–71. *Detroit News,* May 2, 1937.
9. Quoted in Reuther, 202.
10. *Detroit News,* July 7, and July 12, 1937.
11. *Ibid.*, July 16, 1937.
12. Quoted in Reuther, 203.

13. Reuther, 209–11. Sward, 380–84. *Detroit Times,* January 22, 1939.
14. Reuther, *ibid.*
15. Elder's statement can be found in "Deposition of Harry Elder," September 2, 1939, in *The Archives of Labor History and Urban Affairs, R.J. Thomas Collection,* box 8, at Walter P. Reuther Library, Wayne State University, Detroit, Michigan.
16. *Detroit News,* June 28, 1940.
17. *New York Post,* May 25, and 29, 1940. Sward, 299–301.

Chapter 25: Corporations and Conspiracies

1. *Washington Post,* November 9, 1978. Three excellent general studies are August Bequai, *White Collar Crime: A Twentieth Century Crisis,* Lexington, Mass.: 1978; John E. Conklin, *"Illegal But Not Criminal,"* New York: 1977; and Richard Austin Smith, "The Incredible Electrical Conspiracy," *Fortune,* April and May 1961.
2. Joint Economic Committee, U.S. Congress, *The Cost of Crime in 1976,* Washington: 1976, 8.
3. Edwin Sutherland, *White Collar Crime,* Bloomington, Ind.: 1949, 20–24. American Management Associations, *Crimes Against Business,* Washington: 1977.
4. Smith, *Ibid.*
5. Clark Mollenhoff, "Billie Sol Estes," *The Supercrooks,* Roger M. Williams, ed., Chicago: 1973. Raymond Dirks and Leonard Gross, *The Great Wall Street Scandal,* New York: 1974.
6. *New York Times,* May 25, 1975. Release from *Congress Watch, Public Citizen,* Washington, D.C., February 4, 1979. Mark Green, "The Me Decade Meets the Corrupt Seventies," *Politicks & Other Human Interests,* April 25, 1978.
7. *Congress Watch, ibid.*
8. *Washington Post,* May 27, 1977.
9. U.S. District Court for the District of Columbia, *Report of the Special Review Committee of the Board of Directors of Gulf Oil Corporation,* Washington: 1975, 31, 78–79, 163.
10. *Ibid.,* 32–39.
11. *Ibid.,* 35. *Washington Post,* July 20, 1977, and December 24, 1976.

12. *New York Times Magazine,* September 26, 1976. *Newsweek,* February 19, 1979.
13. *Business Week,* March 8, 1976, 29–32. *Wall Street Journal,* April 8, 1977.
14. Confidential memo prepared for U.S. House of Representatives, Subcommittee on Energy and Power, November 28, 1978. *New York Times,* December 11, 1978.
15. Ralph Nader Task Force, "Consumers Lose Billions to Invisible Bilk," in *Crime and the Law,* Washington: 1971, 21.
16. Quoted in Fred Cook, *The Corrupted Land: The Social Mobility of Modern America,* New York: 1966, 39.
17. Quoted in Walter Goodman, *All Honorable Men: Corruption and Compromise in American Life,* Bouton: 1963, 84. See also Mark Dowie, "Pinto Madness," *Mother Jones,* September, 1977.

Chapter 26: The Crime Regulators

1. *Washington Star,* June 8, 1977. Much of the research for the paragraphs concerning the death of Merle Baumgart and the subsequent Justice Department investigation relies on confidential interviews between author Browning and officials of the Justice Department and the Washington Metropolitan Police Department.
2. Confidential interviews.
3. *Washington Star,* June 24, 1977.
4. Knight-Ridder news dispatch in Long Beach, Calif., *Independent,* June 9, 1977.
5. *Washington Star,* June 21, 24, 1977.
6. Confidential interviews. *Washington Star,* July 15, 1977.
7. *Washington Star,* June 8, 1977.
8. Confidential interviews. *Washington Post,* December 22, 1978. *Washington Star,* December 20, 1978.
9. Confidential interviews. *Washington Star,* December 20, 1978.
10. *Ibid.*
11. David Hemenway, "Railroading AntiTrust at the ICC," in Mark J. Green, ed., *The Monopoly Makers: Ralph Nader's Study Group Report on Regulation and Competition,* New York: 1973, 139–57. The President's Council on Wage and Price Stability, *The Value of Motor Carrier Operating Authorities* (mimeograph), Washington: June 9, 1977.

12. American Trucking Associations, *Accounting for Motor Carrier Operating Rights* (brief presented to the Financial Accounting Foundation), Washington: 1974, 5–6. Stephen Chapman, "Busting the Trucking Cartel," *New Republic,* September 30, 1978. *New York Times,* April 11, 1977. *Washington Star,* April 10, 1977.
13. William A. Jordan, "Producer Protection, Prior Market Structure and the Effects of Government Regulation," *Journal of Law and Economics,* vol. XV, no. 1, 151–76.
14. Chapman, *ibid.*
15. *Washington Star,* April 10, 1977.
16. Harry Crews, "The Trucker Militant," *Esquire,* August 1977.
17. *Ibid.* U.S. House of Representatives, *Federal Regulations and Regulatory Reform,* Report of the Subcommittee on Oversight and Investigations, Committee on Interstate and Foreign Commerce, 94th Cong., 2nd Sess., Washington: 1976, 351.
18. Subcommittee Report, 352.
19. *The Packer,* March 26, 1977.
20. Crews, *ibid.*
21. United States of America vs. Austin I. Underdal, Second Supplemental Opposition to Motion to Quash Subpoena Duces Tecum, U.S. District Court, Central District of California, April 8, 1977.
22. *Washington Star,* December 20, 1978. Confidential interviews.

Chapter 27: Organized but also Institutionalized

1. Authors' interviews with investigators, New York State Joint Legislative Committee on Crime, summer 1975. Organized crime expert Hank Messick views La Cosa Nostra as simply a new name for the Mafia, one popularized by Joseph Valachi for the 1963 McClellan hearings and promoted by Hoover for his own propaganda purposes: Hank Messick, *The Silent Syndicate,* New York: 1967, 287. For a more complicated appraisal see Donald R. Cressey, *Theft of the Nation: The Structure and Operations of Organized Crime in America,* New York: 1969, 19–24. See also U.S. Senate, *Hearings Before the Special Committee to Investigate Organized Crime in Interstate Commerce* (sometimes referred to as Kefauver committee), Third Interim Report, 82nd Cong., 1st Sess., Washington: 1951, 150. For Hoover's position, see U.S.

House of Representatives, "Testimony of J. Edgar Hoover," *Hearings Before the Subcommittee on the Departments of State, Justice and Commerce, the Judiciary, and Related Agencies' Appropriations of the House Committee on Appropriations,* 89th Cong., 2nd Sess., Washington: 1966.

2. U.S. Senate, "Testimony of Joseph Valachi," *Hearings Before the Permanent Subcommittee on Investigations* of the Senate Committee on Governmental Operations (sometimes referred to as McClellan committee), 88th cong., 2nd Sess., Washington: 1963.
3. Peter Maas, *The Valachi Papers,* New York: 1968, 112–15. Creesey, 7. Nelli, *Business of Crime,* 179–83.
4. The most useful of the many recent books on syndicate crime, aside from those already noted, are: Robert F. Kennedy, *The Enemy Within,* New York: 1960; Gus Tyler, *Organized Crime in America, A Book of Readings,* Ann Arbor, Mich.: 1962; Fred J. Cook, *The Secret Rulers: Criminal Syndicates and How They Control the U.S. Underworld,* New York: 1966; U.S. President's Commission on Law Enforcement and Administration of Justice, *Task Force Report: Organized Crime,* Washington: 1967; Messick, *Lansky,* New York: 1971; Joseph L. Albini, *The America Mafia: Genesis of a Legend,* New York: 1971; Dwight Smith, *The Mafia Mystique,* New York: 1975; Francis A.J. Ianni, *Black Mafia: Ethnic Succession in Organized Crime,* New York: 1974.
5. Nicholas Pileggi, "Crime at Mid-Century," *New York Magazine,* December 30, 1974. The best general reference on Costello is Leonard Katz, *Uncle Frank: The Biography of Frank Costello,* New York: 1973.
6. Pileggi, *ibid.*
7. *Ibid.*
8. Cressey, 57–58. McClellan committee, part no. 1, 6–8. Nelli, *ibid.,* 261.
9. See Messick, *Lansky.*
10. See Daniel Bell, "Crime as an American Way of Life: A Queer Ladder of Social Mobility," in *The End of Ideology,* New York: 1962.
11. Walter Sheridan, *The Fall and Rise of Jimmy Hoffa,* New York: 1972. Steven Brill, *The Teamsters,* New York: 1978. Dan Muldea, *The Hoffa Wars,* New York: 1978.
12. Brill, chapter 4. *Bergen Record,* November 19–22, 1978.

13. *Bergen Record, ibid.*
14. *Ibid.*
15. *Ibid.*
16. *Ibid.*
17. *Playboy,* November 1963.
18. Murray Kempton, "The Pessimist," *New York Review of Books,* February 22, 1979.
19. *Washington Star,* July 7 and 10, 1977.
20. Authors' confidential interviews with federal and Washington Metropolitan Police Department investigators, 1975.
21. *Ibid.*
22. *Ibid.,* and confidential reports of U.S. Department of Justice, Washington, D.C.
23. Interviews with investigators, New York State Joint Legislative Committee on Crime.
24. Confidential report in files of U.S. Drug Enforcement Administration, Washington, D.C.
25. Authors' interviews with prosecutors in St. Mary's County, Md., district attorney's office.
26. Author Browning's confidential interviews.
27. Confidential report in files of Washington Metropolitan Police Department.
28. Confidential report in files of U.S. Drug Enforcement Administration. Confidential interviews.
29. *Ibid.*

Chapter 28: The Law of the Streets—Dead End

1. *Washington Post,* October 23, 1973.
2. *New York Times,* January 11, 1976.
3. Charles E. Silberman, *Criminal Violence, Criminal Justice,* New York: 1978, 31–32.
4. See James Q. Wilson, *Thinking About Crime,* New York: 1975.
5. Bruce Jackson, *In the Life,* New York: 1972, 166.
6. Joan Petersilia, Peter Greenwood, and Marvin Lavin, *Criminal Careers of Habitual Felons,* Rand Corporation Contract R-2144-DOJ, Santa Monica, Calif.: 1977, 97–105, 114–18. Julian Roebuck, *Criminal Typology,* Springfield, Ill.: 1967, 175. For a

fuller discussion of how contacts are made and careers promoted, see Roebuck and Wolfgang Freese, *The Rendezvous,* New York: 1976.

7. John Allen, *Assault with a Deadly Weapon: The Autobiography of a Street Criminal,* New York: 1977, 1. Silberman, 101–3. Authors' interviews with Vera Institute investigator Orlando Rodriguez on preliminary findings, March 1979.
8. Possibly the most popular description of the dual labor market is Eli Ginzberg, "The Job Problem," *Scientific American,* November 1977. Other more technical economic studies are Marcia Freedman, *Labor Markets: Segments and Shelters,* New York: 1976; Bennett Harrison, "Employment, Unemployment and the Structure of the Urban Labor Market," *Wharton Quarterly,* spring 1972, 4–30; Peter B. Doeringer and Michael J. Piore, "Unemployment and the 'dual labor market,'" *Public Interest,* vol. XXXVIII, 67–79. Particularly useful on criminal activity is Isaac Ehrlich, "Participation in Illegitimate Activities: A Theoretical and Empirical Investigation," *Journal of Political Economy,* vol. LXXXI, 521–65.
9. Allen, *Assault,* 102. Clifford Shaw and Henry McKay, "Social Factors in Juvenile Delinquency," in *National (Wickersham) Commission on the Law Observance and Enforcement, Report on the Causes of Crime,* Washington: 1931, 123.
10. *Pacific News Service,* San Francisco: February 12, 1979.
11. Richard Block, "Homicide in Chicago: A Nine-Year Study," *Journal of Criminal Law and Criminology,* vol. LXVI, no. 4.
12. *The Clay Center [Kansas] Dispatch* (AP report), November 10, 1978.
13. Mark H. Moore, *Buy and Bust,* Lexington, Mass.: 1977, 92–108. Frank Browning, "An American Gestapo," *Playboy,* February 1976.
14. Quoted in Rufus King, *The Drug Hang-up: America's Fifty-Year Folly,* New York: 1972, 39, 54, chapter 15.
15. Browning, *ibid.*
16. King, 65–66.
17. *Washington Post,* November 9, 1976.

Index